D1537540

Party Politics in America

TENTH EDITION

MARJORIE RANDON HERSHEY

Indiana University

PAUL ALLEN BECK

The Ohio State University

Longman

New York San Francisco Boston
London Toronto Sydney Tokyo Singapore Madrid
Mexico City Munich Paris Cape Town Hong Kong Montreal

Senior Executive Editor: Eric Stano
Senior Marketing Manager: Megan Galvin-Fak
Senior Production Manager: Eric Jorgensen
Project Coordination, Text Design, and Electronic Page Makeup: Electronic Publishing
    Services Inc., NYC
Cover Design Manager: Wendy Fredericks
Cover Photo: © Bettmann/CORBIS
Manufacturing Buyer: Al Dorsey
Printer and Binder: The Maple-Vail Book Manufacturing Group
Cover Printer: Lehigh Press, Inc.

Library of Congress Cataloging-in-Publication Data

Hershey, Marjorie Randon.
    Party politics in America / Marjorie Randon Hershey, Paul Allen Beck. --10th ed.
        p.   cm.
    Includes bibliographical references and index.
    ISBN 0-321-09543-X
    1. Political parties--United States. I. Hershey, Marjorie Randon. II. Title.
JK2265 .S65 2003
324.273—dc21

Please visit our website at http://www.ablongman.com

ISBN 0-321-09543-X

1 2 3 4 5 6 7 8 9 10—MV—05 04 03 02

Brief Contents

Detailed Contents

Foreword to
Party Politics in America,
Tenth Edition

W hy should you be interested in studying political parties? The short answer is that virtually everything important in American politics is rooted in *party* politics. Political parties are at the core of American democracy and make it what it is today—just as they have virtually from the Founding.

Why should you use this book to guide you in the search for understanding democratic politics in America? The short answer is that this book is the best guide you can have, and it has been the best guide in this search for quite a long time. Now, let's turn to the longer answers.

I first encountered this text at the same stage in my life you are in now, as an undergraduate—in my case, though, that was way back in the 1960s. I read it in a form called mimeograph—think of it as a very smelly, smudgy Xerox copy—while the second edition was being prepared. At that point, the book was authored by a young, up-coming scholar named Frank Sorauf. Following on the heels of his important study of the impact of political parties on the Pennsylvania legislature,[1] *Party Politics in America* established him as arguably the leading scholar of political parties of his generation. In those days—less so than today—it was common for a "textbook" (that is, a book designed to be used in class) to do more than just tell you what others had written about its subject. Rather, books written for undergraduates were also designed to make a coherent argument about its subject matter —to engage you, the reader, intellectually. So it was then and so, with this book, it still is today.

In the sixth edition, published in 1988, Frank brought in Paul Allen Beck as co-author, a collaboration that continued through the seventh edition. By the eight edition (published in 1997), Sorauf turned the book over entirely to Paul. In 2001, for the ninth edition and then again for the tenth, Marjorie Randon Hershey joined with Beck to create the book you are about to read today. This authorial overlapping brings a high degree of intellectual continuity to *Party Politics in America*. There are three important continuities (the first two of which are things you might want to keep in mind for the exams!). First, Sorauf, Beck, and Hershey very effectively use a three-part division in the discussion of political parties. More specifically, they divide the political party into its electoral, governing, and organizational roles. These three aspects of a party create a coherent system that (sometimes loosely, sometimes more tightly) provides a degree of integration to the diverse workings of any one political

---

[1]Frank J. Sorauf, *Party and Representation, Legislative Politics in Pennsylvania* (New York: Atherton Press, 1963).

party. In those cases, the electoral, governing, and organizational aspects of the political party all pull together. However, as you will learn, there are often strains within and among these three divisions. What, for example, would you do if you were an advisor to the Republican Party faced with the following choice? There is a policy stance that will help your presidential nominee win votes from undecided (typically moderate) voters, and thus perhaps help your party win the presidency. That same stance, however, will hurt your party's candidates for the U.S. House of Representatives in their fund raising campaigns, and thus put at risk the narrow majority they currently hold in the House. Is it more important to hold a majority in the House or to hold the presidency? Should you risk losing potential support from moderate voters to maintain close ties with more extreme groups key to your organizational strength in fund raising?

The second continuity is that Sorauf, Beck, and Hershey see the two major political parties in the U.S. as a system. The two-party system has long played a central role in the historical evolution of American politics (see especially Chapter 7). While this two-party system has important implications for the dynamics of American politics, they also see the two-party system as a part of the intermediary groups in society. By this the authors mean that the parties serve as points of contact between the public and its government (see their Figure 1.1, a figure that I believe has graced the beginning of this book for ten editions now).

The third continuity is that each is a terrific scholar of political parties, and while these continuities have allowed this book to keep its unique intellectual stamp, the transition among authors has also allowed each to bring to the work his or her particular strengths. In the end, this has made the 10th edition of the book richer and stronger than ever before. As I noted earlier, Frank Sorauf used his expertise to explain the role of the political party in government. Since then, he became one of the nation's leading experts on the role of money in politics, and in later editions reflected that increasingly important but perennially controversial subject.[2] Paul Beck brings a distinguished career of scholarship examining the role of political parties in the electorate, adding nicely to Frank's expertise about the governing role.[3] Paul is, like Frank and Marjorie Hershey, an expert on American politics. But Paul is also, more than most of us who study American politics, genuinely knowledgeable about comparative politics. Indeed, he has not only been at the center of the study of "dealignment" from parties in the American electorate (that is, an apparent increase in the people withdrawing from partisan politics), but is also a leading scholar of dealignment in many other nations as well.[4] Marjorie, through her expertise, has made important contributions to one

---

[2]See, for example, Frank J. Sorauf, *Money in American Elections* (Glenview, Ill.: Scott Foresman/Little, Brown College Division, 1988) or *Inside Campaign Finance: Myths and Realities* (New York: Yale University Press, 1992)

[3]He has written a great deal on this subject. One illustration that has long been one of my favorites is his "A Socialization Theory of Partisan Realignment," which was originally published in *The Politics of Future Citizens*, edited by Richard Niemi (San Francisco, Cal.: Jossey-Bass, 1974, pp. 199–219), and reprinted in *Classics In Voting Behavior*, edited by Richard Niemi and Herbert Weisberg (Washington, D.C.: CQ Press, 1992).

[4]Among his many writings, see his edited book with Russell J. Dalton and Scott Flanagan, *Electoral Change in Advanced Industrial Democracies: Realignment or Dealignment?* (Princeton, NJ: Princeton University Press, 1984).

of the most difficult questions to study—how candidates and their campaigns shape and are shaped by electoral forces.[5] This interaction links the two most important components of the party, elections and governance, into a more coherent whole. It has allowed her to bring clarity to what has become an increasingly confused portion of the field. Marjorie also has closely studied the role of gender in politics, a dimension of party politics that has not only been of long-standing importance from at least the granting of women's suffrage, but has also become especially critical with the emergence and growth of the "gender gap."[6] Finally, she has made a long series of contributions to help us understand how to bring meaning to complex events.[7] One special feature of this book is the increased use of narratives from well-known and little-known party figures alike, narratives that serve to bring the subject matter to life.

One issue critical to all who study American politics is the understanding that politics matters in your life, that this is your government, and that the political parties are ways in which you can help shape what your government and elected officials do. This is one of the most important meanings of American political parties. They, and the government they create, are the consequences of you and your political actions. So saying allows me to move more directly to the longer answer about the study of political parties themselves.

At the outset, I mentioned that you should want to study political parties because they are so important to virtually everything that happens in American politics and because political parties are so central to the workings of any democracy. Great, but you are probably asking, "So what questions should I keep in mind as I read this book; what questions will help me understand the material better?" Let me propose three questions as guidelines, ones that are neither too specific nor too general. We are looking, that is, for questions somewhere in between "Are parties good?" on the one hand, and "Why did the House Minority Leader, Tom DeLay (R., TX), speak so strongly against campaign finance reform on February 13, 2002?" on the other hand.

You are well aware that today politicians can appear magnanimous and statesman-like if they say that they will be non-partisan, and if they call for Congress to "rise above" partisan politics to be bipartisan. And yet, essentially every elected official is a partisan, and essentially every elected official chooses to act in a partisan way much of the time. Why do politicians today, you might ask, speak as if they are of two minds about political parties? Perhaps they actually are. And even if you dismiss this rhetoric as just words, it is the case that the public is of two minds about parties, too.

---

[5]See especially her books, *Running for Office: The Political Education of Campaigners* (Chatham, NJ: Chatham House, 1984) and *The Making of Campaign Strategy* (Lexington, Mass: D.C. Heath-Lexington, 1974).

[6]An especially interesting account of the ways the political parties reacted to female suffrage can be found in Anna L. Harvey, *Votes without Leverage: Women in American Electoral Politics, 1920–1970* (Cambridge: Cambridge University Press, 1998)

[7]See, for example, "Constructing Explanations for U.S. State Governors' Races: The Abortion Issue and the 1990 Gubernatorial Elections," *Political Communication* 17 (July-September, 2000), 239–262, "The Meaning of a Mandate: Interpretations of 'Mandate' in 1984 Presidential Election Coverage," *Polity* (Winter, 1995), 225–254, and "Support for Political Woman: Sex Roles," in John C. Pierce and John L. Sullivan, eds., *The Electorate Reconsidered* (Beverly Hills, Cal.: Sage, 1980) 179–198.

This book, like virtually all written about American political parties, includes quotes from the Founding Fathers warning about the dangers of party and faction, often quoting such luminaries as John Adams, Thomas Jefferson, and James Madison. And yet, these very same men not only worried about the dangers of party, they also were the founders and first leaders of our first political parties. So the first question is why are people—leaders and followers, founders and contemporary figures, alike—both attracted to and repulsed by political parties?

Let me suggest two books that might give you additional ways to think about this question. One is Richard Hofstadter's *The Idea of a Party System: The Rise of Legitimate Opposition in the United States, 1780–1840* (Berkeley, Cal.: University of California Press, 1969). This book is a series of public lectures Hofstadter gave in which he roots political parties deeply into the American democratic tradition, arguing that they represent the outward manifestation of a change in philosophic understanding of the relationship between citizens and leaders in this, the world's first practicing democracy. Austin Ranney in *Curing the Mischiefs of Faction: Party Reform in America* (Berkeley, Cal.: University of California Press, 1975) connects Hofstadter's view of the role of philosophic ideas and American democratic practice from our first 60 years to the contemporary era. Ranney was a leading scholar of political parties. But in this case he was also writing this book in reflection upon his time spent as a member of the so-called "McGovern-Fraser Reform Commission," which revised the rules for the Democratic Party, and advocated the reforms that led to the current presidential primary system. Thus, there is both a theoretical and practical dimension to this work.

This question of the purpose of parties in our democracy, both theoretical and practical, leads easily into a second major question that should be in your mind as you work through this book and your course. How does the individual connect to the political party? There are two aspects to this question. One is fairly direct—what do parties mean to the individual and how, if at all, has this changed over time? The great work that laid out this relationship in the modern era is *The American Voter* by Angus Campbell, Philip E. Converse, Warren E. Miller, and Donald E. Stokes (New York: John Wiley, 1960). Many argue that this connection has changed fundamentally. At one extreme, Martin P. Wattenberg has written about the declining relevance of political parties to the voter, such as in his *The Decline of American Political Parties, 1952–1996* (Cambridge, Mass.: Harvard University Press, 1998), using such striking evidence as a dramatic decline in the willingness or ability of citizens to say what they like or dislike about either of our two major political parties. Others disagree with Wattenberg. Larry Bartels, for example, has shown that partisanship remains as influential in shaping the vote as ever.[8] A second dimension of the question is whether any apparent decline, irrelevance, or dealignment of parties reflects growing distancing from the government itself. It is certainly the case that today we hear people say, "The government, they …, " and not, "The government, we…." I suspect few of us think that way, either. It is certainly common to hear politicians call for a tax cut by claiming that doing so will give the people back their money. Such a statement wouldn't make sense if we thought of the government as being composed of us, ourselves, and thus thought of our taxes as sending our money to work in

[8]Larry M. Bartels, "Partisanship and Voting Behavior, 1952–1996," *American Journal of Political Science* 44 (2000): 35–50.

our government, doing our bidding by enacting our preferences into legislation selected by our representatives whom we chose. The question can, however, be cast even more broadly, asking whether or not the people feel removed from social, cultural, economic, and political institutions, generally, with political parties and the government therefore only one more symptom of a larger ill. This, certainly, is a part of the concerns that motivate Robert D. Putnam in his *Bowling Alone: The Collapse and Revival of American Community* (New York: Simon & Schuster, 2000).

The change from a trusting, supportive, identified public to one apparently dramatically less so is one of the great changes that took place in American politics over the last half century. A second great change is what is often called "polarization," a growing distance between the elected officials of the two parties. That is, compared to fifty years ago, today the Democrats are more liberal and consistently more so than Republicans, who in turn are much more conservative than in the Eisenhower administration. While this is not to say that there is anything close to an identical set of beliefs by the members of either party, there is a greater coherence of opinion and belief in, say, the congressional delegations of each party than in earlier times. Even more undeniable is a much clearer divergence between the policy interests and choices of the two parties than, say, fifty years ago. You might refer to Jon R. Bond and Richard Fleisher, eds., *Polarized Politics: Congress and the President in a Partisan Era* (Washington, D.C.: CQ Press, 2000) for a variety of indications of this fact. The question then is not whether there is greater polarization today, the question is whether this relative clarity of polarization matters. As usual, there are at least two ways to understand the question. One is simply to ask whether a more polarized Congress yields different policies from a less polarized one. The readings in Bond and Fleisher generally support that position. Others, for example, Keith Krehbiel in *Pivotal Politics: A Theory of U.S. Lawmaking* (Chicago, Ill.: University of Chicago Press, 1998) and David W. Brady and Craig Volden in *Revolving Gridlock: Politics and Policy from Carter to Clinton* (Boulder, Colo.: Westview Press, 1998) argue that the Founders' creation of checks and balances makes polarization relatively ineffectual in shaping legislation, due to vetoes, compromises necessary between the two chambers, and so on. Even more generally, however, David R. Mayhew has argued in *Divided We Govern: Party Control, Lawmaking, and Investigations, 1946–1990* (New Haven, Conn.: Yale University Press, 1991) that our system generates important legislation regardless of which party is in control, or whether they share power under divided partisan control of government (as, for example, we have in 2002). This carefully considered argument raises the question of whether the party really matters or not. As you might expect, there has been considerable interest in the challenge that Mayhew, Krehbiel, and Brady and Volden have raised. One set of responses can be seen in the Bond and Fleisher volume. Another can be found in Robert S. Erikson, Michael B. MacKuen, and James A. Stimson's book, *The Macro Polity* (Cambridge, UK: Cambridge University Press, 2002).

As you can see, we have now reached the point of very recently published work. We are, that is, asking questions that are motivating the work of scholars today. So, let's get on with it and turn to the book and the study of political parties themselves.

JOHN H. ALDRICH
DUKE UNIVERSITY

Preface

This is a wonderful time to explore party politics. After decades of discussion of party decline, in which some writers even predicted the demise of the American political parties, we now have much fuller information about the nature of the changes that have affected the Democrats and the Republicans—and us. We've learned that both major parties have grown stronger in an organizational sense, especially at the national level, but also in the states and in many localities. The parties in Congress are increasingly polarized and the gulf between Democratic and Republican activists has widened as well, inflamed by intense partisan conflict. Party is back as a powerful influence on voting—at least among the relatively small proportion of Americans who rouse themselves to go to the polls. Intrigued by these changes, students and activists are paying increasing attention to the vital roles of parties in American life.

And yet, even though these changes seem to have reinvigorated the Democratic and Republican parties, they have not recreated the large-scale grassroots organizations that controlled many big cities' governments in the late 1800s. The parties are living in a different world now. It is a world in which voters, not party leaders, decide who the party's candidates will be, powerful interest groups play a big part in the recruiting and funding of candidates, and elections at the local level are usually nonpartisan. So the recent trends have helped revitalize the parties, but only as one of many competitors for influence on candidates and voters.

In preparing this edition of *Party Politics in America,* I have had the great advantage of building on the foundation provided by Frank J. Sorauf and Paul Allen Beck, two of the foremost scholars of political parties. Sorauf created the first edition of this text and continued to strengthen subsequent editions for almost two decades. Beck faced the challenge of moving the book into the late 1980s and 1990s, and did so with the intellectual vision and the meticulous care that has marked his research on parties and voting.

The book that they nurtured has long been known as the "gold standard" of political parties texts. Instructors and students have valued the previous editions because they have provided, quite simply, the most thorough and definitive coverage of the field. From party history to the tripartite nature of the American parties, from conceptions of realignment to the fascinating details of campaign finance, these editions of *Party Politics in America* have been both an essential reference and an invitation to a generation of students. The current edition is designed to build on the book's great strengths—its comprehensive coverage, conceptual clarity and the comparative perspective on the American parties that is so necessary for American students—and to make it even more readable, contemporary and inviting.

This edition of the book, the first as a Longman Classic in Political Science, differs from previous editions in a number of ways. You'll find two new features designed to draw students into the fascination of party politics. One, "A Day in the Life," tells readers the personal stories of individuals, from college students to judges, whose lives have been caught up in the currents of party change. Many of my students see political parties as remote, abstract, and a bit unseemly—something that might interest elderly people, but not teens and twentysomethings. I hope these stories will change their minds. From a young black woman who became a Republican activist to keep the party from being influenced by racists, to the struggle of Senator John Ashcroft's campaign when his Democratic rival died in a plane crash ("How Do You Run Against a Dead Man?"), these are compelling stories that can show readers why studying party politics is worth their time.

In other chapters, the feature titled "Which Would You Choose?" presents students with major debates about the parties: for example, whether encouraging greater voter turnout would help or harm American democracy (see Chapter 8); whether stronger national parties could improve voters' choices or interfere with them (in Chapter 4); and whether legislators ought to be listening mainly to their legislative party leaders or to their constituents (in Chapter 13). These summaries, using the point-counterpoint format with which undergraduates are familiar, could serve as the basis for class debate on these and many other fundamental concerns.

Chapter 3 has been extensively updated to include new research about the structure and activities of state and local parties. Chapters 6 and 7, dealing with parties in the electorate, have been restructured to make them even easier to follow. Discussion of the development of party identification takes place in Chapter 6, so that Chapter 7 can then introduce the ideas of party coalitions, party change, realignment and dealignment. In Chapters 8 and 11, we address the problems and inequities in voting–not just the inadequate voting machines that regularly leave some citizens' ballots uncounted, but the disproportionate burden of poor voting systems on poor communities–that were made so painfully obvious by the Florida vote recounts in 2000 and 2001. Chapter 12 contains an up-to-date treatment of soft money (including the congressional reforms passed in spring, 2002), issue advocacy, and their impact on the parties. In chapter 15, with a discussion of the "semi-responsible parties," we help students understand why even the party polarization of the early 2000s can fall short of the vision of party accountability promoted by reformers for decades.

There are many other changes as well. "Party Politics on the Internet," a section added in the ninth edition to guide students into the engaging world of political parties' Web sites, has been greatly expanded. Students can use it to explore almost two dozen American third parties, from the Prohibition Party (now remade as a Christian right organization) to the Southern Independence Party, as well as major-party organizations from College Democrats and Republicans to the Log Cabin Republicans (a gay and lesbian Republican group). More sites are listed that provide data and opinions about campaign finance, polling, media, and a range of political issues, and the section suggesting possible paper and in-class assignments has also been beefed up.

And, of course, all aspects of the book have been updated with examples and information from the 2000 elections. From data in tables and figures to stories about the campaigns of George W. Bush, Hillary Rodham Clinton, John Ashcroft, and Ralph Nader, the book reflects the excitement of current politics and elections as well as the patterns of party politics over time.

Many people deserve credit for their help with this edition. I am grateful to my colleagues, present and past, in the Department of Political Science at Indiana University, and especially to Bob Huckfeldt, Ted Carmines, John Williams, Leroy Rieselbach, Jerry Wright,

Yvette Alex-Assensoh, Ken Bickers, and Pat Sellers. Members of the department's staff have been indispensable to my efforts: Margaret Anderson, Fern Bennett, Paula Cotner, Scott Feickert, Steve Flinn, Marsha Franklin, Loretta Heyen, Sharon LaRoche, and James Russell. Gary Hetland has been a very capable research assistant. And my thanks go to my graduate and undergraduate students, who have always been the best and most honest judges of what matters in American politics.

It is an honor for me to recognize Austin Ranney, Leon Epstein, and Jack Dennis, who were most responsible for my interest in party politics and for the strength of the training I received in political science. Murray Edelman deserves special mention in that group, not only as a mentor and model for so many of us but also as a much-beloved friend. John Aldrich, one of the most insightful and systematic analysts of political parties, was kind enough to write a Foreword to this edition. Other political scientists have also been among my best and favorite teachers: Bruce Oppenheimer, Gerry Pomper, Tony Broh, Jennifer Hochschild, Burdett Loomis, Richard Fenno, Jeffrey Berry, Ada Finifter, Anthony King, John Kingdon, Mike Kirn, Brian Silver, Jim Stimson, and Brian Vargus. And I am most grateful for the help of Stephanie Curtis, Kathy Frankovic, Curtis Gans, Alan Gitelson, Sheldon Goldman, John Green, Sean Greene, Rick Hardy, Paul Herrnson, Judge Michael Hoff, David Magleby, Bill Mayer, Jeanette Morehouse, Reggie Sheehan, Robin Vuke, Brad Warren, and Jinghua Zou.

Reviewers of the ninth edition—Matthew Corrigan, University of North Florida; Diane Heith, St. John's University; and Joseph K. Unekis, Kansas State University—were generous with their constructive comments. And it continues to be a pleasure to work with the people at Longman, whose great efforts and goodwill did not flag even in the face of the terrorism and anthrax attacks that took place so near them last fall in New York: Editor Eric Stano, Brian VanBuren, and Scott Hitchcock and the other members of the Electronic Publishing Services Inc. production team.

Above all, I am deeply grateful to my family: my husband, Howard, and our daughters, Katie, Lissa, Lani, and Hannah. Everything I do has been made possible by their love and support.

MARJORIE RANDON HERSHEY
BLOOMINGTON, INDIANA
MARCH, 2002

Parties
and Party
Systems

If the writers of the American Constitution were to return today for a look at the government they had designed, they would probably be stunned at its size and scope. Imagine how James Madison might react to a congressional debate on rules governing the cloning of human cells or the taxing of clothes and plane tickets sold on the Internet. Government activity touches every part of our lives, from the number of bacteria allowed in our hamburgers to the questions asked on our drivers' license tests. Who makes these decisions? How can we hold them responsible if their decisions harm us? It is the political system that plays the crucial role in deciding, as in Harold Lasswell's phrase, "who gets what, when, how."[1]

Because government decisions affect almost everything we do, large numbers of groups have mobilized to try to influence these decisions, as well as the selection of the men and women who will make them. In a democracy, the political party is one of the oldest and most important of these groups. It has a great deal of competition, however. Organized interests, such as the National Rifle Association, the Sierra Club, and their fund-raising political action committees (PACs) also try to get their views adopted by government. So do pro-life and pro-choice groups, the Christian Coalition, and People for the Ethical Treatment of Animals. Even organizations whose main purpose is nonpolitical, such as universities, beer manufacturers, and teachers' unions, try to influence government decisions that affect their livelihoods.

All these groups serve as *intermediaries* between citizens and the people in government who make the decisions that affect our lives (see Figure I.1). By bringing together people with shared interests, these groups amplify people's voices when speaking to government. They raise issues that they want government to solve. They bring back information about what government is doing. In these ways, parties and organized interests, along with television and the other media, become the links between citizens and political power.

Different intermediaries specialize in different political activities. Parties focus on nominating candidates, helping to elect them, and organizing the activities of those who win. Most organized interests represent narrower groups; they are unlikely to win majorities, so they try, instead, to influence the views of elected and appointed officials and

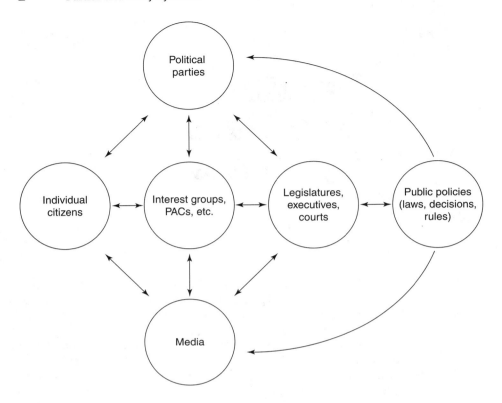

FIGURE I.1   Parties and Other Intermediaries Between Citizens and Government.

even other organized interests. Still others work mainly to affect public opinion and media portrayals of an issue. Groups like these in other democracies may play different roles. The American parties, for example, tend to concentrate on election activities, whereas parties in Europe have been more committed to spreading ideologies and keeping their elected officials faithful to the party's program.

Intermediary groups are in constant competition as they fight to win political power. Parties, of course, compete with one another. They compete with powerful interest groups for the attention of legislators and for a dominant role in political campaigns; in fact, the American parties are not nearly as dominant in the business of campaigning as they were a century ago. They vie with one another for access to the scarce resources of money, expertise, and volunteer help and then, with those resources in hand, for the support of individual citizens and elected officials. Parties, in short, share a number of activities with other kinds of political groups and resemble these groups in some important ways.

They do this, however, in a culture that has mixed feelings about their value. On the one hand, many writers have celebrated the American parties as the "architects" of democratic government and the tools we use to govern ourselves. They have been called the "distinguishing marks" of modern government[2] and the means by which fledgling democracies, from Eastern Europe to Africa, can make the transition to a democratic system.[3]

On the other hand, political parties have been the targets of suspicion and ridicule since this nation began. James Madison and the other founders were very wary of organized factions in their new republic. About a century later, the Progressive movement—reformers intent on rooting out political corruption and returning power to middle-class people like themselves—targeted the parties' "boss rule" as the enemy to overcome. Disgust with party power in the 1960s and 1970s led to another series of party reforms that have helped to reshape current politics. Many Americans remain skeptical and even hostile to the idea of political parties.[4]

The hostile climate of public opinion has led, in turn, to a host of restrictions on how parties can organize and what they can do. Parties have adapted to these rules over time by changing their organizations and the nature of their activities. The political parties of the early 2000s would not be recognizable to politicians of a century ago, and the parties we know today may change dramatically in the coming decades.

The aim of this book is to explore the American parties: how they have developed, how they affect us, and what they are capable of contributing to democratic politics. Given the rise of the Internet, the growth of single-issue groups, and the many other ways in which we can learn about and affect government, it is worth asking whether political parties are really as essential to the survival of a democracy as many have assumed. Are they a boon to both candidates and voters, or do they deserve the distrust with which so many Americans view them? Let us begin by examining the parties as they evolved in and adapted to the American political environment.

In Search of the Political Parties

Try to picture American politics without political parties. Many have found it an attractive thought; George Washington, for example, stated in his Farewell Address: "Let me warn you in the most solemn manner against the baneful effects of the spirit of party," which he considered the "worst enemy" of popular government. A lot of contemporary Americans agree; in survey after survey, many respondents say that they think of political parties with suspicion—like the cat at the bird feeder—when they think of them at all.

Imagine, then, that we heed Washington's message in the coming presidential campaign and magically make the parties disappear. There will be no party organizations to run the primary elections and no party leaders to select or support the candidates. Would we do a better job of choosing a president?

Of course, another way will have to be found to sort through the few hundred thousand presidential wanna-bes and select a very few to run in the general election. Without party primaries and caucuses, who would make that decision? Members of Congress? Not in a system designed to have separated powers. A convention of organized interests such as the National Rifle Association and Handgun Control, Inc.? A panel of judges selected by *People* magazine? The answer is not obvious, though it is obviously vital to our future.

Assuming that problem is solved, many other challenges remain. Strong party organizations help bring voters to the polls. Without any political parties, will voter turnout, already remarkably low in the United States, drop even further? Most people are not very interested in politics, so how will they decide to vote for a candidate if they do not have the guidance that party labels provide? Will they spend hours researching where each candidate stands on the issues, or will they choose the candidate who looks the best on television? When the new president takes office, how will he or she gain majority support for new programs from a Congress elected as individuals, with no party loyalties to link them?

What is this political organization that is so necessary and yet so distrusted? How can we distinguish a party from a temporary alliance of disgruntled politicians, an interest group, or a mass movement? What is included in the concept of party? Is it a group of politicians who share a party label when seeking and holding public offices? Is it the activists who work in the headquarters and on the campaigns? Is it the citizens who regularly vote for candidates bearing one party's label? Or is a party any grouping that chooses to call itself a party, whether Democratic or Boston Tea?

Political parties can be different things to different people. As the following box shows, even analysts do not always agree on a definition of "party." What are the essential features of parties and what makes the parties unique as agents of political power?

What is a Political Party?
Some Alternative Definitions[1]

A party aims to promote certain policies:

> [A] party is a body of men united, for promoting by their joint endeavors the national interest, upon some particular principle in which they are all agreed.

Edmund Burke (1770)

It works to gain power in government:

> In the broadest sense, a political party is a coalition of men seeking to control the governing apparatus by legal means ... [through] duly constituted elections or legitimate influence.

Anthony Downs (1957)

It inspires loyalty among voters:

> [A] political party in the modern sense may be thought of as a relatively durable social formation which seeks offices or power in government, exhibits a structure or organization which links leaders at the centers of government to a significant popular following in the political arena and its local enclaves, and generates in-group perspectives or at least symbols of identification or loyalty.

William Nisbet Chambers (1967)

It is an organization with rules and durability:

> Political parties can be seen as coalitions of elites to capture and use political office.... (But) a political party is ... more than a coalition. A major political party is an institutionalized coalition, one that has adopted rules, norms, and procedures.

John H. Aldrich (1995)

A political party is all of the above:

> Within the body of voters as a whole, groups are formed of persons who regard themselves as party members.... In another sense the term party may refer to the group of more or less professional political workers.... At times party denotes groups within the government.... Often it refers to an entity which rolls into one the party-in-the-electorate, the professional political group, the party-in-the-legislature, and the party-in-the-government.... In truth, this all-encompassing usage has its legitimate applications for all the types of groups called party interact more or less closely and at times may be as one.

V. O. Key, Jr. (1958)

A THREE-PART DEFINITION OF PARTIES

These differing views of party raise a few major themes. Edmund Burke sees a party as a group of like-minded people who share a common set of values or stands on issues. As reasonable as this sounds, policy-based definitions are not often used by students of the American political parties. Parties in the United States are not very ideological or passionately unified on policies, at least in comparison with some European parties. Defining parties solely as groups of ideologically like-minded people also makes it hard to distinguish parties from single-issue and splinter groups.

Most definitions of parties focus on other dimensions. Many scholars, such as Anthony Downs and Leon Epstein, see parties as teams of leaders united in their effort to control government by winning elections and other means. Others, like William Nisbet Chambers and V. O. Key, Jr., prefer a broader definition that includes not only leaders and activists but also ordinary voters. John Aldrich reminds us that parties are not just groups of people; they are institutions that have a life, and a set of rules, of their own.[2]

All these observers agree that officeholders and candidates who share the same party label are a vital part of the parties. Many parties in democratic nations, including the United States, were first formed as groups of political leaders who organized to promote certain programs. It is understandable, then, why some definitions of party center on elected leaders and those who are running to replace them.

But most observers see the American parties as including more than just candidates and officeholders. In some communities, the parties have offices, phone listings, and virtually everywhere, they have official standing under state law. Interested individuals can join them, work within them, become officers, and take part in setting their goals and strategies, just as one would do in a softball league, a sorority, or a Teamsters Union local (or even in yogic flying; see box below). These activists and organizations are central parts of the party, too.

Is This a Party?

In early September 2000, the Natural Law Party formed a coalition with the Reform Party. As one reporter pointed out, with understatement, "They'll have to iron out a few differences in philosophy." Ross Perot, the multimillionaire who founded the Reform Party and ran as its 1996 presidential candidate, stood for such issues as congressional term limits and reduction of the national debt. When Perot declined to run again in 2000, one faction of his party turned to pugilistic conservative commentator Pat Buchanan as its candidate. Anti-Buchanan Reform activists looked for another alternative.

The candidate they found was John Hagelin, who was also the leader of the Natural Law Party. Begun by followers of the Maharishi Mahesh Yogi, a Hindu guru, Hagelin's party calls for conflict-free politics based on Transcendental Meditation (TM). That, they believe, will reduce crime, violence, sickness, and accidents in the United States. An important accompaniment to TM is "yogic flying," in which meditation is said to lift the individual's body off the ground, inch by inch, beginning with "hopping" and, eventually, sailing away.

(box continued)

Some of the more earthbound Reform Party activists struggled mightily to mesh with their new Natural Law allies. "I don't know anything about yogic flying, but I had a sled, an American Flyer, when I was a kid," said Perot's former aide, Russ Verney, at the Natural Law convention. Another worried Reform worker asked Hagelin if he could fly, and was reassured that the answer was no. Whether he was further reassured by the candidate's acceptance speech, in which Hagelin declared that, "the unified field percolates infant universes at the rate of 10 to the 143rd per cubic centimeter per second," was not noted.

Source for the quotations: Dana Milbank, "The Reform Party, Feelin' Guru-vy," *Washington Post,* Sept. 2, 2000, p. C1.

It is tempting to close our definition at this point, and to view the American parties solely as teams of political specialists—elected officials, candidates, party leaders, activists, and organizations—who compete for power and then exercise it. That leaves the rest of the population on the outside of the parties, a position that many citizens may well prefer. It is a neat, well-structured definition that could guide us in examining changes in the form parties have taken over the course of American history.[3]

Yet this definition ignores an important reality about political parties. As intermediaries between government and the public, parties are rooted in the lives and feelings of citizens, as well as candidates and activists. Even though the American parties have no formal, dues-paying "members," many voters develop such strong and enduring attachments to a particular party that they are willing to make their commitment public by registering to vote as a Democrat or a Republican and actively supporting their party's candidates. Further, when observers refer to a "Republican realignment" or a "Democratic area," they see parties that include voters as well as officeholders, office seekers, and activists.

The Progressive movement of the early 1900s, which promoted party registration and the practice of nominating candidates in primary elections, strengthened the case for including a citizen base in a definition of American parties. Voters in primary elections make the single most important decision for their party: who its candidates will be. In most other democracies, only a thin layer of party leaders and activists have the power to make this choice.

Because American voters have the power to nominate the parties' candidates, as well as to elect them, the line that separates party leaders from followers in some other nations becomes blurred in the United States. American voters are not only consumers who choose among the parties' "products" (candidates) in the political marketplace, but also managers who decide just what products will be introduced in the first place. Making consumers into managers has transformed political parties, just as it would revolutionize the market economy. Taking this into account in our definition of parties makes for a messier concept of political party, but a more realistic one in the American setting.

In short, we can most accurately see the major American political parties as having three interacting parts. These three are: the ***party organization***, which includes party leaders and the many activists who work for party causes and candidates; the ***party in*** *government,* comprised of the men and women who run for public office on the party's label and who hold public office; and the ***party in the electorate,*** or those citizens who identify themselves as supporters of the party (see Figure 1.1).[4] We will explore each of these parts separately, keeping in mind that the character of the American parties is defined by the ways they interact, especially in the electoral process.[5]

The Party Organization

Party organizations are groups of people who work to promote *all* of the party's candidates and its perspectives on major issues; this contrasts with individual candidates, whose main concern must be their own chances of winning. Party organizations contain those who hold jobs with titles—the national and state party chairs and officers, the county, city, ward and precinct leaders and committee people—and those who don't, but who are devoted enough to give their time, money, and skills to the party. Some party leaders or activists may be waiting for the right time to run for public office (and thus cross over into the party in government); others have been pressed into service as candidates for Congress or mayor when nobody else wants the job. But many party activists

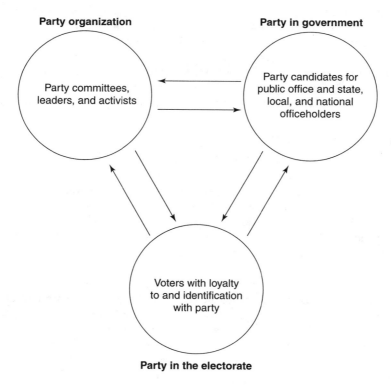

FIGURE 1.1 The Three Parts of American Political Parties.

prefer the tasks of answering phones in the party headquarters and plotting strategy, in contrast with the frenetic days and anxious nights that are the life of a political candidate.

The Party in Government

The party in government is made up of the candidates for public office and those who hold office, whether elected or appointed, who share a party label. The major figures here are presidents, governors, judges, mayors, Congress members, state legislators, bureaucrats, and local officials who share the same party affiliation.

The relationship between the party in government and the party organization is like that of siblings: part devotion and part rivalry. They regularly work together to meet shared goals, but they may have different priorities in reaching those goals. A member of Congress, for example, may be trying to raise as much campaign money as possible because she wants a big victory that will boost her chances of later running for president. At the same time, the party organization's leaders may instead be hoping to convince the same campaign contributors to support more vulnerable party candidates, in the hope of winning a party majority in Congress.

These two parts of the parties also jockey for leadership of the party as a whole. When reporters want to get a "Republican view" on an issue, they will usually interview a source in the White House or a Republican leader in Congress; these members of the party in government are often assumed to speak for the party. The chair of the Republican National Committee, and maybe even the party's platform, may hold a different view on that issue. But presidents and congressional party leaders do not have to clear their pronouncements with the party organization, nor can they be controlled by it. These tensions, which lead the party organization and the party in government to compete for scarce resources, demonstrate why it's helpful to treat them as separate parts of the party.

The Party in the Electorate

The party in the electorate is the least well-defined of the three parts. It consists of the men and women who *see themselves* as Democrats or Republicans: citizens who feel some degree of loyalty to the party, who normally vote for its candidates in primaries and the general election, even if they have never set foot in the party's headquarters or dealt with its leaders and activists. Many of these **partisans** have declared themselves to be a Democrat or Republican when they registered to vote; more than half the states prescribe party registration. But others regard themselves as partisans even if they do not register to vote under a party label.

These members of the electoral party are regular consumers of the party's candidates and appeals. But they are not under the control of the party organization. In general elections, they may vote for one party candidate and reject another; in primaries, they may decide to saddle the party with a candidate the organization can't stand. But they are vitally important as the core of the party's electoral support; without this base, the party would have to work much harder to win power.

This relationship between the party organization and party in government, on the one hand, and the electoral party, on the other, is one of the most striking characteristics of the major American parties. Other political organizations—interest groups such as labor unions and environmental groups—try to attract supporters beyond their members and workers, but these supporters remain outside the group's organization. That is not true of American parties. The party in the electorate is more than an external group to be mobilized. In addition to its power to choose the parties' candidates by voting in primaries, in many states the electoral party helps select local party officials, such as ward and precinct committee leaders. So the major American party is an open, inclusive, semipublic organization. In its combination of organization and electorate, it stands apart from other political organizations and from parties in other democracies.

To further complicate matters, the relationships among the three parts of each major party differ from one state to another. In a few states, the party organization may dominate the party in government, whereas in others, the reverse is the case. The parties also differ from state to state in the extent to which party identifiers can help nominate their party's candidates. Voters in many states must register with the party before election day in order to vote in its primary, while in a few other states a voter can choose among the primary candidates of both parties on the same ballot. The Republicans and the Democrats are so decentralized and diverse that almost every state party has its own distinctive mix.

WHAT PARTIES DO

Political parties in every democracy engage in three sets of activities to at least some degree: they select candidates and contest elections; they try to educate citizens about issues important to the party, and they work to convince elected officials to support particular policies and provide other benefits, such as patronage jobs.[6] Parties and party systems differ in the degree to which they emphasize these individual activities, but no party can completely ignore any of them.

Electing Candidates

Parties often seem to be completely absorbed by their efforts to elect candidates. Electoral activity so dominates the life of the American party that its metabolism follows almost exactly the cycles of the election calendar. Party activity reaches a peak at election time; between elections, most parties go into hibernation. Parties are goal-oriented and in American politics achieving one's goals ultimately depends on winning elections. The three parts of parties may have their differences, but they are brought together in their shared intention to elect party candidates.

Educating (or Propagandizing) Citizens

The American parties carry on a series of loosely related activities intended to teach or propagandize citizens. Clearly, the Democrats and Republicans do not promote all-inclusive ideologies like those of a European Marxist party; some observers even argue that the major American parties are allergic to taking specific stands on issues. They do, however, represent the interests and issue preferences of the groups that identify with and support them. In this sense, the Republicans and Democrats can be seen as the parties of business or labor and of the wealthy or the disadvantaged. Further, party differences on issues have become clearer since the 1960s. In presidential politics alone, the Reagan conservatism of the 1980s, the McGovern liberalism of 1972, and the Goldwater conservatism of 1964 show how ideas can guide the major parties' political activities.

Governing

Almost all American national and state elected officials ran for office as either Democrats or Republicans, and their partisan perspectives affect every aspect of the way government works. The legislatures of 49 states[7] and the United States Congress are organized along party lines. When legislatures face controversial issues, party cohesion may break down. Yet, in general, there is a surprising degree of party discipline in voting on legislation. In executive branches, presidents and governors usually choose cabinet officers and agency heads of their own party. Even the courts show evidence of the organizing and directing touch of the parties, though in more subtle ways.

The American parties, however, don't have a monopoly on any of these three activities. They compete regularly with interest groups, other political organizations, and even the media in all these areas. Even though the parties organize state legislatures and Congress, they must constantly (and often unsuccessfully) battle interest groups and constituency pressures to influence legislators' votes on major bills. In nominating candidates, especially at the local level, parties face tremendous competition from interest groups and powerful local personalities, who may each be sponsoring pet candidates. In promoting issues, the major parties are often overshadowed by the fervor of minor (third) parties, rafts of interest groups and other political groupings, individual public figures, and the media.

The nature of any party's activities affects the balance of power among the party's three parts. American parties' emphasis on election activities, for example, gives the party in government an unusual degree of power, even dominance. It can often leave the party organization in the shadows when competing for the attention of the party in the electorate. In parties more strongly linked to issues and ideologies—European parties, for instance—party organizations are more likely to be able to dictate to the legislative parties.

However, individuals from all three sectors of the party may come together for specific activities. Party organization activists committed to a particular elected official may join with other members of the party in government and with loyal party voters to return that official to office. When the election is won or lost, they will probably drift apart again. These groups of individuals from different parts of a party, drawn together to achieve a particular goal, are like the nuclei of the party.[8] In American politics, alliances and coalitions are far more common within the parties than between them.

THE RESULTS OF PARTY ACTIVITY

Parties have important effects on the functioning of American politics. As the parties work to elect candidates, convince voters, and influence leaders, they help shape the democratic process in many other ways as well:[9]

> First, parties help people make sense of the complexities of politics. Parties simplify issues and elections so that citizens can make sensible choices even when they don't have much information about politics. Voters can use their party attachments as guides for assessing issues and candidates. By helping citizens form political judgments, parties make it easier for people to be politically active. Further, parties preach the value of political commitment. In these ways, they take

part in the political socialization—political learning—of the American electorate by transmitting political information and values to large numbers of current and future voters.

Second, the American parties help aggregate and organize political power. They put together masses of individuals and groups into blocs that are powerful enough to govern or to oppose those who govern. So in the political world, as well as within the individual, parties help to focus political loyalties on a small number of alternatives and then to build support for them.

Because they devote so much effort to contesting elections, the parties dominate the recruitment of political leaders. Biographies of the members of any legislature, a cabinet, or even the courts will show how many of them entered public service through a political party or through partisan candidacy for office. Because the parties work at all levels of government from local to national, they may encourage the movement of leaders from one level to another. Further, because they are constants in the election process, parties help to make changes in government leadership more routine and orderly. In nations where parties are not stable from one election to the next, leadership changes can be much more disruptive.

Finally, the American parties help unify a divided American political system. The government was designed to fragment political power, to make sure that no single group could gain enough of it to become a tyrant. The division between the national government and the states, multiplied by the separation of powers at each level, does an impressive job of fragmenting power. The challenge, of course, is to enable these fragmented units to work together to solve problems. The two major national parties bring a unifying force into American politics. Their ability to bridge the separation of powers has limits, but the major parties can provide a basis for cooperation in a government marked by decentralization and division.

THE SPECIAL CHARACTERISTICS OF POLITICAL PARTIES

We have seen that parties have a lot of competition as intermediaries in politics. *All* political organizations, not just parties, try to organize and mobilize their supporters either to win public office or to influence those who do win. How, then, do parties differ from these other political organizations, and especially from big, nationally organized interest groups?[10]

Parties are Paramount in Elections

Above all, a party can be distinguished from other political organizations by its focus on contesting elections. Other political groups may be involved in elections, even extensively involved. Interest groups encourage candidates to run for office (and discourage others from running), contribute to their campaigns, and get their members to the polls on election day. Other nonparty groups may do the same. The parties, however, are paramount among political groups in contesting elections. Their names and symbols are the ones the states include on most ballots. Candidates are listed on the ballot as "Democrat" or "Republican," not as "National Rifle Association" or "Sierra Club."

They Have a Full-time Commitment to Political Activity

The major American parties, and similar parties elsewhere, are fully committed to political activity; it is the sole purpose of their existence. Interest groups and most other political organizations, in contrast, move freely and frequently from political to nonpolitical activities and back again. The AFL-CIO, for example, is fundamentally concerned with collective bargaining for better pay and working conditions. It may turn to political action to support sympathetic candidates or to lobby Congress for favorable legislation, but its interests are rooted in the workplace. Parties live entirely in the political world.

They Mobilize Large Numbers

An interest group, such as a pork producers' association, does not need millions of supporters in order to try to influence a congressional subcommittee or the Department of Agriculture; it may be able to succeed with only a few strategists and a small, well-mobilized clientele. Because winning elections is so vital to parties' goals, however, parties must recruit and mobilize an enormous range of supporters to win large numbers of races. The result is that in a system such as that of the United States, party appeals must be broad and inclusive; a major party cannot afford to represent only a narrow range of concerns.

They Endure

Political parties, at least in the United States, are also unusually stable and long-lived. Personal cliques, factions, campaign organizations, and even many interest groups are fleeting by comparison. The size and abstractness of the parties, and their ability to transcend individual candidates give them a much longer life. Both major American parties can trace their histories for much more than a century, and the major parties of other Western democracies also have impressive life spans. This remarkable endurance adds to their value for voters. The parties are there as points of reference, year after year, election after election, and candidate after candidate, giving continuity to the choices Americans face and the issues they debate.

They Serve as Political Symbols

Finally, political parties differ from other political organizations by the extent to which they operate as symbols, or emotion-laden objects of loyalty. For millions of Americans, the party label is the chief cue for their decisions about candidates or issues. It helps shape their perceptions and structure their choices; it relates their political values to the real options of American politics.

Remember, however, that the differences between parties and other political organizations are differences of degree. Interest groups do become involved in elections, and the larger organized interests serve as political symbols too. They can recruit candidates and give political cues to their members and friends. The unique American nominating process lets them play an important role in influencing the choice of party candidates. Interest groups also promote issue positions, try to influence officeholders, and (through their political action committees) give money to campaigns. They do not, however, and in most localities cannot, offer their names and symbols for candidates to use on the ballot.

In some respects, the major parties look more like some of the larger interest groups, such as the Chamber of Commerce and the AFL-CIO, than they look like minor or third parties. Most minor political parties are electoral organizations in name only. Their candidates are in no danger of needing a victory speech on election night. Very few minor parties have a lot of local organizations. Their membership base, often dependent on a single issue, may be just as narrow as that of most interest groups. However, minor parties can appear on the ballot, and their candidates can receive public funding where it is available and where they can qualify for it. In these ways (and sometimes *only* in these ways), they can be more like the major parties than the large interest groups.

HOW THE AMERICAN PARTIES DEVELOPED

The world's first political parties developed in the United States and, for more than 200 years, their history has been entwined with the expansion of popular democracy. (For a summary of party history, see the box, "The American Major Parties," in Chapter 2.) The American parties grew up in response to the extension of voting rights. By exploring the parties' development, we can find out how they changed in relation to change in their environment. A key part of this story is the shift in the relative positions of the three parts of the party as first the party in government, then the party organizations, and then both the parties in government and in the electorate enjoyed their period of dominance.[11]

The Founding of American Parties

In the first years of the Republic, the vote was limited in almost every state to those free men who could meet property-holding or taxpaying requirements. Even these relatively small numbers of voters had limited power, as the writers of the Constitution intended. The president was to be chosen not directly by the voters, but indirectly by the electoral college. Each state legislature could choose its own method of selecting that state's electors. Although election to the House of Representatives was entrusted to a direct popular vote, election to the Senate was not. Senators were to be chosen by the respective state legislatures. It was a cautious and limited beginning for democratic self-government.

In their early years, the organizations that were to become the American parties reflected this politics of limited suffrage and indirect elections. They began as caucuses of like-minded members of Congress, concerned only with the political issues that preoccupied the nation's capital. These congressional caucuses nominated presidential candidates and mobilized groups of political leaders to support or oppose the administration of the time. Gradually, during the 1790s, these factions began to take more enduring form. The Federalists, as the dominant group came to be called, were organized around Alexander Hamilton and championed some degree of centralized control over the economy. The opposition, rallying around Thomas Jefferson and James Madison (see box on p. 16), wanted to protect the states' rights from national government interference. These early "parties" were dominated by their party in government.

Officeholders communicated with the voters at home in two ways. Party organization at the grass roots began as "committees of correspondence" between national and local leaders, and each side established a newspaper to propagandize on behalf of its cause. These were the first forms of outreach to the electorate. But the flow of communication was not completely one-sided, from the Capitol to the grass roots. Organized popular protest against the Jay Treaty and other unpopular administration measures, as well as conflict within the various states, fed back to the party in Congress.

When Theory Meets Practice

After the Revolutionary War, James Madison struggled to convince leaders of the new American states that they ought to ratify the Constitution he and others had worked so hard to create. In published letters called *The Federalist,* Madison offered a series of arguments in support of this new Constitution. One was that it would help to overcome the "mischiefs of faction" likely to plague any government. Political parties, Madison thought, were among the worst of these miseries:

> Complaints are everywhere heard from our most considerate and virtuous citizens, equally the friends of public and private faith and of public and personal liberty, that our governments are too unstable, that the public good is disregarded in the conflicts of rival parties, and that measures are too often decided, not according to the rules of justice and the rights of the minor party, but by the superior force of an interested and overbearing majority.[12]

Yet just a few years later, as a member of Congress, Madison helped start a political party. As a member of Congress, Madison disagreed strongly with the guiding figure of the George Washington administration, Alexander Hamilton, on issues of economics and national policy. He led the congressional opposition to the administration, then left Congress and worked with his lifelong friend and ally, Thomas Jefferson, to organize the growing opposition to the administration in the countryside. Their efforts were highly successful; Jefferson won the presidency in 1800, Madison followed him into the top political office, and their political organization, the Democratic-Republican Party, dominated national politics into the 1820s.

How could an anti-party theorist like Madison become a founder of a major political party? Madison probably would not have seen any contradiction between his arguments and his actions. In *The Federalist,* he argued that the Constitution was necessary to contain the natural emergence of factions and to prevent them from undermining democracy. In founding the Democratic-Republicans, he was exercising his right to oppose the policies of one faction by organizing another. Madison's experience, however, suggests that even those who find parties distasteful in theory often learn that they are vital in practice as a means of organizing political power.

One of these incipient parties, the Democratic-Republicans (led by Jefferson), began to look more like a modern-style party by organizing in the states and local communities in time for the 1800 presidential elections. The more elitist Federalists failed to keep up; the result was that they virtually disappeared in most states soon after the defeat of their last president, John Adams, in 1800. In short, the pressures for democratization were already powerful enough by the early 1800s to scuttle an infant party whose leaders in the government could not adapt to the need to organize a mass electorate, especially in the growing states of the frontier.[13]

The Democratic-Republicans, who were the party of agrarian interests and the frontier, quickly established their electoral superiority and held a one-party monopoly for twenty years. They dominated American politics so thoroughly by the time of James Monroe's presidency that the absence of party and political conflict was called the "Era of Good Feelings." In both of his successful races for the presidency (1816 and 1820), Monroe was the only nominee of the Democratic-Republican caucus in the Congress. Despite the decline of one party and the rise of another, however, the nature of party politics did not change much during this period. It was a time when government and politics were the business of an elite group of well-known, well-established men, and the parties reflected the politics of the time. Without party competition, leaders felt no need to establish bigger grassroots organizations, so the parties' further development was stalled.

American politics began to change sharply in the 1820s. By then, most states had eliminated the requirement that only landowners could vote, so the suffrage was extended to all white males, at least in state and federal elections. (Property qualifications lingered in local elections in some places into the twentieth century, where revenues were raised from assessments on property.) The growing pressure for democratization also led governments to make more and more public officials elected, rather than appointed.[14]

The most obvious change in the 1820s, occurring so quickly at the national level that its evolution in the states is often obscured, was the emergence of the presidential election process that has lasted to this day. The framers of the Constitution had crafted an unusual arrangement for selecting the president, known as the electoral college. Each state, in a manner selected by its legislature, would choose a number of presidential electors equal to the size of its congressional delegation. These electors would meet in the state to cast their votes for president; the candidate who received a majority of the states' electoral votes was the national winner. If no candidate received a majority, the president was to be selected by the House of Representatives, with each state casting one vote.

This electoral college was an ingenious invention. By leaving the choice of electors to the state legislatures, the framers avoided having to set uniform election methods and voting requirements, issues on which they strongly disagreed (and which involved, of course, the explosive question of slavery). This also eliminated the need for federal intervention in a question where the states had previously made their own decisions, and which might have produced state opposition. And requiring electors to meet simultaneously in their respective states helped to prevent a conspiracy among electors from different states to put forward their own choice for president.

At first, states used a variety of methods for selecting presidential electors. A few states used popular elections from the beginning, though typically only property owners or taxpayers could vote. The trend toward popular election was uneven; partisan majorities in state legislatures often manipulated the election laws to keep themselves in power. But, by the 1820s, popular election was the most common method, and after 1828, South Carolina was the only state in which the state legislature chose presidential electors.[15]

The growing enthusiasm for democratic practices—the force that propelled this movement toward popular election of presidential electors—also eroded the power of the congressional caucus to nominate a presidential candidate. Caucus nominations came to be criticized as the action of a narrow and self-perpetuating elite. The result was that the congressional party caucus was losing its role as the predominant force within the parties.

The caucus system also began to decline from its own infirmities. The Democratic-Republicans' attempt to nominate a presidential candidate in 1824 ended in chaos. The candidate chosen by the caucus, William Crawford, ran fourth in the actual election, and because no candidate won a majority in the electoral college, the House of Representatives had to choose among John Quincy Adams, Henry Clay, and Andrew Jackson. Although Jackson was the front-runner in both the popular and electoral votes, the House chose Adams. Jackson, in turn, defeated Adams in 1828; by then, the nation had entered a new phase of party politics.

The Emergence of a National Two-Party System

The nonparty politics of the Era of Good Feelings gave way to a two-party system that has prevailed ever since. The Democratic-Republicans had developed wings or factions, which chose divorce rather than reconciliation. Andrew Jackson led the frontier and agrarian wing of the Democratic-Republicans, the inheritors of the Jeffersonian tradition, into what is now called the Democratic Party. The National Republicans, another faction of the old Democratic-Republicans who promoted Henry Clay for president in 1832, merged with the Whigs, and created two-partyism in the United States.

Just as importantly, the parties as political institutions developed even more of a nationwide grassroots base. The Jacksonian Democrats held the first national nominating convention in 1832 which, appropriately, nominated Jackson himself for a second term. (The Whigs and the smaller Anti-Masonic Party had both held more limited conventions a year before.) Larger numbers of citizens were eligible to vote, so the presidential campaign became more concerned with reaching out to the public and was less dominated by a national political leadership; new campaign organizations and tactics brought the contest to more and more people. Jackson was then sent back to the White House for a second term as the leader of a national political party.

Party organization in the states also expanded. Candidates for state and local office were increasingly nominated by conventions of state and local leaders, rather than by the narrower legislative caucuses. By 1840, the Whigs and the Democrats were established in the first truly national party system, and were competitive in all the states.

In short, modern political parties similar to those we know today—with their characteristic organizational structures, bases of loyal voters, and lasting alliances among governmental leaders—had developed by the middle of the nineteenth century.[16] The American parties grew hand-in-hand with the early expansion of the electorate in the United States. Comparable parties did not develop in Great Britain until the 1870s, after further extension of the adult male electorate in the Reform Acts of 1832 and 1867.

The Golden Age of the Parties

Just as the parties were reaching their maturity, they, and American politics, received another massive infusion of voters from a new source: European immigrants. Hundreds of thousands of Europeans—the majority from Ireland and Germany—immigrated to the United States before the Civil War. So many arrived, in fact, that their entry into American politics became a political issue. The newcomers found a ready home in the Democratic Party, and an anti-immigrant third party, the American Party (the so-called Know-Nothing Party), sprang up in response in the 1850s.

The tide of immigration was halted only temporarily by the Civil War. After the war ended, new nationalities came in a virtually uninterrupted flow from 1870 until Congress closed the door to mass immigration in the 1920s. More than five million immigrants arrived in the 1880s (equal to one tenth of the 1880 resident population), and ten million more came between 1905 and 1914 (one eighth of the 1900 resident population).

The political parties played an important role in assimilating these huge waves of immigrants. The newcomers gravitated toward the American cities where industrial jobs were available. It was in the cities that a new kind of party organization, the city "machine," developed in response to the immigrants' needs and vulnerabilities. The machines were impressively efficient organizations. They were also social service systems that helped the new arrivals cope with the challenges of an urban industrial society. They softened the hard edge of poverty, smoothed the way with government and the police, and taught immigrants the customs of their new home. The political machines were often indistinguishable from the government of the city; they were the classic case of "party government" in the American experience. They also were the means by which the new urban working class won control of the cities away from the largely Anglo-Saxon, Protestant elites who had prevailed for so long. As the parties again embodied the hopes of new citizens, just as they had in the 1830s, they reached their high point of power and influence in American history.

The American parties—with the party organization now their dominant part—had reached their "golden age" by the beginning of the twentieth century. Party organization now existed in all the states and localities and flourished in the industrial cities. Party discipline was at an all-time high in Congress and most state legislatures. Parties controlled campaigns for public office; they held rallies, canvassed door-to-door and brought the voters to the polls. They controlled access to many government jobs ranging from street inspectors to members of the U.S. Senate. They were an important source of information and guidance for a largely uneducated and often illiterate electorate. And they rode the crest of an extraordinarily vital American politics; the highest voter turnouts in American presidential history were recorded during the latter half of the nineteenth century. The parties suited the needs and limitations of the new voters and met the need for creating majorities in the new industrial society. This political organization was a good fit to its era.[17]

The Progressive Reforms and Beyond

The drive to democratize American politics continued after the turn of the century. With the adoption of the Seventeenth Amendment, U.S. senators came to be elected directly by the voters rather than by the state legislatures. Women and then blacks finally gained the right to vote, and the voting age was later lowered to 18. Just as important for the parties, however, were changes that would be imposed on them in the name of popular democracy.

The period that parties saw as their "golden age"—the height of their influence on American politics—did not seem so golden to groups of reformers. To Progressive crusaders, party control of politics had led to rampant corruption and government inefficiency.[18] The Progressives attacked party "boss rule" with the direct primary, which gave citizens a voice in choosing the parties' candidates. Presidential nominations were made more open to the public by establishing presidential primaries in the states. Many state legislatures wrote laws to define and limit party organizations, and activists within the parties reformed their national conventions. In all, the Progressive reforms succeeded in wresting control of the parties from their professional organizations.

These reforms were shaped by the impulse to fix the problems of a democratic political system by democratizing the system even more. Because the reformers saw party power as the culprit, they tried to weaken the control that the parties and, especially, the party organizations, had achieved by the late 1800s. And they succeeded; the parties would never regain the exalted position they had enjoyed in the three decades after the Civil War. So the expectations of a democratic society, which first made the parties more public, more decentralized, and more active at the grass roots, later turned on the party organization, leaving it less and less capable of the role it once played in American politics.[19]

It would be too pat to conclude that these changes mark the next shift in power within the party, starting with the party in government, moving to the party organization during the "golden age" of the parties, and now to the party in the electorate. The Progressive reforms did give ordinary citizens new power in party affairs at the expense of the party organizations and their leaders. But, in many cases, these citizens had little attachment to the party itself, making it difficult to view them as the party electorate. Further, the Progressive reforms had the effect of weakening the party's campaign capabilities, which made parties less useful to their candidates. This probably strengthened the position of candidates relative to the party organization and may have made them less vulnerable to popular control.

Not all reforms in traditional party practices have undermined the party organizations. Party rules for the selection of candidates, especially the presidency, have become more uniform across the nation. The Democratic Party, through its national committee and national convention in the 1960s, took the lead in this nationalization of party practices. At the same time, the Republicans were enhancing the capacity of their national party organization to support candidates throughout the country, an activity the Democrats soon tried to match. The result of these two nationalizing thrusts was to strengthen the national party organizations. That has helped shift the balance of organizational power from the grass roots toward the party's national center.

Even with all these changes, the parties remain largely what they were a hundred years ago: the leading political organizations of mass, popular democracy. They developed and grew with the expansion of the suffrage and the popularization of electoral politics. They were and are the invention by which large numbers of voters come together to select their representatives. They rose to prominence at a time when a new electorate of limited knowledge and political sophistication needed the guidance of their symbols. In that way, the modern American party reached its time of glory in the nineteenth century. When people talk today about a supposed decline of parties, it is the standard of that "golden age" against which the decline is measured.

HOW PARTIES ARE SHAPED BY THEIR ENVIRONMENT

This brief excursion into the parties' history reminds us that forces in their environment shape the parties' form and activities. We can't understand the American parties without examining the pressures that affect them. The nature of the voting population is one of the most influential of these forces.

Voters and Elections

As we have seen, the expansion of the right to vote shaped the parties' development. Each new group of voters that enters the electorate challenges the parties to readjust their appeals. As they compete for the support of these new voters, the parties must rethink their strategies for building coalitions that can win elections. Parties in states where black citizens had finally gained the right to vote, for example, learned to campaign differently from the days when they had to appeal to an all-white clientele.

The parties' fortunes are also bound up with the *nature* of American elections. The move from indirect to direct election of U.S. senators, for instance, transformed both the contesting of these elections and the parties that contested them. If the electoral college system is ever abolished and American presidents are chosen by direct popular vote, that change, too, would affect the parties.

A state's election rules have great impact on the parties' activities. Consider, for example, the change from parties' use of conventions to nominate state and congressional candidates to the use of the direct primary. This is a major change in American election law and also an important regulation of the way a party selects its candidates. Even the relatively minor differences in primary law from one state to another, such as differences in the form of the ballot or the timing of the primary, affect the parties. In short, the electoral institutions of the nation and the states set the rules within which the parties compete for votes.

Political Institutions

Very little in the American political system escapes the influence of the two most prominent American institutional features: federalism and the separation of powers. At the national level and in the states, American legislators and executives are elected independently of one another, so it is possible and, in recent decades very likely, for the legislature and the governorship or the presidency to be controlled by different parties. Most other democracies, in contrast, have parliamentary systems in which the legislative majority chooses the officials of the executive branch from among its own members. When that parliamentary majority can no longer hold together, a new government must be formed. An important result of the separation of powers is that American legislative parties can rarely achieve the degree of party discipline and cohesion that is common in parliamentary systems.

This separation between the American executive and the legislature also increases the conflict between executives and legislators of their own party. One reason is that the chief executive and the cabinet secretaries are not also legislative party leaders, as they are in a parliamentary system. Another is that legislators can vote against a president or governor of their party on key issues without fearing that they will bring down the entire government and force new elections. Support for and opposition to executive programs has often cut across party lines in Congress and the state legislatures to a degree rarely found in parliamentary democracies.

The federal system, with its islands of state autonomy from national control, has also left an imprint on the American parties. It has permitted the survival of local political loyalties and traditions. It has spawned an awesome range of public offices to fill, creating an electoral politics that dwarfs that of all other democracies in size and diversity.

By permitting local rewards, local traditions and even local patronage systems, it has nurtured a large set of semi-independent local parties within the two national parties.

Laws Governing Parties

No other parties among the world's democracies are as entangled in legal regulations as are the American parties. It was not always this way. Before the Progressive reforms a century ago, American parties were self-governing organizations, almost unrestrained by state or federal law. For most of the 1800s, for example, the parties printed, distributed, and often—with a wary eye on one another—even counted the ballots. The "Australian" (or secret) ballot changed all of this, giving the responsibility for running elections to government, where it has remained ever since. As noted earlier, during their "golden age," the parties nominated candidates for office using their own rules. The arrival of the direct primary around 1900 severely limited this autonomy, as did more recent reforms of the presidential nomination process that were created by national party commissions but under state laws. In the past, the parties even played an active role in hiring workers for government jobs, a practice that has largely disappeared due to waves of civil service reform and court action.

Both state and, to a limited degree, federal laws govern the parties today, producing an almost bewildering fifty-state variety of political parties. The forms of their organization are prescribed by the states in endless, often finicky detail. State laws set up elaborate layers of party committees and even specify who will compose them, when they will meet, and what their agenda will be. State laws define the parties themselves, often by defining the right to place candidates on the ballot. Most states try to regulate party activities; many, for example, regulate party finances, and most place some limits on their campaign practices. In some states, the parties have tried various strategies to evade the worst of these regulatory burdens. More recently, the federal government has added burdens of its own, including regulating parties' campaign practices and finances. [20]

Political Culture

A nation's political culture is the set of political values and expectations held by its people. It deals with the public's view of what is the political system, what it should be, and what is their place in it.[21] One of the most persistent components of the American political culture is the public's feeling that party politics is an underhanded, dirty business.

We can see evidence of that hostility toward partisan politics by examining public opinion polls. A number of polls have found, for example, that American parents hope their children will not choose politics as their career, and that politicians are viewed, at least generically, as unprincipled and corrupt. Polls report that popular support for the parties is similarly low, even in comparison with other governing institutions, such as Congress, the Supreme Court, or the president—none of which is venerated either. A 1998 survey demonstrated that enthusiasm for the two parties was so limited that, when given a "feeling thermometer" ranging from 0 to 100 degrees on which to indicate their level of positive feeling, respondents could muster no more than an average rating of 55 for the Democrats and the Republicans—a chilly temperature to live in.[22]

These and other elements of the political culture help shape what the parties can be. The widespread view that legislators ought to vote on the basis of their local district's interests, for example, makes it harder to achieve party discipline in Congress and state legislatures. Even the question of what we regard as fair campaigning simply reflects the values and expectations of large numbers of Americans. Whether a strongly worded campaign ad is seen as "negative" or as "hard-hitting and informative" depends on cultural values, not on some set of universal standards. These cultural values affect citizens' feelings about the parties' behavior and, as a result, they influence the behavior itself.

The Nonpolitical Environment

The parties' environment is broader than just their *political* environment. Many factors in their environment affect the parties' functioning. Perhaps no force has been more important for party politics than the emergence of the modern mass media, especially television and the Internet. Because the media can provide so much information about politics and candidates, voters need not depend on the parties to learn about elections and issues. Just as important, candidates can contact voters directly through the media, rather than having to depend on the parties to carry the message for them. That has weakened party control over candidates' campaigns. To add insult to injury, media coverage tends not to pay much attention to the parties themselves. Of course, television attaches great importance to visual images, so it is much more likely to cover individuals—candidates and public officials—than to cover institutions, such as parties, that do not have a "face."

Economic trends can also have a strong and often disruptive impact on the parties. When an economic recession occurs, for example, parties will find it harder to raise money; and the stands the party takes on such questions as taxes, unemployment, and aid to the poor may need to be reevaluated. If the crisis is especially severe, as was the Great Depression of the 1930s, it may even fracture and reorganize the pattern of citizens' party loyalties, end the careers of prominent party leaders, and make a majority party into a weakened minority.

This chapter began as a search for the nature of parties and their activities; it has concluded by looking at how they became what they are. It is important to understand what a political party is, what it does, and, especially, to understand its peculiar three-part nature: the party organization, the party in the electorate, and the party in government. The search for the parties, however, also requires a grasp of the environment in which they have developed and by which they are shaped.

The American Two-Party System

Many Americans think that a two-party system is normal for a democracy. Yet most democracies don't have one. In fact, most nations have either one dominant political party or many parties competing for control of government. One-party systems have appeared in such diverse places as China, the former Soviet Union, and Mexico. In contrast, European democracies typically have multiparty systems in which three, four, or more parties compete with one another, often without any single party being able to win a majority of the votes.[1]

One-party and multiparty systems have been part of the American experience as well. Some states and cities have had a long tradition of one-party rule; in other areas, several parties have flourished at certain times. Minor or third parties and independent candidates have left their mark on American politics, and they continue to do so. Green Party candidate Ralph Nader played a notable role in the 2000 presidential election, accompanied by the largest numbers of third-party candidates for other offices since the 1930s. Ross Perot's independent presidential campaign in 1992 won the support of almost 20 million Americans—the third highest percentage of the popular vote for a minor-party candidate in U.S. history—and was transformed into a third party in 1996. Just three decades earlier, in 1968, Alabama governor George C. Wallace came within 32 electoral votes of throwing the presidential race into the unpredictable hands of the House of Representatives. And recently, at the state level, reporters were captivated by the spectacle of a former professional wrestler named Jesse "The Body" Ventura winning the governorship of Minnesota in 1998 as the candidate of Perot's Reform Party.

These campaigns are colorful enough to capture a lot of media attention; not many governors are nicknamed "The Body," nor have worn a pink feather boa into a public arena. For better or for worse, however, they are rare. For most of American history, most elections have been contested by two parties and only two parties. Even the rapid rise of the Republican Party from its founding in 1854 to becoming one of two major parties two years later, displacing the Whig Party in the process, is the exception that proves the rule. First Democrat versus Whig and then, since 1856, Democrat versus Republican, the United States has had a two-party system in national party competition.

Classifying party systems as one-party, two-party, and multiparty can be limiting. Because this classification focuses simply on counting the number of parties that compete in elections, it overlooks the ways in which minor parties can compete ideologically with the major parties, even if they cannot actually elect candidates. It draws attention to the size of the party's electorate rather than to differences among party organizations, and it ignores the fact that many other types of groups compete politically, in addition to parties. Yet it is a classification that is deeply ingrained in both everyday use and scholarly literature. So as we explore the roots of the two-party system, keep in mind that this classification scheme oversimplifies a more complex political reality.[2]

THE NATIONAL PARTY SYSTEM

The American party system has been essentially a two-party system for more than 160 years. That is a remarkable fact; since the 1830s, almost all partisan political conflict in the United States has been channeled through two major political parties. They rise and fall, they establish areas of strength, they suffer local setbacks and weaknesses, but they endure. Perhaps even more remarkable is that it is so hard to find another democracy in which two parties have dominated a nation's politics so thoroughly and for so long.

Note that this two-party dominance did not exist consistently before 1836 (see box on p. 26). The American party system was unstable until that time. As Chapter 1 showed, the Federalists enjoyed a short period of superiority during the presidency of George Washington, but failed to organize at the state and local level and quickly faded. Their rivals, the Democratic-Republicans, were left with no competition for a time, producing the one-party (or nonparty) politics of James Monroe's presidential terms. As the Washington-centered caucus method of nominations crumbled in the 1820s, however, new national parties appeared, and by 1836 a stable two-party system had emerged. One party, the Democrats, has kept its place in the party system ever since that time. The other party, the Whigs, survived until the 1850s and was replaced almost immediately by the infant Republican Party.

Both the Democratic and Republican parties were briefly divided along sectional lines by the events of the Civil War; they have both changed their issues, appeals, and the coalitions of voters that they assemble. Nevertheless, the Democrats and the Republicans have together made up the American two-party system for the great majority of American history. Thus the two-party drama is long, but its cast of major characters is short.

Throughout this time, the two major parties have been very close competitors, at least at the national level. Of the thirty-four presidential elections from 1868 through 2000, only six were decided by a popular vote spread of more than 20 percent between the two major parties. In other words, in 28 of these presidential elections, a shift of 10 percent of the vote or less would have given the White House to the other party's candidate instead. In fact, almost half (fifteen) of these presidential elections were decided by a spread of less than 7 percent of the popular vote. No president during this time had ever received more than the 61 percent of the popular vote that Lyndon Johnson won in 1964. Some of the closest presidential contests in American history have taken place in the last forty years (2000, which was a virtual tie; 1976; 1968; and 1960).

The American Major Parties

The list of the American major parties is short and select. In over two hundred years of history, only five political parties have achieved a competitive position in American national politics, and one of these five does not fully qualify as a party. Three lost this status; the Democrats and Republicans maintain it to this day.

1. **The Federalist Party, 1788–1816.** The champion of the new Constitution and strong national government, it was the first American political institution to resemble a political party, although it did not fulfill all of the conditions of a full-fledged party. Its strength was rooted in the Northeast and the Atlantic Seaboard, where it attracted the support of merchants, landowners, and established families of wealth and status. Limited by its narrow electoral base, it quickly fell before the success of the Democratic-Republicans.

2. **The Democratic-Republican Party, 1800–1832.** Many of its leaders had been strong proponents of the Constitution, but opposed the extreme nationalism of the Federalists. This was a party of the small farmers, workers, and less-privileged citizens who preferred the authority of the states. Like its leader, Thomas Jefferson, it shared many of the ideals of the French Revolution, especially the extension of the right to vote and the notion of direct popular self-government.

3. **The Democratic Party, 1832–Present.** Growing out of the Jacksonian wing of the Democratic-Republicans, it was the first really broad-based, popular party in the United States. On behalf of a coalition of less-privileged voters, it opposed such commercial goals as national banking and high tariffs; it also welcomed the new immigrants and opposed nativist (anti-immigrant) sentiment.

4. **The Whig Party, 1836–1854.** This party, too, had roots in the old Jeffersonian party, but in the Clay-Adams faction and in opposition to the Jacksonians. Its greatest leaders, Henry Clay and Daniel Webster, stood for legislative supremacy and protested the strong presidency of Andrew Jackson. For its short life, the Whig Party was an unstable coalition of many interests, among them nativism, property, and business and commerce.

5. **The Republican Party, 1854–Present.** Born as the Civil War approached, this was the party of Northern opposition to slavery and its spread to the new territories. Therefore it was also the party of the Union, the North, Lincoln, the freeing of slaves, victory in the Civil War, and the imposition of Reconstruction. From the Whigs it also inherited a concern for business, mercantile, and propertied interests.

Elections to Congress have been even closer. If we turn to percentages of the two-party vote for ease of comparison, we see that the total vote cast for all Democratic candidates for the House of Representatives in a given election is not greatly different from the total vote for Republican candidates; the two parties have stayed roughly in balance for almost seventy years (Table 2.1). In House elections since 1932, there has never been a difference greater than 17 percentage points between the two parties' overall votes, and in most of these elections, the spread was less than 10 percent.

As this quick survey suggests, the two major parties are extremely resilient. Whenever one party has taken a big advantage, in the long run the other party has been able to restore the balance. Although the Democrats seemed to be on the ropes after the Reagan victories of the 1980s and the Republican congressional sweep of 1994, they recovered quickly enough to keep the presidency in 1996 and to continue gaining seats in Congress in 2000. By the same token, the GOP (or Grand Old Party, a nickname that developed for the Republican Party in the late 1800s) confounded the pessimists by springing back from the Roosevelt victories of the 1930s, landslide defeat in 1964, and the Watergate-related setbacks of the mid-1970s.

This pattern of party victories and defeats at the national level is a big part of the story of the American two-party system. But these national trends may hide varying levels of party competition at the state and local levels. So let us explore the degree to which voters can count on two competitive parties in state and local elections—another important issue in the party system.

THE FIFTY STATE PARTY SYSTEMS

The closeness of presidential and congressional elections has often hidden a great deal of one-party dominance below the national level. It was not until 1964, for example—176 years after the Republic formed—that Georgia cast its first electoral votes ever for a Republican presidential candidate and Vermont voted Democratic for the first time since the Civil War. And when we look at individual congressional races, we find that large numbers of candidates are elected to the House of Representatives with a comfortable margin of victory. In 2000, for example, almost half of the winning House candidates got 65 percent or more of the vote, and almost four out of five won with 55 percent of the vote or more.[3]

To measure the competitiveness of the 50 state party systems, however, several practical problems must be resolved. First, which offices should be counted to determine a state's level of party competition: the vote for president, governor, senator, statewide officials, state legislators, or some combination of these? The competitiveness of a state's U.S. Senate seats may be strikingly different from that of its state legislative races. Second, should we count the candidates' vote totals and percentages, or simply the number of offices each party wins? Do we regard a party that averages 45 percent of the vote, but never wins office, any differently from one that averages around the 25 percent mark, but occasionally elects a candidate?

Measuring State Party Competition

The approach used most often to measure interparty competition below the national level is an index originated by Austin Ranney.[4] The Ranney index averages three indicators of party success during a particular time period: the percentage of the popular vote for the parties' gubernatorial candidates, the percentage of seats held by the parties in each house of the legislature, and the length of time plus the percentage of the time the parties held both the governorship and a majority in the state legislature. The resulting scores range

TABLE 2.1 Percentage of Two-Party Vote Won by Republican Candidates and Spread in Percentage of Total Votes for President and House of Representatives: 1932–2000

	Presidential Elections		House Elections	
Year	% Republican of Two-party Vote	% Republican Minus % Democratic of Total Vote	% Republican of Two-party Vote	% Republican Minus % Democratic of Total Vote
1932	40.8	−17.8	43.1	−13.1
1934			43.8	−11.9
1936	37.5	−24.3	41.5	−16.2
1938			49.2	−1.6
1940	45.0	−9.9	47.0	−5.7
1942			52.3	4.5
1944	46.2	−7.5	48.3	−3.4
1946			54.7	9.3
1948	47.7	−4.4	46.8	−6.4
1950			49.9	0
1952	55.4	10.7	50.1	−0.4
1954			47.5	−5.5
1956	57.8	15.4	49.0	−2.4
1958			43.9	−12.8
1960	49.9	−0.2	45.6	−8.8
1962			47.4	−4.9
1964	38.7	−22.6	42.5	−15.3
1966			48.7	−2.7
1968	50.4	0.7	49.1	−1.7
1970			45.6	−8.3
1972	61.8	23.2	47.3	−5.3
1974			41.3	−17.0
1976	48.9	−2.1	42.8	−14.1
1978			45.6	−8.7
1980	55.3	9.7	48.7	−2.4
1982			43.8	−12.7
1984	59.2	18.2	47.2	−5.1
1986			44.9	−9.9
1988	53.9	7.8	46.0	−7.8
1990			46.0	−7.9
1992	46.5	−5.6	47.3	−5.2
1994			53.6	7.0
1996	45.3	−8.5	50.1	0.4
1998			50.4	0.9
2000	49.7	−0.5	50.2	0.4

Sources: Calculated from Harold W. Stanley and Richard G. Niemi, *Vital Statistics on American Politics 1999–2000* (Washington, DC: CQ Press, 2000), Tables 1–7 (for presidential races) and 1–12 (for House elections). Data for 2000 House races are calculated from U.S. Census Bureau, *Statistical Abstract of the United States: 2001* (Washington, DC: Government Printing Office, 2001), p. 239.

from 1.00 (complete Democratic success) through 0.50 (Democratic and Republican parity) to 0.00 (complete Republican success).

Like any other summary measure, the Ranney index picks up some trends more fully than others. One reason is that it is based wholly on state elections. This protects the measure from being distorted by landslide victories and other unusual events at the national level. Yet those national events may foreshadow what will happen in voting for state offices. In the South, for example, growing GOP strength appeared first in competition for national offices and only later worked its way down to the state and local level. In these states, the Ranney index has shown less interparty competition than really exists. A second problem is that the dividing lines between categories are purely arbitrary. There is no magic threshold that separates the category "competitive" from that of "one-party." Finally, any index score will vary, of course, depending on the years and the offices it covers. Nevertheless, its findings provide an interesting picture of state party competition.

Table 2.2 presents the calculations for the Ranney index through the 1998 elections. It shows much more balanced party competition at the state level than had appeared in these calculations earlier in the years since World War II. Note especially that no states are classified as fully one-party. The driving force in this change has been the development of two-party competition in the Southern states, which used to be one-party Democratic, and in formerly one-party Republican states as well. Some regional patterns can still be seen; most states of the Mountain West, for example, remain largely Republican. In fact, these most recent Ranney scores show a shift toward Republican success in the states more generally, with the tipping point coming at the time of the 1994 elections. Because the Democrats had dominated so many states in earlier years, the result has been greater competition between the two parties throughout the 50 states than had existed before.[5]

The differences in two-party competition from state to state can help us explain how competition develops and what nourishes it. Not so long ago, the states with the most competition were those with a more educated citizenry, stronger local party organizations, and larger and more urbanized populations. As the states have become more similar in their levels of interparty competition, the social and political differences between the more and less competitive states surely have narrowed as well.[6]

Competitiveness and Candidate Success

If you were a candidate for elective office, what would these findings about party competition in the states say about your likelihood of winning? For much of the history of the United States, especially throughout the nineteenth century, a candidate's prospects depended on what party he or she represented. Candidates of the dominant party in one-party areas were practically assured of victory. But in more competitive areas, candidates' fates were tied to the national or statewide forces that affected their parties. Even though American candidates have been better able to insulate themselves from their party's misfortunes than have candidates in many other democracies, voters in these more competitive areas could easily turn to the other party as the political winds changed. The result was a lot of party turnover in seats and insecurity for many candidates.

Candidates for many offices since 1900, and especially since the 1950s, have had greater electoral security, mainly because incumbency has become so valuable a political resource. From 1954 through 1988, the average success rates for incumbents seeking

TABLE 2.2 The Fifty States Classified According to Degree of Interparty Competition: 1995–98

One-Party Democratic (none)	Florida (.487)
	Connecticut (.486)
Modified One-Party Democratic	Maine (.464)
	New York (.461)
Hawaii (.775)	South Carolina (.461)
Arkansas (.774)	Indiana (.448)
Maryland (.720)	Colorado (.425)
West Virginia (.689)	Oregon (.413)
Rhode Island (.688)	Alaska (.374)
Georgia (.681)	Iowa (.371)
Louisiana (.680)	Michigan (.369)
Kentucky (.672)	Wisconsin (.364)
Missouri (.665)	Illinois (.363)
Two-Party	*Modified One-Party Republican*
Vermont (.648)	
Massachusetts (.634)	Pennsylvania (.325)
Alabama (.629)	New Jersey (.307)
Mississippi (.625)	New Hampshire (.304)
Oklahoma (.579)	Arizona (.298)
New Mexico (.578)	Utah (.290)
Delaware (.572)	South Dakota (.287)
Tennessee (.566)	Kansas (.264)
North Carolina (.562)	Ohio (.261)
Minnesota (.540)	North Dakota (.245)
Virginia (.536)	Wyoming (.242)
California (.532)	Montana (.225)
Nevada (.516)	Idaho (.199)
Texas (.507)	
perfect competition (.500)	*One-Party Republican (none)*
Washington (.493)	

Source: John F. Bibby and Thomas M. Holbrook, "Parties and Elections," in Virginia Gray, Russell L. Hanson, and Herbert Jacob, eds., *Politics in the American States, Seventh Edition* (Washington, DC: CQ Press, 1999).

reelection were 93 percent in the U.S. House of Representatives and 81 percent in the Senate. These rates peaked in 1988 for the House when more than 98 percent of the incumbents who ran for reelection won, and in 1990 when 29 of 30 senators running for reelection won.[7] (A congressional incumbent in these years probably stood a greater chance of being hit by a truck in Washington, DC traffic than of losing reelection.) Incumbents in most state legislatures were just as likely to keep their jobs.

We do not know for certain why incumbency came to be such a valuable resource in congressional elections. Incumbents certainly benefit from the "perks" of holding office, their name recognition and the attention they receive from the media, the services they can provide to constituents, the relative ease with which they can raise campaign money, and their experience in having run previous successful campaigns. No matter what the reason, it is clear that incumbents had a great deal of job security during this time, even though interparty competition was increasing.

That job security seemed to be at risk in the early 1990s. The popular vote for House incumbents in 1990 dropped below the percentages incumbents had come to treasure in the 1980s, even though most incumbents were still returned to office. The elections of 1992 and 1994 were even harder on incumbents. Because of redistricting, special incentives for retirement, especially strong challengers, and a well-reported scandal, fewer incumbents sought reelection to the House of Representatives in 1992 than at any time since 1954. Those who did met with a success rate of 88 percent in the primaries and general election—the lowest since the post-Watergate election in 1974.

More House incumbents sought reelection in 1994, but "only" 90 percent were reelected in both the primaries and general election.[8] The reelection rate returned to 94 percent in 1996 and 98 percent in 1998 and 2000. So although party competition is increasing nationally and in the states, congressional incumbents still have big advantages in retaining their posts. Yet these high rates of reelection may be a little misleading. Many of the losing incumbents had previously won their districts with comfortable margins, leading their colleagues to wonder whether incumbents really enjoyed the kind of long-term security that their high reelection rates would suggest.[9]

WHAT CAUSES A TWO-PARTY SYSTEM?

We have seen, then, that the American parties are durable, closely competitive with one another at the national level, and increasingly competitive in the states. But why have we had a two-party system for so long, when most other democracies do not? There are several possible explanations for this uniquely American system.

Institutional Theories

The most frequent explanation of the two-party system ties it to the nature of American electoral institutions. Called Duverger's law,[10] it argues that single-member districts with plurality elections tend to produce two-party systems. Plurality election in a single-member district means simply that one candidate is elected to each office, and that the winner is the person who receives the largest number of votes, even if it is not a majority. There are no rewards for parties or candidates that come in second, third, or fourth; even a close second-place finish brings no benefits. The American election system is, for most offices, a single-member district system with plurality election; it offers the reward of winning office only to the single candidate who gets the most votes. So the theory suggests that minor parties will see no point in running candidates if they don't have a shot at winning.

The flip side of Duverger's law is that multimember constituencies and proportional representation result in multiparty systems. A system with multimember constituencies is one in which a particular legislative district will be represented by, say, three or four elected legislators.[11] Each party prepares a slate of candidates for these positions, and the number of party candidates who win is proportional to the overall percentage of the vote won by the party slate (see box on p. 32). Because a party may be able to elect a candidate with only 15 or 20 percent of the votes, depending on the system's rules, small parties are encouraged to keep competing.

Plurality Versus Proportional Representation: How It Works in Practice

Does it matter whether an election uses plurality or proportional representation (PR) rules to count the votes? To find out, let us compare the results of one type of American election in which both rules are used. In presidential primaries—the elections in which party voters choose delegates to the national parties' nominating conventions—the Democrats use PR to select delegates (with at least 15 percent of the vote needed to elect one delegate) and the Republicans generally use plurality election (also called winner-take-all).

Imagine a congressional district that can elect four delegates to the convention, in which candidates A, B, C, and D get the following percentages of the vote. The candidates would win the following numbers of delegates, depending on whether the plurality or PR rule was used:

		Delegates Won	
	% of vote	PR	Plurality
Candidate A	40%	2	4
Candidate B	30%	1	0
Candidate C	20%	1	0
Candidate D	10%	0	0

As you can see, the *plurality* rule increases the delegate strength of the leading candidate (candidate A) at the expense of the other three. The second-place candidate wins nothing, but will still probably run on the chance that he or she could win more votes than candidate A. Under *PR* rules, in contrast, three candidates win delegates in rough proportion to their popular support. So in a typical Democratic primary, the less successful candidates (like candidate C) are encouraged to stay in the nomination race longer, because the PR rules permit them to keep winning at least a few delegates; in a typical Republican primary, only the front-runner will win delegates, so the less successful candidates will probably drop out quickly.

The contrast is even clearer when we compare British elections with the multimember district systems of most European legislative elections. The use of PR in the European elections promotes multiparty politics and coalition governments in which two or more different parties often share control of the executive. In the British parliamentary system, on the other hand, single-member districts operating under plurality rules typically produce a parliamentary majority for one party, giving it sole control of the executive, even if it does not win a majority of the popular vote.

Another institutional explanation is that a two-party system is more likely when a single elected leader holds executive power. The American presidency and the state governorships are the main prizes of American politics and they are indivisible offices that go to only a single party. Many other democracies, using a parliamentary system, select a governing "cabinet" as the executive authority. This cabinet is made up of a number of officeholders, so it can be a coalition that includes representatives of several parties, including minority parties. (In fact, cabinet posts may well be offered to smaller parties in return for the votes needed to produce a majority that can govern.)

In a system with a single executive office, like the American, then minor parties will be weakened because they do not have a realistic chance to compete for president or governor. Even local and regional parties strong enough to elect candidates in their own localities typically find it unrealistic to run a candidate for president. That, in turn, denies a minor party a number of other important opportunities. Without a presidential candidate, a party is not likely to gain the national attention that major parties get and to establish the national spokespersons who increasingly dominate the politics of democracies. Of course, some minor parties try for the presidency anyway. In 1996, the Reform Party focused primarily on the presidential race. But its candidate—Ross Perot, a billionaire willing to spend tens of millions on his campaign—is clearly not typical of most minor parties, no matter how much they may dream of such an opportunity. So the importance of the single, indivisible executive office in the American system strengthens the tendency toward two-party politics.

Political scientist Leon Epstein has identified a third institutional factor—the direct primary—as a force that prevented the development of third parties in areas dominated by one party.[12] Primaries allow voters to choose the parties' nominees, and they have become the main method of selecting party candidates. When disgruntled groups have the opportunity to make their voices heard within the dominant party through a primary, and may even succeed in getting a candidate nominated, the resulting taste of power will probably discourage them from breaking away to pursue a third-party course. Thus, in the one-party Democratic South of an earlier era, where traditional animosities kept most people from voting Republican, factional disputes that under other conditions would have led to third-party development were contained within the Democratic Party by the existence of a direct primary. Similarly, the movement that developed around Ross Perot could have been absorbed by a major party if Perot had chosen to seek that major party's nomination for president.

"Dualist" Theories

Some theorists feel that a basic duality of interest in American society has sustained the two-party system. V. O. Key, Jr. argued that the initial tension between the Eastern financial and commercial interests and the Western frontiersmen stamped itself on the parties as they were forming, and fostered two-party competition. Later, the dualism shifted to North-South conflict over the issue of slavery and the Civil War and then to urban-rural and socioeconomic divisions. A related line of argument suggests that there is a natural dualism within democratic institutions: government versus opposition, those favoring and opposing the status quo, and even the ideological dualism of liberal and conservative. Therefore, social and economic interests, or the very processes of a democratic politics, tend to reduce the contestants to two great camps, and that dualism gives rise to two political parties.[13]

We can see tendencies toward dualism even in multiparty systems, in that the constructing of governmental coalitions clearly separates the parties that make up the government from those that remain in opposition. In France and Italy, for example, the Socialists and other parties of the left, or the various parties of the right and center, often compete against one another in elections, but then come together along largely ideological lines to contest runoff elections or to form a government. What distinguishes two-party from multiparty systems, in short, may be whether this basic tendency toward dualism is expressed in every aspect of the electoral process, or only in the creation and functioning of a government.

The two major American parties play an important role in protecting a two-party system. Their openness to new groups and their adaptability to changing conditions—qualities rare among democratic parties—undermine the development of strong third parties. Just when a third party rides the crest of a new issue to the point where it can challenge the two-party monopoly, one or both of the major parties is likely to absorb the new movement. The experience of the Populists and the Progressives in the early 1900s is a good example, as is the reaction of some Perot followers in time for the 2000 campaign.

Social Consensus Theories

Another possible explanation for the American two-party system is that it reflects a broad consensus on values in American society. Despite their very diverse social and cultural heritage, early on Americans reached a consensus on the fundamentals that divide other societies. Almost all Americans have traditionally accepted the prevailing social, economic, and political institutions. They accepted the Constitution and its governmental structure, a regulated but free enterprise economy, and (perhaps to a lesser extent) American patterns of social class and status.

In traditional multiparty countries, such as France and Italy, noticeable segments of the public have favored radical changes in those and other basic institutions. They have supported fundamental constitutional change, the socialization of the economy, or the disestablishment of the national church. Perhaps American politics escaped these divisions on the essentials because Americans did not have a history of the rigid class structure of feudalism. Perhaps the early expansion of the right to vote made it unnecessary for workers and other economically disadvantaged citizens to organize in order to gain some political power. Or maybe it was the expanding economic and geographic frontiers that allowed Americans to concentrate on claiming a piece of a growing pie, rather than on battling one another. Because the matters that divide Americans are secondary, the argument goes, the compromises needed to bring them into one of two major parties are easier to make.[14]

How can we assess these explanations that have been offered for the existence of two-party politics in the United States? Are the factors they propose really causes of the two-party system or are they effects of it? They are probably, at least in part, effects. Certainly, two major parties will choose and maintain election systems (such as single-member districts) that do not offer easy entry to minor parties. Through their control of Congress and state legislatures, the Democrats and Republicans have made it very hard for third parties to qualify for the ballot and for third-party candidates to receive public funding. The major parties naturally try to get public opinion to buy the alternatives that they are selling.

Yet these effects of the two-party system can also be seen as causes to some degree. Clearly the most important cause is the institutional arrangement of American electoral politics. Without single-member districts, plurality elections, and an indivisible executive, it would have been much easier for third parties to break the near-monopoly enjoyed by the two major parties. The other Anglo-American democracies, such as Britain and Canada, which share the American institutional arrangements, also tend to be dominated by two parties—though third parties are not quite as hobbled in these nations as in the American party system.

The other forces, especially the long-running American consensus on fundamental beliefs and its resulting lack of deep ideological splits, have contributed to the development of the American two-party system as well. Once the two-party system was launched, its very existence fostered the values of moderation, compromise, and pragmatism that helped keep it going. It also created deep loyalties within the American public to one party or the other and attachments to the two-party system itself.

EXCEPTIONS TO THE TWO-PARTY PATTERN

As we have seen, the American two-party system can harbor pockets of one-party politics within some states and localities. There have been other deviations from the two-party pattern. Some areas have developed a uniquely American brand of no-party politics. Third parties or independent candidates have occasionally made their presence felt, as the 2000 presidential election showed. Where do we find these exceptions to two-party politics?

Nonpartisan Elections

One of the crowning achievements of the Progressive movement was to restrict the role of parties in elections by removing party labels from many ballots, mostly in local elections. Roughly three quarters of American towns and cities conduct their local elections on a nonpartisan basis. One state, Nebraska, elects state legislators on a nonpartisan ballot, and many states elect judges in this manner.

Removing party labels from the ballot has probably not removed partisan influences where parties are already strong. The nonpartisan ballot did not prevent the development of a powerful political party machine in Chicago. A resourceful party organization can still select its candidates and work in elections where party labels are not on the ballot, even though it must obviously try much harder to let voters know which are the party's candidates. So in that way, at least, nonpartisanship can add to the burdens of strong local parties.

Typically, however, nonpartisanship has been adopted in areas and at times when partisanship and party organizations were already weakened. The reform was most likely to take root in cities and towns with weak parties and for offices, such as judgeships and school boards, where the traditional American dislike of party politics is most pronounced. In contrast, most Northeastern cities, where strong party machines were the most visible targets of the Progressives, were able to resist the reforms and to continue to hold partisan local elections.

Beyond removing the party label from ballots and adding to the difficulties faced by party organizations, what difference does it make if an election is nonpartisan? The traditional view among political scientists was that a move to nonpartisan elections shifts the balance of power in a pro-Republican direction rather than making politics any less partisan or more high-minded. Without party labels on the ballot, the voter is more dependent on other cues. Higher-status candidates tend to have more resources and visibility in the community, which can fill the void left by the absence of party. In current American politics, these higher-status candidates are more likely to be Republicans.[15] On the other hand, a study of city council races across the nation has challenged this conventional wisdom by showing that the GOP advantage disappears once the partisan attachments of city voters are taken into account.[16]

Pockets of One-Party Monopoly

In the past, the states of the Deep South were the country's most well known examples of one-party domination, though the same could be said of the deeply rooted Republicanism of Maine, New Hampshire, and Vermont. Today, traces of one-party politics can still be found in thousands of cities, towns, and counties in which a mention of the other party can produce anything from raised eyebrows to raised tempers.

Where do we find these one-party areas? Since the 1930s, the major parties, especially in national elections, have divided the American electorate roughly along socioeconomic lines: by income, education, and job status. (More about this can be found in Chapterss 6 and 7.) A local constituency may be too small to contain the wide range of socioeconomic status (SES) characteristics that leads to competitive politics. Thus, we can find "safe" and noncompetitive Democratic congressional districts in the older, poorer, or black neighborhoods of large cities and "safe" Republican districts in the wealthier suburbs. In other words, the less diverse are its people—at least in terms of the characteristics that typically divide Republican voters from Democratic voters—the more likely the district is to foster one-party politics.

Alternatively, there may be some local basis of party loyalty so powerful that it overrides the relationship between SES and partisanship. In the classic one-party politics of the American South, regional loyalties long overrode the factors that were dividing Americans into two parties in most of the rest of the country. Feelings about the Republicans as the party of abolition, Lincoln, the Civil War, and the hated Reconstruction were so intensely negative, even generations after the Civil War ended, that they overpowered the impact of socioeconomic differences. In other areas, the effects of a serious scandal or a bitter strike may linger, leaving only one party as a socially acceptable choice.

Once one party has established dominance in an area, it can be very hard for the weaker party to overcome its disadvantages. These disadvantages begin with stubborn party loyalties. Voters are not easily moved from their attachments to a party, even though the reasons for the original attachment have long passed. Further, a party trying to become competitive may find itself caught in a vicious circle. Its inability to win elections limits its ability to raise money and recruit attractive candidates, because as a chronic loser it offers so little chance of achieving political goals. The Republican Party in the South, for example, found for many years that the Democrats had recruited the region's most promising politicians and had preempted its most powerful appeals.

In addition, the weaker party's ability to attract voters locally is affected by media coverage of its national party's stance. If the Democratic Party is identified nationally with the hopes of the poor and minority groups, its appeal in an affluent suburb may be limited. So a nationalized politics may increasingly rob the local party organization of the chance to develop strength based on its own issues, personalities, and traditions. To the extent that party loyalties grow out of national politics, as many Democrats in the South have learned in recent years, competitiveness may be beyond the reach of some local party organizations.

As if this were not enough, the weaker party faces the hurdle of competing in electoral districts drawn up by the stronger party. The Supreme Court ruled in the 1960s that state legislatures must redraw legislative district boundaries at the beginning of each decade, following the U.S. Census, in order to keep the districts fairly equal in population. The Court halted the decades-old practice of malapportioning those districts to protect or improve the chances of majority party candidates. But majority parties have found remarkably inventive ways to draw districts that preserve their advantage. This is why parties are especially concerned with winning state legislative majorities in the years when district lines must be redrawn. It has sometimes been possible even to manipulate election laws to protect a majority party. Southern Democrats, for instance, were long able to stifle competition by maintaining laws that kept blacks and poor whites from voting.

Third Parties

Two-party politics has also been challenged occasionally by the emergence of a new party or an especially attractive independent candidate. We will explore the recent increase in independent candidates later in this chapter. For most of American history, these challenges have come from other parties, understandably termed "third" or, referring to their impact, "minor" parties.

Third-party challenges have been short-lived in American politics. Only seven minor parties in all of American history have carried even a single state in a presidential election, and only one (the Progressive Party) has done so twice. Theodore Roosevelt and the Progressives, in 1912, were the only minor-party candidacy ever to run ahead of one of the major-party candidates in either electoral or popular votes. The Republicans began as a third party in 1854, but they remained so only briefly; they had replaced the Whigs and became a major party in time to compete in the 1856 presidential election.

In recent years, third parties' prospects have not improved. The combined minor-party vote for president, excluding votes for independent candidates, was only slightly more than 600,000 in 1992, or about 0.6 percent of the total popular vote. In 1996 this total jumped to 9.6 million, or 10 percent, with slightly more than 8 million of those votes going to Ross Perot as the Reform Party candidate. The third-party vote shrank in 2000 to 3.9 million (under 4 percent; see Table 2.3). These numbers are not likely to give much hope to future third-party candidacies.

Third-party successes can be found below the presidential level, but they are as rare as they are fascinating. Of more than a thousand governors elected since 1875, fewer than twenty ran solely on a third-party ticket, and another handful ran as independents.[17] Jesse Ventura's successful candidacy in Minnesota in 1998, received enormous media attention precisely because it was so unusual. Third-party candidates have been more successful in running for Congress, but in only seven election years have they won more than ten seats, and the most recent of those elections was in 1936.

At the state level, we can find the clearest examples of third-party power in the states of the upper Midwest. In the 1930s and 1940s, remnants of the Progressive movement—

TABLE 2.3 Popular Votes Cast for Minor Parties in 2000 and 1996
Presidential Elections

2000		1996	
Parties	*Vote*	*Parties*	*Vote*
Green	2,882,807	Reform	8,085,402
Reform (Buchanan)	448,868	Green	685,128
Libertarian	386,035	Libertarian	485,798
Constitution	98,004	U.S. Taxpayers	184,820
Natural Law/Reform	83,524	Natural Law	113,670
Socialist	7,746	Workers World	29,083
Socialist Workers	7,378	Peace and Freedom	25,332
Libertarian (Arizona)	5,775	Socialist Workers	8,476
Others and Scattered	9,362	Others and Scattered	23,806
Total	3,929,499	Total	9,641,515

Note: Votes for independent and write-in candidates are not included here.

Sources: Federal Election Commission. On the 1996 election, http://www.fec.gov/pubrec/summ.htm. On the 2000 election, http://fecweb1.fec.gov/pubrec/2000presgeresults.htm (accessed Feb. 8, 2001).

the Progressive Party in Wisconsin, the Farmer-Labor Party in Minnesota, and the Non-Partisan League in North Dakota—competed with some success against the major parties. But in these and a few other similar cases, multiparty competition lasted only briefly and ended with a return to two-party politics. Ross Perot hoped to extend his Reform Party into state races in 1996, after having won between 9 and 30 percent of the popular vote in the states as an independent presidential candidate in 1992. But there was not a single winner among the eight Reform Party U.S. Senate candidates and 25 U.S. House candidates in 1996.

Third-party organizers had some success at the local level in 2000. An estimated 1,420 candidates ran on the Libertarian label alone. There were more than 200 Green Party candidates for local office; 32 of them won posts ranging from mayor in five California towns to the drain commissioner of Charlevoix County, Michigan. Minor party activists in some states discussed coming together to deal with the procedural difficulties they all faced.[18] But for every example of third-party victory in local elections, there are thousands of races with no minor-party challenge. The Democratic and Republican parties have monopolized American electoral politics even more fully in the states and cities than at the national level. (For one minor party activist's reaction to this monopoly, see "A Day in the Life" on p. 39.)

The term *third party* refers to all minor parties in the two-party system, but it would be a mistake to treat them as look-alikes. They differ in origin, purpose, and activities. Their variety is as plain as a look at their labels: Socialist Workers, Green Party, Libertarian.[19]

Differences in Scope of Ideological Commitment   Although most minor parties are parties of ideology and issue, they differ in the scope of that commitment. Some have narrow, highly specific commitments: for instance, the Prohibition, Vegetarian, and Right to Life parties. At the other extremes are those with the broadest ideological commitments: the Marxist and conservative parties. One leading minor party in recent years, the

A DAY IN THE LIFE

Competing Against the "Big Guys"

The Democrats and the Republicans, Brad Warren says, have a "death grip" on the American political process. Warren, a tax attorney in Indianapolis, is a Libertarian party activist who ran for the U. S. Senate under that party's banner. "If I need a new pair of socks," he points out, "I can go to dozens of stores and pick from several different brands and dozens of colors—for something as insignificant as socks. But when it comes to politics, which has a monopoly on the lawful use of force in our society, we have only two choices. That is tremendously scary! How do you hold them accountable? If you get angry with the incumbents, you can throw them out, only to reelect the nasty incumbents you had thrown out in the previous election. Four years from now, you'll be throwing out the incumbents you elected today. There's no choice."

Third-party activists, such as Warren, find that they are competing against the "big guys"—the two major parties—on an uneven playing field. A major problem for a third party, Warren says, is simply to get its candidates' names on the ballot. In Indiana, the state legislature used to require any minor party to win just half of 1 percent of the vote for Secretary of State in order to qualify its candidates to get on the state ballot automatically in later elections. The Libertarians met that goal in 1982. The result? The legislature raised the hurdle to 2 percent. Ballot access requirements differ from state to state, making it difficult for a minor party to appear on the ballot in all 50 states.

"Even once you have ballot access," Warren argues, "you will still be excluded from any *meaningful* participation in the election. In practice, we run elections on money, not on votes, and in presidential elections, the Republicans and Democrats divide up hundreds of millions of federal dollars among themselves."

The worst problem for third parties, Warren feels, is getting noticed after the primary election. "I got pretty good media coverage up to the primary election. After the primary, I was nobody. Even though the primary doesn't elect anybody to any office, it *seems to*. It legitimizes the major parties' candidates and delegitimizes everybody else. The media say we have no chance to win, so they won't cover any candidates except the [major] party-anointed ones. The debates typically don't include third-party candidates. Why? Because the commissions that decide who's going to be allowed to participate in debates are 'bipartisan' commissions, made up entirely of Republicans and Democrats, just like the legislatures that write the ballot access laws and the judges who interpret them. We understand that it would be confusing to have too many candidates in a debate. But a party that has gotten on the ballot in all 50 states, like the Libertarians, deserves to be heard."

"The two major parties won't give you any choice," Warren contends. Both parties accept the idea that the government "will take 40 to 50 percent of your resources in taxes, no matter what, so you might as well just try to trample everybody else and get laws passed to get back whatever tax breaks you can. You can't tell the major parties apart without a program."

Libertarian Party, for example, advocates a complete withdrawal of government from most of its present programs and responsibilities.[20] In the middle ground between specific issues and total ideologies, the range is very wide. The farmer-labor parties of economic protest—the Greenback and Populist parties—ran on an extensive program of government regulation of the economy and social welfare legislation. The new Constitution Party argues for less government regulation and lower taxes.

Difference of Origins   The minor parties differ, too, in their origin. Some were literally imported into the United States. Much of the early Socialist Party strength in the United States came from the freethinkers and radicals who fled Europe after the failed revolutions of 1848. Socialist strength in cities such as Milwaukee, New York, and Cincinnati reflected the concentrations of liberal German immigrants there. Other parties, especially the Granger and Populist parties, were homegrown channels of social protest, born of social inequality and economic hardship in the marginal farmlands of America.

Some minor parties began as splinters or factions of one of the major parties. For example, the Progressives (the Bull Moose Party) of 1912 and the Dixiecrats of 1948 objected so strenuously to the platforms and candidates of their parent parties that they ran their own slates and presented their own programs in presidential elections. In fact, the Dixiecrats, an anti-civil-rights faction within the Democratic Party, substituted their own candidate for the one chosen by the party's national convention as the official Democratic presidential candidate in the state.

Differing Tactics   Finally, third parties differ in their tactics. The aim of some of these parties is to educate citizens about their issues; getting votes is merely a sideline. They run candidates because their presence on the ballot brings media attention that they could not otherwise hope to get. Many of these parties serenely accept their election losses because they have chosen not to compromise their principles to win office. The Prohibition Party, for example, has run candidates in presidential elections since 1872 with unflagging devotion to the cause of banning alcoholic beverages, but without apparent concern for the fact that its highest proportion of the popular vote was 2 percent, and that came in 1892.

Some minor parties do have serious electoral ambitions. Often, their goal is local, although today they find it difficult to control an American city, as the Socialists once did, or an entire state, like the Progressives. More realistically, they may hope to hold a balance of power in a close election between the major parties. Ralph Nader, as the candidate of the Association of State Green Parties, probably accomplished that in the 2000 presidential election (see box below). Ross Perot even claimed to be looking for an outright victory in both 1992 (as an independent) and 1996.

Nader's Raiders vs. Al Gore, 2000

Most third-party candidates, in Rodney Dangerfield's immortal words, "don't get no respect." Ralph Nader is an exception. His run for the presidency in 2000 showed the frustrations of a third-party candidacy, but also the potency of a minor party in a close election.

Nader first made his impact on American politics as the author of *Unsafe at Any Speed*, an exposé of the safety hazards of a popular General Motors car.

(box continued)

During his 40-year history as a crusader for consumers' and environmental rights, Nader built the Public Citizen watchdog organization in Washington and the PIRG (Public Interest Research Group) movement on college campuses throughout the nation. In 1996 he made his first run for political office as the Green Party's presidential candidate, though his limited enthusiasm for the job could probably be inferred from the fact that he made a grand total of two campaign appearances.

In 2000, however, Nader announced his intention to create a viable third party that would become a progressive force in American politics. Claiming that both the Democrats and the Republicans were the captives of corporate America, Nader accepted the presidential nomination of the Association of State Green Parties, a breakaway group regarded as more moderate than the Green Party. (It was not hard to be more moderate than the Green Party, which had called for the abolition of the U.S. Senate and the dismantling of the nation's 500 largest corporations.) Nader focused on grassroots organizing, basing his campaign on issues such as environmental protection and opposition to corporate abuses. His party made the enormous effort required to get on the ballot in 45 states and succeeded in recruiting more than 270 candidates, most for local office.

By early summer, Nader had picked up noticeable support. A June, 2000 *USA Today*/CNN/Gallup Poll showed Nader as the presidential choice of 6 percent nationally and 10 percent in California. Many Democrats feared that Nader might get just enough votes in a few key states to tip their electoral votes to Republican George W. Bush. Their concern produced an innovative use of the Internet, in which Web sites sprang up to match Nader supporters in key states willing to vote for Democratic candidate Al Gore, their second choice, with Gore supporters willing to cast their vote for Nader in states where Gore's or Bush's victory was already assured.

As is typical of third-party candidates, Nader's support shrank by about half by election day; he won only 3 percent of the national vote. Yet he may, indeed, have tipped the election to the Republicans. Bush, who lost the national popular vote, finally won the presidency when his tiny, 537-vote victory in Florida gave him all of that state's electoral votes. Nader got 97,488 votes in Florida and exit polls nationally found that about half of all Nader voters would have cast their ballots for Gore (and only about 20 percent for Bush) if Nader had not been a candidate.

Sources: James Dao, "History Could Be the Green Party's Toughest Opponent," *New York Times,* Nov. 2, 2000, p. A25; Evelyn Nieves, "A Party Crasher's Lone Regret: That He Didn't Get More Votes," *New York Times* Feb. 18, 2001, p. 7 sec.4; Associated Press, "Nader Helped Tip Florida to Bush," on the Web, http://www.washingtonpost.com/ac2/wp-dyn/A64639-2000Dec29 (accessed Dec. 30, 2000).

What Difference Do They Make?   Third parties have influenced, maybe even changed, the course of a few presidential elections. By threatening about once a generation to deadlock the electoral college, they have probably kept alive movements to reform it. But beyond their role as potential electoral spoiler, have third parties accomplished anything substantial?

Some argue that minor parties deserve the credit for a number of public policies—programs that were first suggested by a minor party and then adopted by a major party when they reached the threshold of political acceptability. A possible example is the Socialist Party platforms that advocated such measures as a minimum wage for 20 or 30 years before the minimum wage law was enacted in the 1930s. Did the Democratic Party steal the Socialist Party's idea, or would it have proposed a minimum wage for workers even if there had been no Socialist Party? There is no way to be sure. The evidence suggests, however, that the major parties make new proposals in their "time of ripeness," when large numbers of Americans have accepted the idea, and it is thus politically useful for the major party to do so. But the major party might have picked up the new proposal from any of a number of groups: not only minor parties, but also interest groups, the media, or influential public figures.

If the impact of third parties is so limited, then what attracts some voters to them? Note that there aren't many such voters; the self-fulfilling prophecy that a vote for a third party is a wasted vote is very powerful in American politics.[21] Yet some voters do cast third-party ballots. To Steven Rosenstone and his colleagues, this results from the failure of major parties "to do what the electorate expects of them—reflect the issue preferences of voters, manage the economy, select attractive and acceptable candidates, and build voter loyalty to the parties and the political system."[22]

Continued dissatisfaction with the major parties has certainly provided an opening for a formidable third party. When this occurs, however, the normal workings of the American electoral system make it likely that the "third" party will displace one of the major parties (as the Republicans did with the Whigs) or be absorbed by changes in one of the major parties (as happened with the Democrats in 1896 and 1936). So alternatives to the two major parties tend to develop and expand only when the major parties are failing.

The Rise of Independent Candidates

In recent years, dissatisfaction with the two major parties has been expressed in a new way—in support for candidates running as independents, rather than on third-party tickets. The independent presidential candidacy of Ross Perot in 1992 received a larger share of the popular vote than any "third" candidate in history who was not a former president. With 19.7 million popular votes, Perot also outdrew the combined total of all of his third-party opponents in that race—by more than 19 million ballots. Perot failed to win a single state, however, and much of his support seemed to come from voters who were more dissatisfied with the Republican and Democratic candidates than they were attracted to a long-lasting commitment to another party or candidate.[23]

Perot ran for president again in 1996 as the Reform Party candidate. The story of his two candidacies—one as an independent and the other as a third-party candidate—helps us understand some of the advantages of running an independent candidacy now. In his first presidential race, his supporters built a remarkably strong organization. Through its efforts, Perot got on the ballot in all 50 states and mounted an active campaign throughout the nation. The key ingredient in the Perot challenge, however, was money—the millions of dollars from his own personal fortune that Perot was willing to invest in his quest for the presidency. This money financed the organizational efforts at the grass roots and, more importantly, bought large blocks of expensive television time for the candidate's widely viewed "infomercials."[24] No other minor party or independent candidate for president in at least a century has achieved Perot's national visibility.

By 1996, Perot had organized the Reform Party and sought to qualify it for the ballot in all 50 states. This turned out to be much harder than qualifying to run as an independent candidate. In California, which was his toughest challenge, Perot had to get at least 890,000 signatures on a petition by October 1995 to win a place on the state's ballot thirteen months later. He failed. Perot had greater success in most other states, but found it difficult to recruit acceptable Reform candidates for other offices. On election day, Perot got less than half as many votes as a Reform Party candidate than he had four years earlier as an independent.

Why was his third-party effort less successful? Many factors were at work. One may have been simple familiarity; sometimes a candidate does not benefit from letting voters get to know him or her better. Another involved states' election laws, which are generally more restrictive for third parties than for independent candidates. In addition, it is clearly a challenge to nurture an organization to support many candidates, rather than one. Although there are some minor parties that seem to be no more than vehicles for a single candidate, third-party movements usually have to respond to the needs, demands, and personalities of candidates for a variety of offices. In the 2000 presidential campaign, conflicts among Reform Party activists became so intense, especially in trying to select one of several candidates to take Perot's place, that the party's national convention disintegrated into a fistfight and the party split.

Several minor parties, especially the Libertarians and the Greens, have made real efforts since the 2000 election to establish themselves as organizations that extend beyond a relatively small number of candidates. If history is any guide, however, that is a battle they are likely to lose. The result is that when voters consider alternatives to the major parties, independent candidates (especially if they happen to be billionaires) will continue to have real advantages over those who try to form fully-elaborated third parties.

WHAT IS THE FUTURE OF THE AMERICAN TWO-PARTY SYSTEM?

This look at two-party politics and its alternatives leads us to some conflicting conclusions about the future of the two-party system. In important respects, two-party dominance seems to be increasing. The competition between the Democrats and the Republicans, nationally as well as within the states, is more spirited now than it has been in decades. Below the presidential level, one-party politics and third-party successes seem to be less common than they were many years ago.

Yet recent developments threaten the two-party dominance. Wealthy candidates, such as Perot, can get direct access to the media without having to work through a major party, so they can run independent campaigns if they are so inclined. The barriers to ballot access for minor-party and independent candidates, once so substantial, have been lowered in recent years. What will be the result?

The Decline of Minor Parties and the Rise of Independents

The record is clear: third parties are not gaining ground. Third-party members of Congress, common in the early decades of the two-party system, were rare throughout the twentieth century, and especially in recent years (Figure 2.1). Since 1952, only one member of Congress has been elected on a third-party ticket—James Buckley in 1971 as a Conservative Party senator from New York—and he aligned himself with the Republicans after taking office. (Two others have served as independent members of the House

of Representatives but one caucuses with the Democrats and the other is now a Republican.) Minor-party candidates have also fared poorly in state legislative contests during
this period, and local enclaves of minor-party strength have been reduced to a small,
though colorful, handful.

As minor-party strength has declined, independent candidates have become more successful. The presence of independents was responsible for major-party candidates receiving the lowest percentage of the 1992 congressional vote since the 1930s, although this
percentage remained in the high 90s.[25] It is a good measure of the candidate-centered
nature of recent American politics that when voters are inclined to shake off the two-party
habit, they are more likely to support an independent candidate than a minor party.

Minor-party and independent presidential candidates must still satisfy a patchwork
of different state requirements to qualify for the ballot nationwide, though the process
has been eased by court decisions. Even when court action has overturned laws discriminating against independent and third-party candidates, however, the action has typically been piecemeal, requiring petitioners to raise the challenge in each state. And when
activists have persuaded courts to reduce these legal barriers to getting other candidates
on the ballot, third-party leaders must find it ironic that the reductions in these barriers
have benefited their organizations less than they have benefited independent candidates.[26]

The financial hurdles faced by independent and third-party candidates are coming
down. Presidential candidates outside the major-party mainstream can receive public
funding for their campaign if they win at least 5 percent of the popular vote. By that time,
of course, the election is over, so they can use the money only to repay campaign debts,
but they then become eligible for public funding in the next election. Perot's vote in 1996

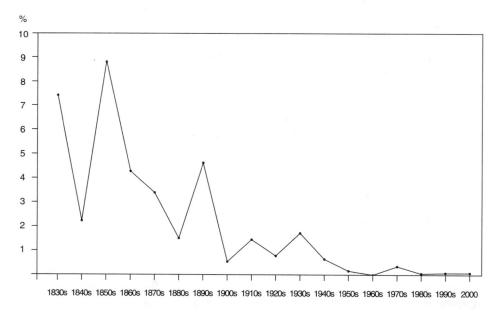

FIGURE 2.1 Third-Party and Independent Members of Congress: 1830s–2000.
Note: Figures are percentages of third-party and independent senators and representatives during each decade.

qualified the 2000 Reform Party candidate, Patrick Buchanan, for more than $12 million in federal funds. Even so, the enormous cost of modern campaigns probably restricts the opportunities to only a few highly visible, or personally wealthy, third-party or independent candidates.

As the Perot example shows, the modern campaign environment offers new advantages for minor-party and independent candidates with money to spend. Television and the Internet provide a national audience to a candidate or party that can afford it. Minor-party and independent candidates can now reach voters throughout the United States without the need for grassroots organizations—if they can pay for the media time or the Web page design. In fact, they can command attention through the very same channels used by the two major parties' candidates.

Quirks in local election laws continue to support a few local third parties. The classic instance is New York's minor parties—notably the Liberals and Conservatives—that survive because they can nominate candidates of a major party to run under their parties' own labels as well.[27] For national impact, minor parties must generally ride the coattails of a well-known, charismatic candidate. It seems most likely, then, that minor parties and independents will follow different paths as they compete for space in the electoral arena.

Increasing Major-Party Competitiveness

The most significant trend we have seen in this chapter, however, is the increasing competitiveness between the Republican and Democratic parties. No regions of the country, and very few states, can be seen as one-party areas any longer. Contests for state offices are more competitive now than they have been in decades, perhaps ever, and presidents have been winning with popular vote percentages that vary less and less from one state to another. They are no longer as likely to carry some states by fat margins while losing others in a similarly lopsided way. The result is a more competitive two-party politics throughout the nation.

Increases in major-party competitiveness have the same roots as the challenges faced by local third parties: the nationalization of life and politics in the United States. It is harder and harder for one major party to maintain its dominance on the basis of regional appeals and traditions, as the Democrats did in the South from 1876 to 1950. Further, the social and economic conditions that support one-party politics are disappearing. As Americans move more frequently, as industry comes to formerly agrarian states, as more and varied people move to the cities, each state gains the diversity of life and interests that supports national party competition. National mass media and national political leaders bring the conflict between the Democrats and the Republicans to all corners of the country. Party voters are increasingly recruited by the appeals of national candidates and issues regardless of the special appeals made by the local party. Most states have moved gubernatorial and other statewide elections to non-presidential-election years in order to mute the influence of these national forces. But this is only a small counterweight to the powerful pull of national politics.

This increase in two-party competition may create some new risks for the American parties. The reduction in pockets of one-party strength tends to remove a source of stability in the party system. When a party has unchallenged dominance in some areas, it can survive even a catastrophic national loss because it is still winning in its own strongholds. Without those one-party strongholds to fall back on, a losing party in the future may find its loss more sweeping and devastating. Further, the increase in competition expands the scope of party activity and thus makes extra demands on party resources. When one-party areas could be written off in a presidential campaign, the area of political combat was reduced. Now the parties must mobilize more resources than ever across more of the states.

The newer challenge of independent candidates also makes elections less predictable and politics less stable. Running by themselves, without anyone else on their "tickets," they are not likely to create an enduring challenge to the Democrats and Republicans. So even though independent candidates can make headlines and the wealthiest among them can buy television time to appeal to voters, they will probably remain no more than periodic threats to the major parties' candidates. To make a sustained challenge that could fundamentally transform the American parties or the party system, these independents (and the Greens and the Libertarians) would need to organize to confront the major parties from the top to the bottom of the ballot. Those who try soon realize that they face a two-party system that may not be greatly beloved, but that is very well entrenched.

The Political Party as an Organization

The parties have a life, as we have seen, that goes beyond the activities and personalities of their candidates. A major party is a network of organizations that exists at all the levels at which Americans elect public officials: precincts, townships, wards, cities, counties, congressional districts, and the states themselves. Both major parties have also set up national committees that concern themselves mainly with presidential and congressional elections. All these party organizations have the official responsibility for making the party's rules and organizing its activities. The next three chapters examine these organizations and the activists and leaders who give them life.

We will focus in these chapters on the "private life" of the party organization, as opposed to its "public life" of recruiting and supporting candidates for office and promoting solutions to public problems. In particular, we will explore these questions: Where does the power lie in the party organizations? What resources do they rely on? What kinds of people are likely to become party activists? How have the organizations changed over time? These internal characteristics of the party influence its ability to act effectively in the larger political system.

American party organizations vary tremendously. Party activists bring a variety of different values and concerns to the party organizations. Parties in various parts of the nation have ranged, throughout American history and, even now, from elaborate organizations to complete somnolence. But by the standards of most Western democracies, the American party organizations would be considered to be fairly weak.

This relative weakness stems from the peculiar nature of the American party. The three sectors of any party—its organization, its candidates and elected officials, and its electorate—compete for dominance. They each have different sets of goals and they each seek control of the party to achieve their own ends. In the American system, the party organizations find it difficult to hold their own in this competition and to get the resources they need to influence elections and promote policies. Weakened by state regulations, the party organizations have rarely been able to exercise any real influence over the party's candidates and officeholders or over party voters. In fact, it is the organizations that are influenced. American party organizations depend on their party in government, which, after all, writes the laws that regulate the organization. They must also devote a great deal of energy to courting and mobilizing the party electorate, who are not formally party members nor, in many cases, even especially loyal to the party in their voting.

This lack of integration among the party's three sectors is typical of *cadre* parties— one of two terms often used to describe the nature of party organizations. Imagine that party organizations are arranged along a continuum. At one end of this continuum is the cadre party, in which the organization is run by a relatively small number of leaders and activists with little or no broader public participation. These officials and activists make the organization's decisions, choose its candidates, and select the strategies they believe voters will find appealing. They focus primarily on electing the party's candidates rather than on issues and ideology. For that reason, the party's activities gear up mainly at election time, when candidates are most in need of the party organization's help. The cadre party, then, is a pragmatic coalition of people and interests brought together temporarily to win elections, only to wither to a smaller core once the elections are over.

At the other end of this scale is the *mass-membership* party, a highly participatory organization in which all three parts of the party are closely intertwined. In this type of party, large numbers of voters become dues-paying members of the party organization and take part in its activities throughout the year, not just during campaigns. A mass-membership party concentrates not just on winning elections but also on promoting an ideology and educating the broader public. The members vote on the party's policies as well as choose its organizational leaders. Members of the party in the electorate are so integral to the party organization that it may even provide them with such nonpolitical benefits as insurance and leisure-time activities. Because the membership-based party organization has great power over candidate selection—it is not limited by the need to give less-involved voters the right to choose party candidates, as happens in a primary election—it can also exercise much greater control over the party in government.

In important ways, the major American parties can be considered cadre parties. As we would expect of cadre parties, most local and state party leaders and activists are not paid professionals but volunteers, whose party activities and those of the party organization ramp up around election time. These organization leaders make relatively little effort to control the party's candidates and elected officials, nor are they likely to succeed if they try. And as is true in other cadre parties, most of the American parties' sympathizers in the public are not involved at all in the party organization; even the most loyal party voters are not normally dues-paying members.

They do not fit the cadre mold perfectly; in practice, parties have a tendency to slither out of precise definitions.[1] For example, the American parties engaged lots of volunteers in the days before the extensive use of television and other mass media, in order to get the campaign help they needed, though they did so without giving these activists much power in the party. But more recently, new technologies, such as television and computers, can free the party organizations from having to depend on platoons of activists.

Recent changes have clearly strengthened the American party organizations. The parties now have the resources to employ full-time professional staffers in their national and state offices. Party organizational power is less decentralized than it used to be. The parties solicit the party electorate more frequently, if only to raise money. Most primary elections are closed primaries in which voters have to declare a party affiliation before they are allowed to select the party's nominees.

Nevertheless, these changes have not made the major American parties into mass-membership organizations. As we've seen in Chapter 2, the nature of the American electoral system leads parties to appeal to majorities, not to smaller voter "niches." In a diverse nation, the result is that the major parties have not been very concerned with ideology or, at times, even with taking very specific stands on issues. Also in contrast to systems with mass-membership parties, the American parties do not monopolize the organization of political interests; rather, they compete in a political system in which voters are already organized by a wealth of interest groups and other nonparty political organizations as well.

Whether they are termed cadre or mass membership, party organizations are at the very center of the political parties. At times in U.S. history when party organizations have grown weaker, the nature of politics in American cities and states has changed. As these organizations have become more robust in recent years, they have altered our politics in ways ranging from campaign fund-raising practices to the nature of political debate. Chapter 3 begins with an exploration of the party organizations closest to home: state and local parties.

The State and Local Party Organizations

Amerian party organizations were often portrayed as military-style political "machines" in the late 1800s and early 1900s—very powerful and even fearsome in their ability to control city governments. In fact, most American party organizations were neither. Later in the 1900s, state and local party organizations were thought by many to be in such a weakened state that they'd probably never recover. That has changed as well. Party organizations in the United States have undergone remarkable transformations in the last century.

What difference does it make if a party organization is vibrant or sickly? As the Introduction noted, in many ways the party organization is the backbone of a political party. It gives the party a way to endure, even as its candidates and elected officeholders come and go. More than the party in government or the party in the electorate, the party organizations are the keepers of the parties' symbols—the unifying labels or ideas that give candidates a shortcut in identifying themselves to voters, and that give voters a shortcut in choosing among the candidates. Without this organization, a party becomes nothing more than an unstable alliance of convenience among candidates, and between candidates and groups of voters—a feeble intermediary, unlikely to be able to accomplish the functions that Chapter 1 described.

We will start to explore the reality of state and local party organizations by viewing them in their environment—in particular, the environment of regulations that have been placed on the state and local parties by state law. Next we turn to the local party organizations, tracing their path from the fabled "political machines" that dominated a number of eastern and midwestern cities beginning in the late 1800s, to the fall and rise of local parties more recently. Finally, we will explore the state parties, as they grew from weakness to relatively greater strength in the closing decades of the twentieth century.

THE PARTY ORGANIZATIONS IN STATE LAW

Americans' traditional suspicion of political parties has led the 50 states to pass a blizzard of rules intended to control their party organizations. Some of these regulations are embedded in state constitutions; others are expressed in a kaleidoscopic variety of state laws.

State Regulations

A recent study indicates the rich variety of state rules governing party organizations.[1] State party committees, it shows, are regulated "lightly" in only 17 states, most of them in the South, Plains states, and upper Midwest. At the other extreme, in 15 states—including California, New Jersey, and Ohio—lawmakers have felt it necessary to tell the state parties everything from the dates on which their central committees must meet to the procedures that must be used to select the parties' local organizations. These extensive state legal rules have not necessarily weakened the parties; some of the strongest party organizations in the nation are also the most tightly regulated. But clearly, these rules can give state governments a set of tools for monitoring and checking their parties.

The party organizations do not face similar kinds of regulations from the federal government. The U.S. Constitution makes no mention of parties. Nor has the Congress tried very often to define or regulate party organizations. Only in the 1970s legislation on campaign finance (and its later amendments) is there a substantial body of national law that affects the parties in important ways.

States do not have complete freedom in regulating the parties. Over the years, the federal courts have frequently stepped in to protect citizens' voting rights (in cases to be discussed in Chapter 8) and to keep the states from unreasonably limiting third-party and independent candidates' access to the ballot (see Chapter 2). More recently, the courts have even begun to overturn some state regulation of party organizational practices. In the 1980s, for example, the Supreme Court ruled that the state of Connecticut could not prevent the Republican Party from opening up its primary to independents if it wanted to. Soon after, the Court threw out California's rules that the state party chair serve a two-year term, that Southern and Northern Californians rotate as party chair, and that parties could not endorse candidates in primary elections.[2] And as we'll see in Chapter 9, a 2000 Supreme Court decision overturned a California state initiative setting up a "blanket primary" on the ground that it violated the party organization's First Amendment right to decide who votes in its primaries. It seems, then, that if the parties choose to challenge the state laws that govern them, they may be able to dismantle much of the regulatory framework that states have imposed on them.

Levels of Party Organization

Though state laws vary, the party organizations created by the states follow a common pattern. Their structure corresponds to the levels of government at which voters elect officeholders. This structure is often pictured as a pyramid based in the grass roots and stretching up to the statewide organization. A pyramid, however, gives the misleading impression that the layer at the top can give orders to the layers below. So picture these party organizations, instead, as they fit into a geographic map (Figure 3.1).

In a typical state, the smallest voting district of the state—the precinct, ward, or township—will have its own party organization, composed of men and women elected to the party's local committee (and called committeemen and committeewomen). Then come a series of party committees at the city, county, and sometimes, even the state legislative, the judicial, and congressional district level. The largest voting district, that of the state itself, is represented by a state central committee. The smallest and the largest of these levels are usually ordained by state laws, but the parties themselves may determine the middle layers.

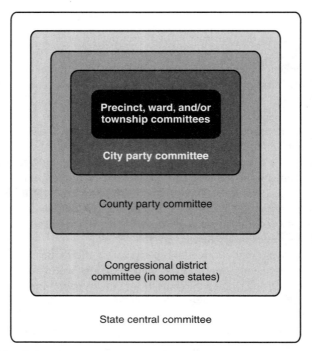

FIGURE 3.1 The Party Organizations in a Typical State.

The Elected Committeeman or Committeewoman

The position of the local committeeman and/or committeewoman is closest to the party's grass roots. These committee leaders are typically chosen at the precinct level. Because there are more than 100,000 precincts in the United States, it would be easy to imagine a vibrant party base made up of at least 200,000 committed men and women. But this exists only in the dreams of party leaders; in reality, many of these local committee positions are vacant because nobody wants to serve in them.

When these positions do get filled, it generally happens in one of three ways. Most committeemen and committeewomen are chosen at local party caucuses or primary elections, but in a few instances, higher party authorities appoint them. In states that choose precinct committeemen and women in the primaries, any voter may nominate him- or herself for the job by filing a petition signed by a handful of local voters. If, as often happens, there are no nominees, the committeeman or woman may be elected by an even smaller handful of write-in votes. In other states, parties hold local caucus meetings in the wards and precincts that are open to any voters of the area who declare themselves attached to the party. These party loyalists then elect the committee leaders in the caucuses; they also generally elect delegates to county and/or state conventions. These local committee positions, in short, are not normally in great demand. So the local parties are far from being exclusive clubs; their "front doors" are often open to anyone who cares to walk in.

What do these precinct party leaders do? State laws often don't say. In areas where local parties are active, their leaders follow patterns that have been carved out over time. In the past, the fabled local committeemen, or "ward heelers," of the American political machine knew the local voters, catered to their needs and problems, introduced the party candidates to them, and promoted the parties' issues—all with the ultimate purpose of turning out a bloc of votes for the party on election day. The main activities of their modern counterparts are similar: registering voters, going door-to-door (called "canvassing") to inform them about candidates, and getting voters to the polls. In the less active local parties, the committeemen and women may do little more than show up at an occasional meeting and campaign for a party candidate or two.

Local Committees   Several layers of party committees are built on top of the precinct level. Collectively, the precinct committeemen and -women often make up the city, town, county, and congressional district committees, or they elect the delegates who do. In a few other cases, these committees are chosen at county conventions, or by the party's candidates for public office. The most important of these is generally the county committee, although in some states the congressional district committees are of comparable importance.

Just as states often regulate the organization of the party, some also regulate its local activities. They may require, for example, that local committees meet within 30 or 45 days after the primary elections, or that they hold their conventions in certain types of public buildings. State law, then, does not view the parties simply as private associations. As Leon Epstein has put it, they are public utilities, sometimes subject to a great deal of state direction.[3]

State Central Committees   The state central committees, too, come in 50 state varieties, some very unified and others full of conflict (see the box on p. 54). In some states, the legislature has let the party organizations decide who will serve on their own state committee. Most state legislatures, however, prefer to make that decision themselves. State law often specifies which lower party committees will be represented on the central committee and whether central committee members will be chosen in the party's primaries, by a party convention, or by some other method.

State law commonly gives party central committees a number of important powers: the responsibility for calling and organizing party conventions, drafting party platforms, supervising the spending of party campaign funds, and selecting the party's presidential electors, representatives to the national committee, and at least some of the national convention delegates and alternates. Some other states give these powers to the party's statewide convention instead, sometimes even giving it the authority to choose the members of the state central committee. And in a few states, the party's state convention actually nominates candidates for some statewide offices—a reminder of the power the party conventions had in the days before the direct primary.

These are the formal organizational structures that state law creates for the state and local parties. From them, we can draw three important conclusions. First, the levels of party organization have been set up to correspond to the voting districts in which citizens choose public officials in that state (for example, city, county, and congressional districts), and the main responsibility of these organizations under state law is to contest

How to Split a State Party: A Race for Party Chair

Except among a few dedicated party activists, interest in the choice of a new state party chair is not normally comparable to interest in the NBA playoffs. Every so often, though, a struggle for the state party leadership becomes so intense—typically because it involves a battle over the party's ideological direction—that it draws national attention. That was the case in 2001 when Ralph Reed, former Executive Director of the Christian Coalition, entered the race for leadership of the Georgia Republican party.

Reed campaigned on the basis of his party-building experience, not on his ideological stance. He promised that he would be a "grassroots chairman," engaged in building a fully staffed GOP organization in every county. Others had different expectations. Backers of the opposing candidates cited a survey by a well-known Republican pollster claiming that Reed's selection would scare moderates away from statewide Republican candidates because, in the words of Emory political scientist Merle Black, "most people think he's way too far to the right." Reed supporters hired another major Republican pollster to critique these findings; he charged that the objections to Reed showed "anti-Christian bigotry" and efforts to exclude people from party leadership because they are "associated with people of faith."

State legislators and members of Congress from Georgia were drawn into the bitter split. A week before the vote, the contest was regarded as too close to call. Reed won the post and emphasized that he would be an "inclusive leader." Republican activists remained fearful (and Democrats hopeful), however, that even though the battle was over, the scars might take a very long time to heal.

Sources: Charles Babington, "Ralph Reed Creates Buzz in Georgia Politics," http://www.washingtonpost.com/ac2/wp-dyn/A12942-2001Apr12 (accessed Apr. 13, 2001); Ralph Reed's campaign Web site (http://www.ralphreedforchairman.com) (accessed Apr. 13, 2001).

elections. State laws, then, see the party organizations as helpers in the state's task of conducting nominations and elections—tasks that before the turn of the twentieth century belonged almost entirely to the parties alone.

Second, the laws indicate that state legislators are ambivalent about what constitutes a party organization. Many of these laws treat the parties as cadre organizations run by a small number of party officials. Yet when they specify that the party's own officials, including local committeemen and -women, must be chosen in a primary election, this gives party voters—and potentially, any voters—a vital, quasi-membership role in the party organization. So state laws help to create a party that is a mix of public and private, rather than a genuinely private group whose members choose its leaders and set its direction.

Finally, the relationships among these state and local party organizations are not those of a hierarchy, in which the "lower" levels take their orders from the higher levels. Instead, through much of their history, the state parties were best described as "a system of layers of organization"[4] or as a "stratarchy,"[5] in which each of the levels has some independent power. In fact, power has traditionally flowed from bottom to top in the local and state parties, as opposed to a hierarchy, where power would be centralized at the top.[6] Party organization is a system of party committees close to, and growing from, the political grass roots. The result is that the party organizations remain decentralized and rooted in local politics, even in the face of recent trends toward stronger state and national committees.

THE LEGENDARY PARTY MACHINES

Perhaps the high point of local party organizational strength in the United States was reached during the heyday of the classic urban political "machine." Machine politics reached its peak at around the turn of the twentieth century when, by one account, a large majority of American cities were governed by machines.[7] The party machine, accounts tell us, was a durable, disciplined organization that controlled the nominations to elective office. It had the hierarchical structure that today's local parties lack. It relied on material incentives—jobs and favors—to build support among voters. Above all, it controlled the government in a city or county.[8] Its colorful history includes the powerful Tammany Hall in New York, the antics of Chicago's "Big Bill" Thompson, and the genial rascality (and mail fraud conviction) of Mayor James Curley of Boston.

Yet for all their power in shaping how we may think of party organizations, the great urban machines were not found in all cities and, like the dinosaurs, they were temporary. The last of the great party machines was Chicago's, and it declined after the death of Mayor Richard J. Daley (the father of the current mayor) in 1976 (see box on p. 56). These dinosaurs were brought down by a number of forces. Some party machines, such as those in Pittsburgh and New York, never recovered from election upsets by middle-class reformers. Others, including those in Philadelphia and Gary, Indiana, lost power when new ethnic groups, especially blacks, became the more effective practitioners of the old ethnic politics.[9]

How The Party Machines Developed

In the late 1800s, large numbers of the immigrants arriving in major American cities had enormous economic and social needs. These newcomers were poor, often spoke no English, and faced a difficult adjustment to their new urban environment. Party leaders in many of these cities—usually Democrats, reflecting that party's history of openness to immigrants—saw the opportunity for an ingenious and mutually beneficial exchange. The populations of immigrants needed jobs, social services, and other benefits that a city government could provide. The party leaders needed lots of votes in order to gain control of city government. If the party could register these new arrivals to vote, their votes could put the party in power; in return, the party, which would then control the many resources that the government had available, could give the new voters the help they needed so desperately.

Jobs ranked high among the newcomers' needs. So the most visible of the benefits offered by party machines were patronage jobs in the city government—those awarded on the basis of party loyalty rather than any other qualifications. During the glory days of the machine, thousands of these patronage positions were at the machine's disposal. By giving patronage jobs to party supporters, the party's leaders could be assured that city workers would remain loyal to the machine and would work to keep it successful at election time by

The Decline of Machine Politics, Chicago Style

For decades, Chicago city government was run by one of the most powerful party "machines" in American history. In its prime, under the leadership of Mayor Richard J. Daley, the Chicago Democratic machine controlled nominations, elections, and the making of public policy in the city. Its dominance was based on control over an estimated 35,000 patronage jobs in government and access to another 10,000 in the private economy. Building from this loyal base by adding families, friends, and relatives, the organization could deliver 350,000 disciplined votes at election time.

With Daley's death in 1976, the machine lost its already-eroding control over Chicago politics and government. Machine candidates were defeated in two successive Democratic primaries, the second of which saw the party polarize along racial lines. It took black Mayor Harold Washington, the narrow victor of the 1983 primary and general election contests, several years to gain even majority support on the Democratic-dominated Board of Aldermen (Chicago's city council). Washington's reelection in 1987 further consolidated his power, but over a Democratic Party riddled with racial conflict, a government with declining numbers of patronage jobs, and a city beset with economic and social problems. Washington's death in 1987 brought about a new round of fierce conflict within the party.

Mayor Daley's son, Richard M. Daley, was able to pull the party together and win his father's post with a substantial majority in 1989; he has been handily reelected since that time. But even with his big election victories, the second Mayor Daley has not been able to restore the Chicago party machine to its glory days. Party organizational influence remains strong at the ward level in influencing citywide council elections, but the Democratic Party organization is not as powerful at the city level.[10]

What broke the back of the Chicago Democratic machine? In part, its decline reflects changes in the political culture, as machine politics became less acceptable and patronage jobs were less plentiful. It may have been weakened by ethnic conflict, as African-Americans sought to get their share of political power that had been dominated so long by other ethnic groups. Perhaps it died along with the first Mayor Daley, whose consummate political skill was once the only glue binding together these antagonistic ethnic, racial, and class groups. Or was it simply an electoral reaction to a decline in the quality of city services? Each of these factors probably contributed to the decline of machine politics in Chicago.[11]

delivering not only their own votes, but those of their friends, family, and neighbors as well. Local party workers also won voter loyalties by finding social welfare agencies for the troubled, or even by providing Christmas baskets or deliveries of coal for the needy.

The machine had favors to offer to local businesses as well. Governments purchase a lot of goods and services from the private sector. If a bank wanted to win the city's deposits, it could expect to compete more effectively for the city's business if it were willing to contribute to the party machine. Insurance agents who hoped to write city policies, lawyers who wanted the city's business, newspapers that printed city notices, even suppliers of soap to city washrooms, all could be drawn into the web of the party machine. In addition, city governments regularly make decisions on matters that affect individuals' and businesses' economic standing, such as building permits and health inspections. If you were helped by one of these decisions, you could expect the machine to ask for your gratitude in the form of contributions and votes at election time. A political leadership intent on winning support in exchange for these so-called "preferments" can use them ruthlessly and effectively to build its political power.

If these preferments were not enough, machines were capable of creating a "designer electorate" by using force and intimidation to keep less-supportive people from voting. Because the party machines controlled the election process, it was also possible, in a pinch, to change the election rules and even to count the votes in a creative manner. One of the indispensable tools of rival party workers in Indianapolis, for example, was a flashlight—to locate ballots that did not support the dominant party's candidates and happened to fly out of the window at vote-counting headquarters in the dark of night.

An important source of the machines' strength was their ability to appeal to ethnic loyalties. Studies in several nations show that when there are competitive elections and mass suffrage, political machines (or organizations similar to them) can flourish in parochial regions where strong family or group loyalties are combined with a great need for immediate, short-term benefits. The rise and fall of the American political machine is closely linked to changes in ethnic-group loyalties in the cities. The machine was a method by which ethnic groups and, especially, the Irish, gained a foothold in American politics.[12]

The classic urban machine, then, was not just a political party organization but also an "informal government," a social service agency, and a ladder for upward social and economic mobility. In some ways, it looked like the local organization of a European mass-membership party, except that the American machine had little or no concern with ideology. It focused on the immediate needs of its constituents and it ignored the issues and ideologies of the larger political environment. Its world was the city and its politics were almost completely divorced from the concerns that animated national politics.

We think of machine politics as flourishing in the biggest cities, but American party machines took root in other areas too.[13] The conditions that led to the development of machines, especially a large, parochially oriented population with short-term economic needs, were also found in small Southern towns and one-company towns. Even some well-to-do suburbs, in defiance of the rule that these organizations take root in poorer areas, have spawned strong machine-style party organizations. In the affluent Long Island suburbs of New York City, for example, a Republican Nassau County political machine developed that controlled local government and politics "with a local party operation that in terms of patronage and party loyalty rivals the machine of the famed Democratic mayor of Chicago, Richard J. Daley."[14]

We cannot be sure how powerful party machines really were, even at their strongest. A Chicago study found, for example, that the party machine distributed public services mainly on the basis of historical factors and bureaucratic decision rules; there was little evidence that services were provided to reward political support in either 1967 or 1977.[15] In New Haven, researchers reported that ethnic loyalties seemed more important to a party machine than even its own maintenance and expansion. The machine, led by Italian politicians, distributed summer jobs disproportionately to Italian youths from nonmachine wards, who rarely took part in later political work, and not to kids from strong machine areas.[16]

Regardless of how well they functioned at the peak of their strength, there is no doubt that the conditions that helped sustain party machines have been undercut. Economic change, as well as political reform, took away the machine's most important resources. Most city jobs are now covered by civil service protection, so the number of patronage jobs that can be used to reward the party faithful (as will be discussed more fully in Chapter 5) has been greatly reduced. Federal entitlement programs, such as welfare and Social Security, have reduced the need for the favors party machines could provide. Economic growth since the Second World War has boosted many Americans' income levels and reduced the attractiveness of the remaining patronage jobs; the chance to work for the sanitation district just doesn't have the cachet that it once may have had. Higher education levels have increased people's ability to fend for themselves in a complex bureaucratic society. And in many areas, the nature of ethnic conflict has changed; racial divisions have overwhelmed the machine's ability to balance competing ethnic groups.

Could Political Machines Reappear?

Yet the conditions that can support machine-style parties have not completely disappeared. Major cities still have economically dependent populations. New immigrant groups have taken the places of the old. Many cities continue to deal with tremendous social service demands at the same time as they are facing a declining tax base. If party machines thrive by offering help with a confusing government bureaucracy, city governments seem more than happy to oblige by providing the confusing bureaucracy. Ethnic strains have not disappeared, even though they may often be overshadowed by black-white conflict.

Where the demand for their services exists, political organizations will respond, even if they have to work within new and tighter constraints. Even past their peak, political machines were very skillful in creatively "interpreting" civil service regulations in order to maintain patronage jobs (for example, Mayor Daley hired thousands of long-term "temporary" employees) and in brokering federal benefits for the poor (the summer jobs distributed by the machine in New Haven were provided through a federal employment training program).

Local governments continue to have large budgets, provide a wide array of services, and play an active regulatory role, so it is still possible to sustain a patron-client form of politics in a supportive political culture. In short, although political machines in their classic (and often exaggerated) form were clearly part of an earlier time, reports of their death may be premature. Party organizations often learn how to adapt to new realities, so functional equivalents to the old-time machines may well emerge.[17]

HOW LOCAL PARTY ORGANIZATIONS HAVE REVITALIZED

The big city machines set the standard for effective party organizations, but it is a standard rarely achieved. At the other extreme—seldom written about because it offers so little to study—is virtual *dis*organization. In such cases, most of the party leadership positions remain vacant or are held by inactive incumbents. A chairman and a handful of loyal party officials may meet occasionally to carry out the most essential affairs of the party. Their main activity occurs shortly before the primary elections, as they plead with members of the party to become candidates, or step in themselves as candidates, to "fill the party ticket." They are not able to raise much money for the campaigns, or to attract media attention. This type of organization has probably always been more common than the machine. Most American local party organizations lie between these two extremes.

Local Parties in the 1970s

We got the first comprehensive look at the range of local party organizations in a 1979–1980 survey of several thousand county leaders (or the equivalent where there were no counties; see Table 3.1).[18] The results showed the distinctive fingerprints of cadre parties. The researchers found that most county organizations (but not all) were headed by a volunteer party chair and executive committee; almost none received salaries for their efforts and only a few had a paid staff to assist them. They had few resources to work with; not many of these local party leaders enjoyed the most basic forms of organizational support, such as a regular budget, a year-round office, or even a telephone listing. They did meet regularly, had formal rules to govern their work, and, together with a few associated activists, made decisions in the name of the party, raised funds, and sought out and screened candidates (or approved candidates who selected themselves). But their activity was far from constant; it peaked during campaigns.

Democratic parties did not differ much from Republicans, on average, in terms of the overall strength of their local organizations. There were considerable differences among states, however, in the organizational strength of their local parties. Some states in the East and Midwest had relatively strong local organizations in both parties, while others—Louisiana, Georgia, Alabama, Kentucky, Texas, and Nebraska—had relatively

TABLE 3.1 Changes in Local Parties' Organizational Strength, 1979–1980 to 1992

The local party organization has (in percent)	Democrats		Republicans	
	1992	*1979–80*	*1992*	*1979–80*
A complete or near complete set of officers	85	90	65	81
A year–round office	45	12	64	14
A telephone listing	68	11	75	16
Paid staff members:				
Full–time	22	3	26	4
Part–time	18	5	36	6
A paid chair	2	—	5	—
Regular volunteer staff	80	—	79	—
A regular annual budget	95	20	97	31
A campaign headquarters	85	55	65	60

Note: The 1979–1980 figures are based on responses from a total of 2,021 Democratic and 1,980 Republican organizations to a mail survey; the 1992 figures are based on telephone and mail responses to a survey of 40 Democratic chairs and 39 Republican chairs in 40 counties nationwide. Some of the differences between the figures may be the result of the different timing of the two surveys in the election cycle. The 1992 study reports on the situation during the general election campaign; the 1979–1980 study covers the period before the general election campaign began.

Source: For the 1979–1980 study, Cornelius P. Cotter, James L. Gibson, John F. Bibby, and Robert J. Huckshorn, *Party Organization in American Politics* (New York: Praeger, 1984), p. 43; for the 1992 study, Paul Allen Beck, Russell J. Dalton, and Robert Huckfeldt, *Comparative National Election Project,* United States study.

weak parties at the county level. In a few states, such as Arizona and Florida, one party was considerably stronger at the local level than the other party. But most often, strong organizations of one party were matched with strong organizations in the other party.[19]

There is persuasive evidence, however, that the county party organizations in 1980 were in the middle of a growth spurt. By asking 1980 county party chairs about the changes in their parties since 1964, researchers found that, on average, local parties had become substantially more involved in five important campaign activities: distributing literature, arranging campaign events, raising funds, publicizing candidates, and registering voters. When the researchers checked in again with these county organizations in 1984, they saw further development, and a national survey in 1988 indicated even higher levels of local party activity. Similar trends were reported in studies over time of local party organizations in Detroit and Los Angeles.[20]

The 1990s: More Money, More Activity

By the early 1990s, although local parties continued to depend on volunteer effort, the biggest change seemed to be in the things money could buy. A study of the county party organizations in 40 representative counties across the nation during the 1992 presidential election found that the basic ingredients for a viable party organization (a permanent office, an office during the campaign, a budget, a telephone listing, a staff) were more widespread in that year than they had been just a few years before. It seems clear that more money has been flowing to local party organizations in recent years, and the result is more energized local parties.

Only one of the 80 Democratic and Republican organizations sampled failed to perform any campaign activities. A majority of each party's local organizations conducted registration drives, transported voters to the polls, ran campaign events, telephoned voters to urge them to support the party ticket, and distributed yard signs and "slate cards" listing the party's candidates.[21] At least some of their efforts seemed to bear fruit; for instance, one study found that more than a third of people regarded as potentially strong candidates for Congress in 1998 had, in fact, been contacted by local party leaders, and that those contacted were more likely to run.[22]

In sum, we have good evidence that county party organizations were stronger and more active in the 1990s than they had been a generation earlier.[23] But because there are so few reliable records prior to the 1960s, it is hard to determine whether these local organizations have regained the levels of vitality that local parties were thought to have achieved a century ago. Even the most active of the present local parties is probably no match for a powerful urban machine. Nevertheless, not many of these local parties are completely dead either. So many counties may now have more robust party organizations than they have ever had.

What accounts for the growing strength of the county parties? The short answer is money. Party organizations at all levels have developed more effective tools for raising money than they have had for some time. Local parties have benefited, in particular, from the willingness of the increasingly well-heeled state parties to share the wealth. But as we will soon see, the nature of these party organizations has changed; rather than serving as the center of election activity, they have become service providers to candidates who often have several other sources of services. So the challenge for the local parties is this: In an age of candidate-centered campaigns, does this growing county organizational presence matter as much as it would have a few decades ago?[24]

THE STATE PARTIES: NEWFOUND PROSPERITY

Throughout the American parties' history, the state committee has rarely had significant power in the party organizations. There have been exceptions, of course. Some powerful, patronage-rich state party organizations developed in the industrial heartland in the late nineteenth century, where they served as the organizational base for U.S. senators (who were appointed rather than elected prior to 1913). Several decades later, Huey Long built a powerful state organization in Louisiana.[25] But in most states, most of the time, the party's state committee has not been the site of the party's main organizational authority.

In recent years, however, state parties have grown in importance. They are richer, more professional and more active now than they have ever been before. There has been a centralization of activity throughout the party structure—a change that has been well documented by capable research. Let us start the story in the years before this change began.

Traditional Weakness

There are many reasons why the state party organizations were traditionally weak. They began as loose federations of semi-independent local party chairmen. These decentralized parties were ripe for factional conflict. Within the states, and therefore within the state parties, there were ample sources of division: rural-urban and regional differences, ethnic and religious differences, loyalties to local leaders, and, especially, conflicts between more liberal and more conservative interests. Because the leadership of the state party organization is a prize that can be won by only one of these factions rather than shared, any consolidation of power at the state level could seriously threaten the losing factions. In the past, with only the few exceptions mentioned above, this threat was often avoided by keeping most of the party's resources out of the hands of the state organization. Power, in other words, was decentralized, collecting in the most viable of the local organizations.

Other forces also weakened the state party organizations. Progressive reforms early in the twentieth century sapped the influence of state parties over nomination and election campaigns for state offices. The Populist influence can be seen even now, in that it is the states where the Populists had greatest strength—the western states, especially the more rural ones—where we still find relatively weak state party organizations.[26]

Due in part to these reforms, candidates could win party nominations in primary elections without party organization support, could raise money for their own campaigns and, thus, run them without party help. Since 1968, the state party's role in the national presidential nominating conventions has been diminished by internal party reforms, especially among the Democrats. It is the voters, rather than the state party organization, who choose convention delegates now; almost all of the delegates come to the convention pledged to a particular candidate for the nomination, rather than controlled by state party leaders. Extensions of civil service protections and growing unionization eroded the patronage base for many state parties. And in what may have been the final indignity for patronage politics, some courts have even prevented the firing of patronage workers when the governing party changes.

The existence of one-party dominance in several states during the first half of the 1900s also kept a number of state parties weak and conflict-ridden. Southern Democratic parties were a notable example (and Southern Republican parties were all but nonexistent). When a single party dominates a state's politics, the diverse forces within the state are likely to compete as factions within that party; the state party organization has neither the incentive nor the ability to unify, as it might if it faced a threat from a viable opposition party. For all these reasons, many state party organizations were described as "empty shells" in the 1940s and 1950s.[27]

Increasing Strength in Recent Years

Since the 1960s, however, state party organizations have become stronger and more active. The state parties began to institutionalize—to become enduring, specialized, well-bounded organizations—during the 1960s and 1970s. In the early 1960s, for example, only 50 percent of a sample of state organizations had permanent state headquarters; two decades later, in 1979–1980, that was true of 91 percent. The number of full-time, salaried, state party chairs doubled during this time, as did the number of full-time staff employed by the parties in nonelection years. These resources—full-time leaders and a stable location—are vital to the development of parties as organizations.[28]

As we found with regard to local parties, the state organizations have continued to expand since then. By 1999, more than half of the state parties surveyed in a careful research study had full-time party chairs, research staff, and public relations directors. Three-quarters had a field staff and 91 percent employed a full-time executive director. The empty shells are being filled. Interestingly, Southern parties—long among the weakest and most faction-ridden—have become some of the strongest state party organizations in the last two decades.[29]

Fund-Raising   State parties have put special effort into developing fund-raising capabilities in recent years. By 1999, according to a study by John H. Aldrich (see Table 3.2), 98 percent of the state parties surveyed held fund-raising events and the same percentage had direct mail fund-raising programs. The Wisconsin Republican state party is a good example; by the late 1990s it had established a computerized marketing center with as many as 35 telemarketers in order to expand the party's small-donor base. State parties used the money to support a variety of races; party candidates for governor, state legislature, and the U.S. Senate and House received contributions from more than four-fifths of these parties. Over 90 percent of the parties surveyed by Aldrich had recruited a full slate of candidates for state races; the parties' new fund-raising skills can be very useful in convincing attractive prospects to run for an office.[30]

The parties are especially active in recruiting candidates for the state legislature, raising funds for them, and helping the candidates raise money themselves. It is the state parties, to a much greater extent than the national or local parties, which offer money

TABLE 3.2 Increasing Organizational Strength among the State Parties

Party Strength and Activity	1999	1979–1980	Difference
Typical Election Year Budget	$2.8 mil.	$340 K	$2.46 mil.
Typical Election Year Fulltime Staff	9.2	7.7	1.5
Conducted Campaign Seminars	95%	89%	6%
Recruited a Full Slate of Candidates	91%	—	—
Operated Voter ID Programs	94%	70%	24%
Conducted Public Opinion Surveys	78%	32%	46%
Held Fund–Raising Event	98%	19%	77%
Contributed to Governor Candidate	89%	47%	42%
Contributed to State Legislator	92%	47%	45%
Contributed to State Senator	85%	25%	60%
Contributed to U.S. Congressional	85%	48%	37%
Contributed to Local Candidate	70%	—	—

Note: 1999 data come from a mail survey conducted by John H. Aldrich and associates of 65 state party chairs (39 Democrats, 26 Republicans). 1979–1980 data are from the mail survey of state parties described in the note to Table 3.1.

Source: For the 1999 data, see Aldrich's "Southern Parties in State and Nation," *Journal of Politics* 62 (2000): 659. The 1979–1980 data are from James L. Gibson, Cornelius P. Cotter, and John F. Bibby, "Assessing Party Organizational Strength," *American Journal of Political Science* 27 (1983): 193–222.

and services to state legislative candidates.[31] In addition, in almost every state these candidates get help from the legislative parties and/or leaders themselves. These state legislative campaign committees have come to play an increasingly important role in legislative campaigns.[32]

The increase in election-year fund-raising between 1980 and 1999 fairly leaps off the page in Table 3.2. Just as important for the development of strong party organizations, fund-raising during nonelection years has been growing as well. The nonelection-year budgets of the state parties climbed from an average (in absolute dollars) of under $200,000 in 1960–1964 to $340,667 in 1979–1980, then to $424,700 by the mid-1980s, and finally to $900,000 by 1999.[33]

Campaign Services   With this increased organizational and financial capacity, the state parties have been able to offer more than just money to political campaigns. They have also devoted their resources to supplying campaign services in the form of training, advertising, polling, and voter-mobilization drives that supplement those of the candidates' own organizations. Now that many state legislative and statewide candidates—even local candidates in some states—need consultants and computers to run a competitive campaign, they increasingly turn to the state party organizations to provide these expensive services.

To fill that need, almost all of the surveyed state parties provided campaign-training seminars. Almost four-fifths conducted public opinion surveys. All of these state parties operated voter identification programs to determine which voters were most likely to support their party's candidates, and also took part in get-out-the-vote drives, as well as joint fund-raising with county party organizations.[34] State parties now frequently provide computers, fax machines, and voter lists to selected candidates. Coordinated campaigns, emphasizing the sharing of campaign services among a variety of candidates, are increasingly being run through the state party organizations. And since 1996, a lot of state party money has been used to pay for issue advocacy ads promoting the party position on issues, which has at least indirect benefits for party candidates.

Republican Advantage   All these studies show that, unlike the situation at the county level, Republican state organizations are considerably stronger than their Democratic counterparts. The Republican parties surveyed by Aldrich have much bigger budgets and bigger and more specialized staffs. Because they are larger and richer, these Republican parties can provide more services to their candidates and local party organizations. For example, Republican state parties are more likely to conduct public opinion polls, employ a field staff and researchers, conduct joint fund-raising with county party organizations, and contribute to local parties than the Democrats are.[35] This GOP advantage reflects to a great degree the extensive subsidies the national party has been able to provide to all of the state parties.

Allied Groups   State Democratic parties, however, hold an important counterweight. Labor unions, especially teachers' and government employees' unions, work closely with their state Democratic party organizations to provide money, volunteer help, and other services to party candidates. In states such as Alabama and Indiana, the state teachers' union is so closely connected with the state party that critics might find it difficult to tell where one stops and the other begins. State Republican parties have close ties to allied groups as well. Small business groups, manufacturing associations, pro-life groups, and Christian conservative organizations often provide services to Republican candidates.

Groups of a variety of types—not just unions and business associations, but also citizen groups, issue organizations, polling and other political consulting firms, and "think tanks"—have become more closely linked with the state party organizations and can provide resources and expertise. So the boundaries of state and local party organizations have begun to blur.[36] The network of the party can be seen as a kind of reservoir of organizations and activists. Drawn from this reservoir are the shifting coalitions that speak and act in the name of the party. A hotly contested governor's race will activate one coalition of partisans and allied groups within the party and a congressional race centering on local issues will activate another. For party leaders, these allied groups can be a mixed blessing, of course; labor unions and business groups have their own agendas and they can be as likely to try to push the state party into locally unpopular stands as to help in the effort to elect party candidates. Nevertheless, allied groups play an increasing role in the expanding network that surrounds the state party. (For an example of these state party coalitions, see Figure 3.2.)

It is not easy to build a powerful state party organization. It requires having to overcome both the grassroots localism of American politics and the widespread hostility toward strong party discipline. Strong and skillful personal leadership by a governor, a senator, or a state chairman helps.[37] So does a state tradition or culture that

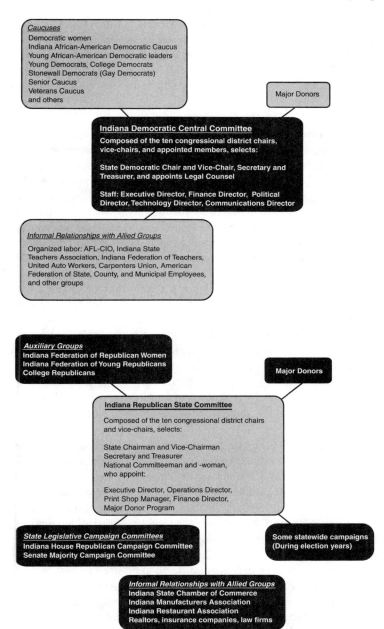

FIGURE 3.2　An Example of the Web of Groups Surrounding a State Party:
The Indiana State Party Organizations, 2001.

Source: Information for this figure comes from the two state party committees (their Web sites are at http://www.indems.org and http://www.indgop.org) and from Brian Vargus, Professor of Political Science at Indiana University-Purdue University at Indianapolis and Director of the Indiana University Public Opinion Laboratory.

accepts the notion of a unified and effective party. State law makes a difference as well. More centralized party organization has flourished in the states in which primary elections are least extensive and in which the party organization has more direct control over who the statewide and congressional candidates will be. Good examples include both Pennsylvania parties, the Ohio Republican party, and the North Dakota Democratic organization.[38]

The Special Case of the South   The most striking case of party organizational development has occurred in the South. Here, several forces—notably Southerners' reaction to national policy change and the resulting development of two-party competition at the state level—have spurred the development of much stronger state parties.[39] As the national Democratic Party showed greater concern for the rights of African-Americans in the 1960s and 1970s, and particularly as the Voting Rights Acts greatly increased the proportion of African-American voters in Southern states, conservative southern Democrats became increasingly estranged from their national party. Southern support for Republican candidates grew, first in presidential elections, later in statewide and U.S. Senate races.

In the 1980s, state legislative candidates could sense the opportunity to run and win as Republicans. By 1994, Republicans were contesting almost a third of the state legislative seats in the South and winning two-thirds of those seats. Between 1994 and 2000, Republicans won the governorship of all but two of the Southern states at least once, and won a majority in at least one house of the state legislature in five Southern states: Florida, Texas, Virginia, and the Carolinas.[40] Republicans, in short, are now approaching parity with the Democrats in state elections—this in a region where, just a few decades before, it was often more socially acceptable to admit to having an alcoholic than a Republican in the family.

National Party Money   The most important ingredient in strengthening the state party organizations, though, has been the national parties' party-building efforts. With more energetic leadership and more lavish financial resources than ever before, since the 1970s the national party committees have worked hard to build the organizational effectiveness of the state parties—and local parties too. The full story of these efforts will be told in Chapter 4, but the central point here is that the state parties have benefited greatly from national party investments. Millions of dollars (since 1980, increasingly in the form of "soft money"[41]) have been channeled from the Democratic and Republican national committees to state party committees, to be used in building up organizational capacity and running party campaigns. In the 1999–2000 election cycle alone, the two national committees transferred almost $250 million to state parties ($129 million from the Republican National Committee and $114.6 million from the Democratic National Committee)—many times the amounts that the national parties infused into the state organizations just a few years earlier. State parties, so recently the poor relations of the formal party organizations, have come into money. Whether their new status has cost them their independence, this time from the national parties, is a question only the future can answer.[42]

SUMMING UP: HOW THE STATE AND LOCAL PARTY ORGANIZATIONS HAVE TRANSFORMED

The story of party organizational strength at the state and local levels is complex. The high point of *local* party organizations was probably reached a hundred years ago, when the parties could be described as:

> ... armies drawn up for combat (in which) financial and communications "sinews of war" were provided by an elaborate, well-staffed, and strongly motivated organizational structure. In the field of communications, a partisan press was dominant.... The "drilling" of voters in this period by their party captains was intense.[43]

Although this description did not apply to party organizations throughout the nation even at that time, it might be impossible to find a local party organization that could be described in these terms today.

Local parties were buffeted by a variety of forces since then. Progressive reforms adopted in the early 1900s undermined party organizations by limiting their control over nominations and general elections, as well as over their valued patronage resources. In recent decades, a number of factors—reforms of the presidential nominating process, the welfare state, the almost total demise of the patronage system, national regulation of previously state-controlled party activities, and greater education of the electorate—undercut the effectiveness of the local parties.[44]

Yet local parties have come a long way toward adapting to these changes. County parties seem to have moved to fill at least some of the void created by the decline of the urban machines. New sources of funding are enabling these county parties to expand their activities. Local party organizations, in short, are demonstrating again their ability to meet the new challenges posed by a changing environment—a resilience that has kept them alive throughout most of American history.

The state party organizations have followed a different route. Traditionally weak in all but a handful of states, the state parties were little more than vessels that could barely contain conflicting local organizations. But state party organizations appear to have grown remarkably robust in recent years, becoming more professionalized than ever before. They are providing campaign and organizational services to local parties that, in an earlier era, would not have dreamed of looking to their state headquarters for help.

In fact, the recent flow of money, resources, and leadership (at least to some degree) from the national party to the state party, and in turn from the state to the local parties, helps to reverse the traditional flow of party power. Through most of their lives, the American parties have been highly decentralized, with power and influence lodged at the base of the organizational pyramid. The parties were hollow at the top, depending on the base for whatever influence and resources they had. Because of the death of urban machines and the birth of vigorous state and national party organizations, we no longer see this extreme form of decentralization. The nationalization of American society and politics has affected the party organizations as well.

Yet ironically, even though they are much stronger now, the formal party organizations at the state and local level probably have less impact on our politics than they once did. There are several reasons. First, they have much more competition for the attention of voters, candidates, and the media. The party organizations are often muscled aside by other groups ranging from independent campaign consultants to organized interests. The campaign communications sent out by the parties merge into a flood of direct mail fund-raising and advertising by citizen groups, corporate and labor PACs, and wealthy individuals, all of whom try to influence voters' choices. Many of these groups encourage individuals to run for office. They give money to candidates. They can offer candidates a means to reach voters and prospective volunteers, independent of the party organization. They have campaign expertise rivaling that of the party's experts.

Second, although most state parties have become much more able fund-raisers, the party's resources are still dwarfed by those of other actors in elections. In state legislative campaigns, for example, this new party money accounts for only about 5–10 percent of the funds received by candidates.[45] Campaigners are happy for every dollar, of course, but these relatively small sums, even with the helpful services that accompany them, may not be enough to entice candidates to listen carefully to the party on legislative matters or any other concerns.

So the increasing organizational strength of the state and local parties has helped them adopt modern campaign skills and recapture a role in candidates' campaigns. But it is not a *dominant* role—not in the way it could have been if party organizations, rather than voters in primaries, selected party candidates. Party organizations rarely *run* the campaigns; instead, their new resources give them more of a chance of competing for the attention of those who do—the candidates—at a time when other competitors (organized interests, consultants and others) have become more effective as well.

Does this mean that the increases in party organizational strength are unimportant? Clearly not. In a very competitive political environment, there's little doubt that it is better to have a stronger organization than a weaker one, and to have more resources rather than fewer. Further, there is evidence that where parties are stronger organizationally (and especially when both parties are strong), citizens are likely to have more supportive attitudes toward parties and partisanship.[46]

In the end, however, despite all the changes in party organization during the last few decades, their most basic structural features have not changed. The American state and local parties remain cadre organizations run by a small number of activists; they involve the bulk of their supporters only at election time. The shift began as a movement from a well-defined cadre party at the local level to a weak cadre party at the local and state levels, and now to a wealthier cadre organization blending easily into a surrounding network of sometimes cooperative, sometimes competitive political forces. The American state and local parties are still a long way from matching the year-round, continuously active lives of parties elsewhere in the world. By the standards of those parties, American party organization continues to be more fluid and fast-changing, more lethargic, except at election time, and more easily dominated by a handful of activists and elected officials.

The Parties' National Organizations

S outh of Capitol Hill, a few blocks from the House and Senate offices, stand the national headquarters buildings of the Democratic and Republican parties. Their upscale quarters show a level of wealth, independence and permanence never seen before in the history of the national parties. Their neighborhoods tell even more about the change in their status. They are now located closer to Congress than to the White House, just as the national parties have moved beyond their traditional job as hand-maiden to the president and into a new role of party building in the states and locali-ties. The older and more imposing GOP headquarters, purchased in 1970 (the Democrats bought theirs in 1984), is testimony to the fact that the Republicans started earlier and have done more to build effective national party organizations.

The change has been remarkable. Only in the earliest years of the American parties, when presidential candidates were nominated by the congressional caucus, were the national parties as important in American politics. Just a few decades ago, the national committees were poor and transient renters—often moving back and forth between New York and Washington, and all but disbanding between presidential campaigns. Leading students of the national committees could accurately describe them as "politics without power."[1] For most of their history, in fact, the national parties were no more than empty boxes on an organizational chart—labels at the top of a party system in which the real power collected at the bottom, as is typical in a decentralized party system.[2]

There is good reason why the parties have long been decentralized, as Chapter 3 indicated. Virtually all American public officials are chosen in state and local elections; even the voting for president is conducted mainly under state election laws. It is the state governments that have been the chief regulators of parties. In years past, most of the incentives parties had to offer, such as preferments and patronage jobs, were available at the local and state levels. All these forces have given the parties a powerful state and local focus that continues to restrain any shift in power within the party organizations. So state and local party organizations pick their own officers, nominate their own candidates, take their own stands on issues, and raise and spend their own funds, without much interfer-ence from the national party.

Yet there are powerful nationalizing forces in American society that have long since affected most other aspects of American politics. The mass media bring the same TV images, reporters, and commentators into homes in all parts of the country. Government in the American federal system became increasingly centered in Washington beginning in the 1930s. Even the other two sectors of the party have been nationalized in the last few decades. Party voters respond increasingly to national issues, national candidates, and national party symbols and positions. And in the party in government, the president and the congressional party leadership have become more than ever the prime spokespersons for their parties.

The party organizations responded more slowly to these nationalizing forces. But since the 1970s there have been striking signs of life in the national committees. Their resources and staffs have grown. They have taken on new roles, new activities and new influence. They have been able to limit the independence of state and local organizations in their one collective function—the selection of delegates to the national conventions. The congressional campaign committees are vital and active. There is, in short, a greater potential for national authority within the major American parties. So although the state and local pull remains strong, the national organizations are an increasingly powerful presence in the parties.

Does this change make a difference in the workings of American politics? Does it affect your own political power? Let us begin by exploring what the national party is and what it is capable of doing.

NATIONAL PARTY COMMITTEES AND OFFICERS

What do we mean by the "national" party? Technically speaking, the party's supreme national authority is the nominating convention each party holds during a presidential election year. The convention's role, however, rarely goes beyond selecting the presidential and vice-presidential candidates and formulating party platforms and rules. It does specify the structure and powers of the national committee, but because the convention meets only once every four years, it cannot exercise continuing supervision over the party's national organization.

The National Committees

Between conventions, the national committees are the main governing institutions of the two major parties. These are venerable organizations: the Democrats created their national committee in 1848 and the Republicans in 1856. For years, Democrats and Republicans had similar rules for representation on the national committee. Every state (and some territories) was represented equally on both national committees, regardless of its voting population or the extent of its party support. Alaska and California, then, had equal-sized delegations to the national party committees, just as they do in the U. S. Senate. That system overrepresented the smaller states and also gave roughly equal weight in the national committees to the winning and the losing parts of the party. In practice, this strengthened the Southern and Western segments of each party, which tended to be more conservative.

Since 1972, when the Democrats drastically changed the makeup of their national committee, the parties have structured their committees differently. After briefly experimenting with unequal state representation in the 1950s, the Republicans have retained their traditional confederational structure by giving each of the state and territorial parties three seats on the committee. By contrast, the Democratic National Committee (DNC), now almost three times the size of its Republican counterpart (RNC), gives weight both to population and to party support in representing the states. California, for example, has twenty seats on the committee and Alaska has four. The two national committees also differ in that the Democrats give national committee seats to representatives of groups especially likely to support Democratic candidates, such as blacks, women, and young people (Table 4.1)—a decision that shows the importance of these groups to the party—as well as to groups of elected officials.

National committee members are selected by the states and, for the Democrats, by these other groups as well. The state parties differ in how they make their decisions, and in many states the two parties choose their national committee representatives differently. They use four main methods of selection: by state party convention, by the party delegation to the national convention, by the state central committee, and by election in a primary. The choice of method makes a difference. The parties' state organizations can usually control the selection of committee members when they are chosen by the state committee and by the state conventions; party organizations are less effective in influencing choices made by primaries or by national convention delegates.

The Officers

The national committees have the power to choose their own leaders. By tradition, however, the parties' presidential candidates can name their party's national chair for the duration of the presidential campaign and the committees ratify their choices without question. The national chair chosen by the winning presidential candidate usually keeps his or her job after the election. So in practice, only the "out" party's national committee actually chooses its own national chair. The committees generally have much greater freedom to select other committee officials—vice-chairs, secretaries, and treasurers. Both national committees also elect executive committees, which include these officers and some other members of the committee.

The chairs, together with the national committees' permanent staffs, dominate these organizations. The members of the full national committees are a collection of state and local party notables who come together only two or three times a year and have little to do as a group. Their meetings are largely for show, and to call media attention to the party and its candidates. The other officers of the party are not especially influential and the executive committees meet only a little more often than the full committees. Like the full committees, the executive committees are composed of men and women whose concern is state (and even local) organizational work, rather than the building of a strong national party apparatus. Thus by tradition, the national chair, with a permanent staff that he or she has chosen, has, in effect, been the national party organization.

TABLE 4.1 Members of Democratic and Republican National Committees: 2000

Democratic National Committee	*Number of Members*
Party Chair and Vice-Chair from each state, D.C., American Samoa, Guam, Puerto Rico, Virgin Islands, and Democrats Abroad	112
Other members apportioned to states on the basis of population (at least two per state, with delegations equally divided between men and women)	200
Elected Officials:	
2 U.S. Senators and 2 U.S. House members (the party leader and one other member of each house)	4
Representatives of Democratic Governors Conference	3
Democratic Mayors Conference	3
Democratic County Officials Conference	3
Democratic Legislative Campaign Committee	3
Democratic Municipal Officials Conference	3
Democratic Lieutenant Governors Association	2
Democratic Secretaries of State Association	2
Democratic State Treasurers Association	2
Representatives of Young Democrats	3
National Federation of Democratic Women	3
Representatives of College Democrats	2
Officers of National Committee	13
(National Chair, General Chair, General Co-chairs, Vice-Chairs, Treasurer, Secretary, Finance Chair, Deputy Chair)	
Additional at-large members appointed by DNC Chair to implement participation goals for blacks, Hispanics, women, youth, Asians, and Native Americans	up to 75
Approximate Total	433
Republican National Committee	
National Committeeman, National Committeewoman, and State Chair from each state and from D.C., American Samoa, Guam, Puerto Rico, and Virgin Islands	165
Total	165

Note: Two Democratic committee officers also are state committee representatives.

Committee Action and Presidential Power

The national committees' role, and that of their chairs, depends on whether the president is from their party. When their party does not hold the presidency, the national chair and committee can provide some national leadership. They bear the responsibility for binding up wounds, healing internal party squabbles, helping pay debts from the losing campaign, raising new money, and energizing the party organization around the country. The "out" party's national chair may speak for the party and the alternatives it proposes. So the national chair and committees play more influential roles, by default, when their party has less control over the national government.

With a party leader in the White House, on the other hand, the national committee's role is whatever the president wants it to be. Presidents came to dominate their national committees early in the 20th century. Their control reached a new peak in the 1960s and 1970s, and has remained strong ever since. James Ceaser, for example, cites the example of Robert Dole, a Republican senator and RNC chair from 1971 to 1973, who was quickly fired by the president when he tried to put a little distance between the party and the president's involvement in Watergate: "I had a nice chat with the President ...while the other fellows went out to get the rope."[3] Some presidents have turned their national committees into little more than managers of the president's campaigns and builders of the president's political support between campaigns. Other presidents, such as Ronald Reagan, have used their control to build up the national committees to achieve party, not just presidential, goals.

In the president's party, the national chair must be congenial to the president, representative of the president's ideological stance and willing to be loyal primarily to the president. Within the opposition party, the chair will need to get along with or at least be trusted by the various factions or segments of the party. Frequently, he or she is chosen for ideological neutrality or for lack of identification with any of the candidates for the party's next presidential nomination. Experience in the nuts and bolts of party and campaign organization is also desirable. In this respect, it is understandable that as the parties came out of the closely fought 2000 election, with the House and Senate closely divided and an expensive race expected in 2002, both parties chose national chairs with a great deal of successful fund-raising experience. The qualifications for the job, then, vary depending on the party's electoral circumstances (see box on p. 74).

THE SUPPORTING CAST OF NATIONAL GROUPS

Clustered around the national committees are a set of more-or-less formal groups that also claim to speak for the national party, or for some part of it. Some are creations of the national committees; others are not. Taken together with the national committee in each party, they come close to constituting that vague entity we call the national party.

Special Constituency Groups

The national party committees sometimes give a formal role in their organization to supportive groups that might not be otherwise well represented. For a long time, both the Democrats and Republicans have had women's divisions associated with their national committees. Both have also had national federations of state and local women's groups: the National Federation of Democratic Women and the National Federation of Republican Women. The importance of these women's divisions has declined markedly in the last 30 years as women have entered regular leadership positions in the parties and served more frequently as convention delegates.

The Young Republican National Federation and the Young Democrats of America also have a long history of representation and support in party councils. The national committees do not control these groups, however, and at times they have taken stands

The National Party Chairs:
Fund-Raising is Job One

Jim Nicholson, chair of the Republican National Committee (RNC) from 1997–2000, had left the RNC in great financial shape. The Committee had millions of dollars in the bank by the summer of 2000, an e-mail list of a million names and a contact list containing information about 165 million voters. Because money was so vital to the party's prospects in the 2000 elections, when George W. Bush became the Republican candidate for president in August 2000, he chose another proven fund-raiser, Virginia Governor Jim Gilmore, to take over as RNC chair.

Gilmore, a former chair of the Republican Governors' Association, had long been a tenacious competitor. After spending three years in Army counterintelligence, Gilmore had applied to the University of Virginia Law School and was turned down. His response was to sit in the admissions office waiting for a position to open in the first-year class. (Fortunately, one did during the second day of his sit-in.) Years later, as the state's attorney general and then governor, Gilmore honed his skills as a money-raiser. He built a large network of contributors, which he tapped to raise millions of dollars for Bush and other Republican candidates in 2000, and he was rewarded by being named one of three co-chairs of Bush's Victory 2000 campaign, before moving to head the RNC. Gilmore was expected to concentrate on the money and to leave the RNC's strategic decisions to Bush's chief advisor, Karl Rove—evidence of the important leadership role presidents play in their party's national committee. Gilmore raised money but resisted White House control. He was forced out after serving for a year and was replaced by former Montana Governor Marc Racicot, a close Bush friend.

Terry McAuliffe, newly-appointed chair of the Democratic National Committee (DNC) in 2000, cut his fund-raising teeth even earlier than Gilmore did. McAuliffe, who started his first company when he was 14, was the top fund-raiser for the 1980 Carter-Mondale presidential campaign at the ripe old age of 22. He later became the DNC's Finance Director, and then National Finance Chair and National Co-Chair for the Clinton-Gore campaign in 1996. McAuliffe claims to have raised a half-billion dollars for Democratic candidates, making him, in the words of New York Times reporter, Richard L. Berke, "the party's premier fund-raiser of the last two decades" (or, in Al Gore's more expansive phrase, "the greatest fund-raiser in the history of the universe"). A home builder and mortgage financier, McAuliffe broadened the Democrats' financial base into the business and legal communities. To Berke, who points out that "the central role of party chairman is always to raise money," the selection of McAuliffe as DNC chair represents the triumph of the "permanent campaign," and, to some extent, of money in politics.

Source: R. H. Melton and Thomas B. Edsall, "Bush Taps Gilmore as RNC Chairman," *Washington Post*, Dec. 22, 2000, p. A1; Mike Allen, "For RNC Head, Bush Turns to Trusted Friend," *Washington Post*, Dec. 6, 2001, p. A12; and Richard L. Berke, "The Man Who Would Be Democratic Chairman Leaves Little to Chance," *New York Times*, February 1, 2001, p. A15.

and supported candidates opposed by the senior party organization. The Young Republicans, for instance, have often taken positions to the right of the regular leadership of their party, and the Young Democrats have frequently stood to the left of their national committee—as they did in 1969, when the Young Democrats' national convention called for liberalization of marijuana laws, for diplomatic recognition of Cuba, and for an immediate and total withdrawal of all American troops in Vietnam. In recent years, the Young Democrats have declined, while the Young Republicans have capitalized on the party's enhanced electoral strength to expand their numbers.

The Party's Officeholders in the States

State governors have long had a powerful voice in their national parties, for several reasons. They hold prestigious offices, earned by winning statewide elections. Many lead, or at least, are supported by their state party organization and some will probably be considered potential candidates for president.

Governors gained a more formal position in the national parties since the 1960s. After the defeat of strongly conservative Republican presidential candidate, Barry Goldwater, in 1964, moderate Republican governors felt the need to counterbalance the conservatives in the party leadership. So they established a full-time Washington office with financial help from the party's national committee, though their influence waned after Republicans won the presidency in 1968. Democratic governors began to press for a role in national party affairs in the 1970s, when their party was in opposition. By 1974, they had won modest representation on the national committee. By the late 1970s and early 1980s then, the governors of both parties had Washington offices and staffs. Their organizational influence in the national parties, however, tends to be greatest in the power vacuum created when their party is out of power.

State legislators and local officials in both parties are organized as well, and are formally represented on the Democratic National Committee, though they do not normally have much influence on either party's national operations. A more influential group is the Democratic Leadership Council (DLC). Founded in 1985, it brings together Democratic elected officials, led by influential members of Congress and governors and some prospective candidates for president. The DLC represents the moderate-to-conservative wing of the party and works to make the party more appealing to Southern and Western voters. It played an important role in Bill Clinton's rise to national prominence leading up to his 1992 nomination for president, and hopes to be at least as influential in the 2004 nomination race.

Congressional Campaign Committees

The most important of all the supporting cast are each party's House and Senate campaign committees (called the "Hill committees" because they used to be housed on Capitol Hill). The House committees were founded in the immediate aftermath of the Civil War; the Senate committees came into being when senators began to be popularly elected in 1913. The Democratic Congressional Campaign Committee (DCCC), the National Republican Congressional Committee (NRCC), the Democratic Senatorial Campaign Committee (DSCC) and the National Republican Senatorial Committee (NRSC) are organized to promote the reelection of their members and the success of other congressional candidates of their party. They are the campaign organizations of the congressional party in government, much as the national committee serves as the campaign organization of the presidential party.

The congressional campaign committees provide party candidates with an impressive range of campaign help, from production facilities for television spots to that most valuable of all resources, money (see box below). They have also become increasingly active in channeling contributions from political action committees to the party's candidates. Although incumbent House and Senate members control these committees, they have resisted the pressures to work only on behalf of incumbents' campaigns; they also support their party's candidates for open seats and challengers who have a chance of winning. In short, they concentrate their considerable resources where they think they are most likely to get the biggest payoff, namely in increasing the size of their party's representation in Congress.

Running for Congress? Here's What the Parties' National Committees Can Do for You

The national party organizations now offer these services to candidates:

- Training for candidates, campaign managers, and other workers in up-to-date campaign techniques and management, fund-raising, research and communications, and field work
- "Issue packages" for selected candidates: information about issues relevant to their campaigns and talking points to use in discussing these issues with constituents
- State-of-the-art TV and radio production facilities, and consultants to help candidates make effective ads at low cost
- Satellite capabilities to let candidates broadcast live interactive programs with constituents
- Contributor lists given to selected candidates, on the condition that these candidates give their own contributor lists to the party after the election
- Party fund-raising events in Washington
- Party leaders' visits to candidate events, live and via satellite uplink, to help candidates raise money and attract votes
- "Hard-money" direct contributions to campaigns*
- "Coordinated spending" to buy polls, media ads, or research for a candidate*
- "Soft-money" support for registration, canvassing, and get-out-the-vote activities*
- "Issue advocacy" ads in support of candidates* and generic ads promoting the party as a whole
- Help in raising money from political action committees (PACs) and individuals

* These will be discussed in Chapter 12.

Sources: Paul S. Herrnson, *Congressional Elections*, 3rd ed. (Washington, DC: CQ Press, 2000), pp. 100–115, and Victoria A. Farrar-Myers and Diana Dwyre, "Parties and Campaign Finance," in Jeffrey E. Cohen, Richard Fleisher, and Paul Kantor, eds., *American Political Parties: Decline or Resurgence?* (Washington, DC: CQ Press, 2001), pp. 143–146.

The congressional campaign committees have become more vibrant forces in recent American politics due to their growing ability to raise campaign money (see the Senate and House columns in Table 4.2). The Republican committees have taken the lead. The stunning success of GOP candidates in the 1994 elections, for example, was due in part to aggressive fund-raising and candidate recruitment by their congressional committees. As the table shows, the Republican Senate and House committees raised almost $100 million in federal ("hard-money") receipts during the 1993–1994 election cycle. Some of these funds went directly to candidates, but the larger part went for candidate recruitment and training, research on opponents and issues, media, opinion polling, ads, and other campaign services.

TABLE 4.2 Political Party Net Receipts: 1975–76 to 1999–2000 (in millions)

	National	Senate	House	State/Local	Total
Democratic Committees					
1975–1976	$ 13.1	1.0	0.9	0.0	$ 15.0
1977–1978	$ 11.3	0.3	2.8	8.7	$ 26.4
1979–1980	$ 15.1	1.7	2.1	11.7	$ 37.2
1981–1982	$ 16.4	5.6	6.5	10.6	$ 39.3
1983–1984	$ 46.6	8.9	10.4	18.5	$ 98.5
1985–1986	$ 17.2	13.4	12.3	14.1	$ 64.8
1987–1988	$ 52.3	16.3	12.5	44.7	$127.9
1989–1990	$ 14.5	17.5	9.1	44.7	$ 85.7
1991–1992	$ 65.8	25.5	12.8	73.7	$177.7
1993–1994	$ 41.8	26.4	19.4	55.6	$139.1
1995–1996	$108.4	30.8	26.6	93.2	$221.6
1997–1998	$ 64.8	35.6	25.2	63.4	$160.0
1999–2000	$124.0	40.5	48.4	149.3	$275.2
Republican Committees					
1975–1976	$ 29.1	12.2	1.8	0.0	$ 43.1
1977–1978	$ 34.2	10.9	14.1	20.9	$ 84.5
1979–1980	$ 76.2	23.3	28.6	33.8	$169.5
1981–1982	$ 83.5	48.9	58.0	24.0	$215.0
1983–1984	$105.9	81.7	58.3	43.1	$297.9
1985–1986	$ 83.8	84.4	39.8	47.2	$255.2
1987–1988	$ 91.0	65.9	34.7	66.0	$263.3
1989–1990	$ 68.7	65.1	33.2	39.3	$205.3
1991–1992	$ 85.4	73.8	35.3	72.8	$267.3
1993–1994	$ 87.4	65.3	26.7	75.0	$245.6
1995–1996	$193.0	64.5	74.2	128.4	$416.5
1997–1998	$104.0	53.4	72.7	89.4	$285.0
1999–2000	$212.8	51.5	97.3	176.6	$465.8

Note: "Soft money" receipts are not included. Beginning with 1987–1988, total receipts do not include monies transferred among the listed committees.

Source: Federal Election Commission at http://www.fec.gov/press/demhrd98.htm and http://www.fec.gov/press/rephrd98.htm. For 1999–2000: http://www.fec.gov/press/051501partyfund/tables/feddem2000.html and http://www.fec.gov/press/051501partyfund/tables/fedrep2000.html (accessed September 9, 2001).

In the 2000 congressional campaigns, the Republican Hill committees began spending earlier than ever before; the NRCC, for example, spent 60 percent more during 1999 and the first three months of 2000 than it had spent in the same period before the 1998 elections. It made extensive use of its ability to swap funds with other party and candidates' committees. Having raised millions in "soft money" (discussed in Chapter 12), which cannot legally be spent on candidates' campaigns, the NRCC traded much of this money to candidates' treasuries and those of other party committees, in return for money these groups raised under federal contribution limits—money that *can* be spent directly on campaigns.[4] Overall, the two Republican Hill committees amassed an impressive $149 million in the two years leading up to the 2000 elections plus about $92 million in "soft money," and had raised another $90 million in soft money alone by the end of 2001, in preparation for the fight to regain control of both the House and the Senate in 2002.

The Democrats followed in a more modest way. The two Democratic committees improved their fund-raising very gradually, from $46 million in 1993–1994 to $61 million in 1997–1998. In 2000, however, the Democratic Hill committees greatly increased their courtship of business and, taking advantage of the closeness of the congressional races, brought in soft money at levels well beyond those reached by these committees in previous years.[5] In both parties, then, the Hill committees are much more active and effective now than they were in the 1970s. In resources and campaigning skills, they have begun to challenge the importance of their national parties' committees.

TWO PATHS TO POWER

The two national parties have traveled two different roads to reach these new levels of effectiveness. The Republicans have followed a service path by building a muscular fund-raising operation in order to provide needed services to their candidates and state parties. The Democrats, in contrast, first followed a procedural path, strengthening their national party's authority over the state parties in the selection of a presidential nominee. The central element in both national parties' development, however, has been their ability to attract thousands of small contributions through mass mailings to likely party supporters; this has given the national parties, which formerly depended on assessments provided by the state parties, an independent financial base.[6] Ironically, then, at a time when some were warning that the parties were in decline, the national party organizations were reaching levels of strength that had never been seen before in American politics.[7]

The Service Party Path

The service party was born when, during the 1960s, a quiet revolution began in the Republican National Committee. The committee's chairman at the time, Ray Bliss, involved the committee more and more in helping state and local parties with the nuts and bolts of party organizational work. Chairman William Brock continued this effort in the mid- to late 1970s, as a means of reviving the party's election prospects after the Republican losses of the post-Watergate years. Bliss and Brock succeeded in fashioning a new role for the Republican National Party by making it into an exceptionally effective service organization for the state and local parties.[8]

There were two keys to success in performing the new service role: money and mastery of the new campaign technologies. Using the new ability to generate computer-based mailing lists, the Republicans began a program of direct-mail solicitations that brought in ever-higher levels of income (see Table 4.2). By the 1983–1984 election cycle, the Republican National Committee and its subsidiaries had raised $105.9 million in hard money—a record for national committee fund-raising that has been broken only twice since then. (Campaign finance is discussed more fully in Chapter 12.) These resources enabled the national Republicans to give unparalleled support to candidates and local party organizations. Their new affluence grew most dramatically in 1979–1980, peaked in 1983–1984 and again in presidential years, beginning with 1995–1996.

The Democratic committees began to follow suit in the midterm elections of 1982. The national Democrats, long mired in debt, began the 1980s badly eclipsed by the Republicans in organizational and service capacity. The good news for the Democrats was that they had dramatically improved their fund-raising capacities (see Table 4.2) and increased their activities in the states and localities. The bad news was that the Republicans were far ahead of them to begin with and were continuing to break new ground. Even so, the Democrats, under the national chairmanship of first Charles Manatt and then Paul Kirk could see that their only feasible course was to become a service party. The national Democrats made no secret of their effort to imitate the Republican success in raising money and using it to buy services. Slowly, they began to catch up; what began as a three-to-one and even five-to-one financial advantage for the Republicans now has been cut by about half (see Figure 4.1).

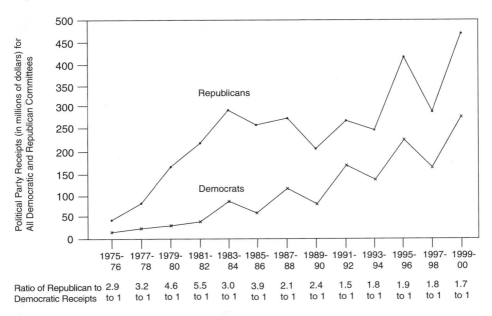

FIGURE 4.1   The Republican Advantage in Fund-Raising: 1975–76 to 1999–2000.
Note: Soft money is not included.

By the mid-1980s, both parties were providing unprecedented levels of aid to candidates and state parties. This assistance included a broad array of services—candidate recruitment and training, research, public opinion polling, data processing, computer networking and software development, production of radio and television commercials, direct mailing, expert consultants, and legal services—and millions of dollars to finance campaigns and to build party organizations. Though the fund-raising rules are complex, national party committees were able to expand their fund-raising markedly in the 1990s by encouraging soft-money contributions, which were then unrestricted in amount (see Chapter 12).

In 2000, for example, the national Republicans established the "Republican Regents" for individuals and corporations who gave at least $250,000 in soft money to the party during a two-year period, which helped produce record soft-money donations; and the Democratic "Jefferson Trust" honored givers of at least $100,000.[9] By 2001, with the national parties' fund-raising in high gear, the Hill committees worked intensively to recruit very attractive candidates for House and Senate races in 2002, but with mixed results; as the DSCC's executive director put it, recruiting strong candidates is "incredibly frustrating. It's simply impossible to bend the wishes of successful, competent people. The irony is that there is no more important function that the parties have than recruitment—and it's the piece of the business we have the least control over."[10]

Concerned with the weakness of party organizations at the grass roots, Republicans have even begun party-building efforts at that level. The Republican National Committee, breaking with its tradition of working only with the state parties, lavished money and assistance in 1984 on 650 key counties containing a majority of the nation's voters. Republican committees again funneled major investments into state legislative races during the spring of 2000 to improve the chances that these legislatures, which would be drawing new legislative districts after the 2000 U.S. Census, would have Republican majorities.

For both parties, the greatest advances in fund-raising and organizational development have come when their party is not holding the presidency. Adversity breeds innovation.[11] These fund-raising advances permitted both national parties to hire increasing numbers of professional staff members, who in turn were able to put new campaign technologies into practice (see Table 4.3). Since the mid-1980s, then, both national parties have become institutionalized as active, well-staffed "service parties" working to support party candidates and state and local organizations throughout the nation.[12]

The Democrats' Procedural-Reform Path

Even before the national Democrats started on the service party path, they had begun to expand the power of the national party organization for other reasons. Reformers supporting the civil rights movement and opposing American involvement in the Vietnam War pressed for change in the Democratic party's positions on these issues. Because the choice of a presidential candidate was the main business of the national party, the reformers focused on changing the rules for selecting presidential candidates. Their aim was to make the nominating process more open and democratic, and in particular more representative of the concerns of people like themselves: blacks, women, and young people. To achieve that goal, they had to attack the confederated structure of the national

TABLE 4.3 The Growth of National Party Committee Staff: 1972–2000

	1972	1976	1980	1984	1988	1992	1996	2000
Democratic Party Committees								
National Committee	30	30	40	130	160	270	264	150
House Campaign Committee	5	6	26	45	80	64	64	75
Senate Campaign Committee	4	5	20	22	50	35	38	40
Republican Party Committees								
National Committee	30	200	350	600	425	300	271	250
House Campaign Committee	6	8	40	130	80	89	64	63
Senate Campaign Committee	4	6	30	90	88	135	150	75

Note: These numbers fluctuate considerably from month to month and year to year. As a general rule, however, size of the national committees peaks in the presidential election year and is smaller in the interelection period.

Source: 1972–1984: Paul S. Herrnson, *Party Campaigning in the 1980s* (Cambridge, MA: Harvard University Press, 1988), p. 39; 1988: Herrnson, "Reemergent National Party Organizations," in L. Sandy Maisel, ed., *The Parties Respond: Changes in the American Party System* (Boulder, CO: Westview Press, 1990), pp. 41–66 at p. 51; 1992: Herrnson, "The Revitalization of National Party Organizations," in Maisel, ed., *The Parties Respond: Changes in American Parties and Campaigns* (Boulder, CO: Westview Press, 1994), pp. 45–68 at p. 54; 1996: Herrnson, "National Party Organizations at the Century's End," in Maisel, ed. *The Parties Respond: Changes in American Parties and Campaigns* (Boulder, CO: Westview Press, 1998), pp. 60–61; 2000: Data were graciously provided by Paul S. Herrnson.

party, which gave each state the power to decide how to select its delegates to the national nominating convention.

In the mid-1960s, these reforms began with efforts to require delegations from southern states to remain loyal to the national Democratic ticket. After the 1968 election, the first of a series of reform commissions worked to dramatically overhaul the party's rules for nominating presidential candidates. (This story is told in more detail in Chapter 10.) In doing so, the Democrats limited the autonomy of the state parties and the authority of state law in determining how convention delegates were to be selected, thus giving the national party the authority over the presidential nominating process.[13] Key court decisions upheld these actions, further solidifying the newfound authority of the national party.

Why would the state party leaders have been willing to go along with this erosion of their independence? Some may still be asking themselves that question. The reformers' success indicates that state Democratic leaders were not sufficiently aware of the threat posed by the reforms; it also reflects the unusual politics of that time and the existence of a power vacuum at the top of the Democratic Party in the 1960s. This change, however, was limited to the Democrats. Republican leaders, consistent with their party's long-standing states' rights orientation, had no real desire to centralize power in their own party organization.[14] Yet ironically, the GOP was still affected by the tide of Democratic party reform, because the bills passed by state legislatures to implement the reforms applied to both parties.

In the early 1980s, the Democrats took stock of the reforms and didn't like what they saw. The newly centralized authority in nominating a presidential candidate and the increased grassroots participation in the nominating process had done little to win elections. Further, it had divided the party and alienated much of the Democratic party in government, many of whom were conspicuously absent from party conventions and conferences in the 1970s. So the national Democrats decided to soft-pedal organizational reforms and move toward the Republican service model. The national committee adopted rules for the 1984 national convention that guaranteed a much greater representation of the party's leaders and officeholders. In addition, in the 1980s, the party rushed to broaden the base of its fund-raising and to provide the means and know-how to recruit candidates and revitalize local parties. When the dust from all of this effort settled, authority over party rules had been nationalized, and what had been two models for strengthening the national party were rapidly converging into one.[15]

WHAT IS THE IMPACT OF THESE STRONGER NATIONAL PARTIES?

The dramatic changes in the national parties have helped beef up the parties' roles in nominating and electing candidates, roles that were seriously undercut a century ago with the advent of the direct primary. To an important degree, the national and state parties (especially the Republicans) have begun to "muscle in" on the campaign support functions that political action committees (PACs) and private campaign consultants had monopolized just a few years ago. It is not likely that party organizations can displace PACs and consultants, but the money and services provided by the national parties have certainly helped raise their profiles in the eyes of candidates. The increasing strength of the national parties also has the potential to alter the relationships within the parties: between the national party and state and local party organizations, the president, and the Congress, as well as among the various segments of the national parties.

The Effects on State and Local Parties

Have the increasing visibility and resources of the national parties led to a shift in power from the state and local to the national party organizations—to centralization rather than decentralization of the parties?[16] Probably not. The Democrats are somewhat more comfortable with centralization; they have more experience than the Republicans in enforcing national rules, and a stronger inclination to accept centralized authority. The structure of representation on the DNC is better able to sustain centralized party power; recall that states are not represented equally on the DNC, but according to size and Democratic support, and that other groups are represented on the committee as well. The Republicans are more wary of centralization. Even so, because of their advantage in fund-raising, the national Republicans have been able to make more of an impact on party organizations at the state and local level. But the forces that encourage a state and local party focus remain strong.

Yet although the parties are far from centralized, the national aid to state and local parties and campaigns and the national intervention in their nomination processes have caused some shift in party power toward the national organizations. When the national parties have a lot of money and services to provide, their suggestions are likely to be taken more seriously by candidates and state and local parties. The result may be more of a national imprint on the issues discussed in state and local campaigns, the kinds of candidates recruited, and the ways in which the parties are organized. State and local organizations that resist the national party's suggestions could find themselves on the short end of the national party's money and help. Those who pay the pipers tend to call the tune.[17] Is this a good thing for American politics? "Which Would You Choose?" on this page, gives you arguments on both sides of this question.

This increased national influence can produce some interesting strains among party organizations at different levels of government. The boxes on pages 84 and 85 tell two contrasting stories about the potential for conflict as well as cooperation between the national parties and their state and local brethren. In the case of the Republican New York Senate nomination in 2000, quiet pressure from the national party probably smoothed the nomination process, though Democrat Hillary Clinton still won the race in the end. But when the DCCC tried to exercise more public pressure on four congressional nominations that year, it prompted intra-party fighting that became a public embarrassment to the national Democrats.

Effects on the Presidency

Is a stronger national party likely to add to the president's power or to serve as a competing power center? Clearly, the increasing resources of the national committees give them

---

WHICH WOULD YOU CHOOSE?

Could a Stronger National Party Help You?

YES! Political parties offer you a valuable shortcut. Government decisions affect almost everything you do, but you may not have time to research dozens of complicated issues (health care, energy prices) and hundreds of candidates in order to vote for those who will act in your interest. A party can do the research for you. If you generally agree with, say, the Republican party, it can offer you a set of issue positions and recommended candidates with no effort on your part. But if each state and local Republican party organization can act independently, and if some of these organizations are more moderate and others are more conservative, then how can you be sure that your state and local Republican candidates will support the positions that drew you to the party? A strong national party could help recruit candidates whose views are consistent with the party's philosophy and help them get elected. It could fund generic ads that promote the party's ideas. And which would you rather have raising campaign money: the national party, or the individual candidates who may soon be voting on bills affecting the donors' interests?

NO! The United States is very diverse; the concerns of Democrats in Omaha may well be different from those in San Francisco, New Hampshire, and the Florida panhandle. If a national party is strong enough to promote a clear set of ideas on what government should be doing, whose ideas should it promote: those of the Omaha Democrats or those of the New Hampshire Democrats? Even if a national party organization confines itself to raising money and giving it to candidates, doesn't that give the national organization a great deal of influence over state and even local candidates? In a nation with a tradition of hostility to "boss rule," couldn't a strong national party raise those fears again?

Cooperation Between National and State Parties

Who Gets to Run Against Hillary?

Hillary Rodham Clinton became the only First Lady ever to run for office in her own right when she announced her plans to seek the U.S. Senate seat from New York in 2000. Although she was a controversial figure, political analysts expected her to be a formidable Democratic candidate. The chance to run against a Clinton tempted a number of Republican officeholders. But a divisive primary pitting high-profile Republicans against one another was not likely to help the party defeat Clinton.

Republican party leaders, then, sought to quietly clear the path to nomination for the strongest possible candidate. Many felt that was the equally controversial mayor of New York City, Rudy Giuliani. The state's Republican governor, George Pataki, felt differently; locked in a "caustic" feud with Giuliani, Pataki was actively seeking an alternative Senate nominee. This fracture in state party leadership split both the party organization and the party in government and led the national Republican party to step in. Working behind the scenes, national as well as state party leaders successfully pressured Pataki to give up his hopes and support Giuliani. The most public sign of the national party's involvement was a dinner held by the National Republican Senatorial Committee (NRSC) at which Republican Senators and major donors endorsed Giuliani as the strongest Republican candidate.

The Republican campaign took a strange twist when Giuliani, beset with personal scandal and newly diagnosed with prostate cancer, decided to quit the race. Again, national party leaders acted quickly to move the state party toward the candidate they felt would be most likely to win the seat for Republicans in the fall. Ironically, that was U.S. Representative Rick Lazio—the candidate Pataki had backed earlier. The NRSC rapidly organized more fund-raising events. Soon after, Lazio was chosen as the party's candidate by its state party convention. Lazio, however, lost to Clinton in the fall.

Sources: Clifford Levy, "Without Enthusiasm, Pataki Endorses Giuliani for Senate," *New York Times*, Aug. 7, 1999; Adam Nagourney, "G.O.P. Senators Rally to Giuliani Candidacy," *New York Times*, Apr. 22, 1999; Mike Allen, "Early Fundraising Start Helps Lazio," *Washington Post*, May 27, 2000, p. A6.

the opportunity for a more independent political role. Beginning in the 1980s, for example, the Republican National Committee came into its own as an important actor in party politics. Federal funding of presidential campaigns, with its strict limits on party spending for presidential politics, freed the national committees from their traditional concentration on presidential elections and allowed them to dedicate their now considerable resources to party-building at the state and local level. At the same time, the party committees carved out new roles in raising soft money for the presidential campaign and channeling this money to the state and local parties for grassroots mobilization activities.

On the other hand, these new capabilities make the national committee an even more attractive resource for presidents. The relationship between the president and the national committee of his or her party has inevitably been close. The president's proposals and

Conflict between National and State and Local Parties—The Perils of Party Pre-Primary Endorsements

Imagine that you are a national party leader hoping to win a majority for your party in Congress. In one congressional district, two candidates are competing for your party's nomination. One candidate is experienced and well respected; the other is well-known, but not as likely to run an effective campaign. You are tempted to offer the national party's endorsement to the stronger candidate before the primary election takes place. Would you do it?

For the first time in years, the Democratic Congressional Campaign Committee (DCCC) decided to publicly endorse four U.S. House candidates in advance of the 2000 Democratic primaries. One was Mike LaPolla, local officeholder running for the party's nomination for an open-seat race in New Jersey. Some county Democratic leaders favored LaPolla, but others were supporting former mayor Maryanne Connelly, who also had the monetary support of EMILY's List, a national group that raises money for pro-choice Democratic women.

LaPolla's primary campaign soon ran into big trouble. A LaPolla campaign ad seemed to portray Connelly as a ditzy game shown contestant; the National Women's Political Caucus demanded that LaPolla take the ad off the air. In the primary election, Connelly eked out the narrowest of victories: 45 percent to LaPolla's 44.7 percent. The DCCC was now in the position of dealing with a Democratic congressional candidate whose nomination it had opposed. Right after the primary, the DCCC faced harsh criticism from other elected Democrats who believed that its process for making pre-primary endorsements was seriously flawed. It also needed to make amends—fast—to Connelly to avoid harming her election chances in the fall. DCCC Chair Patrick Kennedy (D-R.I.) quickly issued a press release saying, "The DCCC supports Maryanne Connelly 100 percent and we will do everything in our power to ensure that she is the next congresswoman from the 7th District." His Republican counterpart expressed the Republicans' "disappointment" with the national Democrats' efforts to drive Connelly out of the Democratic primary. Connelly lost the general election.

The DCCC made three other pre-primary endorsements in 2000. Only two of its endorsed candidates won their primaries. Now: if you were a national party leader, would you have made any pre-primary endorsements?

Sources: Ann Scott Tyson, "On-the-ground Look at Fight for the House," *Christian Science Monitor*, Mar. 14, 2000, p. 3; DCCC Web press release, "DCCC Chairman Kennedy Pledges Full Support for Connelly in NJ-07," June 13, 2000; National Republican Congressional Committee Web press release, "NJ-07 Democratic Candidate Reveals Intimidation and Coercion within Party," Mar. 21, 2000.

record are typically seen as the party's proposals and record in the eyes of citizens and commentators. Not surprisingly then, presidents want the new party power to be at their service, and every president in recent memory has kept his party's national committee on a short leash. RNC Chair Jim Gilmore was edged out in late 2001, for example, because he clashed with the White House over control of the committee. Presidents will certainly want the party committees to mobilize all those members of Congress they recruited, trained, financed, and helped elect to support the president's program. Also, presidents in their first term will want to draw on the assets of the national party for their reelection campaigns, as much as the Federal Election Campaign Act permits. So there is considerable pressure on these stronger national parties to put their capabilities at the service of presidential goals.[18]

The situation is different in the "out" party. During the four years after its presidential candidate has been defeated, a national party suffers constant jockeying for the right to lead. The defeated presidential candidate may or may not remain an important voice within the party, depending on his or her popularity and the credibility of his or her losing campaign. Al Gore, for instance, fell out of the speed-dial lists of many national Democratic leaders after he lost the electoral college vote in 2000. Most often, the leadership of the "out" party falls to its leaders in Congress, supported by the resources of their congressional campaign committees. The reason is that the congressional party, simply because its legislative responsibilities force it to take policy stands, is a logical source of the party's positions and of challenges to the program of the opposition's president. An invigorated national party committee can also help fill the void in national leadership, as can its chair.

Effects on Congress

As we have seen, the congressional campaign committees' resources have expanded in tandem with those of their national committees. The Hill committees have become more and more active in recruiting and supporting party candidates. In the 1990s, for example, the two parties' congressional campaign committees targeted many more races for campaign help than they had in the 1980s. Their help is especially valuable to challengers and candidates for open seats, because incumbents normally find it easy to raise their own campaign resources. In general, however, the committees tend to protect their incumbents when they expect a lean election year and invest in challengers and open seats when a big victory looks likely.

At about the same time as this expansion in the Hill committees' resources, there has also been an increase in the extent to which Congress members cast legislative votes with the majority of their party (as will be discussed in Chapter 13). Did these new campaign resources help convince congressional incumbents to support their party's positions on bills? To this point, the campaign committees have not given out campaign money and services on the basis of a candidate's support for the party's program. But the committees have not been bashful in reminding members, especially newly elected members, that the party played some role in their election success.

The remarkable cohesion of the post-1994 Republican majority in the House surely stems, in part, from the party leadership's financial and other support for Republicans in the 1994 elections. Constituency pressures will always come first in Congress, but the more senators and representatives can count on campaign support from the congressional party, the more open they will be to party-based appeals.[19] This campaign support may also, to some degree, counterbalance pressures on Congress from PACs and the competing centers of party power in Washington—the president and the national party committees.

Relationships within the National Party

There are many opportunities for cooperation among each national party's three main election committees—its national committee and the Senate and House campaign committees—and this cooperation has increased greatly. All three committees benefit, for example, from voter registration and get-out-the-vote drives, and it is often cost-effective for them to work together on candidate recruitment and campaigns. The committees are more competitive, however, in raising and spending their money. They seek financial support from the same contributors (and jealously guard their contributor lists), recruit political talent from the same limited pool and sometimes seek conflicting goals. Resources are scarce in party organizing, so it is not surprising that different organizations from the same party will struggle over them.[20]

THE LIMITS OF PARTY ORGANIZATION

Even the new strength in the national party organizations, however, may not be enough to revive the parties in the minds of many Americans. More professional, service-oriented parties may be better at helping candidates run for office than in stimulating voter attachments to parties or involving people at the grass roots. The strengthening of parties at the center is a fascinating change, but it may not have contributed much to expanding their role in American politics.[21]

Remember that even with these changes, American party organizations remain weak by most standards. In this era of large-scale business, government, universities, and voluntary organizations, the parties cut an unimpressive figure. They lack the top-down control and efficiency, the unified setting of priorities, and the central responsibility we often find in parties in other nations. Where the party organizations of other Western democracies have had permanent, highly professional leadership and large party bureaucracies, most American party organizations have generally done without a professional bureaucracy or leadership. Especially at the local level, the business of American party organization is still often in the hands of part-time activists and inexperienced professionals, which may indicate that its activities do not normally require much specialization or professionalism.[22]

It is not surprising that the American party organization's development remains stunted, even in these times of unprecedented strength at its national level. There is little in American political values that would welcome an efficient or "businesslike" operation of the parties. Americans' traditional fears of party strength combine with legal limits on the parties, the effects of the separation of powers, and the federal structure of our political system to produce a hostile climate for party organizational development. Even the campaign finance reforms since the 1970s have contributed to the weakness of the party organizations by treating them as just another source of campaign money, along with PACs and individuals, rather than as the central organizations in campaign funding, essential to the electoral process.[23]

Besides, a strong organization implies routine and continuity—an arrangement that may be more compatible with a party of unchanging principle, rather than with a party committed to making the adjustments necessary to do well in a pragmatic political system. The American parties are fundamentally flexible and election-oriented, concerned mainly with supporting candidates for office and active mainly during campaigns. For that reason, they have long been led by candidates and officeholders, not by career bureaucrats. So even though they now have active and vibrant national committees, the electoral focus of the American parties may have tipped the scales against the development of any centralized, elaborate party organization. As they have for some time, the American parties remain candidate-centered organizations in a candidate-centered political world.

The Political Party of the Activists

Fighting the bitter cold on a snowy evening in Iowa, thousands of Democrats and Republicans headed for schools, firehouses, and other locations to begin the process of choosing their party's candidate for president in January 2000. These were not state party leaders. Many of them were—or would become—party activists, contributing their time and energy to their party on a purely voluntary basis. Even the paid professional party workers who increasingly staff the national and state offices share many of the attributes of these volunteers. They are not quoted in media accounts or mentioned in state laws. Yet their activity and motivations are at the heart of party politics.

As an organization, the political party is designed to unite people in meeting goals. People who become active in the party organization have their own personal goals as well. Individual party leaders and workers have some reasons—seek some payoffs—for devoting their time to the party's activities, rather than to their church, their service organization, or their golf game. So the party has to be able to work toward its organizational goals while at the same time allowing its individual members to achieve theirs. If it fails to do so, its future as a viable party may be short. How it accomplishes this tricky challenge (and whether it does) is determined by the private life of the party—its internal division of labor and allocation of authority, its communication patterns, and the decision-making processes through which it chooses how to mobilize its resources.

WHAT DRAWS PEOPLE INTO PARTY ACTIVITY?

The American political parties have never operated primarily in a cash economy. They have rarely bought or hired more than a small proportion of the millions of labor hours they need. Even today, in spite of the increasing professionalization of the national and state party headquarters, very few local party organizations have any paid staff members and it is a rare local chairman who draws any salary.[1] The many Americans who volunteer in their local parties get no cash in return for their considerable time and skills. Even the old customs of paying precinct workers on election day, or using government employees as the party's workers at election time, are vanishing. What, then, induces all these people to donate their time and effort to try to meet the party's goals?

In their seminal theory, Peter B. Clark and James Q. Wilson identified three different types of reasons why individuals become active in organizations. *Material incentives* are tangible rewards for activity—direct cash payments or other concrete rewards for one's work. *Solidary incentives* are the intangible, social benefits that people can gain from associating with others, from networking and being part of a group. *Purposive incentives* are intangible rewards of a different kind—based on the sense of satisfaction that comes when people are promoting an issue or principle that matters to them, or feel that they are involved in a worthwhile cause. This typology has been used widely and fruitfully in studying people's motives for becoming and staying involved in party work.[2]

Material Incentives

Historically, the main material inducement to party activity has been the opportunity to share in the "spoils" gained when a party controls the government. These "spoils" have come in the form of patronage and preferments. *Patronage* refers to the appointment of an individual to a government job as a reward for party work. Similarly, the party can provide loyal workers with a base of support if they seek elected office. *Preferments* involve, more generally, granting the favors of government to party supporters. Patronage, access to elected office and preferments have all played important roles in building and sustaining the American party organizations.[3]

Patronage   Since the beginning of the Republic, but especially since the presidency of Andrew Jackson when federal patronage jobs doubled, Americans have been attracted to party work by the prospect of being rewarded with government jobs. Patronage has been used in other nations as well, but no other party system has relied on patronage as systematically and for as long as the American system. In the heyday of the political machine, for example, city governments were staffed almost entirely by loyalists of the party in power—who then faced the prospect of being thrown out of work if their party were turned out of office.[4]

As the price to be paid for their jobs, patronage appointees traditionally "volunteered" their time, energy, and often even a part of their salary to the party organization. Campaign help was especially expected; American party politics is rich with tales of the entire staff of certain government departments being put to work in support of their boss's reelection. Money, too, has always been an important resource in campaigns, and patronage workers have been called upon to "invest" in the party that gave them their jobs. Even now, when such practices are increasingly frowned upon and sometimes even illegal, government employees can still face compelling pressures to contribute time or money to the party. The line between voluntary and expected support is a fine one and it is understandable that at least some public employees choose to remain on the safe side of that line by contributing, even if they are not required to do so.

Despite the explosive growth of government to more than 18 million public employees (about 3 million federal, more than 4 million state, and almost 11 million local), the number of patronage jobs available to the parties has declined dramatically. The main reason is that civil service and merit systems have expanded. The first major step in this process was the establishment of the federal civil service system by the Pendleton Act in 1883, which removed almost 14,000 of the (then) more than 131,000 federal employees from patronage appointment.[5] The number of full-time federal positions filled by political appointees has dwindled over the years to fewer than 10,000 today, many of them high-level policy-making positions.[6] States and cities have followed the same path, but more slowly; large numbers have replaced patronage with appointments made on the basis of competitive exams, at least for employees who are not in policy-making positions.

The Supreme Court has contributed to the dismantling of patronage at the state and local levels. In 1976 and 1980, the Court ruled that some county political employees could not be fired simply because of a change of the party in power. The Supreme Court went further in a 1990 Illinois case, determining that politically based hiring and promotion violated the First Amendment freedoms of speech and association. In each case, the Court acknowledged that party affiliation might be a relevant condition in filling policy-making positions, but not in filling lower-level offices (see box below).[7]

Even where patronage positions remain, it has gotten harder for parties to use them as incentives for party activity. The available patronage jobs are frequently not very attractive to the kinds of activists the party wants to recruit. The politics of patronage worked best among the disadvantaged, who were willing to accept whatever city or county jobs were offered; most patronage positions do not tempt the educated, respected, middle-class leadership the parties would like to attract. And in an age of candidate-centered politics, elected executives are more interested in using patronage to build their own political followings than to strengthen the party organization. As the supply of valuable patronage jobs dwindles, party leaders are probably even more convinced of the old saying that each appointment results in a lot of resentful people who didn't get the job and one ingrate who did.[8]

Even so, patronage is likely to survive as long as it is attractive to both political leaders and their followers. Mayors, governors, and presidents will continue to reserve top policy-making positions for their loyal supporters. Legislatures at all levels of government will remain reluctant to bring their staff employees under the protection of civil service systems. Civil service rules for governmental employees can be bypassed by hiring politically loyal, "temporary" workers outside of the civil service system, or by chan-

---

The Dismantling of Chicago's "Patronage Army"

Unable to defeat a candidate of Chicago's Democratic machine in a race for delegate to the state's 1969 constitutional convention, frustrated reformer Michael Shakman sought judicial relief. He challenged the constitutionality of the city's patronage system in the federal courts. His suit triggered a series of court rulings and resulting consent decrees between 1972 and 1988, through which the city agreed, though grudgingly, to eliminate political hiring and firing for all but the top policy-making positions and to protect city employees from being forced to do political work or make political contributions. To implement these agreements, the courts required the city to develop strict plans for compliance and to submit to yearly external audits of its personnel practices. While politics still influences personnel decisions in Chicago government, the large "patronage army" that once was the hallmark of Chicago politics seems to have been dismantled.

neling party loyalists into jobs in private firms that depend on government business. Honorary positions on government advisory groups will still be coveted as rewards for loyal party service. A few big campaign contributors will continue to be named ambassadors to small and peaceful countries. Wherever political leaders retain discretion over personnel appointments, in short, they will find a way to award them to their trusted political supporters. The promise of such awards, in turn, will keep attracting people to political activity—though not the large numbers who once served as the "foot soldiers" of the traditional political machines.

Keep in mind that some thoughtful observers are sorry to lose the practice of patronage (as unsavory as it now seems) that was central to American political life since early in the nineteenth century. Patronage was a means of keeping party organizations strong as instruments of democracy; without it, parties can find it more and more difficult to recruit the labor they need. Activists who are recruited by parties in the absence of patronage are likely to have other goals; they may demand more ideological payoffs for their participation and that would undermine the pragmatic, inclusive approaches that the parties have taken during most of their histories.

The replacement of political appointees by neutral professionals may actually make governmental bureaucracies less responsive to elected political leaders and perhaps even less sympathetic to the public. When government jobs are filled by civil service procedures (and protected by those procedures), it becomes almost impossible for reform-minded leaders to replace a stodgy or ineffective bureaucracy with more efficient workers. It is easy to forget that patronage was first promoted at the federal level by Andrew Jackson to produce a more democratic and less elitist government, and that career civil service employees today are often criticized as unresponsive to the public they are supposed to serve.[9]

Patronage jobs in government, however, are not the only employment opportunities a party can offer. In recent years, party organizations at the state and national levels have themselves become important employers of professional campaign workers. To provide services to their candidates, party organizations need computer specialists, pollsters, media production experts, field directors, researchers, fund-raisers, strategists, Web-masters, direct mail specialists, and other experts in new campaign techniques. Many activists are attracted to party work by the chance of landing these jobs.

Elected Office   Some women and men become party activists because they see that as a first step toward running for office. About 40 percent of the county chairpersons interviewed in a 1979–1980 national survey hoped to hold public office, and an earlier study found that one third of all state party chairs became candidates for elective office after serving the party.[10] Involvement in the party, like activity in other community organizations, remains an attractive way for aspiring politicians to build a base from which to launch a political career.

A few party organizations keep such disciplined control over their primary elections that, especially at the state and local level, they can and do "give" nominations to public office to loyal party workers. That degree of control over nomination and election to office, however, is rare today. It is far more common for candidates to see the party as one of the bases of support for election or reelection and, in some areas, as the most important one. Candidates need advice, know-how, people (staff and volunteers), and money, and the party remains a likely source of all of these. So the lure of party support in a later campaign for elected office may bring some people into party work.

Preferments   Party activity can lead to tangible rewards other than elective or appointive office. Because public officials can use at least some discretion in distributing government services and in granting government contracts, the potential for political favoritism exists. Many people become involved in party activity and in making contributions to their party in the hope of attracting these favors. A big giver, or "fat cat," might, for example, be hoping to win a government contract to build a new school or library. It is no accident that leaders of the construction industry are so active politically in states and localities that spend millions every year on roads and public buildings.

Preference may take other forms as well. Potential activists may hope for tolerant government regulation or inspection policies, unusually prompt snow and garbage removal, fixed traffic tickets, or admission to a crowded state university. It may also involve the granting of scarce opportunities, such as liquor licenses, cable television franchises, or the calculated "overlooking" of prostitution or drug trafficking, in return for some form of political support. "Preferment," in other words, means receiving special treatment or advantage that flows from the party's holding the decision-making positions in government.

Reformers have promoted a number of safeguards over the years, many of them enacted into law, to limit the discretion available to governments in giving out benefits and buying goods and services from private firms. Examples are: competitive and sealed bidding, conflict of interest statutes, privatization, and even affirmative action. Nonetheless, because the potential benefits are so great for both sides, there always seem to be ways to evade even the tightest controls. There is understandable resistance, in the name of both democracy and efficiency, to sacrificing *all* discretion in order to eliminate *political* discretion. The result is that preferments may have taken the place of patronage as the main material incentive for political activity. Unfortunately for party leaders, however, it is elected officials who grant the preferments, not the party leaders themselves.[11]

Solidary (Social) Incentives

Other motivations for party activity are not as easy to measure as a government job or the awarding of a contract. Many people are drawn to party work by the social contact it provides. In an age when some people's closest relationship is with their computer or their television, the face-to-face contact found at a party headquarters or caucus provides a chance to meet like-minded people and feel a part of an active group. Family traditions may lead some young adults to go to party activities looking for social life, just as others may look to a softball league or a religious organization. The chance to meet local officials whose photos appear in the newspaper may be a draw. For whatever reason, researchers find that a substantial number of party activists cite the social life of party politics as a valuable reward.[12]

These social satisfactions have psychological roots. "Like the theater, politics is a great nourisher of egos," writes one observer. It attracts men and women "who are hungry for attention, for assurance that somebody loves them, for the soul-stirring music of their own voices."[13] The solidarity of party work can help people feel a part of something larger than themselves—a charismatic leader, an important movement, a moment in history. The party can be a small island of excitement in a sea of routine. For some, party activity provides the lure of power; even a precinct committeewoman can dream of herself as a future state chair or a member of Congress.

Purposive (Issue-based) Incentives

To an increasing extent, people are led to party activism by their commitment to particular issues or attitudes about the proper role of government. Someone dedicated to abortion rights, for example, might begin by working for a pro-choice Democratic candidate and then come to see the candidate's party as a vehicle for protecting abortion rights in Congress. A property rights activist may be attracted to the Republican Party by its statements about limited government. Other groups compete for the attention of these activists; the abortion rights supporter, for instance, could also work effectively through organized interests, such as the National Abortion and Reproductive Rights Action League and Planned Parenthood. But parties at all levels have seen an influx of issue-driven activists during the last few decades.

Issue-based party activism has played a vital role in shaping politics at the national level. One of the early ideological triumphs was the capture of the national Republicans in 1964 by conservatives supporting Senator Barry Goldwater for president. Soon after, liberal ideologues left their mark on the national Democratic Party in support of presidential candidates Eugene McCarthy (1968) and George McGovern (1972). Later came the victories of Ronald Reagan and the rise of Christian fundamentalists in the GOP of the 1980s and 1990s. As these examples suggest, it is often the force of an attractive leader that brings ideologically motivated activists into the party. But even in the absence of such a leader, some issues and ideological movements have had enough power to lead activists to switch parties: for example, pro-lifers and Southern conservatives who moved from the Democratic to the Republican Party and who soon made an impact on the issue positions of their new party.[14]

Some people become party activists out of a more general sense of civic obligation, or a belief that citizen participation is essential in a democracy. Researchers who have asked party workers about their motives for serving in the party know the familiar answers. They were asked to volunteer, they say, and they agreed because it was their civic duty. This response often reflects deeply ingrained values, such as local traditions of commitment to political reform and "good government."

Mixed Incentives

No party organization depends on one single incentive and very few people become party activists for only one reason. Most party organizations rely on a variety of incentives. Activists who hope for a political job, or some other preferment, work together with those motivated by a particular issue or by a sense of civic duty. Both may enjoy the sense of solidarity they derive from social contact with like-minded people. There may be different incentives at different levels of the party organization, with higher-level activists sustained more by purposive incentives and lower-level activists attracted by material or solidary rewards.[15] Alternatively, the mix may differ depending on the type of local community, with more traditional cultures giving rise to parties built around material motives and reform-oriented cultures attracting purposive activists.

When we look at the major parties overall, however, we find that issue-oriented incentives—purposive incentives—now seem to be the primary motive for party activism. Most party workers are attracted by a desire to use the party as a means to achieve policy goals.[16] Although we do not have comparable data on earlier periods, there is reason to believe that this was far less true of party workers a generation or two ago.[17] The energy and passion in party organizations come increasingly from issue-driven activists—those on the right in the Republican party and those on the left for the Democrats.

The incentive that recruits people to party work, of course, may not be the incentive that keeps them there. Several studies suggest that activists who come to the party to fulfill purposive goals—to fight for certain issues—are more likely to remain in the party if they come to value the social contact they get from party activism. The motive that sustains their party work, in short, tends to shift to solidary incentives: friendships, identification with the party itself, and other social rewards and satisfactions.[18] (For an example, see "A Day in the Life," p. 95.) It may be that committed issue activists simply burn out, or that the pragmatic American parties, in their effort to remain flexible enough to win elections, cannot provide the level of ideological dedication needed to sustain party workers whose political lives revolve around a set of issues.

HOW DO PARTIES RECRUIT ACTIVISTS?

Parties do not find it easy to recruit people who will work effectively on their behalf. Like almost all other volunteer groups, party organizations have had an increasingly difficult time attracting willing volunteers. Except at the national level, and in some states where there has been an increase in paid positions and exciting professional opportunities, parties often have no effective means of enlisting new activists.

To add to the challenge, state laws often take at least part of the recruitment process out of the party's hands. Rules requiring open party caucuses and the election of party officials in primaries limit the party's control over its personnel. This can lead to the takeover of a local (or even a state) party organization by an intense group of issue activists. At the least, it leaves a party vulnerable to shifts in its direction, as some leaders and activists move on and new, self-recruited leaders take their places.

Finding Volunteers: Is Anybody Home?

In a much-discussed set of writings, political scientist Robert Putnam has shown that there has been a drop in participation in community activities in recent years. Party organizations are not alone in having to search for volunteers; groups ranging from churches to bowling leagues have been starved for participants. Fewer people are involving themselves in the face-to-face activities of politics—attending a political speech or a community meeting—though the lonely activities of check-writing and Internet-surfing are on the increase. Many culprits have been identified, from the numbers of hours Americans spend watching television to the increasing numbers of dual-career families. But the consequences, Putnam argues, are profound: a reduction in the "social capital"—the social connections, values, and trust that enable communities to solve their problems more easily.[19]

Party organizations have a constant need for activists of any kind, so at a time when volunteers are in short supply, the parties are very likely to accept whatever help is available. The nature of parties' recruitment system, then, is pretty haphazard. Some people,

---

A Nontraditional Republican Activist

"I always abhorred party politics," says Robin Vuke. "I thought it was a nasty business. It's unfortunate that we have to be involved in it." And yet Vuke, an African-American woman who graduated from Purdue University in 1990, became a Republican activist. How did it happen?

David Duke, a former Ku Klux Klan leader and friend of the American Nazi Party, had campaigned successfully for a Louisiana state legislative seat in 1989. The following year, he filed as a Republican to run for the U.S. Senate seat of Democrat J. Bennett Johnston. To the embarrassment of Republican leaders, Duke became the leading Republican candidate in the race, and until very close to the election, it appeared that he would force Johnston into a runoff in Louisiana's unusual "blanket primary" (see Chapter 9). "David Duke really scared me," Vuke states. "It was frightening that someone like that could get that far. Everyone has the right to run, but winning state office gives someone a lot of power and to come that close to a U.S. Senate seat...."

"My parents weren't involved in party politics. But my interest in politics was triggered in elementary school. We had a mock presidential election; they brought in a voting machine, we waited till the end of the day to get the results and that experience stuck with me! Then my government teacher in high school really opened my eyes to politics and the analysis of governments. I always saw myself as a behind-the-scenes person. But after Duke's campaign, I felt it was time for me to get involved. I felt there has to be a point where I can affect someone and show that there are good, rational people in the Republican party who are willing to listen."

Vuke then started as an amateur activist; her concerns revolved around issues and principles, rather than the promotion of the party itself. She is pro-choice, very concerned about environmental issues—"values that sometimes run counter to traditional Republican beliefs." Why, then, is she a Republican? "I believe in fiscal responsibility," she says. "I think it's our responsibility as African-Americans to take control of our futures. But that has to be balanced with other commitments I have: to a clean environment, to make sure no one goes without." Vuke's local Republican organization is located in a college town. Do you think she would have felt less comfortable in a Republican local party in Dallas or in rural Wyoming?

As often happens with issue-oriented activists, Vuke has remained in the party for solidarity reasons. "Specific issues come and go," she says. "But now it's really the people who help with the party who keep me here. I don't always agree with everybody in the party. In fact, I found it embarrassing to see the beliefs of the Religious Right gain so much power in the party; I'd like to see us move away from that. I'm in the 'liberal leg' of the party. That can make for a lot of pressure. You can't do anything without criticism. But I wouldn't want to walk away from the party; there are a lot of good people involved, and I want to support them."

fascinated by public policy or by particular issues, recruit themselves. More often, they are persuaded to take part by others. Party leaders and activists may encourage their friends and associates to join them in party work. Over the years, most activists have reported that they first became involved with the party as a result of these informal, personal requests for help.[20]

Events in the larger political world also play an important role in the recruitment of party activists. Some people may be first attracted to party work by a specific candidate or cause and may remain active long after the original reason has disappeared. The nature and direction of the Democratic Party was heavily influenced by the influx of liberals activated by the Vietnam War and the civil rights movement in the 1960s and 1970s. Similarly, the GOP has been energized by religious conservatives, mobilized not only by Barry Goldwater and Ronald Reagan, but also by fundamentalist ministers such as Pat Robertson. Because this recruitment process often depends on the presence of magnetic personalities and powerful issues, it tends to be episodic rather than continuous. It produces generational differences among party activists in which political outlooks may differ considerably, depending on when the individuals became active. More than any other single factor, it defines the ideological direction of the parties.[21]

The result is an extensive, informal recruitment system that selects a particular group of men and women out of the American population. Its main elements are:

- The motives and experiences of the people whom the parties want to recruit.
- The incentives the party can offer for party activity and the value of those incentives.
- The role that state law allows the party to play in recruitment.
- The contacts, opportunities, and events that are the immediate occasions of recruitment.[22]

The components of this system change constantly, and, as they do, they affect the number and types of people who become active. That, in turn, makes a difference. A local Democratic Party whose activists come largely from local labor unions will have different concerns and styles from a local Democratic Party dominated by environmental activists, just as a Republican organization run by local business leaders can differ from one dominated by the Religious Right. Recruitment in any form, however, involves a matching of the motives and goals of the individual with the incentives and expectations of the party organization.

How Are Leaders Recruited?

One way to choose leaders is to recruit from within by promoting especially effective party workers to more responsible positions. A study of Detroit showed this system at work in the 1950s: party leaders had risen exclusively through the avenues of party and public office. One group came up through the precinct positions, another rose through auxiliary organizations (for instance, women's groups, youth organizations, and political clubs), and a third and smaller group moved from the race for public office to a career within the party.[23] Later data suggest, however, that party activists do not invariably inch up the career ladder in the party, position by position. Almost half of a national sample of Democratic and Republican county chairs in 1979–1980, for example, had held no party office before becoming chair.[24] These patterns vary with the nature of the political organization. In party organizations that have relatively open access and easy mobility, careers in the party are developed easily, almost spontaneously. In more disciplined party organizations, party activists must work up the hierarchy in carefully graded steps. Over time with the decline of the old-style hierarchical organizations, career paths have become more varied.

WHAT KINDS OF PEOPLE BECOME PARTY ACTIVISTS?

These various incentives and recruitment processes combine to produce the party activists—the men and women who do the work of the parties. These activists play a wide range of roles in party affairs, from campaigning on behalf of party candidates and serving as delegates to party nominating conventions to answering phones and e-mail at party offices.

Common Characteristics

Although they differ in motivations, American party activists have two characteristics in common that set them apart from the general population. First, they tend to come from families with a history of party activity. Study after study indicates that large numbers of party activists had an adult party activist in their immediate family as they were growing up. Second, activists are relatively high in socioeconomic status (SES); they tend to have higher incomes, more years of formal education and higher-status occupations than does the average American. Lawyers are especially common among the active partisans, just as they are among elected officials.[25] The parties thus attract men and women (in about equal numbers) with the time and financial resources to afford political activity, the information and knowledge to understand it, and the skills to be useful in it.[26]

Some local organizations provided exceptions to this general pattern. The patronage-oriented, favor-dispensing machines in the city centers tended to recruit party workers and leaders who were more representative of the populations with which they worked. For many lower-status Americans, the material incentives the machines could provide were probably the crucial reasons for their activism. When patronage and other material incentives dwindled, the social character of these parties changed. A comparison of county committee members from both Pittsburgh parties in 1971, 1976, and 1983 shows that, as machine control declined, the education levels of party workers increased. The mix of incentives that a party can provide, in short, makes a difference in the social composition of the activists it can recruit.[27]

The social characteristics of Democratic activists differ from those of Republicans, just as the social bases of the parties' voters do. Democratic activists are more likely than their Republican counterparts to be black, union members, or Catholic. But differences in education, income, and occupation have declined in recent years. Although they may come from different backgrounds and certainly hold different political views, the leaders of both parties seem to be drawn disproportionately from the higher status groups in American society—even more now than in decades past.[28] This pattern may not be found to the same degree in other nations' party systems because most democracies have a viable socialist party, which recruits many of its activists from the ranks of organized labor.

Professionals and Amateurs

In addition to their social characteristics, activists' goals and expectations help shape their party organizations. Observers of the American parties often classify party activists into two types, based on the role they play in the organization and the expectations they have for it. One type of party activist is the **_professional_**—the party worker whose first loyalty is to the party itself and whose operating style is pragmatic. A very different type is the **_amateur_**—the issue-oriented purist who sees party activity as only one means for achieving important political goals. Professionals and amateurs differ in almost all of the characteristics important for party activists (see Table 5.1).These two types tend to be more extreme than we are likely to find in reality. Even so, the typology can help us distinguish between traditional party "regulars" and "reformers" in presidential nominating conventions and in party organizations at all levels of government (see box below).[29]

A party organization populated by amateurs will probably behave very differently from a party dominated by professionals. Above all, amateur activists are drawn into the party in order to further some issues or principles; for them, the issue is the goal and the party is the means of achieving it. If the party, or its candidates, pulls back on its commitment to their issue, they may pull back on their commitment to the party. So they tend to be less comfortable with the thought of making compromises in their positions in order to win elections. Further, amateur activists are likely to insist on widespread participation within the party organization in order to put their issue concerns at the top of the party's agenda. When they come to dominate party organizations, they often bring a strong push for reform in both the party's internal business and in the larger political system.

For professionals or pragmatists, on the other hand, the goal is the success of the party in elections; issue positions and candidates are the means of achieving that goal. If

TABLE 5.1 Comparing Professionals and Amateurs

	Professionals	Amateurs
Political Style	Pragmatic	Purist
What do they want?	Material rewards (patronage, preferments)	Purposive rewards (issues, ideology)
Their loyalty is to:	Party organization	Officeholders, other political groups
They want the party to focus on:	Candidates, elections	Issues, ideology
The party should choose candidates on the basis of:	Their electability	Their principles
The style of party governance should be:	Hierarchical	Democratic
Their support of party candidates is:	Automatic	Conditional on candidates' principles
They were recruited into politics through:	Party work	Issue or candidate organizations
Their SES level is:	Average to above average	Well above average

A Tale of Two Democrats: The "Amateur" and the "Professional"

Martin Sheen is a liberal Democrat who plays one on TV. The actor portrays President Josiah Bartlet on NBC's award-winning series "The West Wing." His strong opposition to nuclear testing and support for gun control and environmental protection have long driven Sheen's political involvement. He has been arrested many times while participating in peace and environmental protests. Sheen campaigned for Democratic presidential candidate Al Gore in 2000 and donated his time to make a television ad criticizing candidate George W. Bush's gun control record in Texas; in a media appearance he termed Bush a "moron." But although he supports Democrats, Sheen is primarily concerned about issues. He says, "I don't have a personal interest in politics per se. I have a great interest in the issues that are publicly debated, but I have a far greater interest in social justice and peace. I could never be free to explore that if I was bound to a constituency [by running for office]. If I was bound to a constituency, I would have to foreclose my principles."

Just as Sheen fits the definition of a political "amateur," Robert Strauss is the consummate party "professional." A lifelong Democrat from Texas, Strauss moved up the party hierarchy to become Finance Chair and then Chair of the Democratic National Committee in the 1970s. After Democratic losses in the 1980 election, Strauss and then–Arkansas governor, Bill Clinton, founded the Democratic Leadership Council to encourage the party to appeal to a broad range of viewpoints, just as Strauss had encouraged both conservative Southern Democrats and liberal "new Democrats" to remain in the party during his term as DNC Chair. Strauss has been described as "nonideological," because he is committed to the success of the party rather than to any specific cause. Though he supported Al Gore for the 2000 Democratic presidential nomination, Strauss donated money to the primary campaigns of both Gore and his rival, Bill Bradley. His money and his votes "always go to Democrats because he believes in the party...."

Sources: Sheen quoted on "That's Entertainment," Feb. 3, 2001; Strauss quoted in Susan Feeney, "Texans Making Dual Donations in Presidential Race," *Dallas Morning News,* Aug. 22, 1999, p. 1.

they believe that their party is most likely to win by downplaying an issue, moderating a position, or nominating a candidate who is popular, but not in lockstep with their views on major issues, then that is the course they are likely to favor. The possibility of conflict between amateurs and professionals, as a result, is always present. And the increasing numbers of amateur activists can challenge party leaders; if you were a county party chair, for example, would you prefer to work with a group of activists who were mainly amateurs or mainly professionals?

Differences that are clear in theory, however, do not always carry over into practice. Amateurs may hold different *attitudes* from professionals on such key matters as the importance of party loyalty and the need for compromise. But there is persuasive evidence that these differences in attitudes do not necessarily carry over into behavior. In a study of delegates to state nominating conventions, amateurs were just as likely as professionals to support candidates who seemed electable, rather than those whose ideology they shared.[30] Among county party chairs in 1972, a time when amateurs were thought to hold the upper hand, at least in the Democratic Party, the amateurs did not differ from professionals in their effort to communicate within the party, maintain party morale, or run effective campaigns.[31] It is helpful, in short, not to exaggerate the contrast between professionals and amateurs and the implications of changes in their relative numbers for the parties.

ACTIVISTS' MOTIVES AND THE VITALITY OF PARTY ORGANIZATIONS

In Chapter 3, we saw that party organizations vary a great deal in their effectiveness. Some local parties have impressive success in mobilizing grassroots activity and other resources needed to win elections. Others fall far short. Although the efforts at centralized party-building and funding have improved the integration among national, state, and local parties, communications remain poor within many organizations, and leaders at each level usually operate independently of others. A national survey of local party efforts in the 1992 presidential campaign, for example, found that 22 percent of the county party chairs did not communicate with their local counterparts in the presidential campaign organizations, 21 percent had no contact with their state parties and a majority (61 percent) had no contact with their national parties.[32]

These organizational problems can be traced, in part, to the varying motives, views and levels of commitment of party workers. If the party organization is not able to harness their differing interests in pursuit of a common goal, it will be difficult for the party to remain competitive. Parties' vote-getting success depends to an important degree on their vitality as organizations. Though the effect is not large, evidence shows consistently that a well-organized and active local party can win extra votes for its candidates by mobilizing its supporters and getting them to the polls. In competitive districts, even a small margin produced by party mobilization can be the critical difference between winning and losing.[33]

Because organizational effectiveness makes a difference in elections, let us conclude these three chapters on party organization with some discussion about the relationship between the recruitment of party activists and party organizational strength. Three main questions arise. Under what circumstances, and with what types of recruitment processes are party organizations more effective? Do internally democratic parties, such as those favored by the classic amateurs, strengthen or weaken party efforts? Finally, what are the checks on a strong party organization to keep party leaders and activists from overstepping their bounds?

Party Workers and Organizational Strength

Strong party organizations have been more likely to develop in some types of areas than in others. Because of the population density of cities and the special needs of urban populations, it is not surprising that party organization has often reached its peak in metropolitan areas. These are also areas in which density may make it easier to recruit volunteers and where organizational activities, such as canvassing, are more easily accomplished. Political culture plays a role here, however; canvassing and the use of patronage are more acceptable in some urban areas than in others. Even the mix of amateur and professional orientations within the party organization may vary by political culture. The parties of Berkeley, Manhattan, or suburban Minneapolis may contain more amateurs than those of Columbus, Queens, or Chicago.[34]

As we have seen, party organizations are also stronger where there is close, two-party competition. Areas of one-party politics clearly weaken party organizations—not just that of the entrenched minority party, but of the majority party as well.[35] The role of party recruitment helps explain this finding. Bringing people into a losing party is not an easy job, and it can be almost as difficult to convince volunteers that the party that dominates local politics still has a need for their efforts. Finally, state laws that govern party recruitment can make a difference in organizational strength. Laws that make it difficult for the party to remove or replace inactive officials, to use patronage as an inducement for party work, or to decide which candidates will carry its label hamper the development of strong party organizations.[36]

Activists and Internal Party Democracy

How does the party organization's internal governance affect its strength and effectiveness? Does the increasing number of amateur activists, with their preference for parties that are run democratically, make party organizations more effective or less effective? Note that the image of party bosses who had absolute control over their party apparatus was always a bit of an exaggeration, and continues to exist now only in old movies and works of literature.[37] Even in the era of boss rule, the party leader normally shared power with influential underlings, and the terms of that sharing were deeply rooted in the organization's traditions.

More recently, however, party activists have come to demand a much louder voice in the affairs of the party. In the 1960s and 1970s, much of the ideological fervor of many amateurs was directed at reforming the party's leadership structure, and very little divides amateurs from professionals more than their attitudes toward openness and representation within the party. The amateurs' commitment to internal party democracy follows logically from their desire to achieve certain ideological goals; in politics, the rules determine the outcome, so if activists wanted to change the party's goals, they needed to change its internal rules as well. Thus they had to reform the American parties if they were to reform American society.[38]

It could be argued that their success in making the parties—and especially the Democratic Party—more participatory has weakened the discipline of the party organization. Discipline depends, at least in part, on an organization's ability to reward and punish its active members. An organization in which the leaders are highly accountable to the members, however—as would be the case in a very democratically run party—could find it much harder to insist that party workers do the jobs that the party leadership believes should be done.

In addition, the increase in purposive incentives could pose a problem for a disciplined party. Much of the discipline in the classic party machine resulted from the willingness and ability of party leaders to give or withhold material rewards. A disobedient or inefficient party worker sacrificed a patronage job, or the hope of one. The newer incentives, however, cannot be given or taken away so easily. A local Republican organization is not likely to punish an errant, ideologically motivated activist by ending the party's support of school prayer. Even if it did, the activist can find many other organizations that may be more effective at pursuing that goal, such as religious lobbies or other organized interests.

On the other hand, one could argue that a party organization dominated by amateur activists could be strengthened by its commitment to internal democracy. Rank-and-file activists who are contributing their time and effort in the service of a strongly-held principle and who feel sure that their views are taken seriously by party leaders may be even more likely to work hard on the party's behalf. Granted, it is easier to imagine a strong and disciplined party organization when it is composed of party professionals who are dedicated to the party's success above all else. But the growing importance of issue-based motives for party activism does not necessarily mean a threat to strong party organizations.

Strong party organizations, however, have often been considered a threat to American politics. Since the beginning, American political culture has been dominated by a fear that a few people, responsible to no one, will control the selection of public officials and set the agendas of policy-making in "smoke-filled rooms." The result has been a series of safeguards, both external to and inside the party organizations, to keep the parties from playing too powerful a role in the lives of candidates, elected officials, and voters.

Limits on Strong Parties

One of those "external" safeguards is the simple fact of two-party competition itself. Because they are in competition, each party has an incentive to serve as a check on the other.[39] Thus, the current increase in two-party competitiveness throughout the United States could expose more party organizations to the discipline of the electoral market.

Another "external" check on party organizational strength comes from the use of primary elections. Party reformers promoted the idea of primaries as a way to keep party leaders from appointing, and thus controlling, other party officials, as well as party candidates. But the results have not often satisfied the reformers. Where primary elections are held to choose precinct committee members and other party leaders, there is typically no competition for these offices; in fact, there is often no candidate at all. And efforts to pass laws regulating the workings of party caucuses and conventions have not always succeeded in guaranteeing access to everyone who would qualify to participate.

Yet the reformers have had a few successes. When party caucuses have been required by law to remain open to all qualified partisans, they have sometimes opened the party organization to factional competition, but at other times, to be reinvigorated by new party activists. Further, in every state the direct primary has, at least, forced the parties to face the scrutiny of voters on one key decision: the nomination of candidates for office—at times, in fact, to the detriment of party organizational strength.[40]

"Stratarchy" Rules

In addition to these external controls, the "stratarchy" that is typical of the American parties' structure continues to act as a brake on party organizational power. "Stratarchy," as Chapter 3 mentioned, is a term that describes the relative independence of each level of party organization from all the other levels. Rather than a hierarchical pattern in which the organization is ruled from the top, power in the American parties is diffused through the various levels of party organization. Precinct committee members, city leaders, and county officials freely define their own political roles and nourish their separate bases of party power.[41]

That poses an interesting puzzle. We have just seen, in Chapter 4, the remarkable recent growth in the capabilities of the national and state parties with their fat treasuries and skilled political operatives. Why haven't these stronger national and state party organizations eaten away at the idea of stratarchy and imposed some top-down leadership on the other levels of party? What is it that keeps top party leaders from centralizing organizational power into a hierarchy? These restraints include:

- *Activists' expectations.* Large numbers of party activists expect to participate in their party's decision-making processes. Party organizations, then, often have to tolerate internal party democracy to retain their workers' loyalty.

- *Lower party levels have some control over higher levels.* The leaders of the lower-level party organizations typically make up the conventions that select higher-level party officials. County chairs who choose state officers are forces to be reckoned with in the state party organizations. Similarly, precinct workers or delegates often form or choose county committees.

- *Internal competition.* Party organizations are rarely monoliths. They are often composed of competing organizations or factions. Differences in goals and political styles produce continuing competition in the selecting of party officials and party activities.

- *Officeholders' independence.* Because public officials do not normally rely on the party organization to be nominated or elected, they often create their own power bases within the party; that enables them to compete with party leaders for power over the party organization.

Even with the new resources available in the national parties, the party organizations continue to be marked by a diffusion of power. It is possible that the lure of national party money and advice could bring with it more control and direction from the top, and thus greater party discipline. But given the powerful forces that work against centralized authority in the American parties, this is not likely to happen anytime soon. So top party leaders will continue to have to work hard to mobilize support within their own organization. They do not command, because they cannot. Rather, they bargain, they plead, they reason, and they consult endlessly with leaders and activists at other levels of party organization. They even learn to lose gracefully on occasion. They mobilize party power, not so much by threats as by appealing to common goals and interests.

The traditional worry about the excesses of party power, then, is probably misplaced. There have been few occasions in American history when the parties have been able to corral the kinds of incentives and resources they would need in order to flesh out the party organization that they would like, or that the state laws detail. The thousands of inactive precinct workers and unfilled precinct positions testify to that. The parties have had no alternative but to try to recruit activists who vary in their backgrounds, styles, and motives, with all the challenges and limits that involves. The parties are, after all, the products of their people.

PART THREE

The Political
Party in the
Electorate

If there were a Public Opinion Poll Hall of Fame, surely the first question in it would be: Generally speaking, do you usually think of yourself as a Republican, a Democrat, an independent, or what? The question is meant to classify *party identifiers*—people who feel a sense of psychological attachment to a particular party. If you respond that you do usually think of yourself as a Democrat or a Republican, then you are categorized as belonging to the party in the electorate—the second major sector of the American parties. They make up the core of the party's support: the people who normally vote for a party's candidates and who are inclined to see politics through a partisan's eyes. They are more apt to vote in the party's primary elections and to volunteer for party candidates than are other citizens. They are, in short, the party organization's, and its candidates', closest friends in the public.

Survey researchers have measured Americans' party loyalty since the 1940s. The dominant measure, cited above, has been used in polls conducted by the University of Michigan, now under the auspices of the American National Election Studies (ANES). After asking whether you consider yourself a Republican or a Democrat, the question continues:

[If Republican or Democrat] Would you call yourself a strong [Republican or Democrat] or a not very strong [Republican or Democrat]? [If independent, no preference, or other party] Do you think of yourself as closer to the Republican Party or to the Democratic Party?

Using these answers, researchers classify people into seven different categories of party identification: strong party identifiers (Democrats or Republicans), weak identifiers (Democrats or Republicans), independent "leaners" (toward the Democrats or Republicans), and pure independents.[1]

Note that this definition is not based on people's actual voting behavior. Strong party identifiers usually vote for their party's candidates. But the essence of a party identification is an attachment to the party itself—a commitment distinct from feelings about any particular candidates. Someone can remain a committed Republican, for example, even while choosing to vote for the Democratic candidate in a specific race. Given the large number of elective offices in the United States and the value American culture places on independence, we can often find party identifiers who vote for a candidate or two—or more—of the other party. In the same sense, we do not define the party electorate in terms of the official act of registering with a party. Almost half the states do not have party registration, and in states that do, some voters may change their party attachments without bothering to alter their official registration.[2]

The party electorate's relationship with the other two party sectors—the party organization and the party in government—can be both slippery and frustrating. Clearly, the party cannot survive without the party identifiers' support. Yet the party in the electorate is independent of these other party sectors. Party identifiers are not party "members" in any real sense. The party organizations and candidates see their identifiers as a group of customers to be courted at each election, but largely ignored between elections. Party identifiers, in turn, seldom feel any obligation to the party organization other than to vote for its candidates, if they choose. In these ways, the American parties resemble cadre parties: top-heavy in leaders and activists without any real mass membership, in contrast to the mass-membership parties that have been such an important part of the European democratic experience.

Despite their independence, party identifiers give the party organization and its candidates a continuing core of voter support. The parties do not, in other words, have to start from scratch in every campaign. In their fight to win majorities, parties cannot rely just on their own committed identifiers, of course. They must also attract votes from those with no party attachments and even from some supporters of the other party. Their base, however, is the millions of voters who, by psychologically identifying with that party, comprise its coalition of supporters.

The party in the electorate also largely determines who the party's nominees for office will be by voting in primaries. It is a reservoir of potential activists for the organization. Its members may donate money to the party, or they may work in a specific campaign. They help keep the party alive by transmitting party loyalties to their children. The loyalty that links these groups and individuals to their party can be strong enough to act a filter through which people see and evaluate candidates and issues. It can structure an individual's mental map of the political world.

A party in the electorate is more than a group of individuals, however. It is a coalition of social groups. Our images of the two parties often spring from the types of people the parties have attracted as identifiers. When people speak of the Democrats as the party of the disadvantaged, or of the Republicans as the party of business, they are probably referring, at least in part, to the party in the electorate. The interplay between a party's supporters and its appeals (its candidates, issues, and traditions)—each one shaping and reinforcing the other—comes very close to determining what the parties are.

The three chapters in Part 3 explore the nature and importance of these parties in the electorate. Chapter 6 looks at the development of party identification and its impact on individuals' political behavior. Chapter 7 examines the parties as coalitions of social groups and traces the changes in those coalitions over time. Chapter 8 focuses on the differences between the people who vote and those who do not. These differences have an important effect on the parties' choices in mobilizing their faithful and recruiting new supporters.

Party Identification

Think back to your years in elementary school. If you are like millions of other Americans, by the time you completed sixth grade you could identify yourself as a Democrat, a Republican, or an independent. What led you to develop at least a minimal sense of attachment to a party (or to a rejection of party labels)? Do you still identify with the same party? And what difference does it make? How does the existence of party identification affect the lives of the political parties and the nature of American politics?

Without question, a party identification is a useful shortcut for voters. Politics is complicated, even for political junkies who pay close attention to political news. Americans cope with more elections, and therefore more occasions on which they need to make large numbers of political choices, than do citizens of any other democracy. On any given day, three levels of legislatures—national, state, and local—may be passing laws that affect our lives. It is hard enough for reporters and political activists to keep track of all the action. The challenge is so much greater for other citizens who spend less time thinking about politics (even though their lives are just as greatly affected by political decisions).

It is understandable, then, that most Americans develop an *identification*, or sense of psychological attachment, to a political party.[1] More than 30 percent of Americans call themselves "strong" partisans, and another quarter express some party attachment, though not a strong one. Even among those who at first claim to be independents, more than two-thirds confess to some partisan feeling. This party identification, or party ID, serves as a framework through which individuals see political reality. It gives the individual a predisposition to support Democratic candidates, or Republican candidates, without having to do all the research necessary to make a separate decision on each candidate for office, or to develop an opinion on each bill the legislature considers.

Partisanship can be measured in various ways (see the box on p. 108). However we measure it, people's party ID tells us more about their political perceptions and behavior than does any other single piece of information. A party identification will probably be the individual's most enduring political attachment. For that reason, it often acts as a kind of political gyroscope, stabilizing political outlooks against the buffetings of short-term influences. Where do these party identifications come from?

HOW PEOPLE DEVELOP PARTY IDENTIFICATIONS

Families are the most common source of our first party identifications, as they are of so much else in our early lives. People often say that they are Democrats or Republicans because they were brought up that way, just as they may have been raised as a Methodist or a Jew. As children become aware of politics, they absorb judgments about political parties and typically come to think of themselves as sharing their family's partisanship.

Childhood Influences

Party loyalty often develops as early as the elementary grades. Although they do not usually consciously indoctrinate their children into party loyalty, parents are the primary teachers of political orientations in the American culture (see the cartoon on page 110). Their casual conversations and references to political events are enough to convey their party loyalties to their children. These influences can be powerful enough to last into adulthood, even at times when young adults are pulled toward independence.

This early party identification usually takes hold before children have much information as to what the parties stand for. It isn't until the middle-school and high-school

---

How Should We Measure Party Identification?

The most commonly used measure of party identification classifies people into one of seven types of attachment: strong Democrat, weak Democrat, independent leaning toward Democrats, "pure" independent, independent leaning toward Republicans, weak Republican, and strong Republican. (There are also a very few people who describe themselves as nonpolitical, or who identify with minor parties.) Is this the best way to classify partisans?

This measure produces a continuum of partisanship. But scholars disagree on where "party identifiers" end and "independents" begin. This decision matters, of course, if we want to draw conclusions about the strength of a particular party or about the likelihood of a realignment. So in most tables in this book, the full seven categories are presented, so that readers can draw their own line between partisan and independent. In most of the discussion in these chapters, partisans are defined as strong plus weak party identifiers and the three categories of independents are combined.

Curiously, however, independent "leaners" often behave in a more partisan manner than weak partisans do, especially in voting for their party's candidates. Why is that? It could be that the party identification measure is capturing more than a single attitude toward the parties. Your attitude toward Republicans, for example, could be only partly related to your attitude toward Democrats. Or someone could be attracted both to a particular party and to the idea of political independence. If that is true, then a single continuum may not be the best measure of people's partisan feelings.

Scientists sometimes disagree about how to measure key concepts. This particular controversy focuses on refining, not dismissing, the idea of party loyalties. Generally speaking, the traditional measure of party identification continues to be seen as a valid and reliable measure of party loyalty.[2]

years that students begin to associate the parties with general economic interests—with business or labor, the rich or the poor—and thus to have some reasoning to support the party identification they have already developed. Note the importance of the sequence here. Party loyalty comes first, so it tends to have a long-lasting impact on attitudes toward politics. Only later do people learn about political issues and events, which will then be filtered, at least in part, through a partisan lens.[3]

Once developed, people's party loyalties are often sustained because friends, associates, and relatives typically share the same partisan loyalties.[4] Some people do leave the parties of their parents. Those whose early party loyalty is weak are more likely to change. So are people whose mother and father identified with different parties, or who live in a community or work in a setting where the prevailing party influences differ from their own. But when parents share the same party identification, they are more likely to produce strong party identifiers among their children.[5]

Other agents of political learning tend to support a person's inherited party loyalty or at least do not challenge the family's influence. Schools typically avoid partisan politics; they are probably more inclined to teach political independence than partisanship. During most of the twentieth century, American churches usually steered clear of partisan conflict even at a time when church-connected political parties existed in Europe. Churches and other religious groups have clearly entered the political fray in American politics, but they are not likely to lead young people away from their parents' partisan influence. The American parties themselves do very little direct socialization; they do not maintain the youth groups, the flourishing university branches, the social or recreational activities, or the occupational organizations that some European parties do.

Influences in Adulthood

These influences on children's and teenagers' political learning are more likely to be challenged beginning in young adulthood, when an individual enters any of several new environments: college, work, marriage, a new community, and the unexpected honor of paying taxes. At this point in the life cycle, adults can test their childhood party loyalties against political reality. They can see how their favored party performs in matters that concern them, and they can watch the behavior of the other party as well (see "A Day in the Life," p. 111). Their adult experiences may convince them that their early-learned loyalties are the right ones for them or may undermine those loyalties.[6]

The longer people hold a particular party ID, the more intense it tends to become. Older adults are most likely to hold strong party attachments and least likely to change them. Perhaps party ID is more likely to become a habit after decades of political observations and activity. Or partisanship may grow stronger across the life cycle because it is so useful a shortcut for simplifying the political decision-making of older voters.[7]

There are times, however, when even committed Democrats and Republicans are driven to change their partisanship. During realigning periods, when the issue bases of partisanship and the party coalitions themselves are being transformed, some voters desert the partisan tradition of their parents. (We will look more fully at the idea of realignment in the next chapter.) This happened during the New Deal realignment of the 1930s, and we can find more recent examples of the power of major issues to move some people's partisanship. Older adults may be caught up in the excitement of the moment, but their partisanship, typically reinforced by years of consistent partisan behavior, is much more resistant to change. Thus it is typically young adults who act as the "carriers" of realignment and consequently to whom we should look for early signs of partisan change.[8]

THE STABILITY OF PARTY IDENTIFICATIONS

Large-scale change in party identifications is the exception, however, and not the rule. Most Americans, once they have developed party loyalties, tend to keep them; partisanship becomes a fairly stable anchor in an ever-changing political world. People who do change their party identification normally change only its intensity (for example, from strong to weak identification) rather than convert to the other party. Researchers from the University of Michigan convincingly demonstrated the stability of party identifications by interviewing the same set of individuals in three successive surveys, in 1972, 1974, and 1976. They found that almost two-thirds of the respondents remained in the same broad category of party identification (44 percent were stable strong/weak Democrats or Republicans, 20 percent stable independents) throughout all three surveys. A third changed from one of the parties to independence. Only 3 percent actually changed parties.[9]

The Faithful Republicans

A DAY IN THE LIFE

When Did Your Party ID Change?

U.S. Representative Billy Tauzin (R-Louisiana)

In the Louisiana bayou town where he grew up, W. J. "Billy" Tauzin, the son of an electrical worker, thought of himself as a Democrat, like most of his neighbors. He served as a Democratic state representative from 1971 to 1979 before winning a U.S. House seat in 1980. Though his district was predominantly Democratic, it was also conservative, and so was Tauzin: from 1980 till 1995, his average approval rating from the U.S. Chamber of Commerce was 75%—almost four times higher than his approval rating from the liberal group Americans for Democratic Action.

By 1995, however, the Democratic congressional party had become less accepting of Tauzin's conservative views. In response, Tauzin, long known as an advocate of limited government and private property rights, helped form a coalition of conservative to moderate House Democrats known as the "Blue Dogs." Soon after, he quit the Democratic Congressional Campaign Committee, contending that the DCCC leadership regularly snubbed Blue Dog Democrats. Finally, he announced that he was switching his party affiliation to Republican. Until that point in the 104th Congress, Tauzin had sided with a majority of Democrats against a majority of Republicans on only 20 percent of the votes taken. "We have learned over the course of the last year," he said, "that there is no role for conservatives within the Democratic party. I decided to go with a party that respects my ideas."[10]

U.S. Senator Jim Jeffords (I-Vermont)

"For the past several weeks, I have been struggling with a very difficult decision.... I have spent a lifetime in the Republican party.... I became a Republican not because I was born into the party but because of the kind of fundamental principles that.... many other Republicans stood for: moderation, tolerance, and fiscal responsibility.... [but] Increasingly, I find myself in disagreement with my party.... In the past, without the presidency, the various wings of the Republican Party in Congress have had some freedom to argue and ultimately to shape the party's agenda. The election of President Bush changed that dramatically.... Looking ahead, I can see more and more instances where I will disagree with the President on very fundamental issues: the issues of choice, the direction of the judiciary.... [so] in order to best represent my state of Vermont, my own conscience, and the principles I have stood for my whole life, I will leave the Republican Party and become an Independent. [Party] Control of the Senate will soon be changed by my decision.... My colleagues, many of them my friends for years, may find it difficult in their hearts to befriend me any longer.... But I was not elected to this office to be something that I am not."[11]

Analysts have also found that individuals' attitudes toward the parties—their party identifications—were more stable over two-year periods than their evaluations of prominent political figures or political issues. This set of surveys was conducted during one of the most turbulent periods in recent history, covering Richard Nixon's landslide victory in 1972, the

Watergate scandals that caused Nixon's resignation in 1974, Nixon's subsequent pardon by President Ford, and Ford's own 1976 defeat. It would be hard to find better evidence of the stability of party identification than its consistency during these agitated times.[12]

PARTY IDENTIFICATION AS A FILTER FOR POLITICAL VIEWS

Because of their early development and stability, party loyalties can affect the ways that people view politics. People often develop evaluations of candidates that are heavily colored by their attachment to a party. Whether these images are accurate or not, people tend to *project* favorable characteristics and acceptable issue positions onto the candidates of the party they favor and are *persuaded* to support particular candidates or issues because they are associated with the individual's party.[13]

Projection and Persuasion

When a new political candidate begins to get public notice and before most voters know much about him or her, many partisans in the electorate will react to the candidate positively or negatively based solely on party affiliation. Many people will project their favorable image of the party onto its new candidate and will be persuaded to support him or her. "The stronger the voter's party bias, the more likely he is to see the candidate of his own party as hero, the candidate of the other party as villain."[14] Even when a popular non-politician such as Colin Powell is first mentioned as a possible candidate, evaluations of that person quickly diverge along partisan lines once the name is associated with a party.

Partisan loyalty can have a big impact on people's attitudes, even when it has to compete with other valued loyalties. Democrat John F. Kennedy was only the second Catholic presidential candidate in American history. Catholics tended to view Kennedy more favorably in that election than Protestants did. Catholic Republicans, however, were not as positively disposed toward Kennedy as were Catholic Democrats. Party identification, then, still held its power, even among those with the same religious loyalty. So party identification helps to condition the way people feel about candidates and public officials.[15]

The impact of party ID is selective, however. People are more likely to project their positive view of the party onto a candidate's political traits than onto such purely personal matters as the candidate's personality, appearance, or social characteristics.[16] Further, this projection has limits. Candidates for president who have been defeated in landslides—the last was Democrat Walter Mondale in 1984—were not evaluated very positively even by their fellow partisans. Yet partisanship matters even here; as low as Mondale's standing may have sunk, he could count on more sympathy from Democratic identifiers than from other voters.

Does an individual's partisanship color his or her feelings about political issues as well? That is harder to determine, because it poses a chicken-and-egg problem: which came first, the party ID or the issue position? Democratic identifiers do differ from Republicans in their stands on a large number of issues, as we will see in Chapter 7. We could argue that people are naturally more likely to favor a party that champions their particular beliefs. But there is also a tendency for partisans to adopt their party's positions on issues, especially when those issues are complicated (for example, detailed health care proposals) and remote (i.e., how strongly should we support the government of Taiwan?).

Partisanship as a Two-Way Street

Just as the individual's party loyalty influences his or her perception of political reality, studies have shown that feelings about candidates and issues can affect the individual's party identification as well. In particular, there is powerful evidence that negative reactions to a president's management of the economy (so-called *retrospective evaluations*, in that they refer to past actions rather than hopes for the future) can feed back on party loyalties and weaken or change them. In this way, partisanship could act as a kind of "running tally" of party-related evaluations.[17]

The result is a complex two-way process in which party loyalty affects an individual's evaluations of candidates and issues, and those evaluations, in turn, help to shape the way people view the parties. Even if party identification is usually stable enough to withstand an individual's disappointment in a particular party candidate or in the party's position on an issue or two, an accumulation of these negative experiences can shake an individual's partisanship—as happened over several decades to the long-standing Democratic loyalties of many conservative white Southerners.

PATTERNS OF PARTISANSHIP OVER TIME

When we look at the overall pattern of American party identification over time, we see a remarkable degree of stability, at least in the years since survey data have been available. Table 6.1 shows the responses of Americans to a poll question asked since 1952 by researchers at the University of Michigan: "Generally speaking, do you consider yourself a Democrat or a Republican?"[18] Democrats have held the numerical advantage over Republicans in most years, but the changes in each category of partisanship tend to be fairly limited over time—never more than 7 percent from one survey to the next, and usually around 2 percent.

Even so, the overall pattern shows a change in the 1970s that seemed highly significant to many analysts: a drop in the proportion of party identifiers and a corresponding increase in the percentage of independents. Self-identified Democrats and Republicans, both "strong" and "weak," became a smaller proportion of the survey respondents, and independents and independent "leaners" grew from less than a quarter of the respondents to more than a third. Combined with other events of that time—the political turmoil of the civil rights movement, the protests against American involvement in the Vietnam War, the women's movement, environmental activism—this suggested that partisanship was fading in the United States.

Has There Been a Decline in Partisanship?

Evidence for the "thesis of party decline" was convincing. Even among those who still considered themselves partisans, the strength of party loyalties moderated beginning in the late 1960s (see Table 6.1). A smaller share of the electorate wore the partisan lenses that can color political reality. The consequences were thought to be profound. One prominent analyst saw the American public as "drifting away from the two major political parties,"[19] and others even predicted "the end of parties."[20]

The argument was bolstered by research in other democracies. Across the western industrial world, analysts found a rise in the proportion of independents, a decline in confidence

TABLE 6.1 Party Identification: 1952–2000

	1952	1956	1960	1964	1968	1972	1976	1980	1984	1988	1992	1996	2000
Strong Democrats	22%	21%	20%	27%	20%	15%	15%	18%	17%	17%	17%	19%	19%
Weak Democrats	25	23	25	25	25	26	25	23	20	18	18	20	15
Independents, closer to Democrats	10	6	6	9	10	11	12	11	11	12	14	14	15
Independents	6	9	10	8	10	13	14	13	11	11	12	8	12
Independents, closer to Republicans	7	8	7	6	9	10	10	10	12	13	13	11	13
Weak Republicans	14	14	14	13	14	13	14	14	15	14	15	15	12
Strong Republicans	13	15	15	11	10	10	9	8	12	14	11	13	13
Others	4	4	3	2	2	2	1	3	2	2	1	1	1
	101%	100%	100%	101%	100%	100%	100%	100%	100%	101%	101%	101%	100%
Cases	1793	1762	1928	1571	1556	2707	2864	1614	2236	2033	2478	1714	1785

Note: Based on surveys of the national electorate conducted immediately before each presidential election—in recent years as part of the American National Election Studies (ANES) program. Due to rounding, the percentages do not always add up to exactly 100 percent.

Source: American National Election Studies, Center for Political Studies, University of Michigan; data made available through the Inter-University Consortium for Political and Social Research.

expressed in political parties, and an increase in ***split-ticket voting*** (supporting candidates of more than one party).[21] What caused it? Education levels were steadily increasing in democratic nations; perhaps more educated voters had so much other information available to them that they didn't need parties as a decision shortcut any more. Maybe candidates were becoming more independent of party ties, and influencing other citizens. Or perhaps media coverage of politics stressed nonpartisanship or ignored parties.

These explanations produced even more questions, however. If Americans have more information available than ever before, wouldn't they need a device, like a party ID, to help them sift through it? Even though education levels are rising, one of the things we know with greatest certainty about public opinion is that most of us are not very interested in politics, don't know very much about it, and therefore depend on shortcuts with which to make sense of the voting decisions that face us. We may have a wealth of information, but most of us are not motivated to make use of it. Party identification, then, would probably remain a helpful tool.[22]

And in fact, indicators of partisanship *have* rebounded since the 1970s. At least among those who vote, the decline in party ID has been largely reversed. The distribution of party attachments among voters in the 1990s was not much different from what it had been in the 1950s, which was considered a very partisan time,[23] though the proportion of independents rose markedly in 2000. Perhaps the revival of party attachment in the 1990s was prompted by greater partisanship in Congress and by more partisan political leaders such as Ronald Reagan and former House Speaker Newt Gingrich. Whatever the reason, party remains an influential political attachment.

TABLE 6.2 Voting for Their Party's Presidential Candidates Among Party Identifiers: 1952–2000

	1952	1956	1960	1964	1968	1972	1976	1980	1984	1988	1992	1996	2000
Strong Democrats	84%	85%	90%	95%	85%	73%	91%	86%	87%	93%	93%	96%	97%
Weak Democrats	62	62	72	82	58	48	74	60	67	70	69	82	89
Independents closer to Democrats	60	68	88	90	52	60	72	45	79	88	71	76	72
Independents	—	—	—	—	—	—	—	—	—	—	—	—	—
Independents closer to Republicans	93	94	87	75	82	86	83	76	92	84	62	68	79
Weak Republicans	94	93	87	56	82	90	77	86	93	83	60	70	85
Strong Republicans	98	100	98	90	96	97	96	92	96	98	87	94	97

Note: The table entries are the percentages of each category of partisans who reported a vote for their party's candidate for president. To find the percentage voting for the opposing party's candidate or some other candidate, subtract the entry from 100 percent. Individuals who did not vote for president are excluded from the table.

Source: American National Election Studies, Center for Political Studies, University of Michigan; data made available by the Inter-University Consortium for Political and Social Research.

PARTY IDENTIFICATION AND VOTING

The most important effect of party attachments is their influence on voting. Partisans provide the core support for the candidates of their party. The American electoral system discourages faithful party voting; partisans have to fight their way through long ballots, the culture's traditional emphasis on the individual rather than the party, and its distrust of strong parties. Nevertheless, party identifiers support their party with considerable fidelity.

Party Voting

Party identifiers have been loyal party voters throughout the life of the American National Election Studies (ANES) surveys. A majority in each category of partisanship has voted for their party's presidential candidate in every year, except for weak Democrats in 1972 and independent Democrats in 1980 (both GOP landslide years). Further, strong partisans have always been more faithful than weak or independent partisans (Table 6.2). Even in the Reagan landslide victory of 1984, when voting Democratic clearly ran against the tide, almost 9 out of 10 strong Democrats voted for Reagan's Democratic opponent, Walter Mondale.

Strong Republicans have been the most faithful of party voters in presidential elections. Only twice in forty-five years has their support for the GOP presidential candidate dipped as "low" as 90 percent. The level of party voting among several groups of party identifiers dropped during the late 1960s and 1970s, just as the proportion of strong and weak partisans did. But recent studies find that the impact of party ID on voting behavior increased in each of the presidential elections from 1976 through 1996, reaching a level in the late 1990s higher than in any presidential election since the 1950s.[24] Again, then, the decline in partisanship and party voting was real, but also temporary.

These patterns can also be seen in voting for Congress (Table 6.3). A majority within each group of partisans has voted for their party's congressional candidates in each election, and strong partisans have been the most regular party voters. One key to the Democrats' ability to continue winning congressional majorities in the 1970s and 1980s, even at a time when their electoral base was eroding, may be that they were more faithful than their GOP counterparts in voting for their party's congressional candidates.

Similar results appear in voting at the state and local level through 1984, the last year for which such figures are available. *Straight-ticket voting*—voting for one party's candidates only—declined among all of the partisan groups during these years. But most strong Democrats and strong Republicans remained straight-ticket voters. The stronger an individual's party identification, the more likely he or she was to vote a straight ticket.[25] The curious finding that independents leaning toward a party were more likely to show party loyalty than were weak partisans—a result we often find in presidential and congressional voting—does not occur at the state and local level.[26]

Even though party voting is common in American elections, we still see some fascinating hints of weakened partisanship. For example, even though the majority of party identifiers have been Democrats in the last three decades, Democrats have won the presidency only three times during this period. At no other time in American history has the minority party had so much success at the presidential level. There has also been a lot of variation in partisan "faithfulness" within both parties. For instance, although strong Republicans have faithfully supported their party's presidential candidate, and have

TABLE 6.3 Voting for Their Party's Congressional Candidates Among Party Identifiers: 1952–2000

	1952	1956	1960	1964	1968	1972	1976	1980	1984	1988	1992	1996	2000
Strong Democrats	89%	94%	93%	94%	88%	91%	89%	85%	89%	88%	86%	88%	87%
Weak Democrats	77	86	86	84	73	80	78	69	70	82	82	71	73
Independents closer to Democrats	64	83	84	79	63	80	76	70	78	87	74	69	70
Independents	—	—	—	—	—	—	—	—	—	—	—	—	—
Independents closer to Republicans	81	83	74	72	81	73	65	68	61	64	65	79	67
Weak Republicans	90	88	84	64	78	75	66	74	66	70	63	79	79
Strong Republicans	95	95	90	92	91	85	83	77	85	77	82	97	86

Note: The table entries are the percentages of each category of partisans who reported a vote for their party's candidate for Congress. To find the percentage voting for the opposing party's candidate or some other candidate, subtract the entry from 100 percent. Individuals who did not vote or did not vote for Congress are excluded from the table.

Source: American National Election Studies, Center for Political Studies, University of Michigan; data made available by the Inter-University Consortium for Political and Social Research.

recently become more faithful in congressional elections, that has not been true of weak Republicans. Except for Ronald Reagan's landslide reelection in 1984, weak Republicans' support of their party's presidential candidates in recent years has not returned to the levels achieved in the 1950s. The same is true of their party voting for Congress, even in 1984 (see Tables 6.2 and 6.3).

The most recent congressional midterm elections provide more evidence of this bumpy ride. Republican partisanship was especially strong in 1994 and 1998. Unlike their typical behavior since the 1960s, more Republicans than Democrats supported their party's candidates for the House of Representatives. In both years, Republicans also won a clear majority of the support of independents, but it was probably the extra boost in loyalty from their own partisans that gave them control of Congress for the first time in forty years. In mirror image, Democratic voting fidelity dropped in the 1990s.

Party Versus Candidates and Issues

What causes these ups and downs in the level of party voting? Individuals' voting decisions are affected by the give-and-take of two sets of forces: the strength of their enduring party loyalty (if they have one) and the power of the ***short-term forces*** operating in a given election year. These short-term forces include the attractiveness of particular candidates running that year and the pull of various issues in the campaign. Usually these two sets of forces incline the voter in the same direction; as we've seen, a party identification leads an individual to see the party's candidates and issue stands in a favorable light.

There are times, however, when an especially appealing candidate in the other party, or a particularly appealing issue stance prompts a party identifier to defect and vote for the opposing party. Such split-ticket voting has become more frequent in recent years.[27] Voters don't usually split their tickets out of a conscious desire to create a divided government. Rather, voters are more likely to defect from their party ID because they are attracted to a very visible candidate running a well-funded campaign, most often an incumbent of the other party.[28] In the 2000 elections, for example, Democratic presidential candidate, Al Gore, lost West Virginia with 46 percent of the vote, but popular incumbent Democratic Senator Robert C. Byrd was reelected with 78 percent. Similarly, although Gore won Vermont with 51 percent of the vote, incumbent Republican Senator James Jeffords got 66 percent (and, within a few months, left the Republican Party. Part of his dramatic announcement can be found on p. 111). At times, an issue—an appealing tax cut proposal or a worrisome plan to change Social Security—may lead a voter to desert one or more of his or her party's candidates. The likelihood that voters will temporarily desert their party depends on the degree to which their partisan roots are firmly anchored, as well as on the strength and direction of the forces present in a particular election. In a year when the short-term forces are favoring Republicans, for instance, many Democrats will defect to vote for GOP candidates, but the strong identifiers will remain most steadfast. Of course, the longer these short-term forces pull in the same direction, the greater is the chance that the temporary defectors will become permanent: that voters will change their party ID to bring it into line with their vote.[29]

Although researchers have worked hard to determine the relative importance of party, candidate characteristics, and issues in affecting individuals' voting decisions,[30] the task has been difficult because these three forces are so strongly interrelated. The classic accounts of the dominant role of party ID in the 1950s assumed that party "came first" in the causal ordering: that it influenced people's feelings about candidates and issues, but was not in turn influenced by them. These early studies did not have good measures of how close the voter felt to the candidates on the issues.[31] Now, with new measures available and an understanding that all three of these forces can influence one another, some researchers find that elections since the 1970s have been dominated by the short-run forces: the impact of the issues and candidates in a particular election.[32]

Nevertheless, when we take a longer-term perspective and look at changes in attitudes toward issues and candidates across a four-year period among the same voters, we find that party identification has continuing power to structure the immediate context of the voting decision.[33] So whether we want to explain the general trends of American voting behavior, or the choices of voters in a particular election, party identification plays a prominent role.

Party Identification and Political Activity

Another important effect of party identification is that individuals who consider themselves Democrats and Republicans have higher rates of involvement in political life than do those who call themselves independents. It is the strongest partisans who are the most likely to vote, to pay attention to politics, and to take part in political activities. As in previous years, the 2000 ANES survey shows that strong Democrats and strong Republicans were more likely than weak identifiers or independents to be attentive to politics and highly interested in the campaign, and to follow reports about politics and the campaign on television and in newspapers (Table 6.4).

TABLE 6.4 Political Involvement of Partisans and Independents: 2000

	Democrats		Independents			Republicans	
				Closer to...			
	Strong	Weak	Dem	Neither	Rep	Weak	Strong
Very much interested in politics	54%	30	38	24	42	31	65
Follow public affairs most of time	28%	14	23	14	28	11	32
Great deal of attention to campaign via TV	35%	22	31	18	34	21	43
Read about campaign in newspapers	65%	53	56	40	62	61	74
Voted	84%	76	71	54	78	76	92
Tried to persuade people to vote certain way	44%	26	35	22	38	34	44
Displayed button, bumper sticker, sign	14%	5	7	2	12	10	18
Attended rally or meeting	10%	3	5	2	6	1	8
Contributed money to:							
Candidate	6%	3	8	3	9	4	14
Party	7%	4	5	2	6	4	15

Source: *2000 American National Election Study,* Center for Political Studies, University of Michigan; data made available by the Inter-University Consortium for Political and Social Research.

The strongest partisans are also the most active in other ways. A total of 84 and 92 percent, respectively, of the strong Democrats and Republicans reported having voted in 2000—higher than the turnout levels among weaker partisans or independents.[34] They were also more likely than other citizens to try to persuade other people to vote a certain way, to wear campaign buttons, to display bumper stickers or yard signs, to attend political meetings, and to contribute money to a party. The combatants of American electoral politics, in short, come disproportionately from the ranks of the strong Democrats and strong Republicans.

PARTY IDENTIFICATION AND ATTITUDES TOWARD THE PARTIES

Strong party identifiers tend to see a bigger contrast between the Republican and Democratic parties than do weak identifiers and independents, both in general and on specific policy issues (see Table 6.5). They hold more strongly differentiated evaluations of the two parties' candidates, as well as of the parties' abilities to govern for the benefit of the nation. Strong partisans are more inclined than weaker partisans and independents to contend that their party's president has performed his job well and that a president of the opposing party has performed poorly.[35] In the mind of the strong partisan, in short, the political parties are clearly defined and highly polarized along the important dimensions of politics.

These data do not prove that party identification alone results in greater activity or sharper party images. Other factors also affect people's willingness to become involved in politics. In particular, higher socioeconomic status (SES) and the greater political sophistication and easier entry into politics that it often brings can lead people into political activity. The relatively greater involvement of partisans (and in most years, of Republicans) comes in part from their generally higher SES levels as well as from their more ideological commitment to politics.[36] Even so, party identification has a major impact on people's political activity.

PARTISANSHIP AND PEROT

What happens to party loyalty when an especially attractive third-party or independent candidate enters the race? This is usually a moot point because very few such candidates even show up on the radar screen in any election. Yet one of the biggest

TABLE 6.5 Differences Between the Parties as Perceived by Partisans and Independents: 2000

Percent who see differences between Democratic and Republican Parties	
Strong Democrats	77%
Weak Democrats	69
Independents closer to Democrats	60
Independents	55
Independents closer to Republicans	68
Weak Republicans	71
Strong Republicans	87

Source: 2000 American National Election Study, Center for Political Studies, University of Michigan; data made available by the Inter-University Consortium for Political and Social Research.

TABLE 6.6 Votes for Ross Perot Among Party Identifiers and Independents: 1992 and 1996

Voted for Perot	1992	1996
Strong Democrats	4%	2%
Weak Democrats	18	6
Independents closer to Democrats	23	15
Independents	37	18
Independents closer to Republicans	27	11
Weak Republicans	25	10
Strong Republicans	11	1

Source: 1992 and 1996 American National Election Studies, Center for Political Studies, University of Michigan; data made available by the Inter-University Consortium for Political and Social Research.

stories of the 1992 presidential election was the unprecedented showing of independent candidate, Ross Perot. Unlike most independents, Perot flourished rather than faded as the campaign came to an end. He finished with almost 20 million votes, 19 percent of those cast. Poll results from late spring of 1992 suggested that he might have done even better if he had not temporarily withdrawn from the contest during the summer of 1992.

Electoral conditions were especially ripe for a strong independent or third-party candidate in 1992. The popularity of incumbent President George H. W. Bush was running low, and his Democratic challenger, Governor Bill Clinton, was struggling in the polls also. So there was ample opportunity for a presidential candidate who could appeal to both independents and disgruntled Democrats and Republicans. Perot seemed to be such a candidate. His willingness to spend millions on his campaign gave him the best shot of any non-major-party candidate in almost a century.

In the end, however, the force of party identification limited Perot's support. Very few of Perot's votes came from strong party identifiers. He drew his votes mainly from independents, independent "leaners," and weak Republicans (Table 6.6), as had third-party candidates John Anderson (in 1980) and George Wallace (in 1968) before him.[37] Based on the ANES estimates, a majority of Perot's total vote came from self-identified independents, and he could not construct a winning coalition from such a diverse set of voters.[38] The same was true of Perot's third-party candidacy in 1996. Ralph Nader's well-publicized presidential run in 2000 met the same fate—though even Nader's small proportion of the total vote was probably enough to have tipped the election to Republican George W. Bush.

THE MYTH OF THE INDEPENDENT

It is intriguing that party loyalties govern so much political behavior in a culture that so warmly celebrates the independent voter. There is clearly a disconnect between the American myth of the high-minded independent—the well-informed citizen who is moved by issues and candidates, not parties—and the reality of widespread partisanship. The problem is with the myth.

Attitudinal Independents

One definition of independents refers to those Americans who tell pollsters that they do not identify with a political party. Studies show that they split their tickets more often than other voters do, and they wait longer in the campaign to make their voting decisions. In those ways, they fit the myth. But they fall short of the mythical picture of the independent in most other ways. They are less well informed than party identifiers are, less concerned about specific elections, and less active politically. They are also less likely to vote. In 2000, for instance, independents stayed home from the polls at a higher rate than did party identifiers.

There is an important distinction to be drawn, however, between independents who say they feel closer to one of the two parties (independent "leaners") and those who do not ("pure" independents). The independent leaners usually turn out to be more politically involved (see Table 6.4) and sometimes even more partisan in voting (especially for president) than weak partisans do (see Tables 6.2 and 6.3). It is only in comparison to strong partisans that these partisan-oriented independents fall short. By contrast, the pure independents typically have the most dismal record, with relatively low levels of political interest and information, turnout, and education.[39] It is the pure independents who are the least involved and least informed of all American citizens (see Table 6.4).[40]

Behavioral Independents

We can also define independents in terms of their behavior. In his last work, the unparalleled researcher, V. O. Key, Jr., explored the idea of political independence. The picture of the American voter that was emerging from the electoral studies of the time was not a pretty one; it showed an electorate whose voting decisions were determined by deeply ingrained loyalties—an electorate that had not grasped the major political issues and didn't care that it hadn't.[41]

Key looked for evidence of rational behavior among voters and focused his attention on "party switchers"—those who supported different parties in two consecutive presidential elections—rather than on the self-described independents. Key's switchers came much closer to the flattering myth of the independent than did the self-styled independents. These party switchers, Key found, expressed at least as much political interest as did the stand-patters (those who voted for the same party in both elections). Above all, the switchers showed an issue-related rationality that well fitted the mythical picture of the independent. They agreed on policy issues with the stand-patters toward whose party they had shifted, and they disagreed with the policies of the party from which they had defected.

It is the attitudinal independents, however—those who call themselves independents or voice no party preference—who are the subject of the most research, especially because their numbers have increased in recent years (see Table 6.1). Researchers' conclusion is that they have always been a diverse group containing many of the least involved and informed voters, but also some who resemble the image of the sophisticated independent. The myth that they are a carefully informed and active group of voters who operate above the party fray has withered under the glare of survey research.

PARTY IDENTIFICATION AND PARTY CHANGE

Party identification, then, is a psychological commitment that is often strong enough to guide other political beliefs and behavior. Democratic and Republican partisans see issues and candidates through party-tinted glasses. They are more likely to vote for their party's candidates and are easier to recruit into activism on behalf of the party or its candidates than other citizens are. Yet partisanship functions in a very different context now than it did a century ago.

A More Candidate-Centered Politics

As we have seen in earlier chapters, American politics has changed in some marked ways in the last century. The great majority of Americans still hold a party identification, at least in the sense that they "lean toward" one of the two major parties. But, their party loyalties face more competition for their votes. Almost a century ago, states began adopting the direct primary, in which voters had to choose candidates without the useful guide of a party label. Partisanship remained a helpful short-cut in general elections, but does not differentiate candidates in a party's primary. New campaign and fund-raising technologies developed that were harder for the party organizations to monopolize. Candidates with enough money could find ways, using television, direct mail, and other media, to reach voters directly, over the parties' heads.

During the turbulent years of the 1960s and 1970s, as we have seen, the number of self-identified independents grew and the impact of party identification on people's voting choices declined. Candidates found it helpful to downplay their party label, running instead as individual entrepreneurs. Now, even though party loyalties have regained much of their frequency and influence, candidates still tend to downplay their partisanship or even to emphasize their independence from their own party's leadership as a means of attracting voter support. The consequence is that elections have become less party-centered and more candidate-centered.[42]

In addition, other elements of American politics—organized interests, independent campaign consultants, methods of raising political money—have diversified and strengthened, and so can compete more effectively with party loyalties for the attention and allegiance of citizens. It is not that party identification is weaker now, but that it has more competition from other potential influences on voters. These short-run forces—candidates' characteristics, issues, and the particular events of the current campaign—have important effects on the campaign strategies that party organizations develop (see box on p. 123) as well as on the role of the parties in government.

What have we lost as a result, and what have we gained? A strongly party-identified electorate has a stabilizing influence on politics. When people vote straight-party tickets in election after election, vote outcomes are predictable. Patterns of party support are stable geographically.[43] To the extent that it can be time-consuming and stressful to adapt to political change, predictable elections can be a benefit. When split-ticket voting is more common, we get the patterns of divided party government and more frequent switches in party control of Congress and the presidency that we have seen in the last two decades.

Party Campaign Strategies in the 2000 Presidential Race

The first rule of campaigning is to mobilize your own party identifiers while using issues and candidates' personal characteristics to appeal to independents and partisans of the other party. How you implement this rule depends on whether you are in the majority or the minority party. The job of the majority party is to rally its loyalists by appealing to the party's core issues. Democrats since the 1930s, for example, have stressed the economic issues that gave them their majority status: keeping employment high and protecting people's incomes with strong Social Security and Medicare programs.

The minority party has a different task: to divert attention from these issues by choosing candidates who seem to be "above" politics (Ronald Reagan, for instance, whose attractive personality had wide appeal) or by raising issues that cross party lines (such as the GOP emphasis on patriotism and family values) or that threaten to split the other party's coalition. If the minority party tries to debate the majority party on its core issues, it risks a landslide defeat.

George W. Bush came into the 2000 presidential race with his party's identifiers in the minority. He stressed that he was a "compassionate conservative," in order to appeal to independents and Democrats who valued such issues as education and health care and feared that Republicans were not committed to these issues. Bush also stressed bipartisanship and an end to "partisan bickering," just as a minority-party candidate would logically do.

Democrat Al Gore, on the other hand, emphasized the traditional Democratic core issues of Social Security and Medicare and his concern for "the people, not the powerful." But he also tried to claim credit for the good economic times under Democratic President Clinton. These two strategies weren't always compatible; *Slate* reporter Michael Kinsley parodied Gore's appeal as, "You've never had it so good, and I'm mad as hell about it. Keep the team that brought you this situation, and I'll fight to take back power from the evil forces that have imposed it on you."[44] Using this traditional strategy for a majority party candidate and for a Democrat, Gore almost pulled it off. He won a majority of the popular vote but lost in the electoral college.

The Continuing Significance of Party

Yet we should not underestimate the persistence of party identification. Most Americans—a clear majority if we count only strong and weak identifiers, and almost all Americans if leaners are included as well—still report some degree of attachment to either the Democratic or the Republican Party. Large numbers of Americans are faithful to these loyalties in voting for candidates for office. Voters may stray from the party fold here and there; the abundance of elected offices encourages such defections. But voters continue to perceive candidates, issues, and elections in partisan terms and often vote accordingly.

Probably the most recent dramatic sign of this party influence could be seen in the 1994 congressional elections, which were the most party-oriented contests in years. The Republicans were able to overcome the localism that protected (mainly Democratic) incumbents by appealing to national issues, especially dissatisfaction with the Democratic president. Republican House candidates rallied around a "Contract with America," presented as a set of party pledges. When the Republicans won control of the House in that election (for the first time since 1954), they behaved like a cohesive party. Four years later, party voting remained high among Republicans, though it declined among Democrats.

These congressional elections show that party-dominated contests are still possible, even in the face of the forces competing with parties for voters' attention. Will this continue, or will the instability of modern politics eat away at the parties' base of support? The story continues in the next chapter, where we look more closely at the two major parties' supporting coalitions and their changes over time.

Party Support and Party Realignments

Party identification can have a major influence on your own voting choices, as we have seen, as well as those of large numbers of other Americans. Its impact on the direction of American politics is just as profound. Party identifications are not distributed randomly among Americans. Some social groups lean heavily toward a Democratic Party identification—African-Americans and Jews, for example—and other groups, such as "born again" white Protestants and farmers, are now much more likely to consider themselves Republicans.

The socioeconomic groups that support a party make up what is called the party's *coalition*—the types of people most inclined to favor that party's candidates through good times and bad. These groups' interests, in turn, are likely to affect the party's platform and its strategic choices in campaigns. So the groups in the two parties' coalitions at a particular time are a helpful clue as to which issues dominate the nation's politics at that time. The fact that African-Americans have identified so overwhelmingly as Democrats in recent decades, for example, reminds us that racial issues continue to be powerful in American elections.[1] At various times in U.S. history, sectional or regional conflicts, ethnic and religious divisions, disputes between agriculture and industry, and differences in social class and status have also helped form the basis for differences between the two parties' coalitions, as they have in other Western democracies.[2]

Because the alignment of social groups with parties is so significant in shaping a nation's politics, big and enduring changes in those coalitions, called *realignments,* are well worth exploring.[3] In this chapter, then, we will look at the nature of realignment and other types of party change and tell the story of these changes over time. Then we'll examine the development and nature of the coalitions that currently support the Democrats and the Republicans: from what educational backgrounds, occupations, regions, religions and social groups do these supporters come, and what interests attract them to one party rather than the other? Finally, we will consider whether the parties' coalitions have shifted markedly enough in the last 30 years to constitute another realignment, or whether the current relationship between social groups and parties is something entirely new.

REALIGNMENTS: THE FIVE AMERICAN PARTY SYSTEMS

In the last chapter we saw that although party identification has a major impact on people's voting, the extent of that impact can vary from one individual to another and from one election to the next. Elections can be classified into three types, depending on the degree to which party identifiers vote for their party's presidential candidate:

In *maintaining* elections, the party attachments of the recent past continue without any great change. In these elections, the candidate from the largest party in the electorate wins.

In *deviating* elections, short-term forces (candidates' characteristics or issues) are powerful enough to cause the defeat of the majority party, but the basic distribution of party loyalties is not changed.

In periods of *realigning* elections, the coalition of groups supporting the parties changes in significant ways. The new coalition then endures. These elections typically (but not always) produce a new majority party.

In recent years, deviating elections have been very common; since 1952, the Democratic Party, which has consistently claimed more identifiers than the Republicans, has won the presidency in only five of 13 elections. Prior to that time, if we had survey data with which to measure party identifications since about 1800, scholars believe that we could expect to find long periods of relative stability in the components of each party's coalition—in other words, maintaining elections—punctuated fairly regularly by realigning periods. Unfortunately, survey data were not available until the late 1930s. For earlier years, we can only estimate the composition of the parties in the electorate from aggregated voting returns.[4] These voting patterns, showing changes (realignments) in the levels and the geographical distributions of party support that are then maintained over long periods of time, justify a division of American politics into a series of electoral eras.[5]

Analysts generally agree that the United States has experienced at least five different electoral eras, or *party systems*.[6] In each of these party systems there has been a distinctive pattern of group support for the parties. Each party system can also be distinguished by the kinds of issue concerns that dominated it, and the types of public policies that the government has put into effect. (See Table 7.1 for a summary of each party system.)[7]

The First Party System

The initial American party system (1801–1828)[8] emerged out of a serious conflict between opposing groups within the Washington administration: How much power should the national government exercise, relative to that of the states? Thomas Jefferson and James Madison led one side, advocating a limited national government. In the hotly contested 1800 election, these Democratic-Republicans, as they came to be called, became the first faction in the nation's capital to organize support for its presidential candidate (Jefferson) in the country at large. Jefferson won, the rival Federalists slowly slipped into a fatal decline, and the party of Jefferson then enjoyed more than two decades of almost unchallenged dominance, defined as the ability to control the presidency and Congress.

TABLE 7.1 Years of Partisan Control of Congress and the Presidency: 1801–2002

	House		Senate		President	
	D–R	*Opp.*	*D–R*	*Opp.*	*D–R*	*Opp.*
First party system						
(1801–1828)	26	2	26	2	28	0
	Dem.	*Opp.*	*Dem.*	*Opp.*	*Dem.*	*Opp.*
Second party system						
(1829–1860)	24	8	28	4	24	8
	Dem.	*Rep.*	*Dem.*	*Rep.*	*Dem.*	*Rep.*
Third party system						
(1861–1876)	2	14	0	16	0	16
(1877–1896)	14	6	4	16	8	12
Fourth party system						
(1897–1932)	10	26	6	30	8	28
Fifth party system						
(1933–1968?)	32	4	32	4	28	8
Sixth party system?						
(1969–1980)	12	0	12	0	4	8
(1981–2002)	14	8	10	12	8	14
(1969–2002)	26	8	22	12	12	22

Note: Entries for the first party system are Democratic-Republicans and their opposition, first Federalists and then Jacksonians; for the second party system, Democrats and their opposition, first Whigs and then Republicans; for subsequent party systems, Democrats and Republicans. In 2001, Republicans were in the majority in the Senate for the first five months and Democrats for the last seven, so the Senate is counted as being under Democratic control.

The Second Party System

The next party system (1829–1860) developed when the one-party rule of the Democratic-Republicans was unable to contain all the issues and conflicts generated by a rapidly changing nation. The issues the government faced at this time included how the Union should expand, what the national government's economic powers should be, and, increasingly, how to handle the explosive question of slavery. The Democratic-Republicans split into two factions on these issues. One was a populist Western faction led by Andrew Jackson that would later grow to become the Democratic Party. The other, a more elitist and Eastern faction represented by John Quincy Adams, was eventually absorbed into the Whig Party.[9] Controversy over the 1824 presidential election heightened the strain between the factions. In that election, Jackson received the most popular votes in a four-candidate contest, but lacked an electoral college majority and was denied the presidency by the House of Representatives.

Four years later, Jackson was elected president—the first time popular voting played the key role in determining the winner. As this party system matured, pitting Democrats against Whigs, the nation experienced its first enduring two-party competition. This second party system was class-based, with wealthier voters supporting the Whigs and the less privileged identifying as Democrats. The Democrats dominated as the majority party, growing as the franchise was extended to more and more Americans. Their rule was interrupted only twice, both times by the election of Whig war heroes to the presidency. As the issues of this period grew more disruptive, however, several minor parties developed and the Whigs began to fracture, especially over the issue of slavery.

The Third Party System

One of these third parties—an anti-slavery party called the Republicans—was quickly propelled into major-party status; it was founded in 1854 and had already replaced the seriously divided Whigs by 1856. Its rapid rise signaled the end of the second party system. The intense conflict of the Civil War ensured that the new third party system (1861–1896) would have the most clearly defined coalitional patterns of any party system before or since. War and Reconstruction divided the nation roughly along geographic lines: the South became a Democratic bastion after white Southerners were permitted to return to the polls in the 1870s, and the North remained a reliable base for Republicans. As industrial expansion proceeded, economic issues, and particularly the growth of huge industrial monopolies, became the main focus of the party cleavage.

So sharp was the sectional division that the Democratic Party's only strongholds in the North were in the cities controlled by Democratic machines (for example, New York City's Tammany Hall) and areas settled by Southerners (such as Kentucky, Missouri, and the Southern portions of Ohio, Indiana, and Illinois). In the South, GOP support came only from blacks (in response to Republican President Abraham Lincoln's freeing of the slaves) and people from mountain areas originally opposed to the Southern states' secession. By 1876, when Southern whites were finally reintegrated into national politics, there was close party competition in presidential voting and in the House of Representatives as these sectional monopolies offset one another.[10] Competition was so intense that this period contained two of the four elections in American history where the winner of the popular vote for President lost the vote in the electoral college.

The Fourth Party System

The imprint of the Civil War shaped Southern politics for the next century, but the Civil War party system soon began to fade elsewhere. Under the weight of farm and rural protest and the economic panic of 1893, the third party system dissolved. It was replaced by a fourth party system (1897–1932) that reflected the great differences between the agrarian and industrial economies and ways of life. This new era pitted the Eastern economic "center," which was heavily Republican, against the Western and Southern "periphery," with the South even more Democratic than before. Southern Democrats, out from under the heavy hand of Reconstruction, were able to reinstitute racially discriminatory laws and to prevent blacks from voting in the South. Beginning with William McKinley's defeat of Democratic populist William Jennings Bryan in 1896, Republicans dominated American national politics. Republican rule was disrupted only by an intraparty split in 1912, which gave Democrats an eight-year turn at leadership.

Just as earlier party systems began to weaken a decade or two after they began, the fourth party system showed signs of deterioration in the 1920s, even in the midst of unparalleled Republican successes. The Progressive Party made inroads into major party strength early in the decade, and in 1928 Democratic candidate Al Smith, the first Catholic ever nominated for the presidency, brought Catholic voters into Democratic ranks in the North and drove Protestant Southerners temporarily into voting Republican.

The Fifth Party System

It took the Great Depression of 1929 and the subsequent election of Franklin D. Roosevelt to produce the fifth, or New Deal, party system. During the 1930s, as a means of pulling the nation out of economic ruin, Roosevelt pushed Congress to enact several welfare state programs. These Roosevelt New Deal programs—labor legislation, social security, wages and hours laws—strengthened the Democratic Party's image as the party of the have-nots. By 1936, the new Democratic majority party had become a grand coalition of the less privileged minorities—industrial workers (especially union members), poor farmers, Catholics, Jews, blacks—plus the South, where the Democratic loyalty imprinted by the Civil War had become all but genetic.

The conflicts and costs of these new programs heightened the stakes of socioeconomic status (SES) politics, so the SES stamp on the party division became even more pronounced. The result was to rebuild the Democratic party more clearly than ever before as a party of social and economic reform. Even groups such as blacks, long allied with the Republicans as the party of Lincoln, were lured to the Democratic banner; socioeconomic issues were powerful enough to keep both blacks and Southern whites as wary allies in the Roosevelt coalition. This *New Deal coalition* has shaped the parties' development, to a greater or lesser degree, since then.

It is clear from this brief tour of party history that socioeconomic, racial and regional divisions have had a powerful role in these five realignments of the party system. What is the nature of the two parties' coalitions today? As we explore the fate of the New Deal coalition, we'll ask whether there is convincing evidence that another realignment has taken place, introducing a sixth party system, in the waning years of the twentieth century.

THE SOCIAL BASES OF PARTY COALITIONS

Socioeconomic Status Divisions

Most democratic party systems reflect divisions along social class lines, even if those divisions may have softened over the years.[11] The footprints of SES conflict are scattered throughout American history. James Madison, one of the most perceptive observers of human nature among the nation's founders, wrote in the *Federalist Papers* that economic differences are the most common source of factions.[12] Social and economic status differences underlay the battle between the wealthy, aristocratic Federalists and the less privileged Democratic-Republicans. These differences were even sharper between the Jacksonian Democrats and the Whigs a few decades later, and again, at the time of the fourth party realignment in the 1890s.

The relationship between party and SES established in the New Deal party system can still be seen in American politics today (see Table 7.2, panels A–C). People with lower incomes and less education are more likely to call themselves Democrats than Republicans. In addition, Democrats are more likely to identify themselves as working rather than middle class (see box on p.132). Income, of course, is strongly

TABLE 7.2 Social Characteristics and Party Identification: 2000

	Democrats		Independents			Republicans			
			Closer to Dem.	Closer to Neither	Closer to Rep.			Dem. minus Rep.	Cases
	Strong	Weak				Weak	Strong		
A. Income									
Lower 3rd	24%	16	16	13	10	11	10	19	495
Middle 3rd	18%	16	16	13	14	13	9	12	521
Upper 3rd	17%	14	14	8	15	13	18	0	562
B. Occupation									
Service	16%	20	18	10	12	12	12	12	139
Blue collar	20%	15	16	14	14	9	11	15	221
White collar	15%	17	16	11	13	14	13	5	367
Professional	16%	14	16	10	13	15	15	0	466
Farm	13%	0	7	7	20	27	27	−41	15
C. Education									
No high sch.	26%	20	14	13	8	13	5	28	174
High sch. grad	21%	15	17	16	12	9	10	17	511
College	17%	15	14	9	14	13	16	3	1095
D. Region									
South	21%	15	12	13	13	11	14	11	646
Non-south	19%	15	17	11	13	12	13	9	1139
E. Religion									
Jews	44%	14	21	7	5	5	2	51	43
Catholics	20%	15	15	10	15	11	13	11	457
Protestants	24%	19	13	11	9	13	11	19	618
White "Born-again" Protestants	12%	12	10	10	16	16	23	−15	367
F. Race									
Blacks	46%	22	16	10	3	3	1	64	206
Whites	16%	14	14	12	14	14	15	1	1377
G. Gender									
Female	20%	18	15	12	12	11	12	15	1006
Male	18%	11	15	11	14	14	15	0	779

Note: Totals add to approximately 100 percent reading across (with slight variations due to rounding). Dem. minus Rep. is the party difference calculated by subtracting the percentage of strong and weak Republicans from the percentage of strong and weak Democrats. Negative numbers indicate a Republican advantage in the group.

Source: 2000 American National Election Study, Center for Political Studies, University of Michigan; data made available by the Inter-University Consortium for Political and Social Research.

related to an individual's level of education. Income also underlies some of the effects of religion and race on party identification. The tendency for Protestants to be somewhat higher in SES in the United States helps to explain why they are more likely to identify with the Republican Party than Catholics are. And there is an enormous SES difference between whites and blacks.

Socioeconomic forces, then, continue to leave their mark on American party politics. In fact, some observers argue that, outside the South, less affluent voters have become even more supportive of Democrats in recent decades. The substantial gulf between rich and poor in the United States and the differences between the parties in their stands on issues of special concern to lower-income individuals (such as government-provided health care and social services) may be reinforcing these differences. The result is that, especially in congressional elections, Republicans are even more likely to win races in higher-income districts now, and Democrats are more likely to win in lower-income districts, than they were 20 years ago.[13]

The current relationship between SES and party differs in some interesting ways from that of the New Deal coalition, however. As Table 7.2 shows, although less-educated respondents are much more Democratic than Republican, those with a college education now divide themselves fairly evenly between the parties. The same is true with regard to income and occupation. Those with service jobs (which tend to be lower-paying) and blue-collar jobs remain more likely to be Democrats. Professionals, on the other hand, are no longer distinctively Republican. The identification of many professionals with the Democratic Party is reflected in the support Democratic candidates often receive from teachers' unions and trial lawyers' associations.

These differences should not be overstated. Socioeconomic status has been less important as a basis for party loyalty in the United States than in many other Western democracies,[14] and even at the height of the New Deal, the SES differences between the parties were less clear than the parties' rhetoric would suggest. The electorates of both American parties in the early 2000s contain a significant number of people from all status groups. As a result, the parties don't usually promote blatantly class-based appeals. Their pragmatic, relatively nonideological tone reflects their need to attract votes from a variety of social groupings. Because the SES divisions between the Republicans and Democrats can be muddy, SES is not the only explanation of differences between the parties.

Sectional Divisions

Historically, the greatest rival to SES as an explanation for American party differences has been sectionalism. Different sections of the country have often had differing political interests. When a political party has championed these distinct interests, it has sometimes united large numbers of otherwise different voters.

The most enduring sectionalism in American party history was the one-party Democratic control of the South. Well before the Civil War, white Southerners shared an interest in slavery and an agriculture geared to export markets. The searing experience of that war and the Reconstruction that followed made the South into the "Solid South" and delivered it to the Democrats for the better part of the next century. The 11 states of the former Confederacy cast all their electoral votes for Democratic presidential candidates in every election from 1880 through 1924, except for Tennessee's defection in 1920. Al Smith's Catholicism frightened four of these states into the Republican column in 1928, but the Roosevelt economic programs brought the South back to the Democratic Party for the four Roosevelt elections. Only the beginnings of the civil rights movement had the power to peel away the South from its traditional party loyalties. By 2000, Southerners were no longer distinctive in party identification (Table 7.2, panel D), though traces of the Democratic habit have survived in state and local elections.[15]

How to Tell a Democrat from a Republican During the Holiday Season

- Democrats let their kids open all the gifts on Christmas Eve. Republicans make their kids wait until Christmas morning.
- Republican parents have no problem buying their kids toy guns. Democrats refuse to do so. That is why Democratic kids pretend to shoot each other with dolls.
- Democrats get back at Republicans on their Christmas list by giving them fruitcakes. Republicans rewrap them and send them to in-laws.
- Republicans see nothing wrong with letting their children play "Cowboys and Indians." Democrats don't either, as long as the Indians get to win.
- Republicans spend hundreds of dollars and hours of work decorating the yard with outdoor lights. Democrats drive around at night to look at them.
- Republicans first became Republicans when they stopped believing in Santa Claus. Democrats became Democrats because they never stopped believing in Santa Claus.
- Democratic men like to watch football while their wives, girlfriends, or mothers fix holiday meals. Republican men do, too.

Similarly, the party system has periodically reflected the competition between the economically dominant East and the economically dependent South and West. In the first years of the Republic, the fading Federalists held to an ever-narrowing base of Eastern seaport and financial interests, while the Democratic-Republicans expanded westward with the new settlers. Jackson aimed his party appeals at the men of the frontier, and the protest movements that thrust William Jennings Bryan into the 1896 campaign sprang from the agrarian discontent of the Western prairies and the South. Many of the Populists' loudest complaints were directed at Eastern capitalism, Eastern bankers and Eastern trusts. The geographical distribution of the 1896 presidential vote, with the Democrats winning all but three states in the South and West, but losing all Northern and border states east of the Mississippi River, is a striking example of sectional voting.

Sectional divisions are no longer as obvious. As society has nationalized, the isolation and uniformity that maintained sectional interests are breaking down. Sectional loyalties have not completely disappeared, of course. Southern sectionalism reappeared in a new form in the 1960s, as states of the Deep South supported the Republican presidential candidate, Barry Goldwater, in 1964, and George Wallace in 1968 on the American Independent ticket. Both candidates defended states' rights at a time when many white southerners opposed the national government's efforts to desegregate schools and public accommodations. Even the Democratic Party's decision to nominate two Southerners for president and vice president did not prevent about half the Southern states from voting Republican in 1992 and 1996, and Tennessee Democrat Al Gore lost every Southern state in 2000. The South was solid in voting again, but now in the Republican column.

Yet the rise of Republican strength in the South and Southwest has not dampened two-party competition in the nation as a whole, as regional divisions seemed to do in the fourth and fifth party systems. Instead, two-party competition has increased since the 1960s. In addition, Ross Perot's candidacy in the 1990s never developed a distinctive sectional thrust; Perot is one of the few minor-party presidential candidates not to have drawn upon a sectional base of support. So although we still see some sectional differences between the two parties' coalitions—the "Republican L" for instance, in which recent Republican presidential candidates have concentrated their victories in the Rocky Mountain and Plains states and then across the South—sectionalism has a more subdued influence on the parties now.

It is fair to ask whether sectionalism was ever really a major force in its own right. The term *section* may simply indicate a geographic concentration of voters with other interests—economic or ethnic, for example—who identify with a party because of those other interests. Much sectional voting in the past, for instance, reflected conflicts among crop economies in various agricultural sections. The South, of course, has been more than a descriptive category; its political behavior has been truly sectional, in the sense of having unified interests and an awareness of its own distinctiveness. But the case for sectional explanations weakens as soon as we look beyond the South.

Religious Divisions

There have always been religious differences between the American party coalitions, just as there are in many other democracies.[16] Since the early days of the New Deal party system, Catholics and Jews were among the most loyal supporters of the Democratic Party (Table 7.2, panel E). Some of the relationship between religion and party loyalty is due to the SES differences among religious groupings. Yet religious conviction and group identification also seem to be involved. Internationalism and concern for social justice, rooted in the religious and ethnic traditions of Judaism, have disposed many Jews toward the Democratic Party as the party of international concern, support for Israel, and social and economic justice.[17] The long-standing ties of Catholics to the Democratic Party reflect the party's greater openness to Catholic participation and political advancement. Most of the national chairmen of the Democratic Party in this century have been Catholics and the only Catholic presidential nominees of a major party have been Democrats.

The sources of white Protestant ties to the Republicans are less obvious, probably, in part, because of the enormous diversity of sects and orientations that Protestantism embraces. It may be that the theological individualism of more conservative Protestant denominations inclines Protestants toward the Republican Party, although this tendency was overshadowed for decades by the dominance of SES and sectional interests. In recent years, however, the rise in Protestant fervor for the GOP has been led by the political conservatism of white Protestant fundamentalists, triggered by issues such as abortion and school prayer.[18]

Racial Divisions

Decades ago, the Republican Party—the party founded to abolish slavery, the party of Lincoln, the Civil War, and Reconstruction—was associated with racial equality in the minds of both black and white Americans. Between 1930 and 1960, however, the partisan direction of racial politics turned 180 degrees. It is now the Democratic Party, the

Kennedy, Johnson, and Clinton administrations, the candidacy of Jesse Jackson and Democratic Congresses that blacks see as standing for racial equality. As a result, blacks identify as Democrats in overwhelming numbers today, as they have since at least the 1960s, regardless of their SES, region, or other social characteristics (Table 7.2, panel F). There is no closer tie between a social group and a party than that between blacks and the Democrats. Moreover, racial issues have been responsible for transforming party conflict in the South and, perhaps, in the rest of the nation as well.[19]

Ethnic Divisions

Hispanics are the fastest-growing segment of the U.S. population; the 2000 U.S. census showed that the Hispanic population grew by nearly 60 percent in the previous decade to more than 35 million, rivaling African-Americans as the nation's biggest minority group. Hispanics have long exercised a great deal of voting strength in states such as California, Texas, and Florida. But as their numbers shoot up nationwide, both parties work increasingly hard to attract Hispanic voter support, just as Hispanics seek to gain political influence to the same degree achieved by blacks.

That, however, is easier said than done, largely because Hispanics include many different nationalities with differing interests. The Cuban émigrés who settled in Miami after the Castro revolution took power in the 1950s tend to be conservative, intensely anti-Communist and inclined to vote Republican, whereas the larger Mexican-American population in California is more Democratic-leaning. Republican strategists see Hispanics as potentially responsive to a socially conservative message. Even so, in the words of the chief of staff for a Republican Senator from Oregon, "the machinery of how to go after the Hispanic vote in 2002 is in its infancy."[20]

Gender Divisions

For more than two decades, the votes and stands of adult women have diverged from those of men. In 1980, about 6 percent more women voted for Jimmy Carter than men did. The so-called gender gap grew after that. Women's ratings of President Reagan were much lower than men's and also differed from men's on a number of issues, including greater support for social programs and lesser support for defense spending. By the mid-1980s, the gender difference had extended to partisanship; women were more supportive of the Democratic Party than men were. This partisan gender gap increased in the 1996 election and remained large in 2000 (Table 7.2, panel G). There is evidence that it stems to a greater extent from men becoming more Republican rather than from women becoming more Democratic.[21]

THE ROLE ISSUES PLAY IN THE PARTIES' COALITIONS

These group differences are intriguing and important, but what causes them? Social groups are not "delivered" as a bloc to a party or a candidate by group "leaders." Instead, members of certain social groups—for example, white fundamentalists—may have shared reactions to some major issues and candidates (though the diversity of American society keeps most groups from being very cohesive). These shared reactions may incline them to support one party rather than the other and, over time, that party may come to speak for the hopes and interests of that group, further strengthening the tie between them. So the group basis of party politics is typically rooted in the shared views, within various social groups, of what kind of society we should have and what the government should do to solve particular problems.

Fortunately, we have a huge arsenal of public opinion polls to tell us about the distribution of attitudes on issues within each party's supporting coalition. Table 7.3 shows the preferences of Democratic identifiers, independents, and Republican identifiers on a range of issues that left their mark on recent presidential campaigns. Note the big differences between Democrats and Republicans (seen in the "Dem. minus Rep." column) in attitudes toward programs of the welfare state. Democrats are much more favorable than are Republicans to greater government spending on services and a government role in providing jobs for the unemployed (panels A and B). SES-based issues such as these have been central to the parties' rhetoric and conflict ever since the 1930s.

Is it their socioeconomic status that causes these Democratic identifiers to prefer more government spending on services? Not necessarily. These views may have status roots for some, but other party identifiers hold views that are not consistent with their socioeconomic status. Some well-to-do people, regardless of their partisan loyalty, may feel sympathy for the economic underdog and thus, favor government help to the unemployed; some less-well-off people may be driven by their respect for those who achieve great wealth in the face of great odds and so may oppose government spending on social services. SES is not always a good predictor of people's political attitudes; many other factors make a difference as well.[22]

Party differences are also apparent on non-SES issues, such as civil rights, defense spending and the question of abortion (see Table 7.3, panels C-E). Since the 1960s, for example, party identifiers have been sharply divided in their attitudes toward racial policy, with Democrats much more likely to favor a government role in helping minorities than Republicans are. Other non-SES issues have become important in more recent elections. In 2000, defense and foreign policy issues and concerns about abortion separated Democrats from Republicans to a significant degree. As recently as 1988, however, these issues were not related to party identifications; in fact, they cut across party lines, dividing Democrats from Democrats and Republicans from Republicans.[23]

When an issue cuts across party lines, it can strain the coalitional foundations of a party system. Abortion used to be such an issue. Now, however, pro-choice sentiment is much stronger in the Democratic than the Republican Party. The movement of the abortion issue, from crosscutting to reinforcing partisan divisions, suggests some important changes in the parties in the electorate, which can also be seen in the striking party difference between self-identified liberals and conservatives (Table 7.3, panel F). As one pollster puts it, "We have two massive, colliding force. ... One [i.e., the Republican coalition] is rural, Christian, religiously conservative, with guns at home, terribly unhappy with (then-President Bill) Clinton's behavior. ... And we have a second America [the Democratic coalition] that is socially tolerant, pro-choice, secular, living in New England and the Pacific coast, and in affluent suburbs."[24] Party divisions, then, increasingly reflect differences that have been termed "the culture wars."[25] So to many observers, a combination of social group identities and personal beliefs are increasingly important in creating the divisions between Democratic and Republican identifiers.

TABLE 7.3 Issues, Ideology, and Party Identification: 2000

	Democrats		Independents			Republicans			
	Strong	Weak	Closer to Dem.	Closer to Neither	Closer to Rep.	Weak	Strong	Dem. minus Rep.	Cases
A. Government spending on services									
More	28%	18	18	12	8	8	8	30	575
Same	17%	16	16	11	15	13	13	7	626
Less	4%	8	6	7	22	21	33	−42	281
B. Government role in providing jobs and a good standard of living									
Gov. help	33%	17	18	15	7	7	4	39	307
In between	23%	16	19	10	14	11	8	20	501
Help self	11%	13	11	10	16	16	22	−10	763
C. Government role in improving position of minorities									
Gov. help	35%	16	18	10	7	8	5	38	281
In between	20%	16	18	11	12	13	10	13	678
Help self	12%	15	11	11	17	15	19	−7	589
D. Government spending on defense									
Decrease	22%	20	28	10	8	8	5	29	173
Same	21%	17	16	10	14	11	11	16	677
Increase	14%	12	10	10	14	14	24	−12	552
E. Abortion									
Own choice	22%	18	19	11	12	10	8	22	742
In between	17%	13	13	11	15	14	17	−1	778
Illegal	16%	8	8	16	11	13	17	−6	211
F. Ideological self-identification									
Liberal	34%	20	24	7	8	4	3	47	414
Moderate	19%	20	20	15	14	10	2	27	417
Conservative	9%	8	5	8	18	21	31	−35	618

Note: Totals add to approximately 100 percent reading across (with slight variations due to rounding). Dem. minus Rep. is party difference calculated by subtracting the percentage of strong and weak Republicans from the percentage of strong and weak Democrats. Negative numbers indicate a Republican advantage in the group. Individuals who were unable to describe themselves in ideological terms were not included in the data in panel F.

Source: 2000 American National Election Study, Center for Political Studies, University of Michigan; data made available by the Inter-University Consortium for Political and Social Research.

IS THERE A SIXTH PARTY SYSTEM?

It has been almost 70 years since the beginning of the New Deal—a much longer time than any of the previous American party systems lasted. The patterns of group support that launched the fifth party system can still be seen in polls. But many of these relationships have weakened or changed in recent decades. When we compare the 2000 figures with those from 1960 (Figure 7.1),[26] we find that the SES and sectional differences in partisanship that were so important in the New Deal realignment must now vie for center stage with powerful racial and even gender cleavages (see the box on p. 138). Changing party images and appealing candidates have influenced many Americans to change their party loyalties.[27] Some researchers feel these changes are substantial enough to conclude that the New Deal coalition is now dead.[28]

Evidence of a Realignment

Has there been another realignment of the American parties since the New Deal? To decide, recall the way we have defined realignment: a significant and enduring change in the patterns of group support for the parties, usually (but not always) leading to a new majority party. Has there been a significant and enduring change in the pattern of group

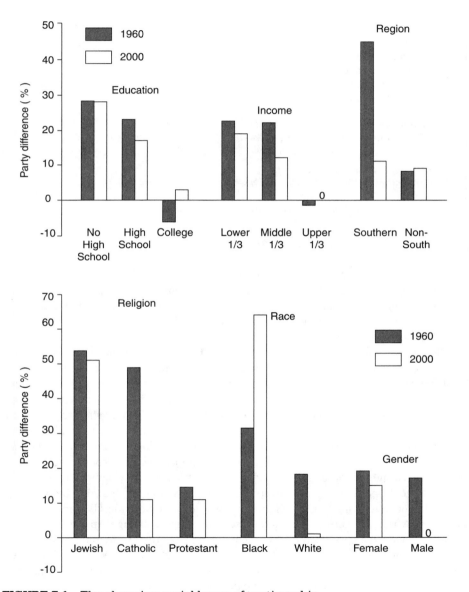

FIGURE 7.1   The changing social bases of partisanship.
Note: Entries are % strong/weak Democrat minus % strong/weak Republican within each group in each year.

The Democratic Coalition in 2000

Percent Reporting a Vote for Al Gore for President:

Income under $15,000	57 %
No high school degree	59
Post-graduate degree	52
African-American	90
Hispanic	62
Jewish	79
Catholic	50
Union member	62
Live in a large city	61
Gay or lesbian	70
Unmarried woman	63
Liberal	80
Abortion should always be legal	70
Government should do more	74
Support stricter gun control laws	62

Source: Voter News Service exit polls, at
http://cnn.com/ELECTION/2000/results/index.epolls.html (accessed Feb. 22, 2002).

---

support for the parties? Figure 7.1 shows several interesting changes. The two parties' coalitions are becoming more similar with regard to religion; there are smaller partisan differences among Catholics and Protestants now than there were in 1960, though Jews remain distinctively Democratic. The party differences between men and women, in contrast, are much greater than they were in 1960.

The most significant changes, however, are those among Southerners and among blacks. The Republican Party's coalition used to be dominated by Northern (and Midwestern) white Protestants. It now gets a substantial share of its identifiers from among conservative Southern whites. African-Americans were predominantly Democratic in 1960. Now, however, they are almost exclusively Democratic. So a Democratic Party that used to draw much of its strength from the South has lost the loyalty of many Southern white conservatives, and blacks have become a much larger proportion of Democratic identifiers.

Do these changes matter? Consider the likely impact on the party's stands on such issues as civil rights, welfare reform and racial profiling. Would a Democratic Party that drew a large proportion of its followers from among Southern whites be likely to support different policies than a Democratic Party whose constituency has become less white and more African-American? In fact, these demographic changes in the Democratic coalition have been paralleled by significant changes in the Democratic platform: for example, from a weak plank on civil rights to a clear stand for affirmative action (as we will see in Chapter 15). If we take seriously the definition of realignment as a change in the party coalitions, these changes are too dramatic to dismiss.

Or Maybe Not

The second element of the definition—a new majority party, or even a clear change in the two parties' share of the electorate—is more elusive. According to the University of Michigan's ANES polling[29] (see Figure 7.2), more Americans called themselves Democrats than either Republicans or Independents throughout the 1952–1964 period. Not even a popular president of the minority party, General Dwight D. Eisenhower, could disturb this Democratic advantage in party identification. (Remember that someone who considers him- or herself a Democrat may choose to vote for a Republican candidate, but still retain a Democratic Party loyalty.)

The Democratic edge began to erode after 1964. Yet Republicans did not immediately benefit. In 1969, analyst Kevin Phillips published a book he believed would be prophetic, titled, *The Emerging Republican Majority*.[30] But in fact, the proportion of Republican identifiers dropped from 1964 through 1980. Even Richard Nixon's landslide victory in the 1972 presidential contest failed to add party loyalists to GOP ranks (nor, interestingly, did Nixon's 1974 resignation after the Watergate scandal[31] reduce the party's 1976 totals). Instead, since the mid-1960s, more Americans have characterized themselves as independents. In this sense, then, there was no sign of a traditional realignment in the late 1960s and 1970s; both parties lost supporters, and neither won an obvious advantage.

The 1980s were a different story. Republican identification was on the rise during the decade in which Ronald Reagan won the presidency twice and the GOP captured the Senate in 1980 for the first time in almost 30 years. In contrast to Eisenhower and Nixon, Reagan's vote-getting popularity seemed to have translated into growth for his party. Democratic strength showed a corresponding decline. Another piece of evidence suggesting a realignment was the Republican surge among young voters who, in the 1980s, became more Republican than Democratic for the first time in the 50 year annals of public opinion polling.[32]

The argument that there was a Republican realignment at this time focuses on the successes of Republican presidential candidates, the growth of the GOP in the once one-party Democratic South and the Republican gains in Congress. In particular, Republican growth in the South has been phenomenal. In the 1980s, the party was able to compete effectively with the Democrats in statewide races and in 1994, there was a GOP majority among the region's U.S. representatives, U.S. senators, and governors for the first time since Reconstruction.[33] In addition to its Southern successes, the size of the Republican *partisan* victory in the 1994 congressional races was unexpectedly large across the nation. Republicans had gained especially from the votes of whites, in particular, Southern whites and high-school-educated white men.[34]

But if the Republican resurgence was really a realignment, why are Republican identifiers (combining "strong" and "weak" Republicans) only about one-quarter of the electorate? True, on the eve of the 1992 presidential election, the percentage of Democratic identifiers was at its lowest level in 40 years; but the surge in GOP party identification had stopped, leaving the electorate even less partisan than before. Then, after some major missteps by the leaders of the new Republican congressional majority, the Democratic vote rebounded in 1996 and 1998, and Democratic Party identification increased a little as well. The most recent readings in the Michigan series show slight drops in the proportions of *both* Democratic and Republican identifiers, and fully 40 percent of the respondents calling themselves independent of party ties. The evidence for a realignment, then, is not strong enough for a conviction.

Evidence of a Dealignment

These ping-pong changes in party loyalties strike many scholars as resembling a different pattern: a *dealignment*, or decline in party loyalties, as opposed to a realignment, in which people develop new party loyalties. To these scholars, it seems clear that the New Deal party system has eroded and Democratic dominance has faded, but the Republican Party has not been able to capitalize fully on the Democrats' losses. In spite of the decline in the percentage of Democratic loyalists since the 1950s, the GOP remains stuck at about the same share of the electorate it had achieved in 1960. Republicans have won the presidency most of the time in recent decades, but these GOP presidents have typically had to deal with a Congress in which at least one house was under Democratic control. Split-ticket voting is fairly common, there has been a steady stream of independent and third-party candidates, and divided government is alive and well in Washington and in most states.[35]

Yet even if there has been a dealignment of the New Deal party system, observers disagree on what will come next. To some scholars, a dealignment is the final phase of a party system, occurring just prior to a realignment. As the electoral conflicts that established the party system begin to age, they argue, voters begin to shake themselves loose from their party identifications, election results become less predictable and new party coalitions can then emerge. It is the newest voters who tend to be the leading edge of such a dealignment; because they don't have the experiences that shaped the partisanship of earlier generations, when the party coalitions were being formed, they are more likely to find the major parties irrelevant to their present needs.[36]

If this argument is correct, then the dealignment will be followed by the emergence of a new party system. Yet the signs of dealignment—the increase in ticket splitting, the shifts in party control at the national level, the rise in self-identified independents—have been present for decades. Why should this particular realignment, if one is in fact coming, be taking so long?

Other observers argue that the long-awaited realignment will never come. Conditions have changed so much, they feel, that a return to a stable party system through realignment is not inevitable. Walter Dean Burnham has written that the American parties have been so weakened by the loss of party control over nominations and the insulation of many state and local elections from national forces, through the scheduling of these elections in off years, that they may no longer be capable of realignment.[37] If so, then dealignment has undermined the foundations of the New Deal party system without building a new party system in its place. This contention, however, does not help us explain why the impact of party ID on voting seems to have been recovering in recent years.

What we are witnessing, in short, is a genuine puzzle about the fate of American party politics. Experts can muster good arguments for three different scenarios: that the party system is in a long-term dealignment, that this dealignment is about to give way to a new realignment of the major parties, or that the realignment has already occurred. It is also possible that the very idea of a realignment is an exception to the more usual pattern, in which some issues (abortion, for example) have a greater capacity than others to

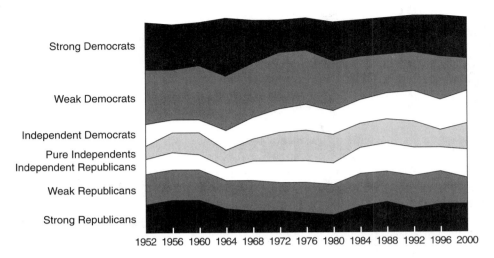

Strong Democrats

Weak Democrats

Independent Democrats

Pure Independents

Independent Republicans

Weak Republicans

Strong Republicans

1952 1956 1960 1964 1968 1972 1976 1980 1984 1988 1992 1996 2000

FIGURE 7.2 Democrats, Republicans, and Independents: 1952–2000.
Note: The data for this figure can be found in Table 6.1 in Chapter 6. The small percentage of "others" (apoliticals and third-party identifiers) is not included.
Source: American National Election Studies, University of Michigan; data made available through the Inter-University Consortium for Political and Social Research.

stimulate people's interest, cut across the existing party lines, and lure some party identifiers to reevaluate and change their party loyalty.[38]

Does it matter which scenario is most accurate? Clearly it does. It will affect the nature and level of political conflict we'll have, the kinds of issues we'll be debating, and the volatility or predictability of our elections. What we *do* know, however, is that at the turn of the millennium, the American electorate is composed of three groups of roughly similar size: Democrats, Republicans, and independents. Both major parties, as well as prospective independent and third-party candidates, have the opportunity of mobilizing voters in the 2004 elections and beyond, and, thus, of shifting the trajectory of American politics.

We know further that, whether we are now living in a realigned sixth party system or the continued dealignment of the New Deal system—and this will be in dispute for some time—the American electorate differs in some significant ways from that of the mid-1900s. It is still dominated by Democratic and Republican Party loyalists. But because these two party camps are so close in size, and because so many Americans consider themselves independent of party, it is also an electorate capable of producing mercurial election results, both within and across elections. And it can sustain third-party and independent candidates for president as well as the divided control of government that has been so characteristic of the American system for the last three decades.

Who Votes— and Why It Matters

In the end, the presidential election of 2000 came down to 537 votes in Florida.[1] That was the margin by which George W. Bush beat his Democratic opponent, Al Gore, in that state. Under Florida's winner-take-all rules, Bush thus won all of its electoral votes—enough to give him a bare majority in the electoral college and, as a result, the presidency. At the same time, about 2.6 *million* Floridians who were registered to vote stayed home from the polls—almost 5,000 times the size of Bush's tiny margin of victory.

Does it matter who votes and who doesn't? Should we care how well the voters reflect the partisanship, social characteristics, and political opinions of the adult population as a whole? It certainly made a difference to Bush and Gore, as well as to thousands of other candidates in close races for other offices. The question of who exercises the right to vote and, more fundamentally, which groups in the population have the right to vote, has been a central concern of the parties throughout their long history.

We have seen that the American parties grew and changed in response to and, in part, stimulated the expansion of the right to vote. As the electorate was expanded to include lower-status people and then women and minorities, the parties were forced to change their organizations and appeals. Parties that failed to adjust to the new electorates—the early Federalists, for example—have become extinct. Others, such as European socialist and labor parties, have gained strength by fighting to secure the suffrage for lower-status voters and then using these voters' support to win political power. The nature of the parties, in short, depends on the nature of the electorate.

Even more, the fate of the parties depends on the active electorate—the types of people who take advantage of their right to vote. Those who vote are rarely a representative sample of all adult citizens; some groups in society are more likely to go to the polls than others are. Because groups have different profiles of support for the parties, as Chapter 7 showed, the composition of the active electorate affects the balance of party power. The remarkably low voter turnout in American elections heightens the impact of these group differences in party support.

THE LOW TURNOUT IN AMERICAN ELECTIONS

It is extremely significant for American elections that so small a percentage of the eligible adult population actually shows up at the polls. Only 51 percent of the eligible electorate cast a ballot for president in 2000. And that was an improvement over 1996, when the turnout rate was 49 percent. These turnout rates have been dropping in recent decades. The only other presidential contests since 1824 in which turnout fell below 50 percent were the first two elections of the 1920s, before many women had become accustomed to their new right to vote. Even fewer people vote in midterm elections; in 1998, only 34 percent of the eligible voters cast a ballot for the top office on the ballot (see Figure 8.1).[2]

These figures hide even lower turnout rates in many states. In the 2000 presidential contest, for example, only 43 percent of the voting-age population cast a ballot in Hawaii in comparison to almost 70 percent in Minnesota. The figures also ignore roll-off, or voting for the most important office on the ballot but not for lesser offices; turnout in the 2000 congressional elections, for example, was about 4 percent less than presidential turnout. An even smaller percentage votes in local elections and party primaries.

These low turnouts have long generated serious debate. Some observers ask: how healthy can our democracy be when fewer than half of its citizens bother to vote?[3] Others have the opposite concern: would American politics be harmed by encouraging the

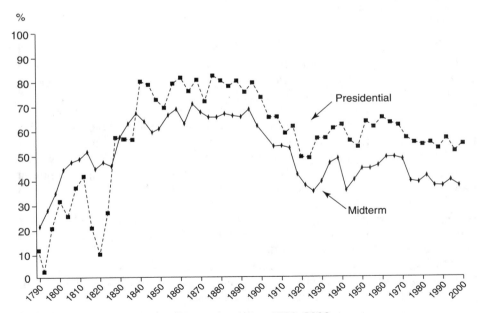

FIGURE 8.1 Turnout in American elections: 1790–2000.
Note: These are the percentages voting for president and for the office with the highest vote in midterm elections. (See note 2).

participation of less interested and, presumably, less informed citizens? Nevertheless, at other times and in other places, democracies have enjoyed much broader participation. Voting turnout in the United States reached an all-time high toward the end of the nineteenth century.[4] In more recent times, turnout in off-year congressional elections peaked at 45 percent in 1962 and 1966, and presidential turnout was as high as 63 percent in 1960. But even these percentages are low in comparison with other countries. In no other democratic nation in the world does such a small share of the electorate take part in choosing the most important government officials.[5]

There are several reasons for low voter participation in the United States. Voter turnout is affected by state laws (and the ways they are applied in practice), economic and social forces, and the nature of the candidates and the competition in a given election. Forces within the individual make a difference as well: people's values, motivation levels, and sense of civic responsibility.

THE EXPANDING RIGHT TO VOTE

The Constitution leaves it to the states to decide who will be eligible to vote. The result is that, even in presidential elections, voting systems vary from state to state, as do rules as to who is eligible to cast a ballot. Since the Civil War, however, the national government has gained the authority, most often through constitutional amendments, to keep states from imposing especially offensive restrictions on voting. Both state and national governments, then, have had a hand in expanding and, sometimes, even restricting the right to vote during the last two centuries.

National Protections for the Right to Vote

White males were given the right to vote earlier in the United States than in any other democracy. In the early 1800s, the states gradually repealed the property, income, and taxpaying qualifications for voting by which they had so severely limited male suffrage.[6] By 1860, no states required propertyholding and only four required substantial taxpaying as a condition for voting. About a century later, the Supreme Court and then, the Twenty-fourth Amendment, finally ended even the small poll tax as a requirement for voting.[7]

Women did not win the right to vote in all states until the twentieth century, and it required federal action. By the mid-1870s, activists had begun to press state governments for women's right to vote; in 1890, when it was admitted to the Union, Wyoming became the first state to grant full voting rights to women. The push for women's suffrage then bogged down, especially in the Eastern states, and women suffragists shifted their hopes to the U.S. Constitution. The Nineteenth Amendment, forbidding states to deny the vote on grounds of gender, was finally ratified in 1920.

The right to vote for black Americans has a more checkered history. Some New England states granted blacks the suffrage before the Civil War. The Fifteenth Amendment, adopted after that war, declared that no state could abridge the right to vote on account of race. But the federal government soon turned its attention to other matters, and Southern states worked effectively to undermine the amendment's purpose by using devices such as poll taxes, outrageous "literacy tests," and outright intimidation to keep blacks from voting. By the early 1900s, black turnout in the South was negligible. It remained that way in most Southern states until the 1960s, when the federal government began to enforce the Fifteenth Amendment and new voting rights laws on the reluctant states.

The most recent change in the legal definition of the electorate has been to lower the voting age to 18. In the 1960s, only a handful of states allowed people under the age of 21 to vote. In 1970, Congress passed a law lowering the minimum voting age to 18 in both state and federal elections. Less than half a year later, the Supreme Court decided that the act was constitutional as it applied to federal elections, but unconstitutional for state and local elections.[8] Congress then passed a constitutional amendment lowering the age to 18 for all elections and it was quickly ratified by the states in 1971.

The national government has taken other steps to expand the electorate. Congress banned literacy, understanding, and "character" tests for registration, and waived residence requirements for voting in presidential elections. The so-called "motor voter" law, passed in 1993, required the states to let citizens register to vote at driver's license bureaus, by mail, and through agencies that give out federal benefits. Voter registration has surged in many areas as a result, although these increases have not been matched by greater voter turnout in most elections.[9]

The Supreme Court has enlarged its own powers in protecting voting rights, citing the Fourteenth Amendment's equal protection clause ("no state shall make or enforce any law which shall ... deny to any person within its jurisdiction the equal protection of the laws") to keep states from discriminating against blacks in defining their electorate. Presumably, this same clause would protect the voting rights of other social groups as well.[10] And the passage of the Twenty-third Amendment in 1961 gave the District of Columbia, whose citizens had been voteless for most of American history, a total of three votes in the electoral college. The District's voters now also elect a nonvoting delegate to Congress and a series of local officials.

LEGAL BARRIERS TO VOTING

These constitutional amendments have limited states' discretion in determining who can vote. So have the political pressures for universal adult suffrage, as well as increased supervision by Congress and the Supreme Court. Over the years, then, the various states have converged on legal definitions of the suffrage that are fairly similar.

Citizenship

Since the 1920s, all states have required that voters be citizens of the United States. As surprising as it may now seem, prior to 1894, at least twelve states permitted noncitizens to vote,[11] although some required that the individual had begun to seek American citizenship. The requirement of citizenship remains the biggest legal barrier to voting. There are millions of adults living in the United States—most of them concentrated in California, Florida, Texas, and New York—who are not eligible to vote until they are "naturalized" as citizens, a process that can take two or three years to complete.

Residence

For most of American history, states could require citizens to live in a state and locality for a certain period of time before being allowed to vote there. Most states had three-layer residence requirements: a minimum period of time in the state, a shorter time in the county, and an even shorter period in the local voting district. Southern states had the longest residence requirements (which kept migrant farmworkers from voting), but other states also had long waits for eligibility. As late as 1970, the median residence requirement among the states was one year in the state, three months in the county, and one month in the voting district.

A few states had begun to lower their residence requirements in the 1950s and 1960s, as society became more mobile; many states set up even lower requirements for new-comers wishing to vote in presidential elections. In 1970, Congress established a national requirement of thirty days' residence within a state for voting in presidential elections. Shortly after, the Supreme Court struck down Tennessee's one-year residence require-ment for state and local elections, indicating a strong preference for a 30-day limit.[12] Since then, almost half of the states have dropped residence requirements altogether and most of the rest have fixed them at one month.

Despite these changes, residency requirements are still a barrier to voting. The United States is a nation of movers. Almost one in every six Americans moved within the United States between March 1999 and March 2000, including about 6 percent who moved to a different county and 3 percent to a different state.[13] Those who have moved recently are far less likely to vote, in part because they must take the time and initiative to find out where and when they need to register (see below). Researchers estimate that with the impact of mobility removed, turnout would be about 9 percent higher.[14]

Registration

One of the biggest obstacles to voting is the registration requirement—the rule in most states that citizens must register in advance in order to vote in an election. During most of the 1800s, voters needed only to show up on election day to cast a ballot, or to be listed on the government's voting roll—the same rules that most European democracies use today. Progressive reformers near the end of the nineteenth century urged states to require advance registration, in order to limit illegal voting in the big cities. That increased the motivation needed to vote, so these registration requirements reduced the high turnout levels of that time.[15]

These requirements have since been relaxed. States differ in what they require and, thus, in the burden they place on citizens. The relevant provisions involve the closing date for registration (which ranges from none to 30 days before the election), the fre-quency with which registration rolls are purged (a few states remove voters from the rolls after missing one election, but most do it only after four years of nonvoting), and the accessibility of registrars.[16] North Dakota does not require its citizens to register at all and six other states permit registering on election day, which tends to increase turnout.

The requirements that remain, however, still make it more inconvenient to vote. The higher these "costs" of voting, the more citizens will choose not to participate in elections. Studies have consistently estimated that turnout in presidential elections would be much higher if all states allowed election day registration, set regular, as well as evening and Saturday hours for registering, and did not purge for nonvoting. The greatest gains would be realized by eliminating the closing date, which would let citizens cast a ballot even if they did not get interested enough to take part until the last, most exciting days of the campaign.[17]

THE SPECIAL CASE OF VOTING RIGHTS FOR AMERICAN BLACKS

Nowhere have legal barriers to voting been more effective than in denying the vote to Southern blacks. Black males got the right to vote nationwide after the defeat of the Confederacy, by the constitutional amendments extending to blacks the rights of citizenship. But when Union occupation troops withdrew from the South as the Reconstruction came to an end, Southern states set about systematically to remove blacks from the active electorate. By the beginning of the twentieth century, they had succeeded.

Systematic Denial of the Right to Vote

The disenfranchisement of Southern black voters is a story of blatant manipulation of the electoral system in order to control election results. It was accomplished by a variety of laws, capricious election administration, and intimidation and violence when these subtler methods were not effective. By these means, blacks were kept away from the polls in the former Confederacy and some neighboring states for almost a century.

Southern states employed an arsenal of weapons to restrict the black vote. Residence requirements were most strict in the South. Most states in that region required payment of a poll tax in order to vote—just one or two dollars, but often demanded well before an election, with the stipulation that the taxpayer keep a receipt and present it weeks later at the voting booth. Many states also required some prospective voters to pass a literacy test, often of both reading ability and understanding. Local voting officials, who were usually hostile to blacks voting, had the power to decide who was "literate" enough to pass the test. These laws were intentionally directed at the poor and uneducated black population. They created huge barriers to voting.

If the law was not enough to discourage blacks from voting, other devices were available. Blacks hoping to register found themselves blocked by endless delays, unavailable or antagonistic registrars, technicalities, and double standards (see box on p. 148). Those who persevered were often faced with economic reprisal (the loss of a job or a home) and physical violence. It is not surprising, in this relentlessly hostile environment, that only 5 percent of voting-age blacks were registered in the 11 Southern states as late as 1940.[18]

The Long Struggle for Voting Rights

For years after the end of Reconstruction, the states and the Supreme Court played a game of constitutional "hide and seek." States would devise a way to disenfranchise blacks, the Court would strike it down as unconstitutional and the states would find another. States were sometimes careful not to disenfranchise poorer whites along with blacks; one method was the "grandfather clause," which automatically registered all men whose ancestors had been eligible to vote before the Civil War.

The "white primary" shows the ingenuity of Southern states determined to avoid black registration. Faced with the threat of black voting in the Democratic primary, some states simply declared the party a private club open only to whites. This was done at a time when the Republican Party was weak to nonexistent in the South, so the candidate who won the Democratic primary was assured of winning the general election. The white

Barriers to Black Registration in the South

In their account of the civil rights movement in the South, Pat Watters and Reese Cleghorn describe how blacks were prevented from registering by simple but effective administrative practices:

> Slowdowns were common. Separate tables would be assigned to whites and Negroes. If a line of Negroes were waiting for the Negro table, a white might go ahead of them, use the empty white table, and leave. In Anniston, Alabama, a report said the white table was larger, and Negroes were not allowed in the room when a white was using it. Another variation was to seat four Negroes at a table, and make three wait until the slowest had finished, while others waited outside in line. These methods were particularly effective when coupled with the one or two day a month registration periods.... In one north Florida county, the registrar didn't bother with any of these refinements, and didn't close his office when Negro applicants appeared. He simply sat with his legs stretched out across the doorway. Negroes didn't break through them.

Source: Pat Watters and Reese Cleghorn, *Climbing Jacob's Ladder* (New York: Harcourt Brace Jovanovich, 1967), pp. 122–123.

primary finally expired, but only after 21 years of lawsuits and five cases before the Supreme Court.[19]

Court action was not nearly as effective against the more informal hurdles faced by blacks trying to vote. So reformers tried legislative and administrative remedies. The federal Voting Rights Act of 1965, extended in 1982, made a frontal assault on these forms of discrimination by involving the national government directly in local registration practices. It authorized the U.S. Justice Department to seek injunctions against anyone who prevented blacks from voting. When the Justice Department could convince a federal court that a "pattern or practice" of discrimination existed in a district, the court could send federal registrars there to register voters. It could also supervise voting procedures in states and counties where less than 50 percent of potential voters had gone to the polls in the most recent presidential election. And it put local registrars under greater regulation and control.[20]

The Growth of Black Registration in the South

This unprecedented federal intervention in state elections, combined with the civil rights movement's efforts to mobilize black voters, enabled the black electorate to grow enormously in the South. Black registration increased from 5 percent of the black voting-age population in 1940 to 29 percent in 1960, and then surged dramatically to 64.5 percent by the 1992 election—a level close to that of white Southerners. White registration also increased during this period, but only from 61 to 68 percent. Black registration levels vary among the Southern states even now, however, depending on the size and socioeconomic characteristics of states' black populations, the states' political traditions, and the barriers they continue to raise to black participation (Figure 8.2).[21]

From Voting Rights to Representation

Even though they are no longer systematically prevented from voting, African-Americans still find it difficult to gain an effective political voice in many areas of the South. In the debate over extending the Voting Rights Act in 1981 and 1982, the major issue was the effort by some states and localities to dilute the impact of black votes or to limit the opportunities for blacks to choose black officeholders. This was most commonly done by redrawing legislative district lines in order to divide black voters among several districts, and by annexing white suburbs to offset black majorities in the cities or towns.

After the 1990 census, the first Bush administration pressed Southern states to redraw congressional district lines so as to create some districts with a majority of black voters. The assumption was that these districts would be very likely to elect black legislators to Congress and, thus, improve the representation of African-Americans. A number of these "majority-minority" districts were created by an interesting alliance of black

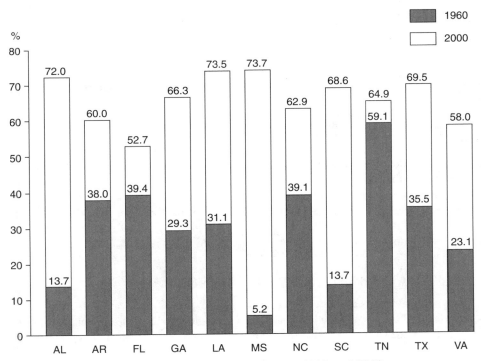

FIGURE 8.2 Black voter registration in the South: 1960 and 2000.

Note: Bars show the percentage of blacks in the two years who were registered to vote.

Source: U.S. Census Bureau

and Hispanic Democrats with white Republicans. The result was to increase the number of congressional seats held by black Americans.

Another effect of these majority-minority districts, however, was to elect more Republicans to Congress from the South—one reason why Republicans supported their creation. Because the districts are fashioned by packing as many (heavily Democratic) black voters into a district as possible, the neighboring districts are left with a higher proportion of whites and Republicans. So, according to one estimate, "for every overwhelmingly black Democratic district created, there is a good chance of creating two or more districts that are overwhelmingly white and Republican."[22] In turn, Democratic state legislatures try to pack the GOP vote into as few districts as possible, and to draw other districts that are 25 to 40 percent black which, coupled with the third or so of white voters who still support Democrats, are very likely to send Democratic representatives to Congress.

In a series of close decisions since the early 1990s, the Supreme Court rejected the most flagrantly gerrymandered of these majority-minority districts. The Court ruled that race can't be the "predominant" factor in drawing district lines, superceding such considerations as county boundaries, compactness and protecting incumbents. But a closely divided Court continues to rule that race can be an element in redrawing district lines, as long as it is not the controlling factor.[23]

Getting Blacks' Votes Counted

As Chapter 11 will show, Americans learned from the 2000 presidential election that, even when people get to the polls, their votes are not always counted. In both Florida and elsewhere in the nation, poorer and minority-dominated districts tend to have older and less reliable voting machines that are more likely to make errors in counting votes. So although it found no evidence of a systematic effort to disenfranchise blacks, the U.S. Commission on Civil Rights reported in 2001 that African-Americans were ten times more likely than whites to have their ballots undercounted or rejected in the 2000 Florida balloting.[24]

These frustrations in using the ballot box to represent blacks' interests are compounded by the fact that as many as 12.5 percent of black males have lost the right to vote because they have felony convictions. The recent spate of mandatory sentences for drug use appear to target drugs used more often by African-Americans and most states deny felons the right to vote, at least while they are serving their sentences.[25] So although voter turnout rates are much higher among Southern blacks now than they were in the mid-1900s, more subtle challenges to blacks' voting rights remain.

POLITICAL INFLUENCES ON TURNOUT

Many political factors also draw voters to the polls or drive them away. These include the importance of the contest, the level of public interest it generates, the amount of competition between the parties, and the efforts of political groups to stimulate more voter turnout.

The Excitement of the Election

American voters face more frequent elections than almost any other population in the democratic world. Within four years, they will be called to the polls to select scores of legislative and executive officeholders (and judges in many states) at the national, state, and local levels. Most of these elections are preceded by primaries. In some areas voters will have to deal with initiatives, referenda, and even an occasional recall election. Americans pay dearly, in the currency of numerous and frequent voting decisions, for the right to keep government on a short electoral leash.

Voter participation varies a great deal depending on the type of election.[26] It is usually highest in presidential elections and lowest in local races. General elections normally attract far more voters than primaries. Initiatives and referenda, the Progressives' devices for allowing voters to decide issues directly, bring out fewer voters than candidate elections. At times, an emotionally charged referendum can provoke a big turnout, but the absence of a personal clash in these questions tends to reduce their allure and they are often complicated enough to confuse many would-be voters.[27]

It is understandable why the more intense general election campaigns for the presidency and governorships entice more voters to participate. The personalities and issues involved are more highly publicized. Because party fortunes are involved, people's party loyalties are aroused, in contrast with the situation of many nonpartisan local elections. Yet, on occasion, a highly personalized mayor's or school board race can make even a presidential contest look dull.[28] An example was the 2001 Democratic primary for mayor of Los Angeles, a lively battle between a longtime party leader and an activist who would have been the first Hispanic-American to lead Los Angeles in more than a century.

Close Competition

Political competition brings voters to the polls. Turnout is higher in areas where the parties and candidates regularly compete on a fairly even basis—for example, in the states in Table 2.2 (in Chapter 2) that fall into the two-party range.[29] Voting participation increases in races that are hotly contested, regardless of the type of office, the nature of the electorate, and the district's historical voting trends.[30] Closely fought races generate excitement and give voters more assurance that their vote will make a difference.

Changes in party competition, historically brought about by realignment, have affected turnout levels. National politics was fiercely competitive in the two decades before 1900; control of government turned on razor-thin margins of victory. The realignment of 1896 brought an abrupt end to this close competition: in the South, the Populist movement was absorbed into the Democratic Party, and outside the South, the Democrats' appeal declined. After the realignment, participation in presidential elections dropped markedly—from almost 80 percent of the voting-age population in prior elections to about 65 percent in the early 1900s. Some scholars argue that the realignment was the culprit; because of the decline in party competition, the parties didn't have as great an incentive to work at mobilizing voters, which resulted in a drop in turnout. Even the realignment of the 1930s failed to restore the competition and high voter turnouts of that earlier era.[31]

There are other possible explanations for this drop in turnout. At around the time of the 1896 realignment, such devices as poll taxes and literacy tests began to increase the "cost" of voting, as did the introduction of the secret ballot and tightened registration requirements.[32] More evidence would be needed to resolve this controversy. But the decline in party competition produced by that realignment probably had at least some role in reducing turnout.

The Representativeness of the Party System

Turnout tends to be much higher in European multiparty systems, where each sizable group in the society is often represented by its own party. The broad, coalitional nature of the two major American parties may make it more difficult for citizens to feel that a party gives voice to their individual needs. One price the United States may pay for its two-party system, then, is lower turnout.[33] The particular types of conflicts that shape the party system—whether social, economic, religious, or racial—can also affect voter involvement. Those citizens who feel that they have a big stake in the prevailing political conflicts are more likely to see a reason to vote—for example, elderly Americans at a time when their Social Security and Medicare benefits, which depend so heavily on government decisions, are consistently an issue in national campaigns.[34]

Organized Efforts to Mobilize Voters

One of the most important findings about voter turnout is that people go to the polls when somebody encourages them to do so. Researchers show that personal canvassing, at least when it uses nonpartisan appeals, does a better job of getting voters to the polls than do mail or phone appeals. Thus, the decline in face-to-face voter mobilization can probably explain some of the drop in voter turnout.[35]

In a nation with low voter turnouts, bringing more voters to the polls has long been an appealing strategy, not only for the parties, but for other groups as well. American history is filled with examples of group efforts to increase turnout. Civil rights groups, as we have seen, helped to achieve dramatic gains in voter registration and turnout since the 1960s, and worked closely with the Democratic Party in the 2000 election to encourage African-Americans to go to the polls.[36] Organized labor mounted a major, and apparently effective, get-out-the-vote drive in 2000, built on union members' contacts with other members and their friends and neighbors.[37] Christian conservatives expanded their influence in the Republican party by developing a base of loyal followers that could be mobilized in elections.

Not all such efforts have been as effective. Mobilizing groups of people for a common cause is hard to do. MTV's "Rock the Vote" campaign, aimed at teens and young adults, for example, has not made much of a dent in the low voting turnout of that age group. And new campaign techniques allowing campaigns to target the people most likely to vote can further entrench existing racial and socioeconomic status (SES) differences between voters and nonvoters.

TURNOUT: INDIVIDUAL DIFFERENCES

We can think about the decision to vote in terms of its costs and benefits to the individual. Each of us pays some costs for the privilege of voting, not in cash but in time, energy, and attention. What we get in return may seem minimal; the influence of a single vote in most elections is likely to be small. From that perspective, it may be remarkable that anyone votes at all.[38] A variety of factors affect the costs and benefits that individuals weigh in choosing whether to go to the polls.

Socioeconomic Status

The biggest difference between voters and nonvoters is their socioeconomic status (SES); lower-status Americans are much less likely to vote.[39] A careful study of voting argues

TABLE 8.1 Personal Characteristics and Voter Turnout: 2000

	Percentage Saying They Voted	
	ANES Survey	U.S.Census
A. Education		
No high school degree	49%	38%
High school graduate	66	52
Attended college	78	63
College or advanced degree	92	77
B. Age		
Under 35	63	44
35 or older	81	66
C. Gender		
Females	74	61
Males	79	58
D. Race		
Blacks	75	57
Whites	77	60
E. Interested in current campaign		
Very much	90	—
Somewhat	74	—
Not much	40	—
F. Party identification		
Strong Democrat	84	—
Weak Democrat	76	—
Independent closer to Democrats	71	—
Independent closer to neither	54	—
Independent closer to Republicans	78	—
Weak Republican	76	—
Strong Republican	92	—

Note: Table entries are the percentage of each group who reported having voted in the 2000 presidential election. The Census does not ask attitudinal questions so it provides no data on partisanship or interest in the campaign.

Source: The ANES data are from the *2000 American National Election Study,* Center for Political Studies, University of Michigan; data made available by the Inter-University Consortium for Political and Social Research. Census data are from the U.S. Census, *Voting and Registration in the Election of November 2000* (Feb. 27, 2002), p. 6; on the Web at *http://www.census.gov/prod/2002pubs/p20–542.pdf* (accessed Mar. 4, 2002).

that education level is the most powerful influence on turnout; the impact of income and occupational differences is minimal once education is taken into account (Table 8.1, panel A). According to this study:

> Education … does three things. First, it increases cognitive skills, which facilitates learning about politics. Schooling increases one's capacity for understanding and working with complex, abstract, and intangible subjects such as politics. This heightens one's ability to pay attention to politics, to understand politics, and to gather the information necessary for making political choices…. Second, better educated people

are likely to get more gratification from political participation. They are more likely to have a strong sense of citizen duty, to feel moral pressure to participate, and to receive expressive benefits from voting. Finally, schooling imparts experience with a variety of bureaucratic relationships: learning requirements, filling out forms, and meeting deadlines. This experience helps one overcome the procedural hurdles required first to register and then to vote.[40]

This relationship between socioeconomic status and voting sounds so obvious that we would expect to see it in other democracies as well. Interestingly, however, the relationship between status and voting is muted in many other democratic nations. In these nations, the disadvantages of low SES seem to be overcome by the efforts of parties and other groups to mobilize lower-SES citizens to vote.[41]

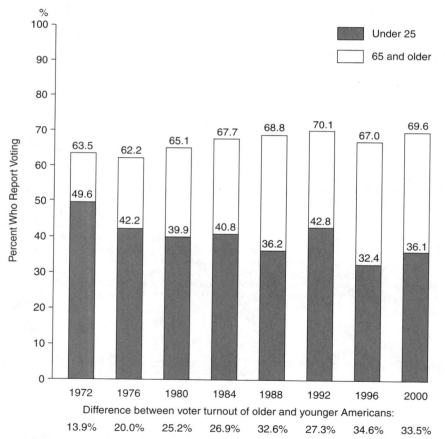

FIGURE 8.3   Voter turnout of younger and older Americans: 1972–2000.
Source: U.S. Census, *Voting and Registration in the Election of November 2000* (Feb. 27, 2002), p. 6; on the Web at *http://www.census.gov/prod/2002pubs/p20-542.pdf* (accessed Mar. 4, 2002).

Youth

After socioeconomic explanations, the next most powerful personal factor in accounting for differences between voters and nonvoters is youth. For a long time, younger Americans have been less likely to go to the polls than almost any other age group in the U.S. (see Table 8.1, panel B, and Figure 8.3). This is largely due to the high "start-up" costs younger people must pay when voting: the difficulties of settling into a community, registering for the first time, and establishing the habit of voting, all at a time when other, more personal interests dominate their lives.[42] The lowering of the national voting age to 18 and the entry of the unusually large "baby boom" generation into the electorate helped to depress voting rates more generally. As a result, campaign agendas became even more attuned to the concerns of older voters—Social Security, Medicare, health care issues—because they are much more likely to go to the polls.

Gender and Race

For many decades after their enfranchisement in 1920, women voted less frequently than men. Women's increasing education levels, however, and changes in women's roles in society have largely eliminated this gender difference (see Table 8.1, panel C). Traditionally, too, blacks have been less likely to vote than whites; this gap still persists, though it is now very small (see Table 8.1, panel D). These racial differences in voting are due almost entirely to the differences in education and occupational status, on average, between whites and blacks.[43]

Social Connectedness

People who have a lot of social ties—those who belong to a variety of organizations and are closely connected with friends and family—are much more likely to participate in elections than others are. Social interaction itself increases the likelihood of involvement in politics. Members of organizations have much higher voting rates than nonmembers; this adds weight to the conclusion that organizations play an important role in mobilizing voters. Voting is also more common among people who are well integrated into the community through home ownership, longtime residence, church attendance, or a job outside the home. Even marriage or the loss of a spouse affects the likelihood that an individual will vote.[44]

Personal Costs of Voting

There are several reasons why the occasion to vote may seem like a threat. For some adults whose political cues are mixed—for example, who have Democratic relatives and a Republican spouse—voting can be stressful. Less-educated citizens may find the length and complexity of the ballot intimidating. Some people refuse to register because the registration rolls are used to choose citizens for jury duty, which they may want to avoid. Or there may be less pressing reasons to avoid voting (see box on p. 157).

Political Attitudes

Attitudes toward politics affect individuals' motivation to vote. Those who find the current campaign more interesting (see Table 8.1, panel E) and who have stronger party loyalties (see Table 8.1, panel F) are more involved in elections. In addition, study after study has shown that a cluster of "civic attitudes" predisposes individuals to vote. The most important of these are perceptions that government is responsive to citizens (or what is termed ***external political efficacy***) and can be trusted to do what is right (***trust in government***) and a sense of responsibility to take part in elections (***citizen duty***).[45] Individuals' attitudes probably interact with the reality of the political system: divided government and separated powers may depress turnout by making it harder for individuals to know who is responsible for what the government does.[46]

THE PUZZLE OF DECLINING VOTER TURNOUT

Since the 1960s, turnout in American elections has declined substantially. Voting in presidential elections fell by almost 15 percentage points from its postwar peak in 1960 (63 percent) to the 1996 low of 49 percent. Turnout in midterm elections also dropped, from a postwar high of 45 percent in 1962 and 1966 to 33 percent in the 1998 House elections.[47]

Explaining the Decline

This decline in voter turnout is puzzling because it has occurred at a time when powerful forces should have propelled turnout upward instead. Educational levels have increased substantially and higher SES is associated with higher voter turnout. The costs of voting have been reduced by liberalized residence and registration rules. New voting methods make it easier to cast a ballot; Oregon, for example, now votes entirely by mail. Earlier generations of women who were not accustomed to voting have been succeeded by generations accustomed to an active political role. Since 1960, groups have worked hard to bring Southern blacks to the polls. Yet turnout has declined, at least outside the South.[48]

One main reason is that the political attitudes that support participation—especially the belief that government is responsive to its citizens (external political efficacy)—have declined since 1960. Alienation and cynicism have increased. When people don't feel connected to the political process, they don't vote. Variations over time in the strength of partisanship have also played a role. These two attitudes contributed separately to the turnout declines from 1960 through 2000, with partisanship accounting for more of the change than efficacy. Their combined effects were even stronger.[49]

Other forces have also taken their toll on voting turnout. Since 1960, the American electorate has become more mobile, less inclined to attend religious services on a regular basis and less likely to be married. These indicate a drop in social "connectedness"— a weakening of the ties binding Americans to the social networks that stimulate participation. Group efforts to turn out the vote through labor-intensive campaigning have declined since the 1960s, as has social movement activism. With this slackening of effort to arouse the electorate, voters had less motivation to go to the polls.[50]

Could Voter Participation Revive?

The decline in turnout seemed to halt in the 1992 and 1994 elections. Although participation was still low by most standards, it reached its highest levels in a decade for midterm contests and in two decades for presidential contests. These two elections proved to be a "blip"; low turnouts returned in 1996 and have remained since then. Yet the reasons for these brief improvements in voter turnout suggest that the long-term turnout decline could be interrupted again.

The excitement of the 1992 election probably explains the surge in presidential turnout in that year. It was the closest election since 1976; public opinion polls showed a tight race through the entire fall campaign. Most states were won by only a small plurality. It was also a genuine three-candidate contest packed with dramatic events, in which independent candidate Ross Perot posed a serious challenge to the major-party standard-bearers. As a result, interest in the election was considerably higher than the 1964 to 1988 average and that buoyed turnout. Perot was able to rally many disaffected Americans who were looking for an alternative to the two traditional parties.[51]

Similarly, the political situation leading up to the 1994 congressional elections probably led more people to the polls. The Republicans seemed to have their best chance in decades to capture the Congress and to gain more governorships and state legislative seats. Media attention focused on the "Contract with America," a statement of conservative principles signed by most Republican congressional candidates in an effort to nationalize the campaign. It was an effective strategy; otherwise, the localism typical of midterm elections would probably have advantaged incumbent Democrats. The result was an unprecedented surge of Republican support. GOP House candidates drew almost 9 million more votes than they had in 1990 and Democrats lost nearly 1 million votes. Such one-sided mobilization is rare; it last appeared in the 1934 election during the realignment that created the New Deal party system.

The 1992 and 1994 campaigns were a hard act to follow. In fact, 1996 and 1998 were business as usual—low turnouts, low political interest. The 2000 presidential election turned out to be the closest in history, but the campaign and the candidates did not seem to engage much public excitement. The lesson of the early 1990s, then, is that when an important race is up for grabs, when the candidates are entertaining and when elections turn on an identifiable set of divisive themes, political interest should increase and carry

Why Didn't You Vote?

Here's why people said they didn't go to the polls in the 2000 election:

I was too busy	21%
Illness or emergency	15
Just not interested	12
Out of town	10
Didn't like the candidates	8
I don't know why	8
Problems with registration	7*
I forgot	4
It was inconvenient	3
Transportation problems	2
The weather was bad	1
Other	10

* Only the answers of registered voters are reported here.

Source: U.S. Census Bureau, *Voting and Registration in the Election of November 2000* (issued Feb. 27, 2002), p. 10, on the Web at *http://www.census.gov/prod/2002pubs/p20-542.pdf* (accessed Mar. 4, 2002).

voter turnout along with it. Without the stimulation of an interesting contest, or the active mobilization of partisans, turnout levels are unlikely to recover. Nonvoting, like voting, becomes a habit that is hard to break.

WHY DO THESE CHANGES IN TURNOUT MATTER?

We have seen, then, that the American parties operate within an electorate that is not representative of the full adult population, nor of all those eligible to vote. This electorate constantly shifts in size and composition. The parties' strategies in winning votes must take these facts into account.

Long-Range Effects

In the long run, the parties have been profoundly affected by the addition of new groups to the electorate. In recent decades, the American parties have absorbed two major new voting groups: blacks and young adults between the ages of 18 and 21. Another such change is occurring now, prompted by a flood of Hispanic and Asian immigrants in recent years, the amnesty for illegal aliens in the 1986 immigration reform law, and incentives for immigrants to become citizens quickly.

These newly enfranchised groups have reshaped the parties. Blacks have flowed into the Democratic Party—more than 80 percent of blacks have voted Democratic in every presidential election since 1964—and this seems to have triggered a countermovement of whites away from the Democrats, particularly in the South.[52] At the same time, the two parties have reshaped their stands on issues ranging from civil rights to welfare reform, as we will see in Chapter 15. The enfranchisement of young voters has had more mixed effects on the parties. The new young voters were more likely to be Democrats than Republicans in the 1970s. That trend reversed in 1984 and 1988, and then re-reversed in the early 1990s. On balance, the youngest voters have tended to pay more attention to the short-term forces of a particular election than to the parties' more fundamental appeals.

Long-term shifts in the geographic distribution of voters have also affected the parties. For instance, the populations of eleven states—all of them in the South and West—grew by more than 15 percent between 1990 and 1999 because of population growth and migration. In addition, the aging of the population has enlarged the group of elderly voters in each successive presidential election. As these groups expand, their distinctive interests carry greater weight in the electorate. If the parties hope to thrive, they must adapt to these changes in a variety of ways, including their positions on issues, the candidates they select, and their strategic choices in campaigns.

The most important, long-term result of these changes is their impact on the political influence of individuals and groups. Casting a vote may not guarantee influence in government, but failing to vote is like asking to be ignored. The implications of this potential loss of influence are all the more serious when the nonvoters differ markedly from the voters. There are more than 70 million adults who have not registered to vote and they tend to have lower socioeconomic status than those who are registered. This lesser turnout probably limits elected officials' incentive to pay attention to the needs of lower-status Americans. Their failure to vote, then, may be partly responsible for the marginalization of disadvantaged people in American politics. The same is probably true of young adults, including college students.[53] Some careful studies contend that nonvoters, in spite of their social backgrounds, tend not to have very different views on issues from those of voters.[54] Yet we can't be sure what nonvoters' political views and aims might be if they were mobilized into political involvement.

Short-Range Effects

In addition to the long-range consequences of changes in the electorate, the parties must deal with short-range changes in turnout from election to election. These increases or decreases in turnout are not likely to benefit all parties and candidates equally, so adding to or reducing turnout becomes a focus of party strategy. Democratic and Republican efforts to attract Hispanic voters in 2000 show how much political strategists appreciate the consequences of mobilization and demobilization.

The conventional wisdom is that big turnouts favor the Democrats. There is reason to believe it. Most nonvoters come from groups—in particular, those of lower socioeconomic status—ordinarily inclined to vote Democratic. That is why proposals to make it easier to register (as did the "motor voter" law), to allow voters to register at the polls, and to make illegal aliens eligible for citizenship are often assumed to benefit the Democrats. It explains why organized labor spends so much money and effort on registration and get-out-the-vote campaigns. It suggests why Republicans tend to prefer that gubernatorial elections be held in non-presidential-election years—because the smaller electorate may be more favorable to Republican candidates. It even explains politicians' belief that rainy weather is Republican weather, in that Republicans will come to the polls anyway.

The conventional wisdom, however, is not subtle enough. Because people who are more interested and involved in politics are more likely to vote, increases in turnout tend to come from the less-involved segment of the electorate. People who are less politically involved are often more responsive to the momentary appeal of a dramatic issue or a popular candidate, whether Democratic or Republican. In fact, Republican presidential candidates have won most of the large-turnout elections in the last five decades.[55] Further, new voters seem to register because of group efforts to mobilize them, rather than because of broad-scale invitations; as an example, Republicans made dramatic gains in voter registration in the Sunbelt during the 1990s because of a large-scale party effort, while Democratic registration hardly increased at all.[56]

Party strategists often nourish the hope that they can affect turnout selectively—that they can bring voters to the polls who will support their candidates and discourage those who won't. In primary elections, they may try to minimize the turnout by selective campaigning, because, in general, the smaller the turnout, the more of it will come from the party's most loyal supporters. In general elections, campaigners may aim their efforts at areas of known party strength to maximize that turnout. It is an interesting challenge for people planning a congressional career that they will face different electorates in alternate elections: the larger turnout of the presidential election followed by the smaller turnout of the midterm election two years later.

THE CHALLENGE TO THE PARTIES

This chapter began by citing one of the most striking facts about current American politics: that even in the most high profile elections, almost half of the potential voters stay home. The case for democracy often rests on the argument that the best decisions are made when the responsibility for decision-making is most widely shared. Full participation in democratic self-governance, then, would seem to be a valuable ideal (see "Which Would You Choose?" on p. 161). Yet American politics falls far short of that ideal—a finding that is all the more bitter when we see that voting turnouts are higher in most other democracies.

If widespread nonvoting is an insult to the democratic spirit, it also raises questions as to whether the major parties—the groups most directly concerned with contesting elections—are doing an effective job of involving the whole electorate. The parties are the organizations that developed to mobilize citizens for political action. They have the great strength, compared with other kinds of organized interests, of being able to recruit large and diverse groups of people into politics. As instruments of mass democracy, it would seem that the parties ought to strive for the greatest possible citizen participation in elections.

If that is so, then the parties have failed. Although they have, at times, actively competed for the support of new voters, the parties do not always seem to relish the challenge of attracting new voting groups, especially those of low status. They have adjusted their strategies to the electorate as it now exists. The party in government, which helps make the rules as to who can vote, has won office with the support of the current patterns of voter turnout; understandably, they don't welcome the uncertainties that a big expansion of the electorate would bring.

The fact that the active electorate in the United States is not as diverse as the nation's population tends to reduce the amount of political conflict and the range of political interests to which the parties must respond. That, in turn, makes it easier for the parties to be moderate and pragmatic. It may be that the American parties can be moderate and nondoctrinaire because they reflect a population that agrees on the fundamental questions. But it is also probably true that these pragmatic parties, accustomed to two-party competition, do not jump at the chance to appeal to the more alienated, less well-educated individuals who are not a part of that moderate consensus. That may be another price we pay for a two-party system.

Many Americans may be happy to pay that price. They may fear that a sudden influx of new and uninformed voters could threaten our democracy. Elections might become more vulnerable to manipulation or unthinking reaction. That seemed to happen in Germany in the 1920s and 1930s, when the Nazi Party, which killed off the democracy Germany had developed, gained power with the support of less-informed and less-involved citizens. Most other Western democracies seem to have avoided these problems even though their electorates are more inclusive; yet the fears remain. We are left, then, with a troubling challenge. Do we have to choose between greater participation and greater political stability? Or are there ways to reconcile our concerns about the quality of democracy with the democratic value of engaging as many of the people as possible in American politics?

WHICH WOULD YOU CHOOSE?

We Need Every Vote ...

Democracy is most vibrant when there is full debate among all viewpoints. When as many people as possible take part in elections, government is more likely to come up with the creative solutions needed to solve public problems.

Politicians pay more attention to the needs of those who vote than to those who don't. So the views and interests of the nonvoters, though real, may well go unrepresented.

The most committed voters tend to be more educated, have higher incomes, and are often more extreme in their viewpoints than other citizens are. These people will thus get more than their share of government benefits and attention from elected officials anxious to get their votes.

It is the more alienated and dissatisfied people who stay away from the polls. They can become ripe for extremist and demagogic appeals. It's better to bring them into the political system where they can voice their concerns in more productive ways.

Let Sleeping Dogs Lie ...

Those who are least likely to vote are also the least interested in government and the least well-informed. Why, then, should we encourage them to have a voice in elections? If they don't care enough to vote, or don't know enough, shouldn't we be grateful that they have abstained?

If people have the right to vote and choose not to, perhaps that means that they are satisfied with things the way they are. If they really wanted change, they'd go to the polls.

If we relax registration and residence requirements to encourage more people to vote, we're opening the floodgates to vote fraud: people voting more than once, or voting under other people's direction.

American democracy has been vibrant enough to survive impeachments, financial scandals, and candidates who lose the presidency even though they won the popular vote. If it ain't broke, why try to fix it?

Parties, Nominations, and Elections

Elections are great political spectacles—ever-changing scenes of crisis and resolution, comedy and tragedy.[1] They are also the main bridge that links the party organizations and identifiers—the first two parts of the American parties, which we've explored in Parts 2 and 3—with the party in government. During campaigns, party activists try to energize party identifiers and get them to the polls in order to support candidates who share the party label. The need to unite around the party's nominees and to work together in the general election are powerful reasons for the three parts of the parties to reconcile their differences—at least until the votes are counted. Elections also link the parties at different levels of government. The process of nominating and electing a presidential candidate binds the state and local parties into at least a brief coalition with the national party. Similarly, a statewide election focuses the energies of local party organizations and leaders within the state.

There is good reason why elections ought to encourage cooperation within the party. When candidates run more capable campaigns, they improve not only their own ability to attract money and other resources, but also that of their party organization. When candidates win, their party's activists stand a better chance of getting action on their issue agenda. When a party's candidate wins the governorship or the local executive office in some areas, then party leaders may gain access to patronage jobs, which in turn can bring more activists into the party organization. In the effort to win, candidates and party activists have to mobilize as many of the party's identifiers as possible. Because victory holds so many attractions for all three parts of the party, it is a powerful lure for them to work together.

All this cooperative activity does not come easily however. Almost every aspect of the electoral process, and especially the nominating process, can also pit the needs of one part of the party against those of another. Whenever primaries are used to select a party's candidates, there will be times when party voters choose a nominee regarded as a disaster by party leaders. Efforts by the party organization to raise money will compete with candidates' own fund-raising. Candidates get to choose which issues they will emphasize, which advisers they will hire and which strategies they will adopt, and these choices will affect the image of the party as a whole, even when the party's leaders,

163

activists, and voters do not share these preferences. Once in office, the party's candidates may have reason to ignore or downplay some questions that are "hot button" issues to party activists.

In addition to the competition within each party, the parties also compete on the larger electoral stage with other political organizations. Groups, such as single-issue organizations, labor unions, religious lobbies, reform groups, corporations, and others, all get involved in campaigns in order to achieve their political goals. Some of these groups work very aggressively to help candidates get nominated, raise money, influence public opinion, and win the election. Democratic state party leaders, for example, will probably have to compete with environmental groups, women's rights groups, civil rights organizations, pro-choice activists and unions representing teachers, trial lawyers, government employees, and a variety of other occupations to get the attention of a Democratic candidate for statewide office.

This competition and cooperation is guided by a set of rules, just as is the cooperation and competition in a basketball game. These rules range from laws to standard practices, and, as they do in basketball, they have a tremendous impact on the parties' electoral activities. One of these "rules" is the widespread use of primary elections, which poses a major challenge to the party organizations in their effort to control the nomination of candidates. Another "rule" is the set of voting systems used in communities across the nation, whose limitations became so painfully obvious in the 2000 presidential race and which can affect Democratic and Republican efforts differently. Yet another is the set of rules that govern campaign fund-raising.

The first two chapters in this section focus on parties' involvement in nominating candidates. Chapter 9 explores the nomination process in general, and Chapter 10 considers the fascinating and peculiar practices through which the parties select their presidential candidates. In Chapter 11, we turn to the role of parties in general elections, and finally, Chapter 12 discusses money in politics. The constant search for dollars to run campaigns gave rise to extensive reform efforts in the 1970s and has prompted more recent debate about the effects of these reforms, leading to the passage of a new campaign finance reform law in 2002. In this chapter we will trace the flow of money into campaigns and consider how it can both expand and contract the influence of parties on their candidates.

CHAPTER 9

How Parties Choose Candidates

In addition to public opinion polls, drive-through restaurants, and other means of democratizing life, Americans invented primary elections. In a primary (more formally known as a *direct primary*), the party electorate chooses which candidates will run for office under the party's label. Then, in a later *general election,* all voters can make the final choice between the two parties' nominees for each office. To American voters neck-deep in primaries during an election season, this may seem like the "normal" way for parties to nominate candidates. It is not; although the idea of a primary election is quickly spreading, candidates in much of the rest of the democratic world are still selected by party leaders, activists, or elected officials, not by voters.[1]

These differences in nomination procedures explain a great deal about the contrasts between American party politics and those of other democracies. The shift to primaries has forced the American parties to develop a different set of strategies in making nominations, contesting elections and trying to hold their candidates accountable after winning public office than we would find in nations that don't hold primaries.

The direct primary permeates every level of American politics. The great majority of states use it in all nominations and the rest use it in most. It dominates the presidential nominating process (see Chapter 10). Even though it is only the first of two steps in electing public officials, it does the major screening of candidates by reducing the choice to two in most constituencies. The nominees chosen in the primary can shape, to a great extent, the party's chance for victory in the general election. In areas where one party dominates, the real choice is made in the primary. What led to the use of this two-step election process? How does it work and how well does it serve the needs of voters, candidates and parties?

HOW THE NOMINATION PROCESS EVOLVED

For the first 110 years of the American Republic, candidates for office were nominated by party caucuses and, later, by party conventions. Critics charged that each of these systems permitted self-selected party "bosses" to choose the party's candidates. The system changed early in the twentieth century when Progressive reformers argued successfully for primary elections, so that the greatest possible number of party supporters could have a voice in deciding who could run under the party's label.

Nominations by Caucus

Once they had evolved beyond legislative coalitions, the parties emerged largely as groups to nominate candidates for public office. In the early years of the Republic, local caucuses (meetings) were held to select candidates for local offices. Frequently, caucuses of like-minded partisans in Congress met to nominate presidential and vice-presidential candidates. Similar caucuses in state legislatures nominated candidates for governor and other statewide offices. These caucuses were informal; the participants were self-selected. There weren't even any procedures for ensuring that all the major figures of the party would take part.

Nominations by Convention

The spread of democratic values made these elite caucuses an inviting target. Followers of Andrew Jackson attacked what they called "King Caucus" as an aristocratic device that foiled popular wishes. In 1832, the Jacksonian Democrats met in a national convention—the first for a major party—and nominated Andrew Jackson for president. Conventions then became the primary means of nominating candidates for the rest of the nineteenth century. The nominating conventions were composed of delegates chosen by state and especially local party leaders, often at their own lower-level conventions.

These large and chaotic conventions looked more broadly representative than the caucuses, but often were not. The selection of delegates and the management of the conventions were guided by the heavy hands of the party leaders. Party insurgents, unhappy with what they considered "bossism," denounced the convention system. The Progressive movement led the drive against conventions, and their journalistic allies, the muckrakers, wrote dispatches about democracy trampled under party leaders' heels.[2]

Nominations by Direct Primaries

The cure offered by the Progressives—the direct primary—reflected their core belief. The best way to cure the ills of democracy, they felt, was to prescribe larger doses of democracy. Robert M. La Follette, who wrote the nation's first statewide primary law in Wisconsin in 1902, argued that the caucus and convention serve only to

> "… give respectable form to political robbery." In a primary, in contrast, "the citizen may cast his vote directly to nominate the candidate of the party with which he affiliates … The nomination of the party will not be the result of 'compromise' or impulse, or evil design … but the candidates of the majority, honestly and fairly nominated."[3]

Some Southern states had adopted primaries at the local level in the years after the Civil War, often to legitimize the nominees and settle internal disputes in their one-party Democratic systems. Then, in the first two decades of the twentieth century, all but four other states turned to primaries for at least some of their statewide nominations. This was a time when one party or the other dominated the politics of many states—the most pervasive one-party rule in American history. It might be possible to tolerate the poor choices made by conventions when voters have a real choice in the general election. But when the nominees of the dominant party have no serious competition, those shortcomings were harder to accept. The convention could choose the most dismal party hack without fear of challenge from the other party. Thus, the Progressives, who fought economic monopoly with antitrust legislation, used the direct primary as their major weapon in battling political monopoly.

Although the primary was designed to democratize the nominating process, many of its supporters hoped it would go further and cripple the political party itself. For them, the best way to weaken party and "boss" rule was to strike at the party organization's chief activity—the nomination of candidates. Primaries took control of the choice of the party's candidates away from party leaders and gave it, instead, to party voters. In fact, some states, such as Wisconsin, took this principle to its logical extreme and adopted a definition of the party electorate so broad that it included any voters who chose to vote in the party's primary on election day.

Primaries were not the first cause of party weakness in the United States; if party leaders had been strong enough throughout the country when primaries were first proposed, they would have been able to keep these primary laws from passing anywhere. But primaries further undermined the power of party organizations. Not only did they greatly limit party leaders' influence on nominations, but they also made it possible for public officeholders without any loyalty to the party organization or its principles to penetrate the party in government. When primaries were used to select party organization leaders, the parties risked losing control even over their own internal affairs. Largely because of the existence of primaries, party leaders in the United States have less control over who will receive the party nomination than in most other democratic political systems.

THE CURRENT MIX OF PRIMARIES AND CONVENTIONS

The use of conventions for nominating candidates is no longer common; it has faded in the face of the primary's democratic appeal. But conventions are still used to nominate candidates in a few states and, most conspicuously, in the contest for the presidency. Because states have the legal right to design their own nominating systems, the result is a mixture of primaries and conventions for choosing candidates for state offices.

All 50 states now use primaries to nominate at least some statewide officials, and 38 of them (plus the District of Columbia) use this method exclusively.[4] In Alabama and Virginia, the party may choose to hold a convention instead of a primary, but only in Virginia has the convention option been used in recent years as a means of unifying the party behind a particular candidate.

The remaining states use some combination of convention and primary. Iowa requires a convention when no candidate wins at least 35 percent of the primary vote. Three states (Indiana, Michigan, and South Dakota) use primaries for the top statewide offices but choose other nominees in conventions. Five (Colorado, New Mexico, New York, North Dakota, and Utah) hold conventions to screen candidates for the primary ballot. A convention is held in Connecticut, but any candidate who has received at least 15 percent of the convention vote can challenge the endorsed candidate in a primary. If there is no challenge, no primary is held.[5] This variety of choices reminds us that, in spite of the national parties' growing strength, party power is still largely decentralized.

TYPES OF PRIMARIES

States also differ in the criteria they use to determine who can vote in their primaries. There are three basic forms, though each has a lot of variations. In the states with so-called "closed" primaries, only voters who have registered their affiliation with a party can participate. Voters in states with "open" primaries have more freedom to choose which party's primary they want to vote in. A few states with "blanket" primaries allow voters to select from among all the candidates for office, Democratic and Republican; they do not restrict voters to the nomination contests of a single party.[6]

Closed Primaries

A slim majority of states hold closed primaries, in which there must be a permanent record of the voter's party affiliation before he or she can vote in that party's primary. In the 11 states with *fully closed* primaries, voters have to register as a Democrat or a Republican prior to the election. Then they receive the primary ballot of only their own party when they enter the polling place on election day. If they want to vote in the other party's primary, they must formally change their party affiliation on the registration rolls sometime before the date of the primary. States with traditionally strong party organizations, such as New York and Pennsylvania, are among those that have been able to keep their primaries closed.[7]

In the other 15 closed-primary states, often called *"semi-closed,"* voters can change their party registration at the polls, or they can simply declare their party preference at the polling place and are given their declared party's ballot. What if, in the latter case, they choose to vote in the primary of a party different from their own? In some states, their declaration can be challenged by one of the party observers at the polls; if so, the voter may be required to take an oath of party loyalty. Some states require voters to affirm that they have voted for the candidates of the party in the past; others ask challenged voters to declare themselves sympathetic at the moment to the candidates and principles of the party; and some ask nothing at all.

These latter provisions make it possible for independents and even the other party's identifiers to vote in a party's primary. From the point of view of the voter, these semi-closed primaries are not very different from an open primary. The difference is important from the party's perspective, however, because in both closed and semi-closed primaries there is usually a written record of party registration, which can then be used by party organizations to target campaigning to their identified supporters.

Open Primaries

Citizens of 20 states can vote in the primary of their choice without ever having a permanent record made as to which party ballot they have selected.[8] There are different types of these open primaries. In *"semi-open"* primaries, used by ten states (most of them in the South), there is no permanent record of a voter's party preference and the voter can pick whichever party's ballot he or she chooses, but he or she will need to ask for a particular party's ballot at the polls. The other ten states hold *fully open* primaries, in which voters receive either a consolidated ballot, or ballots for every party and they select the party of their choice in the privacy of the voting booth. They cannot, however, vote in more than one party's primary in a given election. Many of these states have histories of Progressive strength.

Blanket Primaries

A blanket primary (used in Alaska, California, Louisiana, and Washington in 2000) gives voters even greater freedom. In addition to the fact that they don't need to disclose their party affiliation, they can vote in more than one party's primary; that is, they may choose a Democrat for one office and a Republican for another. Louisiana's version of the blanket primary, sometimes called the "unitary" primary, goes even further. Any candidate who wins a majority of votes in the primary is elected to the office immediately. If no candidate wins an outright majority, then the general election serves as a runoff between the top two vote-getters, regardless of party. The future of the blanket primary is in doubt, however, as the result of a Supreme Court decision in 2000 ruling that these primaries violated the parties' right to freedom of association (see the box below).

WHY DOES THE TYPE OF PRIMARY MATTER?

These varieties of primaries represent different answers to a long-standing debate: is democracy better served by competition between disciplined parties, or by a system in which the parties have relatively little power? Open and blanket primaries reflect the

---

A Wet Blanket for the Blanket Primary

California voters approved an initiative in 1996 that would let them vote for candidates of more than one party in the primary election. Called a "blanket primary," this plan puts all candidates from all parties on the same primary ballot, just as in the general election. Thus, it permits voters who are not affiliated with a party to help choose that party's candidates. Proponents said it would boost voter participation in the primary — and it did — and encourage the choice of more moderate candidates. Party leaders saw it differently; the state's Democratic and Republican parties and two minor parties sued to overturn the law. They claimed that by opening up the primary, the plan prevented the party's loyal supporters from choosing the candidates who best represented their views. That, they said, would keep the party from offering a clear and consistent message to the voters. The result was to violate the First Amendment's guarantee of freedom of association.

The state's lawyers countered that a primary belongs to the voters, not to the parties. A U.S. Circuit Court of Appeals agreed. But in June 2000, the U.S. Supreme Court (in the case of *California Democratic Party v. Jones*) sided with the parties. That gave the right to decide who votes in a primary, at least in California, back to the party organization. The future of the blanket primary is in doubt as a result.

belief that parties and rigid party loyalties are harmful to a democracy. The closed primary, in contrast, suggests that unified parties can benefit us, so it is valuable to give loyal party followers the right to choose their party's candidates.

Party organizations clearly prefer the closed primary, in which voters must register by party before the primary. It pays greater respect to the party's own right to select its candidates. Prior party registration also gives the parties a bonus—published lists of their partisans. Further, the closed primary limits the biggest dangers of open and blanket primaries, at least from the perspective of party leaders: crossing over and raiding. Both terms refer to people who vote in the primary of a party they do not generally support. They differ in the voter's intent. Voters *cross over* in order to take part in a more exciting race or to vote for a more appealing candidate in the other party. *Raiding* is a conscious effort to weaken the other party by voting for its least attractive candidates.

Studies of primary contests in Wisconsin—cradle of the open primary—and other open primary states show that crossing over is common. Partisans rarely cross over in gubernatorial primaries, because that would keep them from having a voice in other party contests. But because only one office is at stake in a presidential primary, both independents and partisans often cross over; in the 2000 presidential race, for example, more Democrats and independents voted in some Republican primaries than Republicans did. Not surprisingly, the candidate preferences of crossover voters may differ a great deal from those of regular party voters.[9]

Organized raiding would be a bigger problem. It is a party leader's nightmare that opponents will make mischief by voting in the party's primary for the least appealing candidate. Studies of open primaries have found little evidence of raiding, however. Voters cross over to vote their real preferences, rather than to weaken the party in whose primary they are participating.[10]

HOW CANDIDATES QUALIFY

States also vary in the ease with which candidates can get their names on the primary ballot and in the support required to win the nomination.

How Do Candidates Get On the Ballot?

In most states, a candidate can get on the primary ballot by filing a petition. State election laws specify how many signatures the petition has to contain—either a specific number, or a percentage of the vote for the office in the last election. States vary a lot in the difficulty of this step. New York, with its complicated law that favors party insiders, has, by far, the strictest requirements for filing (see box on p. 171). In some other states, a candidate needs only to appear before the clerk of elections and pay a small fee. A few states even put candidates on the ballot if public opinion polls show them to have some party support.

These simple rules have consequences for the parties. The easier it is for candidates to get on the ballot, the more likely it becomes that dissident, or even crackpot, candidates will enter a race and engage the party's preferred candidates in costly primary battles. Sometimes, such candidates even win. In states with easy ballot access, citizens can be treated to grudge campaigns, in which people file to oppose the sheriff who arrested them, for instance, or who simply enjoy the thought of wreaking havoc in a primary.[11]

Jump How High? Getting on the Ballot in New York

Five weeks before the New York primary in the 2000 presidential race, a state judge threw Senator John McCain off the primary ballot in much of the state. McCain was one of the two leading contenders for the Republican nomination. The state's Republican establishment, which supported Texas Governor George W. Bush for the nomination, had initiated the action, reportedly in order to help the governor of New York, who hoped to become Bush's running mate.

Under New York's ballot access rules, passed by the state legislature at the request of the state party, candidates have to circulate petitions in each of the state's 31 congressional districts under very restrictive rules. This system, described as "tortuous," is the toughest in the nation. It is especially hostile to candidates who do not have the state party's support; those who do can rely on the party's volunteers to conduct the separate petition drives in each district.

A McCain lawyer said, in reaction to the state judge's decision: "It demonstrates the absurdity of the election law when a candidate such as John McCain, who is a leading candidate in the race, can't get on the ballot in more than a third of the election districts."

Democrats on the State Board of Elections had tried to keep McCain on the ballot in order to set up a more divisive Republican primary. McCain's campaign made good use of the controversy in portraying himself as an outsider running against a corrupt political system. He was later added to the ballot after a successful appeal to a federal judge, who, to the state Republican Party's chagrin, invalidated some requirements for circulating nominating petitions. Imagine battling to get on the primary ballot in New York despite these hurdles—and then dealing with the varying ballot access rules of 49 other states as well!

Source: New York Times stories by Clifford J. Levy: "McCain Off Ballot in Much of Upstate New York," Jan. 28, 2000, p. A1; "McCain on Ballot Across New York as Pataki Gives In," Feb. 4, 2000, p. A1; "Judge Adds McCain to New York Ballot and Rejects Rules," Feb. 5, 2000, p. A1.

Runoffs: When Too Many Candidates Get on the Ballot

What if the leading candidate in a primary gets less than a majority of the votes? In most states' primaries, a plurality is enough. Almost all the Southern and border states, however, hold a runoff between the top two candidates if one candidate does not win at least 50 percent. This Southern institution was developed in the long period of one-party Democratic rule of the South; when there were no Republican candidates, winning the Democratic nomination was the same as winning the general election and intense Democratic factionalism often produced three, four, or five serious candidates for a single office. The runoff was used to ensure a majority winner.

In recent years, the Southern runoff primary has become very controversial. Citing instances in which black candidates who received a plurality in the first primary in the South have lost to whites in the runoff, some have charged that runoffs discriminate against minority groups and are in violation of the Constitution and the federal Voting

Rights Acts. Others have countered that it is the voters, not the runoff, who produce this result, and that, in fact, the runoff helps to force Southern parties to build biracial coalitions. This debate is far from being resolved.[12]

WHAT PARTIES DON'T LIKE ABOUT PRIMARIES

The Progressives designed the direct primary to break the party organization's monopoly control of nominations and, in important respects, it did. In the process, it compromised parties' effectiveness in elections more generally, in several ways.

The Risk of Unattractive Nominees

Party leaders fear that primary voters could choose a weak candidate: one who, because of his or her background or issue stands, may not appeal to the broader voter turnout in the general election. Some candidates can ride strong feelings on a hot-button issue to the nomination, though the voters in November may be more temperate. Imagine the discomfort of party leaders, for instance, when the controversial right-winger Oliver North, who had been convicted on three felony counts for his role in a Reagan White House scandal, won the 1994 GOP nomination for senator in Virginia over a far more electable conservative. North went on to lose the general election. In another classic case, some Democratic Party leaders in southern California even felt the need to disown their own candidate, when a former official of the Ku Klux Klan captured the Democratic nomination for Congress in a multicandidate primary race.

In addition, every election year seems to bring out a few nominees, usually for low-level offices, whose only qualification for leadership is that they have a famous name. In fact, in occasional elections, both candidates have the *same* famous name—as happened for a time in the 2000 Missouri primary, when U.S. House Democratic Leader Richard A. (Dick) Gephardt was challenged by Richard A. (Dick) Gebhardt, a candidate the Minority Leader accused of running as a Republican stalking horse to confuse voters. If the nominations were made by a party convention, it's often argued, convention delegates would know the prospective candidates better, so they would not be prone to these misjudgments.

Difficulties in Recruiting Candidates

Candidate recruitment has never been an easy job, especially for the minority party. The direct primary makes the challenge even more difficult. If an ambitious candidate has the opportunity to challenge the party favorite in the dominant party's primary, he or she is less likely to consider running for office under the minority party's label. So the minority party will find it even harder to recruit good candidates for races it is not likely to win,[13] and the office goes to the other party's nominee by default.[14] Little by little, the majority party becomes the only viable means of exerting political influence and the minority party atrophies.[15]

This argument should not be taken too far. One-party politics has declined in recent years as primaries have become common. (There are still a number of uncontested races in state legislative and other, less visible, elections in many states, however.[16]) And even in areas still dominated by one party, the internal competition promoted by primaries can keep officeholders responsive to their constituents.[17] But primaries make the difficult job of a minority party even tougher. Further, because parties cannot control access to their own primaries, or guarantee the outcome, they have less to offer to candidates they are trying to recruit.

The damage primaries can do to the minority party is an unintended result of this Progressive reform. The Progressives were intent on destroying the party monopoly in nominations, but they certainly didn't aim to make general elections less competitive. A modern-day version of a Progressive reform—the movement to limit the number of terms public officials can serve—could have a similar unintended effect. By preventing an official from staying in office decade after decade, term limits may produce more competition—but probably only in the year when the term limit has been reached and then, only in the majority party's primary in a one-party area. In the other years, competition may be reduced as attractive candidates sit back and wait until the officeholder's term limit has been reached.

Divisive Primaries

Primaries can create conflict that may open up old party wounds:

> A genuine primary is a fight within the family of the party and, like any family fight, is apt to be more bitter and leave more enduring wounds than battles with the November enemy. In primaries, ambitions spurt from nowhere; unknown men carve their mark; old men are sent relentlessly to their political graves; bosses and leaders may be humiliated or unseated. At ward, county, or state level, all primaries are fought with spurious family folksiness and sharp knives.[18]

A divisive primary election can have a number of effects on the party in the short term. Activists who campaigned for the losing candidate in the primary may sit out the general election, rather than work for their party's nominee—though the excitement of the primary may bring in new activists to take their places.[19] Because this is a public fight, the wounds the candidates inflict on one another and on their followers often seem slower to heal.[20] The charges raised by a candidate's primary opponent are often re-used by the opposition in the general election—a source of free campaign help to the other party. Finally, if a bitter primary is expensive, it may eat up much of the money the primary winner would need to run an effective campaign in the general election.

The Democratic Party is famous for its internal disputes. But we can see just as much evidence of the effects of divisive primaries in the Republican Party, especially when candidates linked to the Christian Right challenge Republicans who are more moderate on social issues. Although the Christian Right candidates won many of these primaries in the 1990s, they were less likely than their more moderate rivals to go on to win the general election[21] (see the box on p. 174).

Problems in Holding Candidates Accountable

When candidates are chosen in primaries, rather than by party leaders, the party loses a powerful means of holding its candidates and officeholders accountable for their actions. In England, for example, if an elected official breaks with the party on an important issue, party

Monkeys and Prayers: A Split Primary in Alabama

Divisions between the Christian Right and the more business-oriented wing of the party are becoming increasingly evident in Republican primaries. One of the more colorful examples was the runoff after the 1998 Republican gubernatorial primary in Alabama, pitting incumbent Governor Forrest (Fob) James, an outspoken leader of the Christian Right, against a conservative Republican businessman, Winton Blount. James was a two-term Alabama governor; he had served once as a Democrat in the 1970s and the second time, beginning in 1994, as a Republican. He was well known for his forceful support of teacher-led prayer in the schools, the teaching of creation, and opposition to abortion and same-sex marriage. Blount placed his emphasis on economic development, rather than on social issues.

The race was gritty from the outset. Blount criticized James's colorful antics, which included mimicking a monkey to ridicule a school textbook on evolution. James responded by calling Blount a "fat monkey," and referring to himself as a "God-fearing redneck." James supporter Jerry Falwell, a leader of the Religious Right, contended that "virtually alone among the nation's governors, [James] has stood up and vowed that he will no longer allow liberal judges to deny school children the right to pray."

Alabama's open primary allowed a large number of Democrats to take part in the runoff between Republicans James and Blount. Their votes split, with many blacks supporting Blount and rural whites crossing party lines to vote for James. As often happens in a divisive primary, the bitterness between the two campaigns had an impact on the general election. The two candidates spent so much money in fighting one another that James had difficulty raising funds for his general election race against Democratic Lieutenant Governor Don Siegelman. After Blount's defeat, many big business people threw their support to the Democrat. In the end, as in many other contests, the Christian Right candidate was able to win the primary, but lost the general election to the Democratic candidate.

Sources: Thomas B. Edsall, "In Tuesday's Vote, Bright Spots for Both Parties," *Washington Post,* June 4, 1998, p. A10; Terry M. Neal, "In Alabama, a GOP Squabble," *Washington Post,* June 16, 1998, p. A1.

leaders can usually keep him or her from being renominated. But if the party can't control or prevent the renomination of a maverick officeholder—in the United States, primary voters may continue to vote for mavericks for any of a variety of reasons—then the party really has no way of enforcing loyalty. That, of course, is just what the Progressives had hoped. Thus:

- Primaries permit the nomination of candidates hostile to the party organization and leadership, opposed to the party's platform, or out of step with the public image that party leaders want to project.

- Primaries create the real possibility that the party's candidates in the general election will be an unbalanced ticket if primary voters select all or most of the candidates from a particular group or region.

- Primaries greatly increase campaign spending. The cost of a contested primary is almost always higher than that of a convention.

- Primaries extend political campaigns, already longer in the United States than in other democracies, to a length that can try many voters' patience.

THE PARTY ORGANIZATION FIGHTS BACK

Parties are clearly aware of the threats posed by primary elections, but they are just as aware that a direct attempt to abolish primaries would be futile. So party organizations have developed a range of strategies for trying to limit the damage primaries can cause. The success of these strategies varies; some local parties have neither the will nor the strength to try to affect primary election results, but others have been able to dominate the primaries effectively.

Persuading Candidates to Run (or Not to Run)

The surest way to control a primary is to make sure that the candidate the party favors has no opponent. Some party organizations try to mediate among prospective candidates, or coax an attractive but unwilling candidate to run. If they have a strong organization, they may be able to convince less-desirable candidates to stay out of the race by offering them a patronage position or a chance to run in the future. Alternatively, they may threaten to block a candidate's access to campaign money. It is difficult for a party organization to gain this level of control of nominations, though this is the norm in most of the world's other democracies.

Endorsing Candidates

A number of state parties go beyond this informal influence on candidate selection and offer some form of pre-primary endorsement to the candidates they prefer. In ten states, at least one of the parties holds a party convention, with the blessing of state law, to formally endorse candidates for state office. Usually, a candidate who gets a certain percentage of the convention's vote automatically gets his or her name on the primary ballot. In several of these states, however, candidates who are not endorsed by the party can still be listed on the primary ballot, if they file petitions that request it. In some other states, such as Illinois, Ohio, and Michigan, party leaders meet informally to endorse some candidates; and in California, such endorsements are made by a group of party activists called the California Democratic Council.

What influence do these endorsements have on the voters in primary elections? The record is mixed. Formal endorsements can often discourage other candidates from challenging the party's choice in the primary. Since 1980, however, when there has been competition in the primary the endorsed candidate has won only about half the time—a big drop from the success rate of endorsed candidates in the 1960s and 1970s.[22] In some states, legal requirements make the endorsement less valuable; the parties in Utah, for example, are required by state law to endorse two candidates for each office. And in other states, laws have been passed to prevent parties from endorsing candidates in advance of the primary.

When the parties are restricted to offering informal endorsements before the primary, their effectiveness is limited. These informal endorsements are not listed on the primary ballot. As a result, only the most politically attentive voters are likely to know that the party is supporting a particular candidate and they are the ones least in need of the guidance provided by an official party endorsement.[23]

Providing Tangible Support

If the party is not able to prevent a challenge to its preferred candidates, then it must fall back on more conventional approaches. It may urge party activists to help the favored candidates circulate their nominating petitions and leave the other candidates to their own devices (as John McCain learned in the 2000 New York primary). It may make party workers, money, and expertise available to the chosen candidates. It may publish ads announcing the party's endorsees, or print handy reference cards that forgetful voters can take right into the polling booth. On the day of the primary, the party organization may help to get the party's voters to the polls. This is more likely to happen in areas where the political culture is favorable to the party; in other areas, voter sensitivity to party intervention (or "bossism") may dictate that the candidates appear untouched by party hands.

Party efforts to influence primary elections vary from state to state and within states. It is probably safe to say that the most common nominating activity is the recruiting of candidates. Efforts to dissuade would-be nominees are less common. The parties' efforts are complicated by the fact that, in most parts of the country, parties are only one of a number of groups seeking out and supporting men and women to run for office. Local business, professional, farm, and labor groups, civic associations, ethnic, racial, and religious organizations, and other interest groups and officeholders may also be working to recruit candidates. The party organizations that seem best able to control candidate recruitment are generally the parties that also endorse and support candidates in the primary itself.

CANDIDATES AND VOTERS IN THE PRIMARIES

Two facts help make the primaries more manageable for the parties: often only one candidate files for each office in a primary, and the vast majority of voters do not vote in them. The party may be responsible for one or both of these situations; there may be no competition in a primary, for example, because of the party's skill in persuading and dissuading potential candidates. No matter why they occur, however, the result is that nomination politics can be more easily controlled by aggressive party organization.

Many Candidates Run Without Competition

In every part of the United States, large numbers of primary candidates win nominations without a contest. Probably the most important determinant of the competitiveness of a primary is the party's prospects for victory in the general election; candidates rarely fight for the right to face almost certain defeat. Primaries also tend to be less competitive when an incumbent is running, where parties have made pre-primary endorsements and where the state's rules make it harder to get on the ballot.[24]

The power of incumbency to discourage competition is another of the ironies of the primary. In an election where voters cannot rely on the party label to guide their choices, name recognition and media coverage are important influences. Incumbents, of course, are more likely to have these resources than are challengers. To dislodge an incumbent, a challenger will often need large amounts of campaign money, but few challengers can raise large campaign budgets. By weakening party control of nominations through the direct primary, then, Progressive reformers may have unintentionally made it harder to defeat incumbents.

... And Voters Are in Short Supply

If competition is scarce in the primaries, so are voters. One important fact about primaries is that most people don't vote in them. In a study of gubernatorial primaries from 1968 to 1998, the authors found that, even in competitive states, only half as many people voted in the primaries—in both parties—as in the general election.[25]

How can we explain such low turnout? One reason is that there is no competition in so many primary races. Turnout tends to be lower in the minority party's primary, in primaries held separately from the state's presidential primary, and in elections where independents and the other party's identifiers are not allowed to vote.[26] In addition, the fact that no one is elected in a primary probably depresses turnout; a race for the nomination lacks the drama inherent in a general election that is followed by victorious candidates taking office. (There are some notable exceptions, though; see "A Day in the Life.")

Because it is such a small sample of the eligible voters, the primary electorate is distinctive in several ways. Many primary voters are strong party identifiers and activists, which makes them more responsive to party endorsements and appeals on behalf of certain candidates. As would be expected, people who vote in primaries have higher levels of education and political interest. They are often assumed to hold more extreme ideological positions than those of other party voters. While early studies of Wisconsin's open primary found little support for that assumption, more recent research (coming largely from presidential primaries, which will be considered later) suggests that it is accurate.[27] Even if the ideological positions of primary voters turn out not to be distinctive, the intensity of their ideological commitment may be.

Primary voters often make unexpected choices. Because all the candidates come from the same party, partisan loyalties cannot guide the voters' choices. The primary campaign often gets little media coverage, the candidates are often not well known and the issues, if any, may be unclear. The presence of an incumbent in the race may be the only continuing, stabilizing element. Thus, the voter's choice in a primary is not as well structured or predictable as that in a general election. Many voting decisions are made right in the polling booth, where a famous name or a candidate's location on the ballot can make a difference. It is small wonder that parties are rarely confident about primary results, and public opinion pollsters prefer not to forecast them.

Southern primaries in earlier years were the one great exception to the rule that turnouts are low in primaries. From the end of Reconstruction to the years right after World War II, the South was overwhelmingly a one-party Democratic area. Winning the Democratic nomination was tantamount to winning the office itself. Therefore, candidate competition centered in the Democratic primary and turnout in primary elections was relatively high—often even higher than in the general elections.

As the Republican Party has become stronger and more competitive in the South, however, the Democratic primaries have lost their special standing. The general election has become more significant. The result is that participation has declined in primaries, even at a time when the mobilization of blacks into Democratic Party politics should have increased competition within the party. Republican primaries are attracting more voters now, because their candidates' prospects in the general election have greatly improved. But the GOP increase has not been large enough to compensate for the drop in Democratic turnout. So turnout in Southern primaries has become less and less distinctive.[28]

THE IMPACT OF THE DIRECT PRIMARY

Americans have had nearly a century of experience with the direct primary. On balance, how has it affected us? Has the primary democratized nominations by taking them out of the hands of party leaders and giving them to voters? Has it weakened the party organizations overall? In short, have the Progressives' hopes been realized?

More Than Just "The Lesbian Candidate for Congress"

Soon after finishing law school, Tammy Baldwin won a seat on the county board of supervisors. At age 30, she moved on to the Wisconsin state legislature, where she was the youngest woman and the first openly gay person to serve in that body. Six years later, when the Republican U. S. Representative in her district announced his intention to retire, she entered the Democratic primary to replace him.

It was a risky decision. The district's previous Democratic incumbent had endorsed another of the four candidates for the nomination. Even many Democrats considered Baldwin to be too liberal to win, though if elected, she would represent the city known by some as the People's Republic of Madison. But she was forthright about her background and orientation, arguing that, as a woman, she would take on issues that most congressmen would not. In particular, she called for tougher environmental regulations, publicly financed day care, and long-term care for the elderly.

Baldwin's sexual orientation was inevitably an undercurrent in the campaign. By 1998, there were gay members of Congress, but all had gone public about their homosexuality *after* having been first elected to the House. Tammy Baldwin didn't make an issue of her sexual orientation, but neither did she try to hide it. In fact, it offered one political advantage: she was able to raise a large campaign budget through her appeals to gay and women supporters. Anti-gay rhetoric was not common in the primary race, but stereotyping was; it took more than a month for her campaign manager to persuade newspapers to stop referring to the candidate as "Tammy Baldwin, the lesbian candidate for Congress."

Was she expecting to win? "Well, you know, throughout my political career," she says, "I've always been dealing with the skeptics and the cynics, who say, 'This isn't going to be our best candidate to win the primary.' And, you know, 'She's too progressive, she's too young, she's a woman, she's a lesbian.' … Hey, folks, this is a democracy, and in a democracy the cynics don't decide who's elected to office unless you let them—unless they're the only ones who vote. We decide. And that's a message that pervaded the entire campaign—stop listening to those people who say, 'you can't, you shouldn't, it won't work,' and start deciding that we can do it."[29] And she did; after narrowly winning the Democratic primary, Baldwin won the general election and went to Congress in 1999. She was reelected in 2000 by a narrow margin.

Has It Made Elections More Democratic?

It is clearly true that more people take part in primaries than take part in conventions or caucuses. In that sense, the process has been made more democratic. But the democratic promise of primaries is cut short by the number of unopposed candidates and the low levels of voter turnout. If voters are to have meaningful alternatives, then there must be more than one candidate for an office. And if the results are to be meaningful, people must go to the polls.

By its very nature, however, the primary tends to reduce participation. Would-be candidates are discouraged by the cost of an additional race, the difficulty of getting on the primary ballot, and the need to differentiate themselves from other candidates of the same party. The large number of primaries and the frequent lack of party cues reduce the quantity and quality of voter participation. If widespread competition for office and extensive public participation in the nominating process were goals of the primary's architects, then their hopes have not been realized.

Nor has the direct primary fully replaced party leaders in making nominations. Caucuses and conventions are still used, most visibly in presidential nominations, though they are more open than they used to be. And as we have seen, parties can influence the competition in primaries. If only 30 or 40 percent of registered voters go to the polls, then 15 or 20 percent will be enough to nominate a candidate. Parties count on the fact that a large part of that group will probably be party loyalists who care about the party leaders' recommendations. Thus strong party organizations—those able to muster the needed voters, money, activists, and organization—can still have a big influence on the results.

Even so, trying to influence primary elections is very costly and time-consuming, even for strong parties. The Jacksonian tradition of electing every public official from senator to surveyor means that party organizations need to deal with large numbers of contests. The time and expense forces many parties to be selective in trying to affect primaries. Parties sometimes stand aside, because picking a favorite in the primary might heat up old resentments or open new wounds. Of course, the biggest fear of party leaders is that if they support one candidate in a primary and the other candidate wins, as happened in two Democratic congressional races in 2000 (see p. 85 in Chapter 4), they could lose all influence over the winning officeholder.

In some ways, then, the primary has been a democratizing force. In competitive districts, especially when no incumbent is running, voters have the opportunity for choice envisioned by the reformers. In all districts, the primaries place real limits on the power of party leaders. Parties, even strong ones, can no longer whisk just any warm body through the nomination process. The primary gives dissenters a chance to take their case to the party's voters, so it offers them a potential veto over the party leaders' preferences (as "A Day in the Life" shows).

How Badly Has It Harmed the Parties?

On the other hand, is it possible to say that the direct primary has strengthened democracy in the United States if it weakens the political parties? From the risk of divisive primary races to the added campaign funding and voter mobilization they require, primaries strain party resources and create headaches for party leaders and activists. Although we've seen the methods used by some state party organizations to maintain some control over their primaries, by making pre-primary endorsements, or holding conventions to nominate some candidates, the bottom line is this: when a party organization cannot choose who will carry the party label into the general election, the party has been deprived of one of its key resources.

The direct primary has redistributed power within the parties. The Progressives' goal was to shift the power to nominate candidates from the party organization to the party in the electorate. But a funny thing happened along the way. Because candidates (especially incumbents) can win the party's nomination even when they defy the party organization, the idea of party "discipline" loses its credibility. Just as the direct primary undercuts the ability of the party organization to recruit candidates who share its goals and accept its discipline, it prevents the organization from disciplining partisans who already are in office. The primary, then, empowers the party's candidates and the party in government at the expense of the party organization. This sets the United States apart from many other democracies, in which the party organization has real power over the party in government.

Primaries also contribute to the decentralization of power in the American parties. As long as the candidates can appeal successfully to a majority of local primary voters, they are free from the control of a state or national party and its leaders. In all these ways, the direct primary has influenced more than the nominating process; it has helped to reshape the American parties.

Even beyond the parties, another unintended effect of the direct primary is the expanded political power of the media. Television has become an essential tool in most campaigns but especially in primary campaigns, where voters can't rely on the party label to guide their choice. That increases the cost of campaigns (see Chapter 12). It would be sad news for Progressive reformers if, in their effort to wrest control of elections from the party bosses, their real impact was to hand that control to an even more unresponsive group of bosses: media consultants and the special interests who fund political campaigns.[30] Surely the last thing these reformers wanted was to promote a system in which incumbents and wealthy special interests got an extra boost in elections.

Is the Primary Worth the Cost?

How party candidates should be nominated has been a controversial matter since political parties first appeared in the United States. It raises the fundamental question of what a political party is. Are parties only alliances of officeholders—the party in government? That seemed to be the prevailing definition in the early years, when public officials selected their prospective colleagues in party caucuses. Should the definition be expanded to include the party's activists and leaders? The change from a caucus to a convention system of nominations, where the party organization played its greatest role, reflects this change in the definition of party.

Or should we extend the idea of party well beyond the limits accepted by most other democracies to incorporate the party's supporters in the electorate? If so, which supporters should be included: only those willing to register formally as party loyalists, or anyone who wants to vote for a party candidate in a primary election? The answer has evolved over the years toward the most inclusive definition of party. Even though the Supreme Court insists that the parties' freedom of association is vital, the "party," especially in states with an open or blanket primary—and, in practice, in the semi-closed primary states—has become so permeable that its boundaries are hard to locate.

The implications of this choice and of the choice of a nominating system go well beyond an interesting debate. The Progressives used their definition of party and their preference for the direct primary as a weapon with which to wrest control of the party and, ultimately, the government from the party organization regulars, just as the Jacksonians used the convention system to gain control from the congressional party leaders. Because of the importance of nominations in the political process, those who control the nominations have great influence on the political agenda and, in turn, over who gets what in the political system. The stakes in this debate, as a result, are extremely high.

CHAPTER 10

Choosing the Presidential Nominees

The system Americans use to nominate a president is unique. It takes almost a year, costs hundreds of millions of dollars and differs from the way in which every other democratic nation chooses its executive. In fact, it differs from the process by which candidates for almost every other major office are selected in the United States. Understanding this process takes us a long way toward understanding the relationship between the parties and the presidency itself.

Presidential candidates are formally nominated by the parties' national conventions every four years. But the convention delegates simply ratify candidate choices that have actually been made weeks, or even months, before the convention's opening gavel, by voters in their states' delegate selection events. The great majority of states use primary elections—whose benefits and drawbacks we explored in the last chapter—for that purpose. (The process is shown in the box on p. 182.)

This heavy reliance on primaries can be traced to a Democratic Party upheaval in 1968. Prior to that time, the use of primary elections in presidential nominations had waxed and waned. After Wisconsin adopted the first presidential primary in 1905, other states quickly followed and within a decade a majority of states were using this method of nomination. But the movement soon faded. Advocates may have lost faith in the effectiveness of primaries; opponents probably worked hard to get rid of them and restore party leaders' control over nominations. By 1936, only 14 states were still using presidential primaries. That number had hardly changed by 1968.[1]

In that year, however, in the furor over the Democratic Party's presidential nomination, the primary movement was given new life. Reform rules led states to adopt presidential primaries. By the 1980s, a decisive majority of convention delegates were selected in primary elections. Even in states that retained the caucus-convention system, the rules were changed to increase participation greatly.

How a Presidential Candidate Is Nominated

Step 1: Voters cast a ballot in their states for the candidate they want their party to nominate for president. Most states hold primary elections for this purpose; a few use participatory caucuses and state conventions.
Timing: Between late January and early summer of each presidential election year.

Step 2: Delegates representing the chosen candidate(s) are sent by each state's party voters to that party's national convention.
Timing: By tradition, the party that does not currently hold the presidency has its convention first, usually in July; the other party's is held in August.

Step 3: The two major parties' conventions ratify the choice of presidential candidate made in the nominating season (Step 1) and the candidate's choice of a vice-presidential nominee, and adopt a party platform.

Step 4: The two major parties' candidates run against one another in the general election.
Timing: The first Tuesday after the first Monday in November.

WHAT SPARKED THE REFORMS?

For years, the state parties had the power to decide how they would choose their delegates to the national conventions that select the parties' presidential candidates. Party leaders dominated the process and often even picked the state's delegates. In most states, the selection was done through a series of party-controlled caucuses, or meetings, beginning at the local level and culminating in statewide party conventions. Even in many states that held primaries, voters could take part in only a "beauty contest" among presidential candidates; the delegates who went to the national convention to choose a presidential candidate were selected elsewhere. A fascinating story began to unfold in 1968, however, in which the national Democratic Party took control of the delegate selection process away from the state parties.

Turbulence in the Democratic Party

The 1968 Democratic convention was a riotous event. Struggling with the painful issues of civil rights and American involvement in the Vietnam War, the convention nominated the party leaders' choice, incumbent Vice President Hubert Humphrey, as the Democratic presidential candidate. Insurgent forces within the party protested that Humphrey's nomination betrayed the wishes of Democratic voters in the primaries. To try to make peace with their critics, the national party leaders agreed to change the methods by which convention delegates were selected.

A commission chaired by Senator George McGovern of South Dakota (and later by Representative Donald Fraser of Minnesota) recommended, and the Democratic National Committee and the next Democratic convention approved, major changes for the 1972 nominating process. One of the striking elements of this story is the remarkable ease with which Democratic Party leaders accepted rule changes that greatly reduced their influence on the awarding of the party's greatest prize, the presidential nomination.[2]

In trying to comply with the complicated new rules imposed by the national Democratic Party, many states substituted primary elections for their traditional caucus-convention systems.[3] The few caucuses that remained were bridled by strict party rules requiring delegates to be selected in timely, open and well-publicized meetings. Techniques formerly used by state party organizations to control the caucuses were outlawed. In the process, not only were the delegate selection rules radically changed, but also the principle was established that the national parties, rather than the states or the state parties, determine the rules of presidential nomination.[4]

Once the reform genie was let out of the bottle, it proved hard to contain. The Democrats tinkered with their presidential nomination process in advance of almost every election for the next 20 years. First, they used national party leverage to make the process more open and more representative of women, blacks, and young people. (The quotas that were first used to accomplish that goal produced bitter debate, however, and were eliminated.) Then, the Democrats "fine-tuned" the rules so that voter support for candidates was more faithfully represented in delegate counts; ever since 1992, candidates in primaries or caucuses who win at least 15 percent of the vote are guaranteed a share of the state's delegates proportional to their vote total. And to bring party leaders (and their "peer review" of candidates for the nomination) back into the process, many elected and party officials were guaranteed a vote at the convention as uncommitted "superdelegates."

The result has been a stunning transformation of the process by which the Democrats select their presidential nominees. Many state legislatures responded to the new Democratic requirements by changing state election laws for both parties. When states decided to run a primary for one party, for example, they typically did it for both. Thus the Republicans became the unwilling beneficiaries of the Democratic reforms. Republicans have preserved their tradition of giving state parties wide latitude in developing their own rules, however, which has kept the national party out of much of the rules debate. So even while being swept up in the movement toward primaries, state Republican parties have tended to stay away from proportional representation; instead, they have retained statewide winner-take-all primaries. Nor have the Republicans followed the Democrats' lead in formally reserving delegate seats for party and public officials or developing affirmative action programs for women or minorities.

Presidential Primaries Today

Presidential primaries are now used in more than four fifths of the states, including most of the largest. The proportion of delegates selected in primaries has reached a high plateau in the Republican Party and continues to climb for the Democrats (see Table 10.1). Because the decision to use primaries or caucuses is made by states and state parties, though, these numbers fluctuate from one presidential election to the next.

In the primaries, the popular vote determines how the state's delegates are apportioned among the presidential candidates. In earlier years, primary voters in some states were permitted to select only the convention delegates themselves, without any assurance as to which presidential candidates these delegates supported. Now, however, the

TABLE 10.1 The Growing Number of Presidential Primaries: 1968–2000

	Democrats		Republicans	
Year	No. of states	Percent of delegate votes	No. of states	Percent of delegate votes
1968	17	41	16	43
1972	23	65	22	56
1976	29	75	28	67
1980	30	71	33	75
1984	24	54	28	63
1988	33	67	34	72
1992	35	67	38	79
1996	34	62	41	81
2000	38	64	42	83

Note: Includes all 50 states plus Washington, D.C., but not the territories (American Samoa, Guam, Puerto Rico, Virgin Islands) or Democrats Abroad. Includes only primaries used to select and/or bind delegates (i.e., not primaries that were purely advisory). Delegate percentages include Democratic superdelegates.

Source: Michael G. Hagen and William G. Mayer, "The Modern Politics of Presidential Selection," in William G. Mayer, ed., *In Pursuit of the White House 2000* (New York: Chatham House, 2000), pp. 11 and 43–44. Figures for 2000 were kindly provided by Mayer.

names of the presidential candidates normally appear on the ballots, and the candidates, or their agents, usually select the members of their own delegate slates. This all but guarantees that the popular vote for candidates will be faithfully translated into delegates committed to the respective candidates at the national convention, even though there are no laws requiring delegates to support the popular vote winner in their state.[5]

Most party leaders prefer some form of closed primary (see Chapter 9). Democratic Party reform commissions have tried several times to ban open primaries, which allow non-Democrats to have a voice in the selection of party candidates. The open primary has survived these assaults, however. After a long struggle, the national party allowed Wisconsin to return to its cherished open primary in 1988 and the other states that hold open primaries need no longer fear a veto by the national party.[6]

In fact, in the 2000 nominating season, even the closed primaries did not look very closed. In the rush to move their presidential primaries to the early weeks of the nominating season, as we will see later, several states separated their presidential primary from the rest of their primary elections. This helped state parties protect their favorites for lower-level offices from the crossover voters attracted by presidential contests. In the most notable case, California held two simultaneous primaries in 2000: a unified ballot for president, in which any voter could select a candidate of any party, and a separate closed primary, in which, for example, only self-identified Republicans' votes would be counted to elect Republican presidential convention delegates and candidates for other offices.

Some Party Caucuses Remain

States that have not adopted presidential primaries use a longer process that begins with precinct caucuses. These are very different experiences than primaries for their participants;

they involve face-to-face debate among voters who gather in local schools and other public buildings, often for several hours. Their purpose is to choose delegates to higher-level caucuses, typically at the county, congressional district, and, then, the state level. It is only at the state-level conventions where the final delegate slate for the national convention is determined. The much-publicized Iowa caucuses, for example, began with precinct meetings in January 2000 at which front-runners George W. Bush and Al Gore were heralded the winners, even though Iowa's national convention delegates were not chosen until the state conventions in June.[7]

The selection of delegates in the caucus states attracted little media coverage until 1976, when a virtually unknown Democratic governor, Jimmy Carter, made himself a serious presidential candidate by campaigning intensively in Iowa and winning an unexpected number of delegates. When caucuses do not get much media attention, party leaders have an easier time controlling their outcomes. But when a state's caucuses attract controversy, the party leaders' influence fades. A classic case occurred in 1986, when Michigan GOP leaders scheduled their precinct caucuses two years before the 1988 state convention, in order to boost the influence of their brand of moderate Republicanism in national nomination politics. Their efforts backfired when supporters of Pat Robertson, a leader of the Christian Right, flooded the local caucuses and threw the state's nomination process into turmoil for the next two years.

THE RACE TO WIN DELEGATE VOTES

To a presidential candidate, the marathon of primaries and caucuses is do-or-die; no recent presidential candidate who did poorly in the nominating season has been resurrected by his party's national convention. Every presidential nomination in both parties since 1956 has been won on the convention's first ballot, and since 1968, that first-ballot nominee has always been the winner of the most delegates in the primaries and caucuses. How does a candidate get to that coveted spot?

Candidates' Strategic Choices

It takes years to prepare for a presidential race. Almost all serious candidates enter the contest at least a year before the presidential election and begin raising money much earlier than that. They must make endless strategic choices as to which states to contest and how much effort and money to put into each one. Even when these hard choices are made, they will probably need to be reconsidered many times; "conventional wisdom" in a presidential race can change from week to week.

The most important factor to be weighed in making these choices is the nature of the opposition. Front-runners, for example, normally need to demonstrate overwhelming support in the early delegate selection events. Otherwise, their supporters' and contributors' confidence may be so badly undermined that their hopes for the nomination vanish. George W. Bush entered the nomination season in January 2000 with more campaign money than any other candidate in American political history—$67 million—and the widespread expectation that he would coast to the Republican nomination. After he lost the very first primary in New Hampshire to Senator John McCain, his advisers were forced to rethink his approach. In turn, McCain's success after New Hampshire shows how a candidate with less initial support can improve his or her chances for the nomination, simply by exceeding expectations in an early and heavily reported contest.

Money and organization are critical to a candidate's chances. A very few presidential candidates—Bush is the most notable example—have been able to raise enough money to resist the lure of federal matching funds for their campaigns (see Chapter 12). The others must follow the rules that can give them access to those matching funds. First, they must build nationwide campaign organizations in order to qualify for the federal money and then they must decide how to allocate their funds and personnel. Public funding will not cover (or permit) full-blown campaigns in every state. The early primaries and caucuses necessarily attract the greatest candidate spending, but candidates must then set priorities; legal restrictions on the federal funds prevent candidates from raising money quickly from a few sources, as they were used to doing in the years before the reforms.

All these decisions must take into account the rules of the process as set down by the parties and the states. A candidate who expects to do especially well among independents will need to concentrate resources in states with open primaries, in which independents and other partisans can vote, as John McCain did in 2000 (see box below). These rules of the game differ from party to party. Because Democrats require a "fair reflection" of candidate strength in the selection of delegates, a candidate with significant support will not be shut out in any state. The Republican Party permits winner-take-all primaries, however, and many state Republican Parties hold them, so it is still possible for a Republican candidate to win 49 percent of the votes in a state and come away without a single delegate.[8]

A Tale of Two Primaries

In politics, as in everything else, the rules affect the results. Consider the rules that governed primary elections in the race for the 2000 Republican presidential nomination. Michigan's Republican contest is an *open primary*, in which voters do not have to declare a party affiliation to take a Republican ballot. In fact, in an exit poll conducted by Voter News Service, only 47 percent of the voters in the Republican primary were Republicans! Texas Governor George W. Bush got the votes of Republicans by a margin of more than two to one, but Arizona Senator John McCain received enough independent and Democratic votes to win the primary.

New York held a *closed primary* two weeks later. There, 72 percent of the Republican primary voters were Republicans, according to the exit poll, and almost all of the others called themselves independents. Eighty-four percent of the Bush voters said they were Republicans; 34 percent of the McCain voters were independents. Bush won the primary and clinched the nomination that day.

Source: R. W. Apple, Jr., "On a Rocky Road, the Race Tightens," *New York Times*, Feb. 23, 2000, p. A1 (on Michigan), and *http://www.nytimes.com/library/pol* (on New York; accessed Feb. 24, 2000).

Win Early or Die

The strongest imperative is the need to win early. Victories early in the nominating process create momentum; they bring the resources and support that make later victories more likely. Early successes attract more media coverage for the candidate and, in turn, more name recognition among voters. The candidate looks more and more credible, so it is easier to raise money. The other candidates in the race fall further and further behind.

In fact, the earliest wins take place even before the first delegates are selected. Journalists want to get the scoop on who will eventually win the nomination and they start making guesses long before the first primary and caucus are held. Their main indicator of a likely winner is the candidates' fund-raising success in the year before the election. In this so-called "money primary," as one researcher suggests, many analysts "are ready to proclaim the race over—before a single vote is cast."[9] The "money primary" gives the advantage to candidates who have built a big campaign organization and stockpiled a lot of campaign money at a time when the coming presidential race is not yet even on the radar screen for most Americans.[10] So the list of prospective candidates has already been pared down by the time that Iowa and New Hampshire voters choose their convention delegates.

Then, once these first delegate selection events have taken place, the contest for the nomination tends to wrap up very quickly. The nomination process has become highly "front-loaded." A number of states have moved their primaries forward to the first weeks after New Hampshire and Iowa to benefit from the attention attracted to these early delegate selection events, not to mention the campaign spending that comes with it. The stampede among states to occupy an early position in the 2000 election calendar was so intense that both the Democratic and Republican nominations were wrapped up in the first six weeks of a five-month nominating season. Between late January and March 14, 34 states held their primaries or caucuses in at least one party, including California, Florida, New York, and Texas; and 75 percent of the delegates had been selected by the end of March (see box on p. 188).[11] And in 2004, as a result of a rules change by the Democrats, the nominating calendar will be even more front-loaded.

What Is the Party's Role?

The party organizations have interests at stake in the selection of delegates, but not necessarily the same interests as those of the aspiring presidential candidates. State and local parties want a nominee who will be best able to bring voters to the polls to support the party's candidates for state and local offices; a weak presidential candidate may hurt their chances. Party leaders also generally prefer early agreement on a presidential candidate; a hotly contested race often heightens conflict within local and state parties, which can weaken the party effort in the general election.[12]

Historically, the state parties protected their interests by selecting delegates uncommitted to any candidate and then casting the state's delegate votes as a bloc for a particular nominee or platform plank. The impact of swinging a bloc of delegates to one side or another could be dramatic and increased the state party's influence at the convention. But the current nominating system prevents the state parties from engineering an uncommitted delegation. In most primary states, it is the candidates who set up their delegate

Front-Loading the Nomination Process

Before Californians were able to express their preferences in the 1996 presidential primaries, the race for the parties' nominations was effectively over. Why were the voters in the nation's biggest state not consulted? Because their primary was held in late March, and by the end of March, primaries had already been held in states containing almost two-thirds of the parties' national convention delegates.

Front-loading was even more prominent in 2000. By the end of March 7—a day on which an avalanche of 16 states held primaries or caucuses—almost 40 percent of the Democratic convention delegates and 45 percent of the Republicans had been selected. (One of those March 7 primaries was California's, which had determined not to be left behind again.) The Democratic and Republican nominees had been effectively decided—Al Gore and George W. Bush, respectively—and it was a full eight months until the general election.

This front-loading of the calendar has had important implications for the nomination process; for one, it increased the importance of early money. That meant candidates had to start raising serious money even earlier than in past years. Bush, for example, had raised $67 million before the first caucuses were held and spent all but about $20 million of it by the end of February 2000. There was not enough time for a long-shot candidate to get enough bounce from an early primary or caucus, to raise the money needed to compete in California or New York. In such a foreshortened nomination season, the cost of strategic miscalculations, such as John McCain's attacks on Christian conservative leaders, could be extremely high. This "rush to judgment," as two political scientists call it, makes the nominating system "less deliberative, less rational, less flexible and more chaotic."[13]

slates, so the delegates' first loyalty is to the candidate. In caucus states, delegates committed to a candidate simply have greater appeal to caucus participants than do uncommitted delegates. And because of the front-loading of the nomination events, for delegates to remain uncommitted while one candidate is locking up a majority of convention votes would be to lose all influence over the nomination.

Party leaders, then, have a harder time protecting the party's interests in a nominating process that is dominated by the candidates and their supporters. The Republicans have tried to respond by preserving winner-take-all rules in state primaries and other practices of the pre-reform era. The Democrats followed a different path, deciding in 1984 to set aside delegate seats at the national convention for elected and party officials. These so-called *superdelegates*—all Democratic governors and members of Congress, current and former presidents and vice presidents, and all members of the Democratic National Committee—were meant to be a large, uncommitted bloc totaling almost 20 percent of all delegates, with the party's interests in mind. But because the nomination race has concluded so quickly in recent years, the superdelegates have not been able to play an independent role in the nominating process.[14]

VOTERS' CHOICES IN PRESIDENTIAL NOMINATIONS

The move to primaries has greatly increased citizen participation in the process of nominating a president. What determines the level of voter participation and what guides the voters' choices in these contests?

Who Votes?

Turnout varies a great deal from state to state and across different years in any one state.[15] The first caucuses (Iowa) and the first primary (New Hampshire) usually bring out a relatively large number of voters because of the media attention to those early contests. More generally, turnout tends to be higher in states with a better-educated citizenry, higher percentages of registered voters and a tradition of two-party competition—the same states that enjoy higher general election turnout. The nature of the contest matters too. Voters are most likely to participate in early races that are closely fought, where the candidates spend more money and the excitement is high, all of which increase voter interest in the election.[16]

Are Primary Voters Typical?

Yet turnout is lower in primary than in general elections. Are the people who turn out to vote in the primaries—and who therefore choose the nominees for the rest of the public—typical of other citizens? Critics of the reforms have charged that they are not and, thus, that candidates are now being selected by an unrepresentative group of citizens.

We can explore this question in several ways. When we compare primary voters with nonvoters, we find that those who vote in primaries are, in fact, better educated, wealthier, and older—but then, so are general election voters. A more appropriate comparison is with party identifiers, because primaries are the means by which the party electorate chooses its nominees. Using this comparison, few important differences appear. There is still a tendency for voters in primaries to be slightly older, better educated, more affluent, better integrated into their communities, and less likely to be black or Hispanic. But their positions on key policy issues are similar to those of other party identifiers.[17] So there is not much support for the argument that primary voters are less representative of the party than are other groups of voters.

Do Voters Make Informed Choices?

Another criticism of the primaries is that voters do not make very well-informed decisions. Compared with voters in the general election, primary voters have been found to pay less attention to the campaign and to have less knowledge about the candidates. Especially in the early contests, voters are influenced by candidate momentum, as bandwagons form for candidates who have won by a large margin, or even just exceeded reporters' expectations. Candidates' personal characteristics influence voters in the primaries, but issues often have only minor impact. The result, so this argument goes, is a series of contests decided mainly on the basis of short-run, superficial considerations.[18]

Most analysts think that this indictment of the primaries goes too far. They feel that voters respond with some rationality to the challenge of having to choose among several candidates in a short campaign without the powerful guidance provided by party labels. Primary voters make decisions based on candidates' chances of winning, personal and demographic characteristics, and whatever inferences can be drawn about their policy positions.[19]

Is it rational for voters to be drawn to a presidential candidate who is gathering momentum in the primaries? Some would say yes—that party voters don't always see many big differences among their party's candidates and just want to pick the candidate who has the best chance of winning the nomination and the presidency. Momentum seems to make a difference especially when voters are being asked to sort through a pack of candidates they know little about,[20] and when there is no well-known front-runner.[21] Even then, the candidates who move to the head of the pack are usually subjected to more searching evaluations, which give voters more reasons to support or oppose them. Momentum is probably least influential in the campaigns of incumbent presidents and vice presidents; because they are better known, their candidacies are less likely to be affected by the ups and downs of the polls, unless their chances of winning drop substantially.

In short, even though primary voters often base their decisions on less information than do general election voters, their choices are not necessarily irrational. In contests that pit a party's candidates against one another, issue differences among candidates are likely to be minor. It should not be surprising, then, that other factors, including candidates' characteristics and issue priorities, as opposed to issue positions, would become important. The basis for voters' decisions in primaries may not differ very much from those in caucuses or general elections.[22] Besides, the questions raised about the quality of voter decision making in primaries could be raised just as easily about the judgment of the party leaders who selected candidates under the earlier caucus-convention system.

SUMMING UP: PRIMARY VERSUS PARTY SELECTION

Both the current primary-dominated system and the earlier caucus-convention system have attractive and unattractive qualities. Talented and engaging candidates have been nominated by both, and so have less distinguished candidates. The earlier nominating system, not surprisingly, favored mainstream candidates, those who were more acceptable to the party's leaders and its activists, including some candidates who had earned their nomination through party loyalty, rather than through either their personal appeal or their skills at governing. Primaries are more likely to advantage candidates whose names are well-known to the public and those who have the support of issue activists and ideological extremists.[23]

One clear result of the reforms is that the politics of choosing delegates has become more open and more similar in all states, whether they use primaries or caucuses and conventions. As the media coverage of nominations has become national in scope and the delegate selection is more open, candidates are forced to run more nationalized campaigns. The consequence is a more homogeneous nomination politics. The campaign ad run by a candidate in New York may well be reported to television viewers in South Dakota; it is harder for candidates to tailor their appeals to specific local areas. The quiet agreements that were once made to swing an uncommitted delegation are no longer functional; they have been replaced by the public promises designed to sway voters in a primary.

Because of this very openness, a primary's results confer a lot of legitimacy on the winning candidates. Primary victories may be just as important to candidates for their symbolic value, then, as for the delegates they award. Primaries give candidates a chance to demonstrate their public support, raise more campaign money, and demonstrate their stamina and resilience, to a greater extent than they could in the older party-dominated system. Candidates' performance in the primary contests may not be a good indicator of their likely competence in the White House, but they do give voters at least some measure of the candidates' (and their advisers') ability to cope gracefully under pressure.

ON TO THE NATIONAL CONVENTIONS

Once the states have chosen their delegates through primaries and caucuses, the Democrats and Republicans assemble as national parties in conventions. These mass meetings bring together the party organization and activists, and the party in government. But the traditional purpose of the convention—to select the party's presidential nominee—has already been accomplished in those primaries and caucuses. Aside from formally approving the candidates who have won the most delegates, what is left for the convention to do?

Roots of the Conventions

The national party convention is a venerable institution, but it began as a power grab. In 1832, the nomination of Andrew Jackson as the Democratic-Republican candidate for president was a foregone conclusion. But state political leaders wanted to keep Henry Clay, the favorite of the congressional caucus, from being nominated as vice-president; they preferred Martin Van Buren. So these leaders pushed for a national convention to make the nominations. In doing so, they wrested control of the presidential selection process from congressional leaders. By the time the Republican Party emerged in 1854, the convention had become the accepted means through which a major party's candidates for president and vice-president were selected.[24] The GOP held its first convention in 1856. Ever since then, the two major parties have held national conventions every four years.[25]

What Conventions Do

The conventions are creatures of the parties themselves. They are subject to no congressional or state regulation and even the federal courts have been reluctant to intervene in their operation. Responsibility for them falls to the national party committees and their staffs, although an incumbent president strongly influences the planning for his (or, someday, her) party's convention.

Months before the convention, its major committees begin their work (see box on p. 192). What these committees decide can be overruled by the convention itself, which acts as the ultimate arbiter of its own structure and procedures. Some of the most famous battles on the floor of the convention have involved disputes over committee recommendations. The convention warms up with the keynote address by a party "star," tries to maintain momentum and suspense as it considers the platform, and reaches a dramatic peak in the nomination of the presidential and vice-presidential candidates. This general format has remained basically the same for decades.

Key Committees of the National Party Conventions

The national conventions have four important committees:

Credentials deals with the qualifications of delegates and alternates. In earlier years, fierce battles sometimes took place over the seating of delegations—for example, in the 1964 Democratic convention, when the all-white Mississippi delegation was challenged as being unrepresentative of Mississippi Democrats. Now, the state procedures are regularized, so this committee is no longer as crucial.

Permanent Organization selects the officials of the convention, including the chair, secretary, and sergeant at arms.

Rules sets the rules of the convention, including the length and number of nomination speeches. Disputes can occur over procedures for future conventions.

Platform (or Resolutions) drafts the party's platform for action by the convention. Because internal party battles focus increasingly on issues, this committee takes on special importance.

Approving the Platform   In addition to nominating candidates, the convention's main job is to approve the party's ***platform***—its statement of party positions on a wide range of issues. The platform committees begin public hearings long before the convention opens, so that a draft can be ready for the convention. The finished platform is then presented to the convention for its approval. That approval is not always forthcoming; platforms have caused some spirited convention battles because many of the delegates care deeply about this single statement of the party's beliefs. In 1980, Democrats held a 17-hour debate over economic policy that was the last gasp of Senator Ted Kennedy's ill-fated challenge to President Carter. In more recent conventions, struggles over the abortion issue have taken place or have threatened to disrupt convention goodwill.[26]

Party platforms are like foreign films: referred to, but rarely seen. Even party leaders often ignore them; Republican Senate Majority Leader Robert Dole admitted during his 1996 presidential campaign that he had not read his party's platform. Rather than a statement of continuing party philosophy, the platform is actually an expression of the policy preferences of majorities that can be assembled around each of its planks. The platform is also a campaign document intended to position the party favorably for the general election in the fall.

Even though platforms are an attempt to satisfy various party constituencies, they do define the major differences between the parties. In recent years, the Democratic and Republican platforms have disagreed on a number of issues, most notably abortion, taxes, collective bargaining rights, gun control, racial policy, deficit spending, and American involvement in the world (see Chapter 15). The party platform is important, its leading scholar says, "because it summarizes, crystallizes, and presents to the voters the character of the party coalition."[27] Yet platforms are also shaped by the fact that they are drafted and approved in conventions, whose main goal is to pick a presidential candidate. Because the party's presidential nominee generally controls the convention, the platform has usually been a reflection of his views—or at least of the bargains he has been willing to strike for other gains or to preserve party harmony.[28]

Formalizing the Presidential Nomination   The vote on the party's nominee for president begins with nominations made by delegates, shorter seconding speeches and brief but passionate demonstrations by the candidate's supporters. These events are sedate compared with the rambunctious conventions of earlier years. The presence of media coverage encourages party leaders to aim for a carefully crafted picture of the party's strength and vision; this tends to deprive conventions of much of the sense of carnival and drama that were central to their tradition.

Once the nominee (or, in rare cases, the nominees) has been presented, the secretary calls the roll of the states (and other voting units), asking each delegation to report its vote. The result in recent times has taken only one ballot—far from the days when, in 1924, the Democrats plodded through 103 ballots in sultry New York's Madison Square Garden, before John W. Davis won the majority needed for the nomination. Yet a convention that requires more than one ballot to choose the presidential nominee is still a possibility—perhaps especially for the Democrats because of their use of proportional representation in the primaries and caucuses.

In the past, when a convention had more than one candidate for the nomination and the first ballot did not produce a majority, intense negotiations would follow. The leading candidates would need to protect their image as likely winners by keeping other candidates from chipping away their supporters and by negotiating for the votes of delegates who had come committed to minor candidates. It is hard to imagine how these negotiations could work in conventions today; because the delegates are tied to candidates rather than to state party leaders, who could play the traditional role of broker? The leading candidates might choose to negotiate among themselves for the nomination. Another possibility is that the uncommitted superdelegates would broker a majority for one candidate.[29]

Approving the Vice-Presidential Nominee   The day after the presidential nominee is chosen, the secretary calls the roll again to select the vice-presidential candidate. This process, too, is ceremonial; presidential nominees almost always choose their own running mates and conventions routinely ratify their choice.[30] This method of selecting vice-presidential candidates has drawn criticism—not so much because they are hand-picked by the presidential nominee as because the decision is often made by a tired candidate and then sprung, at the last minute, on convention delegates. George H. W. Bush's nomination of Indiana Senator Dan Quayle in 1988 was attacked on these grounds. But without any viable procedure to replace it, this choice and the responsibility for a poor selection will remain in the hands of the party's presidential nominee.

Launching the Presidential Campaign   The final business of the conventions is to present their party's presidential choice to the American voters. The nominating speeches and the candidates' own acceptance speeches are the opening shots of the fall campaign. Most nominees generally get a boost in public support (a "convention bounce") from this campaign kickoff. For the candidates at least, then, the most important role of the convention is as a campaign event.

WHO ARE THE DELEGATES?

Convention delegates are among the most visible of the party's activists. They help to shape the public's image of the two parties. Who the delegates are says a great deal about what the parties are.

Apportioning Delegate Slots among the States

It is the parties that determine how many delegates each state can send to the convention. The two parties make these choices differently. The Republicans allocate delegates more equally among the states; the Democrats weigh more heavily the size of the state's population and its record of support for Democratic candidates.

These formulas affect the voting strength of various groups within the party coalitions. The GOP's decision to represent the small states more equally with the large states has advantaged its conservative wing. In contrast, by giving relatively more weight to the larger states with stronger Democratic voting traditions, the Democrats have favored the more liberal interests in their party. Even if these delegate allocation formulas have only marginal effects on the balance of forces within the parties, many nominations have been won—and lost—at the margin.

How Representative Are the Delegates?

The delegates to the Democratic and Republican conventions have never been a cross section of American citizens, or even of their party's rank and file. Whites, males, the well educated, and the affluent have traditionally been overrepresented in conventions. Reflecting their different coalitional bases, since the 1930s, Democratic delegations have had more trade unionists and African-Americans, and Republican conventions have drawn more Protestants and business entrepreneurs.

Demographics   Since the nomination reforms, the delegates of both parties, but especially the Democrats, have become more representative of other citizens, in some ways. The Democrats used affirmative action plans after 1968 to increase the presence of women, blacks, and for a brief time, young people; since 1980, they have required that half the delegates be women. The percentage of female delegates at Republican conventions has gone up somewhat during this period, as well, but without party mandates. The Democratic National Committee has urged its state organizations to recruit more low- and moderate-income delegates, but the low political involvement levels of these groups and the high price of attending a convention stand in the way. So conventions remain meetings of the affluent and well educated (see Table 10.2).[31]

Political Experience   We might assume that delegates would be recidivists, making return appearances at convention after convention. But that was not the case even before the 1970s reforms; even then, a comfortable majority of delegates at each convention were first-timers. With the move to primaries, the percentage of newcomers jumped to about 80 percent before declining. The decline became more marked when the Democrats granted convention seats to politically experienced superdelegates.

Even if many delegates are new to conventions, however, the great majority are long-time party activists. In 2000, for example, most of a random sample of convention

TABLE 10.2 How Representative Were the 2000 Democratic and Republican Convention Delegates?

	Dem. Delegates	Dem. Voters	All Voters	Rep. Voters	Rep. Delegates
Gender					
Female	48%	57%	54%	52%	35%
Race					
Black	19%	17%	10%	2%	4%
White	64	74	81	90	85
Hispanic	12	6	**	**	6
Education					
HS graduate or less	6%	50%	46%	40%	4
Some college	19	27	28	29	19
College grad	25	14	16	18	31
Postgraduate	49	10	11	11	46
Household Income					
Under $25,000	3%	35%*	29%*	21%*	2%
Over $75,000	57	15	19	25	57
Religion					
Protestant	47%	48%	53%	63%	63%
Evangelical or Born-again[†]	12	24	**	37	27
Catholic	30	28	25	19	27
Jewish	8	2	1	0	2

* under $30,000   ** data not available   [†] asked in a separate question, so percentages for "religion" do not add up to 100 percent.

Source: Data on convention delegates were collected by the CBS News/*New York Times* poll during June, July, and August 2000. Voter data are from a CBS News poll conducted from July 13–17, 2000. The nationwide sample of 954 adults, interviewed by phone, included 728 registered voters. Data were kindly provided by Kathleen Frankovic and Jinghua Zou of CBS News.

delegates reported that they had been party activists for at least 20 years, and a majority said they currently hold party office.[32] In spite of the high turnover, then, these national party meetings still bring together the activists of the state and local party organizations and the leaders of the party in government.

Issues and Ideology   Another way in which convention delegates differ from the average party voter is that the delegates are much more involved in politics, more aware of issues, and more ideologically extreme. Democratic delegates are more liberal than Democratic voters and much more liberal than the average voter; Republican delegates tend to be further to the right than either their party voters or voters generally. The distance between delegates and their party's voters varies from issue to issue. As Table 10.3 shows, Democratic delegates in 2000 came closest to the views of Democratic voters (and all voters) on the issues of environmental protection and trigger locks on handguns, but were at least about 20 points more liberal on a number of other big issues. Republican delegates were most similar to Republican voters, as well as all voters, in

TABLE 10.3 Views on Issues: Comparing Delegates and Voters in 2000

	Dem. Delegates	Dem. Voters	All Voters	Rep. Voters	Rep. Delegates
Government should do more to solve national problems	73%	44%	33%	21%	4%
Abortion should be permitted in all cases	63	34	26	16	10
Death penalty for murder	20	46	51	55	60
Require gun manufacturers to put child safety locks on handguns	94	91	84	76	48
Favor affirmative action to remedy past discrimination	83	59	51	44	29
Medicare should cover prescription drugs for the elderly	58	39	37	36	34
Must protect the environment even if jobs in your community are lost	63	72	64	57	32
Tax-funded vouchers to help parents pay tuition for private/ religious schools	10	41	47	53	71
Individuals should be allowed to invest a portion of their Social Security taxes on their own	23	44	53	61	89

Note: Figures are the percentage of each group who agreed with the statement.

Source: Same as in Table 10.2.

their support for the death penalty and opposition to abortion and prescription drug coverage under Medicare, but scored well to the right on other questions.

The degree to which delegates hold more extreme views than party voters bears on a long-standing debate about the nominating process. Democrats who promoted the 1970s reforms were motivated, in part, by the argument that the old caucus-convention system, dominated by party leaders, did not represent the views of grass-roots party supporters. In turn, the critics of the reforms contend that the delegates selected under the new rules are even more out of step ideologically with party voters and the electorate in general.

The reality is that the reforms have not made the conventions more representative of the views of party identifiers. Prior to 1972, it was the Republican conventions whose delegates appeared to be more ideologically out of step with party voters, and even more compared with the general voting public.[33] The Democratic reforms first seemed to reverse that pattern. Democratic delegates in 1972 were more ideologically distant from their party identifiers than Republican delegates were and even farther away from the public, and some charged that the reforms were at fault.[34] But these disparities on issues seem to have been reduced in later Democratic conventions, especially after the introduction of superdelegates.[35]

The real effect of the reforms has been to link the selection of delegates more closely to candidate preferences. As a result, when an ideologically committed candidate does well in the primaries and caucuses, more ideologically oriented activists become convention delegates. At those times, conventions may be less representative of the party in the electorate. However, they may offer clearer choices to voters.

Amateurs or Professionals?   The reforms were also expected to result in delegates with a different approach to politics. Using the terms described in Chapter 5, some convention delegates can be described as amateurs, others as professionals. Amateurs are more attracted by issues, more insistent on internal party democracy, less willing to compromise and less committed to the prime importance of winning elections. Professionals, in contrast, are more likely to have a long-term commitment to the party and to be more willing to compromise on issues in the interest of winning the general election.

There is some evidence that the Democratic Party's reforms had, as intended, reduced the presence of party professionals between the 1968 and the 1972 conventions.[36] As we have seen, however, the party later moved to reverse this trend, particularly by adding superdelegates. Research shows that even after the reforms, delegates have remained strongly committed to the parties and their goals.[37] It may be that for both professionals and amateurs, involvement in this highly public party pageant strengthens delegates' commitment to the party's aims.

Who Controls the Delegates?   It would not matter how representative delegates are if they act as pawns of powerful party leaders. In fact, for most of the history of party conventions, that is exactly how the state delegations behaved. Top state party leaders and some big-city mayors had a commanding presence, especially at Democratic conventions.

Now, however, strong party leaders no longer control the convention by dominating their state delegations. When the Democrats eliminated their long-standing unit rule in 1968, through which a majority of a state delegation could throw all of the delegation's votes to one candidate, they removed a powerful instrument of leadership control. In addition, by opening up the delegate selection process after 1968, both parties also made it difficult for elected leaders to claim delegate seats without committing early to a presidential candidate, which they were reluctant to do. Democratic elected leaders were much less likely to become convention delegates after 1968, until they gained delegate slots as superdelegates beginning in 1984.

Perhaps the most powerful force preventing state party leaders from controlling the conventions is the fact that so many delegates in both parties now come to the conventions already committed to a candidate. That makes them unavailable for "delivery" by party leaders. If anyone controls the modern conventions, then, it is the party's prospective nominee for president, not leaders of the state parties.

THE CHANGING ROLE OF MEDIA COVERAGE

In addition to all these changes in the convention's power centers and delegates, media coverage of conventions has changed significantly. On one hand, conventions have been reshaped and rescheduled to meet the media's needs. The result, as Byron Shafer puts it, is a "bifurcated politics" in which the convention is one thing to delegates in the meeting hall and quite another to the millions catching a glimpse of it on television.[38] On the other, ironically, media attention to the conventions has declined sharply in recent years.

Beginning with the first televised national party conventions in 1948,[39] TV journalists and politicians found ways to serve one another's needs. In the early days of television before the convenience of videotape, networks were desperate for content with which to fill broadcast time. So they covered the party conventions live, from gavel to gavel. For television news, the convention became a major story, like a natural disaster or the Olympics, through which it could demonstrate its skill and provide a public service. Reporters swarmed through the convention halls, covering the strategic moves of major candidates, the actions of powerful figures in the party and the complaints of individual delegates. Even the formerly secret work of the platform committee came to be done in the public eye.

For the party leaders, television coverage offered a priceless opportunity to reach voters and to launch the presidential campaign with maximum impact. So they reshaped the convention into a performance intended as much for the national television audience as for the delegates. Party officials gave key speaking roles to telegenic candidates, speeded up the proceedings and moved the most dramatic convention business into prime-time hours. More and more, the aim of the convention shifted from the conduct of party business to the wooing of voters.

These two sets of goals, however—the networks' interest in a good story and the parties' interest in attracting supporters—steadily began to conflict. Once the nomination reforms took effect, the choice of the parties' presidential candidates was settled before the convention started. That took most of the drama and suspense out of the conventions. To keep their audience, media people searched the conventions for new sources of excitement, such as potential conflicts or disputes. But party leaders had no interest in making their disputes public; that would interfere with the positive message they were trying to convey. As the conventions' audience appeal continued to decline, the major networks reduced their coverage to broadcast only the most significant events. Although convention "junkies" still can turn to C-SPAN, MSNBC, or other cable sources for comprehensive convention coverage, the number of hours of coverage on ABC, CBS, and NBC fell from about 60 per convention in 1952 to little more than an hour a night in 2000.[40]

Media coverage, of course, is not always a boon for the parties. Television's capacity to dramatize and personalize can make a convention come to life for its audience, as it did in covering the struggles in the Democratic convention hall and streets of Chicago in 1968, which led to the nomination reforms. But the sight of bloody demonstrators and angry delegates did not help the Democratic Party attract voter support for its candidates that year. TV cameras can encourage some participants to use the convention as a podium to advance their own causes even if they risk undermining the party's interests. For better or worse, the televised conventions of 2000 had become a shadow of their former selves, in which a shrinking audience watched snippets of roll-call votes, shots of people wearing funny hats, and intense discussions among media commentators.

Do Conventions Still Have a Purpose?

Since the nomination reforms, then, conventions have greatly changed. They are no longer the occasions when the major parties actually select their presidential nominees. That happens in the primaries and a few caucuses; the conventions simply ratify the results. The national conventions have lost much of their deliberative character and independence; genuinely brokered nominations and last-minute compromises seem to belong to the past.

In another way, however, the conventions have become more significant. Because candidates must mobilize groups of activists and voters in order to win primaries and caucuses and because many of these groups are concerned with particular policies, the nomination reforms have made issues all the more important in convention politics. Many delegates arrive at the convention committed not only to a candidate, but also to a cause. Ideological factions and their aims, then, have become new centers of power in the conventions. The pressures exerted by Christian conservatives at Republican conventions in the 1990s and 2000 on behalf of such causes as school prayer and opposition to abortion and homosexuality are a good illustration.

In spite of all these changes—or perhaps because of them—the national conventions are living symbols of the national parties. They provide a unique occasion for rediscovering common traditions and interests, and for celebrating the party's heroes and achievements. Conventions motivate state and local party candidates, energize party workers and launch presidential campaigns. They may not win Emmy awards for compelling viewing, but they frequently remind party activists, and even some party identifiers, why the party matters to them.

SHOULD WE REFORM THE REFORMS?

The reforms of the presidential nominating system are part of a long pattern in American politics: efforts by reformers to break up concentrations of party power. As we have seen with regard to delegate selection and the national conventions, however, the reforms have had many unintended as well as intended effects. Is there a good argument for further effort at reform?

Pros and Cons of the Current System

The drawbacks of the reformed system are serious. Primaries can create internal divisions in state party organizations that may not heal in time for the general election. The low turnouts in primaries and caucuses may increase the influence of well-organized groups that are on the ideological extremes: the right wing of the Republican Party and the left wing of the Democrats. The results of a few early contests in states not very representative of the nation have a disproportionate effect on the national outcome.[41] Candidates must invest such an enormous amount of time, energy, and money before the presidential campaign has even begun that the ultimate winner can arrive at the party convention personally and financially exhausted. And by the time most voters know enough about the prospective nominees to make an informed choice, the nominations have already been decided.

Yet there is no going back to the old system. As the reformers charged, it was usually controlled by state and local party leaders who were often out of touch with the electorate. It kept many party voters and even party activists out of the crucial first step in picking a president. It violated the desire for a more open, democratic politics. And it did not help presidential candidates learn how to prepare for the most powerful leadership position in the world.[42] By comparison, the system of primaries and a weaker convention seems more secure in public opinion.[43]

What Could Be Done?

Could the reforms' drawbacks be fixed by more reforms? One possibility is to create regional nominating events, in which the states in a given region would all schedule their primaries on the same day. That might bring more coherence to the welter of state contests, by limiting the number of dates on which they could be held and reducing the enormous strain on the candidates.

For a time in the late 1980s and 1990s, one regional primary existed; most Southern states chose to hold their primaries early in March on a date referred to as Super Tuesday. The aim of these states was to draw greater attention to Southern concerns in the nominating process and to encourage the nomination of moderate candidates acceptable to the South. By 1996, New England states also scheduled their primaries on this date. In 2000, six Southern and Southwestern states attempted another Southern primary, but the front-loading of other states' events reduced its impact.

Regional primaries, however, have drawbacks too. Which region would go first? Even if the order were rotated from one election to the next, the first region to vote, with its peculiarities and specific concerns, would have a disproportionate effect on the nominations. Regional primaries could still produce all the complaints listed above, from internal party divisions to low turnouts. And given the fact that the only major war fought on American soil was a regional dispute—the Civil War—some might ask whether it is wise to encourage regional divisions.

A Republican Party committee proposed a variation of a regional primary system in 2000. Under this plan, four multistate primaries would be held during a four-month period. The smallest states would vote in the first primary, in order to give less well-known candidates a chance to build support. Because the largest states with the most delegates would vote last, the nomination would not be locked up too early. Understandably, though, the large states were not thrilled about taking a back seat in the selection of a presidential candidate and the idea was dropped.

Another option might be to hold a national primary in which all the states' delegate selection events were held on the same day. But this would serve the interests of neither the parties nor the states. States would lose their chance of becoming key players in the nomination race. The parties would lose control over presidential selection, throwing the contest for the presidency wide open to any candidate who could mobilize a national constituency (and a great deal of money). A national primary could be accomplished only by ending the long tradition of state and party control over the presidential nomination process—and for all of the reforms we have seen in recent decades, there is little chance that will happen.

CHAPTER 11

The General Election

When media consultant Peter Fenn found himself on the same airplane as former U.S. Senator Tom Eagleton, the two began trading stories about past campaigns. "Eagleton spoke wistfully of shooting his [television] commercials during the summer break [in Congress during the 1970s], all positive, and airing them during October." To Fenn, who advises current candidates on their media ads, it was like a story about pioneers moving their covered wagons West.[1] In contrast to the days when a campaign's advertising consisted of a half-dozen TV commercials planned in leisurely meetings, consultants like Fenn live in a world of point-counterpoint instant responses, daily tracking polls and pop-up ads on Internet sites.

The world of campaign politics has been transformed in the last two decades. Now, if you plan to run for statewide or national office (or even local office in many areas), you would expect to hire a laundry list of professional political consultants, ranging from pollsters to media specialists, direct mail experts, Web page designers, fund-raisers, accountants, and others. They will do the work—for a fee, of course—that would have been done for free (or at least for no monetary payment) in the days when state and local party organizations were the main planners and managers of campaigns.

It would be easy to assume, as a result, that the traditional grassroots party organization has become technologically obsolete—that it has been superseded by newer, more efficient, and more powerful campaign techniques. But the party organizations are highly adaptable. Throughout their history, the Democratic and Republican Parties have responded to change; that in part accounts for their long lives. Instead of relegating the parties to the sidelines, then, we need to examine their current role in political campaigns.

The impact of changing technologies also brings up a fundamental fact of political life: campaigns operate within a broader context, determined by a number of forces beyond the campaigners' immediate control. Before we can understand the changes in campaigning, we need to take a look at the context. We have already discussed much of it—parties' organizational strength, political activists, party loyalties, voter turnout, and the rules governing party nominations. We will later examine other aspects of it, including campaign finance rules and the role of the party in government. In this chapter, we

201

will begin with the legal context of campaigns: how elections are regulated. We cannot hope to understand the electoral game without examining the rules.

ELECTIONS: THE RULES OF THE GAME

The rules in politics, as well as everything else, are never neutral. Each rule of the electoral game—for example, how votes must be cast or when elections must be held—not only limits a campaign's choices, but also affects each of the different parties and candidates differently. Some rules benefit certain types of candidates, parties, or party systems; other rules would have different effects. Over the years, reformers have worked hard to change the rules in order to weaken the parties, just as the parties have tried to tinker with the rules to gain strength. Overall, the reformers have won these rules battles more often than the parties have.

The Secret Ballot

American elections did not always use secret ballots. In the early nineteenth century, in many areas, voters simply told the election officials which candidates they preferred. Gradually, this "oral vote" was replaced by the use of ballots printed by the parties or candidates. The voter brought the ballot of a particular candidate or party to the polling place and put it in the ballot box. The ballots of different parties were different in appearance, so observers could tell how an individual had voted. That was not accidental; if party leaders in urban machines had done a voter a favor in exchange for a vote, they wanted to be sure they had gotten their money's worth. This type of ballot also discouraged ticket-splitting—voting for candidates from different parties for different offices.

To discourage vote buying, a new ballot system then came into widespread use. Called the Australian ballot after the country where it originated, these ballots were printed by the government and marked by the voter in secret. The reform quickly swept the nation in the 1890s. By the early twentieth century, its success was virtually complete; only South Carolina waited until 1950 to adopt it. Because the ballot is administered and paid for by the government, this reform involved the government in running elections, which opened the door to government regulation of the parties. It has also enabled voters to split their tickets easily.[2]

The Format of the Ballot

The *format* of this secret ballot varies from state to state, however, which makes a difference in the role of the parties.

Office-Bloc Ballots   In earlier years, many states used a party-column ballot, in which the candidates of each party are grouped together so that voters could see them as a party ticket. That encourages straight-ticket voting (i.e., voting for all of a party's candidates for the offices being filled). More and more, however, states have adopted an office-bloc ballot form, which groups the candidates according to the office they seek. The result is to make split-ticket voting more likely.[3]

The Order of Candidates' Names   Other aspects of the ballot format can affect a candidate's chance of winning. It is a curious fact that some voters are more likely to select the first name on a list of candidates than they are to select a name listed later.[4] So some states randomly assign the order in which candidates' names appear on the ballot, or even rotate the order among groups of ballots; in other states, incumbents' names appear first. The decision to list incumbents first increases their already substantial electoral advantages. The order of the candidates' names probably matters most in primaries and other nonpartisan contests, when voters can find no information about the candidates on the ballot itself.

A related decision must be made in general elections: Which party's candidates should be listed first for each office? States often give the preferred position to the majority party and almost always give more prominence to the major parties than to minor parties. On the other hand, the election rules in almost every state allow voters to write in the names of people not listed on the ballot. Write-in candidates hardly ever win, but rules permitting their existence give independent candidates at least a small avenue into the election process.[5]

The Long Ballot   Another important "rule" is that American voters traditionally face a lengthy ballot. We elect large numbers of state and local officials who would be appointed in other democracies. In many areas, voters also cast ballots on issues. In an exhausting example in 2000, voters in Salem, Oregon, were faced with 26 statewide measures (ranging from gun control to whether public schools should be prohibited from promoting homosexual behavior), 13 land annexations, and 3 tax and bond issues, in addition to an array of statewide elected offices.

Voters would need a great deal of information about candidates and ballot measures in order to cast a meaningful vote in such an election. Many citizens consider this an invitation to stay away from the polls. Those who do vote may find that the cost is too high to gather the necessary data, so they selectively abstain. This partial voting, called roll-off, is most often seen on minor offices and referenda, where as many as 20 or 30 percent of the voters abstain.[6] The voter fatigue caused by the long ballot leads people to use various shortcuts to make their choices; party identification, of course, is one.

Voting Systems

Most of us assume that, even if a ballot is long, it is easy enough to understand: you choose a candidate, push a button, or pull a lever and that candidate gets your vote. At least, we *would* have made that assumption until the aftermath of the 2000 presidential race. Recounts prompted by the closeness of the vote showed that on 1.5 to 2 million ballots—about 2 percent of all those cast—the counting machines had found no presidential vote, or votes for more than one candidate; these voters' ballots, then, were not counted. Some of these "undervotes" or "overvotes" could have been intentional, but studies showing that these problems occurred much more frequently in some types of voting machines (such as punch card systems) than in others suggest that the voting system itself may have been the culprit (see box on p. 204).[7]

If We Can Count Craters on Mars, Why Can't We Count Votes Accurately?

Here's some of what we learned from the 2000 elections about the voting systems used in the United States:[8]

- In a nation where the latest hand held computer is considered a staple of many professions, almost a third of all voting in the United States is done on punch-card machines, where voters must punch out a perforated rectangle (called a "chad") next to the candidate's name. Sometimes, however, the chad doesn't fall out or is pushed back in as the voter moves down the ballot. When that happens, the voter's choice can't be read by the voting machine. That's called an "undervote," and the voter may as well have stayed home.

- In some counties, the ballot format was confusing enough that some voters, whether intentionally or not, cast ballots for more than one candidate ("overvotes"). Those votes couldn't be counted either.

- New York City voters use pull-a-lever voting machines so old that they aren't made any more. The 900-pound machines each have 27,000 parts and must be pulled on and off trucks to get to the polls. Not surprisingly, they break down. Similar machines in Louisiana can be rigged using pliers, a screwdriver, a cigarette lighter, and a Q-Tip. The late Louisiana Senator Earl Long used to say that he wanted to be buried in Louisiana so he could keep voting.

- Indiana's voting registration lists include hundreds of thousands of people who are ineligible to vote because they are dead, felons, or have registered more than once. Alaska has more registered voters than people of voting age.

- In Oregon, all votes in the 2000 election were cast by mail. An estimated 40 percent of California's votes were cast absentee. Counties vary a lot in their requirements for an absentee ballot. Voting absentee can increase the chance of cheating, when people mark their ballots at "ballot parties" or forge signatures of registered voters.

In other cases, analysts charged that confusing ballot layout, such as the so-called "butterfly ballot" used in Palm Beach County, Florida, led many voters to cast their ballot for a different candidate than they had intended (see Figures 11.1 and 11.2). This was an especially worrisome issue in Florida, which decided the election for Bush by a margin of only 537 votes. There were other problems as well, for example: voters turned away from polling places or misinformed about voting procedures, malfunctioning voting machines, and outright fraud.

Why does this happen? There are about 191,000 voting precincts in the United States. They contain about 700,000 voting machines tended by almost 1.5 million poll workers who are typically poorly paid, lightly trained partisan volunteers.[9] Simple human error is as likely to occur in running elections and counting votes as it is in any other large-scale activity. Because of the complexity and decentralization of this system, vot-

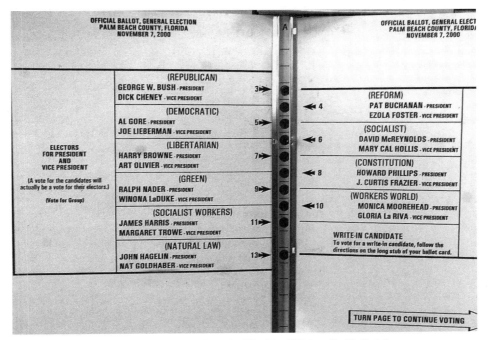

FIGURE 11.1   The Famous Palm Beach, Florida "Butterfly Ballot."
Designed by a Democratic official in Palm Beach County, this ballot format was intended to make it easier for visually challenged older voters to read the ballot. As shown in this graphic by Daniel Niblock of the South Florida *Sun-Sentinel* (showing the angle at which most voters would have seen the ballot), the problem was that the punch card holes did not always line up with the candidates' names, and that in order to vote for Al Gore, whose name was second on the list of candidates, voters had to punch the *third* hole.

Source: http://www.sun-sentinel.com/graphics/news/ballot.htm . Reprinted by permission from the South Florida Sun-Sentinel.

ers in one state, even in one county, may well be treated differently from voters in another. In particular, counties differ in their ability to pay for the most reliable (and most expensive) voting systems. The result is that error-prone voting systems are more likely to be found in poorer counties, which are more likely to vote Democratic.

During the 2001 state legislative sessions, more than 1500 state legislative bills were proposed to reform elections and modernize voting systems. But the cost of these reforms cooled the ardor of most reformers; upgrading every precinct with the more reliable optical scanning systems, like those widely used for grading exams, would cost billions of dollars. Besides, the urgency of the need inevitably drained away because elections, though a vital function of government, take place only occasionally; thus, they are more likely to be ignored than are the ever-present demands on local budgets for more road repair, trash pickup, and police.

THE PALM BEACH BALLOT

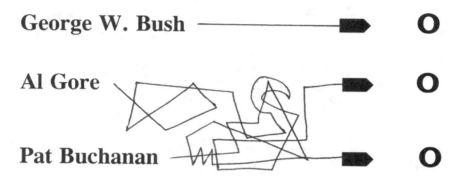

FIGURE 11.2   The "Butterfly Ballot" as seen by some critics.
Source: Adapted from *http://www.justsaywow.com/butterflyballot-new.cfm* (accessed March 1, 2002).

Single-Member Districts

American officeholders are usually elected from single-member constituencies by plurality election. In other words, only one person per constituency is elected to a city council, a state legislature, or mayor's office; and the candidate who wins the most votes (the plurality) is elected. Multimember districts are uncommon.[10]

These rules have important consequences for the American parties. As discussed in Chapter 2, single-member districts and plurality elections discourage minor political parties (and candidates). A third party that wins 10 or 20 percent of the vote under these rules will not elect any candidates. In contrast, in several European democracies that use proportional representation, such a party can win legislative seats and cabinet positions. Plurality rules affect the major parties as well. A party that is ideologically distinctive takes the risk that it may not be able to win a plurality and thus, might not elect any candidates. U.S. election rules, then, encourage parties to broaden their appeal in order to win.

Further, plurality elections deprive the party of one means of influence over its candidates. In electoral systems with multimember districts using proportional representation rules, the voters cast a ballot for a list of party candidates rather than for individual candidates. The parties then divide the seats according to the percentage of the votes they polled, as was described in Chapter 2.[11] The parties determine which candidates will be at, or near, the top of the list, and thus, will be most likely to win office—a powerful incentive for candidates to take their party organization seriously. In contrast, the prevailing single-member plurality rules for American elections help to reinforce the two-party system of broadly based parties, as well as the independence of candidates and officeholders from their parties.

Election Calendars

Even a feature so seemingly innocuous as when elections are held can have important consequences for the candidates and the parties. Since 1845, federal elections have almost always been held on the first Tuesday after the first Monday in November of the even-numbered years. To save money, many statewide and local elections have traditionally been held at the same time.

Scheduling elections for various offices at the same time on the same ballot links the electoral fates of their candidates. A voter's decision on one contest can affect his or her other choices on the same ballot. This is termed a *coattail* effect: the ability of candidates at the top of the ticket to carry into office "on their coattails" other candidates on the same party ticket.[12] As a result, candidates for lesser offices have an incentive to want the strongest possible candidates at the top of the party ticket, to ensure that those coattails are long and sturdy.

Parties often prefer to enhance this linkage because it fosters party cohesion. Progressive reformers, not surprisingly, worked to weaken it, using devices such as office bloc ballots and nonpartisan elections. Some incumbents and other candidates have also found it preferable to insulate their campaigns from the powerful and distracting forces present in federal contests. Most states now elect governors and other top state officials in the second year after a presidential election at the same time as the midterm congressional contests. Most local elections are scheduled at some other time, when no federal offices are on the ballot. This practice of insulating elected officials from one another limits the possibilities for coattail effects and has also worked to reduce the cohesiveness of the party in government.[13]

Election Districts

Candidates' strategies are also affected by the size and composition of the district they hope will elect them. Small, compact districts encourage a level of face-to-face campaigning that simply is not possible in a large, sprawling constituency where voters may be reachable only through the mass media. The partisan composition of a district influences, in a different way, what the parties and candidates do. By setting the initial odds of victory or defeat, it determines the quality of the candidates who are attracted to the race and, often, the amount of effort that candidates and parties will feel the need to expend. Districts with lopsided majorities in favor of one party discourage activity by minority-party candidates; districts that are well-balanced between the parties can prompt spirited campaigns by both candidates and parties.

In a broader sense, the peculiar American institution of the Electoral College produces another kind of electoral district effect. Since the 1830s, victory in the presidential race has required winning a majority of the state electoral votes, rather than getting the most popular votes across the nation. Presidential candidates develop their strategies accordingly. Candidates normally concentrate their attention on the states with the largest number of electoral votes and the greatest interparty competition, which are generally the largest and most diverse states. They typically write off the less populous states and those they are unlikely to win regardless of their efforts.[14] That can make a difference in the issues they choose to address and the groups to which they appeal.

Throughout much of its history, the vote in the Electoral College has magnified the popular vote margin of the winning candidate, so it seemed to be a benign (though strange) way to increase the winner's legitimacy. The day after the 2000 presidential election, however, Americans woke up to discover that the winner of the popular vote, Al Gore, had narrowly lost the presidency, because he had fallen five votes short in the Electoral College. Although that had happened only three times before in the nation's history, all in the 1800s, the shock waves led to a serious discussion of the impact of this election rule—though not to any real action to change it.[15]

POLITICAL EFFECTS OF ELECTION LAW

Most important, the "rules" of American elections have tended to focus attention on the candidates, rather than on the parties. The American electoral process has few institutions, such as parliamentary-cabinet government or proportional representation, which can encourage the voter to see elections as contests between parties for control of government. Rather, features such as the layout of the ballot and even single-member districts (in the absence of a parliamentary system) focus voters' choices on a series of contests between individual candidates. Nonpartisan elections for local offices have reduced the parties' visibility in elections even further, and the separate scheduling of contests at different levels of government makes it difficult for the parties to coordinate their campaigns and their programmatic emphases.

Who Benefits?

Clearly, then, the rules are not neutral in their impact; they are always likely to advantage some contestants more than others. For example, if polling places close at 6:00 P.M., so that factory and office workers find it difficult to get to the polls on time, then the Democratic Party may lose a disproportionate number of votes. If the state makes it relatively easy to vote absentee, that can benefit any local party well-organized enough to distribute absentee ballots to its supporters. Ballot formats that may confuse less-educated voters and those with limited English skills can often work to the advantage of Republican candidates.

Legislative Redistricting

One obvious way in which parties and officeholders try to change the rules to benefit themselves has been through the drawing of constituency lines. Every ten years, after the national census, state legislatures and other governmental bodies must redraw the boundaries of congressional and state legislative districts in order to take into account changes in population size and distribution. How these opportunities have been turned to political advantage is a continuing story of the creativity and resourcefulness of American politicians.

Partisan Redistricting Through Malapportionment and Gerrymandering

Two methods have traditionally been used to turn redistricting opportunities into political gains. The first and most obvious has been simply to ignore population changes. Many states used this tactic for most of the twentieth century by refusing to shift legislative districts and, thus, political power, from the shrinking rural and small-town populations to the growing cities. By the 1960s, many state legislatures and the U.S. House of Representatives better represented the largely rural America of 1900 than the urban nation it had become. Such ***malapportionment*** worked to the disadvantage of Republicans in the South and Democrats elsewhere—and of the needs of cities everywhere. In a series of decisions in the early 1960s, however, the U.S. Supreme Court ended these inequities by requiring that legislative districts be of equal population size. As the courts have applied the "one person, one vote" rule to all types of legislatures, they have closed off this way to exploit the rules of the electoral game.[16]

It is still possible, however, to *gerrymander*—to draw district lines in a way that maximizes one party's strength and disadvantages the other party. That can be done by dividing and, thereby, diluting pockets of the other party's strength to prevent it from winning office. Alternatively, if the other party's strength is too great to be diluted, then a gerrymander can be accomplished by consolidating that party's voters into a few districts and forcing it to win elections by large, wasteful majorities. The party in power when it is time to redistrict is probably always tempted to gerrymander; whether it succeeds often depends on the actions of the federal government (see box below).

Redistricting: The Mark of Zorro

A "gerrymander" occurs when a state's legislative district lines are redrawn by the party in power in order to give it a bigger share of legislative seats than its share of votes. The term came from a governor of Massachusetts, Eldridge Gerry, who signed a bill redrawing the state's districts to favor the minority Democrats. One of the redrawn districts had the shape of a salamander, so the district was mockingly termed a gerrymander.

Gerrymandering is almost inevitable when states redraw their legislative districts to take account of population changes. If a state has eight congressional districts, how many different ways could you draw the lines so as to divide the state into eighths? If you keep the state's biggest city, which is heavily Democratic, in a single district, you probably insure the election of a Democratic member of Congress. If you divide the city among three districts, each including many Republican suburbs, you reduce the chance for a Democrat to win.

During the 1990s round of redistricting, many new districts were created that rivaled Gerry's salamander in their strange shapes. For instance, a Louisiana congressional district, as it was originally drawn, was labeled the "mark of Zorro" because it cut a Z-shaped swath from the top nearly to the bottom of the state to find enough black voters for a black-majority district. Legislators now use computer programs to maximize their chance of gaining partisan advantage from redistricting. Blatant gerrymanders are no longer as common, but during 2001, state legislative majorities were doing their best to gain partisan advantage without generating too much negative publicity.

Federal Involvement in Redistricting   Even after federal courts had worked their way through a series of cases to give meaning to the prescription of "one person, one vote," they still resisted entering the "political thicket" of gerrymandering. No matter how much the courts insisted on "precise mathematical equality" among legislative districts, they rarely rejected plans for equal-sized districts on the ground that the lines were drawn to favor one party.[17] That began to change in the early 1980s with the passage of extensions of the Voting Rights Act. The aim of the legislation was to protect the voting rights of minorities who had suffered from decades of disenfranchisement. The act required a number of states, including all Southern states, to get prior approval of any changes in their election laws—from redistricting plans to voting laws—by officials of the U.S. Department of Justice. Justice rejected nine state redistricting plans after the 1980 census.[18]

As we have seen in Chapter 8, the federal government went much further in the 1990s. The 1982 Voting Rights Act required states to construct legislative districts that would maximize the chance for black and Hispanic candidates to win office. Republicans in many states joined with black Democrats, with the encouragement of the first Bush administration, to create new districts with clear black and Hispanic majorities. These new *majority-minority districts* did bring more black and Hispanic representatives into Congress and state legislatures.

But the plan also helped Republicans to expand the inroads they were already making into previously Democratic strongholds, especially in the South. Because Democratic-leaning black and Hispanic voters were concentrated in a few majority-minority districts, Republican candidates had a better chance to win the newly constructed districts nearby, which were now less Democratic.[19] That created an interesting dilemma for minority voters, most of whom are Democrats: did the increasing number of black and Hispanic faces in Congress make up for the Republican gains that came along with them? This question has become less pressing now that the Supreme Court has ruled that although race can be *one* factor in drawing congressional districts, it can't be the *predominant* factor.

Do Parties Still Gain from Gerrymandering?   Gerrymanders don't always work the way they were intended, however. California Democrats reaped major advantage from a gerrymander in the 1980s, but an equally notorious redistricting in Indiana designed to benefit Republicans had a short-lived effect. And although the great majority of state legislatures redrawing district lines after the 1990 census were Democratic-controlled, just four years later, Republicans won a majority of the congressional districts they created. So, except for the creation of majority-minority districts, the effects of redistricting are not always substantial, especially after the first few years.[20]

It may be that increased media coverage of redistricting has helped to restrain legislators' enthusiasm for the more outrageous gerrymanders. Greater scrutiny by the Justice Department can also limit parties' ability to win big from redistricting. When courts have the final say in redistricting plans—for example, in states with divided government, where the efforts to redistrict have deadlocked—they are often more willing to draw district lines across counties and other political divisions, and thus, across the lines of local party organization. This makes it harder, in yet another way, for party organizations to maintain a role in electoral politics.

CAMPAIGN STRATEGY

These "rules" of American elections structure the environment of political campaigns. They are, however, among the only certainties in modern political campaigning.[21] Most American campaigns lurch from one immediate crisis to the next. They are frequently underorganized, underplanned, underfinanced, and understaffed; consequently, they often play by ear with a surprising lack of information. If the great majority of voters had strong party loyalties, of course, this would not matter; the majority party would turn out its voters and win. But as attractive as that may sound (at least to candidates of the majority party), the life of a campaigner is much more unpredictable.

In designing a campaign strategy, the most critical variables are the nature of the district and its voters, the type of office being sought, the candidate's skills and background, the opponent, the availability of money and other resources, and the party organizations and other organized groups in the constituency. The first big task of campaign strategists is to evaluate the opportunities and the hazards embedded in each of these factors and to determine which ought to be exploited and which need to be downplayed. "Early" is the operative word here; within two months after they had been reelected in 2000, for example, two U.S. House members announced they had formed campaign committees for Senate races in 2002.[22]

Once a campaign's strategists have identified its likely strengths and weaknesses, they must choose how to spend each unit of their scarce time, energy, and money, in order to achieve the greatest possible return in terms of votes. If the candidate's party is in the majority in a district where party voting is common, the campaign can spend most of its resources on appeals to party voters and get-out-the-vote drives. If that is not the case, how can they most effectively attract independents without losing their base of party identifiers? Can they afford television and radio ads and, if so, do the audiences of various stations coincide well enough with the election district to make this spending cost-effective? Is theirs a district in which money can be raised successfully through direct mail appeals, or do donors insist on meeting the candidate face to face?[23]

The two most important factors conditioning the campaign's decisions are incumbency and the competitiveness of the race. Incumbents, even in years when hostility toward the government is high, have enormous advantages in running for reelection.[24] Congressional incumbents, as we have seen, probably have a better chance of being mugged in Washington, D.C., than of losing their next race. Incumbents of any office are greatly advantaged by having put together a successful campaign for that office at least once before. Part of that campaign organization is likely to remain in place between elections, some of it perhaps employed as members of the incumbent's office staff. Incumbents normally have greater name recognition, more success in attracting media coverage, and greater appeal to campaign contributors than do most of their potential competitors.

The result is that challengers—candidates who run against incumbents—face a predictable spiral. Especially if they have not won any political office before, challengers do not start with an experienced organization, proven fund-raising skills, or the other incumbent advantages. In the days when party organizations dominated campaigns, this might not have been a problem. Now it is. One obvious answer might be to purchase an experienced campaign organization by hiring political consultants. But most challengers do not have the money to do that. Thus the cycle begins: the challenger lacks an existing organization and enough money to attract the interest of well-known consultants, so he or she cannot reach many voters; and without these two vital resources, a challenger is not likely to raise enough money to be able to afford either one.

Candidates for open seats (those where no incumbent is running) often have the means to break out of this spiral, especially when the office they seek is prominent. Those who choose to run for the most visible offices—governorships, Congress, the presidency, major city offices—typically start with considerable name recognition, which increases because of the attention given to the race. They can raise enough money for extensive media campaigns. Their major challenge will be to spend their money most effectively and to succeed in defining themselves to the voters before their opponents get the opportunity to define them.

The great majority of campaigns in the United States, however, are far less visible. The means they use to reach voters will depend, in part, on the prevailing political practices of their constituency; in some areas, state legislative candidates rely on yard signs and door-to-door campaigning to make their names known, while in others, full-scale media assaults planned by professional consultants are expected of any serious candidate.

CAMPAIGNING IN THE NEW MILLENNIUM

Within less than a generation, changes amounting to a revolution have altered much of American political campaigning. In particular, campaigns have found effective ways to apply advances in polling, media use, and computer technology. With the new technologies have come the new campaign professionals: specialists in an ever-widening range of political skills whose services are available to candidates who can afford the price.

Professional Consultants

Professional campaign consultants come from a variety of backgrounds. Some have been involved in party or other political work since they were old enough to pick up a phone. Others got their start in university graduate programs or in professional campaign management institutes. Not only have they prospered in American politics, they have also exported their campaign expertise to the rest of the democratic world. Pollster Stan Greenberg, for instance, signed on to Al Gore's presidential campaign in 2000 after having worked on campaigns for prime minister in England in 1997, Germany in 1998, and Israel in 1999.[25]

Campaign consultants come in all sizes and varieties. Some are general consultants, similar to the general contractors who oversee the construction of a building; others concentrate on the minutiae of mailing lists or Web page design. Some are experts in the development of media messages, others in how and where to place media ads. Some can provide organizational skills and, sometimes, even lists of local party people and possible volunteer workers; they can organize rallies, coffee parties, phone banks, and hand-shaking tours of shopping centers. Some provide lawyers and accountants to steer the campaign away from legal shoals and to handle the reporting of campaign finances to state and federal regulators. Some are publicists who write speeches and press releases, some sample public opinion and some are skilled in raising money.

As a sign that it is a developing profession rather than just a collection of talented talkers, the consulting business has become more specialized and has even begun to police itself through a national association. The growth of its influence has been dramatic. There is no better testimony to the takeover of so many campaigns by professional consultants, displacing the candidate loyalists who made these decisions in earlier years, than the fact that the names of some of these campaign professionals—for example, James Carville, Alex Castellanos, Geoff Garin, David Garth, Stan Greenberg, Peter Hart, Mary Matalin, Joe Napolitan, Ed Rollins, Lance Tarrance, Bob Teeter—have become as familiar as some of the candidates for office, at least in political circles.[26]

Professional consultants typically work for several different campaigns during the same election cycle. It is not uncommon for a consulting firm to handle a collection of Senate, House, and gubernatorial races in a given election year, and many of these firms like to stabilize their business by taking nonpolitical clients as well. As "hired guns," they work independently of the party organizations. Yet they almost always work with clients from only one of the parties—some consultants restrict themselves even further to one wing, or ideological grouping, within the party—and they normally maintain a cooperative relationship with that party's leaders and organization. In fact, national party committees often play an important matchmaking role in bringing together consultants and candidates.

Sources of Information

Computers   Experienced candidates develop a picture of their constituency in their minds. As the result of years of contact with constituents, they know what kinds of people support them and how they believe they can trigger that support again. In past years, this "theory" of the campaign would have guided the candidate's strategy—even if the beliefs were inaccurate or the constituency had changed.

Computer technology now provides a much more sophisticated check on the candidate's beliefs. Computerized records can produce much faster and more accurate answers to questions about voter behavior than even the most experienced party workers can. Ever since the first sophisticated use of computers in campaigns, in John F. Kennedy's 1960 presidential race,[27] computer technology has made it possible to process an incredible amount detail in an instant—that is, if anybody is available to compile the information. A local party can computerize reports from canvassers so that they can quickly compile lists of voters to contact on election day. Fund-raisers can merge mailing lists from groups and publications whose members may be predisposed to favor their candidate, and then produce targeted mailings within hours. Using computerized records, "oppo" researchers can locate statements made by the opponent on any conceivable issue.

Polls   No new avenue to political knowledge has been more fully exploited than the public opinion poll.[28] Candidates poll before deciding whether to run for an office, to assess voters' views and to probe for weaknesses in the opposition. When the campaign begins, polls are used to determine what issues are uppermost in voters' minds and how the candidate's first steps are affecting his or her "negatives" and "positives." Consultants use polls to decide whether the campaign ads should emphasize party loyalties or ties with other party candidates. Close to the end of the race, tracking polls can follow the reactions of small samples of voters each day, to measure immediate responses to a campaign event or a new ad or appeal. In fact, polls have become so ubiquitous in campaigns, even in local elections, that stealth volleys of attack ads have been disguised as polls.

Not all candidates have access to poll data. The expense of sophisticated polling puts it beyond the reach of many candidates. Recent technical support efforts by the national party organizations (reviewed in Chapter 4), however, have made some poll data available even to low-budget campaigns.

Methods of Persuasion

Campaigns are exercises in mass persuasion. Each candidate seeks to define him- or herself to the voters as a trustworthy and qualified representative. Because of the large size of most election districts, the predominant means of persuasion are the mass media: television, radio, newspapers, and the Internet. Even old-style communications are pursued with the media in mind: a candidate takes the time to address a rally or meeting largely in the hope that it will produce a brief report on the local TV news. Early in the campaign, candidates fight to buy choice TV time and billboard space for the concluding weeks of the campaign. As the campaign progresses, the candidates' faces, names, and slogans blossom on billboards, newspaper ads, radio and TV spot announcements, and even on yard signs, brochures, shopping bags, and potholders.

Television   Television is the medium of choice for most campaigns, as long as its audience is reasonably well matched to the candidate's constituency. Time on TV often consumes most of the campaign's money. In the early and inexpensive days of television, candidates bought large chunks of time for entire speeches that were carried nation- or statewide. Now, however, campaign messages are compressed into 30- or 60-second spot ads that can be run frequently or targeted to a particular audience. The writing, producing and placing of these spots (after the pro football game? before the evening news?) has become a central focus of campaigns, as have the fund-raising activities needed to pay for them. Thus what was a long, stem-winder of a speech by the candidate in a sweaty hall 50 or 60 years ago is now a few carefully crafted visual images and a very simple text put together by professionals.[29]

Because of the high cost of network television, candidates and consultants look for alternatives. The cost of advertising on cable television stations is often lower than on the networks and may also be more efficient for local campaigns, whose constituencies are too small to warrant buying time in major media markets. Many cable stations have more specialized "niche" audiences than do the major networks; this permits campaigns to target their messages (called *narrowcasting*). In addition, it makes good sense for campaigns to maximize their exposure on the "free media" of television newscasts and newspaper columns. When newscasts provide coverage of a candidate, the information may seem more credible and "objective" than if it is conveyed through the campaign's own spot ads.

Some candidates do a masterful job of attracting free media coverage that transmits the images they want voters to see. John McCain, for example—who began a run for the Republican presidential nomination in 2000 in relative obscurity—gained flattering media coverage by remaining almost constantly available to reporters aboard his "Straight-Talk Express" campaign bus. Unaccustomed to such a refreshing degree of candor, television and print reporters transmitted positive images of McCain's personal history and political stances that probably helped the candidate vault over the other lesser-known Republican candidates and become the chief alternative to the front-runner, George W. Bush.

To get media coverage, campaigns need to provide material that the media want. In particular, the campaign's information and its visuals must meet the media's definition of what constitutes "news."[30] If "news" is that which is different from the norm, dramatic and controversial, then a candidate is not likely to earn media coverage with yet another rendition of a standard stump speech. Dave Barry offers this illustration: "Let's consider two headlines. FIRST HEADLINE: 'Federal Reserve Board Ponders Reversal of Postponement of Deferral of Policy Reconsideration.' SECOND HEADLINE: 'Federal Reserve Board Caught in Motel with Underage Sheep.' Be honest, now. Which of these two stories would you read?"[31] Candidates who depend on free media will be driven to stage campaign events that make for good television, using the tamer, political equivalent of the underage sheep: dramatic confrontations, visits to natural disasters or other tragedies, or meetings with very well-known or telegenic people.

Direct Mail   Ironically, in the midst of all this high-tech effort, computers have brought the postal service back to the center of the campaign. Computers can produce personalized, targeted letters by the millions. They are effective both for campaigning and for fund-raising; the well-written letter seeking money is also an appeal for the candidate seeking the funds. Direct mail appeals raise the emotional temperature of a campaign. Reporter E. J. Dionne quotes a prominent direct mail specialist: "The one thing direct mail letters are not is dispassionate. 'You've got to have a devil,' said Mr. (Roger) Craver. 'If you don't have a devil, you're in trouble.' ... 'You need a letter filled with ideas and passion... It does not beat around the bush, it is not academic, it is not objective.'"[32] The direct mail campaign is an effort to build a list of reliable contributors and supporters who can be counted on to respond whenever the campaign calls. Some veteran campaigners have "called" for long periods of time, using their contributor list as a base for moving on to higher office.

Internet and E-Mail   The newest means of campaign persuasion is the Internet, first used by candidates and consultants in 1996. By now, every major campaign has a Web site, as do many local races. Some of these sites are elaborate and professionally designed; others make use of the skills of Web-savvy teenagers. Internet technology permits the combination of Web pages and electronic mail to create interactive Web sites; campaigns can then communicate with visitors to their site via e-mail.

In the 2000 elections, the Republican National Committee worked to develop a computerized version of a phone tree, in which a core group of Republican supporters each created an e-mail distribution list to send campaign information to other supporters, who in turn spread the information more widely and, of course, almost simultaneously. Campaigns can also load their spot ads online and distribute them nationally through the Internet, without the cost of buying TV time. Because not all voters have ready access to the Internet, however, online campaigning is more likely to benefit candidates who seek the voters most likely to be "wired": young, highly educated, more affluent people. Its use is also limited by its audience's interests; only about a quarter of the likely voters among these Internet users have searched online for information about candidates.[33]

Traditional campaign techniques are certainly not obsolete. Shaking constituents' hands at factory gates is still a common campaign activity, even when the television cameras do not show up. Candidates still seek endorsements from local groups, meet with newspaper editors and look for gimmicks with which to penetrate the consciousness of busy citizens. The old ways are very much alive. The new campaign technologies have simply layered on a sophisticated set of tools that demand expert knowledge and a great deal of money.

The Old Standby: Negative Campaigning

Attacks on the opponent have also gone high-tech. It has become a staple of political consulting that, when a candidate is falling behind in the polls, one of the surest ways to recover is to "go negative" and launch attacks on his or her opponent. Negative campaigning is nothing new in American politics, of course; politicians since the earliest days of the Republic have been the focus of vicious attacks. Concern about negative campaigns has increased recently, however, because they can be spread much more quickly and widely by the new media; rumors about a candidate's personal life that were once circulated mainly within political circles can now be accessed on the Internet in Honolulu and Fairbanks.

Does negative campaigning work? The findings are mixed. Some researchers find that negative ads are particularly memorable and that a negative campaign drives down turnout because it increases voter cynicism. Others find no advantage in effectiveness and no evidence of turnout decline.[34] One of the biggest challenges in tracing the impact of negative ads is the difficulty of defining "negative"; what one person considers irrelevant mudslinging is helpful, "comparative" information to another. But there are campaigns, such as the 2000 race for mayor of Los Angeles—in which bogus fund-raising calls claimed that one candidate wanted more lenient treatment for criminals and another was entirely dependent on Jewish money—that few people would have trouble characterizing as negative.

Effects On Presidential Campaigns

The newest campaign technologies and trends are especially visible in presidential races. Because of the vast size of the United States, it is not surprising that presidential campaigns are run largely through the mass media, especially television. With a media-based campaign, presidential candidates can communicate efficiently with a national audience, reaching more potential voters than they could ever hope for with any series of local campaign appearances. The sheer size of the campaign also means that it will be difficult for candidates to assess how they're doing without extensive use of professional pollsters, in contrast to their earlier counterparts' heavier reliance on the reports of local politicians.

Local appearances remain important for the free media coverage they generate. But the modern presidential campaign is an incredibly complex operation integrating national media, coordination with local party and organization leaders, and fleets of paid professional consultants. The extensive use of media is made possible in presidential races by sums of money that few other candidates can command. Ironically, it is also made necessary by the limits on campaign spending that go along with public funding of these campaigns (as we will see in the next chapter).[35]

DO CAMPAIGNS MAKE A DIFFERENCE?

With so much money, energy, and professional advice invested in campaigns, it is easy to assume that they have a big impact on voters' choices. If they didn't, why would candidates bother? Reporters, too, invest a lot of time covering the strategies, the surprises, and the drama of the competition.[36] And yet, researchers find that election results can usually be predicted pretty well from conditions that existed before the campaign began, such as the distribution of party loyalties in the district, economic conditions and the incumbent's poll ratings. That doesn't leave much room for the events of a campaign to help determine the outcome. Instead, it seems to suggest that, at most, campaigns simply remind voters of these longer-lasting conditions and, in this way, help them move toward a largely preordained outcome.[37]

How can we determine how much influence campaigns have? It is hard to measure the effects of any single campaign activity, much less all the elements of the campaign combined. Did George W. Bush win the presidency in 2000 because of the tax cut he proposed, his criticism of President Clinton's behavior, or his engaging personality? Observers' answers often vary depending on the observer's own agenda (see box below). Researchers have used a variety of methods to measure campaign impact, and, not surprisingly, they have come up with a variety of conclusions.

The Argument that Campaigns Matter

A long line of evidence suggests that party canvassing in campaigns—going door-to-door to tell voters about the party's candidates—has a small but meaningful effect on both turnout and voters' choices. Studies spanning half a century have found that traditional grassroots precinct work by party activists can boost the party's voter turnout.[38] Precinct work, some have reported, probably has more influence in local elections than in presidential races, because there are fewer alternative sources of information in the local contests. Research also shows that personal contacts activate voters more often than mailed propaganda does, and door-to-door canvassing has more influence than telephone calls.[39] With regard to voters' other decision—their choice of candidates—most recent

---

Why Did George W. Bush Win?

Many conservative Republicans argued: because Bush was so clearly associated with conservative principles, such as personal morality and individual responsibility.

To many moderate Republicans: because Bush ran as a *compassionate* conservative, stressing issues such as education and health care rather than as a right-winger.

To moderate Democrats: because Al Gore moved too far to the left, emphasizing a populist appeal, rather than the more centrist message of budget discipline and responsibility.

To liberal Democrats: Gore led in the polls only when he linked himself to traditional liberal Democratic programs, such as Social Security and Medicare, and with "the people, not the powerful." When he abandoned these themes, voters couldn't distinguish him from Bush.[40]

Or ... He didn't. Gore won the popular vote. It was the Electoral College, and a Supreme Court decision stopping further hand recounts in Florida, that decided the election for Bush.

research indicates that where a party is active, its vote share can increase by at least a few percentage points, which could be the critical margin in a close race.[41]

Television news and advertising—and the money that pays for it[42]—may have even greater influence on voters' decisions than canvassing does. To Austin Ranney, candidates recognize that in a society in which most voters would rather stay home and watch TV than go to a political rally,

> appearing on television is the closest candidates can get to all but a handful of their constituents and provides by far the most cost-effective campaigning device they have. Moreover, ... while eye-to-eye contact and a warm handshake between politician and voter may be best, having the politician's voice and face appear in living color on the tube a few feet away from the constituent in his own living room is surely second best.[43]

Television is clearly the predominant source of political information in the United States. By the early 1960s, television had replaced newspapers as Americans' most important and credible source of political news; TV has been the leading news source ever since.[44] And it has supplanted the parties in providing campaign information. Only 36 percent of a national sample reported being contacted by either party during the 2000 campaigns. By contrast, 82 percent of the respondents paid at least some attention to television news about the campaign.[45] This widespread exposure to TV news and campaign ads can make a difference, especially when it gives viewers new information about a candidate.[46]

The Argument That They Don't

However, there are several reasons why even televised campaigning may have only a limited effect. First, television news and advertising offer viewers a wide range of conflicting messages about candidates—positive, negative and neutral information and opinions, all mixed together. The inconsistency of these messages makes it harder for media coverage to change viewers' minds about candidates.[47] Besides, we know that American voters pay selective attention to media and other campaign communications, just as they do to most other experiences. People usually see events through a filter of stable, long-lasting orientations, the most stable of which is party identification. They tend to surround themselves with friends, information, and even personal experiences (such as rallies and meetings) that support their beliefs and loyalties.[48]

So even though most voters are exposed to campaigns on TV, they may pick and choose among the mix of differing messages and ignore those that conflict with their existing beliefs and opinions. Most campaign communications, then, probably have the effect of activating and reinforcing the voter's existing political inclinations, as they always have. That can explain why so much campaign effort is directed at getting people out to vote—to act on their existing beliefs and opinions—rather than at trying to change their voting decision.[49]

Yet news coverage of campaigns can have a more subtle influence. By the kinds of issues and events they emphasize, the media affect what people come to consider important in a campaign; this process is known as *agenda-setting.* In directing viewers' attention in this way, media coverage "primes" viewers to look for some qualities in candidates, rather than others.[50] News coverage of the 2000 presidential race, for example, focused intently on Al Gore's boasts and exaggerations, rather than on

George Bush's, and on Bush's slips of the tongue rather than Gore's.[51] This kind of media influence is indirect and thus hard to measure, but its effects on election results could be profound.

Did September 11 Change American Campaigning?

Some observers wondered whether the terrorist attacks on the World Trade Center and the Pentagon on September 11, 2001, might have limited the impact of campaigns even more severely. The immediate public and political response—the drive for national unity that produced displays of flags, patriotic slogans, and outpourings of community support—posed a real challenge for candidates for office in the fall of 2001. Races for mayor in New York, governor in New Jersey and Virginia, and several special House elections would be held two months later. Yet it seemed inappropriate to mount strong partisan attacks in the wake of the national tragedies. In fact, all the national party committees suspended major fund-raising events and many candidates even put their electioneering on hold.

But not for long. A week after the Pentagon was attacked, candidates for governor in that state, Virginia, were back on the air with gentle, patriotic campaign ads. The trauma of the attacks probably did mute some of the harsh rhetoric that would have been expected so close to an election, and led many incumbents, so often happy to run "against the system" of which they are a part, to emphasize their experience in government instead. But by January, 2002 the process was largely back to normal; partisanship in Congress was intense (see Chapter 13) and fund-raising had reached a fever pitch in advance of the 2002 elections.

Even in the face of an overwhelming shock to the nation, then, and even though they know that campaign activities have limited effects on voters, candidates and activists continue to make every effort to persuade and mobilize. Campaigning, after all, is their only means of providing new information to prospective voters, of trying to motivate likely supporters, and of getting the money to do these things. For people as intensely involved as prospective office-holders and other political activists, in a system in which party identification is not ironclad, there simply is no reasonable alternative.

Some Tentative Answers

There is a lot left to learn about the effects of campaigns on voters. It seems clear that face-to-face campaign contact and media coverage has at least some impact on voter turnout and voters' decisions. As a general rule, campaign communications are most effective in bringing weak partisans back into the fold when they have had doubts about their party's candidate.[52] Now, in the information-rich environment of current campaigns and among the large numbers of independents, the potential for campaigns to shape voters' perceptions of candidates may be higher than it has ever been. And there are times when dramatic events during a campaign may actually decide the outcome (see "A Day in the Life"). But the impact of campaigns will continue to be limited by the same forces that have always constrained it: voters' tendency to pay attention mainly to the messages they already agree with, and their ability to tune out most political messages altogether.

A D A Y I N T H E L I F E

How Do You Run Against a Dead Man?

The campaign was a "clash of the titans," according to University of Missouri political scientist Rick Hardy. Republican U.S. Senator John Ashcroft had previously served as Missouri's governor and attorney general; he had never lost a race. In 2000, he was running for reelection against the state's current governor, Democrat Mel Carnahan. Like Ashcroft, Carnahan "had politics in his blood." He had been Missouri's treasurer and lieutenant governor and he came from an old political family. The race was close—and bitter—but by mid-October, it appeared that Ashcroft was beginning to pull ahead in the polls.

Everything changed on October 16. Mel Carnahan's campaign plane crashed. The governor, his son, and his top aide were killed. As the shock wave receded, Missourians faced a novel challenge. It was too late in the campaign for the Missouri Democratic Party to nominate another candidate, so Carnahan's name would have to stay on the ballot. If Carnahan got a majority of votes, the Democratic lieutenant governor announced, he would appoint Carnahan's widow, Jean, to fill the seat. In a poignant announcement from her home, Mrs. Carnahan said that she'd accept.

Imagine that you are John Ashcroft. You have three weeks left to campaign before Election Day. Your opponent's supporters are urging voters to "keep the fire lit" by voting for Carnahan so that his widow can take his place. Continued Republican control of the Senate could hinge on the outcome of this race. How are you going to respond? A negative campaign is out of the question; it's not usually considered good form to attack a dead man. But how can you run a positive campaign when media coverage of the race is concentrating entirely on the tragedy of Carnahan's death?

"John Ashcroft was in a political straightjacket," said Hardy. "He had to put his campaign in abeyance. If he had continued campaigning, he would have come off as the 'heavy'; it would have been tacky. So he laid low. But politics abhors a vacuum," and the media, national as well as local, zoomed in on Jean Carnahan's losses and her unique situation. Soon, her dead husband was moving ahead in the polls. "Ashcroft wasn't running against Mel Carnahan anymore," Hardy noted. "He was running against a martyr, against Mrs. Carnahan, and against the media. Mel Carnahan became more popular in death than he had been in life."

Ashcroft's supporters, after watching in great frustration, finally took some steps. A widely respected former senator, Republican John Danforth, reminded Missourians to look at Ashcroft's record and accomplishments. That hardly made a dent. Then, a week before the election, Hardy says, "Ashcroft decided to take a statewide bus tour with other Republican 'heavyweights' to speak about his record. He was surrounded by hordes of media people—but all they were asking (and reporting) was whether he had called Mrs. Carnahan yet. He couldn't control the agenda. And when a politician can't control the agenda ..."

Ashcroft narrowly lost the election. If you had been in his shoes, would you have run those last three weeks of your campaign differently?

THE PARTIES' ROLE IN CAMPAIGNS

While campaigners are trying to influence voters, party organizations are trying to influence the campaigns. Although the realities of American politics force most candidates to run under a party label, nothing forces them to let the party organization control, or even participate in, their campaigns. The direct primary allows candidates to run without the party organization's approval. Electoral rules, ranging from the office-bloc ballot to the separation of national from state elections, encourage candidates to run as individuals, rather than as members of a party ticket. Even the new campaign technologies can help candidates resist party influence. Because tools such as direct mail appeals and television advertising are available to any candidate who can pay for them, these technologies let candidates communicate with voters without the party's help.

If they are going to have a role in campaigns now, party organizations have to earn it. They no longer have the traditional lure of platoons of party volunteers to offer as canvassers. As we saw in Chapter 5, voluntary organizations of all types, parties included, are having more and more trouble enticing busy Americans to volunteer their time.

Adapting to New Realities

Instead, party organizations have expanded their role in campaigns by using their fundraising prowess to provide new technologies and other services to candidates. The large sums of money that have flowed into the national parties in the past two decades have helped them stimulate greater activity in the state and local parties and assist individual campaigns directly.[53] Some of this money has been used by party organizations to hire professional campaign consultants—pollsters, media experts, and others. Parties have often served as placement offices for these consultants, matching them up with needy campaigns and even sustaining them during the lean years between campaigns.

The effort seems to have worked. With their newfound wealth and the services it can buy, the national parties have become more visible to campaigns at all levels. The infusion of millions of dollars of "soft money" into state and local parties, as well as these parties' own improving fund-raising capabilities, have helped them expand their campaign roles even more.[54] Yet the nature of this expanded party role, relying on money and sophisticated technology, is likely to differ a great deal from the kind of party role that is based on face-to-face contact between party volunteers and campaign personnel. Further, these new service activities are not likely to result in a more effective grassroots party organization.[55]

The Continuing Struggle Between Candidates and Party Organizations

In addition to the new resources that party organizations have been able to offer to campaigns, it might well be more efficient, at least in an economic sense, for the parties to organize campaigns on behalf of their candidates. The party organization could distribute literature for a number of candidates at the same time and mount voter registration drives to help the entire ticket. It could coordinate Election Day activities: setting up a headquarters, providing poll-watchers to oversee the voting, offering cars to get people to the polls, and checking voter lists to alert nonvoters late in the day.

This efficiency, however, would necessarily be bought at the cost of limiting each candidate's independence. A party organization may feel that it is best positioned to raise money for the whole party ticket, in order to prevent its candidates from competing for contributors. An individual candidate, however, may think that he or she can raise more money in an independent effort. The party may prefer renting billboards to celebrate the full party ticket, but some candidates on that ticket may believe they're more likely to win votes if they go it alone. Although the party organization would try to stimulate party loyalty in voters, not all candidates find this helpful to their own chances of winning, especially when they are running in districts dominated by the other party.

The current relationship between party organizations and their candidates' campaigns, then, can be both tense and competitive. The two "sides" have interests that are never entirely in harmony. The first commitment of any candidate is to win his or her own race, no matter how dismal its chances are. The party, in contrast, takes a broader view. It is selective in its commitment, because it wants to spend as few of its scarce resources as possible on the races it considers hopeless. Other sources of tension heighten these conflicts. In the days when most activists were drawn to the party for material or solidary reasons (see Chapter 5), they were probably satisfied with victory itself; their goals were to hold public office and get the patronage that flowed from it. Now, however, large numbers of activists seek more than just victory; they want candidates and officials who will fight for specific issues and policy goals after winning. To achieve their own goals, then, the workers of the party organization try to assert greater control over the party's candidates in ways that tie those candidates' hands.

The result is a continuing struggle between party organizations and candidates—the party in government—for control of campaigns. This struggle has great significance: whoever controls the running of campaigns controls the parties. In modern American politics, the candidates are winning the fight. Even if the parties have more to offer candidates than they did just a few years ago, party organizations still contribute only a fairly small percentage of candidates' overall campaign spending. In contrast, European parties often provide more than half the funding used by most candidates.

The new campaign techniques that we have explored in this chapter have helped reinforce the move toward candidate-centered, rather than party-centered, politics. Because candidates can use the Internet, television, and direct mail independently of their party organization, they can develop ties with their constituents that are free of party loyalty and party organizational control. By controlling their own campaigns, candidates are free to form alliances with political action committees, single-issue groups, and other nonparty organizations, which enhance the ability of these groups to influence public policy. In short, it underscores the power of the party in government relative to that of the party organization. It also poses an important question: If the parties can be effective means of holding elected officials accountable for their actions, then how much accountability do voters get from a candidate-centered politics?

Financing the Campaigns

Candidate George Washington was known to be a big spender. When Washington ran for the Virginia House of Burgesses in 1757, long before the American colonies put their armies under his direction in the Revolutionary War:

> he provided his friends with the "customary means of winning votes": namely 28 gallons of rum, 50 gallons of rum punch, 34 gallons of wine, 46 gallons of beer, and 2 gallons of cider royal. Even in those days this was considered a large campaign expenditure, because there were only 391 voters in his district for an average outlay of more than a quart and a half per person.[1]

Washington was, by all accounts, a very well qualified candidate, yet he still felt that he needed to spend freely in order to win. Two and a half centuries later, fund-raising is a much bigger job; television advertising, after all, costs a lot more than 50 gallons of rum punch and takes greater expertise to prepare. Money has never been more important in American elections than it is today. As candidates have come to depend on paid professionals and television, money has become key to mobilizing the other resources needed for a viable campaign. So candidates, especially for statewide and national office, are not likely to be taken seriously unless they start with a big campaign budget or a proven talent for raising funds.

Until the campaign finance reforms of the 1970s, much of the collecting and spending of campaign money took place in secret. Candidates were not required to disclose the way they raised funds and contributors were often reluctant to be identified publicly. The few laws governing campaign contributions were full of loopholes and were regularly ignored. Large amounts of money could be raised and spent for many state and local contests without any public accounting at all.

As a result of the 1970s reforms, we now have a flood of data about campaign spending and contributions.[2] The Federal Election Commission (FEC) produces mountains of reports on the contributions and spending in U.S. House, Senate, and presidential campaigns. Yet the mind-boggling complexity of campaign finance makes it difficult to grasp even with—or perhaps because of—all these data. Regulation varies from state to state and from the state to the federal level. And it is constantly under assault by candidates and contributors who are adept at finding loopholes through which they can pursue their aims.

Despite all this change, the basic questions remain the same. How much money is spent to elect candidates to office and who spends it? Who contributes the money? What is the party's role in funding campaigns? How effective were the campaign finance reforms in checking the power of money in politics and what are the challenges we still face?

HOW BIG HAS THE MONEY BECOME?

Total campaign spending at all levels, including both nominations and general elections, would seem to have exploded since 1960. According to the most authoritative source on campaign funding, candidates at all levels of office spent a total of about $3.9 *billion* in 2000,[3] a 22-fold increase during these 40 years.[4] Spending took giant leaps in 1980 and 1988, and again in 1996 and 2000.

Yet when we adjust for inflation, which has reduced the purchasing power of the dollar during this time, the increase is not nearly as impressive. Campaign spending actually dropped from 1972 to 1976 as a temporary result of reforms of the process, before surging in the next election. Even the well-funded candidacy of Ross Perot did not boost spending in 1992. The fourfold increase in *real* spending since 1960 is not trivial, however, and as we will see, the ingenuity of campaigners, parties, and interest groups in finding new sources of campaign money may fuel an even bigger jump in the coming elections.

Presidential Campaigns

The most expensive campaigns for public office in the United States are those for the presidency (Table 12.1). In fact, the table greatly underestimates total spending in the 2000 presidential race. By 2000, a great deal of party and interest group money was spent on "issue advocacy" ads (to be discussed later in this chapter), whose funding does not have to be reported to any federal agency. So although we know that the candidates themselves spent $607 million in that election, the total spending, if we were able to count interest group money, would be much higher.

The cost of presidential campaigns varies depending on the amount of competition for each party's presidential nomination and the willingness of the candidates to refuse federal funding (and its accompanying fund-raising limits) and raise all their campaign money themselves. George W. Bush decided to do just that in the 2000 nomination race and had pulled in almost $80 million in contributions before even half of the primaries were over. By November, Bush had run the most expensive campaign in American history.

Congressional Campaigns

Individual House and Senate races are run on much smaller budgets, though their collective cost has surpassed that of the presidential race in recent years (Table 12.2).[5] The total spending is higher in House contests simply because there are many more House races in a given year than there are Senate races. During the past 30 years, the actual

TABLE 12.1 Total Spending by Candidates, Parties, and Groups in Presidential General Elections: 1960–2000

Year	Expenditures (in millions)		Percentage change since previous election	
	Actual	Inflation-Adjusted	Actual	Inflation-Adjusted
1960	$30.0	$30.0	—	—
1964	60.0	57.3	+100.0%	+91.0%
1968	100.0	85.2	+66.7	+48.7
1972	138.0	97.8	+38.0	+14.8
1976	160.0	83.3	+15.9	−14.8
1980	275.0	99.1	+71.9	+19.0
1984	325.0	92.6	+18.2	−6.6
1988	500.0	125.4	+53.8	+35.4
1992	550.0	116.3	+10.0	−7.3
1996	700.0	132.4	+27.3	+13.8
2000	607.0*	**	**	**

*The 2000 figure is not comparable to the earlier figures because it includes only the candidates' spending. The reason is that money spent by interest groups and parties on issue advocacy, which became a much bigger proportion of total spending in 2000, is not reported to the Federal Election Commission.

** These figures cannot be calculated, because total spending for the 2000 election is not known.

Note: Estimates are for two-year cycles ending in the presidential election years. Inflation-adjusted figures are computed by deflating the actual expenditures by changes in the price level as measured by the Consumer Price Index (yearly averages) using 1960 as the base year.

Source: John C. Green, ed., *Financing the 1996 Election* (Armonk, NY: M.E. Sharpe, 1999), Table 2.5, p. 19, for actual spending; and Candice J. Nelson, "Spending in the 2000 Elections," in David B. Magleby, ed., *Financing the 2000 Election* (Washington, DC: Brookings, 2002), Table 2–1, for 2000. CPI deflator is based on Table No. 691 in U.S. Bureau of the Census, *Statistical Abstract of the United States: 2001* (Washington, DC: U.S. Government Printing Office, 2001), p. 451.

spending figures for both types of campaigns have trended upward. When we examine the figures adjusted for inflation, however, the picture changes: real spending in congressional races has gone down almost as often as it has gone up. Major increases appear only in the hotly contested 1978 and 1992 elections, and then again in 2000—and the total for the 2000 elections would be even higher if all party and interest group spending on these races were included. Campaign costs at the state and local level have grown substantially as well.

Even so, these figures tell only part of the story. The increase in total campaign spending has outstripped increases in the cost of most other items in the economy, but it still doesn't match the amounts some large corporations spend each year to advertise soap and cigarettes (see box on p. 227). Although few would dispute the benefits of soap, our futures are affected even more by the choices we make in state and federal elections. So, to the extent that campaigns give us the opportunity to assess the views of incumbents more accurately and to learn about the strengths and weaknesses of the candidates who would replace them, the amounts spent on campaign advertising could be considered a real bargain.[6]

TABLE 12.2 Total Spending by Candidates in Congressional Campaigns, 1971–1972 to 1999–2000

	Expenditures (in millions)				Percentage change since previous election			
	Actual		Inflation-Adjusted		Actual		Inflation-Adjusted	
Year	House	Senate	House	Senate	House	Senate	House	Senate
1971–1972	$46.5	$30.7	$46.5	$30.7	—	—	—	—
1973–1974	53.5	34.7	45.4	29.4	+15.1	+13.0	−2.4	−4.2
1975–1976	71.5	44.0	52.5	32.3	+33.6	+26.8	+15.6	+9.9
1977–1978	109.7	85.2	70.3	54.6	+53.4	+93.6	+33.9	+69.0
1979–1980	136.0	102.9	69.1	52.3	+24.0	+20.8	−1.7	−4.2
1981–1982	204.0	138.4	88.3	59.9	+50.0	+34.5	+27.8	+14.5
1983–1984	203.6	170.5	81.8	68.5	−0.2	+23.2	−7.4	+14.4
1985–1986	239.3	211.6	91.4	80.8	+17.5	+24.1	+11.7	+18.0
1987–1988	256.5	201.2	90.8	71.2	+7.2	−4.9	−0.7	−11.9
1989–1990	265.8	180.4	85.2	57.8	+3.6	−10.3	−6.2	−18.8
1991–1992	406.7	271.6	121.3	81.0	+53.0	+50.6	+42.4	+40.1
1993–1994	406.2	319.0	114.7	90.0	−0.1	+17.5	−5.4	+11.1
1995–1996	477.8	287.5	127.5	76.7	+17.6	−9.9	+11.2	−14.8
1997–1998	452.5	287.8	113.6	72.2	−5.3	0.0	−10.9	−5.9
1999–2000	572.3	434.7	139.1	105.6	+26.5	+51.0	+22.4	+46.3

Note: Estimates are for two-year cycles ending in the presidential and midterm election years. Inflation-adjusted figures are computed by deflating the actual expenditures by changes in the price level as measured by the Consumer Price Index (yearly averages) using 1972 as the base year.

Source: John C. Green, ed., *Financing the 1996 Election* (Armonk, NY: M.E. Sharpe, 1999), Table 2.7, p. 23 for actual spending through 1995–1996; for 1997-2000, FEC news release, *http://www.fec.gov* (accessed May 15, 2001). CPI deflator is the same as that listed for Table 12.1.

WHO SPENDS THE CAMPAIGN MONEY?

In most other democracies, the parties do most of the campaign spending. In contrast, most campaign money in American elections is spent by the candidates' own campaign organizations and by a variety of interest groups and individuals who flood the media with advertising. But parties play a growing part in campaign funding as well.

Presidential Campaigns

Imagine that you've thought about running for president. How much money would you need to raise? In 2000, it took hundreds of millions of dollars just to get out of the gates. Candidates' campaigns for their parties' nominations cost a grand total of $326 million, including $224.7 million spent by Republican candidates and $88 million by Democrats prior to the parties' nominating conventions (see Table 12.3). Because Bush chose to forgo the federal matching funds allowed for primary campaigns under campaign finance laws and, therefore, to avoid their fund-raising limits, his campaign was able to spend $89 million of that total. One of his opponents for the

Campaign Spending: Too Much or Too Little?

What will $3.9 billion buy in the United States?

- Less than three-fifths of the cigarette advertising and promotion run in 1998
- Less than a year's advertising (in 1999) for General Motors plus Proctor & Gamble
- Six percent of the amount spent in 2000 on gambling
- About one-fourth the amount Americans paid for athletic shoes in 2000
- About a third of Americans' annual spending on pornography
- All the political campaigns run at all levels of government by and for all candidates in 2000

Sources: http://www.lungusa.org/data/smoke/smoke1.pdf (American Lung Association, on cigarette advertising); *http://www.cmr.com/news/2000/032900_2.html* (on GM and Proctor & Gamble); *http://grossannualwager.com* (on gambling); *http://www.sgma.com* (on athletic shoes), (all accessed Feb. 27, 2002); Forrester Research (Cambridge, MA; on pornography).

Republican nomination was Steve Forbes, a wealthy businessman, who spent almost $48 million through the early Republican primaries (all but $10 million of that from his own funds) before folding his tent and leaving the race. Al Gore, who ran for the Democratic Party nomination against former Senator Bill Bradley, accounted for just $42.5 million of the total nomination spending.

The price goes up in the general election, but the candidates get more of their own campaign budgets from our federal tax dollars. Since the campaign finance reforms of the 1970s, every major party candidate has accepted federal funds to run his general election campaign. (The story of these reforms—and the many loopholes that have eviscerated them—will be told later in this chapter.) To get the federal money, candidates must agree to raise no other funds (with the exception of money they need to pay the lawyers and accountants required to fill out the FEC forms). Thus, in 2000, the Bush and Gore general election campaigns were able to spend $67.6 million each, plus the money needed for accountants and lawyers.

The money spent by candidates, however, is only a small part of the total cost of the general election campaign. Most of the campaign communications are funded by groups and individuals other than the campaigners themselves. The implications are important. The candidates' campaigns are (largely) under their own control; spending by other groups in the election is not and, thus, may emphasize appeals that the candidate would prefer to avoid. Even the "friendly fire" laid down by the parties' committees and supportive interest groups can pose a real problem for candidates, simply by diverting voters' attention from the campaign's own agenda.

Who are the other big spenders? The major party organizations funded much of their national conventions and also spent a great deal in the general election on advertising, consultants, and other services to support their party's candidate, in both coordinated

TABLE 12.3 What It Cost to Nominate and Elect a President: 2000

	Amount (in millions)	
I. Prenomination Receipts and Spending	Raised	Spent
All Republican candidates	$232.7	$224.7
Bush	94.5	89.1
Forbes	48.1	47.8
McCain	45.0	44.6
All Democratic candidates	95.9	88.0
Gore	49.2	42.5
Bradley	42.1	41.1
Third party candidates	14.4	13.3
Independent expenditures by political action committees		1.2
Communication costs		3.3
Issue advocacy ads by interest groups, individuals, and parties		*
II. Conventions		
Public funding for party conventions		29.5
Private funding		*
III. General Election		
Public funding for major party candidates		$135.2
Public funding for Reform Party candidate		12.6
Private funding for minor party candidates (mainly Nader)		5.7
Parties' coordinated expenditures		26.7
Parties' soft money, issue advertising		at least 58*
Issue advocacy ads by interest groups and individuals		*
Independent expenditures		14.7
Communication costs		*
Compliance costs		18.6
Recount funds		11.2*

* unreported or incompletely reported

Source: Calculated from John C. Green and Nathan S. Bigelow, "The 2000 Presidential Nominations: The Cost of Innovation," in David B. Magleby, ed., *Financing the 2000 Election* (Washington, DC: Brookings, 2002), p. 55; and Anthony Corrado, *"Financing the 2000 Presidential General Election,"* in Magleby, ed., *Financing the 2000 Election,* pp. 87–102. The data are drawn from the FEC.

expenditures and soft money. (We will look more closely at these types of spending later.) In addition, party organizations, individuals, and PACs are permitted to spend as much as they choose in support of or opposition to a candidate; under the law, this spending must be done without the knowledge or cooperation of any candidate. These ***independent expenditures*** vary a lot from election to election.[7]

Communication costs involve spending by organizations to urge their workers or members to vote for a particular candidate; labor unions account for most of this money. Labor unions, corporations, and membership associations also spent millions on "nonpartisan" voter mobilization—mainly in programs to register voters and get them to the polls on Election Day. Again, labor unions were the big spenders here.[8]

Congressional Campaigns

Candidates for Congress in 2000 spent a total of a little over $1 billion in the primaries and general elections (see Table 12.2). That was a major increase over the $740 million spent in the midterm elections of 1998 and the $764 million spent in the last set of Senate and House races in a presidential election year (1996). The candidates themselves are the biggest spenders in most congressional contests, so our attention will be focused primarily on them.[9]

One of the cardinal rules of modern campaign finance is that incumbent officeholders vastly outspend their challengers in campaigns for Congress. In the 1991–1992 electoral cycle, the spending edge for incumbents was almost 1.8 to 1; it had grown even more by 1999–2000, especially in House races. But the partisan direction of this advantage has changed. Until 1994, most congressional incumbents in most election years were Democrats, so Democratic candidates were normally able to outspend Republicans in congressional elections. But the electoral tides were running Republican in 1994; Republican candidates increased their spending by almost 25 percent overall, which put them ahead of the Democrats, and the Republican Party won majorities in both the House and the Senate for the first time since 1954. Their status as the majority party gave the Republicans an even greater financial advantage going into the next two congressional elections. When the two parties' prospects looked more similar in 2000, the Republican edge was reduced.

Looking beneath these totals, we see a great deal of variation in individual campaigns. The biggest spender in the 1999–2000 Senate races was New Jersey Democrat Jon Corzine, a former investment banker and multimillionaire who won an open seat after spending $63 million. All the candidates in the unusual New York Senate race between First Lady Hillary Rodham Clinton and Representative Rick Lazio spent a total of $92 million, of which Clinton and Lazio's campaigns together accounted for more than $70 million. The smallest campaign bank account belonged to Republican incumbent Olympia Snowe of Maine, whose reelection campaign cost just under $2 million. The average Senate candidate spent $5.6 million in the 2000 general election (compared with $3.6 million in 1998), and it cost an average of $3.6 million even to lose a race.[10]

Corzine was only the latest entry in what has been a remarkable escalation in spending on Senate campaigns. North Carolina's Senator Jesse Helms had set the record in the 1980s, spending $13.4 million to keep his job. In 1994, Republicans Oliver North and Michael Huffington, the losing Senate candidates in Virginia and California, respectively, spent $20.6 million and $28 million in their efforts to beat Democratic incumbents. But in 2000, Corzine spent more than $34 million *in the primary election alone* to defeat a prominent New Jersey Democrat for nomination to the U.S. Senate—a reported $141 per vote—and contributed $60 million of the $63 million spent by his campaign overall. The average 2000 House general election campaign, by contrast, cost "only" about $670,000—way up from about $493,000 in 1998. A growing number of House candidates are running million-dollar campaigns, however, and in 2000, the House race between incumbent James Rogan and Democrat Adam Schiff, which cost $18.5 million, of which the candidates raised and spent $11.5 million, set the all-time record.

The candidates are not the only important spenders in congressional campaigns. The parties invest money in races for Congress in addition to the sums they give directly to candidates. The House and Senate campaign committees, national committees, and state and local committees spent $50.6 million on behalf of candidates of their parties in 1999–2000; Republican committees outspent the Democrats. Corporations, labor unions, and other groups also invest money directly in campaign activities. The money is intended to encourage their members to oppose or support particular candidates and to get them to the polls.[11]

State and Local Campaigns

We know much less about spending practices in the thousands of campaigns for state and local office, mainly because there is no central reporting agency comparable to the FEC. The range in these races is tremendous. Many state and local candidates win after spending a few hundred dollars. On the other hand, in the spring of 2001, 11 candidates running for a single seat on the Los Angeles city council reported spending a total of $1.4 million—and that was a week before the primary election was held. That fall, Michael R. Bloomberg spent $69 million of his own money to become mayor of New York, which was about $68.7 million more than the job's annual salary.[12]

Campaigns for governor in big states often cost as much as, or more than, races for the U.S. Senate; California typically sets the records. Successful contests for the state legislature in large states can require more than $100,000 and spending in these contests seems to be growing faster than for any other office. Again, the most expensive contests are usually found in California. By 1998, it cost an average of $500,000 to win a seat in the lower house of the California legislature, and some particularly competitive races drove that cost up far more. Even state supreme court elections are becoming big-spending contests; the average candidate for a state supreme court seat in 2000 raised almost half a million dollars, much of it from trial lawyers who have a big stake in the judges' rulings.[13]

WHAT IS THE IMPACT OF CAMPAIGN SPENDING?

Money does not buy victory—but it certainly doesn't hurt, either. In the general election for president, both sides have enough money to reach voters with their messages, so the candidate with the largest war chest does not gain an overwhelming advantage. Money matters more in the nomination race for president, especially in buying the early visibility that is so vital to an underdog. Nevertheless, a big budget did not make Steve Forbes a front-runner, and once a candidate has qualified for federal matching funds, the advantage money can confer narrows considerably.

In other races, as well, there are times when unique circumstances can propel a candidate to victory even when he or she has campaigned for office on a shoestring. Recall the case of Jesse Ventura, a former professional wrestler, who ran as the Reform Party candidate for governor of Minnesota in 1998. Ventura won the three-way race after spending only $200,000 on his campaign, while his Democratic and Republican rivals spent about $6 million between them. Ventura's forceful personality, the novelty of his campaign, and other unusual aspects of the race brought free media attention that helped substitute for a big campaign budget.

The best evidence we have about the impact of campaign spending refers to congressional races. Researchers find that money makes a real difference in these elections. The more challengers can spend when they run against incumbents, the better their chances of victory. The same is not always true for incumbents. Gary Jacobson found that the more incumbents spend, the worse they do in the race. It is not that incumbent spending turns voters off, but rather that incumbents tend to spend a lot when they face serious competition. A big budget for an incumbent, then, signals that he or she has (or expects) an unusually strong challenger.

Other researchers have questioned this conclusion. They argue that when incumbents spend more, they do get a return in terms of votes. The dispute turns on thorny questions about the proper way to estimate the impact of spending, but there is general agreement on two points. First, House incumbents rarely face a serious challenge for reelection. Second, when they do have a strong opponent, incumbents may not be able to survive the challenge by pouring more money into their reelection effort.[14]

These findings have important implications for current efforts to reform campaign spending. If both incumbents and challengers have a better chance of winning as their campaign spending increases, then reforms that limit campaign spending may not advantage either one. But if challengers get more votes when they spend more, while incumbents' chances decline or are unaffected by increased spending, then putting a ceiling on campaign spending—especially if it is a low ceiling—would benefit incumbents. It seems likely that challengers need to spend more just to compensate for all the advantages incumbents enjoy: greater name recognition, more media coverage, greater experience, and so on. Most members of Congress seem to agree that spending limits would, in fact, favor incumbents. Therefore, in congressional debates about campaign finance reform, members of the majority party are more likely to favor a spending cap in congressional races.

The impact of some other spending is less clear. Communication costs incurred by labor unions overwhelmingly support Democrats, but labor support can be the kiss of death in some areas, especially when opponents make it a campaign issue. It is just as difficult to measure the effects of "nonpartisan" voter registration and get-out-the-vote drives. They are nonpartisan on the surface, but the unions, corporations, and associations that mount them usually do so in the confidence that they are mobilizing voters strongly in favor of one party or ideological preference.

WHERE DOES THE MONEY COME FROM?

Candidates raise their campaign funds from five main sources: individual contributors, political action committees, political parties, the candidates' own resources, and public (tax) funds. There are no other sources from which candidates can raise large amounts of money. Campaign finance reform, then, can't do much more than mandate a different mix among these five or try to eliminate one or more of these sources altogether (Table 12.4).

Individual Contributors

It is one of the best-kept secrets in American politics that individuals, not parties or PACs, still dominate campaign finance—at least in the form of contributions to candidates.

TABLE 12.4 Sources of Campaign Funds for Presidential and Congressional Candidates (in millions)

| | Presidential, 1999–2000 | | | | | |
| | Democrats | | Republicans | | Total | |
	Nomination	General	Nomination	General	Nomination	General
Individuals	$66.6	$0	$157.4	$0	$235.0	$5.7
Candidates	>.1	0	43.0	0	52.3	0
PACs	>.1	0	2.0	0	2.0	0
Party Coordinated	0	13.5	0	13.2	0	26.7
Public Funds	29.0	67.6	24.5	67.6	53.5	147.8
Legal, Accounting, Recount	0	11.1	0	7.5	0	29.8
TOTAL	$95.9	$92.2	$232.7	$88.3	$342.8	$210.0

| | Congressional, 1999–2000 | | | | | | |
| | Democrats | | Republicans | | Total | | Grand |
	House	Senate	House	Senate	House	Senate	Total
Individuals	$145.9	$97.5	$166.9	$152.5	$315.6	$252.1	$567.7
Candidates							
Contributions	2.4	18.3	3.7	.1	6.3	18.7	25.0
Loans	23.2	82.3	36.8	6.3	61.9	89.0	150.9
PACs	98.1	18.7	94.7	33.2	193.4	52.0	245.4
Party	1.0	.4	1.7	.5	2.7	.9	3.6
Party Coordinated	3.3	5.1	4.4	10.8	7.7	16.0	23.7
Public Funding	0	0	0	0	0	0	0
Other	.9	.3	.6	.2	1.5	.5	2.0
TOTAL	$286.7	$230.4	$317.7	$203.8	$610.4	$437.0	$1,047.3

Note: Candidate loans are personal loans by the candidate to her or his campaign. The total columns include funds for Democratic, Republican, and other candidates.

Source: For the presidential campaign, FEC data calculated from David B. Magleby, ed., *Financing the 2000 Election* (Washington, D.C.: Brookings, 2002), pp. 55, 62, 70, 89, 93; for Congress, *http://www.fec.gov/press/051501congfinact/ tables/allcong2000.html* (accessed Mar. 2, 2002).

Although public funding has reduced the role of the individual donor in presidential general elections, individuals still fund most of the nomination races, both by their contributions and through the federal matching funds they generate. Individuals also donate the largest portion of congressional campaign funds. In 1999–2000, individuals accounted for 52 percent of the contributions to House candidates and 58 percent of all of the money given to Senate candidates. Data on state elections are harder to obtain, but individual givers probably provide the majority of funds here, too.[15]

There have been changes, however, in the nature of the individual contributor. Before the 1970s campaign finance reforms, congressional and presidential candidates were allowed to take large sums of money from individual givers. Two notable examples were insurance magnate W. Clement Stone, and multimillionaire Richard Mellon Scaife, who donated a total of $3 million to the reelection campaign of President Richard Nixon in 1972. Well-supported fears that these "fat cats" were getting something in return for their money—preferential treatment ranging from tax breaks to ambassadorships—led Congress to set a maximum of $1,000 on donations to any single candidate for federal office.

For the next two decades, these limits seemed to work. Because of the reforms, congressional campaigns were financed not by a handful of big givers, but by large numbers of people making small donations. That was also true of the nomination phase of presidential campaigns. These small contributors are not very representative of the American electorate. Generally speaking, they tend to be older, more involved in politics, more conservative, and wealthier than the average American.[16] But they resemble the typical American voter much more closely than the Stones and the Scaifes did.

Campaigns, then, had to learn new ways of separating prospective contributors from their money. When the "fat cats" were the preferred funding source, they were wooed by personal visits and phone calls with the candidate. Group events, such as star-studded dinners or a briefing from a top adviser, also brought in large sums. The small contributors, however, are usually found and solicited by mail. With computerized mailing lists and the technology for personalizing letters, direct-mail consultants can often raise a lot of money; mailing lists of dependable donors have become one of the most treasured resources in modern campaigning. In contrast to earlier elections, when individual contributors had typically been more generous to Democratic congressional candidates than to Republicans, the GOP has maintained the edge since it took over control of Congress in 1994.

These small contributors have continued to be very important to campaign fundraisers. But with the rise of soft money and issue advocacy ads, as we will see shortly, the fat cats were back. From the late 1970s through 2002, campaign finance loopholes allowed wealthy donors to funnel large sums into candidates' campaigns via the party organizations. As a result, the influence they could exert over candidates revived as well.

Political Action Committees

Political action committees (PACs) are political groups, other than party organizations, whose purpose is to raise and spend money to influence elections. Most PACs have been set up by corporations, labor unions, or trade associations; these "parent" groups can help support a PAC as it begins its work of raising money. The others have no sponsoring organizations; the so-called *nonconnected* PACs are most likely to be ideological groups of the right or the left. PACs spend the money they raise in several different ways. Some, especially the ideological PACs, may use it in independent expenditures or issue ads (see below). Other PACs give the money directly to candidates and party organizations.

Only 608 PACs existed in 1974, but by the end of 2000 that number had climbed to 4,499. The greatest growth over time has come in the number of corporate and nonconnected PACs. Corporate PACs climbed from 15 percent of the 1974 total to 38 percent by 2000, and nonconnected PACs grew from 0 to 30 percent during this same period. The number of labor and trade association PACs increased as well.[17] There have also been big recent increases in giving by "leadership PACs"—those set up by incumbents to distribute money to other candidates. Members of Congress give campaign funds to other candidates, in order to solicit their support in elections for party leadership positions in Congress or because their Hill committee has insisted that they "share the wealth."[18]

A number of factors account for that growth. Most important was the reform legislation of the post-Watergate years. The ***Federal Election Campaign Act (FECA)*** of 1974, responding to the scandals involving wealthy individual donors, set the limit on individual contributions far below that for PACs. That made it more efficient for campaigns to raise money from PACs than from individuals. The new law also explicitly permitted corporations doing business with government to have PACs. (A previous law had stated that government contractors could not contribute directly or indirectly to federal campaigns.) Federal court decisions and the FEC confirmed the legality of PACs and the right of sponsoring organizations to pay their overhead expenses as long as the PAC's political funds are collected and kept in a separate fund; the sponsoring organization cannot use its regular assets and revenues to make political contributions. Once their legality was clarified and their fund-raising advantages became obvious, their numbers exploded.

Although PACs are an important source of campaign contributions, they are not always the big spenders that they may seem. In presidential general election campaigns, the candidates get most of their funding from federal tax money. PACs can contribute to presidential candidates during the nominating season, but these contributions have been modest in recent years ($2.6 million in 1999–2000). PACs can also make independent expenditures for or against presidential candidates. They did so to the tune of $6.1 million in the 1999–2000 electoral cycle—a big increase over their independent spending in 1996. They can air issue ads as well.

But the bulk of PAC contributions go to congressional candidates. PACs gave a total of $245.4 million to House and Senate candidates in 1999–2000 (Table 12.4), a 19 percent increase over the prior election cycle. Of the 1999–2000 total, the largest amounts came from corporate PACs (34 percent) and PACs of trade associations (28 percent; most of these are business-related as well). Nonconnected PACs added 15 percent, and labor PACs gave 20 percent. Even these large numbers, however, accounted for only a quarter of all the money received by congressional candidates in 1999–2000 (23 percent).

Another limit on their power is that PACs are not monolithic; their contributions come from several thousand different PACs representing diverse and even competing interests. Although corporate PACs are the largest PAC givers, often donating almost twice as much to Republicans as to Democrats, there are both business and labor PACs among the biggest PAC spenders (see Table 12.5). Further, because labor PACs give almost all of their money to Democratic candidates, they help to compensate for the Republican edge in corporate contributions. Other types of PACs give to candidates from both parties.

Candidates pursue the PACs at least as seriously as they pursue individual contributors. Both parties' congressional and senatorial campaign committees work hard to connect their candidates with PACs likely to be sympathetic to their causes. Campaigners also seek PAC help directly, assisted by the directories that list PACs by their issue positions, the size of their resources and their previous contributions. Incumbent Congress members invite PACs or the lobbyists of their parent organizations to fund-raising parties in Washington, at which a check earns the PAC people hors d'oeuvres, drinks, and, they hope, legislative gratitude. PACs take the initiative as well. Unlike most individual donors, they are in the business of making political contributions and they don't necessarily wait to be asked.[19]

TABLE 12.5 The Top-Ten (Plus One) List of the Biggest PACs (in Contributions to Federal Candidates, 1999–2000)

| Rank | PAC | Contributions to federal candidates | | |
		Democrats	Republicans	Total
1.	Realtors PAC	$1.4 million	$2.0 million	$3.4 million
2.	Association of Trial Lawyers of America PAC	2.3	.3	2.7
3.	International Brotherhood of Electrical Workers PAC*	2.5	<.1	2.6
4.	American Federation of State, County & Municipal Employees*	2.5	.1	2.6
5.	Teamsters Union*	2.4	.2	2.6
6.	National Auto Dealers PAC	.8	1.7	2.5
7.	Laborers Union*	2.0	.2	2.2
8.	Machinists/Aerospace Workers Union PAC*	2.2	<.1	2.2
9.	United Auto Workers PAC*	2.1	<.1	2.2
10.	American Medical Association PAC	1.0	1.0	2.0
11.	National Beer Wholesalers Association PAC	.4	1.5	1.9

Note: *Labor union PACs. Totals do not always add up to 100 percent due to rounding error.

Source: http://www.opensecrets.org (accessed Mar. 2, 2002). Opensecrets is a nonprofit group that tracks PAC spending and lobbying. Its data are drawn from FEC reports.

What do PACs buy with their donations to congressional campaigns? Most PAC money is intended to gain access for the giver: the assurance that the legislator's door will be open when the group needs to plead its case on a bill. The result is that most PAC contributions go to incumbents—in 2000, almost three-quarters of all PAC spending. Challengers get only a small share of the PACs' largesse; there is little advantage, after all, in getting access to a likely loser. PAC money, like individual donations, therefore flows to the party with the most incumbents, and since the 1994 elections, that has been the Republicans. Party competition in the 2000 House and Senate races was so close, however, that only a bare majority of PAC money at the federal level went to Republican candidates.

It seems likely that their contributions do help them get access to lawmakers. What elected officials will fail to listen to representatives of interests that provided money for their campaigns? It is harder to determine, however, how hard they listen and whether the PAC's concerns will influence their legislative behavior. There is not much evidence that PAC contributions affect the recipients' roll call votes.[20] But legislators who receive PAC money do seem to become more active in congressional committees on behalf of issues that interest their PAC donors.[21]

There are many reasons why PAC money rarely "buys" votes. A single PAC can give no more than $5,000 directly to a member of Congress in each election or $10,000 for the primary and general election together; in fact, the great majority of PACs give much less. Most PACs, then, can be considered "small" contributors. PACs give most of their money to incumbents, who normally have a relatively easy time raising other campaign funds. In addition, PACs generally choose to support legislators who have shown that they are already favorable to the PAC's interests, rather than to uncommitted legislators. That limits the opportunity for PAC money to change legislators' votes.

In some cases, their limited success may be due to their structure as organizations. Many large PACs are set up as federations; their local members, who provide most of these PACs' money, may want to support local incumbents even when those incumbents are not helpful to the national PAC.[22] PACs' influence is also limited because they have so much competition—from party leaders, constituents, and other PACs—for the ear and the vote of a legislator. Their influence tends to be greatest when they represent powerful interests in the legislator's constituency, when they are not in conflict with his or her party's position, and when the benefit they want is of little concern to anyone else (such as a small change in the tax laws that gives a big break to a particular corporation).

Party Organizations

At the time of the 1970s reforms, the party organizations' role in campaign finance could easily have been overlooked. But party money—or, more accurately, money raised by the party organizations from individuals, PACs, and other interests—now plays an increasingly important role in campaigns. That role varies during the nominating season, as Chapters 9 and 10 indicate. Parties invest a lot of resources in their presidential nominating conventions. And, especially in the last decade, they have injected ever-growing sums of soft money into campaigns.

The parties' direct contributions are only a small part of the candidates' campaign budgets. In 1999–2000, for example, Republican committees gave $2.3 million directly to candidates and Democrats contributed $1.4 million. More substantial are the two parties' *coordinated expenditures*—the funds they spend on behalf of their candidates, typically for services such as polls, television and radio ads, and consultants' fees. Federal law limits the national parties' coordinated expenditures in each race: in the 2000 House campaigns, each party was permitted to spend $33,780 per election (with the primary and general elections counted as separate contests). In Senate campaigns, it varied with the size of the state's voting-age population: from $67,560 in Delaware to $1.6 million in California. Counting direct contributions by the party's national committee, the relevant congressional campaign committee, and the state party, plus two elections' worth of coordinated spending, each party could spend almost $100,000 in a House race and much more in a Senate race.

Overall, in the 2000 election cycle, the two parties' coordinated expenditures were about seven times larger than their direct contributions. Coordinated spending is particularly useful to the party, not only because it allows the party organizations greater opportunities to contribute, but also because party committees have more control over how the money is spent than they do in making direct contributions to candidates. Even these coordinated expenditures, however, amounted to only about 2 percent of the candidates' total spending in 1999–2000.

"Soft money," which will be discussed below, has been a much bigger portion of the party money that goes into congressional and other campaigns—many times the size of the parties' coordinated expenditures. When they began to raise soft money in a big way in 1996, both national parties almost doubled their fund-raising compared with their 1992 totals. The national Republicans made another big jump in fund-raising by 2000, and the Democrats' success in raising soft money permitted them to remain within striking range of the Republicans' totals.

The Candidates Themselves

Candidates have always spent their personal wealth on their campaigns, and that has been especially true in recent years. Take the example of Jon Corzine; FEC reports show that he invested more of his own money in his New Jersey Senate campaign than Ross Perot spent in seeking the presidency in 1992. (A placard held by a supporter of Corzine's primary opponent, referring to Corzine's reputed $400 million fortune, read, "Make him spend it all!") In 1999–2000, congressional candidates bankrolled their campaigns to the tune of $25 million plus $150.9 million in loans, representing 17 percent of all their campaign money (Table 12.4). Nineteen House candidates each contributed at least half a million dollars to their own campaigns in 2000. The averages can be greatly inflated by a few wealthy candidates, however. In 1993–1994, for example, just one candidate, Michael Huffington of California, accounted for almost a quarter of the total personal contributions and loans.

Public Funding

Finally, public funding is available for presidential campaigns if the candidate wishes to accept it—and thus, of course, to accept the spending limits that come with it. Congress voted in the early 1970s to let taxpayers designate a dollar (now $3) of their tax payments to match small contributions to candidates for their party's presidential nomination and to foot the total bill for the major-party nominees in the general election campaign. The intent was to reduce campaign corruption by limiting the role of private funds. In 2000, public matching funds in the nomination race and the general election campaign totaled $208.3 million. Public funds comprised the majority (62.5 percent) of Al Gore's spending in the nomination race and the general election, but only 35 percent of George Bush's funds. Congress has chosen not to extend public funding to its own races.

MONEY IN STATE AND LOCAL CAMPAIGNS

Evidence suggests that state and local campaigns generally follow the same pattern as those at the national level. Individual contributors are the most important source of candidates' campaign funds, followed by PAC contributions, and then, at greater distance, by party and personal funds. Also following the national example, several states and even some cities (such as New York) were providing public funding for candidates by the late 1990s. Some set campaign spending limits that were not much higher than the public funding to restrict the role of private money in these campaigns. In other states, the public funding covers only a small portion of the campaign's costs and often goes to parties, rather than candidates. But public support for these programs, as seen by taxpayers' willingness to direct their tax money to these funds, has declined sharply.[23]

There are a few interesting differences, however, between federal, state, and local campaign finance. One is that individual contributions are relatively more important in local campaigns because parties and PACs play a lesser (though expanding) role at this level. There are exceptions, of course; in Oregon, Pennsylvania, and Washington, PACs have provided at least a third of the campaign funds for legislative candidates, compared to 13 percent in Wisconsin and 12 percent in Missouri.[24] In addition, in an increasing number of states, legislative leaders and caucuses are giving money to their party's state legislative candidates. Because many states do not limit campaign contributions in state legislative contests, such donations can play a significant role in a candidate's campaign.[25]

REFORM OF THE CAMPAIGN FINANCE RULES

For years, campaign finance laws in the United States were a flimsy structure of half-hearted and not very well integrated federal and state statutes. Periodically, reformers tried to strengthen legal controls over the raising and spending of campaign money. A new episode of reform was under way in the early 1970s, when the Watergate scandals broke over the country. The revulsion caused by these fund-raising scandals produced the most extensive federal legislation on the subject in the history of the Republic—the Federal Election Campaign Act (FECA) amendments. The Supreme Court, acting in 1976, invalidated some of these 1974 reforms. Congress then revised the law and amended it again in the late 1970s. The resulting legislation has two main parts: limits on campaign contributions and spending, and a system of public funding for presidential campaigns.[26]

Contribution Limits

The law limits the amounts of money an individual, a political action committee, and a party organization can give directly to a candidate in each election (primary or general) in a given year. Legislation passed in 2002 raised the limits for the first time in almost 30 years (see Table 12.6). These limits apply only to federal campaigns—those for president and Congress. Corporations and labor unions are not allowed to contribute directly, but they may set up PACs and pay their overhead and administrative costs. The money contributed under these regulations is called **hard money**—contributions that fall under the "hard limits of the federal law."

TABLE 12.6 Limits on Campaign Contributions Under Federal Law

	Limit on Contributions		
	Individual	*Political Action Committee*	*Party Committee*
To candidate or candidate committee per election	$2,000	$5,000*	$5,000*
To national party committee per year	20,000	15,000	no limit
To any nonparty committee (PAC) per year	5,000	5,000	$5,000
Total per 2-year election cycle	95,000	no limit	no limit

*If the political action committee or the party committee qualifies as a "multicandidate committee" under federal law by making contributions to five or more federal candidates, the limit is $5,000. Otherwise the PAC is treated as an individual with a limit of $2,000. Party committees can contribute up to $17,500 to Senate candidates.

Note: These are the limits on so-called "hard money" contributions.

Source: Updated from Federal Election Commission, *Campaign Guide* (June 1985).

Spending Limits

Spending by presidential candidates was also limited by the 1970s reform. Those who accept federal money in the race for their party's nomination must also accept spending limits in each of the 50 states. These limits are set according to the state's voting-age population and, in 2000, ranged from a high of $13.1 million in California to a low of $675,000 in the smallest states. In the general election campaign, presidential candidates who accept federal subsidies can spend no more than the law permits.

The intrepid congressional incumbents tried to limit spending in House and Senate campaigns, as well, but the Supreme Court would not agree. The Court's majority accepted the arguments of a group of strange bedfellows, including conservative New York Senator James Buckley, liberal Democratic Senator Eugene McCarthy, and the New York Civil Liberties Union; they contended that the law's restrictions on campaign spending infringed on the rights to free speech and political activity. So, in *Buckley v. Valeo*,[27] the Court ruled that Congress could limit campaign spending only for candidates who accepted public funding. Congress could apply spending limits to its own campaigns, then, only as part of a plan for subsidizing them. That would mean subsidizing their challengers' campaigns as well. For congressional incumbents, who are normally quite capable of outraising their challengers, that was not an attractive prospect.

Public Disclosure

A vital part of the FECA reform was the requirement that contributions and spending be disclosed publicly. The principle was that if voters had access to information about the sources of candidates' cash, they could punish greedy or corrupt campaigners with their ballots. All donations to a federal candidate must now go through and be accounted for by a single campaign committee; before the reforms, candidates could avoid full public disclosure by using a complex array of committees. Each candidate must file quarterly reports on his or her finances and supplement them with reports ten days before the election and 30 days afterward. All contributors of $200 or more must be identified by name, address, occupation, and name of employer.

Earlier legislation had tried and failed to achieve this goal. Required reports were sketchy at best and missing at worst. The new legislation improved the quality of reporting, however, by creating the Federal Election Commission (FEC) to collect the data and to make them available. Some members of Congress still try to undercut the disclosure of campaign finance data by regularly threatening to reduce the FEC's funding. But the commission's public files, available on the Internet (at *http://www.fec.gov*) as well as on paper, have provided a wealth of campaign finance information for journalists and scholars.

Public Funding of Presidential Campaigns

Although Congress has not yet been willing to fund its own challengers from the public treasury, since 1976 it has provided public funding for presidential candidates. To get the money, a candidate for a party's presidential nomination must first raise $5,000 in contributions of $250 or less in each of 20 states, as a way of demonstrating broad public support. After that, public funds match every individual contribution up to $250. In addition, the Democratic and Republican parties each received $13.5 million in 2000 to help pay for their national conventions. The candidate nominated in each convention receives money for the general election campaign from tax funds. The figure rises every year with increases in the Consumer Price Index; it reached $67.6 million in 2000.

Minor parties fare less well. They receive only a fraction of that total and, then, only after the election if they have received at least 5 percent of the vote. Once they have reached that milestone, however, they have qualified to receive their payment before the next presidential election. Because Ross Perot won 8 percent of the vote as the Reform Party's presidential candidate in 1996, the party's candidate in 2000 was guaranteed to receive $12.6 million in advance of that campaign. That clearly enhanced the attractiveness of the Reform Party's nomination. No other minor party has ever qualified for public funding, however. Because of the need to pay cash for many campaign expenses, this provision of FECA adds to the difficulty of financing even a modest third-party campaign.

THE LOOPHOLES THAT ATE THE REFORMS

This set of reforms was far-reaching. Yet, not long after the legislation was passed, those affected by it began to find and exploit loopholes in its provisions. Seeds were planted by FECA amendments in 1979 and by FEC and Supreme Court action, which have steadily eaten away at the framework of the FECA reforms.

Independent Spending

If an interest group or individual runs a campaign ad in support of a candidate and works with the campaign in doing so, then the law treats that ad as a campaign contribution. But as long as the individual or group does not coordinate its advertising with a candidate's campaign, then it is regarded by the Supreme Court as *independent spending,* and the group is permitted to spend unlimited amounts of money on it. The Court majority's logic in the case of *Buckley v. Valeo* was that free speech is fundamental to American democracy and since "free" speech normally costs money to disseminate through radio, TV, and other media, Congress cannot limit the amount that groups, individuals, or parties can spend on campaign ads that are run independent of a candidate's campaign.

Independent spending poses a number of challenges. For one, it can easily promote irresponsible campaign attacks. If a *candidate* launches an outrageous attack, voters can protest by supporting his or her opponent. But, if an independent spender runs an outrageous ad, who can be held responsible? The independent spender can't be punished at the polls; he or she isn't running for anything. And because independent spenders, by definition, are not supposed to be coordinating their efforts with a candidate, is it fair to punish the candidate for the offensive ad? So they are free to make whatever charges they wish and the candidate they favor can't be held accountable.

From the candidate's perspective, the ads run by an independent spender may prove to be a mixed blessing. The spending, because it must be made independently of the candidate's campaign, may not convey the messages the campaign would prefer. In fact, at times it may work to the candidate's disadvantage. A group called Americans for Job Security, for instance, spent $2 million to defeat Democratic House member Frank Pallone in 1998—twice Pallone's entire campaign budget—but flooded the airwaves with such negative ads that the opposing candidate felt it may have helped Pallone win reelection.[28]

Finally, from a regulator's perspective, the problem is to determine how independent the spending really is. The 2000 presidential race was beset with an unusually heavy volume of these ads, from advocates on both sides of issues ranging from abortion to gun control. A high-tech executive put more than a million dollars into newspaper and Internet ads lambasting Bush on education,[29] and a wealthy Bush supporter spent about $2.5 million in the primaries on an ad praising Bush's environmental record. These sky-high expenditures were legal, because they claimed to be independent of the presidential candidates' campaigns. But were they? Short of an admission of guilt, how would you prove collusion between an independent spender and a presidential campaign?

Soft Money

When Congress provided public funding for presidential general election campaigns, candidates accepting the money were required to limit their overall spending. Presidential candidates, then, put their scarce dollars into the campaign techniques they regarded as most effective: TV, radio and newspaper advertising, and direct mail. There was little money to spare for such traditional campaign paraphernalia as bumper stickers, leaflets, and campaign buttons. Local and state parties complained; the buttons and bumper stickers, they argued, were vital in helping them drum up enthusiasm among party loyalists. So as a means of strengthening state and local parties, the new law in 1979 exempted from federal regulation any money raised and spent by state and local parties for party-building, voter registration, and get-out-the-vote activities—even though these activities would inevitably help bring out voters who could then cast votes in presidential and congressional elections. This came to be called *soft money.*[30]

The law was interpreted to allow unlimited contributions not only to be donated to state and local parties, but also to pass through national party committees on their way to the state parties. So although FECA permitted individuals to give no more than $1,000 each to a federal candidate per election, citizens could also give unlimited amounts of money to party organizations as soft money. These funds couldn't be spent directly on federal campaigns, but they could pay for any nonfederal portion of a campaign effort and they had a tendency to migrate wherever they were needed. In effect, then, soft money became a way for individuals and PACs to launder large contributions through a party organization. Indeed, much of the soft money came from individuals who gave large sums. Fat cats, in short, had reentered the building. It was not the law's stated intention for soft money to become an end run around the limits on hard money. But the difficulty of monitoring the uses of these funds made it so. Soft money could be raised not only from individuals and PACs, but from corporations' profits and labor union dues as well—funds that cannot be donated directly to federal candidates under FECA.[31]

Tremendous sums of money have flowed through the soft-money conduit in recent years (see box on p. 242). In 1999–2000, for example, the major national party committees raised $495 million in soft money—almost twice the amount raised in the last presidential election cycle. Much of this total was generated by the efforts of the Democratic National Committee ($101.9 million) and the Republican National Committee ($113.1 million). Soft money had become so attractive a source of funding—especially

The New Fat Cats: Soft-Money Donors in 2000

The Democratic and Republican Parties almost doubled their "take" of soft money in the 1999–2000 election cycle, compared with 1997–1998. Five corporations and five labor unions each gave more than $2 million. The unions donated almost exclusively to the Democrats; they included the American Federation of State County and Municipal Employees (a public employees' union; $5.9 million), the Service Employees International Union ($4.3 million), Carpenters and Joiners ($2.9 million), Communications Workers of America ($2.4 million), and United Food and Commercial Workers ($2.1 million). The corporations split their giving more evenly. Although Philip Morris ($2.4 million) donated the bulk of its money to Republicans, AT&T ($3.8 million), Freddie Mac (a mortgage corporation; $2.4 million), and Microsoft ($2.3 million) tilted Republican less heavily, and Global Crossing (telecommunications; $2.1 million) gave a little more than half its donations to the Democrats.

Note: These are FEC data; totals reflect contributions made by individuals associated with the company or union as well as official company contributions.

Source: Center for Responsive Politics, *http://www.opensecrets.org* (accessed October 14, 2001).

for the Democrats, who now find it more difficult to attract hard money—that in 2000, it comprised almost half of the total receipts of the Democratic Party and about one-third of the Republicans' (see Figure 12.1).

In early 2002, after four years of trying, congressional reformers succeeded in passing legislation that would ban most soft money; the ban would take effect right after the 2002 elections. National party committees would no longer be able to accept soft money, and contributions to state and local parties would be capped at $10,000. The immediate result, of course, was to set off an unprecedented drive by both national parties to soak up every possible drop of soft money contributions before the November 2002 deadline. The likely long-term effects are not as obvious. If the soft money had been used mainly to beef up the party organizations' capabilities, then its loss would be very painful. But most of the time, the parties have been little more than a pipeline by which big soft-money contributions have moved from the givers to the candidates. Opponents of the reform filed suit soon after it was signed into law. The only certainty is that campaign specialists are working to adapt to the change, so that big money can continue to flow into federal campaigns.

Issue Advocacy Ads

Soft money has been used to fund a number of different campaign efforts. It can pay a portion of the party organization's overhead expenses and activities (such as registration and get-out-the-vote drives); it has been transferred to state and local parties for their use, and it can fund issue advocacy ads and generic party advertising. An *issue advocacy* ad is a campaign advertisement that does not include the terms "elect," "vote for," or "support." As long as an ad does not use these "magic words," the courts define it as "issue advo-

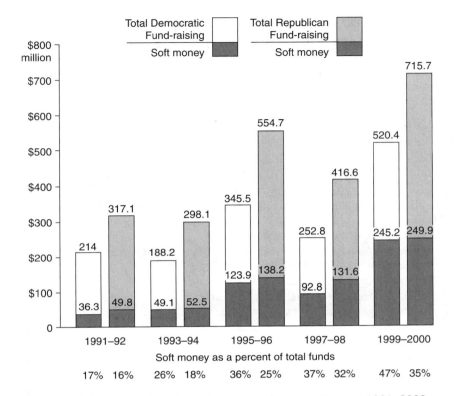

FIGURE 12.1   Increasing Party Dependence on Soft Money: 1991–2000.

Note: Bars represent total party fund-raising and the portion of it received in the form of soft money for each election cycle.

Source: FEC data, from *http://www.fec.gov/press/051501partyfund/051501partyfund.html* (accessed Sept. 10, 2001).

cacy" instead of election advertising, or "express advocacy." Therefore, the courts say, it is not subject to FECA's reporting requirements, or spending limits; instead, it falls under the First Amendment's right to freedom of expression and cannot be regulated.

Here are two examples of ads that were considered "issue advocacy" by courts in 1996 and 2000; thus, they could be funded with unlimited amounts of money and fully coordinated with the candidate's campaign, with no need for the sponsoring organization to disclose its receipts or spending:

"Congresswoman Andrea Seastrand has voted to make it easier to dump pollutants and sewage into our water. Fact is, it's time to dump Seastrand, before she dumps anything else on us." (Sponsored by the Sierra Club)[32]

[video: pictures of babies, one wearing a Yankee ball cap] "In New York, all babies like these have something in common. They've lived here longer than Hillary Rodham Clinton." (Sponsored by the American Conservative Union)[33]

These certainly sound like campaign ads. But because they don't use the "magic words," they give these groups, as well as corporate and union givers, party organizations and big individual donors, a perfectly legal way around the limits imposed by FECA (see Figure 12.2). Why does that make sense? Because the Supreme Court has ruled that even though citizens need to protect themselves against the corruption that can result from campaign contributions, it is even more important to protect individuals' and groups' right to express their ideas freely. They certainly did in 2000; the volume of issue ads funded by interest groups and parties threatened to drown out the voices of the candidates.

"527" Groups

In recent years, almost 2,000 political groups have formed to take advantage of a provision in tax law (which gave them their name: the "527s") allowing them to raise and spend unlimited amounts of money on campaigns without disclosing their contributors or spending, as long as they do not expressly call for the election or defeat of specific candidates. By mid-summer in the 2000 campaign, these groups had already spent more than $130 million on political donations and campaign ads, and were expected to account for 10 to 20 percent of all election spending.[34]

Some of these groups are traditional PACs whose campaign advertising is easy enough for voters to identify. Others carry such generic labels as Citizens for Better Medicare, a group formed by drug companies. This group spent an estimated $40–65 million in the 2000 election, including about $8 million on an ad campaign opposing prescription drug coverage under Medicare, yet it didn't have to disclose its contributors or its spending, under IRS rules. Another group, called the Republican Leadership Coalition, spent almost $2 million on ads encouraging Democrats to vote for Ralph Nader for President, rather than Al Gore; the group's executive director explained, "I don't think he (Bush) could have gotten away with it the way we did."[35]

Congress voted in the summer of 2000 to require such groups to disclose their contributors and expenses. But they still get favorable treatment under tax law, and they are still able to raise and spend unlimited amounts of money for campaign ads, which are protected as free speech. And after Congress acted, some of these groups reorganized themselves as for-profit organizations to avoid the need for disclosure.

WHAT HAVE THE REFORMS ACCOMPLISHED?

With loopholes this size, there was reason to wonder by the end of the 2000 campaign if the reforms were on life support. As one expert observer noted, "In the world we live in today, practically speaking, there are no limits on what you can give to a campaign.... We're looking at a shrinking pie of reportable money, and it's frightening."[36] Have the reforms had any lasting impact?

Intended and Unintended Effects

In fact, the reforms did achieve *most* of the goals they were intended to reach. They slowed the growth of campaign spending in presidential races—at least in spending by the candidates' own campaigns. Between 1960 and 1972, presidential campaign expenditures had shot up by 225 percent; from 1972 to 1996, however, real spending increased

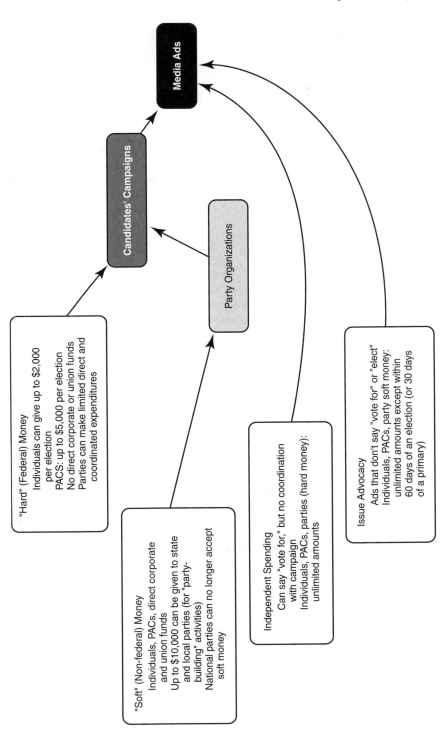

FIGURE 12.2 How Money Flows Into Federal Campaigns.

Source: Adapted from "Types of Contributions," *Congressional Quarterly Weekly Report (CQ Weekly)*, May 13, 2000, pp. 1086–1087 and "The Bill at a Glance," *Washington Post*, March 21, 2002. This is the status of the regulations beginning November 6, 2002 unless court challenges to the reforms are successful.

by only 36 percent, and in three of the eight elections, spending actually declined. The reforms also opened much of the campaign finance process to public scrutiny.

Like all reforms, however, the campaign finance laws of the 1970s have had some unintended effects—and some worrisome ones. One of the biggest is the ever-expanding imbalance between hard money contributions to candidates, which are sharply limited, and the unlimited spending that soft money, issue advocacy ads, and independent expenditures have made possible. In the early days of the reforms, the limits on hard-money contributions made small donations more valuable to candidates than ever. That had the beneficial effect of broadening the base of campaign finance. But it also affected the climate of campaign communication. To raise enough money through small contributions, candidates and parties turned to experts in direct mail fund-raising, which is designed to reach a broad range of prospective donors. Direct mail is most effective when it makes dramatic and even inflammatory appeals. These raise the temperature, but not the tone of campaign debate.

Over time, the emphasis on small contributions posed other challenges as well. Candidates complained that the limits on these hard money contributions were too low. The cap of $1,000 on individual donations was not raised until 2002, though inflation had eroded its value during that time. So, to an increasing extent, these relatively low ceilings made soft money and independent spending all the more attractive to parties and candidates. We have already explored some of the dangers posed by these forms of spending.

The growth of soft money and independent spending has had partisan implications as well. Republican candidates tend to be favored by the groups that do independent spending—at first, wealthy individuals and ideological PACs, and more recently corporate and trade association PACs and the parties themselves. So the net effect of independent spending has probably been to pad the existing Republican advantage in congressional campaign spending. Republicans also have an edge in raising soft money. But Democratic fund-raisers have done a more effective job of matching the Republicans in soft money—because of the Democrats' traditional ability to raise large sums from labor unions and some wealthy individuals—than in hard money, so in this avenue of the money chase, the partisan imbalances have been more limited. A soft money ban, then, will probably increase the Republican advantage in fund-raising, by increasing the value of their edge in hard money contributions and independent spending.

Incumbents and wealthy candidates have also benefited from the reforms. The rise of PACs has added to the already considerable advantages held by incumbents in congressional races. And although candidates who are affluent enough to bankroll their own campaigns have always been sought after in politics, the courts' explicit statement that candidates are allowed to spend unlimited amounts of their own money on their campaigns has made them even more attractive to party and interest group leaders.

In the long run, then, the reformers' efforts have failed to meet one of their major goals: reducing the influence of "interested money" by broadening the base of campaign funding. Currently, less than 5 percent of Americans give money to political campaigns, and only one-quarter of 1 percent give $200 or more.[37] All the rest of the money given to campaigns comes from groups—corporations, labor unions, and other organized interests—that want something specific from government. In 2001, for example, with the parties balanced so closely in Congress, fund-raising began right after the ink was dry on the previous election results. One Republican dinner raised a record $20 million in a single evening, most of it in soft money. Some of the biggest givers, including telecommunications companies (for the Republicans) and trial lawyers (for the Democrats), had major interest in pending legislation.

Effects on the Parties

For the first two decades after FECA was passed, the prevailing view was that the reforms had harmed the party organizations. By limiting the parties' direct contributions to presidential and congressional candidates, some argued, the party organizations were treated as no more privileged in the campaign process than were PACs or other groups. In addition, the public funding of presidential campaigns goes to the candidates themselves, not to the parties, as it does in most other democracies. That creates more distance between the party organization and the presidential campaign.

Since 1996, however, we have seen that loopholes in the reforms—particularly the provisions for soft money and issue advocacy—have given the national parties the means to raise much more money than ever before. That, in turn, has opened a major new avenue for expanding party money in campaigns. In 17 of the most competitive House and Senate races in 2000, party organizations spent more on TV and radio advertising than the candidates did.[38] Most of this party advertising was paid for by soft money. So were the beefed-up voter mobilization programs so prominent at the conclusion of the campaign. Very little of the party-funded issue advocacy even mentions the party labels, so it may not be helping to strengthen the parties' ties with voters, but it is certainly very significant to candidates.[39]

State and local parties, energized by money received from the national parties and by their own success in fund-raising, have become more actively involved in campaigns as well and even in the labor-intensive grassroots work that was the staple of party organizations in an earlier era. Soft money, then, has allowed the parties to become more equal partners with the candidates than had been the case in more than half a century. Further, party organizations have used some of these new riches to invest in long-term state and local party-building.

Has this new party money given the state and national party organizations the ability to tell their candidates how to campaign? Does it give party organizations a voice in how their members of Congress vote on legislation? If so, that would change the balance of power within the American parties. But the conclusion of this story has not yet been written. Soft money has given the party organizations a valuable tool. As it shrinks, and moves from the national to the state and local parties, national party committees must search for new methods of influencing candidates' campaigns.[40]

State Regulation and Financing

Even more complicated than this tangled federal reform is the fabric of 50 different sets of state regulations. The Watergate scandals triggered a reform movement in many states during the 1970s. The wave of new campaign finance laws focused mainly on requiring public disclosure; there was little effort at that time to limit campaign contributions or to restrict the fund-raising practices that were commonly used in the state.

Since that time, the movement has broadened. As the federal government has pushed a number of conflict-filled social and economic issues (abortion policy, for example) back to the states, there has been a big increase in interest group activity and PAC formation at the state level. More state legislatures have worked to regulate the size of campaign contributions from PACs, individuals, labor unions, and corporations. As of 1998, 38 states limited campaign contributions by individuals—a right upheld by the Supreme Court in 2000. The same number either prohibited, or limited, union donations; almost as many put limits on PAC giving and even more regulated corporate contributions.[41] Some states have even limited contributions from the candidates themselves—a step the Supreme Court would not let Congress take in federal elections. More than half the states limit party contributions to campaigns.

A growing number of states, now nearly half, have ventured into public funding for state elections. Four states—Arizona, Maine, Massachusetts, and Vermont—approved public financing systems in initiatives between 1996 and 2000. In ten of these states, the payments go to the political parties, which can spend the money on behalf of candidates. Another ten give the funding directly to the candidates, and in three states, public funding goes to both the parties and the candidates. The level of the funding provided is not large, however, and is not typically accompanied by limits on campaign spending.[42] And in most states, as at the federal level, the agencies designed to enforce these regulations are small and poorly-funded.

Continuing Efforts at Reform

The unintended effects of the 1970s reforms—and some of the intended effects as well—continue to create pressures for new reforms. Concern about the effects of PACs has led to proposals to lower the limits on PAC contributions, limit the amount congressional candidates could accept from PACs, or even eliminate PACs altogether. Some reformers hope to restrict the amount of money a candidate can raise from outside his or her state. Others keep looking for a way to reduce independent spending without running afoul of the Supreme Court's interpretation of the First Amendment.

Above all, reformers have targeted soft money. When a U.S. Senator called soft money "that armpit of today's fundraising,"[43] and a prominent lobbyist wrote that soft money and issue ads "are making a joke of contribution limits and are allowing some of the wealthiest interests far too much power and influence,"[44] it was clear that many participants felt that the explosive increase in soft money had drained the meaning from the reforms.

The effort to cap or eliminate soft money was at the center of a series of reforms proposed by Senators John McCain (R-AZ) and Russ Feingold (D-WI), joined by Christopher Shays (R-CN) and Martin Meehan (D-MA) in the House. The proposals had been given a wink and a nod in Congress for several years during the 1990s; House members would vote for the bill knowing that it would be killed in the Senate. And not surprisingly: few of us would voluntarily turn off the spigot that provides us with ready cash in time of need.

Finally, however, the right conditions came together—the switch to Democratic control in the Senate, McCain's own dogged determination—for the Senate to pass the McCain-Feingold bill in the summer of 2001. Then a corporate scandal broke out just in time to push a House majority into supporting the bill again. The new law not only bans soft-money contributions to national parties and caps contributions to state and local party organizations, but also bans issue advocacy ads within 60 days of a general election and 30 days of a primary. The ink on the legislation was barely dry when two lawsuits mobilized to challenge its provisions, on the familiar ground that it violated the free speech and freedom of association clauses of the First Amendment.

Reform advocates were overjoyed by this victory—the first important change in the campaign finance regulations since 1979. Even so, campaign finance reform was not regarded as a "voting issue" for many citizens; big spending in campaigns had become so common that voters were numb to its effects. The successful push for a bill to limit soft money after 2002, then, has probably taken the steam out of further reform efforts for the near future.[45]

MONEY IN POLITICS, AMERICAN STYLE

The American way of campaign finance reflects the American way of politics. Our campaigns cost more than those of most other democracies for many reasons: the sheer size of our constituencies, the many elective offices at various levels of government, and the localism of American politics. Candidates play a dominant role in U.S. campaign spending just as the party in government dominates the American parties. The importance of media in American campaigns reflects the importance of media in American lives.

Campaign finance in Britain works very differently. The British election campaign runs for only about three weeks, and candidates and parties cannot buy media time for ads during this period. Instead, British party leaders get free time on the government-run BBC network. British campaigns are organized around their national party leaders, but there is considerable integration between the local parliamentary candidate and the leader, rather than the largely separate campaigns of American congressional and presidential candidates. Because the average constituency in the House of Commons has less than one-fifth as many people as the average American congressional district, smaller sums of money are spent, generally under the control of the party organizations.

One of the most important of these differences is the dominance of candidates in American campaign fund-raising. The patterns of campaign funding described in this chapter allow current elected officials to escape the control of their party organizations. That is one reason why Congress members and state legislators are reluctant to change campaign finance laws: they like the independence that the current rules bring. Even the parties' fund-raising organizations at the national and state levels—the legislative campaign committees, for example—are controlled by elected officeholders, rather than party leaders. The 1970s reforms gave the parties an expandable role and they have expanded it with enthusiasm. But it is much less than would be necessary to establish strong and disciplined parties with power over their candidates and officeholders.

We pay a price for this candidate-dominated system of campaign finance. If the party organization does not control campaign funding, then the party in government loses a big reason to remain unified and responsible as a team. When a party's candidates and officeholders have so much independence from their party organization, party activists find it much harder to achieve their legislative goals. As the costs of campaigning rise, the sector of the party that has greatest access to cash resources can secure its dominance of the party as a whole. To this point, the advantage is clearly with the candidates and officeholders.

But the story is broader than the struggle between these two segments of the American parties. More generally, the limited results of the reforms remind us that money will always have an important impact on elections. Campaign finance reforms designed to limit and channel that impact often seem like sandcastles in the face of big waves. The most foolproof restrictions become challenges for the resourceful campaigner and contributor to overcome. Reformers are often able to alter the flow of money, at least temporarily, though sometimes in ways they did not anticipate or approve. But they will never be able to eliminate it.

PART FIVE

The Party in Government

A merica's first political parties began as factions in the government.[1] The ***party in
government*** has dominated the American parties ever since. As we discussed in
Chapter 1, the boundaries of the party in government include *any elected or appointed
public officials* who see themselves as part of the party. The Republican Party in Congress is easy enough to identify: it consists of everyone elected to the House or the Senate as a Republican. But the Republican Party in government ranges far beyond this
group, to encompass a Republican president, Republican identifiers who work for federal, state, and local administrative agencies, Republican governors and state legislators,
Republicans who serve in local elective and appointive office, and even judges (and
Supreme Court Justices) who see themselves as Republicans. More than the party in the
electorate and the people who work for the party organization, it is these legislative parties and the party in the executive and the judiciary that structure partisan political conflict and shape our images of the Democratic and Republican Parties.

Unlike their counterparts in many other democracies (especially those with parliamentary systems), however, the American parties in government are only loosely organized as coalitions. Each legislator represents a different constituency and usually pays
more attention to the constituency than to his or her party leaders. The design of the federal government, with a Congress elected separately from the president, fractures the
party in government and prevents it from setting the government on a coherent policy
path. And because they have been elected independently of their co-partisans at the federal level, state and local officeholders can have very different ideas as to what a Democratic or a Republican Party in government ought to be doing. As a prominent scholar
has written, this is one of the most significant features of our politics: "What kind of
party is it that, having won control of government, is unable to govern?"[2]

For decades, reformers have dreamed of an alternative. One of the most discussed
is the idea of ***party government***, or ***responsible parties***. The argument is that American
democracy would be strengthened if the parties were to offer clearer and fuller statements of their proposed policies, nominate candidates pledged to support those policies,
and then see to it that their winning candidates enacted those programs.[3] The parties,

then, would let voters choose not only between candidates but, more importantly, between alternative sets of policies and be assured that the winning set would be put into effect. That would change and greatly strengthen the parties' role in American politics. Parties would become the main link between citizens and the uses of government power. Voters, the argument goes, would be better able to hold their government accountable.

Could this work in the United States? Probably not. Because of the separation of powers, Republicans can hold a majority in Congress while a Democrat sits in the White House, or one party can dominate the House while the other controls the Senate. In fact, in recent years, divided control of government has been the norm. We can also find a variety of goals and motives within each party. Party activists may be dedicated to certain policy goals, but they may also be motivated by personal rewards or the thrill of victory. Some party voters support the party in order to get certain policies enacted; others are attracted by personalities, traditional party loyalties, or the power of incumbency. Candidates and elected officials seek not only to put policies into effect, but also to earn the perks of power and less tangible rewards.

None of the three sectors of the parties, then, is wholly committed to winning office in order to enact party policies into law. Even if they were, their concerns might differ. Would the party's program be decided by the party organization, by its candidates and elected officials, or by the party electorate? And if the party in government were to set the party's policies, could we expect that the legislative party would agree on goals with its colleagues in the executive? You can see how difficult it would be for all parts of a party to reach agreement on a coherent set of proposals, not to mention passing it into law and enforcing it.

Several European parties behave more like responsible parties. In Britain, for example, the parliamentary government encourages the kind of legislative party unity that the advocates of responsible parties have in mind. The House of Commons selects the government's chief executive, the prime minister, from its own ranks; he or she must then keep a legislative majority in order to stay in office. That creates a powerful incentive for party government. The party in government then tries to carry out a program that was adopted with the help of party leaders, activists, and members at party conferences. But even though the uniquely American governmental design keeps the Democrats and Republicans from following that path, recently both American parties have become more focused on policy goals than they have been in decades. More and more citizens are being attracted to party work because of particular issues that concern them, so pressure builds for greater party responsibility.

At the same time, the major parties have become more central to the government's functioning. Congress and state legislatures now divide more along party lines than they have in decades. Partisanship has a major influence on the staffing of top executive offices and the appointment of judges. Thus, government policies change depending on the makeup of the party in government and the party winning the presidency is usually able to carry out much of its party platform.[4] It would be too strong to call the result an American twin of British party government, but we are probably safe in acknowledging it as a distant cousin.

The chapters in Part Five address these questions of party influence in government. Chapters 13 and 14 examine the roles of the parties in the organization and operation of the legislature, the executive branch and the courts. Chapter 15 looks at the degree to which party government can be said to exist in American politics and the reasons why policy has become a more central focus of both parties.

Parties in Congress and State Legislatures

When President Bush proposed a $1.6 trillion tax cut in March of 2001, the headlines could have read, "Conservatives in Congress Promote Tax Cut; Liberals Oppose." They could have read, "Westerners in Congress Advance Tax Cut; Easterners Oppose." Both headlines would have been largely accurate. Instead, the headlines were these:

"Republicans in the House Advance Plan for Tax Cuts" (*New York Times*)

"Democrats Tout $900 Billion Tax Alternative" (*Washington Post*)

Party ties are central to the workings of Congress and most state legislatures. That is even truer today than it was for most of the 1900s. Congress and state legislatures are organized by party. Members of each of the four congressional parties—the House Democrats, House Republicans, Senate Democrats, and Senate Republicans—show increasing levels of internal unity, and issue differences between the Republicans and Democrats are as high as they have ever been.

Yet at the same time, we find that a number of legislators cross party lines and vote against elements of their parties' platforms, sometimes even on big issues. In a number of congressional districts, voters continue to send these party "mavericks" back to Congress and state legislatures. And although the Democrats differ dramatically from the Republicans in Congress in their positions on many important issues, there is very little evidence that the party *organizations* have influenced them to do so. In fact, even the parties' leaders in Congress are limited in their ability to discipline legislators who break ranks.

Any signs of weakness in the legislative parties should come as no surprise. One of the most basic rules of American politics, the separation of powers, undermines efforts at party unity. In a political system without a separation of powers—a parliamentary regime, such as that of Great Britain—a majority party in the legislature must unite in support of its leaders in the government. When those leaders cannot muster a majority in parliament, either the governing cabinet must be reshuffled or the legislature must be dissolved and its members sent home to campaign for their jobs again. This creates powerful pressures for the legislative party to remain united.

American legislators do not face these pressures. They can reject the proposals of a president, a governor, or a legislative leader of their own party without bringing down the government and having to face a new election. They probably will not pay a high price in their constituency for doing so. And yet, in Congress and many state legislatures in the early 2000s, high levels of party competition and distinctive profiles of party support within constituencies are encouraging members of each legislative party to hang together. How is this happening, even though the institutional rules and the formal powers of party leaders don't require it? Let us start the story with a look at the leadership of legislative parties.

HOW THE LEGISLATIVE PARTIES ARE ORGANIZED

Almost all members of Congress and state legislators are elected as candidates of a major party.[1] Once they take office, however, there are enormous differences among the legislative parties that they create. In a few states, the legislative party hardly exists; in others, it dominates the legislative process through almost-daily party caucuses. The parties in most state legislatures and in Congress fall somewhere in between these extremes.

Party Organization in Congress

Every two years, at the beginning of a new congressional session, the members of each party come together in both houses of Congress. These party meetings (called *caucuses* by the Democrats and *conferences* by the Republicans) nominate candidates for Speaker of the House or president pro tempore of the Senate and set up procedures for appointing party members to congressional committees. Thus these party meetings do the initial work of organizing the House and Senate. They select the leadership of the party (the leaders, whips, policy committees) and structure the chamber itself (the presiding officer and the committees). (The party leadership positions are described in the box below.) In this way, the organization of the two parties and the organization of the House and Senate are woven together into what appears to be a single fabric.

This system of organization is dominated by the majority party. The majority party's candidate becomes Speaker of the House. The Vice President of the United States is the formal presiding officer of the Senate, but it is the majority party that manages floor action—to the degree that floor action can be managed in that highly democratic institution. The majority party chooses the chairs of all the standing committees in both houses. It hires (and fires) the staff of these committees and of the chambers. Most of each committee's members come from the majority party, by a margin that is usually larger than the majority's margin in the chamber.

The majority party, in short, controls the action in the committees and on the floor. From the early 1950s until 1994, the Democrats held this position in the House; since then and for much of the period since 1980 in the Senate, the Republicans have been in charge. This system was sorely tested in 2001 when, in what was justifiably called "uncharted territory," the Senate split 50-50 between the two parties. After a few months' experience with power-sharing under a Republican "majority" (because Republican Vice President Dick Cheney had the power to break any tie votes), one Republican senator renounced his party ties and became an independent. For the first

---

Party Leadership Positions in the House and Senate

Each party creates its own leadership structure in each house of Congress; the individual leaders are elected by the entire party membership of the chamber. At the top of the hierarchy is the party leader (called the **majority** or **minority leader**, depending on whether the party controls the chamber). In the House of Representatives, the **Speaker** ranks above the majority leader as the true leader of the majority party. These party leaders have assistants called **whips** and **assistant whips** who try to mobilize party members to vote the way the party leadership wants.

Each congressional party also has several specialized leadership positions. There is a **caucus** or **conference chair** to head the meeting of all party members. Other chairs are selected for the **Steering Committee** (among all but the Senate Republicans, where it is called the Committee on Committees), which assigns party members to committees; the **Policy Committee,** which advises on legislative action and policy priorities; the **Campaign Committee,** which provides campaign support to the party's congressional candidates; and any other committees the legislative party may create.

---

time in American history, party control of a house of Congress switched in the middle of a legislative session (see box on p. 256).

Changes in House Party Leaders' Power

Because party leaders in Congress are chosen by the votes of all members of their legislative party, their power is, in effect, delegated to them by their party caucus (or conference) and they serve subject to its approval.[2] There have been important changes over time in the willingness of the party rank and file to accept strong leadership. In addition, some party leaders have wielded more power than others, in part, due to their personal characteristics.

The Revolt Against "Czar" Cannon   Years ago, power in the House of Representatives was highly centralized in the hands of the Speaker. In the first decade of the 1900s, powerful Speaker Joe Cannon chaired the Rules Committee, the "traffic cop" through which he could control the flow of legislation to the floor. He appointed committees and their chairs, putting his lieutenants in the key positions, and generally had the resources and sanctions necessary for enforcing party discipline.[3] In 1910, however, dissidents from within his own party combined with the minority Democrats to revolt against "Czar" Cannon, and for decades after that, Speakers could not command such a powerful institutional position. Instead, they had to operate in a much more decentralized House in which party discipline could be maintained only through skillful bargaining and strong personal loyalties. Successful Speakers during this era, such as Sam Rayburn and Tip O'Neill, were consummate brokers rather than czars.[4]

The 50-50 Majority

After the last recount of the 2000 elections was completed, the new Senate emerged deadlocked, with 50 Democrats and 50 Republicans. In both houses of Congress, the chamber's business is organized and its committees are chaired by members of the majority party. But which party was that? Because the Vice President is the tie-breaker in the Senate and he was a Republican, the 50 Senate Republicans claimed the right to lead. The 50 Democrats, however, insisted on a number of concessions—and under the Senate's rules, they could have brought the chamber's work to a halt if those were not granted. These concessions included an equal sharing of committee positions, staff resources, and office space in an unprecedented power-sharing agreement.

Partisan conflict in the chamber was high, however, and the agreement quickly began to fray at the edges. Both parties' leaders probed for members of the other party who might be persuaded to break ranks. In an institution that encourages freewheeling independence, that didn't take long. Republican Senator John McCain pushed for campaign finance reform, an issue his Senate party leaders did not want on the agenda. The situation was fluid and confusing. "We're still testing the waters to figure out who the hell is in charge," said a top Senate GOP aide. "And we're learning quickly that it isn't us."[5]

That turned out to be prophetic. In May, after expressing his unhappiness at the party leadership's treatment of Republican moderates, Vermont Senator James M. Jeffords announced that he was leaving the Republican Party to become an Independent who would caucus with the Democrats. The result was a Democratic majority of 50-49-1. Within two weeks, Republicans gave up the chairs of every Senate committee but one to Democrats (Jeffords himself now chaired the Environment and Public Works committee), and South Dakota Democrat Tom Daschle became the majority leader. Democrats got a one-seat edge on almost every committee. The solid Republican front—President Bush and a Republican House and Senate—gave way to the more usual situation of divided government. And the agenda changed; a patients' bill of rights, for example, which Bush and the Republicans opposed but the Democrats favored, jumped to the front of the line in the Senate.

Growing Party Coordination   Party coordination has increased more recently, however, especially in the House. The Republicans took a tentative step in this direction in the late 1960s, by giving rank-and-file party legislators more opportunity to influence party policy through the party conference. In the 1970s, the Democrats, under the prodding of the reform-minded Democratic Study Group[6] and the wave of liberals elected in the wake of the Watergate scandals of 1974, took more serious steps toward the same goal by strengthening both the party caucus and the party leadership.

Next came a direct assault on the party leaders' main competitors for power in the House: the chairs of the standing committees that deal with proposed legislation. These committee chairs were selected using the *seniority rule,* which directed that the most senior member of the majority party on a committee automatically became that committee's chair.[7] Because of this rule, members of the majority party could win a chairmanship simply by being reelected to Congress over and over again, even if they did not support their party leadership's position on issues—in fact, even if they voted with the *other* party more often than with their own. That gave experienced party members a base of power in Congress independent of the party leaders. Committee chairs were capable of using that power in an autocratic manner.

In a bid to enhance its own power and to give rank-and-file Democrats more rights on their committees, the Democratic caucus moved to revise the seniority rule in the mid-1970s. The caucus granted itself the power to challenge and even oust committee chairs by secret ballot. Soon after, some chairs were, in fact, challenged in the caucus and a few were defeated and replaced by the caucus's choice, who was not always the second most senior party member.[8] The effect was to increase the party leaders' authority by reducing that of the committee chairs. The reform, then, fundamentally changed the structure of authority within the Democratic-run House.[9]

The power to assign members to committees was vested in the new Steering and Policy Committee chaired by the Speaker. The Speaker was also allowed to choose, subject to caucus approval, the chair and other Democratic members of the Rules Committee, whose independence had formerly been a real thorn in the side of the party leadership. The whip system—a set of deputies responsible for informing their party colleagues about the party's stands and for finding out how many members are supporting those stands—was made more responsive to party leaders as well. And the whip system became much more elaborate; it now includes a substantial number of the party's Congress members.[10]

Policy Leadership   The reforms, then, gave the legislative party in the House, with its strengthened leadership, an opportunity to use its new power on behalf of policy goals. It is usually the party leadership, not the caucus, that sets party policy. This is especially true in the large and unwieldy House of Representatives. The floor leaders and other powerful party figures consult widely throughout the party, but the final codification of party policy, the sensing of a will or consensus, rests primarily on the leaders' judgment.[11]

In order for the legislative party to become an instrument of policy, however, most individual party members in the House would have to be willing to use the party caucus for collective party purposes and party leaders would have to be willing and able to play an active coordinating role.[12] As both parties in the House became more ideologically homogeneous during the 1970s and 1980s, the chances of accomplishing the former were increased. With changes in the Southern electorate, fewer conservative Democrats were being elected to Congress and their strongholds of committee power were fading. Democratic House members, then, were more cohesively liberal than had been the case in earlier decades. At the same time, congressional Republicans, energized especially by the conservative policy leadership coming from the White House under Ronald Reagan, became more ideologically unified as well.

When parties are ideologically cohesive and polarized on issues, it is easier for the caucus to agree on a party position on legislation. So parties become more willing to grant power to the legislative party leaders, including the power to pressure straggling legislators to fall in line, because the members can better trust their leaders to reflect the interests of the party in Congress.[13] Speaker Jim Wright, during his brief tenure as party leader in the late 1980s, took advantage of these opportunities to become one of the most assertive Democratic leaders in decades. His successor, Thomas Foley, was not as inclined to aggressive partisanship; Foley returned to a more collegial style before being defeated for reelection in the Republican surge of 1994.[14]

The Gingrich Revolution

Ironically, given that the Democrats in the House had been the agent of stronger legislative party leadership during the 1970s and 1980s, it was a Republican who brought party leadership to its recent pinnacle of power. The Republican minority had been bystanders to the Democratic procedural reforms of the 1970s and 1980s. But the 1994 election produced landmark changes. Republicans won a majority of House seats that year, after a campaign centered on their "Contract with America," a set of pledges of comprehensive policy change made most visible by the party's leader in the House, Representative Newt Gingrich.

The election of a number of new conservative members had made the House Republicans even more cohesive. Most of these newcomers had gotten campaign help from Gingrich and, together with their more senior colleagues, credited him with engineering their party's takeover of the House—the first Republican House majority in 40 years. But the Republicans had only a slender majority in the House and they faced a Democrat, Bill Clinton, in the White House. In order to try to achieve the goals of their "contract," GOP members were willing to accept strong party leadership and discipline.[15] They elected Gingrich Speaker and gave him unprecedented authority to pursue the Republican agenda.

One of the most important tools given to the Speaker by the House Republican conference was the power to select committee and subcommittee chairs who were committed to bringing the desired legislation to the floor. Gingrich was more than willing to exercise that power. Why did the committee chairs, the chief losers in this extraordinary usurpation of committee power, agree to it? The new Republican majority was so homogeneously conservative that the change may well have been propelled by dedication to the party's policy agenda—or by the chairs' personal loyalty to Gingrich or perhaps even fear for their political careers if they resisted. It was a giant step in the expansion of party power in the House and Gingrich became the strongest Speaker in modern times.[16]

The result was a level of party discipline with which "Czar" Cannon would probably have felt very comfortable. On the ten sections of the Contract with America, out of a possible 2,300 Republican voting decisions (ten provisions times 230 Republican House members), there were a grand total of only 111 "no" votes—5 percent of the Republican votes in the House in opposition to the leadership's position. And to a greater extent than had been seen in almost a century, that party discipline was directed toward achieving the congressional party's policy goals.

... and Its Aftermath

Later in 1995, however, Gingrich's aura of invincibility started to crumble. When a standoff on the national budget between President Clinton and the House Republicans led to a shutdown of the government, Gingrich and his colleagues got the blame. The Speaker was dogged by charges of ethics violations and declining popularity ratings. House Republicans had become frustrated by his uneven leadership style. An aborted effort to oust him from the Speaker's position in 1997 had quiet help from some House party leaders. Then, when the Republicans lost a net of five House seats in the 1998 election, there were widespread demands among the House Republicans for new leadership; this was only the second time since the Civil War that the party not in control of the White House lost seats in a midterm election. Gingrich resigned three days later, leaving many to wonder whether he had been better suited to be the leader of a contentious minority than of the day-to-day demands of a majority.

Gingrich's successor, Dennis Hastert of Illinois, was not as inclined by temperament to demand unshakable party discipline, and his party colleagues, in 1999, were not as inclined to give it. But although committee chairs have been allowed to take the lead on most legislation, the Republican Party leadership has maintained control over the chairs' selection. The Gingrich reforms included a six-year term limit on committee chairs. Those who hoped to head committees after the first term-limited chairs had to step down in 2001 were in the unusual position of having to submit to interviews by Hastert and other party leaders, as well as to the judgment of the party's backbenchers before the appointments were made. So even in the post-Gingrich era, the traditional pressures for committee independence continue to be more closely balanced by centralized party power.

Parties in the "Individualist Senate"

Clearly, the job of a House party leader is challenging. But the work of the Senate's party leaders is more like herding cats. By the mid-1970s, Barbara Sinclair tells us,[17] the U.S. Senate had moved from an institution governed by elaborate "rules" of reciprocity, specialization, and apprenticeship, in which powerful committees dominated the legislative work, to a much more individualistic body. Increasingly, and with avid media attention, members of the Senate established themselves as national spokespersons on various policy questions. Once they had become political "stars," these senators expected to participate more fully in the Senate's work, on their way to, many hoped, greater glory and higher office.

By the late 1980s, that individualism had led to a big increase in use (or the threat) of the peculiar Senate institution of the filibuster—the right of extended debate, used to talk a bill or a nomination to death if the votes weren't available to defeat it in any other way. Senators are also able to plaster a bill with non-germane amendments (those not pertinent to the bill) as a means of stalling it or getting other favored bills through. By the same time, the election of Ronald Reagan had led to greater party polarization in the Senate, just as it had in the House.

The combination was potentially explosive. Issues reaching both houses of Congress were often contentious. Add to this a more partisan Senate and a set of rules that permitted any member to tie up the work of the institution for an indefinite period, and the result is a desperate need for a legislative traffic cop. Increasingly, it has been the party leadership in the Senate that has tried to direct the traffic. The Senate's rules do not allow the centralization of power in the party leadership that was seen in the House in the 1990s, however.[18] So the Senate's majority and minority party leaders consult extensively with their party colleagues, rather than command them, to build the unanimous consent agreements that allow bills to be brought to a vote without risking a filibuster by an unhappy senator.

That has been an extremely difficult job. Small, organized groups of partisans intent on blocking a bill have become the main obstacles to these unanimous consent agreements. In fact, a central element in the minority party's strategy since the 1990s has been its ability to use the Senate's elaborate rules to take control of the legislative agenda from the majority party.[19] And as the parties in the Senate have become more polarized, individual senators are more inclined to expect their party leaders to promote the legislative party's interests, both inside and outside the Senate chamber.

Parties in the State Legislatures

As in Congress, the legislative parties organize the legislatures in almost every state.[20] They structure everything from the legislative leadership to its committees. The power of the legislative parties varies, however, depending on the legislature's rules and on the personal skills and resources of the party leaders. In some state legislatures, daily caucuses, binding party discipline, and autocratic party leadership make for a party every bit as potent as the Republicans in the 1995 U.S. House. In others, especially the traditionally one-party states, party organization is weaker than it was in Congress before the reforms of the 1970s. There are states, for example, in which a majority party's caucus has split, either because of ideological differences or personal rivalries. In other states, the pressure of electoral realignment has produced a bipartisan legislative leadership— as in Florida in the late 1980s, when conservative Democrats joined with a growing minority of Republicans to choose the leadership of the state senate.

More typically, however, the party leaders chosen by state legislators have great power over the day-to-day workings of the legislature. They do not usually have to defer to powerful steering committees or policy committee chairs; it is a major source of power for these party leaders that they can appoint the members, as well as the chairs of these committees, often with little or no attention to the members' seniority. Whether a legislator is picked to lead or join a committee, then, can be made to depend on his or her support for the legislative party leader personally, or for the party's views on issues the committee will consider. Yet even this substantial power is now more likely to be exercised in consultation with legislative "backbenchers." Members of state legislatures have become less tolerant of autocratic leaders, so the job of party leader is now "more complex and more challenging than in the past."[21]

Party leaders exercise their influence, in part, through the party caucus. Caucuses can be used for a number of purposes. In many states with strong two-party systems, party leaders call caucus meetings to give members information about upcoming bills, learn whether their membership is united or divided on an issue, and encourage legislators to support the party's position. Leaders in a few of these states even try, occasionally, to get the caucus to hold a "binding" vote on some important issues—a vote that calls on all members to support the party's position. Where the state parties are not as strong, it is more common for the party caucus simply to offer information, or allow leaders to hear members' opinions, but not to try to build consensus.[22]

In sum, although the parties' legislative organizations look pretty similar across the states—their party leadership positions are fairly uniform—they differ in their behavior. The power of state party leaders varies substantially, even between the two houses of the same state legislature. So does the influence and effectiveness of the party caucus.[23]

THE USES OF PARTY INFLUENCE

How do legislative parties and their leaders exercise their power? What resources can they use to influence their members' behavior—and what types of behavior do they try to influence?

Carrots and Sticks

Legislative party leaders have a variety of tools available in trying to shape the behavior of their party colleagues. But these tools often are not enough. The most powerful form of influence would be to remove a maverick legislator from his or her seat in the House or Senate. Party leaders do not have that power, however. Only the legislator's constituents can do that, and they are not likely to serve as the agents of the congressional party leadership. So representatives and senators can normally vote against their party's leadership or against major bills proposed by their party's president, without fear of losing their jobs. The Democrats who voted in 2001 for a Republican-backed overhaul of the bankruptcy system and the Republicans who voted to ban soft money in campaigns, over the objections of their party's leadership, were not penalized by their parties for doing so. Unless members are willing to accept party discipline, their party leaders (who, after all, are elected by the members) will find it difficult to impose.

Even the in-your-face disloyalty of supporting the other party's presidential candidate in the general election has not been punished consistently in Congress. In 1965, the House Democratic caucus stripped committee seniority from two southern Democrats who had supported the Republican presidential candidate, Barry Goldwater, the year before. In 1968, the same fate befell Representative John Rarick, a Democrat from Louisiana, for supporting George Wallace. In 2000, however, a conservative southern Democrat, Representative Ralph Hall from Texas, endorsed Republican George W. Bush for president and faced no sanctions from his party.

Perhaps the most famous example of the weakness of party penalties is the story of Phil Gramm, elected as a Democratic representative from Texas. The House Democratic leadership gave Gramm, a conservative, a seat on the prestigious House Budget Committee, in return for his promise to cooperate with the party leadership. But in 1983, members of the Democratic caucus were outraged to learn that Gramm had leaked the details of secret Democratic Party meetings on the Reagan budget to Republican House members. The caucus took away Gramm's seat on the Budget Committee. The object of this party discipline did not accept his punishment, however. He resigned his seat, went back to Texas and then ran—as a Republican—in the special election held to replace him. His constituents reelected him to the House and later to the Senate, as a Republican. In fact, he was soon back on the House Budget Committee, courtesy of the Republican leadership! As long as legislative party leaders cannot keep a party maverick from being renominated and reelected, and in districts where voters are not impressed by a legislator's party loyalty, party influence will be limited.

Even this punishment of removing legislators from their committee positions is used only rarely. Several of Gramm's Southern Democratic colleagues had voted for the Republican budget in 1983, but were not disciplined in any way. Republican Speaker Newt Gingrich made veiled threats in 1995 to remove some GOP committee chairs from their positions when they stood in the way of action on the party's Contract with America. His maneuver worked; the chairs became more compliant. If it hadn't, Gingrich would have had to call on an unusual level of party conference support in order to make good on his threats.

In sum, the House and Senate party leaders have a fairly short list of punishments at their command in trying to unify their parties and they can use those punishments only as long as their party colleagues are willing to accept them. So the party organizations in Congress rely on carrots much more than these fairly weak sticks to increase party cohesiveness. Party leaders can offer desirable committee assignments, help in passing a member's bills, or even provide additional office space, in order to cultivate party support. They can promote pork barrel projects in the member's district. Through their personal relationships with party colleagues, they can try to persuade members to support the party's stands—through careful listening and dialogue, like Senate Democratic Majority leader Tom Daschle in 2001, or through more hard-edged persuasion, like his Republican counterpart, Trent Lott.

Party leaders have other persuasive resources as well. Some researchers—not all—find that junior members of Congress are more likely to vote with their party than are more senior members, perhaps because the newer legislators have greater need for the information or other resources that party leaders can provide.[24] By using their control of floor activities, party leaders can set the agenda so as to maximize party unity on important matters.[25] They can also provide campaign help: for example by giving speeches and raising money for a member's reelection effort. The parties' congressional campaign committees, with their newfound riches, have been a major factor in promoting party cohesion in Congress.[26]

PARTY INFLUENCE ON LEGISLATIVE VOTING

How well do these carrots and sticks work in practice? The first place to look is at the votes cast by Congress members on proposed bills. Roll-call votes are not the only important actions Congress members take. Yet the public nature of the roll-call vote makes it a good test of the party's ability to influence its members.

Party can influence legislators' votes in two ways: through the direct impact of the party leaders' tools of persuasion and as a result of the ability of a member's partisanship to structure issues and to create loyalties within his or her own mind. In both senses, party has a lot of competition in trying to influence legislators' votes on any given issue. There may be contending demands from organized interests and financial contributors back home, as well as from friends in the legislature. In a broad sense, there may be constituency pressure. The wishes of a president or governor may be pressed on the legislator and he or she is likely to have personal experiences with, and beliefs about, policies. On many issues, all or most of these pressures point in the same direction. When they don't, party loyalty may understandably give way.

How Unified Is Each Legislative Party?

Researchers use two kinds of measures to determine the role of the party in roll calls. The first, *party voting*, is the proportion of roll calls on which most Democrats vote one way on a bill and most Republicans vote the other way. The second, *party cohesion* (or *support*), is the percentage of legislators who vote with their party's majority on these party votes. We can begin with party voting, but first we have to define it.

Party Votes   One way to measure party voting discipline in legislatures is to use the toughest test: any legislative roll call in which at least 90 percent of one party's members vote yes and 90 percent or more of the other party vote no. By such a strict test, party discipline appears regularly in the British House of Commons, but not nearly as often in American legislatures. Under Czar Cannon, about a third of all roll calls in the House met this standard of party discipline. From 1921 through 1948, that had dropped to only 17 percent[27] and it declined steadily to about 2 to 8 percent in the 1950s and 1960s.[28] During approximately the same period, in the British House of Commons, this striking party division occurred on almost every roll call.

Since the 1990s, we have seen an increase in party-line votes, especially on issues where there are clean ideological divisions between the two parties. During the 2001 congressional session, for example, both houses were dramatically divided by party on issues such as President Bush's trillion-dollar tax cut and on a rule proposed earlier by President Clinton that would have required action by businesses to prevent repetitive stress injuries (see Figure 13.1). With the exception of the Senate Democrats in both instances, the legislative parties were highly united and highly polarized on these issues.

The "90 percent versus 90 percent" standard is too strict, however, for a look at the American legislative experience over time. So researchers have focused on a less-demanding measure: the ***party vote,*** or the percentage of roll calls on which the *majority* of one party opposed a majority of the other. By this measure, the 1990s produced the highest levels of congressional party voting in many years.

Let us start where senators think we should: with the Senate. During the late 1960s and early 1970s, a majority of Democrats opposed a majority of Republicans in only about one-third of all Senate roll-call votes.[29] By 1995, the figure was 69 percent—the highest recorded in the Senate since these measurements started in 1954. The figure dropped to 49 percent in 2000, but not because the two parties were less polarized. Instead, the Senate and House were so closely divided that party leaders avoided bringing highly partisan issues to a vote unless they felt confident of winning. When these issues *did* come to a vote and a majority of Republicans opposed a majority of Democrats, the former voted with their party's position 89 percent of the time in 2000, compared with 88 percent for the Democrats—very comparable to the levels recorded since 1996.

Party voting has been even more prevalent in the House at times.[30] From its twentieth-century lows in 1970 and 1972 (27 percent), it reached levels in the mid-1980s not seen since the partisan divisions over New Deal legislation in the 1930s (Figure 13.2).[31] In the rancorous 1995 session, party voting reached a 50-year high of 73 percent in the House. Those levels could not be sustained after 1995—the figure was down as far as 43 percent in 2000. But as was the case in the Senate, on votes where a majority of Republicans did oppose a majority of Democrats, 88 percent of Republicans voted with their party, as did 82 percent of Democrats.

What has caused the changes over time in levels of party voting? In the 1800s, congressional party voting was substantial (though still far below that of the British Parliament). This was a time when party competition existed in most congressional districts, party leaders wielded considerable legislative authority and Congress was far less professional. After 1900, following what Nelson W. Polsby has termed the "institutionalization" of Congress and what Walter Dean Burnham has seen as a "disaggregation" of party,[32] party voting dropped dramatically. The New Deal realignment of the 1930s increased the frequency of party voting, but still not to the levels seen in much of the previous century. And again, in the late 1990s, for reasons we will discuss shortly, party voting had reached its highest levels in modern times.[33]

Case 1: Cut taxes by about $1.4 trillion, as proposed by President Bush?

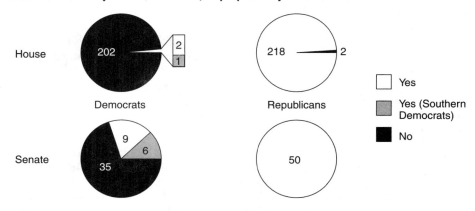

Case 2: Stop a Clinton administration ergonomics rule (to prevent repetitive stress injuries)?

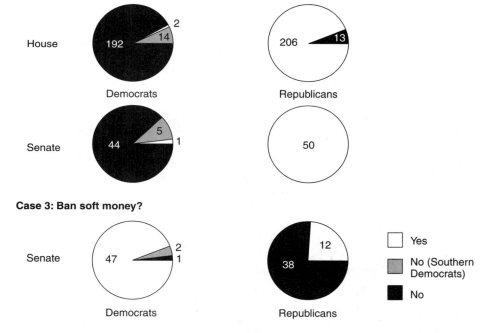

Case 3: Ban soft money?

Case 4: Amend the Constitution to let Congress ban flag desecration?

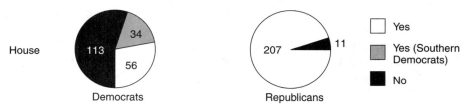

FIGURE 13.1   Party Unity and Disunity in the 2001 Congress.

Note: The figure shows the numbers of Democrats (including Southern Democrats) and Republicans in the Senate and House casting "yes" and "no" votes on the bills named.

Source: Calculated from *Congressional Quarterly Weekly Report:* Mar. 31, 2001, p. 744; Apr. 14, 2001, p. 853 (taxes); Mar. 10, 2001, pp. 560 and 564 (ergonomics); Apr. 7, 2001, p. 797 (campaign finance); and July 21, 2001, p. 1806 (flag desecration).

There is a lot of variation among the state legislatures in levels of party voting: both across the states and within a given state from one political generation to the next. We are most likely to see party voting in states where the two parties are closely balanced in strength in the legislature (so the majority party has good reason to remain united) and where the two parties represent distinctive groups of voters. For example, party voting is usually prevalent where Democratic strength is concentrated in the big cities with districts containing many union members and black voters, and Republican state legislators tend to represent suburban and rural districts that are predominantly white and conservative. These divisions are most often seen in the legislatures of urban, industrialized states. The result is an issue-oriented politics that reflects those divisions. Just as the party

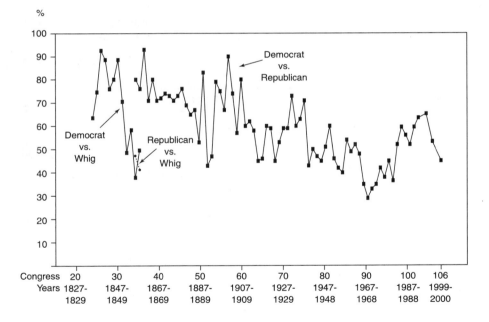

FIGURE 13.2   Party Voting in the House of Representatives: 1835–2000.

Note: Entries are the percentage of roll-call votes on which a majority of one party opposed a majority of the other party for both sessions combined.

Source: For 24th through 36th Congresses, Thomas B. Alexander, *Sectional Stress and Party Strength* (Nashville, TN: Vanderbilt University Press, 1967). For 37th through 93rd Congresses, Jerome B. Chubb and Santa A. Traugott, "Partisan Cleavage and Cohesion in the House of Representatives, 1861–1974," *Journal of Interdisciplinary History* 7 (1977), 382–383. Beginning with the 94th Congress, data come from *Congressional Quarterly Weekly Report (CQ Weekly),* reported in December or early January issues.

in Congress is more likely to accept strong party leadership when it is more homogeneous, the same can be true in state legislatures. Party voting in Southern states, then, such as Texas and Florida, has been increasing in the 1990s.[34]

Party Cohesion   To what extent do legislators support their party on party votes? As is shown in Figure 13.3, party cohesion has been on the rise in the last 30 years. This is another reflection of the major change we have discussed in the composition of the Southern Democratic representatives. In the 1960s and 1970s, conservative Southern Democrats often crossed the aisle to vote with Republicans in the House and Senate, and their defections were tolerated by the decentralized party leadership of that time. This cross-party alliance, known as the ***conservative coalition,*** came together to oppose civil rights bills and Democratic labor and education proposals from the 1940s to the mid-1980s.

By that time, however, the Democratic Party's supporting coalition in the South was in the process of being reshaped. The Voting Rights Act, bringing southern blacks into the electorate, was resulting in the election of more moderate and liberal Democrats to Congress. The policy disagreements between Northern and Southern Democrats were starting to fade. So the conservative coalition of Northern Republicans and Southern Democrats grew weaker, leaving the Democratic Party more cohesive than it has been in decades. Party cohesion continued to increase during the Clinton presidency—especially among the Republicans once they took control of Congress in 1995.

The result has been a remarkable degree of clarity in the issue differences between the congressional parties. Consider, for example, reports by a liberal group, Americans

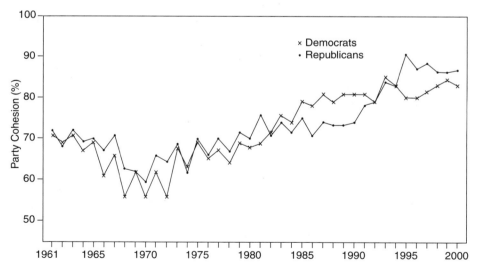

FIGURE 13.3   Party Cohesion on Party Votes: 1961–2000.

Note: Entries are the average percentages of members voting in agreement with a majority of their party on party votes. Party votes are votes in which a majority of one party voted against a majority of the other party. Figures for the House and Senate are combined.

Source: CQ Weekly, Jan. 6, 2001, p. 67.

for Democratic Action (ADA), about how often legislators voted with the ADA's position on 20 key votes. The median score for Democratic senators in 1999 was 100 percent and that of the Republicans was zero. The House pattern was almost as stark.[35] In addition to the constituency changes, the organizational reforms discussed earlier in the chapter, which reduced the power of committee chairs and strengthened the power of party leaders, made it easier for the Democratic leadership to unify its party and to fend off Republican appeals to more conservative Democrats.[36]

The conservative coalition in the 1990s and 2000s has resembled the Cheshire cat. Its substance has faded,[37] but the smile remains. This cross-party alliance could be seen in support of the North American Free Trade Agreement (NAFTA) during the Clinton era. And you can see in Figure 13.1 that, when the Democrats in Congress do split, it is the Southern Democrats who are the main source of disunity within the party.

When Are the Parties Most Unified?

The parties are more unified on some issues than others. Students of Congress and state legislatures find that three kinds of concerns are most likely to prompt high levels of party voting and party cohesion: those touching the interests of the legislative party as a group, those involving support of or opposition to an executive program, and those concerning the issues that divide the party voters.

On Issues That Touch the Interests of the Legislative Parties   These are the issues that often spur the greatest party unity. Among the clearest examples are the basic votes to organize the legislative chamber. In Congress, for example, it is safe to predict 100 percent party cohesion on the vote to elect the Speaker of the House. In 2001, when the 107th Congress began, Republican Dennis Hastert got all of the Republican votes for Speaker and only one single Democratic vote (from Ohio Representative James A. Traficant, Jr., perhaps best known for concluding his House speeches with "Beam me up." Traficant was promptly expelled from the Democratic caucus and stripped of his committee assignments as the result of his vote for Hastert[38]). The parties also tend to be very cohesive on issues affecting their numerical strength. In a 1985 vote on whether to award a congressional seat to Democrat Frank McCloskey or Republican Richard McIntyre after a disputed Indiana election, for instance, House Democrats voted 236 to 10 to seat McCloskey and Republicans voted 180 to 0 for McIntyre.

Discipline runs high in state legislatures over issues such as laws regulating parties, elections and campaigning; the seating of challenged members of the legislature; and the creation or alteration of legislative districts. Whatever form these issues take, they all touch the basic interests of the party as a political organization: its organizational structure, its system of rewards, or its competitiveness.

On the Executive's Proposals   Legislators often rally around their party's executive or unite against the executive of the other party. The reaction may not be as marked as it would be in a parliamentary system, because American presidents freely court the support of the other party, but the partisanship is obvious. Figure 13.4 traces the support that each legislative party has given to the president on issues he clearly designated a part of his program. From 1966 through 2000, Republicans supported Republican presidents

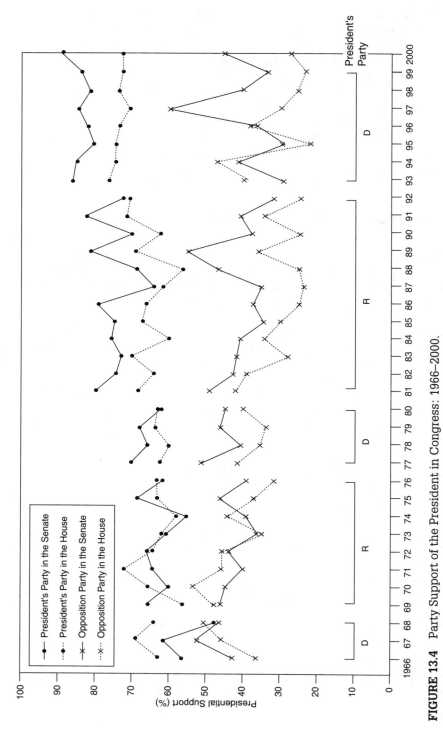

FIGURE 13.4   Party Support of the President in Congress: 1966–2000.

Note: Entries are percentages of the time that members supported the announced position of the president.

Source: Data from *CQ Almanac* for each year through 1989, and from *CQ Weekly* for 1990–2000 (typically reported in December issues).

and Democrats supported Democratic presidents on about two-thirds of these votes; the only time party support fell below 50 percent occurred among Senate Democrats in 1968, as Lyndon Johnson's presidency was eroding.

Conversely, the opposition party's support for a president's program almost always fell below 50 percent during these years and typically averaged around 40 percent. And the figure shows increasing partisanship in Congress during the last two decades.[39] The Clinton presidency is an excellent example. In the early years of Clinton's first term, Democrats' support for their president was higher than it had been since the mid-1960s, and Republicans' support was relatively low. The president became an even more powerful partisan trigger in 1998, when Clinton was impeached by the House for lying about his sexual relationship with a White House intern. Sparked by some strongly antagonistic congressional party leaders on both sides of the aisle, the House vote to impeach and the Senate vote to acquit Clinton were close to being party-line votes. In 2000, Clinton's last year as president, there was a difference of about 50 percentage points between Republicans' and Democrats' support of the president's position in the Senate and House.

This executive-oriented cohesion in Congress, which appears in the state legislatures as well, indicates that governors and presidents are increasingly seen as representatives of their party and its performance. Legislators of the president's or the governor's party know that they threaten their party and their own political future if they make their party's executive look ineffective. It may also stem from the benefits that the executive can offer legislators: personal support in campaigning and fund-raising or support for programs that help the legislator's district. And it can result from a similarity of views and constituencies between the congressional party and its president.

Even so, there are times when legislators decline the opportunity to support their chief executive because of other pressures and demands. Republican Senator John McCain's commitment to campaign finance reform, forged before he ran against George W. Bush for the presidential nomination in 2000, led him to press for a vote his chief executive did not want on that issue, and we have seen that Senator James Jeffords left the Republican Party in 2001 after expressing his belief that Bush and his party were not paying attention to moderate Republican voices. Although the legislative party's disloyalty to its president can be a major embarrassment to the president and a source of tension between the White House and Capitol Hill, it does not carry the threat of a new election or a new leader as it does in a parliamentary system.

On Policies Central to the Party System   Legislative parties are especially cohesive on issues that represent the fundamental lines of division between the parties in the electorate. At the time of the Civil War, the questions of slavery and Reconstruction generated the greatest party conflict and internal party cohesion. These issues were displaced by conflicts between agrarian and industrial interests in the realignment of 1896. Now, the parties are most cohesive on the issues of the welfare state—the role of government in the economy and in people's personal lives—that have dominated the party system since the 1930s.

In many state legislatures, for instance, an attempt to change the rules governing the hiring of teenagers by local businesses will pit one unified party against another, with the legislators' pro-labor or pro-management stands reinforced by their roots in their home districts and by their own values. Other such issues include social security, welfare, and insurance programs; labor–management relations; environmental issues; the rights of women and minority groups; and aid to agriculture and other sectors of the economy. In Congress, a similar set of issues—social welfare, government management of the economy, and agricultural assistance—has produced the most cohesive partisan voting over the years.[40]

Because these issue divisions are particularly sharp in the early years of a new party system, we might expect to see the greatest party cohesion at the times when a realignment has reshaped the fault lines of American party politics.[41] The trend line in Figure 13.2 confirms that party voting in the House has generally peaked during party realignments. These realignments focus attention on national rather than local issues, so they overcome the inherent localism of Congress. In doing so, realignments promote party unity on the issues most central to the new party system and thereby permit a degree of party discipline that is rare in American politics. This newly "responsible" majority party is then in a position to enact the major policy changes that we have come to associate with realignments.[42] Party voting and cohesion tend to decline as the prevailing party system ages and dealignment sets in.[43]

Other Sources of Unified Parties

As we saw in the cases of Speakers Cannon and Gingrich, party voting also tends to peak at times when the congressional party leadership is more centralized. Both of these forces—greater party voting and more centralized party leadership—may stem from a common cause: an increase in the homogeneity and polarization of the party in the electorate and party activists. But vigorous party leadership can work to maintain party unity. Daily caucuses and the party pressures of a powerful governor or party leader enhance cohesion in some of the states today. Even when party leadership is strong, however, it may be more concerned with keeping the legislature working smoothly than with passing particular party policies.

The level of competition between the two parties bears an interesting relationship to party voting. At the level of the individual legislator, those from marginal districts— where the two parties have relatively equal shares of the electorate—are less likely to vote with their legislative party than are those from "safer" districts. Legislative districts may be marginal because both parties have strong organizations and appealing candidates; many marginal districts have party constituencies that differ from the typical supporters of that party. Both of these circumstances force the legislator to be more than usually sensitive to the constituency, and the voters often don't reward a record of loyal party voting.

At the level of the legislature as a whole, however, close party competition may increase party voting. When a party dominates a legislative body, it can become flabby and vulnerable to disintegrating squabbles among regional or personal cliques. That was true of many legislative parties in the South during the period of one-party Democratic rule. And we have seen that representatives from the one-party South were those most responsible for undermining the cohesion of the Democratic majority in Congress in much of the post–World War II period.

THE LIMITS ON PARTY POWER

Party voting, in short, is alive and well now in Congress and most state legislatures. But can it be sustained at times when a party's legislators are not as inclined to coordinate their action on public policy? Each legislative party has a policy committee designed to serve as a broadly based instrument for crafting party policies. These committees, however, are often collections of whatever blocs and wings exist in the party rather than unified instruments for action. Nor have the party caucuses or conferences always served to unite the party on behalf of policies. They do meet to discuss important issues, but only occasionally do they "bind" their members on a bill.

Further, the policies created by party leaders in this process are *legislative* party policies to a greater extent than they are "party policy" more broadly. They rarely flow from the party's national platform; instead, they reflect the needs and demands of constituencies represented by the legislative party's members, as well as the need to support or oppose a president. They are the product of a negotiated compromise among the goals of the party members who hold committee power, the party leaders themselves, the rank and file of the legislative party, and (in one party) the president. Legislative party policy, in short, is normally created as much to serve the individual reelection needs of each party member as to implement any coherent party philosophy.[44]

WHEN CONSTITUENCY INTERFERES WITH PARTY UNITY

We have seen that constituency and activist pressures are a major influence on party voting and cohesion in Congress and the state legislatures. At times and on certain issues, these pressures can undermine party unity. When party voters in a district hold different views from the national or state party on a big issue, a representative will usually need to bend to constituency wishes in order to get reelected, even if that means opposing his or her legislative party's position. Party leaders rarely insist on the member's party loyalty in such situations. Racial issues have been good examples; U.S. House members during the late 1950s did not stray far from their constituents' preferences on civil rights, especially in the South where constituency pressures were intense.[45]

In the current Congress, small groups within both parties resist the influence of their legislative party leaders and cling to more moderate positions "because they are convinced that is what their constituents want."[46] Within the Democratic Party, a dominantly Southern group of about 30 conservative House Democrats calling themselves the "Blue Dogs" often votes with the Republicans on tax and many social issues. On the Republican side, several moderates, many of them from the Northeast, often break with their party on environmental, fiscal, and social issues. Because both the House and Senate were split almost evenly between Republicans and Democrats in 2001, these moderates, though few in number, enjoyed increased influence in both party caucuses. As long as the American parties cannot protect legislators from constituency pressures and as long as what it means to be a Democrat in Alabama is not the same as what it means to be a Democrat in Alaska or New York, then party cohesion will suffer.

Comparing Party Power in Congress and State Legislatures

These constituency pressures exist within state legislatures too. Yet parties in some state legislatures are clearly more disciplined and cohesive than the parties normally are in Congress. Let us examine these contrasts to sum up the conditions most likely to produce strong legislative parties.

Greater Political Homogeneity   The first condition is the extent to which the various constituencies of a legislative party resemble one another in their preferences and differ from the constituencies of the other party. Greater party unity in some state legislatures reflects the greater homogeneity of state parties. There is a narrower spectrum of interests and ideologies in any given state party than in that same party at the national level. That means fewer possible sources of internal conflict. In some cases, the state's political culture is more tolerant of party discipline over legislators than in the nation as a whole. For example, legislative party strength has long flourished in Northeastern states, such as Rhode Island, Connecticut, Pennsylvania, and New Jersey, where we find stronger party organizations, more patronage, weak primaries, and a political culture that seems more willing to accept centralized political control.

No Competing Centers of Power   The more independent a legislature's committees are—for example, when committee influence comes from seniority or some other criterion than party loyalty—the less they owe to parties and their priorities. In Congress, the committees were traditionally autonomous centers of legislative power, set up to screen the great mass of legislative proposals for the relatively few nuggets of legislative gold. Much of the real business of Congress goes on in them. When their chairs were chosen by seniority, they became centers of power alternative to and independent from the legislative party leaders.

In the typical state, on the other hand, because the legislature is less attractive as a career, legislators accumulate less seniority[47] and seniority is used far less often as a criterion for allocating positions of power. State parties are freer to appoint their party loyalists to powerful legislative positions, so the committees generally operate as instruments of party power. In this way, Congress, since 1995, may be coming to resemble the patterns of power in many state legislatures, or the Congress of the late nineteenth and early twentieth centuries.

Stronger Party Organization   State and local party organizations often have more influence on state legislators than the party's national committee does on members of Congress. In the states the party organization and the legislative party are more likely to be allies. Party leaders have become more active in recruiting candidates for the legislature in many states, and some may be able to convince local activists and voters to oppose the renomination of candidates disloyal to the party (though that ability can always be undermined by primary elections). Further, it is not as rare in the states—as it is in Washington, where serving in Congress is a full-time job—for state and local party leaders to *be* legislative leaders as well.

State and local parties are also important to state legislative candidates because of the campaign money the parties can provide. State legislative campaigns are more likely than congressional campaigns to depend on the party organization for financial support for several reasons. First, the states that provide public funding for campaigns are as likely to channel that money through the parties as to give it directly to candidates. Second, many states place no ceilings on party contributions to campaigns, so parties can make substantial investments, if they wish—as they have been able to do at the federal level through the use of soft money. Third, the parties' legislative campaign committees help out in most states, and legislative party leaders' personal PACs help in some.[48] And given the shortage of campaign funds at this level, many candidates look beyond the legislative campaign committees to the state parties themselves for campaign money and services and the state parties are better prepared to respond now than they have been in past years.

Party leaders in many state legislatures also control other resources that are vital to their colleagues. Through their power over the legislative agenda, they can help a member get a desired bill passed. And although we often think of pork-barrel projects as efforts by individual legislators to curry favor with voters, these projects can be offered or withheld by legislative party leaders to help maintain the loyalty of their party colleagues, as happens in at least some parliamentary democracies.[49] Pork-barrel projects in the member's home district, which can be moved up or down on the agenda by a party leader or even a president, are the main material incentives for party discipline in Congress. In some states, these material rewards—which also include patronage and other forms of governmental preference—are more abundant than in the national government.

Lesser Legislative Professionalism Congress has evolved into a highly professional legislative body. Each member controls a sizable and well-paid personal staff and a considerable budget, which are used to meet personal legislative and reelection needs. Congress now meets almost continuously and the office has become a full-time job with high pay (an annual salary of $141,300 in 2000) and good benefits.

State legislatures have become much more professional in recent years, but very few provide ordinary members with levels of support that even approach those in the Congress. Staff and budget resources are usually minimal. Most state legislators are lucky to have as much as a private office and a personal secretary. The labor that a party leader can provide to help perform the tasks of legislative life, then, can be very valuable. Many state legislatures meet for only part of the year and pay so little that most members must hold other jobs and live only temporarily in the capital. With such limited personal resources, state legislators in most states find it harder to operate independently of their party leaders than members of Congress do. When a state legislator depends on the party leadership for needed resources, he or she has a greater incentive to listen when a leader calls for party discipline.[50]

LEGISLATIVE PARTIES: FIGHTING FOR POWER

Parties are at the very center of the legislative process. Some even view them as "legislative leviathans" that dominate the business of Congress in order to benefit their individual members.[51] Party affiliation does more to explain the legislative behavior of state legislators and Congress members than any other single factor in their environment.[52] Yet, despite their central position, most American legislative parties are only moderately unified when compared with those of other nations. The legislative party leaders must compete with the efforts of big givers, single-issue groups, powerful state and local leaders, and legislative committee chairs for the ability to organize legislative majorities.

This is another instance in which the fragmenting institutions of American government have left their mark. Because of the separation of powers, there is no institutional need for a party to remain internally unified, as there is in parliamentary systems.[53] Under certain conditions—in particular, times when the party's legislative constituencies are more alike in their preferences and more different from those of the other party—the legislative parties will be more unified. But these conditions and this polarization are not likely to last indefinitely.[54]

Even at times when American legislative parties have been very cohesive, that does not necessarily result in a party-dominated government. The reason is inherent in the nature of the American parties: the party in government has only limited ties to the party organization. The parties in Congress and the state legislatures are not controlled by— or always even in contact with—the party's national, state, or local party committees. American legislative parties find it easy to keep the party organization and its commitments to particular policies at arm's length. The legislative parties control most of their own rewards and punishments in the form of party campaign help and legislative carrots and sticks. So when the legislative parties are able to muster some degree of discipline, it is usually on behalf of a set of proposals that originated in the executive or within the legislative party itself, rather than in the party organization.[55]

What difference does this make in the ongoing effort to sustain a democracy in the United States? It clearly underscores the fact that the primary relationship in American legislatures is between representatives and their constituents, rather than between legislators and their party leaders or party organizations (see "Which Would You Choose?"). Most Americans, suspicious of party influence, would probably be cheered by that thought. Yet it comes at a fairly high cost. This close relationship leaves legislators vulnerable to the squeaky wheels—the organized groups within constituencies—who press their demands, but whose interests may be very different from those of the average citizen. The people who are *least* able to press their demands on their legislators—the unorganized, the politically apathetic—are exactly those whose concerns legislative parties and, in fact, all parties, have the capacity to represent.

WHICH WOULD YOU CHOOSE?

Should your senator or Congress member listen more closely to the party or to the constituents?

TO THE CONSTITUENTS   This sounds like a no-brainer. If we elect members of Congress, they ought to represent the interests of their constituents, right? We have a single-member-per-district system with candidate-centered campaigns; that encourages us to focus on the qualities of individual candidates, rather than on the party's platform or plans. We vote for a candidate, he or she goes to Washington and is then supposed to do whatever we ask. Why should the legislator listen to the party leadership?

TO THEIR PARTY   This constituent-centered approach sounds good, but it isn't realistic. How are members of Congress supposed to know what their constituents want with regard to railroad subsidies, Superfund, or the American relationship with China? And if those who do contact their senator on these issues are not typical of the rest of us, is it their constituency opinion that he or she should represent? Isn't it better for the two major parties to offer competing answers to these issues, press their legislative party colleagues to pass these policies and then let voters decide whether they like the results? That asks less of us as voters and probably corresponds better to the (minimal) time we're willing to spend on politics. Besides, suppose most constituents are easily satisfied by parochial benefits from Congress, such as new highways and bridges. By taking a longer view and holding their Congress members to it, the parties can look beyond local concerns to a broader national interest.

TO BOTH   As we've seen, when the various constituencies that a party's legislators represent become more similar in views and more different from the constituencies of the other party, then legislators don't have to choose between constituents and party. At these times, members can vote with their party colleagues and also speak for the interests and the voters who, in their view, sent them to the legislature. So party and constituency are not necessarily in conflict.

The Party in the Executive and the Courts

By December 7, 2000—a full month after election day—the United States still didn't know whom it had elected President. That decision awaited action by two courts. The Florida Supreme Court, all of whose members had been appointed by Democratic governors, ruled in favor of Democratic candidate Al Gore, who had argued that a hand recount of ballots in Florida should be allowed to continue. But the U.S. Supreme Court followed with a ruling that shut down the recount on December 12, thus effectively handing the presidency to Republican George W. Bush. In the U.S. Supreme Court's close decision, all five of the justices who voted to support Bush had been appointed to their posts by Republican Presidents.[1]

This looks suspiciously like partisan behavior—but how could that be, in high courts that most Americans prefer to see as nonpartisan? Could it have been a remarkable coincidence? Is it time to set aside the notion that the courts are "above party politics"? Or is there some other explanation for the apparent link between the interests of individual justices and the presidential candidate of their party?

In fact, as we will see in this chapter, American presidents, governors, and judges have been drawn into party politics since the early years of the Republic. When the presidency emerged as a popularly elected office in the early 1800s, it became possible for a president to become a party leader at the national level, just as many governors had long been in their states. Now, given the prominence of chief executives in American politics, it would be hard for a president or governor to avoid the dominant leadership role of her or his party.

And although the framers of the Constitution designed an independent federal court system with lifetime appointments and a clear separation from the legislative branch, hoping that it would be "above" the bruising battles of partisanship, one of the most famous partisan confrontations in American history involved the federal judiciary. An early Chief Justice of the U.S. Supreme Court, John Marshall, made use of a case in 1803 to rule that the Court had the power to declare acts of Congress unconstitutional—and managed to thwart the Jefferson administration in the process. (Marshall was a committed Federalist).[2] In this brilliant piece of political maneuvering, as well as in the high-stakes conflicts today over the nomination of federal judges, we see ample evidence of party considerations in the courts.

In many ways, partisanship has penetrated more deeply into the executive and judicial branches in the United States than it has in other Western democracies. As we have seen in Chapter 2, the push for popular democracy led to the long ballot on which Americans elect judges, statewide administrative officials (such as state school superintendents and attorneys general), and even local administrators, ranging from surveyors to coroners. When judges and administrators are elected to office rather than appointed, the door is open to party influence in their elections. And the extensive use of patronage in earlier years encouraged the use of party ties in choosing appointees to administrative offices. These tendencies have remained, even in the face of later reforms intended to insulate judges and bureaucrats from partisan pressures.

What difference does it make if the reach of party extends into administrative agencies, courtrooms, and executive offices? If parties affect the recruitment and selection of these officeholders, do they also influence the ways judges and administrators use their powers? Do bureaucrats who are Democrats make different decisions from their Republican brethren? If you go to court as a criminal defendant, will you get a different ruling from a Democratic judge than you would from a Republican? And if this is so, does it result from active attempts by party organizations to affect the behavior of executives and judges in order to promote the party's views on public policies? Or is it simply that people who consider themselves Republicans tend to share similar attitudes toward political issues and similar views of human nature, whether they serve as county surveyors or Supreme Court justices? And is the same true of those who identify as Democrats?

PRESIDENTS AND GOVERNORS AS PARTY LEADERS

American presidents were not always the dominant leaders that they are today. But in the twentieth century, the expansion of the right to vote and the tremendous growth of mass communications pulled political executives into the public spotlight. The needs of radio and then television led them to focus on individual elected officials, such as presidents and governors, rather than on more faceless institutions such as Congress and courts. Presidents, in particular, became symbolic public figures, thought to have great power and be capable of arousing the most passionate loyalties and hatreds. We can see an increase in personal leadership, even in nations with parliamentary systems; their election campaigns increasingly center on the potential prime ministers.[3]

In addition to their status as popularly elected leaders, presidents draw power from their leadership of a mass political party. Presidents, governors, and mayors rarely serve in formal party leadership posts; other party colleagues hold these jobs. Rather, a chief executive's role as party leader is a subtle combination of several partisan roles.

Party Leader as Representative of the Whole Constituency

It's at least worth arguing that the president represents the only truly national constituency in the United States. House districts are local and particularistic; Senate constituencies collectively overrepresent the rural areas of the country. When we sum all these congressional districts to form a whole, we find a constituency that differs in interesting ways from the one represented by a president. The states that dominate the president's constituency are those with the most electoral votes: the large, urban, industrial states containing the nation's biggest cities. The nature of his or her "district" often leads a president to accept more extensive governmental action in solving national problems than the congressional party is likely to do.

Similarly, American governors represent the entire state, in contrast to the local ties of the state legislators. Other public officials may also have statewide constituencies; some states have made the state treasurer, attorney general, state insurance commissioner, and state Supreme Court justices into elected officials. Unlike these lesser-known officials, though, the governor is recognized by voters as the executive and must develop a policy record and a concern for the problems of the whole state. For a public that views politics chiefly in personal terms, a governor often comes to personify the party on the statewide level, just as presidents do at the national level and big-city mayors often do in their localities. As a senior House Democratic aide commented about the national executive, "The president becomes the face of your party."[4] Executive programs, then, are seen as party programs.

Party Leader as Organizational Leader

American executives have the luxury of being able to choose whether or not to involve themselves in their party's organizational efforts. Most recent presidents, however, have taken their party leadership role seriously, even to the extent of spending time raising money for the party's candidates. Bill Clinton remained an active Democratic fund-raiser as president, helping to attract contributions not only for Senate and House candidates, but in contests for governor as well.[5] Although George W. Bush limited his party fund-raising activities in the early months of his administration, while Congress debated bills that would have overhauled the campaign finance system, Bush quickly returned to the task, in order to "help build the party and ... help elect and reelect legislators who support his agenda."[6] The benefit to his party was great, because presidents are remarkable fund-raisers. In a single fund-raising event in Birmingham that featured President Bush, for example, guests donated $1.75 million for the 2002 campaign of Republican Senator Jeff Sessions of Alabama—the bulk of the $2.4 million that Sessions was able to raise during a six-month period—even though Sessions had no major opponent.[7]

Presidents can do a great deal more for their party organizations as well. The state or national party organization often finds itself in the difficult position of trying to convince a reluctant but attractive prospect to run against an entrenched incumbent of the other party or to ask a House member to give up a safe seat in order to challenge a potentially vulnerable opposition senator. When the unwilling target of the party's affections is invited to dinner at the White House to hear how personally important the race is to the President of the United States, the party's job gets easier. White House leverage is also useful in clearing a path for the party's preferred nominee. In the spring of 2001, for instance, Vice President Dick Cheney persuaded a Minnesota Republican to give up a bid for the state's 2002 Senate nomination—just 90 minutes prior to the scheduled press conference at which he was to announce his candidacy—to clear the way for a candidate the party regarded as stronger. "I was de-cruited," explained the suddenly retired candidate.[8]

In a more formal sense, the president's major influence on the party organization rests in his control of the party's national committee. The president is free to shape the national committee's role—even if only to turn it into his or her own personal campaign organization—and to choose its chair. Earlier presidents often included their national party's chairman in their cabinet and relied on the chair's advice on the intricacies of party politics. They frequently drew on the national committee and state party organizations in selecting members of the president's immediate White House staff.[9] Now, however, presidents such as Bush and Clinton choose cabinet members and White House staff to help them govern and to protect their own political positions, rather than to serve the needs of the party organization. This practice has become so entrenched that the Democratic National Committee chair during the Johnson administration, Robert Strauss, was heard to complain, "If you're a Democratic Party chairman when a Democrat is president, you're a goddam clerk."[10]

In particular, presidents' relationships with state and local party organizations have weakened. Presidents are less inclined now to do the kind of "party-building"—strengthening state parties and their leadership—that presidents routinely did early in the twentieth century. Although President Reagan campaigned unusually hard for Republican candidates, for example, the Republican National Committee's extensive party-building efforts were largely independent of the White House. So the involvement of presidents in their party's organizational leadership is currently directed more to building the president's own successes by recruiting and helping fund candidates who will support the president's legislative priorities, than it is to building the party as a whole.

Party Leader as Electoral Leader

The political successes or failures of executives, especially presidents and governors, affect the electoral fates of other candidates of their party. A good example was Ronald Reagan's win in 1980 and landslide reelection in 1984, which were accompanied by higher than normal levels of success for other Republican candidates. Republicans gained control of the Senate in 1980 for the first time since the 1952 election, and Republican House candidates received a higher percentage of the votes cast in 1980 and 1984 than in the preceding and following midterm elections, when Reagan was not on the ballot.

Coattail Effects   This link between presidential success and party victories is traditionally explained by the metaphor of *coattails*. Presidents ran "at the top of the ticket," the explanation goes, and the rest of the party ticket came into office clinging to their sturdy coattails. (Nineteenth-century dress coats did have tails.) This coattail effect was very common in the nineteenth century because the parties printed their own ballots, so a voter was limited to casting a ballot for an entire party ticket. Since World War II, however, coattail effects have declined.[11] Incumbent Congress members are better able now to insulate themselves from outside electoral forces, including presidential popularity, by increasing attentiveness to their districts and because their campaign resources are normally so much greater than those of their challengers.

We can see the limits of the coattail effect in the last two decades. Even though Republican George H. W. Bush defeated Michael Dukakis in 1988 by 54 to 46 percent in the popular vote and Republican House candidates got a 1 percent gain in votes, the party actually lost two seats in the House of Representatives. Vote gains in congressional elections do not translate perfectly into gains in House seats; this moderates the effect of coattails. Bush's successor, Bill Clinton, seemed to have even shorter coattails. In Clinton's 1992 victory in a three-candidate presidential race, Democratic House candidates ran well ahead of their presidential candidate. When he won reelection in 1996, with an improvement of 6 percent in his vote share, Democrats gained nine seats in the House, but lost two in the Senate and Clinton was not able to restore Democratic control in either house of Congress.

Nevertheless, presidents can develop coattails in particular races even now. At times, presidential coattails have extended beyond House races to some Senate elections, in spite of the high visibility of most Senate candidates. Coattail effects can reach into elections to state legislatures as well; from 1944 through 1984, when a president ran strongly in a state, the president's party typically did better in state legislative contests on the same ballot.[12] Presidential coattails were not as strong in state legislative races as they could be in congressional elections. Even so, many states decided to move their state legislative elections to years when the presidency was not on the ballot, to insulate state elections from presidential politics.

Coattails Even Without the Coat   In fact, presidential leadership is so prominent in voters' eyes that a president can influence election results for other contests, even when he is not on the ballot. During the campaign prior to a midterm congressional election, voters' expressed intentions to vote for candidates of the president's party vary in tandem with their levels of approval of the way the president is handling his job. And in the midterm election itself, at least since the late 1930s, the gains or losses of the president's party are strongly related to voters' approval of the president.[13] Drops in President Clinton's approval rating at the time of the 1994 midterm election coincided with big Democratic losses in the House and Senate. Clinton's public approval was on the upswing in time for the 1998 congressional elections—ironically, in that he was just a few weeks away from being impeached by the House—because, in part, of public discomfort with the unremitting pursuit of impeachment by the Republican congressional majority, and Democratic congressional candidates reaped the benefit.

Very frequently, however, presidents' standing in public opinion is weaker at the midpoint of their terms than it is at the beginning or the end. Analysts have often commented that since the Civil War, the pattern of party ups and downs in elections resembles a sawtooth: the party that wins a presidential election almost always suffers a decline in its share of House seats in the next congressional election. This intriguing sawtooth pattern may be due in part to declining public enthusiasm for a president in the middle of his term. So the 1998 congressional elections were one of the rare midterms when the presidential party did *not* lose seats in the House of Representatives. Or it may suggest that, just as a popular presidential candidate can boost the chances of his party's candidates in the presidential year, his absence from the ticket may deprive them of this advantage at midterm.[14]

A Broader Perspective on Electoral Influence   In sum, there are several important ways in which a president is the electoral leader of his party. Presidential coattails vary in strength, but they indicate that at least some voters seem to be influenced by the president's performance when they cast ballots for other offices. The candidates for these other offices—both the president's partisans and their opponents—take this relationship into account as they plan and run their campaigns.[15]

The weakening of presidential coattails certainly dilutes his power as party leader and his influence in Congress. Yet even if the president's popularity accounts for only small percentage shifts in the congressional vote, these small shifts can make a big difference in party strength in Congress. From 1952 to 1970, each shift of 1 percent in the popular vote added or subtracted about eight seats in the House of Representatives.[16] Although House seats have become less responsive to popular vote changes since then, the tight balance between Democrats and Republicans in both the House and the Senate allows even a small change in seats to have a big impact on legislation.

In the years between elections as well, popular support is a valuable resource for the chief executive in getting Congress to go along with his programs. In the first year of the Reagan administration, for example, President Reagan's popularity in the country was one reason for his considerable success on the Hill, just as President Clinton's unpopularity made it harder for him to steer health care reform through a Democratic Congress. Members of Congress apparently assume that being linked with the proposals of an unpopular president will hurt them electorally—and with good reason. There is evidence that citizens who disapprove of the president's performance vote in larger numbers in midterm elections than those who approve and that their disapproval leads them to vote for the other party and its candidates.[17] People's evaluations of a president or governor also seem to affect the way they view the parties more broadly. An especially attractive president can add luster to a party's public image for years by making a big positive impression on young adults who are just entering the electorate. Ronald Reagan seems to have done that for the Republican Party.

Limits on Presidential Leadership

The ties between chief executives and their party have real limits, however. Some governors and presidents would prefer to appear "above" party politics and not to work with the party organization and its people.[18] Even those who are comfortable with a party leadership role may find that the pressures to act as a president, governor, or mayor of "all the people" constrain their natural partisanship. George W. Bush found himself in that situation during his first year in office, when the horrific terrorist attacks on the World Trade Center and on several prominent political leaders made a partisan posture seem quite inappropriate.

The Executive-Centered Party

Even so, a president normally heads and sometimes even unifies the national party, as most governors do in their state parties.[19] So it is no exaggeration to describe the American parties as executive-centered coalitions. If the party in government dominates the American political party, the executive dominates the party in government. No other leader can compete with presidents, governors and mayors in representing the party to the public, in commanding a broad range of tools of influence, or in enjoying as much legitimacy as the center of party leadership.

PARTY LEADERSHIP AND LEGISLATIVE RELATIONS

This central role of the executive would surprise anyone whose knowledge of American politics is limited to a reading of the Constitution. The writers of the Constitution gave the presidency a paltry grant of power—not enough to hold his or her own in struggles with Congress. Even in the fields of national defense and foreign policy where presidents have more independent power than they do in domestic politics, a president is likely to face challenges from Congress. Faced with this shortage of formal powers, presidents have learned to rely heavily on other sources of power. These include the leverage they get from their position as party leader, as well as the ties they share with their co-partisans in Congress.

How Executives Try to Influence Legislatures

As was clear in the Clinton and Bush administrations, presidents make frequent use of their persuasiveness, their command of the media, and whatever prestige they may have at the time in trying to get Congress to go along with their objectives. They appeal to their co-partisans' party attachments; they refer to whatever lingering patronage or preferments they can command (a judicial appointment here, a government project there), and their ability to influence upcoming elections. Members of the president's party know that if they make him look bad, they might also make themselves and their party look bad, and that can encourage them to rally around the president on important votes, even if they would prefer to vote differently. When a president has vetoed a bill, for example, members of his party have sometimes rallied to the president and voted to uphold his veto, even if that requires them to reverse their original support of the bill.

Legislative Support for Executives

As presidents would attest, however, Congress is often stubbornly resistant to presidential leadership. Even when their party controls the Congress, recent presidents have often been unable to win congressional approval of their proposals. President Carter had only about a 75 percent success rate with a Democratic Congress and President Clinton scored only about 10 percent higher during his first two years in office, when the Democrats held majorities in both the House and Senate.

Divided Control of Government   Presidents get much less support, of course, when Congress is in the hands of the opposing party, as the pitched battles between President Clinton and the Republican Congress in the 1990s demonstrate. And unhappily for modern presidents, divided government has been the rule, not the exception, in the last three decades. During the same period, almost all of the states have also experienced divided party control of the legislature and the governorship. (You'll find more on divided government in the next chapter.)

In times of divided government, it can be risky for presidents and governors to rely heavily on partisan appeals. Because of the close party division in many legislatures and the unreliability of some legislators of their own party, American chief executives must also curry favor with some legislators in the opposing party. That requires them to walk a fine line, using partisan appeals to legislators of their own party and nonpartisan, or bipartisan, appeals to those in the opposition. There are times—the early Reagan years are a good example—when especially effective presidential leadership can get even a Congress controlled by the other party to go along with what he wants. (Reagan was helped in these years, of course, by the fact that his party did control the Senate.) And Bill Clinton deftly used the veto and threats of the veto to get the Republican Congress to accept many of his initiatives after 1995.[20] But American presidents have never been able to gain as much support in Congress as prime ministers naturally enjoy in parliamentary systems.

As Figure 14.1 (below), shows, presidential success rates varied quite a lot during the last five decades, but success rates have dropped a bit in recent years.[21] In addition to the challenge of divided government, changes in congressional elections have also been a factor here, including weaker and more variable presidential coattails and the high

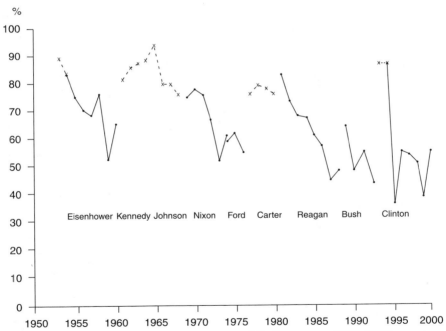

FIGURE 14.1 Presidential Success in the U.S. Congress: 1953–2000.

Note: The entry for each year is the percentage of time members of both the House and the Senate voted in support of the announced position of the president. Years in which the president's party controlled both houses of Congress are indicated by an "x" and connected by dotted lines. Years in which the opposition party controlled at least one house of Congress are indicated by a "." and connected by solid lines.

Source: Congressional Quarterly Weekly Report, Dec. 31, 1994, 3654, and, for 1995–2000, other end-of-the-year *CQ Weekly* issues.

reelection rate of congressional incumbents. Members of Congress have gotten extremely good at cultivating their constituency by attending closely to its interests and providing more services to individual constituents; this helps to protect them from the heavy hand of the president's electoral impact,[22] and also, as a result, from the president's persuasive powers. So recent presidents may be tempted to put less emphasis on their role as party leaders and more on other components of their influence.

Governors, on the other hand, can often exercise much greater and more direct party organizational power over the legislators of their party. Many state legislatures do not use seniority rules, so some governors can take an active part in selecting committee chairs and party floor leaders when the legislative session begins. Some governors lead powerful state party organizations; legislators who cross them may risk undermining their legislative career as well as their ambitions for higher office. In short, the average governor has greater control over party rewards and incentives than a president does. On the other hand, governors are not as visible as presidents are, so their coattails and prestige are likely to be less potent than those of presidents.

PARTY INFLUENCE IN EXECUTIVE AGENCIES

The president is the tip of an iceberg. Below the surface, huge and powerful, lies the rest of the executive branch. The bureaucrats who work there in cabinet-level departments such as Defense and in other federal agencies, such as the Environmental Protection Agency (EPA), are charged by the Constitution with carrying out the laws Congress passes. In spite of a burst of deregulation in the 1980s and 1990s, these executive agencies still regulate vast areas of the economy—food safety, prescription drugs, radio and TV, and pollution, for example—under congressional mandates that require a lot of interpretation.[23] The bureaucrats who implement these laws, therefore, must make important decisions on public policy; they shape policy by applying it. It is they, for example, who determine whether the eggs you ate last week were inspected for contamination and whether your next car will need an air bag. Because of their power, we need to ask whether presidents, governors, and mayors are able to hold these administrators responsible for implementing a party program—or any program at all.

Bureaucrats Have Constituents Too

Perhaps the biggest problem executives face in enforcing party discipline on their subordinates is the same problem faced by legislative party leaders: constituency pressure. Just as legislators try to meet the needs of their constituents, administrators often identify with the needs of the groups their agencies deal with. Top-level administrators know that their best political protection is the support of their client groups. The Environmental Protection Agency, for instance, works very closely with the industries it regulates. If its rulings in applying the Clean Air Act enrage automobile manufacturers and oil companies, the EPA will be in the political hot seat. Party loyalties do not compete very well with the power of these constituencies; in the executive as well as the legislative branch, the party has less to give and less to take away than the constituency does.[24]

Many other factors limit an executive's ability to unify an administration and hold it accountable for achieving a party's policy goals. Several of these limits were put in place by Progressive reforms enacted early in the twentieth century:

- Legislatures can protect top-level bureaucrats from presidential influence (and, through the president, party influence) by giving them terms longer than that of the president, by limiting the president's (or governor's) power to remove them, or by requiring that they be chosen through a merit system, rather than a political appointment process.

- Legislatures can prevent party control of an administrative agency by requiring that its leadership include members of both parties. The Federal Election Commission board, for example, must be composed of three Democrats and three Republicans—and at least *four* board members must agree to investigate any suspected campaign finance abuse. (This, of course, is as much a prescription for inactivity as it is for bipartisanship.)

- Top administrators in many states are elected. So voters may choose, say, a Republican for governor and a Democrat for state treasurer to work together in an uneasy alliance. Even if both officials are of the same party, their offices are often politically and constitutionally independent.

- Most American executives are term-limited; presidents can run for only two terms and most governors can serve only one or two consecutive terms. As the end of their term approaches, their authority over other officeholders diminishes.

- Finally, executives must often share power with others. The practice of senatorial courtesy gives the U.S. Senate a say in presidential appointees. In forming a cabinet, presidents also cannot ignore the preferences of groups within the party that contributed to the president's victory.

Holding Bureaucrats Accountable

Some high-level administrators are easier to hold responsible for promoting a party program than others, however. The people appointed to head cabinet departments—the biggest and best-known parts of the executive branch, such as State, Health and Human Services, and Defense—have often had a long history of party activity, so they are likely to feel some degree of commitment to the party's goals and programs. All but one of the members of President Clinton's cabinet had been active in Democratic Party politics, either as elected officeholders, candidates for office, appointees to political positions in previous Democratic administrations, or campaign strategists. (The remaining cabinet member was Republican Defense Secretary William Cohen, selected to offer partisan balance.) The same has been true under President George W. Bush, whose cabinet appointees in 2001 included a Republican state party chair, the wife of a Republican House member, a former director of the National Republican Senatorial Committee, two Republican governors, two other Republican elected officials, four political appointees in previous Republican administrations—and, for balance, a Democratic House member.

So party remains a source of talent, even a recruiter of talent, for modern adminis-trations. Presidents are no longer as explicitly partisan as they once were in making cab-inet appointments; they no longer use these positions as rewards for loyal *party* service. Instead, they look for individuals with experience in the areas of policy they will admin-ister and loyalty to the president's *own* aims.[25] Nevertheless, most presidential appointees have been active partisans, whose values and political careers have been shaped to a sig-nificant degree by their party.

Just below this top level, however, officeholders are less likely to have party and gov-ernmental experience. These officials are most often chosen for their administrative skills and experience, and only secondarily for their political credentials. The party organiza-tion's role in their selection may extend only to verifying that they are politically accept-able (that is, not offensive) in their home states. Yet they continue to come largely from the party of the president and the party link can produce a commitment to a common outlook.[26]

Administrations with an ideological mission, such as the Reagan administration, have worked hard to ensure this common political outlook. They try to fill executive positions with ideological sympathizers, not just co-partisans and to charge them with the mission of carrying out the president's policies. In such cases, tension is likely to develop between the party loyalists and the ideologues in the administration's top leadership. Appointing ideological sympathizers can produce a cohesive administration, but it can weaken the party's impact and undermine the president's influence with co-partisans in the Congress.

In all these ways, it is a formidable problem to establish political control over the executive bureaucracy, especially at the national level. Modern presidents can make only about 3,500 political appointments—fewer appointive positions than some governors have—to try to gain control of an executive branch employing several million civilian employees. Many of the president's men and women are novices with little time to "learn the ropes" and little hope of gaining the necessary support of career bureaucrats. As Hugh Heclo has shown, together they comprise "a government of strangers": a set of execu-tives whose limited familiarity and interaction with one another keep them from acting as an effective team and who are therefore likely to be overwhelmed by a huge, frag-mented and more or less permanent bureaucracy.[27]

Not surprisingly then, recent presidents, and especially Republican presidents, have relied more and more on their immediate White House staff and the Office of Manage-ment and Budget when they try to mobilize the executive branch to achieve their policy goals.[28] Party can help in organizing an administration, serving as both a recruitment channel for executive talent and a common bond between the executive and top bureau-crats. But it does not have the power to hold the executive branch responsible for carry-ing out a party program.

Changing Political Outlooks in the Federal Bureaucracy

Even though the executive's party is not able to enforce party discipline, the federal bureaucracy (and many state bureaucracies) nevertheless shows some responsiveness to partisan forces over the long run. As the federal government expanded in the 1930s, Pres-ident Roosevelt drew people into the career bureaucracy who were committed to his pro-grams. They then became a bulwark against later efforts to weaken these programs, especially as these dedicated New Dealers came to be promoted to more and more senior positions in their agencies.

By 1970, Joel Aberbach and Bert Rockman found that nearly a majority of these career bureaucrats said they normally voted Democratic and only 17 percent usually voted Republican. In federal social service agencies, even the administrators who were not Democrats said that they favored liberal policies. Republican President Richard Nixon, in office at that time, thus faced a federal bureaucracy that had little sympathy for his conservative agenda. His administration spent a lot of time trying to control the bureaucracy by appointing White House loyalists to top bureaucratic positions.[29]

By 1992, however, the bureaucratic environment had changed. In the intervening two decades, Republicans had held the White House for all but four years. And when Aberbach and Rockman returned to interview career administrators in comparable positions to those they interviewed in 1970, they now found slight Republican pluralities, although the career executives were still much more Democratic and liberal than the Reagan and Bush political appointees. As older civil servants retired, a new generation, less committed to New Deal and Great Society programs, had been recruited into senior executive positions. Changes in civil service laws, further, allowed positions formerly reserved for career employees to be filled by political appointees who could be carefully screened by the White House. The bureaucracy was no longer as unsympathetic to Republican initiatives. But the inherent difficulties of controlling even a sympathetic bureaucracy remained.[30]

In sum, although there is party influence in the executive branch, most presidents and governors use their party leadership role to promote their own programs and their own reelection, not the programs of their party. To the extent that the executive's goals are similar to those of their party, of course, the party's program benefits. Many governors do use some patronage appointments purely to boost their state party and presidents may use some cabinet appointments to recognize various groups within their party. But for most American executives, the goals and interests of their party organization are secondary to their own policy goals and political careers.

TRACES OF PARTY IN THE COURTS

Courts and judges are affected by party politics as well. Most American judges—even most Justices of the U.S. Supreme Court—are political men and women who took office after careers that involved them in some aspect of partisan politics (see the box on p. 288). Although reformers have tried to insulate the judicial system from politics and especially from party politics, the selection of judges continues to be shaped by partisanship in elections and through appointments. Because of the nature of the judiciary, however, the influence can be subtle.

Judicial Voting Along Party Lines

Hints of party influence appear when we examine the voting in American appellate courts. Several studies show that in cases such as those involving workers' compensation, judges split into partisan blocs. In a study of state courts, in comparison with Republican judges, Democratic judges were found to decide more often for the defendant in

The Partisan Backgrounds of U.S. Supreme Court Justices

Justices Appointed by Republican Presidents:

William H. Rehnquist (Chief Justice; appointed by Nixon) was a Republican Party official in Phoenix. He was later appointed Assistant Attorney General in the Republican administration of President Nixon.

John Paul Stevens (Ford) is a registered Republican, though he was never active in Republican Party politics.

Sandra Day O'Connor (Reagan) was a Republican Party committeewoman and legislative district chair in Phoenix. She served two full terms as a Republican state senator in Arizona and became Republican Majority Leader in the State Senate.

Antonin Scalia (Reagan) was named General Counsel for the Office of Telecommunications Policy in the Republican Nixon administration and then Assistant Attorney General under Republican Gerald Ford.

Anthony Kennedy (Reagan) was a Republican activist and campaign donor in California and then became a legal adviser to Reagan as Governor.

David H. Souter (GHW Bush) was never active in party politics, but was appointed Deputy Attorney General and then Attorney General in New Hampshire, in both cases by Republican governors.

Clarence Thomas (GHW Bush) served on the staff of Missouri's Republican Attorney General and as Assistant Secretary for Civil Rights and Director of the Equal Employment Opportunity Commission in the Republican Reagan administration. Thomas's wife is a senior aide to the House Republican Majority Leader.

Justices Appointed by a Democratic President:

Ruth Bader Ginsburg (Clinton) had no formal party positions or appointments prior to her nomination to the Court.

Stephen G. Breyer (Clinton) was a special assistant to the Assistant Attorney General under Democratic President Lyndon Johnson, assistant special prosecutor in the Watergate investigation, and Special Counsel and then Chief Counsel to the Democratic-led Senate Judiciary Committee.

criminal cases, for the government in tax cases, for the regulatory agency in cases involving the regulation of business, and for the claimants in workers' compensation, unemployment compensation, and auto accident cases[31]—just as we might expect in comparing the views of Democratic and Republican activists outside the courtroom.

Similarly, in recent redistricting cases, U.S. District Court judges have tended to uphold plans enacted by their party more than those enacted by the opposing party.[32] That was often the case in 2001 when state legislatures deadlocked over redistricting plans, which were then kicked to the courts. Judges show much less party cohesion than members of legislatures do and it appears only in certain types of cases. Yet it does appear; Democratic judges rule differently under some circumstances than their Republican colleagues.

What accounts for this apparent partisanship? Very little of it is probably due to overt efforts by party leaders to influence court decisions. That does happen occasionally at the state and local level—as in the rare judge who continues to be deeply immersed in party politics even after going on the bench. In a few counties, the local district or county judge slates candidates for office behind the scenes. A judge who is closely tied to the local party may provide a reservoir of patronage for the party organization through guardianships, receiverships in bankruptcy, and clerkships that can be given to party loyalists who are attorneys.[33] In most areas, however, explicitly partisan activity by a judge or pressure by a party leader to decide a case in a certain way would now be seen as violating the norms of the judicial system.

What Causes Partisan Behavior on the Courts?

A much better explanation for the impact of party on judges' behavior is simply that judges, like most other well-educated people, hold party identifications and bring these partisan frames of reference to their work on the court. Just as the two parties reflect different sets of values, so do their identifiers, including those who become judges. Two judges might vote together on the issue of regulating business because of the values they share about the proper role of government in the economy. Those same values led them years earlier to join the same party or were developed out of experience in the same party. In other words, it is not usually the external pressure provided by a party organization or leader, but rather the party *in* the judge that leads judges with similar partisan backgrounds to the same decisions. (See "A Day in the Life," on p. 290)

Those who appoint judges to their positions are well aware of the importance of judges' value systems. They know that the law is often not "cut and dried," that judges often have discretion in deciding cases, and that the choices they make may reflect, at least in part, their own experiences and beliefs. So the selection of judges, especially for the higher courts that receive the most challenging cases, has traditionally taken into account the values and attitudes of the candidates.

Party Considerations in Judicial Appointments

Parties can affect the selection of judges in several ways. In many states, party organizations have the opportunity to recommend or at least to advise on the nominations of prospective judges. That gives them a means to advance party goals by encouraging the appointment or election of judges who believe in the party's values. It also permits them to further the careers of lawyers who have served the party loyally. Even when party organizations don't have that opportunity, the nomination of judges by a governor or a president permits the influence of the party in government on judicial appointments.

Federal Judges   Presidents nominate candidates for federal judgeships; Congress has the right to confirm or deny them. Because prospective judges' party and ideology serve as important indicators of their attitudes and, thus, potentially affect their decisions in some kinds of cases, every American president during the twentieth century has made at

A DAY IN THE LIFE

Can Partisan Elections Produce Impartial Judges?

"Many of us joked that we went to law school because we watched 'Perry Mason' on TV when we were children," says Circuit Court Judge E. Michael Hoff. "The role of a lawyer was an attractive role; I wanted to be a lawyer for a long time. But I had never thought about becoming a judge.

"While I was practicing law, I served occasionally as a judge pro tem—a kind of 'substitute judge' in cases where the juvenile court magistrate had previously been involved as a deputy prosecutor and so had to recuse herself. That got me interested in the process.

"I was also involved at that time as an active member of the local Democratic Party. I worked in several elections as an election official, went to candidates' fund-raising events, and served as a volunteer attorney for the party, in one instance representing a candidate in a recount. I knew a lot of people who were local officials. Then a friend who was also active in the local party told me that a group of people was trying to recruit candidates and asked if I'd consider running for judge. The occupant of the judgeship had retired. So the party was essential in my selection.

"Beginning in February, I started campaigning door-to-door, talking to people who were likely voters in the Democratic primary. Running for office is an exciting experience, but not an easy one. It's very hard to go up to a group of people and start introducing yourself; it didn't come naturally to me. But I went knocking on doors almost every day after work until it got dark, and I won the primary in May and then beat a very good Republican candidate in November.

"Does my political affiliation affect me on the bench? On one hand, a lot of the decisions you have to make as a judge don't have much to do with partisan matters: for example, when you decide where a child ought to be placed or how to interpret a contract. On the other hand, judges do have a lot of discretion in many of the decisions they make. Someone's personal philosophy will inevitably influence him or her in exercising this discretion—for instance, in cases where you have to decide: should I enforce this lease and evict a tenant in mid-January? Decisions on sentencing criminals can certainly be related to someone's philosophy. This is not, however, the same thing as a judge making a certain decision *because* the judge is a Democrat, or a Republican, or a Libertarian. Any good judge would avoid that like poison, and the judges I know care about their jobs and want to do them well.

"Should judges be elected to office? I think they definitely should. I don't see any reason why judges shouldn't be elected by the people they serve. Supreme Court and appeals judges are different; I can see the logic in having commissions appoint them. For other judges, however, although I believe that they should be elected, I can see the argument for electing them on nonpartisan ballots. It's a little strange to require that judges run on partisan ballots and run along with other people who have to make strictly political decisions, and then ask judges to behave on the bench in a completely nonpartisan manner."

least 80 percent of his judicial appointments from within his own party (see Table 14.1). The average is higher than 90 percent.

Recent presidents have differed in the extent to which ideological and party considerations have affected their judicial appointments. The Reagan and first Bush administrations took special care to screen candidates for their dedication to conservative principles. In fact, since 1980 the Republican platform has pledged to nominate only those prospective judges who believe in the sanctity of human life—in other words, those who oppose abortion. These administrations modified the tradition of allowing the presidential party's senators to select candidates for district and appellate judgeships; senators were asked to submit three names for consideration and the administration made the final choice.[34]

As a result, Reagan and Bush appointees were even more ideologically distinctive (as well as more likely to have been active in party politics) than average among recent presidents. By contrast, the Clinton administration gave a larger role to Democratic senators and other party leaders in suggesting judicial nominees and was less concerned with ideological screening. Clinton also appointed a somewhat lower percentage of federal

TABLE 14.1 Partisan Appointments to Federal District and Appellate Courts: Presidents Grover Cleveland to George W. Bush

	Percentage from the President's Party
Cleveland	97.3
Harrison	87.9
McKinley	95.7
T. Roosevelt	95.8
Taft	82.2
Wilson	98.6
Harding	97.7
Coolidge	94.1
Hoover	85.7
F. Roosevelt	96.4
Truman	93.1
Eisenhower	95.1
Kennedy	90.9
Johnson	94.5
Nixon	92.8
Ford	81.2
Carter	88.8
Reagan	92.7
G.H.W. Bush	88.6
Clinton	87.1

Source: Harold W. Stanley and Richard G. Niemi, *Vital Statistics on American Politics 1999–2000* (Washington, DC: CQ Press, 2000), Table 7.6, p. 278. Updated numbers on the Clinton administration were kindly provided by Sheldon Goldman; see Goldman, Elliot Slotnick, Gerard Gryski, and Gary Zuk, "Clinton's Judges: Summing Up the Legacy," *Judicature* 84 (2001), pp. 244 and 249.

judges from his own party than most of his predecessors did and was less inclined to choose judges with records of party activity.[35]

Senate action on the president's nominations to federal judgeships has become increasingly partisan during the last two decades. The first shots were fired in the 1980s and early 1990s, when Senate Democrats and their allies waged major battles over the confirmation of two conservative nominees to the Supreme Court: Robert Bork and Clarence Thomas. (In fact, the former case gave rise to a new verb: when an intense, usually partisan campaign has been mustered against a nominee, he or she is said to have been "Borked.") By the end of the Clinton administration, the level of partisan animosity over judicial appointments was so high that Republican Senate leaders were refusing to schedule debate on some of the president's nominees. In one especially dramatic case, Clinton nominated an African-American lawyer to the Fourth Circuit Court of Appeals, regarded as the most conservative circuit court in the nation. To avoid the threat that the Senate would stall the nomination indefinitely, Clinton appointed his nominee while the Senate was not in session.[36] Examples of bare-knuckles partisanship continued in 2001, when the situation was reversed and the Senate's Democratic leaders sat on the judicial nominations of the Republican president.[37]

State Court Judges   State court judges are selected in a very different manner. As of 2000, states use five different methods of selection. Governors appoint the judges in six states and in another five, the legislature chooses them. In 13 states, all candidates for judgeships must run in partisan elections, though at times, both parties will endorse the same candidate, who is often the choice of the state bar association. Fourteen states try to take partisanship out of the selection process by electing their judges on a nonpartisan ballot. (In some of these states, however, it is common for each party to endorse its own slate of candidates publicly, so the "nonpartisanship" is a sham.) The remaining 12 states use the merit, or "Missouri," plan in which judges are first selected (usually by the governor) from a list compiled by a nonpartisan screening committee and then must run in a retention election within several years of their appointment.[38]

Most of these alternatives leave room for partisan influence. Even when the voters do the choosing, in practice many of the candidates will be incumbents who have been appointed to their posts by a partisan official. Judicial terms tend to be long ones—often as long as ten years. Those elected to them are typically middle-aged or older. When an elected judge leaves the bench because of death or illness, the governor normally fills the vacancy until the next election—at which the appointee, with the advantage of even a brief period of incumbency, usually wins a full term. Of course, the security of a long term and a high probability of reelection can free judges from party pressures. But these pressures are so often already internalized in the judge's values and preferences that a long-term judgeship merely allows them to flourish.[39]

So the selection process is one reason why we see party differences in judges' rulings. Another major reason is that in the American system there is no special training process for judges—no exam to take, no advanced degree in "judgeship." Any lawyer can be a judge if he or she can win election or appointment to the job. In many European countries on the other hand, someone prepares to be a judge through study, apprenticeship, and then by scoring well on a special civil service exam. Under those circumstances, party organizations will find it much harder to affect the selection of judges. But even so, those who become judges will still have political preferences, many of which will have been shaped by their party identification and their earlier partisan experiences.

THE PARTY WITHIN THE EXECUTIVE AND THE JUDGE

When we talk about party influence on executives and judges, then, the best explanation for this influence is that executives and judges are people who hold political values and commitments, and those values tend to differ according to the individual's party affiliation. Democrats tend to hold different beliefs about government and the economy than Republicans do (more on this in Chapter 15), and Democratic judges and bureaucrats, similarly, hold different views from Republican judges and bureaucrats. These party differences are reinforced by partisan elements in the process by which presidents and governors, top executive officials, and most judges are chosen. But we rarely see much evidence of direct influence by the party organization on bureaucrats and courts; the parties don't have the means to enforce party discipline in the executive or judicial branches.

Efforts have been made—the use of the merit system to appoint officials, for instance—to wring partisan considerations out of the selection process. There is good reason to do so. When judgeships are elected, candidates can receive campaign money from private interests, just as other candidates can. In elections from 1994 to 1998, as one example, judges who won seats on the Texas Supreme Court raised about $11 million in campaign contributions; more than a third of the money came from corporate law firms, many of whom try cases before that court.[40] When people suspect that partisan forces are active, as some inevitably believed about the case that opened this chapter, understandably public confidence in courts and administrative agencies can be undermined. But there is no way to eliminate individuals' beliefs and values—including their partisanship—from their selection as administrators or judges or from their behavior in administrative agencies and in court.

The Semi-Responsible Parties

In the late spring of 2001, Republicans held a majority of the elective offices in the federal government. George W. Bush was in the White House, completing his third month as president. There were Republican majorities in both the House and the Senate, so Republicans chaired all of the standing committees of Congress. The time was ripe for turning Republican Party initiatives into public policy. In one of the first of these initiatives, Bush proposed, as the Republican platform had promised, that students in failing public schools should get taxpayer-funded vouchers to pay their tuition at a private school.[1] When this Republican initiative appeared in the president's education bill ... it failed to attract enough congressional support and was dropped. Say, what?

American party politics is a paradox. On the one hand, we have seen in earlier chapters that the parties pervade the political process. Even when there is no obvious influence of party organization or leaders, party considerations can weigh heavily in the decisions made by voters, legislators, bureaucrats and even judges. Yet compared with many European parties, the Democrats and Republicans have very limited ability to control the actions of elected and appointed officials. They lack the most powerful tools for mobilizing elected officials behind a unified set of party policies. So even when a party has won a majority in government, it still can't guarantee that the party's promises to the nation—the pledges it has made in its platform—will be carried out.[2]

Parties are among the best means available to citizens for controlling their government. If the American parties are not strong enough to hold elected officials accountable, then doesn't that put American democracy at risk? A series of observers believe that it does. Bolstered by an early report constructed by some leading academic experts on political parties,[3] they argue that the answer is to create a system of more "responsible" parties. The governing party in this system would translate a coherent political philosophy into government action and would then be held responsible for the results. That, they argue, would improve the American system of governance.

Others see a more limited problem with party politics. For decades, the American parties have been assailed as being too much alike in their platforms, too centrist, and not clear and specific enough on major issues.[4] Conservative Republican activists in the 1964 presidential campaign pleaded for a platform that would be "a choice, not an echo" of the Democrats. In his third-party candidacy in 1968, George Wallace scoffed that there was "not a dime's worth of difference" between the major parties. John McCain campaigned in the 2000 Republican primaries on the charge that both parties were tied to the demands of moneyed special interests, just as Ross Perot had claimed in 1992 and 1996.

These two sets of critics—the scholars who favor party government and the ideologically oriented activists—have different perspectives, but at heart they make the same point. They both want the parties to offer clearer and more specific platforms, and they want the winning party to put its principles to work in public policy. And to some extent, their complaints have been answered. Both parties have become more distinctive in their stands on important issues in the last two decades. The Democratic Party is more uniformly liberal now, after many Southern conservatives moved away from their traditional Democratic allegiance and into the Republican Party, and the Republicans have followed a more clearly conservative path. Have they become more like "responsible" parties, and does that make them better able to serve the needs of a democracy?

THE CASE FOR RESPONSIBLE PARTY GOVERNMENT

The idea of *party government*, or *responsible parties*, offers a vision of a democracy that contrasts sharply with the traditional American commitment to limited government and the equally traditional American hostility to powerful political parties. Champions of party government believe that we need a strong and decisive government—and, in particular, a strong executive—to solve social and economic problems. Our political institutions, they feel, may have been well suited to the limited, gingerly governing of the early years of American history, but do not serve us well today, when we need more vigorous government action. Undisciplined parties containing diverse interests only make the problem worse.

But this strong government must be held accountable to the public. The current system doesn't permit that, they charge; in fact, it keeps citizens from having a real voice in American politics. Individuals rarely have the time or the information to play an active political role, or even to find out what their elected representatives are doing, so they depend on parties to present them with coherent alternatives and to hold elected officials accountable for their actions. When parties are unable to do that, voters drift from one meaningless decision to another.[5] In a system of candidate-centered politics in which power in government is often divided between the parties, there can be no genuine public control. The result, they argue, is that well-financed minorities—corporations, labor unions, single-issue groups—find it easy to step in and get what they want from government.

How Would Party Government (Responsible Parties) Work?

The best way to deal with this problem, party government advocates say, is to restructure the American parties. The parties would then play the primary organizing role in government and would, in the process, reinvigorate the other institutions of popular democracy. The process of party government would work like this:

- Each party would draw up a reasonably clear and specific statement of the principles and programs it favors. It would pledge to carry out those programs if the party won.

- The parties would nominate candidates loyal to the party program and willing to enact it into public policy if elected.

- Each party would run a campaign that clarifies the programmatic differences between the two parties, so that voters would grasp these differences and vote largely on that basis.

- Once elected, the party would hold its officeholders responsible for carrying out the party program. It would discipline them if they failed to do so. Voters could then determine if they approved of the results and decide whether to keep or throw out the governing party at the next election.

In this system of responsible parties, then, the party's main focus would be on the set of policies it has pledged to put into effect. Winning elections would not be an end in itself, nor would it center on the right to distribute patronage or pork barrel. Nominations and elections would become no more—and no less—than a means to achieve certain public policy goals.[6] For this to happen, all the elected branches of government would have to be controlled by the same party at a particular time. The party would bind the divided institutions of government into a working whole, as happens in parliamentary democracies.

What qualifies the party to play this crucial role? In the words of a prominent party scholar, it is because:

> ... the parties have claims on the loyalties of the American people superior to the claims of any other forms of political organization ... the parties are the special form of political organization adapted to the mobilization of majorities. How else can the majority get organized? If democracy means anything at all it means that the majority has the right to organize for the purpose of taking over the government.[7]

Only the parties, their supporters believe, are stable and visible enough to take on this kind of responsibility. So parties would hold a privileged position in politics compared with interest groups, their major rivals as intermediaries between citizens and government.[8]

Those who argue for party government do not always agree on the purposes that they feel a strong, decisive government should serve. Many conservatives, once suspicious of a powerful central government, grew to like it better when conservative Presidents Reagan and Bush used their power to try to make Congress reduce domestic spending and eliminate liberal programs. Similarly, liberals who were frustrated by the separation of powers developed greater enthusiasm for the principle when Congress proved capable of checking Reagan's initiatives. It is much easier to like party government, apparently, when your party is in charge. But in any case, proponents of party government feel that a central government pulled together by strong parties would give the public a bigger voice in politics.

THE CASE AGAINST PARTY GOVERNMENT

The advocates of party government are persuasive, but most American political scientists and political leaders remain unconvinced. Their concerns about party government and responsibility take two forms. One is the argument that party government would not produce desirable results. The other is that it simply would not work in the American context.[9]

It Would Increase Conflict

First, these skeptics fear that the nature of party government—its dedication to providing clear alternatives on major issues—would stimulate a more intense and dogmatic politics. Compromise would become more rare. Legislators, they say, would be bound to a fixed party position; they would no longer be free to represent their own constituents and to negotiate mutually acceptable solutions. That would weaken the deliberative character of American legislatures.

Critics of party government also fear that a system that makes parties the primary avenue of political representation could undercut or destroy the rich variety of interest groups and other nonparty organizations. Without these other means of representing the nation's diversity, the two major parties might be seriously overloaded. Minor parties would be likely to pop up, which would further fragment the American system. In short, they fear that politics and legislatures would be dominated by a number of doctrinaire, unyielding political parties, none of them strong enough to govern yet none willing to let others govern.

It Wouldn't Work in American Politics

The second major argument against responsible parties is that the idea could not take root in the United States because it is not compatible with American political culture. The biggest problem here is the design of the American government itself.[10] The principles of separation of powers and federalism were intended to prevent tyranny, by dividing constitutional authority among the various levels and branches of government. The separation of powers, for example, allows voters to give control of the executive branch to one party and the legislative branch to the other. Elections for Congress take place on a different schedule from presidential elections, so congressional candidates can insulate themselves, to some extent, from presidential coattails. Federalism permits different parties to dominate in different states. Any change in these basic principles—for example, a switch to a parliamentary system, which would give the party a powerful reason to remain united in the legislature—would require major revision of the Constitution.

Divided Government   In recent years, American voters have made enthusiastic use of the separation of powers. Prior to 1950, the president's party controlled both houses of Congress most of the time. But since then, ***divided government*** has prevailed—the situation in which a president or governor faces at least one house of the legislature controlled by the other party. As you can see in Table 15.1, there have been only two years since 1980 when control of the federal government *wasn't* shared by the two parties. Divided party control has existed in most state governments, as well, since the early 1980s.[11]

TABLE 15.1 Party Control of Government at the National Level, 1951–2002

Year	President	Party in control of the: House	Senate	Divided Government
1951–1952	D	D	D	
1953–1954	R	R	R	
1955–1956	R	D	D	x
1957–1958	R	D	D	x
1959–1960	R	D	D	x
1961–1962	D	D	D	
1963–1964	D	D	D	
1965–1966	D	D	D	
1967–1968	D	D	D	
1969–1970	R	D	D	x
1971–1972	R	D	D	x
1973–1974	R	D	D	x
1975–1976	R	D	D	x
1977–1978	D	D	D	
1979–1980	D	D	D	
1981–1982	R	D	R	x
1983–1984	R	D	R	x
1985–1986	R	D	R	x
1987–1988	R	D	D	x
1989–1990	R	D	D	x
1991–1992	R	D	D	x
1993–1994	D	D	D	
1995–1996	D	R	R	x
1997–1998	D	R	R	x
1999–2000	D	R	R	x
2001–2002	R	R	D*	x

*The Senate was Republican-controlled for the first five months of 2001, until Republican Senator James Jeffords left the Republican Party and the Democrats gained majority control.

Note: D=Democratic control; R=Republican control; x=president, House, and Senate controlled by different parties.

Source: Harold W. Stanley and Richard G. Niemi, *Vital Statistics on American Politics 1999–2000* (Washington, DC: CQ Press, 2000), pp. 34–38.

Until the 1950s, the rare instances of divided government at the federal level usually resulted from very close elections or times when the president's party lost control of one or both houses of Congress in a midterm election. In more recent decades, the main cause of divided government has been split-ticket voting. At the national level, many voters have been willing to split their votes between Republican presidential candidates and Democratic candidates for Congress, most of them incumbents seeking reelection. For a time in the 1990s, the pattern was reversed; voters chose a Democratic president and Republicans for the House and Senate—but the result was a federal government just as divided. Ticket splitting has also been a cause of divided control of government in the states.[12]

Divided government makes responsible party government impossible. By giving control of different branches of government to opposing parties, it requires agreement between the parties for successful policymaking—or what James Sundquist has labeled "coalition government."[13] Negotiation and bargaining are necessary ingredients for government action in any democratic system. But when both Democrats and Republicans have their fingerprints on every major piece of legislation, voters are deprived of their most effective tool for controlling government: the ability to determine which party is responsible for bad policies and to throw that party out of office and replace it with the opposition.

To party government advocates, the prevalence of divided government helps to explain why the federal government has failed to respond effectively on a number of major concerns from health care to energy. The critics disagree. They contend that unified party government doesn't necessarily produce more significant legislative accomplishments, that the federal government has a lot of practice in coping with shared party power,[14] and even, that American voters prefer it that way.[15] The jury is still out regarding some aspects of this question. But it is clear that divided government and the resulting "coalition politics" are high hurdles for those who would like to see responsible parties.

The Gingrich Experiment: A Temporarily Responsible Party

Americans did get at least a whiff of party responsibility in the mid-1990s. In a move spearheaded by House Republican minority leader, Newt Gingrich, the great majority of Republicans running for House seats in 1994 signed a statement they called a "Contract with America." In it, they pledged that if the voters would give the Republicans a House majority, they would change the way Congress worked and would guarantee a vote on each of ten pieces of legislation, all embodying conservative principles, within the first 100 days of the next Congress. The statement concluded, in words that would gladden the hearts of party government advocates: "If we break this contract, throw us out. We mean it."

The Republicans did win a majority of House seats in 1994. And they delivered on their promise; once in office, the new Republican leadership used its iron control of the House agenda to hold votes on each of those bills before the self-imposed deadline expired. Levels of voting cohesion on these pieces of legislation were higher than they had been in decades. That, however, is when party government stalled. The Senate Republican majority had not committed itself to the Contract with America and it did not feel bound to consider these bills promptly or to pass them when they came up. The House Republicans' efforts were further stymied by divided government; a Democratic president had the power to veto any legislation that made it through both houses.

What can we learn from this experiment? It is clear that the separation of powers is a mighty roadblock in the path of party government. Even the commitment of a legislative party to a set of clear and consistent principles is not enough to produce responsible party government, as long as the president and the other house of Congress are not willing to go along. And there is reason to doubt that most voters appreciated the experiment; although Republicans kept their House majority in the next elections in 1996, so did the Senate Republicans who had not signed the Contract with America, and the Democratic President was reelected as well.

There are many other obstacles to achieving party government in the United States. Because voters in primaries choose their candidates, parties lack the power to insist that their nominees be loyal to the party's program. Even legislators who often buck their party's leaders or its platform are able to keep their jobs, as long as their constituents keep voting for them. Changes in campaign finance have given candidates and office-holders even greater freedom from their party organization, which makes it harder to create and promote a unified party "team" in elections. Critics of the responsible parties model have also argued that:

- American voters are not issue-oriented enough to be willing to see politics only through ideological lenses.

- The diversity of interests in American society is too great to be contained within just two platforms.

- The parties themselves are too decentralized to be able to take a single, national position on an issue and then enforce it on all their officeholders.

- Americans distrust parties too much—as seen by their frequent efforts to reduce party influence in politics—to be willing to accept increased party power.

The idea of a responsible governing party, in other words, seems to the critics to ask too much of the voters, the parties themselves, and the institutions of American government.

SEMI-RESPONSIBLE PARTIES: PARTY COHESION AND IDEOLOGY

There is little chance, then, for genuine party government to emerge in the United States. Even so, it might still be possible to nudge the parties in the direction of greater account-ability. The challenge would be to unite the party organization with party voters and the party in government behind a clear and consistent party program—in short, to make the parties more cohesive. Perhaps the only feasible way for a party to grow into a more cohe-sive unit in modern American politics is if its various parts were to come to agree volun-tarily on a party program, an ideological position, or at least, on a set of shared interests. Because their shared commitment to that program would be voluntary, it would not vio-late the separation of powers, or require a basic change in the form of the federal gov-ernment. What is the chance that ideological parties could develop in American politics?

Are the American Parties Ideological?

When analysts refer to an *ideological party*, they mean a party with clear and consistent principles on questions ranging from the purpose of government to the pitfalls and pos-sibilities of human nature. Good examples include: European Socialist parties, the old-style Communist parties, and the Muslim fundamentalist parties that have arisen in Middle Eastern nations. The principles of an ideological party offer straight answers to questions such as these: What should the power relationships in the society look like? How should the society be governed and what values should the government try to achieve? What are the appropriate means to use to achieve these values?[16]

Throughout their histories, however, the American parties have tended to be prag-matic rather than ideological, focusing on concrete problems rather than on protecting the purity of their principles. It is true that the Republican Party had ideological roots, founded on the principle that slavery was an illegitimate exercise of power in a moral society. But the party moved away from those roots as slavery ended and Republicans tried to hold together a national constituency as a majority party.

Why have the major American parties been so free of ideology? Most important, there are only two of them to divide up a tremendous array of interests in American politics. In a system with several parties, a party can cater to one particular ideological niche in the voting public and still hope to survive. In a diverse two-party system, such specialized appeals can be made only by minor parties—or by a major party with a death wish. With so many different interests and people to represent, the American parties have been called "catch-all" parties.[17] It has also been argued that Americans are unusually free of the kinds of deep-seated animosities that fuel an ideological politics in other democracies[18]—though this may surprise observers of American presidential campaigns.

Do They At Least Offer Clear Choices?

But although the two parties are not as ideological as are many European parties, they do, nevertheless, differ clearly in their stands on specific policies. We can see these differences in the platforms they adopt every four years at their national nominating conventions (see box on pp. 302-4), in their candidates' speeches, and in the policies they pursue when they win.[19] It would have been hard during the 2000 presidential campaign, for example, to mistake the tax-cutting proposals of Republican George W. Bush for the spending on social programs recommended by Democrat Al Gore. These differences have grown out of the realigning periods that shaped the different American party systems (see Chapter 7); the Republican dread of an all-powerful federal government and the Democratic commitment to expanding federal social programs have been central principles of the two parties since the New Deal.

Both major parties have become more concerned with issues in the last few decades, more cohesive, and, as a result, more like ideological parties. A major contributor was the issue of civil rights. As issues of racial justice emerged as an important focus of national policy debate, white Southerners deserted the Democratic Party in increasing numbers and took with them their more conservative views on a variety of other issues as well. This lowered the biggest barrier to unity within the Democratic Party on several issues.[20] As you saw in Chapter 13, the Democratic congressional party votes more cohesively now than it has in decades. The Republicans have also become more united on conservative principles.

A major step in this direction occurred with the election and reelection of Ronald Reagan in the 1980s. Reagan, a candidate strongly identified with the conservative wing of the Republican Party, demonstrated the appeal of a simple vision based on one major principle: less government involvement in social welfare programs. The clarity of his message appealed even to voters who were not persuaded by its content. His principled assault on the role of government as it had developed since the New Deal gave a more ideological tone to American politics than it had witnessed in decades. Since then, more issue-oriented leaders have been selected in both parties and have gained a platform to pursue a more ideologically driven agenda. At the same time, as Chapter 5 notes, political ideas—purposive values—have become more prominent in bringing people into party work.

As a result, a change in party control can now make a noticeable difference in public policy. When Vermont Senator James Jeffords left the Republican Party in mid-2001

What the Democrats and Republicans Stand For: The 2000 Party Platforms

These selections from the 2000 platforms show some of the most important differences between the major parties.

Abortion

> **Democrats:** "The Democratic Party stands behind the right of every woman to choose, consistent with *Roe v. Wade,* and regardless of ability to pay."

> **Republicans:** "The unborn child has a fundamental individual right to life which cannot be infringed.... We oppose using public revenues for abortion and will not fund organizations which advocate it."

Civil Rights

> **Democrats:** "We continue to lead the fight to end discrimination on the basis of race, gender, religion, age, ethnicity, disability, and sexual orientation.... We support the full inclusion of gay and lesbian families in the life of the nation."

> **Republicans:** "We support the traditional definition of 'marriage' as the legal union of one man and one woman, and we believe that federal judges and bureaucrats should not force states to recognize other living arrangements as marriages.... We do not believe sexual preference should be given special legal protection or standing in law."

Defense

> **Democrats:** "... ensuring peace and security for Americans today does not just mean guarding against armies on the march. It means investing in building the global peace. It means addressing the fact that more than 1 billion of the Earth's inhabitants live on less than $1 a day—inviting social dislocation, violence, and war."

> **Republicans:** "A strong and well-trained American military is the world's best guarantee of peace ... today, only nine years after the tremendous victory in the Persian Gulf War, the U.S. military faces growing problems in readiness, morale, and its ability to prepare for the threats of the future. The administration has cut defense spending to its lowest percentage of gross domestic product since before [World War 2]."

Education

> **Democrats:** "What America needs are public schools that compete with one another and are held accountable for results, not private school vouchers that drain resources from public schools and hand over the public's hard-earned tax dollars to private schools with no accountability."

> **Republicans:** "Raise academic standards through increased local control ... empower needy families to escape persistently failing schools by allowing federal dollars to follow their children to the school of their choice [including private and religious schools]."

Environment

> **Democrats:** "The Republicans have tried to sell off national parks; gut air, water, and endangered species protections; let polluters off the hook; and put the special interests ahead of the people's interest.... We must dramat-

ically reduce climate-disrupting and health-threatening pollution in this country, while making sure that all nations of the world participate in this effort."

Republicans: "We believe the government's main role should be to provide market-based incentives to innovate and develop the new technologies for Americans to meet—and exceed—environmental standards.... We will safeguard private property rights by enforcing the Takings Clause of the Fifth Amendment and by providing just compensation whenever private property is needed to achieve a compelling public purpose."

Guns

Democrats: "A shocking level of gun violence on our streets and in our schools has shown America the need to keep guns away from those who shouldn't have them—in ways that respect the rights of hunters, sportsmen, and legitimate gun owners.... We should require a photo license I.D., a full background check, and a gun safety test to buy a new handgun in America."

Republicans: "We defend the constitutional right to keep and bear arms.... We oppose federal licensing of law-abiding gun owners and national gun registration as a violation of the Second Amendment."

Hate Crime

Democrats: "Hate crimes are more than assaults on people, they are assaults on the very idea of America. They should be punished with extra force. Protections should include hate violence based on gender, disability, or sexual orientation."

Republicans: "We believe rights inhere in individuals, not in groups."

Health Care

Democrats: "Instead of the guaranteed, universal prescription drug benefit that Democrats believe should be added to Medicare, Republicans are proposing to leave to insurance companies the decisions about whether and where a drug benefit might be offered, what it would include, and how much it would cost."

Republicans: "We need to build on the strengths of the free market system, offer seniors real choices in coverage, give participants flexibility, and make sure there are incentives for the private sector to develop new and inexpensive drugs.... Every Medicare beneficiary should have a choice of health care options ... no more governmental one-size-fits-all."

Labor

Democrats: "Unions have given working people the chance to improve their living standards and have a voice on the job.... We must ... protect workers' rights to organize into unions by providing for a more level playing field between management and labor during organizing drives, and facilitating the ability of workers to organize and to bargain collectively."

Republicans: "We therefore support the right of states to enact Right-to-Work laws [which would require that any workplace be open to non-union as well as union employees, even if the nonunion employees benefited from union negotiations without paying union dues]."

Privatizing Government Services

> **Democrats:** "Democrats do not believe that privatization is a panacea. Some services are inherently public."

> **Republicans:** "If public services can be delivered more efficiently and less expensively through the private sector, they will be privatized."

Taxes

> **Democrats:** "The Bush tax slash ... would let the richest one percent of Americans afford a new sports car and middle class Americans afford a warm soda. Democrats seek the right kind of tax relief—tax cuts that are specifically targeted to help those who need them the most."

> **Republicans:** "We cheer [the Republican Congress'] lowering of the capital gains tax and look forward to further reductions.... To guard against future tax hikes, we support legislation requiring a super-majority vote in both houses of Congress to raise taxes."

Trade

> **Democrats:** "We need to make ... sure that all trade agreements contain provisions that will protect the environment and labor standards, as well as open markets in other countries."

> **Republicans:** "The old liberal approach—using the threat of stifling regulations to redistribute wealth and opportunity—will work no better than it ever has, and perhaps much worse, in the new economy."

Welfare

> **Democrats:** "We changed the nation's welfare system—transforming the program into one that encourages and promotes work. Since 1993, the welfare rolls have fallen to their lowest levels in over 30 years."

> **Republicans:** "The Republican Congress mandated charitable choice in the welfare reform law of 1996, allowing states to contract with faith-based providers for welfare services on the same basis as any other providers. The [Clinton] administration has done its utmost to block the implementation of that provision, insisting that all symbols of religion must be removed or covered over. ..."

You can find the full text of the platforms at *http://www.democrats.org/about/platform.html* (for the Democrats), and *http://www.rnc.org/gopinfo/platform* (for the Republicans).

and caused the Republicans to lose their one-vote Senate majority, the agenda of the Senate changed very quickly. A patients' rights bill, for example, which was regarded as dead in the water under Republican control, went to the head of the legislative line after the Democrats took over, and several environmental measures took on new life as well. The switch in party control was enough to cause a change in the tactics and sometimes the personnel of the rafts of lobbyists who promote their groups' wish list of public policies.[21]

But Internal Variations Remain

Even these clear differences on major issues, however, do not add up to the kinds of sharply articulated, all-encompassing political philosophies that are found in genuinely ideological parties. Nor do the American parties insist that their elected officials and identifiers obey these principles faithfully. They permit, and the localism of American politics encourages, their leaders and followers to be drawn into the party for whatever reasons they choose, without having to pass any kind of ideological "litmus test" to enter.

The result is that some internal divisions remain within each party. Economic conservatives in the Republican Party, for instance, stress reducing the size of government, while the party's social conservatives argue for greater government intervention to protect against pornography, abortion, and homosexuality.[22] These divisions often affect the construction of the party's platform as they did in 2000, when George W. Bush's advisers were forced into negotiations with the party's right wing over the platform plank on abortion.[23] After the election, one of Bush's priorities was to maintain peace among the different wings of the party, from anti-tax and Christian conservative groups to those who favored more moderate policies on education and immigration.

The Democrats have at least as long a history of internal variation. After the Bush victory, for example, a number of moderate Democrats strongly criticized Al Gore's campaign on the ground that he should have stressed more centrist themes, such as the economic growth that had taken place under the Clinton-Gore administration. Voices from the more liberal wing of the party strongly disagreed, arguing that Gore did best when he emphasized the liberal goals of defending Social Security, Medicare, and a higher minimum wage.[24] These recriminations reflected years of dispute between party moderates and liberals; recall the response of former Senator Eugene McCarthy to the accusation that he had split the Democratic Party: "Have you ever tried to split sawdust?"[25]

Yet there is no doubt that both parties have become more cohesive in recent years and their positions on issues have become more distinct—at least among party leaders and activists and members of the party in government. What about party voters? Is it true, as some ideologues have charged, that a large number of Americans are committed to ideological principles and have turned away from the major parties because the Democrats and Republicans are not willing or able to provide clearly defined ideological alternatives? Or are party voters bored with, or even alienated by, the programmatic concerns of many party activists?

IDEOLOGY AND THE AMERICAN VOTER

Popular and media commentary certainly make it seem as though the American public is ideologically oriented. Reports of election results often use the terms "liberal" and "conservative" to describe voters' choices. It has been common, for example, to explain the Republican electoral successes since 1980 and the emergence of more moderate Democratic leaders as a response to what is regarded as a more conservative mood among American voters.[26]

How Ideological Is the American Public?

Careful study of American political attitudes since the 1950s, however, raises serious doubt that most voters can be described as "ideological." An ideological voter, like an ideological party, would not just hold clear attitudes toward a variety of individual issues, but would connect those attitudes into a coherent structure. Since the early days of opinion research, when analysts have compared an individual's attitudes toward several different issues, such as welfare and foreign policy or taxes and civil rights, they have found fairly low levels of consistency.[27] And it has been one of the staples of American survey research that large numbers of respondents say they want both a smaller government with lower taxes, *and* a government that spends more and provides more services in areas such as defense, health care, environment, and education—understandable goals, but not a likely foundation for ideological thinking.[28]

Most of us, according to convincing recent research, hold in our minds a mix of conflicting considerations about politics, in general, and even about particular issues. Our views of politics are not like a set of fixed points—an unqualified "yes" on all forms of affirmative action, a definite "no" to taxcutting—that are unyielding, because they are based on extensive study. Rather, we might feel that affirmative action can help those who need it *and* that it can give an unfair advantage. We can be pulled toward one of these views under some conditions and toward another view under other conditions. Thus, most people react to issues with a degree of ambivalence[29]—a sharp contrast with the more stable, predictable response of an ideologue.

Studies show that only a small (but growing) minority of the public spontaneously refers to liberal or conservative ideological principles in discussing their political views, though much larger numbers use those terms if a pollster includes them in the question. And even when people call themselves liberals or conservatives, their definitions of these terms may startle a political scientist—think, for example, of the respondent in an early public opinion study who defined "liberalist" as meaning a person who liked both parties.[30] Further, the label they choose for themselves may have little to do with the positions they take on specific issues or with their party choice. In a recent survey, for instance, only 55 percent of the Republicans called themselves conservatives and 54 percent of Democrats said they were liberals.[31]

Instead, for most Americans, politics revolves around concrete problems and pragmatic efforts to solve them. Even in the case of Ronald Reagan, who campaigned for president as a principled conservative, voters' judgments turned more on their ***retrospective evaluations*** of presidential performance—their feelings as to whether the most recent presidency had turned out well—than on Reagan's issue positions. In fact, many voters supported Reagan in spite of his conservative policy positions, rather than because of them; in both 1980 and 1984, most voters preferred the policy stands of Reagan's opponent.[32] In the 2000 presidential election, as well, the drag of Bill Clinton's ethical lapses and the importance of such personal qualities as honesty and leadership also suggested a focus on the candidates' character, even for many survey respondents who said they were mainly concerned about specific policy issues.[33]

Voters' choices tend to be results-oriented, retrospective evaluations, not ideological judgments. So parties and candidates try to stitch together winning coalitions by appealing to a range of qualities: the candidates' personal characteristics, group interests, single issues, and feelings toward the party in power—but rarely by using ideological appeals. Even though Americans are more likely now to see a difference between the two parties on issues, and Republican and Democratic identifiers are increasingly polarized in their attitudes toward candidates and issues,[34] ideological thinking has not been common enough within the American public to provide a dependable foundation for responsible parties.

Responsible party government may not require an ideologically oriented public. Even in nations that have ideological party systems, the political thinking of the average citizen is not typically as highly structured as that of political activists and leaders; it is the institutional arrangements and the leaders' perspectives that sustain party government.[35] In American politics, however, none of these supports for responsible party government are especially strong or stable.

The Dilemma of Ideology

In recent years, then, an interesting gulf has opened up within the parties. Leaders, activists, and some voters seem to be increasingly concerned with programmatic questions, and both parties appear to be more united around consistent positions: the Democrats more liberal and the Republicans more conservative. Yet most voters remain more interested in pragmatic questions. Thus, ideological concerns are distributed unevenly within the parties.

Differences by Social Class   An individual's level of education is closely related to his or her affinity for ideological thinking. The abstractions and the verbal content of ideologies come more easily to people with higher levels of formal education.[36] Because education levels are closely related to income and job status, ideological concerns are most often found among the affluent, well educated, upper-middle-class in American politics—the people most likely to become party activists.

Differences among Activists, Candidates, and Voters   The ideological gulf between party activists and party voters is deepened by the related tendency for activists to take more extreme positions on many issues than do party voters. Studies of delegates to the two national parties' nominating conventions have consistently found Democratic activists on the liberal end of the liberal-conservative continuum and Republican activists on the conservative end, with both parties' voters much closer to the center. Figure 15.1 shows these patterns dramatically in opinions about government activism, private school vouchers, and affirmative action. In fact, in the case of vouchers (and among the Democrats on the other two issues as well), each party's activists are more distant from their own party's voters than the two parties' voters are from one another.[37]

A party's candidates and officeholders often find themselves caught in between: closer to the left or right than the party's voters, but not as extreme as its activists. That can put candidates in a difficult position. If they try to muffle their conservative or liberal views, they risk alienating their party's activists. But if they express those views candidly, more moderate voters may choose not to support them in the next election. It is no wonder that many candidates often prefer to remain ambiguous when asked about issues in their campaigns and resist the push toward clearer, more ideological commitments within the parties.[38]

Government should do more to solve national problems. (% agree)

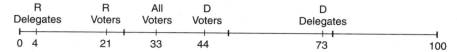

Parents should get tax-funded vouchers to help pay tuition for their children to attend private/religious schools. (% disagree)

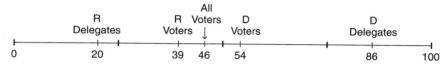

To remedy past discrimination, we should make special efforts to help minorities to get ahead. (% agree)

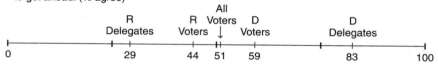

R = Republican
D = Democrat

FIGURE 15.1   Party Activists, Party Identifiers, and the Public on Key Issues, 2000.

Source: The data can be found in Chapter 10, Table 10.3. "Delegates" are delegates to the parties' national presidential conventions.

These differences between more ideological activists and more flexible candidates can aggravate the tensions among the party organization, the party in government, and the party's voters. The ideologues in both parties complain periodically about the moderation of the party in government. Liberal Democrats often objected to the more centrist policies of Democratic President Clinton, and although George W. Bush has done an effective job of calming the fears of social conservatives about his core values, right-wing groups (and moderates as well) remain watchful.[39]

The dilemma of ideology, then, is not whether the American parties can become genuinely ideological parties. That is very unlikely. The problem is whether the increasing ideological commitment of their activists and of many of their officeholders can be sustained without alienating their more pragmatic supporters. If party voters welcome the significant differences that they see between the Democratic and Republican Parties on policy, then there is not much risk of alienation.[40] But it is at least as likely that large numbers of Americans, whose interest in politics is low, will find these sharpened party differences to be more of a turnoff than an incentive to learn more.

WHEN IS PARTY GOVERNMENT MOST LIKELY?

Responsible parties are hard to achieve. Even the British Parliament, so often cited as a model by proponents of party government, has rarely developed the cohesion and the binding party discipline that a "pure" responsible party government would require.[41] The parties in some American state legislatures can be very disciplined, but normally in support of a program drawn up by the governor or the legislative party leaders, not by the party organization. Occasionally, however, the American parties may approach the ideal of responsible party government. Under what conditions is this more likely to occur?

When There is Strong Presidential Leadership

At times, strong presidential leadership can produce a fairly cohesive program that becomes a party program. Especially when the president's party controls both houses of Congress, that program can be translated into law. Some presidents—Ronald Reagan and Lyndon Johnson are good examples—have been able to push Congress to enact large parts of the party platform on which they ran for office. In addition, strong, party-oriented presidents can draw attention to party differences and act as reference points for voters' approval or disapproval. But the result is that the president's performance, not the program of the party as a whole, guides voters' decision-making. So although this presidential government offers some features of a responsible party system, it does not necessarily produce the unified parties and clear ideological alternatives that the reformers demand.

In Times of Crisis

At critical times in American history, the parties have divided in ways that were, if not truly ideological, at least determinedly programmatic. In the 1936 presidential election, for example, the Democrats and the Republicans offered dramatically different solutions to a nation devastated by the Great Depression. The hardships of that economic collapse probably focused voter attention to an unusual degree on the possible remedies that public policy could provide. This, combined with a campaign centered on the pros and cons of the Roosevelt program for social and economic change, may well have produced something close to a mandate in the election for both the president and Congress. When strong presidential leadership is combined with crisis conditions, then perhaps, a degree of responsible party government can be achieved, at least for relatively short periods of time. This is not likely to happen when the crisis comes in the form of an external threat, however; the terrorist attacks of September 11, 2001 resulted in an effort at bipartisan cooperation, though partisan conflict resumed within a month or so.

During Party Realignments

It is during party realignments that the American political system seems to have approached the requirements for party government most closely. During realignment periods, the party coalitions have tended to divide more clearly along a single line of political cleavage, and party leaders, activists and voters seem to reach their highest levels of agreement with one another, and their greatest differences with the other party.[42] Realignments typically produce a unified federal government with the same party controlling both houses of Congress, the presidency and a judiciary that, through the president's appointment power, comes to reflect the new majority. On only five occasions in American history has one party enjoyed control of Congress and the presidency continuously for more than a decade and each time, this control was first established during a realignment.

Unified party control does not guarantee that the policy-making branches of the government will cooperate with one another. But cooperation is certainly more likely when a president is dealing with a majority of his own party in Congress—especially if its members feel they owe their positions to their party label, as often is the case during a realignment—than when Congress is controlled by the opposition. Moreover, during realignments, party cohesion in Congress is especially high. So it is not surprising that major bursts of comprehensive policy change have typically followed realignments.[43] These wholesale realignments of the party system and the atmosphere of crisis and the strong presidential leadership that have accompanied them have brought the United States as close to responsible party government as we have ever been able to achieve.

Even during realignments, however, the American version of party government has been a pale imitation of its European counterparts. In previous U.S. realignments, party commitment to a set of shared ideological principles has fallen short of the level that would be necessary for truly responsible parties. The realignment of the 1930s, for example, produced a majority Democratic Party by linking a liberal northern wing, attracted to the party because it represented the hopes of disadvantaged groups and championed the developing welfare state, and a conservative Southern wing that often opposed both of these goals. The president at the time, Franklin D. Roosevelt, had a congressional majority large enough to achieve many of his policy goals. But he faced persistent opposition within his own party throughout his long career in the White House.

In short, even when they are most unified around a single political agenda during a realignment, the American parties are broad coalitions of differing interests and goals. They have never been sufficiently united in a set of common principles to be able to overcome the institutional forces—federalism and the separation of powers—that tend to disunite them.

PARTY GOVERNMENT AND POPULAR CONTROL

This chapter tells a complicated story. To many analysts, the idea of party government, or responsible parties, has continuing appeal. When parties stand for clear principles and voters are offered clear choices in elections, it is easier for citizens to hold government responsible for the policies it produces. That may make for a stronger and more vibrant democracy.

The major American parties are not ideological parties like many in Europe. But the congressional parties and, to some extent, the parties in the electorate have become more cohesive in the last two decades than they have been in a very long time. At the federal level and in many states, the level of party conflict over basic principles of public policy is very high. The national party committees never have been stronger than they are today, nor more engaged in coordinating the activities of the state and local parties, and financing federal and nonfederal campaigns.

Yet if the parties are to become more accountable—more like responsible parties in a system of party government—clear differences on issues are not enough. There must be some set of basic principles or values that can connect different issues into a single logical structure, some means by which voters and leaders are able to distill the large number of policy issues into one major dimension or a few, so that voters can easily understand and predict the party's stands, and so that the party's supporting coalition remains constant from one issue to the next. There must be some standard by which issues that crosscut the party coalitions can be relegated to the Siberia of the party's agenda.

This level of structure and coherence will be harder and perhaps impossible to achieve. In addition, political candidates remain pretty much on their own in gaining their party's nomination and running in the general election. Candidates still have the responsibility of raising most of their campaign money. Increases in candidate spending and in issue advocacy ads encourage voters to respond to candidates as individuals not as elements of a party ticket. All these forces give candidates greater independence from their parties than the increase in party resources can counteract. And no amount of party money can buy an exception to the rules of federalism and the separation of powers.

It doesn't seem likely then that the American parties—and the American voters— can meet the demands that the classic model of party responsibility would impose on them. The increased party cohesion may be enough to produce an enhanced level of responsibility. But the party organizations have not grown into the central role that the reformers so valued: that of drawing up a party program and enforcing it on candidates and officeholders. Many would find that to be cause for celebration. Others would remind us that, in a system of government as fragmented as that of the United States, semi-responsible parties make it even harder to accomplish one of the basic tasks of a democracy: holding public officials accountable for their actions.

The Place of Parties in American Politics

B y the 1970s, the American parties appeared to be in decline on a number of fronts. Because their troubles had started a decade or two earlier in response to long-term changes in American society, it was easy to assume that the decline was permanent. By the time their decay had become the central theme of books and articles about the parties, however, there were clear signs of party resurgence. The parties have grown into different types of organizations than they once were. But in this changed form, they continue to be an important part of the American political landscape.

To conclude this look at the American parties, let us examine these changes in relation to a simple, but profound truth: political parties are powerfully shaped by the world around them.[1] Parties affect presidents, legislatures, citizens, election rules, interest groups, and campaign finance, but they are also influenced by these forces. The changes in party power and functions over time can be better understood by looking at the relationships between parties and their environment.

PARTIES AND THEIR ENVIRONMENT

Political parties influence their environment in a variety of ways. Party organizations and the parties in government decide how candidates will be nominated and who will have the opportunity to choose them. Through their own performance and the messages they offer, parties affect public attitudes about the Democrats and the Republicans and about politics more generally. The parties mobilize citizens, converting resources such as money and loyalties into various forms of influence. They play a major role in the process that links citizens' beliefs, demands, and fears on the one hand, and public policies on the other.

Yet the impact of their environment on the parties is probably even more extensive. Three types of environmental factors have been especially important in helping to shape the American parties as well as those in other Western democracies. They include the nature of the electorate, the nation's basic governmental institutions and rules, and the forces that mold the broader society (Table 16.1).[2]

TABLE 16.1 How Their Environment Influences the American Parties

Types of Influences	Examples
1. Nature of the electorate	Expansion of the right to vote, citizens' political interest and knowledge, social characteristics of the electorate (distributions of age, race, income, education)
2. Political institutions and rules	
(a) Institutions	Federalism, separation of powers, nature of the presidency, single-member districts
(b) Electoral processes	Direct primary, nonpartisan elections
(c) Laws and regulations	Laws governing campaign finance, structure of party organization, merit system
3. Social forces	
(a) National events and conditions	State of the economy, war, other national problems
(b) Other political intermediaries	Types of other organized interests, nature and importance of television and other media, independent consultants
(c) Political culture	Attitudes toward parties, politics, and politicians

The Nature of the Electorate

Characteristics of the electorate affect the parties in many ways. One of the most basic is that the nation's rules governing who will have the right to vote condition the party's activities; dropping the minimum voting age to 18, for example, produced a change in the parties' target audience. Social conditions, such as levels of education, affluence, and age distributions, help to determine who will exercise that right and, therefore, which groups' concerns will dominate the party system. In the case of age, we have seen in Chapter 8 that people 65 and older vote at a rate about twice that of people 24 and younger. It should come as no surprise then, that Social Security and Medicare are much more frequent campaign issues than are college loans. The societal "fault lines" that divide the electorate into opposing groups—race is one of the best and most persistent examples in American politics—have had an important role in defining the party system as well.

Over time, changes in the American electorate have traced the rise of mass popular democracy in the United States. From an extremely limited suffrage—the small proportion of white male adults who owned property—the right to vote has evolved to include a much broader adult suffrage. Political awareness has expanded as a much greater proportion of the public has gained the privilege of more years of education and as the media have made political information much more accessible. And perhaps as a result, people's expectations that their views *ought to be* taken into account in public policy have increased. At the same time, new opportunities have been created for voters to participate in political decisions, through primary elections, referenda, and other means. But for a variety of reasons, people's interest in politics and feelings of political effectiveness have not followed suit. So ironically, as these opportunities for participation have expanded, voter turnout has declined, especially among lower-income Americans.[3]

Political Institutions and Rules

The second cluster of environmental influences on the parties includes the main institutions and "rules" of government. Most important here is the basic framework of political institutions: whether the government is federal or unitary, whether it is parliamentary or has separated powers, and how its positions of power are structured. Then there are the laws that regulate the parties and their activities, from those prescribing the party's organizational arrangements to laws regulating campaign spending. We have discussed, for example, the effects of the separation of powers, the direct primary, and the use of plurality elections in single-member districts on the development and cohesion of the parties.

The American parties have been subjected to more regulation than have parties in other nations. The direct primary limits their role in the selection of candidates to a degree unknown in most other democracies, and American state laws defining the party organizations have no parallel in the democratic world. The effect of this regulation—and in most cases its aim—is to put limits on the party organization; an unintended consequence is to boost the power of the party in government relative to that of the party organization. But with the important exception of the direct primary and a few other rules,[4] changes in the institutional aspects of the parties' environment have probably been less dramatic than have the changes in the nature of the electorate. In fact, these institutional forces have remained more stable during the last century in the United States than they have in most other democracies.

Societal Forces

A third set of environmental influences refers to events and trends in the larger society that affect politics at a particular time. The horrors of the World Trade Center attack and other terrorist acts in the United States, the relocation of U.S. industries to Mexico and other nations, and the rise and fall of energy prices have had powerful effects on the nation's agenda. Thus they have become part of the parties' agenda, as well, and they affect the types of goals that individuals feel can be achieved through the parties. So even though these events and trends are often beyond the parties' influence, they affect the parties' supporting coalitions, their platforms and their behavior more generally.

Other societal forces include the number and character of organized interests in the nation, the types and behavior of the media, and other means of representing interests. If individuals find other, more effective ways to pursue their political goals than through the parties, they will use them. If the "hot line" of a local newspaper is better able to track down a reader's Social Security check that has gotten lost in the bureaucracy or if an interest group is more vocal in opposing abortion or gay rights, then why should the individual try to achieve her political aims through a party? The nature of the parties at any given time, then, depends in part on the available alternatives to parties and the competition among them.

All these elements of their environment have contributed to the unique character of the American parties. But the most extensive and systematic changes have probably involved the nature of the electorate. Thus, as we summarize the dramatic changes that have occurred in the parties' structure, supporting coalitions, and strength during the last four decades, we will pay special attention to their relationship to changes in the electorate.

PARTY DECAY IN THE 1960s AND 1970s

A fundamental and unique feature of the American parties is that the three party sectors are bound together only loosely. The party organization has never been able to involve large numbers of party identifiers in its structure and activities, nor has it been successful in directing the campaigns or the policy-making of the party in government. The party decline that was becoming apparent in the 1960s, then, affected the three sectors very differently.[5]

The Parties in the Electorate

During a time of upheaval in many of aspects of American life, voters' loyalty to their parties weakened substantially in the late 1960s and 1970s. Increasing numbers of adults began to think of themselves as independents, rather than party identifiers. Those who remained attached to a party no longer relied on that identification as much as they once did; voters were less and less willing to delegate their choices in elections to a party's judgment. The parties, then, found themselves with smaller numbers of less loyal identifiers.

One result was a surge in ticket-splitting. Beginning in the late 1960s, the percentage of Americans who reported voting for a presidential candidate of one party and a House candidate of the other began to grow. That percentage had doubled by 1972, and similar increases occurred in ticket-splitting between Senate and House races and in state and local elections. By 1968, almost half of the respondents in national surveys said they had voted for more than one party's candidates in state or local elections, and by 1974 that figure topped out at 61 percent. At the aggregate level, the number of congressional districts selecting a presidential candidate of one party and a congressional candidate of the other party exceeded 30 percent for the first time in history in 1964 and had reached 44 percent early in the next decade.[6]

In place of party identification and as education levels increased, some voters became more responsive to the increasingly issue-oriented candidacies of the time. The campaigns of Barry Goldwater in 1964, Eugene McCarthy and George Wallace in 1968, and George McGovern in 1972 prompted greater awareness of political issues in parts of the electorate. For other voters, the most effective appeals were those of a candidate's personality and media image. The handsome faces, ready smiles, and graceful lifestyles that television screens so fully convey attracted some of the support that party symbols once commanded.

Voters became more inclined, then, to respond to candidates as individuals, rather than as members of a particular political party. Independent candidates for president—McCarthy in 1976, John Anderson in 1980—and for governor gained greater success than in previous years as a consequence of this decline in party voting. Because candidates and issues change far more frequently than parties, the result was a less stable and predictable pattern of voting.

Party Organizations

The last of the great party machines were fading in the 1960s and 1970s. The famous Daley machine in Chicago was ripped apart in a series of tumultuous struggles after Richard J. Daley's death in 1976 and then stripped of its patronage base. Party organizations could no longer depend on the patronage and preferments that once were so vital in recruiting party activists. Instead, more people were being drawn into party activism because of their commitment to particular issues. These were better-educated people and they demanded greater participation in the party's decisions. Some of these new activists thought compromise was a dirty word; to them, standing for a set of principles was more important than winning an election. If their party did not satisfy their ideological goals, they stood ready to leave it for other groups—particular candidates' campaigns and single-issue organizations—that were more individually tailored to meet their needs.

Other aspects of the party organization were under fire as well. As the use of the direct primary spread, party organizations gave up their control over nominations to whoever chose to vote in the primary. By the time a primary season had ended, the party's presidential nominee had been determined, so its presidential nominating convention no longer had much of a deliberative role. As grassroots activists came to expect a bigger say within the party organization, its own internal decision-making was no longer under the party leaders' control. This was particularly true of the Democrats who in 1972 and 1976 nominated presidential candidates who were well outside the mainstream of their own party.

In addition to their declining influence over nominations, by the 1960s and 1970s the party organizations had lost their central role in campaigns. Candidates now built their own campaign organizations, raised their own campaign money, and made their own decisions on how to spend it. The campaign assets they once received from their local party organizations—public opinion data, strategic advice, fund-raising, willing helpers—could now be obtained directly from pollsters, the media, public relations experts, issue-oriented activists, or campaign consulting firms that were, in effect, "rent-a-party" agencies. The campaign finance reforms gave candidates an incentive to try to raise nonparty money at a time when the technologies for doing so were becoming more widely available.

In fact, in comparison with these independent consultants, the campaign skills that local party organizations could offer their candidates were fairly primitive. The national parties began to develop expertise in newer campaign technologies during the 1970s and to share their resources with state and local parties. But the consultants and the other nonparty providers of campaign expertise had already established a beachhead. The state and local party organizations, in particular, saw their influence on candidates wane.

The party organizations in the 1970s remained much more decentralized than did life and politics in the United States. Voters were looking more and more to national political leaders and symbols, but the party organizations still tended to be collections of state and local fiefdoms. Even in the face of the new vigor in their national committees—stronger organizations and more central authority—the real power in the parties seemed likely to remain at the local level.

The Party in Government

Elected officials came to depend more than ever on direct appeals to voters in the 1960s and 1970s. That was not surprising; they had been freed from reliance on the party organization by the direct primary, by their direct access to the media, and by the money they could raise and the volunteers they could attract independent of the party's efforts. Because of split-ticket voting, candidates didn't even need to rely on party identification. Through personal style, personal appeals, and personal funds, they developed a "personal vote" independent of party.[7]

It became harder than ever before to unseat an incumbent, especially in Congress. The cycle perpetuated itself; because there was not as much chance of beating an elected official, serious challengers did not appear as frequently. When they did, party organizations were not vigorous enough to provide challengers with the campaign resources they so desperately needed. Holding public office became more of a profession—a lifetime career—even at the state and local level, where political professionals had formerly been rare.

As incumbents became more secure electorally—even though many did not feel that way—the congressional parties enjoyed greater freedom from the party organizations. Even the legislative party's leaders found it harder to marshal their troops on behalf of the legislative party's bills or the programs of the party's president. Party-line voting in Congress fell to an all-time low in the late 1960s and early 1970s. But it was a perverse kind of freedom. Protected from the demands of party activists and party organizations, legislators were thus more exposed to other pressures, mainly from large numbers of organized interests.

When the legislative party lacks cohesion and strength, the executive party rushes into the vacuum. Presidents and governors began to exercise greater power and leadership. More than other elected officials, they came increasingly to personify the party and its programs to the voters. The parties, then, could be viewed as executive-centered coalitions during the late 1960s and 1970s. This was especially true of national politics and, in particular, of the ability of presidents to dominate their national party organizations. Presidents did not depend on their party organizations for much; in fact, with the help of federal campaign money after 1974, presidential candidates were able to run their campaigns free of obligation to the party organization at any level. Yet just as the dominance of the parties by chief executives became clear, divided government became the norm. That undercut executives' power by permitting the opposition party to block their leadership.

Shifting Power Centers in the Three-part Party

These changes produced a major shift of power within the parties. Power flowed from the decentralized party organization to the individual members of the party in government, especially the executives. The changes also accentuated a shift in influence away from the parties and toward rival political intermediaries, especially organized interests and the mass media.[8]

At the core of these changes was the increasing isolation of the party organization, not only within the parties but also in American politics more generally. The organizations had enjoyed their days of glory, but they ultimately failed to keep the wholehearted loyalty of many party voters. Isolated from the electorate and without its broad-based support or participation, party organizations and their leaders became even more vulnerable to suspicions that they were run by irresponsible bosses plotting in smoke-filled rooms. Visions of "boss rule" were as much alive at party conventions in the 1960s and

1970s—particularly the 1968 and 1972 Democratic conventions—as they were in the early 1900s. But ironically, the resources the party organizations had in the early 1900s, which could have justified the charge of boss rule at that time, were largely eroded by the 1960s and early 1970s.

The result was a peculiar kind of political party. It seems reasonable that the vital core of any party would be a vibrant party organization. The party organization, after all, is the only sector of the party whose interests go beyond the winning of individual elections. It is the party organization that sustains the party when its candidates lose their races. It is the organization that links the party's officeholders and office seekers; it can call them to collective action of the type that political parties were created to achieve. Without it, party candidates become individual entrepreneurs seeking individual goals in a political system that requires collective decisions. The decline of the party organizations was clearly a major force in the decline of the parties more generally.

PARTY RENEWAL

This marked decline was not the end of the story, however. The American parties responded to these challenges in the 1980s and 1990s, just as they had adapted to changing circumstances at other times in the past. The steady decay of the parties was stopped and even reversed. But some of the changes that took place in the 1960s and 1970s have left their imprint even now. In some important ways, then, the parties have had to adjust to a new role in American politics.

Change in the Parties' Electoral Coalitions

The slow, steady change in the two parties' supporting coalitions, discussed especially in Chapter 7, has led to regularly recurring speculation that a party realignment has taken place. The symptoms that normally precede a realignment began to be present in the early 1960s: dropping levels of voter turnout, a weakened impact of party loyalties on people's voting, more ticket-splitting, greater support for third-party or independent candidates, less predictable elections and divided government.[9]

When Republicans won both the presidency and the Senate in 1980 and gained control of the House in 1994—the first time since 1954 that there was a Republican majority in both Houses of Congress—some concluded that the long-awaited realignment had finally taken place. There is no doubt that one condition of a realignment has been fulfilled. The party coalitions have clearly changed from those of the New Deal period; black Americans are now steadfastly Democratic, white Southerners have moved into the GOP's ranks in large numbers and religious conservatives—Southern and non-southern—are now a distinctive force within the GOP. The most striking feature of this new alignment has been the decline of Democratic strength in the South (see Figure 16.1). And as we have seen, the proportion of party identifiers has rebounded since the 1970s, and there is much greater parity between Republican and Democratic identifiers than there has been since the 1930s.

Yet if this is a realignment, it doesn't look like the realignment of the 1930s. Elections continue to be volatile. Republican House candidates, who appeared to be powerhouses in 1994, seemed more like desperate survivors in 1998. The proportion of the public calling themselves independents remains high. New parties and independent candidacies have aroused a lot of public interest and attracted a notable percentage of the vote in 1992 and 1996. Public opinion polls do not show any signs of great public enthusiasm for the major parties or their conventions, or for that matter, many other aspects of American politics. And even a full-fledged realignment, in a world of primaries, would not give back the party organizations' power to nominate their candidates. Lasting change in the parties' coalitions could not guarantee an end to the more candidate-centered electoral world that has resulted.[10]

Whether or not they led to a realignment, the events of the 1960s and 1970s resulted in a continuing challenge to American party loyalties. Large numbers of voters now rely on sources other than the parties—the media, single-issue groups, increasingly diverse primary groups—for their information about politics. In earlier times, these sources may have helped to reinforce partisan views and loyalties; now they often do not.[11]

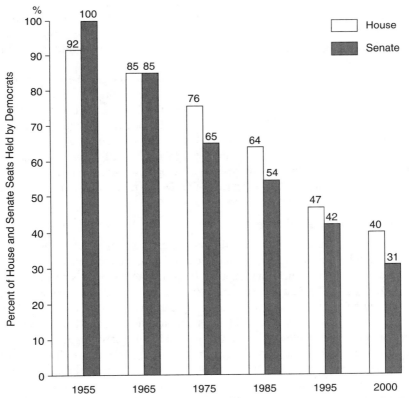

FIGURE 16.1   Eroding Democratic Strength in the South: U.S. House and Senate Seats, 1955–2000.

Note: Data points are the percentage of U.S. senators and House members from the 13 Southern states who are Democrats.

Source: Data for 1955–1995 from *Congressional Quarterly Weekly Report*, Nov. 12, 1994: 3231. Data for 2000 calculated from Harold W. Stanley and Richard G. Niemi, *Vital Statistics on American Politics 1999–2000* (Washington, DC: CQ Press, 2000), Tables 5.10 and 5.11, pp. 213–238.

This variety of sources can encourage people to create their political commitments as they would a patchwork quilt: an issue from this group, a candidate from that party. Yet even with this formidable competition, parties remain important markers on most people's political map. Levels of party identification rebounded in the 1990s and partisanship is at least as strong an influence on people's voting now as it was before the 1960s and 1970s.[12]

The Rise of More Cohesive Parties in Government

Well before the current revival of partisanship in the electorate—and thus a possible cause of it—the parties in government had begun a revival of their own. By the 1970s, the long decline in party cohesion in Congress had stopped and the organizational seeds had been sown for greater party strength. By the 1980s, with stronger and more assertive leadership, the congressional parties had become more cohesive than they had been since the early part of the century. As historically one-party areas (such as the South) became competitive, each of the congressional parties grew more homogeneous, which made it easier for them to offer distinctive alternatives on major issues. Recall the example of the House Republicans' Contract with America and the House Democrats' response to it. In a number of states, as well, legislative parties were becoming more unified and taking clearer positions on issues.

Parties also took on greater importance in the executive branch. The Reagan administration came into office in 1981 as the most ideologically committed in decades. Reagan's leadership placed conservative principles at the top of the GOP's agenda and solidified the hold of his brand of conservatives on the party. The Democrats, though more internally diverse, became more unified in response. By the mid-1990s, there was intense partisan warfare in Washington between a programmatically committed Republican majority in Congress and an activist Clinton White House. The battles continued in 2001 between a conservative Republican president and a razor-thin Democratic majority in the Senate.

The New "Service" Parties

These are dramatic changes. Even more dramatic, however, has been the renaissance of the party organizations. Faced with a more candidate-centered politics, both parties retooled their national organizations to provide services to the party's candidates. With bigger budgets and professional staffs skilled in applying the latest campaign technologies, they have become more active in recruiting candidates for office. They have distributed their resources not only to candidates, but also to state and local parties; these resources, including valuable soft money, have enabled the party organizations to step up their role in campaigns, at least in comparison with the recent past. The infusion of resources is both timely and necessary; as two-party competition spreads, state and local parties need to become more effective just to keep up with the competition.

The new service party, however, differs a great deal from the grassroots organizations of earlier years. Because its main role is to support candidates, it is not very visible to voters. Nor is its impact on candidates assured. In the big-spending world of campaign finance, the party organizations do not bring enough money to the table to be able to dominate political campaigning—or at times even to be heard very clearly. The service party is one of many forces trying to win the attention of candidates. To succeed it must compete with independent campaign consultants, interest groups, and others. As service parties, then, the party organizations are no longer as distinctive as they used to be, in the sense of providing campaign resources that no other group could deliver.[13]

The party organizations, in short, are more vigorous now than they have been in years. But instead of building on their old sources of strength, they have adapted to new conditions and taken on a new form: that of the service party. These service parties live in a political world in which they compete increasingly with other transmitters of political symbols and information: media, organized interests and PACs, candidates' organizations, and social movements. They vie with these groups to provide campaign money for candidates, to influence elected officials, and to get citizens registered and mobilized to vote on Election Day.[14]

THE FUTURE OF PARTY POLITICS IN AMERICA

These trends are vital to us because political parties are vital to us. Parties have the potential to do a lot of good for a democracy.[15] They give political leaders a reason to work together and a set of shared interests that goes beyond personalities. When parties take clear stands on issues, they clarify political choices for the public. That helps voters learn about politics at lower cost to them. Parties can bring voters to the polls, which helps to legitimize a democracy. Perhaps most important, parties organize majorities, which are necessary for governing. Interest groups do a good job of representing intense minorities. But there are not many alternatives to the parties for organizing majorities in a reasonably stable way.

And therein lies the problem. We need parties but we don't like them. We don't feel influenced by them, even though we are. When asked, most of us claim that issues and candidates' personal qualities have the biggest impact on our votes. Yet it's clear that partisanship is closely related to our attitudes toward issues and candidates and is the source of much of their influence.[16]

A Changing Intermediary Role

Parties are the only political organizations whose names go on the ballot alongside those of candidates. A candidate for U.S. Senate is identified in the polling booth not as a Sierra Club member, nor as a pro-lifer—and usually not even as an incumbent—but rather as a Democrat or Republican. Parties developed in part out of voters' need for a guide, a shortcut, to the confusing choices that elections require. The willingness of large numbers of voters to respond to that party label is what has made it so valuable. When the party label is able to produce stable and enduring loyalties to the party and to dominate voting decisions, then it is clear that parties serve as key intermediaries between citizens and the wider political world.

The value of the party label in elections is probably greatest when a mass electorate has just begun to develop and has serious need for information. As the electorate matures, its needs change. One explanation for American voters' decreased reliance on party loyalties in the 1960s and 1970s was that voters are better educated and better informed now than they were 60 or 80 years ago. This may better prepare them to sift through a broader range of political messages without the need for party labels as a guide.[17]

Current voters also have a great deal of exposure to information through the mass media, which tend to emphasize candidates' personal characteristics and styles rather than their party. Most current voters have grown up with media that feed them great visuals, but fairly small snippets of content. Many have grown accustomed to thinking of politics in terms of the personalities and personal images that the mass media carry so effectively. It is not that media coverage ignores political parties; the media that activists and elected officials rely on continue to refer frequently to the parties in their domestic political coverage.[18] But more popular media—and especially the entertainment media that also affect people's views about politics—are more likely to be party-free.

Further, citizens have larger numbers of political organizations now to help them reach their goals. Early in the twentieth century someone concerned about environmental quality would probably have had to pursue his or her goals through a political party; not many groups focused specifically on resource conservation, much less pollution control. Now, however, in tandem with the growing reach of government into most aspects of private life, a huge array of organized interests has developed that permit individuals to establish a "designer link" with the political system. If someone prefers to see politics entirely from the perspective of gun rights or gay rights, several groups exist to make that possible. There is no need to compromise or to support a coalition of other groups' needs and a range of candidate styles, as a party loyalty would require.

Yet Americans still need cues or labels to help them make sense of politics—perhaps even more now, because of the blizzard of information available to them. Granted, the parties' traditional dominance has been eroded by competition from organized interests and the media. It has never been easy for two broad-based, pragmatic political parties to handle the tremendous diversity of goals among American voters and it is not getting any easier. But the story of this book is that although they have always struggled within a hostile environment, the major American parties have found ways to adapt to a long history of challenges, and they continue to do so, regaining strength in somewhat changed form.

Domination by the Party in Government

In their glory days at the beginning of the twentieth century, the American parties may have been dominated by their party organizations, but no longer. Now the parties are ruled by their candidates and officeholders—by the party in government. More and more, it is the members of the party in government who run the campaigns, control the party's image, and govern in office without much pressure from their party organizations.

A party dominated by its officeholders and office seekers differs in several basic ways from a party led by its organization (Figure 16.2). Where the party in government dominates, almost by definition the party's focus is electoral, because the party's officeholders are primarily concerned with winning elections. Elected officials work to control the resources necessary for election victory. Once they win, they govern so as to create a record of accomplishment in office and to increase their chances of reelection.

In contrast, when a party is dominated by its organizational sector, it is the party organization that speaks for the party, chooses its candidates, and maintains some degree of leverage over its legislators. The result is that the issue commitments or ideologies of the organization's activists have much greater influence on the party as a whole than in

When the Party Organization Dominates:

1. It is the party organization's activists who set the party's goals.

2. The party organization controls the nomination of candidates and much of the election campaign.

3. The legislative party is relatively unified.

4. There is a great deal of coordination among the three party sectors.

5. Party voters can be more fully integrated into the party organization.

6. The party's activities are mainly electoral, but policy-based as well.

When the Party in Government Dominates:

1. The party is unified, if at all, by the executive party's goals and programs.

2. The party organization has little control over candidates' nominations and campaigns.

3. The legislative party is not very unified over time.

4. The three party sectors can, and often do, act independently of one another.

5. Party voters do not have a formal role in the party organization.

6. The party's activities revolve amost exclusively around elections.

FIGURE 16.2   Which Sector of the Party Dominates: What Difference Does It Make?

a party dominated by its candidates and officeholders. Perhaps the best examples of party organizational dominance were the early working-class parties of the European parliamentary democracies, although they, too, have come under more control by their officeholders in recent years.[19]

These two types of parties differ in their ability to create strong links among the party organization, the party in government, and the party electorate. In the party dominated by its organization, ties of loyalty and party discipline bind the three sectors closely together. Much of the party's electorate becomes part of the organization through membership in it. Candidates are tied closely to the party organization, because they are indebted to it for their nomination and for its campaign help. In the classic urban party machines, the party organization and its candidates were united in their pragmatic dedication to winning elections. In the responsible party model, these two sectors could be held together by loyalty to the same principles or by the organization's ability to discipline elected officials by denying them renomination.

In the party controlled by the party in government, by contrast, the focus is on whatever is needed to win. Alliances can be made and broken depending on their contribution to that goal. The dominant party in government is free to form alliances with interest groups or other organizations, rather than to work with its own party organization. In fact, it is free to ally with members of the opposition party if that will enhance its chances of winning; we have seen how Southern Democrats, for example, frequently allied with Republicans in Congress during the 1950s and 1960s in a "conservative coalition."

In addition, its candidates and elected officials tend to make contact with party voters without relying on the party organization—and for good reason, since the organization typically has few resources to offer its candidates. As we have seen, this was particularly true of the American parties during the 1950s and 1960s. Thus, the party organizations were ignored by many candidates during the campaign and had little influence on them afterward. The congressional parties, for instance, set up their own campaign committees in Congress, from which they received their party resources, so they were able to ignore the national party organizations.

The differences between these two types of parties affect the character of a democratic system. A party that is dominated by its candidates and public officials is not likely to provide the continuity needed to maintain public accountability. On the other hand, where the party organization dominates, the party can be something more than the sum total of the candidates who run on its label. It can be strong enough to exert policy leadership, perhaps even approaching the model of the responsible party. It can provide leadership in the recruitment of public officials and offer a stable cue to millions of voters. That in turn can bolster officeholders' responsibility to their constituents. The collection of a party's candidates and elected officials are not likely to have the incentive to join together in this way; only the party organization has the necessary commitment to all the party's goals and to the party itself.

What causes some parties to be dominated by their party organizations and others to be led by their elected officials and candidates? Several environmental factors seem to make a difference:

- The institutions of government play an important role. A parliamentary system demands that the parties be disciplined and unified; a system of separated powers does not. In practice, nations with parliamentary forms of government are more likely to have organization-dominated parties.

- American electoral law (primaries and the regulation of campaign finance, for example) favors the party in government, giving it easy access to nomination and great freedom from the party organization in waging campaigns.

- State governments have seriously hindered the state party organizations, making it difficult for them to develop large memberships, requiring them to use unwieldy organizational forms and to remain open to penetration by outsiders. This reformist urge, which has been so antiorganization in its goals, has all but ignored the party in government.

Once one sector of the party comes to dominate, moreover, it can usually keep control through the laws and customs that govern party practices. The development of sophisticated new campaign techniques offers a good example. In a number of democratic nations with parliamentary systems, party organizations have used their power to promote laws that limit candidates' independent access to these campaign technologies—for instance, by mandating that free television time goes to the party organizations which then dole it out to their candidates, rather than to the candidates directly. The party organization, then, administers the new campaign tools, which buttresses its central role. In the United States, however, the dominant party in government has no reason to reduce its power by passing laws that turn over control of these campaign tools to the party organizations; therefore, the television time and other valuable tools remain available directly to candidates and officeholders.[20]

Other forces in the American political environment have reinforced the dominance of the party in government. Many aspects of the Progressive reforms were intended to weaken the party organizations. The result, however unintended, was to give a decided advantage to the party in government. Even the increasing role of organized interests and the media further undercuts the party organizations. Under such an assault, what is remarkable is not that the party organizations' role has eroded, but that they have survived at all.

The Need for Strong Parties

Democracy is unthinkable without parties. But political life in the United States without the dominance of two major parties is no longer unthinkable. Much of American local politics has been, at least officially, nonpartisan for some time. At the state and national levels, divided government, independent candidates, and third (and fourth and fifth) parties have become familiar parts of the political landscape.

The consequences of a multiparty system would be profound.[21] More disturbing, however, would be a politics in which parties played a much smaller role. It is no exaggeration to suggest that the quality of American democracy would be weakened. Among the many links between citizens and government in American society, only the parties have the incentive to create majorities, in order to win a wide range of elections over a long period. That, in turn, gives the parties—to a greater extent than interest groups, PACs, or even elected officials—good reason to pay attention to those citizens who are not activists or big campaign contributors. Walter Dean Burnham writes,

> Political parties, with all their well-known human and structural shortcomings, are the only devices thus far invented by the wit of Western man which, with some effectiveness, can generate countervailing collective power on behalf of the many individually powerless against the relatively few who are individually—or organizationally—powerful.[22]

It is the parties that mobilize sheer numbers against the organized minorities who hold other political resources. The parties do so in the one political arena where sheer numbers count most heavily: elections. Because of that, parties traditionally have been the means by which newly enfranchised, but otherwise powerless groups gained a foothold in American life. The old-style urban machines, for example, provided the tool by which recent immigrants won control of their cities from older, largely white, Anglo-Saxon Protestant elites.

In other periods of American history as well, the party has been the form of political organization most available to those citizens who lack the resources to make a real impact on public decisions using other means. In a less party-driven, more fluid politics, where bargaining takes place among many more types of political organizations and millions more uncommitted voters, the well-organized minorities with critical resources, such as money, insider knowledge, and technological expertise, would probably have an even greater advantage than they do now. We can see from research on nonpartisan elections, for instance, that the elimination of the party symbol and of the party as an organizer in these elections has probably helped wealthier and higher-status groups of both the right and the left to dominate these elections.[23] That may be one reason why the participation declines of the last few decades have been somewhat greater among lower-status and less educated Americans; they may feel less represented by a politics in which the parties are no longer dominant.[24]

Some might argue that the development of more ideological parties could pose the same problem. To the extent that an ideological perspective is more likely to be found among the better educated and activist citizens, the parties might become focused on issues that were even less important and less comprehensible to the less involved, less educated voters.

Finally, weakened parties would rob the political system of an effective means for creating governing coalitions. Without at least moderately strong parties, it becomes harder to mobilize majorities that can come together in support of policies. Individual candidates, freed from lasting party loyalties, would have to re-create majorities for every new legislative proposal. The result could be political immobility in which legislatures splinter into conflicting and intransigent groups. This can further undermine public confidence in democratic politics. Laws and policies would continue to be made. But they would be made by shifting coalitions made up of interest groups, campaign contributors, bureaucrats, and elected officials acting as free agents. These coalitions would be less permanent and less identifiable to the public—and therefore, much harder to hold accountable—than the parties have been and can be.

We should not exaggerate the parties' traditional contributions to democratic politics. Although no democracies so far have survived without parties, it is possible for a mature political system to develop workable alternatives to stable, two-party politics. But in a diverse nation, the challenge is whether any of the alternatives could pull together the pieces of a fragmented politics and separated political institutions as effectively as the parties have done. It is risky, to say the least, to move toward a politics without parties, whose hazards would not be known until it was too late for them to avoided.

How to Make the Parties Stronger

Because parties bring so much value to American democracy, some analysts have considered ways to expand the parties' role in political life. Larry J. Sabato, a prominent student of the American parties, has offered a number of suggestions.[25] Citing poll data showing that a majority of respondents would like the parties to be more active as civic organizations in helping people deal with government, he proposes that the party organizations could create party "mobile units" to offer help to citizens in areas where the U.S. House (and perhaps the state) representative is from the other party. That would allow the party organization, not just the members of the party in government, to be responsible for constituent service. Sabato notes that this idea was especially attractive to respondents who described their commitment to party as having declined in the last five years and who said they were not registered to vote—those, in short, more likely to be alienated from American politics.[26]

Another way for the parties to strengthen their connection with citizens is to use the increasing pot of party money to air campaign ads that promote the party as a whole, rather than just its individual candidates. In particular, such advertising could strengthen the meaning of party by stressing the link between the party's stands and viewers' and readers' daily lives. An independent group, called the Republican Ideas Political Committee, sponsored such an ad in Kansas City during the 2000 presidential campaign, claiming that Republican policies would help families who wanted to send their children to private schools.[27] To this point, however, the bulk of both parties' money goes to fund ads that do not even mention the party itself.

CONCLUSION: THE PARTY DILEMMA

The American parties face a range of difficult problems. The American electorate is more and more varied. The breakdown of traditional group ties encourages greater individualism. Voters respond with more differentiated loyalties. The great majority of voters maintain an identification with a political party, but they also respond to candidates and issues, stylistic matters and national trends. The result is a more diverse, complicated politics that no single set of loyalties and no single set of political organizations can easily contain.

The parties cannot be all things to all citizens. They can't represent the individual agenda of each citizen while trying to build a majority coalition. It is very difficult for them to be pure in their issue stands and still make the compromises necessary to build coalitions and govern. They find it hard to offer policy alternatives in elections without engaging in the partisan conflict and competition that many Americans find so distasteful. They cannot unite their officeholders and office seekers in common cause while giving candidates full electoral independence and freedom. They cannot depend on unwavering party loyalty in an electorate that wants to choose candidates individually.

These conflicting expectations are not likely to be resolved. The American parties will continue to need to adapt to them while facing attack from a rich assortment of critics. The parties' distinctive character has sustained them longer than any other tool of democratic politics. For the sake of accountability in governance, even the most independent-minded citizens have a stake in sustaining vigorous party politics in the United States.

Party Politics
on the Internet

The Web pages of the two major parties and a variety of minor parties can provide a fascinating glimpse into the world of each party's politics and can serve as the basis for some interesting assignments. Here are the main sites of the Democrats, the Republicans, and *twenty* American minor parties for you to explore. Later in this section you'll find a listing of other sites on party politics and a number of sample assignments using all these sites.

http://www.democrats.org

This is the official Web site of the Democratic National Committee. It contains party news, statements by Democratic elected officials, and, at campaign time, information about Republican candidates (as seen through DNC eyes). There are links to the state Democratic Parties and the party's most recent national platform, as well as several State of the State addresses by Democratic governors. Visitors can find out how to receive e-mail updates from the DNC, enroll in campaign training seminars, and register to vote. Job and internship opportunities at the DNC are listed.

http://www.rnc.org

The Republican National Committee's official Web site provides news about national politics, the RNC, and a range of party activities. Information about Democratic candidates is posted here at election time, and the site includes the party platform, a discussion of its history and rules, and material about party stands on a range of issues. There is also a listing of allied groups, such as the College Republican National Committee. Links enable the visitor to contact state Republican organizations, donate money, and register to vote. Video clips are available on the site.

http://www.reformparty.org

This is the site of the dominant branch of the Reform Party, founded in the mid-1990s by Ross Perot. Since Perot's exit from the party, it has taken a sharp turn to the right. The party's platform is posted here, along with a statement of party history and current party news. Visitors to the site can register to vote, contribute online, join the party's e-mail lists, and learn about party candidates. There are links to several state Reform Parties.

http://www.americanreform.org

The American Reform Party is an anti-Perot group that split off from the main body of the Reform Party in 1997. The site contains a history of the organization, position papers, a party platform, and links to state groups. You can join a list server on issues and get information on how to contribute online and by regular mail.

http://www.americanheritageparty.org
An explicitly Christian party, the American Heritage Party promotes the Bible as a blue-print for political action, and opposes abortion, group-based civil rights, gun control, property taxes, and government welfare programs. Its Web site emphasizes its statement of principles and states its aim to establish voter clubs at the local level, in addition to its existing party organization in Washington state.

http://www.dsausa.org/dsa.html
The Democratic Socialists of America's site offers a statement of the party's principles and links to information about socialism in the United States and in other nations. There are video clips, reports about local parties' activities, and an invitation for members to form other local parties and to join Young Democratic Socialists.

http://www.greens.org/na.html
The Green Parties of North America list their platform, which emphasizes environmental issues, peace, and social justice, on this Web site. The site includes a series of party publications, e-mail services, listings of its election results since 1986, and, at election time, its current candidates. There are links to state Green Parties and to Campus Greens.

http://www.usiap.org
A western party, the Independent American Party wants smaller government and an emphasis on Christian values, patriotism and property rights. The site contains a variety of issue positions and links to a few affiliated state party organizations.

http://www.lcr.org
The Log Cabin Republicans are the largest national gay and lesbian Republican organization. Their site includes legislative information, material about party conventions and Republican candidates, and a newsletter. Candidate endorsements are listed at election time. Links exist to various local chapters and to "donor clubs."

http://www.lp.org
The Libertarian Party believes in complete freedom from government and taxes. Its home page provides news about party candidates and party principles. There is a link to a quiz, "Are You a Libertarian?" You'll also find a statement of the party's history and activities and a list of state chapters. Interested visitors can sign up for the party's e-mail announcement list, register to vote and contribute online. The site includes a sample letter that sympathizers can send to their friends to encourage interest in the Libertarian Party.

http://www.natural-law.org
The Natural Law party says it wants to "bring the light of science into politics" and espouses Transcendental Meditation and other new-age practices. The site includes the party platform, news and party events, information about issues such as genetic engineering, and a link to the Student Natural Law Party Club. You'll find video and audio clips, party endorsements of candidates, links to party representatives in the states, and an opportunity to join the party's e-mail list.

http://www.newparty.org
The New Party is a progressive, grassroots party concerned mainly with local elections in a variety of cities. It promotes "fusion"—the listing of candidates on multiple party

lines. The site features materials about the party's principles, its chapters and candidates. There are links to other progressive organizations such as feminist and civil rights groups and a page to make on-line contributions.

http://www.prohibition.org

Founded in the mid-1800s to oppose the manufacture and sale of alcoholic beverages, the Prohibition Party has taken on a new life as a pro-life, anti-gay, pro-prayer party. Its Web site displays a palm tree and a camel, apparently to symbolize that the party is an "oasis" of constitutional rights and moral values. It discusses the party's 1999 national convention and its nomination of a presidential candidate. There are no links or mentions of any further activity.

http://www.cpusa.org

This is the home page of the Communist Party USA. Posted here are position papers stating the party's stands against joblessness, racism, and poverty and a list of party-related newspapers and journals. There are e-mail addresses for joining the national party and contacting state parties, audio links, listings of party events and links to a variety of groups with similar aims.

http://www.sp-usa.org

The century-old Socialist Party USA stands for principles of democratic socialism, including full employment and an internally democratic party organization. It is an anti-communist socialist group, unlike several other socialist parties. Its Web site lists a variety of socialist publications, local activities and a speakers' bureau. Its efforts are predominantly local, centering on demonstrations as well as some local campaigns. It lists regular-mail addresses for state socialist parties. Site visitors can find information about joining and sending contributions offline and about internships in the New York area.

http://www.slp.org

The Socialist Labor Party bills itself as the original Socialist party in the United States, founded in the late 1800s. It no longer runs candidates for president, but does take part in a few local races. Its Web site discusses its principles, links to a newsletter and to socialist writings, and provides e-mail links to several local chapters.

http://www.themilitant.com

The Socialist Workers Party broke away from the Communist Party decades ago and now espouses a pro-Castro viewpoint. It runs local candidates in some areas as well as a candidate for president. Its Web site is a newsletter presenting party views on current issues.

http://www.southernparty.org

Founded in 1998, the Southern Party argues for the sovereignty, and eventually the independence, of the southern states. Its home page displays the "stars and bars"—one of the Confederate flags during the Civil War—and also disavows the activities of hate groups. The site features position papers, press releases, and a listing of state parties (which include, interestingly enough, Delaware and New Mexico). There is information about contributing to the party offline.

http://www.southernindependentparty.com

A splinter group of the Southern Party, the Southern Independence Party has the same goals as its former colleagues; it broke off in 2000 as the result of personal disputes. Its site contains a party platform; material about the Civil War; links to state sites (no Delaware listing, but hopes for a future in New Mexico); a list of articles, speeches, and other publications; and a slightly different version of the "stars and bars" on its flag. There is an e-mail link with the Southern Independence Party's Young Confederates.

http://www.USTaxpayers.org *also reachable at* http://www.Constitutionparty.com
Formerly the U.S. Taxpayers Party, the Constitution Party favors limited government, and opposes abortion, gun control, immigration, taxes, and gay rights. The site offers press releases, a list of party events, its platform, and a place to order campaign materials. There are audio clips, links to state party organizations, and online opportunities to volunteer for the party and make contributions.

http://www.wethepeople-wtp.org
The We the People Party views itself as a coalition of independents organized to take part in the 2004 presidential race. Its primary concern is campaign finance reform. The site contains a statement of principles, a free membership application, and a page encouraging visitors to express their concerns, as well as party newsletters. The creation of two founders, it is located in New Hampshire.

http://www.workers.org
The Workers World Party has a 40-year history in the United States since it split off from the Socialist Workers Party. The WWP is an anti-capitalist organization with a pro-Cuba, pro-China approach to communist politics. Its site contains news of issues that the organization finds interesting, events, and a listing of local parties.

Here are some other Internet sites through which you can get information about political parties, elections, and voting:

Campaign Finance:

http://www.commoncause.org
Common Cause monitors a variety of political issues. You can research your own members of the U.S. House and Senate, get campaign finance data, and learn about campaign finance reform.

http://www.fec.gov
This is the Federal Election Commission's Web site. In addition to information about the Commission itself, it provides access to current and past campaign finance data in federal (presidential and congressional) races, as well as a variety of reports about those data.

http://www.opensecrets.org
The Center for Responsive Politics, a nonpartisan research group, maintains this site to provide information on money in politics. Its databases include presidential and congressional races, political action committees, soft money, lobbyists, and news links of various kinds.

Politics and Political Issues:

http://www.govote.com
This site has a wealth of information on elections, issues, and other political news. It permits visitors to see poll results and take part in discussion groups about a variety of issues. There are links to federal and state government offices.

http://www.heritage.org
The Heritage Foundation is a conservative think tank; its site provides current political news and detailed analyses of policy issues from a conservative perspective.

http://www.mojones.com
Mother Jones, a liberal publication that appears on the Web as well as in hard copy, covers American politics and issues and also contains a lot of international news.

http://www.nga.org
You can find state election results at the site of the National Governors' Association, as well as NGA positions on issues of interest to the states. Job opportunities are listed here too. The home page of the Council of State Governments, *http://www.statesnews.org,* has more information on state policy issues.

http://politics.com
You'll find links to news stories about politics, roll-call votes taken in the current sessions of the U.S. House and Senate, and information about what Congress is doing on the day you check the site.

http://www.rollcall.com
Roll Call is a newspaper that covers Congress and Capitol Hill. Its site provides news about current legislative action and "insider" information about Congress.

http://www.speakout.com
This is a nonpartisan site that offers argument and details on a range of political issues, the chance to take part in and view poll results, and a discussion of political activism on these issues.

http://www.vote-smart.org
Project Vote Smart provides information on federal and state candidates, including biographical data, interest group ratings, voting records and candidates' responses to questions about their issue priorities. It offers data on campaign finance, tracks legislation in Congress, and tells site visitors how to register to vote. It also contains survey results from a study of 18- to 25-year-olds.

Polling:

http://www.gallup.com/index.html
Here you'll find the most recent Gallup polls and links to reports on previous polls conducted by the Gallup organization.

http://www.people-press.org
The Pew Research Center for the People and the Press conducts polls about politics, policy, and public attitudes toward the media. Its site contains a lot of polling data and analysis and a description of ten types of voters, with which you can compare your own attitudes and demographics.

http://www.tarrance.com/battleground/default.asp
The Battleground Poll is a collaboration between Democratic pollster Celinda Lake and Republican strategist Ed Goeas. The site offers public opinion polling data and strategic analyses from both parties' perspectives.

http://www.umich.edu/~nes/
The National Election Studies, based at the University of Michigan, have been conducted since 1952 to provide information on public opinion, political participation, and voting behavior. Students can view and download survey data from current and earlier studies and find research reports.

Media Sites:

http://www.cnn.com/ALLPOLITICS
Here are links to current and recent news stories from CNN and *Time* magazine.

http://cagle.slate.msn.com/comics/editorialcontents.asp
You'll find dozens of current political cartoons on this site, including some from Canada and other nations.

http://www.Washingtonpost.com
Major national newspapers such as the *Washington Post* can be read on the Internet. The Post is notable for the excellence of its political coverage. See also the *New York Times* at *http://www.nytimes.com* and the *Los Angeles Times* at *http://www.latimes.com.*

SAMPLE ASSIGNMENTS USING THESE WEB SITES:

- Pick two political issues that interest you. Use the Democratic and Republican Parties' Web sites to determine where they stand on these issues. How clear are their stands and how much difference do you find between them? Do they offer you a distinct choice?

- Compare the positions of the two major parties with those of two minor parties. How easy is it to find out where the minor parties stand on these issues that interest you? How different are their stands from those of the Democrats and Republicans? What would be the advantages and disadvantages for American politics if these alternatives were more widely publicized?

- What can you learn from these sites about the parties' organizations? At what levels of government do the major parties have organizations? Where do the minor parties have chapters or branches, other than at the national level?

- What kinds of activities do the Democrats and Republicans sponsor? To what extent do minor parties offer similar activities to their sympathizers?

- Does a party's Web site show evidence that the party offers material rewards for activists or solidary or purposive rewards (see Chapter 5)? Which type of rewards seems to be most common? Do you find more emphasis on purposive rewards in the major parties' Web sites or in the minor parties'? What about solidary rewards?

- Which do the Democrats' and Republicans' home pages stress most: their candidates' experience and personal qualities, or the party's issue stands?

- Do the two major parties seem to be targeting particular groups in the population, such as women, Hispanics, or others? Which ones? Do the Democrats and Republicans target the same groups or different groups?

- What kinds of news stories do various parties feature on their home pages? Why do you think they chose these stories? If the same news item is posted on more than one party's site, is it treated differently or explained differently by the two parties?

- Are the statements on these Web sites predominantly positive—that is, presenting the party's own beliefs—or predominantly negative, in the sense of criticizing other parties' or groups' actions and views? Do you find the major parties' statements to be more positive (or negative) than those of the minor parties? the liberal parties' statements to be more positive (or negative) than those of the conservative parties?

- In comparison with the breadth of the major parties, why is the universe of minor parties so splintered? There are, for example, five socialist parties listed here. How do they differ from one another, and how substantial are their differences? What about the differences among the several conservative minor parties? Why would there be two Southern parties? Do you find anything in these Web sites that helps explain this proliferation?

- Are there any major issue positions or views of the world that you do *not* find represented by any party, major or minor? What are they, and why would you expect them to be omitted?

- Using the American National Election Studies Web site, familiarize yourself with the results of survey questions on citizens' feelings about the parties. When you read a survey question, predict what you expect the responses to be. Compare your prediction with the actual data. Have the responses changed over time?

- Use this American National Election Studies Web site to create cross-tabulations: How do Democratic and Republican identifiers compare in their views on various issues? Are there big differences among strong identifiers, weak identifiers, and independent leaners? Which group expresses the greatest interest in politics? Would you have expected this finding?

- Using the Opensecrets site, check out the information on soft money (see Chapter 12). Which party would you expect to raise the most soft money? Compare your prediction with the actual data. How do the parties spend their money?

- What interest groups would you expect to give Democrats in Congress high ratings? Republicans? Go to the VoteSmart site and test your guesses against their findings.

- Using the *Washington Post*'s Web site (or that of any other major newspaper or broadcast media outlet), read articles, columns, and editorials about political issues. Are the major parties mentioned? If so, what aspects of the parties' activities are emphasized? Are political candidates mentioned more frequently than parties are, or the reverse? Do you find any mention of minor parties?

Endnotes

PART 1

1. This is the title of Harold Lasswell's pioneering book, *Politics: Who Gets What, When, How* (New York: McGraw-Hill, 1936).
2. E. E. Schattschneider, *Party Government* (New York: Rinehart, 1942), p. 1.
3. See Herbert Kitschelt, Zdenka Mansfeldova, Radoslaw Markowski, and Gabor Toka, *Post-Communist Party Systems* (New York: Cambridge University Press, 1999), and, on party influence on voters' choices, Timothy J. Colton, *Transitional Citizens* (Cambridge: Harvard University Press, 2000).
4. Austin Ranney provides an excellent account of these antiparty attitudes and reforms in *Curing the Mischiefs of Faction* (Berkeley: University of California Press, 1975).

CHAPTER 1

1. These definitions come from: Edmund Burke, "Thoughts on the Cause of the Present Discontents" (1770) in *The Works of Edmund Burke* (Boston: Little, Brown, 1839), vol. I, pp. 425–426; Anthony Downs, *An Economic Theory of Democracy* (New York: Harper & Row, 1957), p. 24; William Nisbet Chambers, "Party Development and the American Mainstream," in Chambers and Walter Dean Burnham, eds., *The American Party Systems* (New York: Oxford University Press, 1967), p. 5; John H. Aldrich, *Why Parties? The Origin and Transformation of Party Politics in America* (Chicago: University of Chicago Press, 1995), pp. 283–284; and V. O. Key, Jr. *Politics, Parties, and Pressure Groups* (New York: Crowell, 1958), pp. 180–182. For an extended discussion of key issues in defining political parties, see Leon Epstein, *Political Parties in Western Democracies* (New Brunswick, NJ: Transaction Books, 1980); Gerald Pomper, *Passions and Interests: Political Party Concepts of American Democracy* (Lawrence: University of Kansas Press, 1992); Giovanni Sartori, *Parties and Party Systems* (New York: Cambridge University Press, 1976), pp. 3–38; and Joseph Schlesinger, *Political Parties and the Winning of Office* (Ann Arbor: University of Michigan Press, 1991), pp. 5–10.
2. See Pomper, *Passions and Interests*, for another approach to defining parties.
3. For a good example, see John H. Aldrich, *Why Parties?* especially Chapter 1. Aldrich's definition centers on elected leaders and party leaders; he does not see a mass base as central to a definition of party.
4. V. O. Key, Jr., used this "tripartite" conception of political parties to organize his classic political parties text, *Politics, Parties, and Pressure Groups*. Key attributed the concept of party-in-the-electorate to Ralph M. Goldman, *Party Chairmen and Party Factions, 1789–1900* (Chicago: University of Chicago Ph.D. dissertation, 1951), Chapter 17.
5. On this point, see Denise L. Baer and David A. Bositis, *Elite Cadres and Party Coalitions: Representing the Public in Party Politics* (Westport, CT: Greenwood Press, 1988), pp. 21–50; and Pomper, *Passions and Interests*, pp. 3–5.
6. See Joseph A. Schlesinger, "The Primary Goals of Political Parties: A Clarification of Positive Theory," *American Political Science Review* 69 (1975): 840–849, on parties' electoral goals.

7. State legislative elections in Nebraska are nonpartisan, although the candidates' partisan ties are obvious to many voters, and statewide officials (such as the governor and attorney general) are elected on a partisan ballot.

8. This image is Joseph A. Schlesinger's in "The New American Political Party," *American Political Science Review* 79 (1985): 1152–1169.

9. See Theodore Lowi, "Toward Functionalism in Political Science: The Case of Innovation in Party Systems," *American Political Science Review* 57 (1963): 570–583; and A. James Reichley, *The Life of the Parties* (New York: Free Press, 1992), pp. 1–2 and 414–415.

10. John Aldrich sees parties as organizations created by rational politicians to solve their most challenging collective action problems: to organize officeholders into an enduring and cohesive group supporting key policy principles, to forge durable majorities, and to mobilize voters in elections and other political activity on behalf of their cause. See Aldrich, *Why Parties?* especially Chapters 2 and 9.

11. Among the best histories of American party development are William N. Chambers, *Political Parties in a New Nation* (New York: Oxford University Press, 1963); Chambers and Burnham, *The American Party Systems;* Everett C. Ladd, Jr., *American Political Parties* (New York: Norton, 1970); Reichley, *The Life of the Parties*; and John H. Aldrich, *Why Parties?*

12. Quoted in *The Federalist* (New York: Mentor Books, 1961), p. 77. *The Federalist* is the collection of 85 essays written to justify the new Constitution and published as letters to the editor in New York newspapers in 1787 and 1788 under the pen name of Publius. Their authors were Alexander Hamilton, James Madison, and John Jay; Madison was clearly the author of the paper quoted here.

13. See John H. Aldrich and Ruth W. Grant, "The Antifederalists, the First Congress, and the First Parties," *Journal of Politics* 55 (1993): 295–326; Joseph Charles, *The Origins of the American Party System* (New York: Harper & Row, 1961); and John F. Hoadley, *Origins of American Political Parties 1789–1803* (Lexington: University of Kentucky Press, 1986).

14. For a detailed account of the extension of the suffrage, see Chilton Williamson, *American Suffrage: From Property to Democracy* (Princeton: Princeton University Press, 1960).

15. For a more complete account, see Neal R. Peirce and Lawrence D. Longley, *The People's President: The Electoral College in American History and the Direct Vote Alternative* (New Haven: Yale University Press, 1981).

16. Aldrich in *Why Parties?* Chapter 4, and Reichley in *The Life of the Parties*, Chapter 5, provide excellent descriptions of how mass parties first appeared in the decades after the 1820s. Martin Van Buren, leader of the Albany, New York, Regency machine and the eighth president of the United States, is credited as being the lead architect in the creation of the Democratic Party, the first of the mass parties.

17. For a more complete account of parties during their golden age, see Reichley, *The Life of the Parties*, Chaps. 6–11.

18. A spirited (and disapproving) account of the development of American parties at this time is found in Moisei Ostrogorski, *Democracy and the Organization of Political Parties, Volume II: The United States* (Garden City, NY: Anchor Books, 1964, originally published in 1902).

19. On the various episodes of party reform in American history and their impact, see Austin Ranney, *Curing the Mischiefs of Faction* (Berkeley: University of California Press, 1975). Richard Hofstadter provides a good account of the Progressive movement in *The Age of Reform* (New York: Vintage Books, 1955).

20. Government regulation of political parties is so extensive that Leon Epstein has referred to them as public utilities rather than as the private associations they were during the nineteenth century. See his *Political Parties in the American Mold* (Madison: University of Wisconsin Press, 1986), pp. 155–199.

21. The best discussions of the concept of political culture remain Gabriel Almond and Sidney Verba, *The Civic Culture* (Princeton: Princeton University Press, 1963), and Lucian W. Pye and Sidney Verba, *Political Culture and Political Development* (Princeton: Princeton University Press, 1965). Daniel Elazar applies the idea of political culture to American state and local politics in *American Federalism: A View from the States* (New York: Crowell, 1972), Chapter 4.

22. Some results of this survey, conducted by the American National Election Studies at the University of Michigan, can be found in The NES Guide to Public Opinion and Electoral Behavior, located on the Internet at *http://www.umich.edu/~nes/nesguide/toptable/tab2b_2.htm*

CHAPTER 2

1. See Kenneth Janda, *Political Parties: A Cross-National Survey* (New York: Free Press, 1980), and Arend Lijphart, *Electoral Systems and Party Systems: A Study of Twenty-Seven Democracies, 1945–1990* (New York: Oxford University Press, 1994), for comprehensive studies of other party systems.

2. See Giovanni Sartori, *Parties and Party Systems* (New York: Cambridge University Press, 1976), for a critique of the traditional classification of party systems.

3. See *Congressional Quarterly Weekly Report* (*CQ* Weekly) (November 11, 2000), p. 2652. House races were highly competitive through the mid-1890s but competitiveness declined after that. See James C. Garand and Donald A. Gross, "Changes in the Vote Margins for Congressional Candidates: A Specification of Historical Trends," *American Political Science Review* 78 (1984): 17–30, and Donald A. Gross and James C. Garand, "The Vanishing Marginals, 1824–1980," *Journal of Politics* 46 (1984): 224–237.

4. Interparty competition refers to competition between the parties, as opposed to competition within a particular party (termed "intra-party"). See Austin Ranney, "Parties in State Politics," in Herbert Jacob and Kenneth Vines, eds., *Politics in the American States* (Boston: Little, Brown, 1965), p. 65, for the first index measurements. For an alternative index based on state legislative races, see Thomas M. Holbrook and Emily Van Dunk, "Electoral Competition in the American States," *American Political Science Review* 87 (1993): 955–962.

5. See Chapter 2, "The Growth in Two-Party Competition," in Malcolm E. Jewell and Sarah M. Morehouse, *Political Parties and Elections in American States* (Washington, DC: CQ Press, 2001).

6. On this change between 1970 and 1980, see Samuel C. Patterson and Gregory A. Caldeira, "The Etiology of Partisan Competition," *American Political Science Review* 78 (1984): 691–707.

7. These figures are drawn from Paul R. Abramson, John H. Aldrich, and David W. Rohde, *Change and Continuity in the 1996 Elections* (Washington, DC: CQ Press, 1998), Chapter 9 and especially Table 9.1. On the advantage of incumbency in state legislative races, see John M. Carey, Richard G. Niemi, and Lynda W. Powell, "Incumbency and the Probability of Reelection in State Legislative Elections," *Journal of Politics* 62 (2000): 671–700.

8. All the losing candidates in 1994 were Democrats, however, which suggests that party considerations were more important than incumbency. Data from 1994–1996 come from Abramson *et al., Change and Continuity*, and for 1998 and 2000 from *CQ Weekly* postelection figures. On the influence of incumbency on elections, see Gary C. Jacobson, *The Politics of Congressional Elections*, 5th ed. (New York: Longman, 2001), Chapter 3; Paul S. Herrnson, *Congressional Elections*, 3rd ed. (Washington, DC: CQ Press, 2000), Chapter 9; Stephen Ansolabehere, James M. Snyder, Jr., and Charles Stewart III, "Old Voters, New Voters, and the Personal Vote: Using Redistricting to Measure the Incumbency Advantage," *American Journal of Political Science* 44 (2000): 17–34; and, on state legislative elections, Jewell and Morehouse, *Political Parties and Elections*, pp. 202–208.

9. Gary C. Jacobson, "The Marginals Never Vanished: Incumbency and Competition in Elections to the U.S. House of Representatives, 1952–82," *American Journal of Political Science* 31 (1987): 126–141. On how redistricting and scandals make incumbents vulnerable to defeat, see Monica Bauer and John R. Hibbing, "Which Incumbents Lose in House Elections: A Response to Jacobson's 'The Marginals Never Vanished,'" *American Journal of Political Science* 31 (1987): 262–271.

10. See Maurice Duverger, *Political Parties* (New York: Wiley, 1954). E. E. Schattschneider offers an institutional explanation in *Party Government* (New York: Rinehart, 1942). On the influence of electoral institutions on the number of parties in a nation, see Octavio Amorim Neto and Gary W. Cox, "Electoral Institutions, Cleavage Structures, and the Number of Parties," *American Journal of Political Science* 41 (1997):149–174.

11. Many American state legislatures used to have multimember districts. In 1955, 58 percent of all state legislative districts were multimember; this number had declined to 10 percent by the 1980s. See Richard Niemi, Simon Jackman, and Laura Winsky, "Candidates and Competitiveness in Multimember Districts," *Legislative Studies Quarterly* 16 (1991): 91–109.

12. Leon Epstein, *Political Parties in the American Mold* (Madison: University of Wisconsin Press, 1986), pp. 129–132.

13. See, for example, V. O. Key, Jr., *Politics, Parties, and Pressure Groups*, 5th ed. (New York: Crowell, 1964), pp. 229 ff.

14. See Louis Hartz, *The Liberal Tradition in America* (New York: Harcourt, Brace and World, 1955). Yet this "consensus" is full of mixed feelings: See Stanley Feldman and John Zaller, "The Political Culture of Ambivalence," *American Journal of Political Science* 36 (1992): 268–307.

15. See Willis D. Hawley, *Nonpartisan Elections and the Case for Party Politics* (New York: Wiley, 1973).

16. Susan Welch and Timothy Bledsoe, "The Partisan Consequences of Nonpartisan Elections and the Changing Nature of Urban Politics," *American Journal of Political Science* 30 (1986): 128–139.

17. On third-party and independent governors through 1992, see J. David Gillespie, *Politics at the Periphery* (Columbia: University of South Carolina Press, 1993). More recent information is available on the Federal Election Commission (FEC) Web site, http://www.fec.gov.

18. See Michael Janofsky, "Town Becomes a Laboratory for Rule by Greens," *New York Times* on the Web, *http://www.nytimes.com/2001/01/03/politics/03GREE.html* (accessed Jan. 2, 2001), and Janofsky, "Minor Parties in Colorado Agree to Cooperate," *New York Times* on the web, *http://www.nytimes.com/2001/01/15/politics/15DENV.html* (accessed Jan. 15, 2001).

19. Among the best books on American third parties are Steven J. Rosenstone, Roy L. Behr, and Edward H. Lazarus, *Third Parties in America*, 2nd ed. (Princeton: Princeton University Press, 1996); Paul S. Herrnson and John C. Green, *Multiparty Politics in America*, 2nd ed. (Lanham, MD: Rowman and Littlefield, 2002); and Daniel A. Mazmanian, *Third Parties in Presidential Elections* (Washington, DC: Brookings Institution, 1974).

20. For more on the Libertarians, see Joseph M. Hazlett II, *The Libertarian Party* (Jefferson, NC: McFarland and Company, 1992).

21. We can see the degree of voter skepticism in the fact that almost all third-party presidential candidates since 1900 have received less support on election day than they did in pre-election polls; see Rosenstone, Behr, and Lazarus, *Third Parties in America*, p. 41.

22. *Ibid.*, p. 162.

23. See Paul R. Abramson, John H. Aldrich, and David W. Rohde, *Change and Continuity in the 1992 Elections* (Washington, DC: CQ Press, 1994), and Herbert B. Asher, "The Perot Campaign," in Herbert Weisberg, ed., *Democracy's Feast: The 1992 U.S. Elections* (Chatham, NJ: Chatham House, 1994), Chapter 6.

24. FEC figures show that the Perot organization invested almost $73 million in the 1992 campaign (June 28, 1994 report). According to reporter Richard L. Berke (*New York Times*, Oct. 27, 1992, p. A11), as much as $46 million of this money was spent on television.

25. See J. David Gillespie, quoted in the *Washington Post National Weekly Edition*, Sept. 19–25, 1994, p. 13.

26. See Clifton McCleskey, "Parties at the Bar: Equal Protection, Freedom of Association, and the Rights of Political Organizations," *Journal of Politics* 46 (1984): 346–368; and Lee Epstein and Charles D. Hadley, "On the Treatment of Political Parties in the U.S. Supreme Court, 1900–1986," *Journal of Politics* 52 (1990): 413–432. For up-to-date reports on ballot access by minor parties and independents, see Richard Winger's *Ballot Access News* at *http://www.ballot-access.org*.

27. See Howard A. Scarrow, *Parties, Elections, and Representation in the State of New York* (New York: New York University Press, 1983).

PART 2

1. For more on the distinction between cadre and mass membership parties, as well as the difficulties of drawing these distinctions in practice, see Alan Ware, ed., *Political Parties: Electoral Change and Structural Response* (New York: Basil Blackwell, 1987).

CHAPTER 3

1. Larry J. Sabato and Bruce Larson, *The Party's Just Begun,* 2nd ed. (New York: Longman, 2002), pp.176–177. The data were compiled from Andrew M. Appleton and Daniel S. Ward, *State Party Profiles: A 50-State Guide to Development, Organization, and Resources* (Washington, DC: CQ Press, 1997), Appendix.

2. The case citations are *Tashjian v. Republican Party of Connecticut,* 479 U.S. 1024 (1986); and *Eu* (Secretary of State of California) *v. San Francisco County Democratic Central Committee et al.,* 103 L. Ed. 2nd 271 (1989). For a review of earlier federal court decisions in this area, see Clifton McCleskey, "Parties at the Bar: Equal Protection, Freedom of Association, and the Rights of Political Organizations," *Journal of Politics* 46 (1984): 346–368. On deregulation of parties in California, see Roy Christman and Barbara Norrander, "A Reflection on Political Party Deregulation Via the Courts: The Case of California," *Journal of Law and Politics* 6 (1990): 723–742.

3. A public utility is a government-regulated provider of services, such as an electric company or a water company. Leon Epstein, *Political Parties in the American Mold* (Madison: University of Wisconsin Press, 1986), pp. 155–199.

4. V. O. Key, Jr., *Politics, Parties and Pressure Groups* (New York: Crowell, 1964), p. 316.

5. Samuel J. Eldersveld, *Political Parties: A Behavioral Analysis* (Chicago: Rand McNally, 1964).

6. The organization of American political parties raises questions about what Robert Michels calls the "iron law of oligarchy"—that organizations are inevitably controlled from the top. See Robert Michels, *Political Parties* (Glencoe, IL: Free Press, 1949; originally published in 1915); and Eldersveld, *Political Parties.*

7. These estimates on the number of machines governing American cities at various times during their heyday come from M. Craig Brown and Charles N. Halaby, "Machine Politics in America, 1870–1945," *Journal of Interdisciplinary History* 17 (1987): 587–612.

8. These are the characteristics David Mayhew uses to define traditional party organizations; when they hold overall control of a city or county at the local level, they are called machines. See Mayhew's *Placing Parties in American Politics* (Princeton: Princeton University Press, 1986), pp. 19–21.

9. For an interesting comparison of reform movements in three cities, see Kenneth Finegold, *Experts and Politicians: Reform Challenges to Machine Politics in New York, Cleveland, and Chicago* (Princeton, NJ: Princeton University Press, 1995).

10. For more on this point, see Timothy B. Krebs, "The Determinants of Candidates' Vote Share and the Advantages of Incumbency in City Council Elections," *American Journal of Political Science* 42 (1998): 921–35.

11. The colorful politics of Chicago has stimulated a rich literature, probably the richest on the subject of party politics in any American city. An early study of the Chicago machine is Harold Foote Gosnell's classic *Machine Politics: Chicago Style* (Chicago: University of Chicago Press, 1939). Good studies of the Daley years are Edward C. Banfield, *Political Influence* (New York: The Free Press, 1961); Milton Rakove, *Don't Make No Waves, Don't Back No Losers* (Bloomington, IN: Indiana University Press, 1975); and Thomas M. Guterbok, *Machine Politics in Transition: Party and Community in Chicago* (Chicago: University of Chicago Press, 1980). For perspectives on the post-Daley years, see Paul Kleppner, *Chicago Divided: The Making of a Black Mayor* (DeKalb, IL: Northern Illinois University Press, 1985); William J. Grimshaw, *Bitter Fruit: Black Politics and the Chicago Machine* (Chicago: University of Chicago Press, 1992); and Kenneth Finegold, *Experts and Politicians.*

12. Steven P. Erie makes a persuasive argument that the great urban machines were principally organizations of, by, and for the Irish, who proved unwilling to accommodate other ethnic groups. See his *Rainbow's End: Irish-Americans and the Dilemmas of Urban Machine Politics, 1840–1985* (Berkeley: University of California Press, 1988). Not all machine cities had major European immigrant populations, however; see John F. Bibby, "Party Organizations 1946–1996," in Byron E. Shafer, *Partisan Approaches to Postwar American Politics* (New York: Chatham House, 1998), pp.142–185.

13 For an insightful discussion of the conditions for machine politics here and abroad, see James C. Scott, "Corruption, Machine Politics, and Political Change," *American Political Science Review* 63 (1969): 1142–1158. Amy Bridges offers a useful perspective on the development of American machines in *A City in the Republic: Antebellum New York and the Origins of Machine Politics* (New York: Cambridge University Press, 1984).

14. See Anne Freedman, *Patronage: An American Tradition* (Chicago: Nelson-Hall, 1994), Chapter 5.

15. Kenneth R. Mladenka, "The Urban Bureaucracy and the Chicago Political Machine: Who Gets What and the Limits to Political Control," *American Political Science Review* 74 (1980): 991–998.

16. Michael Johnston, "Patrons and Clients, Jobs and Machines: A Case Study in the Uses of Patronage," *American Political Science Review* 73 (1979): 385–398.

17. See Raymond Wolfinger's "Why Political Machines Have Not Withered Away and Other Revisionist Thoughts," *Journal of Politics* 34 (1972): 365–398, and Theodore Lowi, "Machine Politics—Old and New," *Public Interest,* Fall 1967, pp. 83–92.

18. The results of this survey are reported in James L. Gibson, Cornelius P. Cotter, John F. Bibby, and Robert J. Huckshorn, "Whither the Local Parties?" *American Journal of Political Science* 29 (1985): 139–160; and Cornelius P. Cotter, James L. Gibson, John F. Bibby, and Robert J. Huckshorn, *Party Organization in American Politics* (New York: Praeger, 1984).

19. Cotter *et al.*, *Party Organization in American Politics,* pp. 49–53. The states with strong and weak local organizations, respectively, are virtually the same ones cited in Mayhew's survey of party strength in the late 1960s. See Mayhew, *Placing Parties in American Politics.*

20. See Cotter *et al.*, *Party Organization in American Politics*, p. 54, for the 1964–1980 comparison. The 1964 figures come from Paul Allen Beck, "Environment and Party," *American Political Science Review* 68 (1974): 1229–1244. The 1984 data are found in James L. Gibson, John P. Frendreis, and Laura L. Vertz, "Party Dynamics in the 1980s: Change in County Party Orga-

nizational Strength, 1980–1984," *American Journal of Political Science* 33 (1989): 67–90. Evidence on 1988 was gathered by John Kessel and William Jacoby and reported in Charles E. Smith, Jr., "Changes in Party Organizational Strength and Activity 1979–1988," Ohio State University, unpublished manuscript, 1989. On Detroit and Los Angeles, see Samuel J. Eldersveld, "The Party Activist in Detroit and Los Angeles: A Longitudinal View, 1956–1980," in William J. Crotty, ed., *Political Parties in Local Areas* (Knoxville: University of Tennessee Press, 1986), pp. 89–119.

21. This study of local party organizations was conducted by Paul Allen Beck, Russell J. Dalton, Audrey Haynes, and Robert Huckfeldt as a part of the American component in the Cross-National Election Project. For early reports on the results of this study, see Beck, Dalton, Haynes, and Huckfeldt, "Local Party Organizations and Presidential Politics," in Birol Yesilada, ed., *Comparative Political Parties and Party Elites* (Ann Arbor: University of Michigan Press, 1999), pp. 55–79; and "Presidential Campaigning at the Grass Roots," *Journal of Politics* (1997): 1264–1275.

22. See L. Sandy Maisel, "American Political Parties: Still Central to a Functioning Democracy?" in Jeffrey E. Cohen, Richard Fleisher, and Paul Kantor, eds., *American Political Parties: Decline or Resurgence?* (Washington, DC: CQ Press, 2001), pp. 112–114.

23. See also John Frendreis, Alan R. Gitelson, Gregory Flemming, and Anne Layzell, "Local Political Parties and the 1992 Campaign for the State Legislatures," paper presented at the 1993 Annual Meeting of the American Political Science Association.

24. John J. Coleman, "The Resurgence of Party Organization? A Dissent from the New Orthodoxy," in Daniel M. Shea and John C. Green, eds., *The State of the Parties: The Changing Role of Contemporary American Parties* (Lanham, MD: Rowman and Littlefield, 1994), pp. 282–298.

25. A. James Reichley cites Illinois, Michigan, Ohio, Pennsylvania, and Wisconsin as having had powerful state organizations near the turn of the twentieth century. See Reichley's *The Life of the Parties* (New York: Free Press, 1992), pp. 144–160 and 268–272.

26. See Malcolm E. Jewell and Sarah M. Morehouse, *Political Parties and Elections in American States*, 4th ed. (Washington, DC: CQ Press, 2001), p. 4.

27. See Jewell and Morehouse, p. 1. The argument that two-party competition is a vital basis for an organized party system and a vibrant democracy can be found in V. O. Key, Jr., *Southern Politics in State and Nation* (Knoxville: University of Tennessee Press, 1984; originally published in 1949). John H. Aldrich evaluates Key's argument in "Southern Parties in State and Nation," *Journal of Politics* 62 (2000): 643–670.

28. These findings come from a study of state party organizations conducted in 1979–1980 by John F. Bibby, Cornelius P. Cotter, James L. Gibson, and Robert J. Huckshorn. See Huckshorn and Bibby, "State Parties in an Era of Political Change," in Joel L. Fleishman, ed., *The Future of American Political Parties* (Englewood Cliffs, NJ: Prentice-Hall, 1982), pp. 70–100; and Gibson, Cotter, Bibby and Huckshorn, "Assessing Party Organizational Strength," *American Journal of Political Science* 27 (1983): 193–222.

29. Reported in Aldrich, "Southern Parties," p. 655.

30. On Wisconsin's Republican organization, see Jewell and Morehouse, *Political Parties and Elections in American States*, p. 52. On the 1999 survey of many state party organizations, see Aldrich, "Southern Parties," 655–659.

31. Jewell and Morehouse, *Political Parties and Elections*, p. 211.

32. See Anthony Gierzynski, *Legislative Party Campaign Committees in the American States* (Lexington, KY: University of Kentucky Press, 1992).

33. These estimates come from Huckshorn and Bibby, "State Parties in an Era of Political Change," Gibson, Cotter, Bibby, and Huckshorn, "Assessing Party Organizational Strength," and Aldrich, "Southern Parties," p. 656.

34. See Jewell and Morehouse, *Political Parties and Elections*, p. 49, and Aldrich, "Southern Parties," pp. 656–657.

35. Aldrich, "Southern Parties," Table 7, pp. 656–657.

36. This notion of the state and local parties fits Mildred Schwartz's conceptualization of the party as a network of interactions in *The Party Network: The Robust Organization of Illinois Republicans* (Madison: University of Wisconsin Press, 1990).

37. For an example, see John H. Kessel, "Ray Bliss and the Development of the Ohio Republican Party During the 1950s," in John C. Green, ed., *Politics, Professionalism, and Power* (Lanham, MD: University Press of America, 1994), pp. 48–61.

38. These were also identified as among the strongest state organizations in 1979–1980 by Cotter *et al., Party Organizations in American Politics,* pp. 28–29.

39. Aldrich argues in "Southern Parties," however, that although increasing party competition is part of the story of party organizational development in the South, the nature of southern society was more important.

40. Jewell and Morehouse, *Political Parties and Elections*, p. 36. Other parts of this complicated story are told by Aldrich, "Southern Parties"; Edward G. Carmines and James A. Stimson, *Issue Evolution* (Princeton: Princeton University Press, 1989); and Joseph A. Aistrup, *The Southern Strategy Revisited: Republican Top-Down Advancement in the South* (Lexington: University Press of Kentucky, 1996).

41. "Soft money" refers to campaign contributions given to the parties (national and state) ostensibly to support party-building activities such as registration and get-out-the-vote drives. For more on soft money, see Chapter 12.

42. On the role of the national parties in state-party building, see John F. Bibby, "State Party Organizations: Coping and Adapting," in L. Sandy Maisel, ed., *The Parties Respond* (Boulder, CO: Westview, 1994), pp. 21–44, especially pp. 36–43. Funding figures for 1999–2000 come from the Federal Election Commission Web page, at: *http://www.fec.gov/press/051501partyfund/tables/nat2state.html* (accessed Feb. 12, 2002).

43. Walter Dean Burnham, *Critical Elections and the Mainsprings of American Politics* (New York: Norton, 1970), p. 72.

44. See Alan Ware, *The Breakdown of the Democratic Party Organization 1940–80* (Oxford, England: Oxford University Press, 1985).

45. See Jewell and Morehouse, *Political Parties and Elections*, p. 214. On the growth in parties' use of up-to-date campaign skills, see Bibby, "State Party Organizations: Coping and Adapting."

46. See John J. Coleman, "Party Organizational Strength and Public Support for the Parties," *American Journal of Political Science* 40 (1996): 805–824.

CHAPTER 4

1. Cornelius P. Cotter and Bernard C. Hennessy, *Politics without Power: The National Party Committees* (New York: Atherton, 1964). For a comprehensive history of the national committees, see Ralph M. Goldman, *The National Party Chairmen and Committees* (Armonk, NY: M. E. Sharpe, 1990).

2. See E. E. Schattschneider, *Party Government* (New York: Rinehart, 1942), pp. 129, 132–133.

3. James W. Ceaser, "Political Parties—Declining, Stabilizing, or Resurging," in Anthony King, ed., *The New American Political System* (Washington, DC: American Enterprise Institute, 1990), pp. 87–137 at p. 115. See also Sidney M. Milkis, *The President and the Parties: The Transformation of the American Party System Since the New Deal* (New York: Oxford University Press, 1993).

4. See Jonathan D. Salant, "NRCC Boosts Spending on House Races," *Washington Post*, July 5, 2000, on the Web at *http://www.washingtonpost.com* (accessed July 13, 2000).

5. See Karen Foerstel and Derek Willis, "DCCC Rakes in New Money As Business Hedges Its Bets," *CQ Weekly*, July 15, 2000, pp. 1708–1712.

6. For a description of this earlier system, see Cotter and Hennessy, *Politics without Power*, pp. 180–182. For more on modern party finance, see Frank J. Sorauf and Scott A. Wilson, "Political Parties and Campaign Finance: Adaptation and Accommodation Toward a Changing Role," in L. Sandy Maisel, ed., *The Parties Respond: Changes in American Parties and Campaigns*, 2nd ed. (Boulder, CO: Westview Press, 1994), pp. 235–53; and David B. Magleby and Candice J. Nelson, *The Money Chase* (Washington, DC: Brookings, 1990).

7. It is fascinating to compare David Broder's *The Party's Over* (New York: Harper and Row, 1972), an early statement of the party decline thesis, with *The Party Goes On* by Xandra Kayden and Eddie Mahe, Jr. (New York: Basic Books, 1985) or *The Party's Just Begun*, 2nd ed. by Larry J. Sabato and Bruce Larson, (New York: Longman 2002).

8. Excellent accounts of the roles of Brock and especially Bliss in party building at the national level are contained in John C. Green, ed., *Politics, Professionalism, and Power: Modern Party Organization and the Legacy of Ray C. Bliss* (Lanham, MD: University Press of American, 1994). On the role of Charles Manatt and others in putting the Democratic National Party on the same path, see A. James Reichley, *The Life of the Parties* (New York: Free Press, 1992), pp. 353–381.

9. See Don Van Natta, Jr. and John M. Broder, "The Few, the Rich, the Rewarded Donate the Bulk of G.O.P. Gifts," *New York Times*, Aug. 2, 2000, p. A1; and Ceci Connolly, "In Final Funding Drive, Parties Eye 'Hard' Cash," *Washington Post*, Sept. 21, 2000, p. A16.

10. Quoted in Adam Clymer, "2 Parties on the Prowl to Claim the Senate in '02," *New York Times* on the Web, June 23, 2001 (accessed June 23, 2001).

11. John H. Kessel, "Organizational Development of National Party Committees: Some Generalizations and Supporting Evidence," *Vox Pop: Newsletter of Political Organizations and Parties* 7, no. 3, p. 1.

12. F. Christopher Arterton calls them "service vendor" parties, and Paul Herrnson refers to them as "intermediary" parties. See Arterton's "Political Money and Party Strength," in Joel Fleishman, ed., *The Future of American Political Parties* (Englewood Cliffs, NJ: Prentice-Hall, 1982), pp. 101–139; and Paul S. Herrnson, *Party Campaigning in the 1980s* (Cambridge: Harvard University Press, 1988), Chapter 3, p. 47.

13. On Democratic Party reform, see Austin Ranney, *Curing the Mischiefs of Faction: Party Reform in America* (Berkeley: University of California Press, 1975); William J. Crotty, *Decisions for the Democrats: Reforming the Party Structure* (Baltimore, MD: Johns Hopkins University Press, 1978); and Byron E. Shafer, *The Quiet Revolution: The Struggle for the Democratic Party and the Shaping of Post-Reform Politics* (New York: Russell Sage Foundation, 1983).

14. A reform committee, the Rule 29 Committee, was mandated by the 1972 Republican National Convention, but its recommendations for RNC review of state party "positive action" programs were rejected by the RNC and later by the 1976 convention. In general, the GOP has been far more protective of states' rights for the parties than have the Democrats. See John F. Bibby, "Party Renewal in the Republican National Party," in Gerald M. Pomper, ed., *Party Renewal in America* (New York: Praeger, 1981), pp. 102–115.

15. For comprehensive accounts of the increased strength of the national parties, see Reichley, *The Life of the Political Parties*, pp. 353–381; and Paul S. Herrnson, "The Revitalization of National Party Organizations," in Maisel, *The Parties Respond,* pp. 45–68.

16. For a good description of the traditional relationships of state party leadership and the national parties, see Robert J. Huckshorn, *Party Leadership in the States* (Amherst: University of Massachusetts Press, 1976), Chapter 8.

17. See Leon D. Epstein, *Political Parties in the American Mold* (Madison: University of Wisconsin Press, 1986), p. 237; and Xandra Kayden, "The Nationalization of the Party System,"

in Michael J. Malbin, ed., *Parties, Interest Groups, and the Campaign Finance Laws* (Washington, DC: American Enterprise Institute, 1980), pp. 257–282.

18. Party-presidential relations during the Reagan years are discussed in A. James Reichley, "The Rise of National Parties," in John E. Chubb and Paul E. Peterson, eds., *The New Direction in American Politics* (Washington, DC: Brookings Institution, 1985), pp. 175–200. On Gilmore, see R.H. Melton and Dan Balz, "Gilmore Resigns RNC Post, May Run Again in Va.," *Washington Post*, Dec. 1, 2001, p. A1.

19. The national committees may also exert considerable influence over the management of a campaign, particularly for nonincumbents, who are most in need of their assistance, through their power to withhold services and funds. See Herrnson, *Party Campaigning in the 1980s*, p. 59.

20. Herrnson, *Party Campaigning in the 1980s,* pp. 41–42.

21. This observation is made by Reichley, *The Life of the Party,* pp. 377–381. See also John J. Coleman, "The Resurgence of Party Organization? A Dissent from the New Orthodoxy," in Daniel M. Shea and John C. Green, eds., *The State of the Parties* (Lanham, MD: Rowman and Littlefield, 1994), pp. 311–328.

22. See, for example, Epstein, *Political Parties in the American Mold,* p. 200.

23. This point is made by Ceaser in "Political Parties—Declining, Stabilizing, or Resurging?" p. 120.

CHAPTER 5

1. A 1992 national survey of county party organizations conducted by Paul Allen Beck, Russell J. Dalton, Audrey Haynes, and Robert Huckfeldt found that only 24 percent of the county organizations had paid staff and fewer than 4 percent had paid chairs. This is higher than in 1980, when a national survey put these figures at 10 percent and 2 percent respectively, but it still shows how reliant the local parties are on volunteers. See Cornelius P. Cotter, James L. Gibson, John F. Bibby, and Robert J. Huckshorn, *Party Organizations in American Politics* (New York: Praeger, 1984), pp. 42–43, for a report on the 1980 study.

2. See Peter B. Clark and James Q. Wilson, "Incentive Systems: A Theory of Organizations," *Administrative Science Quarterly* 6 (1961): 129–166, for the original development of this theory; and James Q. Wilson, *The Amateur Democrat* (Chicago: University of Chicago Press, 1960) and *Political Organizations* (New York: Basic Books, 1973), Chapter 6, for the application to political organizations.

3. For a lively account of the use of patronage and preferments, see Martin and Susan Tolchin, *To the Victor* (New York: Random House, 1971).

4. See A. James Reichley, *The Life of the Parties* (New York: Free Press, 1992), pp. 55–56, 67–68, 88–92, and 202–220; Martin Shefter, *Political Parties and the State* (Princeton, NJ: Princeton University Press, 1994); and Anne Freedman, *Patronage: An American Tradition* (Chicago: Nelson-Hall, 1994).

5. These figures are cited in Stephen Skowronek's study of the reform of the federal bureaucracy. See his *Building a New American State* (New York: Cambridge University Press, 1982), p. 69.

6. All are listed in a publication unofficially known as the "Plum Book" (its official title is *U.S. Government Policy and Supporting Positions*), compiled alternately by the House Committee on Government Reform and Oversight and the Senate Committee on Governmental Affairs.

7. The 1976 case is *Elrod v. Burns,* 427 U.S. 347; the 1980 case is *Branti v. Finkel,* 445 U.S. 507; and the 1990 case is *Rutan v. Republican Party of Illinois,* 111 L. Ed. 2d 52.

8. On the problems of using patronage, see Frank J. Sorauf, "State Patronage in a Rural County," *American Political Science Review* 50 (1956): 1046–1056; W. Robert Gump, "The Functions

of Patronage in American Party Politics: An Empirical Reappraisal," *Midwest Journal of Political Science* 15 (1971): 87–107; and Michael Johnston, "Patrons and Clients, Jobs and Machines: A Case Study of the Uses of Patronage," *American Political Science Review* 73 (1979): 385–398.

9. The case for patronage—in particular, that it helps in achieving democratic control of the bureaucracy—has been stated over the years in *The Washington Monthly* and in the dissenting opinions to the Supreme Court's *Elrod, Branti,* and *Rutan* decisions. The case against patronage is well put in Freedman, *Patronage: An American Tradition,* Chapter 5.

10. For the 1979–1980 results, see Cotter, *et al., Party Organizations in American Politics,* p. 42; the figures on state chairs are for 1962–1972 and come from Robert J. Huckshorn, *Party Leadership in the States* (Amherst: University of Massachusetts Press, 1976), p. 37.

11. This point is made by Reichley in *The Life of the Parties,* p. 313.

12. See William Crotty, ed., *Political Parties in Local Areas* (Knoxville: University of Tennessee Press, 1986). The importance of solidary incentives is illustrated well in George V. Higgins's novel, *Victories* (New York: Holt, 1991).

13. John Fischer, "Please Don't Bite the Politicians," *Harper's* (Nov. 1960), p. 16.

14. A 1988 study of county leaders of the Bush campaign organization found that 32 percent of them had switched to the GOP from the Democratic Party, typically to align their ideological convictions with their party; see John A. Clark, John M. Bruce, John H. Kessel, and William Jacoby, "I'd Rather Switch than Fight: Lifelong Democrats and Converts to Republicanism among Campaign Activists," *American Journal of Political Science* 35 (1991): 577–597. Studies of conversions among Democratic and Republican state party convention delegates in 1980 and 1984 corroborate the strong ideological bases of party-switching. See Mary Grisez Kweit, "Ideological Congruence of Party Switchers and Nonswitchers: The Case of Party Activists," *American Journal of Political Science* 30 (1986): 184–196; and Dorothy Davidson Nesbit, "Changing Partisanship among Southern Party Activists," *Journal of Politics* 50 (1988): 322–334.

15. Samuel Eldersveld, *Political Parties: A Behavioral Analysis* (Chicago: Rand McNally, 1964), p. 278 and Chapter 11.

16. See Barbara C. Burrell, "Local Political Party Committees, Task Performance and Organizational Vitality," *Western Political Quarterly* 39 (1986): 48–66; John C. Green, John S. Jackson, and Nancy L. Clayton, "Issue Networks and Party Elites in 1996," in John C. Green and Daniel M. Shea, eds., *The State of the Parties,* 3rd ed. (Lanham, MD: Rowman and Littlefield, 1999); and John H. Aldrich, *Why Parties?* (Chicago: University of Chicago Press, 1995), pp. 171–173 and 186–187.

17. The fact that Eldersveld finds little change between 1956 and 1980 in the incentives for party activity in Detroit and Los Angeles, though, should rein in sweeping generalizations about motivational change. It is possible that what may distinguish modern from traditional party workers is the direction of their ideology, not its intensity. See Samuel J. Eldersveld, "The Party Activist in Detroit and Los Angeles: A Longitudinal View, 1956–1980," in Crotty, *Political Parties in Local Areas,* Chapter 4.

18. Among others, see M. Margaret Conway and Frank B. Feigert, "Motivation, Incentive Systems, and the Political Party Organization," *American Political Science Review* 62 (1968): 1159–1173.

19. See Robert D. Putnam, *Bowling Alone: The Collapse and Revival of American Community* (New York: Simon & Schuster, 2000).

20. Henry E. Brady, Kay Lehman Schlozman, and Sidney Verba, "Prospecting for Participants: Rational Expectations and the Recruitment of Political Activists," *American Political Science Review* 93 (1999): 153–168. See also James A. McCann, Ronald B. Rapoport, and Walter J. Stone, "Heeding the Call: An Assessment of Mobilization into H. Ross Perot's 1992 Presidential Campaign," *American Journal of Political Science* 43 (1999): 1–28.

21. See Paul Allen Beck and M. Kent Jennings, "Political Periods and Political Participation," *American Political Science Review* 73 (1979): 737–750, and their "Updating Political Periods and Political Participation," *American Political Science Review* 78 (1984): 198–201. See also Steven E. Finkel and Gregory Trevor, "Reassessing Ideological Bias in Campaign Participation," *Political Behavior* 8 (1986): 374–390.

22. For similar theories of recruitment, see Lewis Bowman and G.R. Boynton, "Recruitment Patterns among Local Party Officials," *American Political Science Review* 60 (1966): 667–676; and C. Richard Hofstetter, "Organizational Activists: The Bases of Participation in Amateur and Professional Groups," *American Politics Quarterly* 1 (1973): 244–276.

23. Eldersveld, *Political Parties,* pp. 142–143.

24. Cotter *et al.*, *Party Organizations in American Politics*, p. 42.

25. On the prominence of lawyers in American politics, see Heinz Eulau and John D. Sprague, *Lawyers in Politics* (Indianapolis: Bobbs-Merrill, 1964).

26. The relatively high status of party activists is documented in Sidney Verba and Norman H. Nie, *Participation in America* (New York: Harper Row, 1972), Chapter 8, for campaign activists; in Crotty, *Political Parties in Local Areas,* pp. 45, 72, 94–95, and 162–163, and Cotter, *et al.*, *Party Organizations in American Politics,* p. 42, for local leaders; in Ronald B. Rapoport, Alan I. Abramowitz, and John McGlennon, *The Life of the Parties* (Lexington: The University of Kentucky Press, 1986), Chapter 3, for state convention delegates; and in Warren E. Miller and M. Kent Jennings, *Parties in Transition* (New York: Russell Sage Foundation, 1986), pp. 67–85, for national convention delegates—findings that are confirmed by news organizations' surveys of contemporary convention delegates and county party officials.

27. See Michael Margolis and Raymond E. Owen, "From Organization to Personalism: A Note on the Transmogrification of the Local Political Party," *Polity* 18 (1985): 313–328.

28. See Martin Plissner and Warren J. Mitofsky, "The Making of the Delegates, 1968–1988," *Public Opinion* 11 (Sept./Oct. 1988): 45–47, on characteristics of delegates to the national nominating conventions through 1988; data from a survey of convention delegates in 2000 (see Chapter 10) show that the Democrats remained highly atypical of the rank and file of their party and more like Republicans in both income and education. See also Malcolm E. Jewell and Sarah M. Morehouse, *Political Parties and Elections in American States*, 4th Ed. (Washington, DC: CQ Press, 2001), p. 86.

29. This distinction between amateurs and professionals is developed in Clark and Wilson, "Incentive Systems"; Wilson, *The Amateur Democrat;* and John W. Soule and James W. Clarke, "Amateurs and Professionals: A Study of Delegates to the 1968 Democratic National Convention," *American Political Science Review* 64 (1970): 888–898.

30. Walter J. Stone and Alan I. Abramowitz, "Winning May Not Be Everything But It's More Than We Thought: Presidential Party Activists in 1980," *American Political Science Review* 77 (1983): 945–956.

31. Michael A. Maggiotto and Ronald E. Weber, "The Impact of Organizational Incentives on County Party Chairpersons," *American Politics Quarterly* 14 (1986): 201–218.

32. The 1992 national survey of county party organizations was conducted by Paul Allen Beck, Russell J. Dalton, Audrey Haynes, and Robert Huckfeldt. These data are from the study's codebook.

33. On the effects of party effort, see Gerald H. Kramer, "The Effects of Precinct-Level Canvassing on Voter Behavior," *Public Opinion Quarterly* 34 (1970–1971): 560–572; William J. Crotty, "Party Effort and Its Impact on the Vote," *American Political Science Review* 65 (1971): 439–450; John P. Frendreis, James L. Gibson, and Laura L. Vertz, "The Electoral Relevance of Local Party Organizations," *American Political Science Review* 84 (1990): 225–235; and Robert Huckfeldt and John Sprague, "Political Parties and Electoral Mobilization," *American Political Science Review* 86 (1992): 70–86.

34. See Daniel Elazar, *American Federalism: A View from the States* (New York: Crowell, 1972), Chapter 4, for the distribution of individualistic, moralistic, and traditionalistic political cultures throughout the nation.

35. This has not always been the case. In the 1960s and 1970s, some researchers found no relationship between competition and party strength; see Cotter, *et al.*, *Party Organizations in American Politics*, pp. 83–95. But in more recent years, party competitiveness has gone hand in hand with increasing organizational strength. See John H. Aldrich, "Southern Parties in State and Nation," *Journal of Politics* 62 (2000): 643–670; and Jewell and Morehouse, *Political Parties and Elections in American States*, pp. 92–99.

36. The original statement is in V. O. Key, Jr., *American State Politics* (New York: Knopf, 1956), Chapter 6.

37. The most notable fictionalized accounts of real-life "bosses" are to be found in Edwin O'Connor, *The Last Hurrah* (Boston: Little, Brown, 1956); and Robert Penn Warren, *All the King's Men* (New York: Harcourt, Brace, 1946).

38. Wilson, *The Amateur Democrat*, Chapter 5. These reform orientations are sometimes rooted as much in the deprivations of being out of power as in principled opposition to the concentration of power in a political machine. For some evidence of this in a Chicago reform club, see David L. Protess and Alan R. Gitelson, "Political Stability, Reform Clubs, and the Amateur Democrat," in William Crotty, ed., *The Party Symbol* (San Francisco: Freeman, 1980), pp. 87–100.

39. This theory is elaborated in Anthony Downs, *An Economic Theory of Democracy* (New York: Harper & Row, 1957).

40. Key, *American State Politics*; and Walter Dean Burnham, *Critical Elections and the Mainsprings of American Politics* (New York: Norton, 1970), p. 75.

41. The classic discussion of the idea of stratarchy can be found in Eldersveld, *Political Parties,* pp. 99–100.

PART 3

1. The concept of party identification and the most familiar measures of it were introduced in Angus Campbell, Philip E. Converse, Warren E. Miller, and Donald E. Stokes, *The American Voter* (New York: Wiley, 1960), Chapter 6.

2. For a discussion of some alternatives in identifying party loyalists, see Everett C. Ladd and Charles D. Hadley, "Party Definition and Party Differentiation," *Public Opinion Quarterly* 37 (1973): 21–34; and Steven E. Finkel and Howard A. Scarrow, "Party Identification and Party Enrollment: The Difference and the Consequence," *Journal of Politics* 47 (1985): 620–642.

CHAPTER 6

1. Researchers find that in newer democracies including Russia and the Ukraine, majorities of citizens have already begun to develop party identifications, even in the face of overwhelmingly negative attitudes toward political parties more generally, presumably because they find parties necessary. See Arthur H. Miller and Thomas F. Klobucar, "The Development of Party Identification in Post-Soviet Societies," *American Journal of Political Science* 44 (2000): 667–685; and Ted Brader and Joshua A. Tucker, "The Emergence of Mass Partisanship in Russia, 1993–1996," *American Journal of Political Science* 45 (2001): 69–83.

2. See John R. Petrocik, "An Analysis of the Intransitivities in the Index of Party Identification," *Political Methodology* 1 (1974): 31–47; Ralph W. Bastedo and Milton Lodge, "The Meaning of Party Labels," *Political Behavior* 2 (1980): 287–308; and Herbert F. Weisberg, "A Multidimensional Conceptualization of Party Identification," *Political Behavior* 2 (1980): 33–60.

3. Paul Allen Beck and M. Kent Jennings, "Family Traditions, Political Periods, and the Development of Partisan Orientations," *Journal of Politics* 53 (1991): 742–763. See also Fred I. Greenstein, *Children and Politics* (New Haven: Yale University Press, 1965); and Robert D. Hess and Judith V. Torney, *The Development of Political Attitudes in Children* (Chicago: Aldine, 1967), especially pp. 80–81.

4. On the partisan homogeneity of social networks, see Robert Huckfeldt and John Sprague, *Citizens, Politics, and Social Communication* (New York: Cambridge University Press, 1995), especially Chapter 7; and Robert Huckfeldt and Paul Allen Beck, "Contexts, Intermediaries, and Political Behavior," in Lawrence C. Dodd and Calvin Jillson, eds., *The Dynamics of American Politics: Approaches and Limitations* (Boulder, CO: Westview Press, 1994), pp. 252–276.

5. Arthur S. Goldberg, "Social Determinism and Rationality As Bases of Party Identification," *American Political Science Review* 63 (1969): 5–25.

6. Morris P. Fiorina, *Retrospective Voting in American National Elections* (New Haven: Yale University Press, 1981), p. 102. On the role issues may play in disrupting the transmission of partisanship from parents to children, see Robert C. Luskin, John P. McIver, and Edward G. Carmines, "Issues and the Transmission of Partisanship," *American Journal of Political Science* 33 (1989): 440–458; and Richard G. Niemi and M. Kent Jennings, "Issues and Inheritance in the Formation of Party Identification," *American Journal of Political Science* 35 (1991): 970–988.

7. See William Clagett, "Partisan Acquisition vs. Partisan Intensity: Life-Cycle, Generational, and Period Effects," *American Journal of Political Science* 25 (1981): 193–214. On the strengthening of partisanship with age, see Paul R. Abramson, "Developing Party Identification: A Further Examination of Life-Cycle, Generational, and Period Effects," *American Journal of Political Science* 23 (1979): 78–96; and W. Phillips Shively, "The Development of Party Identification among Adults," *American Political Science Review* 73 (1979): 1039–1054.

8. For the view that realignments are due to the mobilization of young and other new voters, see Kristi Andersen, *The Creation of a Democratic Majority 1928–1936* (Chicago: University of Chicago Press, 1979); and James E. Campbell, "Sources of the New Deal Realignment," *Western Political Quarterly* 38 (1985): 357–376. For an alternative view emphasizing the conversion of older voters to new partisan loyalties, see Robert S. Erikson and Kent L. Tedin, "The 1928–1936 Partisan Realignment: The Case for the Conversion Hypothesis," *American Political Science Review* 75 (1981): 951–963. The role of young people in partisan change is discussed in Warren E. Miller, "Generational Changes and Party Identification," *Political Behavior* 14 (1992): 333–352.

9. See Paul Allen Beck, "The Dealignment Era in America," in Russell J. Dalton, Scott C. Flanagan, and Paul Allen Beck, eds., *Electoral Change in Advanced Industrial Democracies* (Princeton, NJ: Princeton University Press, 1984), pp. 244–246.

10. CNN/Time All Politics, *http://www.cnn.com/ELECTION/CQ.profiles/LA03HOUSETAUZIN. html* (accessed July 11, 2001).

11. "Declaration of Independence," statement of Senator James Jeffords, May 24, 2001, *http://www.senate.gov/~jeffords/524statement.html* (accessed Apr. 10, 2002).

12. Philip E. Converse and Gregory B. Markus, "Plus ça change . . . : The New CPS Election Study Panel," *American Political Science Review* 73 (1979): 32–49. Even greater stability in partisanship, as expected because of the shorter time period, was found from January to November during the 1980 presidential campaign. See Donald Philip Green and Bradley Palmquist, "Of Artifacts and Partisan Instability," *American Journal of Political Science* 34 (1990): 872–902, and "How Stable is Party Identification?" *Political Behavior* 16 (1994): 437–66.

13. On the political impact of the psychological processes of projection and persuasion, see Bernard R. Berelson, Paul F. Lazarsfeld, and William N. McPhee, *Voting* (Chicago: University of Chicago Press, 1954), pp. 215–233; and Benjamin I. Page and Richard A. Brody, "Pol-

icy Voting and the Electoral Process: The Vietnam War Issue," *American Political Science Review* 66 (1972): 979–995.

14. Donald E. Stokes, "Some Dynamic Elements of Contests for the Presidency," *American Political Science Review* 60 (1966): 23.

15. On the importance of party as a shortcut in candidate evaluations, see Pamela J. Conover and Stanley Feldman, "Candidate Perceptions in an Ambiguous World: Campaigns, Cues, and Inference Processes," *American Journal of Political Science* 33 (1989): 912–940; and Wendy M. Rahn, "The Role of Partisan Stereotypes in Information Processing about Political Candidates," *American Journal of Political Science* 37 (1993): 472–496.

16. Roberta A. Sigel, "Effects of Partisanship on the Perception of Political Candidates," *Public Opinion Quarterly* 28 (1964): 483–496.

17. See Fiorina, *Retrospective Voting*; Benjamin I. Page and Calvin C. Jones, "Reciprocal Effects of Policy Preferences, Party Loyalties and the Vote," *American Political Science Review* 73 (1979): 1071–1089; and Michael B. MacKuen, Robert S. Erikson, and James A. Stimson, "Macropartisanship," *American Political Science Review* 83 (1989): 1125–1142.

18. Beginning with the first large-scale presidential-year survey in 1952, researchers at the University of Michigan have continued to conduct surveys of the American electorate in presidential and midterm election years, most recently under National Science Foundation auspices as the American National Election Studies (ANES). The seminal work on party identification, based on the 1952 and 1956 surveys, is reported in Angus Campbell, Philip E. Converse, Warren E. Miller, and Donald E. Stokes, *The American Voter* (New York: Wiley, 1960).

19. Martin P. Wattenberg, *The Decline of American Political Parties, 1952–1994* (Cambridge: Harvard University Press, 1996), p. ix.

20. Richard G. Niemi and Herbert F. Weisberg, eds., *Controversies in American Voting Behavior* (San Francisco: W. H. Freeman, 1976), p. 414.

21. For an excellent summary, see Russell J. Dalton, Ian McAllister, and Martin P. Wattenberg, "The Decline in Party Identification and the Consequences of Dealignment: The Evidence from 20 OECD Nations," paper presented at the 2000 American Political Science Association Annual Meeting, Washington, DC.

22. See James H. Kuklinski, Paul J. Quirk, Jennifer Jerit, and Robert F. Rich, "The Political Environment and Citizen Competence," *American Journal of Political Science* 45 (2001): 410–424; and Paul M. Sniderman, "Taking Sides: A Fixed Choice Theory of Political Reasoning," in Arthur Lupia, Mathew D. McCubbins, and Samuel L. Popkin, eds., *Elements of Reason* (New York: Cambridge University Press, 2000).

23. Larry M. Bartels, "Partisanship and Voting Behavior, 1952–1996," *American Journal of Political Science* 44 (2000): 35–50, and David G. Lawrence, "On the Resurgence of Party Identification in the 1990s," in Jeffrey E. Cohen, Richard Fleisher, and Paul Kantor, eds., *American Political Parties: Decline or Resurgence?* (Washington, DC: CQ Press, 2001), pp. 30–54.

24. Bartels, "Partisanship and Voting Behavior."

25. A study of voting for five statewide offices in Ohio found that party ID was the best predictor of straight-ticket voting. See Paul Allen Beck, Lawrence Baum, Aage R. Clausen, and Charles E. Smith, Jr., "Patterns and Sources of Ticket Splitting in Subpresidential Voting," *American Political Science Review* 86 (1992): 916–928.

26. One possible explanation for the greater partisanship of independent "leaners" is that the when independents are asked to indicate whether they consider themselves Democrats or Republicans, they tend to name the party for which they plan to vote that year. On the other hand, these independent "leaners" may actually be partisans who don't choose to admit it. For persuasive evidence on this point, see Bruce E. Keith, David B. Magleby, Candice J. Nelson, Elizabeth Orr, Mark Westlye, and Raymond E. Wolfinger, *The Myth of the Independent Voter* (Berkeley, CA: University of California Press, 1992).

27. See Barry C. Burden and David C. Kimball, "A New Approach to the Study of Ticket-Splitting," *American Political Science Review* 92 (1998): 533–544. Malcolm E. Jewell and Sarah M. Morehouse point out, however (in *Political Parties and Elections in American States* [Washington, DC: CQ Press, 2001], p. 277), that this increased level of split-ticket voting—measured by the proportion of congressional districts carried by one party for president and the other for the House seat—has now existed for the past 40 years.

28. Beck, Baum, Clausen, and Smith, "Patterns and Sources of Ticket Splitting," and Burden and Kimball, "A New Approach."

29. Philip E. Converse, "The Concept of a Normal Vote," in Angus Campbell, Philip E. Converse, Warren E. Miller, and Donald E. Stokes, eds., *Elections and the Political Order* (New York: Wiley, 1966), pp. 9–39.

30. For example, see Norman H. Nie, Sidney Verba, and John R. Petrocik, *The Changing American Voter* (Cambridge, MA: Harvard University Press, 1976), Chapters 10, 16, and 20 (especially pp. 373–378); and Frederick Hartwig, William R. Jenkins, and Earl M. Temchin, "Variability in Electoral Behavior: The 1960, 1968, and 1976 Elections," *American Journal of Political Science* 24 (1980): 353–358.

31. For the classic view, see Campbell, Converse, Miller, and Stokes, *The American Voter*; and Arthur S. Goldberg, "Discerning a Causal Pattern among Data on Voting Behavior," *American Political Science Review* 60 (1966): 913–922.

32. Page and Jones, "Reciprocal Effects of Policy Preferences, Party Loyalties and the Vote."

33. Gregory B. Markus and Philip E. Converse, "A Dynamic Simultaneous Equation Model of Electoral Choice," *American Political Science Review* 73 (1979): 1055–1070.

34. Overall turnout in 2000 among citizens of voting age was estimated at 51 percent. Reported turnout levels in the 2000 ANES survey are considerably higher for reasons specified in Chapter 8.

35. These differences are documented in Paul R. Abramson, John H. Aldrich, and David W. Rohde, *Change and Continuity in the 1996 Elections* (Washington, DC: CQ Press, 1998), Chapter 8, especially Table 8.5 and Figure 8.1.

36. Sidney Verba and Norman H. Nie analyze the unusually high political participation of Republican identifiers in *Participation in America* (Chicago: University of Chicago Press, 1987), Chapter 12. The changing relationships between ideology and campaign activity are examined in Paul Allen Beck and M. Kent Jennings, "Political Periods and Political Participation," *American Political Science Review* 73 (1979): 737–750.

37. For comparisons of the support for Wallace, Anderson, and Perot among white party identifiers, see Paul R. Abramson, John H. Aldrich, and David W. Rohde, *Change and Continuity in the 1992 Elections* (Washington, DC: CQ Press, 1995), Table 8.9, p. 245. For more on the Perot candidacy, see Herb Asher, "The Perot Campaign," in Herbert F. Weisberg, ed., *Democracy's Feast* (Chatham, NJ: Chatham House, 1995), Chapter 6.

38. Although it is easy to picture independents as potential supporters of a new party or independent candidate, in reality independents are so varied in their feelings about issues and politics that they are unlikely to merge into the supporting coalition for any single candidate. On the range of attitudes among independent voters, see Keith, Magleby, Nelson, Orr, Westlye, and Wolfinger, *The Myth of the Independent Voter.*

39. See Petrocik, "An Analysis of Intransitivities in the Index of Party Identification," pp. 31–47; and Keith, Magleby, Nelson, Orr, Westlye, and Wolfinger, *The Myth of the Independent Voter.*

40. See Keith, Magleby, Nelson, Orr, Westlye, and Wolfinger, *The Myth of the Independent Voter.* In fact, the myth of the independent as the highly informed, sophisticated voter was laid to rest even in research on the 1952 and 1956 elections by Campbell, Converse, Miller, and Stokes in *The American Voter.*

41. V. O. Key, Jr. (with the assistance of Milton C. Cummings), *The Responsible Electorate* (Cambridge, MA: Harvard University Press, 1966).

42. See Martin P. Wattenberg, *The Rise of Candidate-Centered Politics: Presidential Elections of the 1980s* (Cambridge, MA: Harvard University Press, 1991); and Morris P. Fiorina, "The Electorate at the Polls in the 1990s," in L. Sandy Maisel, ed., *The Parties Respond* (Boulder, CO: Westview, 1994), pp. 123–142.

43. V. O. Key, Jr. and Frank Munger characterized the century-long stable voting patterns of Indiana counties as "standing decisions" to support a particular party. See their "Social Determinism and Electoral Decision," in Eugene Burdick and Arthur J. Brodbeck, eds., *American Voting Behavior* (Glencoe, IL: Free Press, 1959), pp. 281–299.

44. Quoted in Marjorie Randon Hershey, "The Campaign and the Media," in Gerald M. Pomper, ed., *The Election of 2000* (New York: Chatham House, 2001), p. 55.

CHAPTER 7

1. See, for example, Robert Huckfeldt and Carol Weitzel Kohfeld, *Race and the Decline of Class in American Politics* (Urbana: University of Illinois Press, 1989).

2. For a comprehensive treatment of these various cleavages, see Seymour Martin Lipset and Stein Rokkan, "Cleavage Structures, Party Systems, and Voting Alignments," in Seymour Martin Lipset and Stein Rokkan, eds., *Party Systems and Voter Alignments* (New York: Free Press, 1967), pp. 1–67.

3. This definition of realignment, focusing on changes in the party coalitions or parties in the electorate, is the one most commonly used. See V. O. Key, Jr., "A Theory of Critical Elections," *Journal of Politics* 17 (1955): 3–18; Walter Dean Burnham, *Critical Elections and the Mainsprings of American Politics* (New York: Norton, 1970); and James L. Sundquist, *Dynamics of the Party System* (Washington, DC: Brookings Institution, 1973). For one alternative view of what constitutes a realignment, see Jerome M. Clubb, William H. Flanigan, and Nancy H. Zingale, *Partisan Realignment: Voters, Parties, and Government in American History* (Beverly Hills, CA: Sage, 1980). Another view is that realignment is elite rather than mass-based—the product of the changing party loyalties of American industrial and business interests. See Thomas Ferguson, *Golden Rule: The Investment Theory of Party Competition and the Logic of Money-driven Political Systems* (Chicago: University of Chicago Press, 1995).

4. Aggregate election returns have some drawbacks as indicators of a realignment. They are affected by short-term forces (for example, candidate appeal, issues, and levels of turnout) as well as long-term party loyalties. They reflect geographical divisions more clearly than SES-based divisions. It is helpful, then, to examine aggregate election results together with other data in defining realignment periods.

5. Not all scholars are persuaded that the idea of realignment captures the essence of American electoral change, especially in recent years. For differing views, see Edward G. Carmines and James A. Stimson, *Issue Evolution* (Princeton, NJ: Princeton University Press, 1989); Byron E. Shafer, ed., *The End of Realignment? Interpreting American Electoral Eras* (Madison: University of Wisconsin Press, 1991), and Allan J. Lichtman, "The End of Realignment Theory—Toward a New Research Program for American Political History," *Historical Methods* 15 (1982): 170–188. Peter F. Nardulli, in "The Concept of a Critical Realignment, Electoral Behavior, and Political Change," *American Political Science Review* 89 (1995): 10–22, argues that the important changes are not national in scope, but subnational.

6. For similar classifications of American political history from the realignment perspective, see Burnham, *Critical Elections;* William Nisbet Chambers and Walter Dean Burnham, eds., *The American Party Systems* (New York: Oxford University Press, 1967); Clubb, Flanigan, and Zingale, *Partisan Realignment;* Charles Sellers, "The Equilibrium Cycle in Two-Party Politics," *Public Opinion Quarterly* 30 (1965): 16–38; and Sundquist, *Dynamics of the Party System.*

7. Comprehensive treatments of the different party systems may be found in Paul Goodman, "The First Party System," in Chambers and Burnham, *The American Party Systems*, pp. 59–89; Richard McCormick, *The Second American Party System: Party Formation in the Jacksonian Era* (Chapel Hill: University of North Carolina Press, 1966); and, for the party systems since the 1850s, Sundquist, *Dynamics of the Party System*. Especially valuable accounts of the development of the first three party systems may be found in John H. Aldrich, *Why Parties? The Origin and Transformation of Party Politics in America* (Chicago: University of Chicago Press, 1995), Chapters 3–5.

8. Realignments typically unfold over a period of time, so it is a bit misleading to mark them as beginning in a specific year. For convenience, however, we will locate the beginning of each party system in the year in which the new majority party coalition first took office.

9. Because of the tremendous diversity of groups and interests in the United States, American party coalitions are never simple or predictable on issue grounds. In this second party system, the Democrats were composed not only of Western populists but also of the New York political organization run by Martin Van Buren, who was attracted to the party because of interstate rivalries and the promise of political patronage. Such odd alliances have been a hallmark of the American two-party system.

10. The third party system actually contained two distinct periods. From the end of the Civil War in 1865 through 1876, Democratic voting strength in the South was held in check by the occupying Union army and various Reconstruction policies and laws. So to reflect the true party balance during this time, it is helpful to differentiate between 1861–1876 and the more representative 1877–1896 period.

11. The classic statement of the role of social class in the elections of the Western democracies appears in Seymour Martin Lipset, *Political Man* (New York: Doubleday, 1960), especially Chapter 7. Also see Richard Hamilton, *Class and Politics in the United States* (New York: Wiley, 1972).

12. See Madison's *Federalist* 10: "The most common and durable source of factions has been the various and unequal distribution of property."

13. See Jeffrey M. Stonecash, *Class and Party in American Politics* (Boulder, CO: Westview Press, 2000), pp. 13 and 139, and Chapter 4.

14. See Robert A. Alford, *Party and Society* (Chicago: Rand McNally, 1963); and Russell J. Dalton, Scott C. Flanagan, and Paul Allen Beck, eds., *Electoral Change in Advanced Industrial Democracies* (Princeton, NJ: Princeton University Press, 1984). For an appraisal of class voting in the Western world during the past century from the perspective of working-class support for a left-wing party, see Adam Przeworski and John Sprague, *Paper Stones: A History of Electoral Socialism* (Chicago: University of Chicago Press, 1986).

15. For more on this phenomenon, often called "split-level partisanship," see Charles D. Hadley, "Dual Partisan Identification in the South," *Journal of Politics* 47 (1985): 254–268; and Richard G. Niemi, Stephen Wright, and Lynda W. Powell, "Multiple Party Identifiers and the Measurement of Party Identification," *Journal of Politics* 49 (1987): 1093–1104.

16. Richard Rose and Derek Urwin have shown that religion rivals social class as a basis for partisan loyalties in the Western democracies. See their "Social Cohesion, Political Parties and Strains in Regimes," *Comparative Political Studies* 2 (1967): 7–67.

17. Steven M. Cohen and Charles S. Liebman, "American Jewish Liberalism," *Public Opinion Quarterly* 61(1997): 405–430.

18. See Ted G. Jelen, *The Political Mobilization of Religious Belief* (Westport, CT: Praeger, 1991); David C. Leege and Lyman A. Kellstedt, eds., *Rediscovering the Religious Factor in American Politics* (Armonk, NY: M. E. Sharpe, 1993); and Kenneth D. Wald, *Religion and Politics in the United States* (New York: St. Martin's Press, 1987).

19. On black political behavior, see Patricia Gurin, Shirley Hatchett, and James S. Jackson, *Hope and Independence: Blacks' Response to Electoral and Party Politics* (New York: Russell Sage

Foundation, 1989); and Katherine Tate, *From Protest to Politics* (Cambridge, MA: Harvard University Press, 1994). On possible explanations for racial differences in issue attitudes, see Donald R. Kinder and Nicholas Winter, "Exploring the Racial Divide: Blacks, Whites, and Opinion on National Policy," *American Journal of Political Science* 45 (2001): 439–453.

20. Quoted in Eric Schmitt, "Hispanic Voter Is Vivid in Parties' Crystal Ball," *New York Times*, Apr. 9, 2001, p. A14.

21. Karen M. Kaufman and John R. Petrocik, "The Changing Politics of American Men: Understanding the Sources of the Gender Gap," *American Journal of Political Science* 43 (1999): 864–887. See also Paul R. Abramson, John H. Aldrich, and David W. Rohde, *Change and Continuity in the 1996 Elections* (Washington, DC: CQ Press, 1998), pp. 236–237.

22. See David O. Sears, Richard R. Lau, Tom R. Tyler, and Harris M. Allen, Jr., "Self-Interest vs. Symbolic Politics in Policy Attitudes and Presidential Voting," *American Political Science Review* 74 (1980): 670–684. For an alternative view, see Paul Sniderman and Thomas Piazza, *The Scar of Race* (Cambridge, MA: Harvard University Press, 1993).

23. For a discussion of the crosscutting nature of some of these issues, see Warren E. Miller and Teresa E. Levitin, *Leadership and Change: The New Politics and the American Electorate* (Cambridge, MA: Winthrop, 1976).

24. Quoted in Thomas B. Edsall, "Political Party Is No Longer Dictated By Class Status," *Washington Post*, Nov. 9, 2000, p. A37.

25. See Geoffrey C. Layman, *The Great Divide: Religious and Cultural Conflict in American Party Politics* (New York: Columbia University Press, 2001).

26. Data from 1960 are more appropriate for this comparison than data from 1964, when the Democratic landslide victory produced a temporary surge in Democratic partisanship across most of the social groups. The 1960 figures are taken from Warren E. Miller and Santa A. Traugott, *American National Election Studies Sourcebook, 1952–1986* (Cambridge, MA: Harvard University Press, 1989).

27. For demonstrations of how attitudinal and behavioral deviance from one's partisanship can undermine it, see Fiorina, *Retrospective Voting in American National Elections;* and Benjamin I. Page and Calvin C. Jones, "Reciprocal Effects of Policy Preferences, Party Loyalties and the Vote," *American Political Science Review* 73 (1979): 1071–1089.

28. On social group changes in the party coalitions, see John R. Petrocik, *Party Coalitions* (Chicago: University of Chicago Press, 1981); and Harold W. Stanley and Richard G. Niemi, "The Demise of the New Deal Coalition: Partisanship and Group Support, 1952–1992," in Weisberg, *Democracy's Feast,* pp. 220–240. Stanley and Niemi, in particular, feel that the New Deal coalition has eroded so much that it is no longer visible.

29. Chapter 6 describes the seminal work on party identification done by the University of Michigan's American National Election Studies beginning in 1952. See Angus Campbell, Philip E. Converse, Warren E. Miller, and Donald E. Stokes, *The American Voter* (New York: Wiley, 1960).

30. Kevin P. Phillips, *The Emerging Republican Majority* (New Rochelle, NY: Arlington House, 1969).

31. The Watergate affair began in 1972 when burglars with ties to the Nixon reelection campaign were arrested for breaking into the offices of the Democratic National Committee. Two years later, President Nixon resigned from office; he was about to be impeached by the House of Representatives for trying to cover up his role in the affair.

32. On the party loyalties of young people during this time, see Helmut Norpoth, "Under Way and Here to Stay: Party Realignment in the 1980s?" *Public Opinion Quarterly* 51 (1987): 376–391; and Warren E. Miller, "Party Identification, Realignment, and Party Voting: Back to Basics," *American Political Science Review* 85 (1991): 557–570.

33. For more on the case for realignment, see Aldrich, *Why Parties:* Chapter 8; Earl Black and Merle Black, *Politics and Society in the South* (Cambridge, MA: Harvard University Press,

1987); and Michael F. Meffert, Helmut Norpoth, and Anirudh V. S. Ruhil, "Realignment and Macropartisanship," *American Political Science Review* 95 (2001): 953–962.

34. "Voting for the US House of Representatives 1984–1996: The Group Story," *The Public Perspective* (1997): 24. The data come from Voter News Service.

35. For more on the case for dealignment, see Paul Allen Beck, "Incomplete Realignment: The Reagan Legacy for Parties and Elections," in Charles O. Jones, ed., *The Reagan Legacy* (Chatham, NJ: Chatham House, 1988); Walter Dean Burnham, *The Current Crisis in American Politics* (New York: Oxford University Press, 1982); and Martin P. Wattenberg, *The Decline of American Political Parties 1952–96* (Cambridge: Harvard University Press, 1998).

36. See Paul Allen Beck, "The Electoral Cycle and Patterns of American Politics," *British Journal of Political Science* 9 (1979): 129–156. Martin P. Wattenberg argues that Americans' attitudes toward the parties are characterized more by neutrality than by rejection; see Wattenberg, *The Decline of American Political Parties*. But Stephen C. Craig finds evidence that Americans are in fact becoming more negative toward the parties; see Craig's "The Decline of Partisanship in the United States: A Reexamination of the Neutrality Hypothesis," *Political Behavior* 7 (1985): 57–78.

37. Burnham, *Critical Elections,* Chapters 4 and 5.

38. For a persuasive discussion of this dynamic evolutionary process of party change, see Carmines and Stimson, *Issue Evolution.*

CHAPTER 8

1. This was the result certified by Florida Secretary of State Katherine Harris on November 26, 2000, the deadline set by the Florida Supreme Court for counting and recounting the state's votes. It is one of a number of vote totals that came out of the recount process, and that continued to emerge from recounts sponsored by news and other organizations.

2. Because of the difficulties in estimating American turnout, most "official" turnout figures *underestimate* it. The percentages in Figure 8.1 follow the method of Walter Dean Burnham, which carefully corrects for this underestimation, so they are a little higher than the widely reported turnout figures. Their denominator is an effort to estimate the *eligible* population; it is the adult population of voting age minus the number of aliens living in the United States (noncitizens have been prevented from voting by all states since 1924). The numerator of the turnout fraction is the number of voters who cast a vote for president or for the office with the highest vote in midterm elections. Estimated turnout would be slightly higher if we had a reliable way to include in the numerator blank or spoiled ballots, write-in votes for the office with the highest vote total, and voters who did not vote for that office, and to exclude from the denominator citizens who are not eligible to vote in various states because they are inmates of prisons or mental hospitals. For a discussion of the problems in estimating turnout, see Walter Dean Burnham, "The Turnout Problem," in A. James Reichley, ed., *Elections American Style* (Washington, DC: Brookings Institution, 1987), pp. 97–133, especially footnote 1.

3. See Benjamin Barber, *Strong Democracy: Participatory Politics for a New Age* (Berkeley: University of California Press, 1994). One empirical study discounts the threat that nonvoters can pose for democracy; see Stephen Earl Bennett and David Resnick, "The Implications of Nonvoting for Democracy in the United States," *American Journal of Political Science* 34 (1990): 771–802.

4. Walter Dean Burnham, "The Changing Shape of the American Political Universe," *American Political Science Review* 59 (1965): 7–28.

5. G. Bingham Powell, Jr., "American Voter Turnout in Comparative Perspective," *American Political Science Review* 80 (1986): 17–44. Also see Burnham, "The Turnout Problem,"

p. 107. Only Switzerland has had lower national turnout levels than the United States, but national elections are less important than local contests there.

6. "Suffrage" means the right to vote. On the early development of the American electorate, see Chilton Williamson, *American Suffrage: From Property to Democracy* (Princeton, NJ: Princeton University Press, 1960).

7. The Supreme Court case overturning the poll tax was *Harper v. Virginia State Board of Elections,* 383 U.S. 633 (1966).

8. *Oregon v. Mitchell,* 400 U.S. 112 (1970).

9. See, for example, Raymond E. Wolfinger and Jonathan Hoffman, "Registering and Voting with Motor Voter," *PS: Political Science and Politics* 34 (2001): 85–92.

10. The legal and constitutional issues involved in defining the electorate through the 1960s are covered in Richard Claude, *The Supreme Court and the Electoral Process* (Baltimore, MD: The John Hopkins University Press, 1970).

11. Paul Kleppner, *Continuity and Change in Electoral Politics, 1893–1928* (Westport, CT: Greenwood Press, 1987), pp. 165–166.

12. The landmark Supreme Court cases dealing with residency requirements are *Dunn v. Blumstein,* 405 U.S. 330 (1972); and *Burns v. Fortson,* 410 U.S. 686 (1973).

13. U.S. Census Bureau, Table A., Annual Moving Rates By Type of Move: 1990–2000, found at *http://www.census.gov/prod/2001pubs/p20–538.pdf* (accessed July 30, 2001).

14. Peverill Squire, Raymond E. Wolfinger, and David P. Glass, "Residential Mobility and Voter Turnout," *American Political Science Review* 81 (1987): 45–65.

15. See Philip E. Converse, "Change in the American Electorate," in Angus Campbell and Philip E. Converse, eds., *The Human Meaning of Social Change* (New York: Russell Sage Foundation, 1972), pp. 263–337; Walter Dean Burnham, "Theory and Voting Research: Some Reflections on Converse's 'Change in the American Electorate,'" *American Political Science Review* 68 (1974): 1002–1023; and Frances Fox Piven and Richard A. Cloward, *Why Americans Don't Vote* (New York: Pantheon Books, 1988).

16. A state-by-state list of registration requirements is reported each year in *The Book of the States* (Lexington, KY: The Council of State Governments). See Robert L. Dudley and Alan R. Gitelson, *American Elections: The Rules Matter* (New York: Longman, 2002), pp. 7–15.

17. Ruy A. Teixiera estimates that turnout would be 7.8 percent higher without the most burdensome requirements; see his *The Disappearing American Voter* (Washington, DC: Brookings Institution, 1992), Chapter 4. See also Raymond E. Wolfinger and Steven J. Rosenstone, *Who Votes?* (New Haven, CT: Yale University Press, 1980), pp. 61–78; and Glenn E. Mitchell and Christopher Wlezien, "The Impact of Legal Constraints on Voter Registration, Turnout, and the Composition of the American Electorate," *Political Behavior* 17 (1995): 179–202.

18. The story of black disenfranchisement in the South is well told by V. O. Key, Jr., in *Southern Politics in State and Nation* (New York: Knopf, 1949). See also J. Morgan Kousser, *The Shaping of Southern Politics* (New Haven: Yale University Press, 1974); and Donald R. Matthews and James W. Prothro, *Negroes and the New Southern Politics* (New York: Harcourt, Brace and World, 1966).

19. The white primary was finally overturned by the Supreme Court in *Smith v. Allwright,* 321 U.S. 649 (1944). Not only is this a landmark case in the area of black voting rights, but it is also significant in establishing that political parties, though they have the right to handle their own affairs (under the "freedom of association" clause of the First Amendment), are not free to violate constitutional bans on discrimination.

20. Chandler Davidson and Bernard Grofman, eds., *Quiet Revolution in the South* (Princeton, NJ: Princeton University Press, 1994). On black turnout in the South generally, see Harold W. Stanley, *Voter Mobilization and the Politics of Race* (New York: Praeger, 1987).

21. See Matthews and Prothro, *Negroes and the New Southern Politics;* H. Douglas Price, *The Negro and Southern Politics* (New York: New York University Press, 1957); David Campbell

and Joe R. Feagin, "Black Politics in the South: A Descriptive Analysis," *Journal of Politics* 37 (1975): 129–162; and Lester M. Salamon and Stephen Van Evera, "Fear, Apathy, and Participation," *American Political Science Review* 67 (1973): 1288–1306.

22. Thomas B. Edsall, "Parties Play Voting Rights Role Reversal," *Washington Post,* Feb. 25, 2001, p. A1.

23. The principle that race can't be the predominant factor was established in a Georgia case in *Miller v. Johnson* (1995), and the ruling that race can nevertheless be an element in redistricting, involving a North Carolina district, is found in *Easley v. Cromartie* (2001). On the impact of majority-minority districts, see David T. Canon, *Race, Redistricting, and Representation: The Unintended Consequences of Black Majority Districts* (Chicago: University of Chicago Press, 1999), and David Lublin, "Racial Redistricting and African-American Representation," *American Political Science Review* 93 (1999): 183–186.

24. The Civil Rights Commission's study is discussed in Robert E. Pierre and Peter Slevin, "Fla. Vote Rife With Disparities, Study Says," *Washington Post*, June 5, 2001, p. A1. When levels of income, education, and the design of the ballot were taken into account by another study, predominantly black precincts in Florida had more than three times as many rejected ballots as majority white precincts. See Ford Fessenden, "Ballots Cast by Blacks and Older Voters Were Tossed in Far Greater Numbers," *New York Times*, Nov. 12, 2001, p. A17.

25. Associated Press, "Crimes Keep Many Blacks From Voting," *http://www.nytimes.com/aponline/politics/AP-Felons-Voting.html* (accessed Sept. 21, 2000).

26. See, for example, Robert A. Jackson, "The Mobilization of U.S. State Electorates in the 1988 and 1990 Elections," *Journal of Politics* 59 (1997): 520–537.

27. See David B. Magleby, *Direct Legislation: Voting on Ballot Propositions in the United States* (Baltimore, MD: Johns Hopkins University Press, 1984); and Thomas E. Cronin, *Direct Democracy* (Cambridge, MA: Harvard University Press, 1989).

28. For systematic explanation of variations in turnout across the election calendar and for different combinations of contests, see Richard W. Boyd, "Election Calendars and Voter Turnout," *American Politics Quarterly* 14 (1986): 89–104, and "The Effects of Primaries and Statewide Races on Voter Turnout," *Journal of Politics* 51 (1989): 730–739.

29. Jae-On Kim, John R. Petrocik, and Stephen N. Enokson, "Voter Turnout among the American States: Systemic and Individual Components," *American Political Science Review* 69 (1975): 107–123.

30. Steven J. Rosenstone and John Mark Hansen, *Mobilization, Participation, and Democracy in America* (New York: Macmillan, 1993), pp. 177–188; Gregory A. Caldeira and Samuel C. Patterson, "Contextual Influences on Participation in U.S. State Legislative Contests," *Legislative Studies Quarterly* 3 (1982): 359–381; Samuel C. Patterson and Gregory A. Caldeira, "Getting Out the Vote: Participation in Gubernatorial Elections," *American Political Science Review* 77 (1983): 675–689; and Gregory A. Caldeira, Samuel C. Patterson, and Gregory A. Markko, "The Mobilization of Voters in Congressional Elections," *Journal of Politics* 47 (1985): 490–509.

31. Walter Dean Burnham, "The Changing Shape of the American Political Universe" and "Theory and Voting Research: Some Reflections on Converse's 'Change in the American Electorate.'" Also see Paul Kleppner, *Who Voted?* (New York: Praeger, 1982).

32. Converse, "Change in the American Electorate"; and Jerrold G. Rusk, "The American Electoral Universe: Speculation and Evidence," *American Political Science Review* 68 (1974): 1028–1049. See also Walter Dean Burnham *The Current Crisis in American Politics* (New York: Oxford University Press, 1982), pp. 121–165.

33. Sidney Verba, Norman H. Nie, and Jae-On Kim, *Participation and Political Equality* (Cambridge, UK: Cambridge University Press, 1978); and Powell, "American Voter Turnout in Comparative Perspective."

34. Of course, this is why turnout may change as the result of a realignment. For an insightful discussion of how the nature of political conflict affects participation, see E. E. Schattschneider, *The Semi-Sovereign People* (New York: Holt, Rinehart, and Winston, 1960).

35. See Alan S. Gerber and Donald M. Green, "The Effects of Canvassing, Telephone Calls, and Direct Mail on Voter Turnout: A Field Experiment," *American Political Science Review* 94 (2000): 653–663; and Rosenstone and Hansen, *Mobilization, Participation, and Democracy in America.*

36. On the mobilization of black voters, see Rosenstone and Hansen, *Mobilization, Participation, and Democracy in America,* pp. 188–196 and 219–224; Lawrence Bobo and Franklin D. Gilliam, Jr., "Race, Sociopolitical Participation, and Black Empowerment," *American Political Science Review* 84 (1990): 377–394; Frederick C. Harris, "Something Within: Religion as a Mobilizer of African-American Political Activism," *Journal of Politics* 56 (1994): 42–68; Katherine Tate, "Black Political Participation in the 1984 and 1988 Presidential Elections," *American Political Science Review* 85 (1991): 1159–1176; and Richard Timpone, "Mass Mobilization or Governmental Intervention: The Growth of Black Registration in the South," *Journal of Politics* 57 (1995): 425–442.

37. Juliet Eilperin, "Battle for the House: Labor on the Front Lines," *Washington Post,* Aug. 29, 2000, p. A1.

38. See John H. Aldrich, "Rational Choice and Turnout," *American Journal of Political Science* 37 (1993): 246–278.

39. Sidney Verba and Norman H. Nie, *Participation in America* (New York: Harper and Row, 1972), pp. 125–137. See also Teixiera, *The Disappearing American Voter,* Chapter 3.

40. Wolfinger and Rosenstone, *Who Votes?* pp. 35–36.

41. Verba, Nie, and Kim, *Participation and Political Equality.*

42. Verba and Nie, *Participation in America,* pp. 145–147. Of course, chronological age indexes the varying political experiences of different generations in addition to people's place in the life cycle, but scholars have found little evidence that generation has an independent impact on turnout. On this point, see Rosenstone and Hansen, *Mobilization, Participation, and Democracy in America,* pp. 136–141.

43. Bobo and Gilliam, "Race, Sociopolitical Participation, and Black Empowerment."

44. Verba and Nie, *Participation in America,* Chapter 11, examines the effects of organizational membership. On the impact of getting married or losing a spouse, see Laura Stoker and M. Kent Jennings, "Life-Cycle Transitions and Political Participation: The Case of Marriage," *American Political Science Review* 89 (1995): 421–436; and Rosenstone and Wolfinger, *Who Votes?* See also Nancy Burns, Kay Lehman Schlozman, and Sidney Verba, "The Public Consequences of Private Inequality: Family Life and Citizen Participation," *American Political Science Review* 91 (1997): 373–389.

45. See Rosenstone and Hansen, *Mobilization, Participation, and Democracy in America,* pp. 141–156; and Verba and Nie, *Participation in America,* pp. 133–136.

46. See Mark N. Franklin and Wolfgang P. Hirczy de Mino, "Separated Powers, Divided Government, and Turnout in U.S. Presidential Elections," *American Journal of Political Science* 42 (1998): 316–326.

47. See Census data at *http://www.census.gov/population/socdemo/voting/proj00/tab02.txt.*

48. See Richard A. Brody, "The Puzzle of Participation in America," in Anthony King, ed., *The New American Political System* (Washington, DC: American Enterprise Institute, 1978), pp. 287–324.

49. Paul R. Abramson and John H. Aldrich, "The Decline of Electoral Participation in America," *American Political Science Review* 76 (1982): 502–521; and Paul R. Abramson, John H. Aldrich, and David W. Rohde, *Change and Continuity in the 1992 Election* (Washington, DC: CQ Press, 1995), pp. 114–120.

50. Studies by Teixeira, *The Disappearing American Voter,* Chapter 1, and Rosenstone and Hansen, *Mobilization, Participation, and Democracy in America,* Chapter 7, all discuss the role of feelings of efficacy but argue that the biggest added effects are due to declines in social connectedness (both studies) and electoral mobilization (Rosenstone and Hansen). For a more general account of the deterioration of social connectedness in the United States, see Robert D. Putnam, *Bowling Alone: The Collapse and Revival of American Community* (New York: Simon & Schuster, 2000).

51. See Stephen M. Nichols and Paul Allen Beck, "Reversing the Decline: Voter Turnout in the 1992 Election," in Herbert F. Weisberg, ed., *Democracy's Feast* (Chatham, NJ: Chatham House, 1995), Chapter 2.

52. Edward G. Carmines and James A. Stimson, *Issue Evolution* (Princeton, NJ: Princeton University Press, 1989). See also Claudine Gay, "The Effect of Black Congressional Representation on Political Participation," *American Political Science Review* 95 (2001): 589–602.

53. See Verba and Nie, *Participation in America,* Part III; and Bennett and Resnick, "The Implications of Nonvoting for Democracy in the United States."

54. Wolfinger and Rosenstone, *Who Votes?* Chapter 6; and Teixeira, *The Disappearing American Voter,* Chapter 3.

55. See James DeNardo, "Turnout and the Vote: The Joke's on the Democrats," *American Political Science Review* 74 (1980): 406–420; the exchange between DeNardo and Harvey J. Tucker and Arnold Vedlitz, "Does Heavy Turnout Help Democrats in Presidential Elections?" *American Political Science Review* 80 (1986): 1291–1304; and Jack H. Nagel and John E. McNulty, "Partisan Effects of Voter Turnout in Senatorial and Gubernatorial Elections," *American Political Science Review* 90 (1996): 780–793.

56. *Congressional Quarterly Weekly Report,* Jan. 13, 1996, pp. 97–100.

PART 4

1. See Murray Edelman, *Constructing the Political Spectacle* (Chicago: University of Chicago Press, 1988).

CHAPTER 9

1. On the spread of the primary to other democracies, see R. K. Carty and Donald E. Blake, "The Adoption of Membership Votes for Choosing Party Leaders: The Experience of Canadian Parties," *Party Politics* 5 (1999): 211–224; and Russell J. Dalton, Ian McAllister, and Martin P. Wattenberg, "The Decline in Party Identification and the Consequences of Dealignment: The Evidence from 20 OECD Nations," paper delivered at the 2000 American Political Science Association Annual Meeting, Washington.

2. For the story of the convention system and the early years of the direct primary, see Charles E. Merriam and Louise Overacker, *Primary Elections* (Chicago: University of Chicago Press, 1928). On the early spread of the direct primary, see V. O. Key, Jr., *American State Politics: An Introduction* (New York: Knopf, 1956), pp. 87–97.

3. Robert M. La Follette, *La Follette's Autobiography* (Madison, WI: R. M. La Follette, 1913), pp. 197–198.

4. Some states allow third parties to nominate their candidates through conventions.

5. *The Book of the States 2000–01* (Lexington, KY: The Council of State Governments, 2000), pp. 164–165. For more on nomination methods, see Malcolm E. Jewell and Sarah M. Morehouse, *Political Parties and Elections in American States,* 4th ed. (Washington, DC: CQ Press, 2001), Chapter 4.

6. For an account of variations within these broad categories, see Craig L. Carr and Gary L. Scott, "The Logic of State Primary Classification Schemes," *American Politics Quarterly* 12

(1984): 465–476; and Steven E. Finkel and Howard A. Scarrow, "Party Identification and Party Enrollment: The Difference and the Consequence," *Journal of Politics* 47 (1985): 620–652.

7. The numbers of states in each category are drawn from Jewell and Morehouse, *Political Parties and Elections in American States*, pp. 103–106. Note that experts disagree on these definitions and on the dividing line between an "open" and a "closed" primary.

8. A 1986 Supreme Court decision (*Tashjian v. Republican Party of Connecticut,* 106 S. Ct. 783 and 1257) upheld the Connecticut party's attempts to establish an open primary by overriding the state's closed-primary law. This decision affirms the authority of the party, rather than the state, to control its own nomination process and may clear the way for other state parties to regulate participation in their primaries as they wish. Most state parties would prefer a closed primary to an open one, however.

9. See David Adamany, "Crossover Voting and the Democratic Party's Reform Rules," *American Political Science Review* 70 (1976): 536–541. Also see Ronald D. Hedlund and Meredith W. Watts, "The Wisconsin Open Primary: 1968 to 1984," *American Politics Quarterly* 14 (1986): 55–74; and Gary D. Wekkin, "The Conceptualization and Measurement of Crossover Voting," *Western Political Quarterly* 41 (1988): 105–114.

10. Alan Abramowitz, John McGlennon, and Ronald Rapoport, "A Note on Strategic Voting in a Primary Election," *Journal of Politics* 43 (1981): 899–904; and Gary D. Wekkin, "Why Crossover Voters Are Not 'Mischievous' Voters," *American Politics Quarterly* 19 (1991): 229–247.

11. Access to the major-party ballot has become easier as a result of court action in recent decades. In key early cases, the U.S. Supreme Court invalidated a Texas law requiring candidates to pay both a flat fee for candidacy and a share of the cost of the election (up to $9,000) and overturned the California scale of filing fees because they did not provide an alternative means of access to the ballot (such as a petition) for candidates unable to pay. The cases were *Bullock v. Carter,* 405 U.S. 134 (1972); and *Lubin v. Panish,* 415 U.S. 709 (1974). The monthly newsletter *Ballot Access News* reports current efforts to change the rules governing ballot access, especially for third parties and independents. It can be found on the Internet at *http://www.ballot-access.org.*

12. That blacks are disadvantaged by runoff primaries is challenged by Charles S. Bullock, III, and A. Brock Smith in "Black Success in Local Runoff Elections," *Journal of Politics* 52 (1990): 1205–1220. For more on the discriminatory impact of runoff primaries, see Harold Stanley, "The Runoff: The Case for Retention," *PS: Political Science and Politics* 18 (1985): 231–236; and Charles S. Bullock, III, and Loch K. Johnson, *Runoff Elections in the United States* (Knoxville: University of Tennessee Press, 1991).

13. See Jewell and Morehouse, *Political Parties and Elections in American States*, pp. 119–120.

14. Followers of Lyndon LaRouche, a fringe candidate, have cleverly taken advantage of these situations by filing as the only candidates for minority party nomination in one-party areas. If the major-party candidate then stumbled on the way to what seemed to be sure victory, this put LaRouche's candidates in position to win the office.

15. See Key, *American State Politics: An Introduction*, Chapter 6, p. 195.

16. About a third of all state legislative races have been uncontested in recent years. On the phenomenon of uncontested races, as well as candidate recruitment more generally, see L. Sandy Maisel, Linda L. Fowler, Ruth S. Jones, and Walter J. Stone, "Nomination Politics: The Roles of Institutional, Contextual, and Personal Variables," in L. Sandy Maisel, ed., *The Parties Respond* (Boulder, CO: Westview, 1994), pp. 148–152.

17. See John G. Geer and Mark E. Shere, "Party Competition and the Prisoner's Dilemma: An Argument for the Direct Primary," *Journal of Politics* 54 (1992): 741–761.

18. Theodore H. White, *The Making of the President 1960* (New York: Atheneum, 1961), p. 78.

19. See Emmett H. Buehll, Jr., "Divisive Primaries and Participation in Fall Presidential Campaigns," *American Politics Quarterly* 14 (1986): 376–390; Walter J. Stone, "The Carryover Effect in Presidential Elections," *American Political Science Review* 80 (1986): 271–280; and Martin P. Wattenberg, "The Republican Presidential Advantage in the Age of Party Disunity," in Gary W. Cox and Samuel Kernell, eds., *The Politics of Divided Government* (Boulder, CO: Westview, 1991), Chapter 3.

20. Several studies have found that divisive primaries depress general election support for most offices except for the House of Representatives. See Patrick J. Kenney, "Sorting Out the Effects of Primary Divisiveness in Congressional and Senatorial Elections," *Western Political Quarterly* 41 (1988): 765–777; Patrick J. Kenney and Tom W. Rice, "Presidential Prenomination Preferences and Candidate Evaluations," *American Political Science Review* 82 (1988): 1309–1319; and James I. Lengle, Diana Owen, and Molly W. Sonner, "Divisive Nominating Mechanisms and Democratic Party Electoral Prospects," *Journal of Politics* 57 (1995): 370–383. Lonna Rae Atkeson reports, however, that divisive primaries have only modest effects on general election results; see "Divisive Primaries and General Election Outcomes: Another Look at Presidential Campaigns," *American Journal of Political Science* 42 (1998): 256–271. Some differences in findings stem from differences in the way "divisive" is defined.

21. See Paige Schneider, "Factionalism in the Southern Republican Party: The Impact of the Christian Right," paper delivered at the 1997 Southern Political Science Association Annual Meeting, Norfolk, VA.

22. Jewell and Morehouse, *Political Parties and Elections in American States,* pp. 109–110.

23. See Maisel, Fowler, Jones, and Stone, "Nomination Politics," pp. 155–156.

24. On the factors that promote or suppress competition in the primaries, see Tom W. Rice, "Gubernatorial and Senatorial Primary Elections: Determinants of Competition," *American Politics Quarterly* 13 (1985): 427–446; Harvey L. Schantz, "Contested and Uncontested Primaries for the U.S. House," *Legislative Studies Quarterly* 4 (1980): 545–562; Jewell and Morehouse, *Political Parties and Elections in American States*, pp. 118–120, and Andrew D. McNitt, "The Effect of Preprimary Endorsement on Competition for Nominations: An Examination of Different Nominating Systems," *Journal of Politics* 42 (1980): 257–266.

25. Jewell and Morehouse, *Political Parties and Elections in American States*, p. 123.

26. Malcolm E. Jewell, "Northern State Gubernatorial Primary Elections: Explaining Voting Turnout," *American Politics Quarterly* 12 (1984): 101–116; and Patrick J. Kenney, "Explaining Turnout in Gubernatorial Primaries," *American Politics Quarterly* 11 (1983): 315–326.

27. The early studies are Austin Ranney and Leon D. Epstein, "The Two Electorates: Voters and Non-Voters in a Wisconsin Primary," *Journal of Politics* 28 (1966): 598–616; and Austin Ranney, "The Representativeness of Primary Electorates," *American Journal of Political Science* 12 (1968): 224–238. See also Patrick J. Kenney, "Explaining Primary Turnout: The Senatorial Case," *Legislative Studies Quarterly* 11 (1986): 65–74. On different results in presidential primaries, see John G. Geer, "Assessing the Representativeness of Electorates in Presidential Primaries," *American Journal of Political Science* 32 (1988): 929–945.

28. Jewell and Morehouse, *Political Parties and Elections in American States*, pp. 124–125.

29. Ruth Conniff, "Tammy Baldwin," *The Progressive, http://www.progressive.org/baldwin9901.htm* (accessed Aug. 15, 2001). See also David T. Canon and Paul S. Herrnson, "Professionalism, Progressivism, and People Power," in Michael A. Bailey, Ronald A. Faucheux, Paul S. Herrnson, and Clyde Wilcox, eds., *Campaigns & Elections: Contemporary Case Studies* (Washington, DC: CQ Press, 2000), pp. 83–92.

30. A study of gubernatorial nominations showed that more money was spent on campaigns and the spending was more related to the outcome in states where party organizations did not make pre-primary endorsements. Sarah M. Morehouse, "Money versus Party Effort: Nominating for Governor," *American Journal of Political Science* 34 (1990): 706–724.

CHAPTER 10

1. After the movement to nominate state officials in primaries had begun in 1902, it seemed only natural to involve voters in the selection of presidential candidates as well. But the national conventions remained in place, and even where presidential primaries were adopted, they only supplemented rather than displaced the traditional convention system. On the history of the nomination process, see John S. Jackson III and William J. Crotty, *The Politics of Presidential Selection,* 2nd ed. (New York: Longman, 2001), Chapters 3 and 4.

2. See Byron E. Shafer, *Quiet Revolution* (New York: Russell Sage Foundation, 1983); James W. Ceaser, *Presidential Selection* (Princeton, NJ: Princeton University Press, 1979); William J. Crotty, *Party Reform* (New York: Longman, 1983); Nelson W. Polsby, *The Consequences of Party Reform* (Oxford: Oxford University Press, 1983); and Austin Ranney, *Curing the Mischiefs of Faction: Party Reform in America* (Berkeley, CA: University of California Press, 1975).

3. Michael G. Hagen and William G. Mayer, "The Modern Politics of Presidential Selection: How Changing the Rules Really Did Change the Game," in William G. Mayer, ed., *In Pursuit of the White House 2000* (New York: Chatham House, 2000), pp. 1–55.

4. In a case involving the Wisconsin open primary, the Supreme Court upheld the power of the national party to refuse to seat delegates chosen under a state law that violated its rules. See *Democratic Party of the United States v. La Follette,* 450 U.S. 107 (1981).

5. On the shift to candidate-oriented delegate loyalties, see Byron E. Shafer, *Bifurcated Politics: Evolution and Reform in the National Party Convention* (Cambridge, MA: Harvard University Press, 1988), pp. 181–184.

6. For an account of the struggle between the Wisconsin Democrats and the national party over open primaries, see Gary D. Wekkin, *Democrats versus Democrats* (Columbia: University of Missouri Press, 1983).

7. On the Iowa caucuses, see Peverill Squire, ed., *The Iowa Caucuses and the Presidential Nominating Process* (Boulder, CO: Westview, 1989).

8. These strategic considerations are discussed in John H. Aldrich, *Before the Convention* (Chicago: University of Chicago Press, 1980); and Paul-Henri Gurian and Audrey A. Haynes, "Campaign Strategy in Presidential Primaries," *American Journal of Political Science* 37 (1993): 335–341.

9. Matthew Robert Kerbel, "The Media: Old Frames in a Time of Transition," in Michael Nelson, ed., *The Elections of 2000* (Washington, DC: CQ Press, 2001), p. 119, quoting the *Los Angeles Times.*

10. See Harold W. Stanley, "The Nominations: The Return of the Party Leaders," in Michael Nelson, ed., *The Elections of 2000* (Washington, DC: CQ Press, 2001), p. 28.

11. See William G. Mayer, "The Presidential Nominations," in Gerald M. Pomper, ed., *The Election of 2000* (New York: Chatham House, 2001), pp. 13–16.

12. Studies of the effect of divisive primaries on a presidential race are cited in endnotes 19 and 20 of Chapter 9.

13. Hagen and Mayer, "The Modern Politics of Presidential Selection," p. 40.

14. Differences between "superdelegates" and regular delegates are examined in Richard Herrera, "Are 'Superdelegates' Super?" *Political Behavior* 16 (1994): 79–92; and Priscilla L. Southwell, "The 1984 Democratic Nomination Process: The Significance of Unpledged Superdelegates," *American Politics Quarterly* 14 (1986): 75–88.

15. Turnout rates in nomination contests are very difficult to estimate. The turnout rate cannot be counted as a percentage of the voters registered with that party because many states do not have party registration. Should it be based on the potential general election electorate for that party? That number surely is affected by who the nominee is. Is it the total voting-age population? Party turnout from that base depends upon how much competition there is in each

party's primary or caucus. The best estimate of turnout under these circumstances, although hardly ideal, is a comparison of two different calculations—the one based on general election voters for that party, the other on the voting-age population.

16. See Patrick J. Kenney and Tom W. Rice, "Voter Turnout in Presidential Primaries: A Cross-Sectional Examination," *Political Behavior* 7 (1985): 101–112; Barbara Norrander and Gregg W. Smith, "Type of Contest, Candidate Strategy, and Turnout in Presidential Primaries," *American Politics Quarterly* 13 (1985): 28–50; and Barbara Norrander, "Selective Participation: Presidential Voters as a Subset of General Election Voters," *American Politics Quarterly* 14 (1986): 35–54.

17. Larry M. Bartels, *Presidential Primaries and the Dynamics of Public Choice* (Princeton, NJ: Princeton University Press, 1988), pp. 140–148; John G. Geer, "The Representativeness of Presidential Primary Electorates," *American Journal of Political Science* 32 (1988): 929–945; and Barbara Norrander, "Ideological Representativeness of Primary Voters," *American Journal of Political Science* 33 (1989): 570–587.

18. See Scott Keeter and Cliff Zukin, *Uninformed Choice* (New York: Praeger, 1983); John G. Geer, *Nominating Presidents: An Evaluation of Voters and Primaries* (New York: Greenwood Press, 1989); Barbara Norrander, "Correlates of Vote Choice in the 1980 Presidential Primaries," *Journal of Politics* 48 (1986): 156–166; and J. David Gopoian, "Issue Preferences and Candidate Choice in the 1980 Presidential Primaries," *American Journal of Political Science* 26 (1982): 523–546.

19. Samuel L. Popkin, *The Reasoning Voter* (Chicago: University of Chicago Press, 1991), especially Chapters 6–8.

20. Bartels, *Presidential Primaries and the Dynamics of Public Choice.*

21. For a persuasive analysis of strategic voting in primaries, in which voters temper their "sincere" preferences with calculations of their candidate's viability, see Paul R. Abramson, John H. Aldrich, Phil Paolino, and David W. Rohde, "'Sophisticated' Voting in the 1988 Presidential Primaries," *American Political Science Review* 86 (1992): 55–69.

22. A similar blend of preferences and strategic calculations has been found to influence the decisions of participants in the Iowa caucuses and convention. See Walter J. Stone, Ronald B. Rapoport, and Alan I. Abramowitz, "Candidate Support in Presidential Nomination Campaigns: The Case of Iowa in 1984," *Journal of Politics* 54 (1992): 1074–1097.

23. Hagen and Mayer, "The Modern Politics of Presidential Selection," pp. 17–21.

24. Credit for the idea of a national party convention goes to a long-forgotten minor party, the Anti-Masons, who brought together their supporters in a Baltimore meeting in 1831 to nominate a candidate for president.

25. The best account of the evolution of the national party conventions is Shafer, *Bifurcated Politics.* On pre-1960 conventions, see Paul T. David, Ralph M. Goldman, and Richard C. Bain, *The Politics of the National Party Conventions* (Washington, DC: Brookings Institution, 1960).

26. Party platforms first appeared in the 1840s, and all of them through 1976 are available in one volume: Donald B. Johnson, *National Party Platforms, 1840–1976* (Urbana: University of Illinois Press, 1978). For summaries of more recent platforms, see post-convention issues of *CQ Weekly.*

27. Gerald M. Pomper, *Elections in America* (New York: Dodd, Mead, 1968), p. 201. Pomper updates his conclusion that parties generally try to fulfill most of their platform pledges in his "Party Responsibility and the Future of American Democracy," in Jeffrey E. Cohen, Richard Fleisher, and Paul Kantor, eds., *American Political Parties: Decline or Resurgence?* (Washington, DC: CQ Press, 2001), pp. 170–172.

28. Candidates, especially the winning candidate, play a more important role in platform development now than ever before. See L. Sandy Maisel, "The Platform-Writing Process: Candidate-Centered Platforms in 1992," *Political Science Quarterly* 108 (1993–1994): 671–699.

29. In *Bifurcated Politics* (pp. 333–337) Shafer discusses the possibility, in a "deviant" year, of the nomination decision returning to the convention.

30. See Lee Sigelman and Paul J. Wahlbeck, "The 'Veepstakes': Strategic Choice in Presidential Running Mate Selection," *American Political Science Review* 91 (1997): 855–864 on the factors that help explain presidential nominees' choice of running mates.

31. See Howard L. Reiter, *Selecting the President* (Philadelphia: University of Pennsylvania Press, 1985), Chapter 4.

32. These figures come from the CBS News/*New York Times* delegate polls taken in June–August 2000. The data were provided by Kathleen Frankovic and Jinghua Zou of CBS News.

33. The classic account of this relationship, in which delegates to the 1956 conventions were compared to Democratic and Republican identifiers from a national survey, is found in Herbert McClosky, Paul Hoffman, and Rosemary O'Hara, "Issue Conflict and Consensus among Party Leaders and Followers," *American Political Science Review* 54 (1960): 406–427.

34. See Jeane Kirkpatrick, *The New Presidential Elite* (New York: Russell Sage Foundation and Twentieth Century Fund, 1976).

35. For comparisons of convention delegates with their respective party identifiers since 1972, see John S. Jackson III, Barbara L. Brown, and David Bositis, "Herbert McClosky and Friends Revisited: 1980 Democratic and Republican Party Elites Compared to the Mass Public," *American Politics Quarterly* 10 (1982): 158–180; Warren E. Miller and M. Kent Jennings, *Parties in Transition* (New York: Russell Sage Foundation, 1986), Chapters 7–9; Denise L. Baer and David A. Bositis, *Elite Cadres and Party Coalitions* (New York: Greenwood Press, 1988), Chapter 8; and Shafer, *Bifurcated Politics*, pp. 100–107.

36. See John W. Soule and Wilma E. McGrath, "A Comparative Study of Presidential Nomination Conventions: The Democrats 1968 and 1972," *American Journal of Political Science* 19 (1975): 501–517. The seminal study is John W. Soule and James W. Clarke, "Amateurs and Professionals: A Study of Delegates to the 1968 Democratic National Convention," *American Political Science Review* 64 (1970): 888–898.

37. Denis G. Sullivan, Jeffrey L. Pressman, Benjamin I. Page, and John J. Lyons, *The Politics of Representation: The Democratic Convention 1972* (New York: St. Martin's, 1974); Kirkpatrick, *The New Presidential Elite;* Thomas H. Roback, "Motivations for Activism among Republican National Convention Delegates," *Journal of Politics* 42 (1980): 181–201; and Denise Baer and David Bositis, *Elite Cadres and Party Coalitions*, Chapter 7.

38. Shafer, *Bifurcated Politics*, Chapter 8.

39. Don Hewitt, then a photo editor who had been asked by CBS to help with convention coverage, responded incredulously, "You mean people are going to sit at home and watch little pictures in a [7-inch] box? ... I don't believe it!" Hewitt, who later became executive producer of the network's "60 Minutes," evidently became a believer. See Roger Simon, "Philadelphia Story," *U.S. News & World Report,* Aug. 7, 2000, pp. 30–41.

40. See the figures cited in Shafer, *Bifurcated Politics,* Chapter 8, especially p. 280. Harold W. Stanley reports, as well, that the network evening news programs devoted only half as much airtime to the presidential nominations during 1999 as they had in 1995. See his "The Nominations: The Return of the Party Leaders," in Michael Nelson, ed., *The Elections of 2000* (Washington, DC: CQ Press, 2001), p. 35.

41. Iowa and New Hampshire, whose citizens comprise only 2.9 percent of the U.S. population, receive a disproportionate share of the media coverage in the nomination process. On the New Hampshire primary, see Emmett H. Buell, Jr., "The Changing Face of the New Hampshire Primary," in William G. Mayer, ed., *In Pursuit of the White House 2000* (New York: Chatham House, 2000), pp. 87–144.

42. A good statement of the case against the 1970s party reforms may be found in Polsby, *Consequences of Party Reform*. The case for party reforms is best articulated in William J. Crotty, *Decision for the Democrats* (Baltimore: The Johns Hopkins University Press, 1978).

43. See Michael W. Traugott and Margaret Petrella, "Public Evaluations of the Presidential Nomination Process," *Political Behavior* 11 (1989): 335–352.

CHAPTER 11

1. Peter Fenn, "Interactive Engagement," *Campaigns & Elections* (2000): 25.

2. Jerrold G. Rusk, "The Effect of the Australian Ballot Reform on Split Ticket Voting: 1876–1908," *American Political Science Review* 64 (1970): 1220–1238.

3. The best account of the effects of ballot form on voting remains Angus Campbell, Philip E. Converse, Warren E. Miller, and Donald E. Stokes, *The American Voter* (New York: Wiley, 1960), Chapter 11.

4. Joanne M. Miller and Jon A. Krosnick, "The Impact of Candidate Name Order on Election Outcomes," *Public Opinion Quarterly* 62 (1998): 291–330.

5. States have typically protected the parties by making write-ins inconvenient, however. In addition, most states have so-called sore-loser laws that prevent candidates who have lost their party's primary from qualifying for the general election ballot as an independent.

6. Walter Dean Burnham, "The Changing Shape of the American Political Universe," *American Political Science Review* 59 (1965): 7–28; and Rusk, "The Effect of the Australian Ballot Reform on Split Ticket Voting," p. 1237. Roll-off can be decreased by the use of electronic voting machines that use a blinking light to alert voters when they haven't completed the whole ballot; see Stephen M. Nichols and Gregory A. Strizek, "Electronic Voting Machines and Ballot Roll-off," *American Politics Quarterly* 23 (1995): 300–318.

7. Guy Gugliotta, "Study Finds Millions of Votes Lost," *Washington Post,* July 17, 2001, p. A1. For more detail, see the Washington Post, *Deadlock: The Inside Story of America's Closest Election* (Washington, DC: Public Affairs, 2001).

8. On these problems, see Robin Toner, "For Those Behind the Scenes, It's Old News That Elections Are Not an Exact Science," *New York Times,* Nov. 17, 2000, p. A23; David S. Broder, "In Need Of an Overhaul," *Washington Post,* Dec. 6, 2000, p. A35; Dan Keating, "Absentee Voting Practices Vary Widely Despite Fla. Law," *Washington Post,* Dec. 12, 2000, p. A38; Times Staff Writers, "A 'Modern' Democracy That Can't Count Votes," *Los Angeles Times,* Dec. 11, 2000, p. A1.

9. Robin Toner, "For Those Behind the Scenes, It's Old News That Elections Are Not an Exact Science."

10. For a good survey of the effects of various types of districts, see Howard D. Hamilton, "Legislative Constituencies: Single-Member Districts, Multi-Member Districts, and Floterial Districts," *Western Political Quarterly* 20 (1967): 321–340.

11. On proportional representation, see Douglas W. Rae, *The Political Consequences of Electoral Law* (New Haven, CT: Yale University Press, 1967); and Arend Lijphart, *Electoral Systems and Party Systems: A Study of Twenty-Seven Democracies, 1945–1990* (New York: Oxford University Press, 1994).

12. The classic study of presidential coattails is Warren E. Miller, "Presidential Coattails: A Study in Political Myth and Methodology," *Public Opinion Quarterly* 19 (1955–56): 353–368. See also Jeffery J. Mondak, "Determinants of Coattail Voting," *Political Behavior* 12 (1990): 265–288.

13. Walter Dean Burnham, *Critical Elections and the Mainsprings of American Politics* (New York: Norton, 1970), p. 94; and V. O. Key, Jr., *American State Politics: An Introduction* (New York: Knopf, 1967), pp. 41–49 and 52–84.

14. George Rabinowitz and Stuart Elaine MacDonald, "The Power of the States in U.S. Presidential Elections," *American Political Science Review* 80 (1986): 65–87; and Larry M. Bartels, "Resource Allocation in Presidential Campaigns," *Journal of Politics* 47 (1985): 928–936.

15. Fascinating exchanges on this issue can be found in Paul Schumaker and Burdett A. Loomis, eds., *How Should We Elect our President? The Electoral College and Beyond* (New York: Chatham House, 2001).

16. The landmark Supreme Court cases are *Baker v. Carr,* 369 U.S. 186 (1962); *Reynolds v. Sims,* 377 U.S. 533 (1964); and *Wesberry v. Sanders,* 376 U.S. 1. In fact, in *Karcher v. Daggett* (462 U.S. 725 [1983]), the Supreme Court struck down a New Jersey plan because by creating districts that differed in population size by seven tenths of one percent from the average, it violated the constitutional requirements of "precise mathematical equality."

17. For example, the Supreme Court chose not to invalidate notorious gerrymanders in Indiana (*Davis v. Bandamer,* 478 U.S. 109 [1986]) and California (*Badham v. Eu,* 488 U.S. 1024 [1989]). Earlier, however, in *Gomillion v. Lightfoot,* 364 U.S. 339 (1960), the Court had struck down an Alabama gerrymander in which a city's boundaries were redrawn to exclude blacks.

18. Chandler Davidson and Bernard Grofman, eds., *Quiet Revolution in the South* (Princeton, NJ: Princeton University Press, 1994), especially Chapter 1.

19. Kimball Brace, Bernard Grofman, and Lisa Handley, "Does Redistricting Aimed to Help Blacks Necessarily Help Republicans," *Journal of Politics* 49 (1987): 169–185; and Kevin A. Hill, "Does the Creation of Majority Black Districts Aid Republicans? An Analysis of the 1992 Congressional Elections in Eight Southern States," *Journal of Politics* 57 (1995): 384–401. Another study shows that although racial redistricting cost the Democrats state legislative seats in the South, the shift toward Republican votes among white voters has had a greater impact; see David Lublin and D. Stephen Voss, "Racial Redistricting and Realignment in Southern State Legislatures," *American Journal of Political Science* 44 (2000): 792–810.

20. For differing views, see Gary W. Cox and Jonathan N. Katz," The Reapportionment Revolution and Bias in U.S. Congressional Elections," *American Journal of Political Science* 43 (1999): 812–841; Amihai Glazer, Bernard Grofman, and Marc Robbins, "Partisan and Incumbency Effects of 1970s Congressional Redistricting," *American Journal of Political Science* 31 (1987): 680–707; Richard G. Niemi and Laura R. Winsky, "The Persistence of Partisan Redistricting Effects in Congressional Elections in the 1970s and 1980s," *Journal of Politics* 54 (1992): 565–572; Richard G. Niemi and Alan I. Abramowitz, "Partisan Redistricting and the 1992 Congressional Elections," *Journal of Politics* 56 (1994): 811–817, and Andrew Gelman and Gary King, "Enhancing Democracy through Legislative Redistricting," *American Political Science Review* 88 (1994): 541–559. On California, see Bruce E. Cain, "Assessing the Partisan Effects of Redistricting," *American Political Science Review* 79 (1985): 320–334; on Indiana, see John D. Cranor, Gary L. Crawley, and Raymond H. Scheele, "The Anatomy of a Gerrymander," *American Journal of Political Science* 33 (1989): 222–239.

21. See Paul S. Herrnson, *Congressional Elections: Campaigning at Home and in Washington,* 3rd ed. (Washington, DC: CQ Press, 2000); Marjorie Randon Hershey, *Running for Office: The Political Education of Campaigners* (Chatham, NJ: Chatham House, 1984); John H. Kessel, *Presidential Campaign Politics* (Chicago: Dorsey, 1988); Lucius J. Barker and Ronald W. Walters, *Jesse Jackson's 1984 Presidential Campaign: Challenge and Change in American Politics* (Champaign: University of Illinois Press, 1979); L. Sandy Maisel, *From Obscurity to Oblivion: Running in the Congressional Primary* (Knoxville: University of Tennessee Press, 1986); Jack W. Germond and Jules Witcover, *Mad as Hell: Revolt at the Ballot Box, 1992* (New York: Warner Books, 1993); and Mary Matalin and James Carville, *All's Fair: Love, War, and Running for President* (New York: Random House, 1994).

22. Ben White, "It's Never Too Soon to Start a Senate Race," *Washington Post*, Feb. 18, 2001, p. A18.

23. For an examination of how presidential candidates allocated one scarce resource, campaign visits, among various constituency groups, see Darrell M. West, "Constituencies and Travel Allocations in the 1980 Presidential Campaign," *American Journal of Political Science* 27 (1983): 515–529.

24. Herrnson, *Congressional Elections*; and Gary C. Jacobson, *The Politics of Congressional Elections*, 5th ed. (New York: Longman, 2001).

25. Robin Toner, "A Political Pulse-Taker Is Back, Without Missing a Beat," *New York Times*, Aug. 28, 2000, p. A10. See also John M. Russonello, "The Making of the President ... in the Philippines, Venezuela, France ...," *Public Opinion* 9 (1986): 10–12.

26. Among the many books on the subject, see especially Sidney Blumenthal, *The Permanent Campaign* (New York: Simon and Schuster, 1980); and Larry J. Sabato, *The Rise of Political Consultants* (New York: Basic, 1981); as well as the magazine *Campaigns and Elections*.

27. Described in Ithiel de Sola Pool, Robert P. Abelson, and Samuel Popkin, *Candidates, Issues, and Strategies* (Cambridge, MA: MIT Press, 1964).

28. James A. Thurber and Candice J. Nelson, eds., *Campaign Warriors* (Washington, DC: Brookings, 2000).

29. On the use of television advertising in modern campaigns, see Kathleen Hall Jamieson, *Packaging the Presidency: A History and Criticism of Presidential Campaign Advertising* (New York: Oxford University Press, 1996); Montague Kern, *Thirty-Second Politics: Political Advertising in the Eighties* (New York: Praeger, 1989); and Darrell West, *Air Wars: Television Advertising in Election Campaigns, 1952–96*, 2nd ed. (Washington, DC: CQ Press, 1997).

30. For a discussion of the routines of media coverage, see Doris A. Graber, *Mass Media and American Politics*, 5th ed. (Washington, DC: CQ Press, 1997), Chapter 4.

31. Dave Barry, "Scandal Sheep," *The Boston Globe Magazine*, Mar. 15, 1998, pp. 12–13.

32. E. J. Dionne, Jr., in the *New York Times*, Sept. 7, 1980.

33. Michael Cornfield, "A User's Guide to 'the Digital Divide,'" *Campaigns & Elections* (2000): 47.

34. On the impact of negative advertising, see Kathleen Hall Jamieson, *Dirty Politics: Deception, Distraction, and Democracy* (New York: Oxford University Press, 1992); Richard R. Lau and Lee Sigelman, "Effectiveness of Negative Political Advertising," in James A. Thurber, Candice J. Nelson, and David A. Dulio, eds., *Crowded Airwaves* (Washington, DC: Brookings, 2000), pp. 10–43; Richard R. Lau and Gerald M. Pomper, "Effectiveness of Negative Campaigning in U.S. Senate Elections," *American Journal of Political Science* 46 (2002): 47–66; and Stephen Ansolabehere and Shanto Iyengar, *Going Negative: How Campaign Advertising Shrinks and Polarizes the Electorate* (New York: Free Press, 1995). These findings are evaluated in a symposium in the *American Political Science Review* 93 (1999): 851–909.

35. Mathew D. McCubbins, ed., *Under the Watchful Eye* (Washington, DC: CQ Press, 1992); and Thomas E. Patterson, *Out of Order* (New York: Knopf, 1993).

36. For years, the media have covered elections as though they were strategic games or "horse races"; see, for example, Patterson, *Out of Order*, pp. 53–133 and Marjorie Randon Hershey, "The Campaign and the Media," in Gerald M. Pomper, ed., *The Election of 2000* (New York: Chatham House, 2001), pp. 48–49, 55–57, 65–66.

37. Andrew Gelman and Gary King, "Party Competition and Media Messages in U.S. Presidential Elections," in L. Sandy Maisel, ed., *The Parties Respond*, 2nd ed. (Boulder, CO: Westview, 1994), pp. 255–295; and Thomas M. Holbrook, "Campaigns, National Conditions, and U.S. Presidential Elections," *American Journal of Political Science* 38 (1994): 973–998.

38. See Peter W. Wielhouwer and Brad Lockerbie, "Party Contacting and Political Participation, 1952–90," *American Journal of Political Science* 38 (1994): 211–229; Robert Huckfeldt and

John Sprague, "Political Parties and Electoral Mobilization," *American Political Science Review* 86 (1992): 70–86; Phillips Cutright and Peter H. Rossi, "Grass Roots Politicians and the Vote," *American Sociological Review* 23 (1958): 171–179; Daniel Katz and Samuel J. Eldersveld, "The Impact of Local Party Activity upon the Electorate," *Public Opinion Quarterly* 25 (1961): 1–24; and Raymond E. Wolfinger, "The Influence of Precinct Work on Voting Behavior," *Public Opinion Quarterly* 27 (1963): 387–398.

39. Samuel J. Eldersveld, "Experimental Propaganda Techniques and Voting Behavior," *American Political Science Review* 50 (1956): 154–165; and John C. Blydenburg, "A Controlled Experiment to Measure the Effects of Personal Contact Campaigning," *Midwest Journal of Political Science* 15 (1971): 365–381.

40. See Charles Babington, "Democrats Split on What Went Wrong," *Washington Post,* Jan. 25, 2001, p. A6; Carter Eskew, "The Lessons of 2000," *Washington Post,* Jan. 30, 2001, p. A17, and David S. Broder, "Party's Fault Lines Likely to Surface," *Washington Post,* Jan. 21, 2001, p. A22 for a variety of alternative explanations of the election result.

41. See, for example, John P. Frendreis, James L. Gibson, and Laura L. Vertz, "The Electoral Relevance of Local Party Organizations," *American Political Science Review* 84 (1990): 225–235. For a different view, see Gerald H. Kramer, "The Effects of Precinct-Level Canvassing on Voter Behavior," *Public Opinion Quarterly* 34 (1970): 560–572; and William J. Crotty, "Party Effort and Its Impact on the Vote," *American Political Science Review* 65 (1971): 439–450.

42 The definitive discussion is by Jacobson, *The Politics of Congressional Elections,* pp. 41–46.

43. Austin Ranney, *Channels of Power: The Impact of Television on American Politics* (New York: Basic Books, 1983), p. 90.

44. Harold W. Stanley and Richard G. Niemi, *Vital Statistics on American Politics 1999–2000* (Washington, DC: CQ Press, 2000), Table 4.5, p. 173.

45. American National Election Study, *The NES Guide to Public Opinion and Electoral Behavior,* Tables 6C.1a and 6D.1, at *http://www.umich.edu/~nes/nesguide* (accessed Feb. 24, 2002).

46. See, for example, Daron R. Shaw, "The Effect of TV Ads and Candidate Appearances on Statewide Presidential Votes, 1988–96," *American Political Science Review* 93 (1999): 345–61; see also the sources cited in Carroll J. Glynn, Susan Herbst, Garrett J. O'Keefe, and Robert Y. Shapiro, *Public Opinion* (Boulder, CO: Westview, 1999), pp. 436–441.

47. Russell J. Dalton, Paul A. Beck and Robert Huckfeldt, "Partisan Cues and the Media: Information Flows in the 1992 Presidential Election," *American Political Science Review* 92 (1998): 111–126. On the variety of media assessments of the 1996 presidential candidates, see Stanley and Niemi, *Vital Statistics on American Politics,* pp. 188–189.

48. See Robert Huckfeldt and John Sprague, "Networks in Context: The Social Flow of Political Information," *American Political Science Review* 81 (1987): 1197–1216; and Paul Allen Beck, "Voters' Intermediation Environments in the 1988 Presidential Contest," *Public Opinion Quarterly* 55 (1991): 371–394.

49. The classic studies of the mobilizing effects of campaigns include Paul Lazarsfeld, Bernard Berelson, and Hazel Gaudet, *The People's Choice* (New York: Columbia University Press, 1948); and Bernard Berelson, Paul Lazarsfeld, and William McPhee, *Voting* (Chicago: University of Chicago Press, 1954).

50. On agenda-setting, see Donald Shaw and Maxwell E. McCombs, *The Emergence of American Political Issues: The Agenda-Setting Function of the Press* (St. Paul, MN: West, 1977). On priming, see Joanne M. Miller and Jon A. Krosnick, "News Media Impact on the Ingredients of Presidential Evaluations," *American Journal of Political Science* 44 (2000): 295–309. For evidence on both priming and agenda-setting, see Shanto Iyengar and Donald Kinder, *News That Matters* (Chicago: University of Chicago Press, 1987).

51. See Hershey, "The Campaign and the Media."

52. Shanto Iyengar and John R. Petrocik, " 'Basic Rule' Voting: Impact of Campaigns on Party- and Approval-Based Voting," in James A. Thurber, Candice J. Nelson, and David A. Dulio, eds., *Crowded Airwaves* (Washington, DC: Brookings, 2000), p. 142.

53. Paul S. Herrnson, *Party Campaigning in the 1980s* (Cambridge, MA: Harvard University Press, 1988).

54. Soft money refers to contributions to the national parties that would be illegal under federal law if they stayed at the national level. See Frank J. Sorauf, *Inside Campaign Finance* (New Haven, CT: Yale University Press, 1992), pp. 146–152.

55. A. James Reichley, *The Life of the Parties* (New York: Free Press, 1992), pp. 377–381.

CHAPTER 12

1. George Thayer, *Who Shakes the Money Tree?* (New York: Simon and Schuster, 1973), p. 25.

2. Among the best studies of modern campaign finance are Frank J. Sorauf, *Inside Campaign Finance: Myths and Realities* (New Haven, CT: Yale University Press, 1992); and, on state campaigns, Michael J. Malbin and Thomas L. Gais, *The Day After Reform* (Albany, NY: Rockefeller Institute, 1998). The standard accounts of campaign finance before modern times are Louise Overacker, *Money in Elections* (New York: Macmillan, 1932), and *Presidential Campaign Funds* (Boston: Boston University Press, 1944); and Alexander Heard, *The Costs of Democracy* (Chapel Hill: The University of North Carolina Press, 1960).

3. This is the best estimate of Candice J. Nelson, "Spending in the 2000 Elections," in David B. Magleby, ed., *Financing the 2000 Election* (Washington DC: Brookings, 2002), Chapter 2; it includes spending by presidential and congressional candidates, party spending in hard dollars, soft money, issue advocacy spending, and spending in state elections, judicial elections, and on ballot initiatives. A more precise figure is impossible because spending on state and local campaigns and issue ads is not reported to the Federal Election Commission.

4. Since 1960 a definitive series of books on campaign finance has been published by Herbert Alexander and a succession of colleagues. The most recent book in this series is Magleby's *Financing the 2000 Election.*

5. This table does not include all of the spending on congressional elections. Although much of the money spent by parties' congressional campaign committees goes directly to the candidates and is therefore reflected in their totals, these committees also make "coordinated expenditures" for candidates and spend money directly on issue advertising in many campaigns. Substantial amounts are also spent independently by political action committees, other interest groups, and individuals. There are increasing numbers of campaigns, then, in which the candidates' spending is less than that of party organizations and interest groups.

6. See John J. Coleman and Paul F. Manna, "Congressional Campaign Spending and the Quality of Democracy," *Journal of Politics* 62 (2000): 757–789.

7. The Supreme Court ruled in *Buckley v. Valeo*, 424 U.S. 1 (1976), that such campaign spending was a First Amendment right and was therefore exempted from campaign spending regulations.

8. For more on 2000 presidential campaign finance, see Anthony Corrado, "Financing the 2000 Elections," in Gerald M. Pomper, *et al.*, eds., *The Election of 2000* (New York: Chatham House, 2001), pp. 92–124; and Magleby, *Financing the 2000 Election.* Unless otherwise noted, specific figures cited in this chapter come from FEC reports.

9. Just because money is spent "by" the campaign does not mean that it is spent "on" the campaign itself. Campaigns have a number of expenses beyond those meant to persuade voters to support their candidate. On this point, see Stephen Ansolabehere and Alan Gerber, "The Mismeasure of Campaign Spending: Evidence from the 1990 U.S. House Elections," *Journal of Politics* 56 (1994): 1106–1118.

10. The FEC data reported in this paragraph are drawn from the Center for Responsive Politics, *http://www.opensecrets.org/2000elect/storysofar/index.asp* (accessed Sept. 12, 2001). The average figures include major party candidates only.

11. For the FEC's figures, see *http://www.fec.gov/*. For more on recent congressional campaign spending, see Magleby, *Financing the 2000 Election*; and Paul S. Herrnson, *Congressional Elections,* 3rd ed. (Washington, DC: CQ Press, 2000).

12. Patrick McGreevey, "5th Ditrict Candidates Set Record for Spending," *Los Angeles Times,* Apr. 7, 2001, p. B7. On Bloomberg, see Michael Cooper, "At $92.60 a Vote, Bloomberg Shatters An Election Record," *New York Times,* Dec. 4, 2001, p. A1.

13. See Malcolm Jewell and Sarah M. Morehouse, *Political Parties and Elections in American States* (Washington, DC: CQ Press, 2001), p. 11. On state supreme court races, see Neil A. Lewis, "Gifts in State Judicial Races Are Up Sharply," *New York Times,* Feb. 14, 2002, p. A27.

14. These differing conclusions are well represented in an exchange in the *American Journal of Political Science.* See Donald Philip Green and Jonathan S. Krasno, "Salvation for the Spendthrift Incumbent: Reestimating the Effects of Campaign Spending in House Elections," 32 (1988): 884–907; Gary C. Jacobson, "The Effects of Campaign Spending in House Elections: New Evidence for Old Arguments," 34 (1990): 334–362; and Donald Philip Green and Jonathan S. Krasno, "Rebuttal to Jacobson's 'New Evidence for Old Arguments,'" 34 (1990): 363–372.

15. For a discussion of campaign spending in the states, see Malbin and Gais, *The Day After Reform*; and Frank J. Sorauf, *Money in American Elections* (Glenview, IL: Scott, Foresman, 1988), Chapter 9.

16. Benjamin A. Webster *et al.*, "Competing for Cash: The Individual Financiers of Congressional Elections," in Paul S. Herrnson, ed., *Playing Hardball* (Upper Saddle River, NJ: Prentice-Hall, 2001), pp. 41-69.

17. The figures are for the number of PACs registered at the federal level and come from the end-of-year reports of the Federal Election Commission. Data for 1999–2000 are from *http://www.fec.gov/press/053101pacfund/tables/pacsum00.htm* (accessed Sept. 10, 2001).

18. Larry J. Sabato and Bruce A. Larson, *The Party's Just Begun,* 2nd ed. (New York: Longman, 2002), pp. 84–88.

19. For a more extensive discussion of the role of PACs in campaign financing, see Sorauf, *Inside Campaign Finance,* Chapter 4. See also Larry J. Sabato, *PAC Power: Inside the World of Political Action Committees* (New York: Norton, 1984).

20. See, for example, Gregory Wawro, "A Panel Probit Analysis of Campaign Contributions and Roll-Call Votes," *American Journal of Political Science* 45 (2001): 563–579.

21. On access, see Laura I. Langbein, "Money and Access: Some Empirical Evidence," *Journal of Politics* 48 (1986): 1052–1064. On committee involvement, see Richard L. Hall and Frank W. Wayman, "Buying Time: Moneyed Interests and the Mobilization of Bias in Congressional Committees," *American Political Science Review* 84 (1990): 797–820.

22. John R. Wright, "PACs, Contributions, and Roll Calls: An Organizational Perspective," *American Political Science Review* 79 (1985): 400–414.

23. See Malbin and Gais, *The Day After Reform,* Chapter 4; and Ruth S. Jones, "State Public Campaign Finance: Implications for Partisan Politics," *American Journal of Political Science* 25 (1981): 342–361.

24. The figures come from William E. Cassie, Joel A. Thompson, and Malcolm E. Jewell, "The Pattern of PAC Contributions in Legislative Elections: An Eleven State Analysis," paper delivered at the Annual Meeting of the American Political Science Association, Chicago, 1992.

25. See Arnold Fleischmann and David C. Nice, "States and PACs: The Legacy of Established Decision Rules," *Political Behavior* 10 (1988): 349–363.

26. See Sorauf, *Inside Campaign Finance,* Chapter 7; and Robert E. Mutch, *Campaigns, Congress, and the Courts* (New York: Praeger, 1988).

27. *Buckley v. Valeo,* 424 U.S. 1 (1976).

28. See Philip D. Duncan, "Incumbent in the Cross Hairs," *Campaigns & Elections* (1999), on the Internet at *http://www.camelect.com.*

29. See Derek Willis, "Private Parties' Last-Minute Spending Spree," *CQ Weekly,* Nov. 11, 2000, p. 2624.

30. More generally, soft money can be defined as any campaign funds that are not subject to regulation by FECA; for that reason, they are also referred to as "nonfederal" money.

31. On soft-money contributions in the 2000 campaign, see Corrado, "Financing the 2000 Elections"; see also Diana Dwyre and Victoria A. Farrar-Myers, *Legislative Labyrinth: Congress and Campaign Finance Reform* (Washington, DC: CQ Press, 2001).

32. Malbin and Gais, *The Day After Reform,* pp. 11–12.

33. Quoted in Diana Dwyre, "Campaigning Outside the Law: Interest Group Issue Advocacy," in Allan J. Cigler and Burdett A. Loomis, eds., *Interest Group Politics,* 6th ed. (Washington, DC: CQ Press, 2002). p. 146.

34. See John Solomon, "AP: Groups Spend To Sway Elections," Nov. 4, 2000, *http://www. washingtonpost.com/ac2/wp-dyn/A11961–2000Nov4,* accessed Nov. 5, 2000.

35. Solomon, "AP: Groups Spend."

36. Larry Makinson, executive director of the Center for Responsive Politics, quoted in Karen Foerstel and Peter Wallsten with Derek Willis, "Campaign Overhaul Mired in Money and Loopholes," *Congressional Quarterly Weekly Report (CQ Weekly),* May 13, 2000, p. 1084.

37. Foerstal and Wallsten, "Campaign Overhaul."

38. Mike Allen, "Interest Groups a Force in Congressional Elections," *Washington Post,* Feb. 5, 2001, p. A5.

39. See Jonathan Krasno and Daniel Seltz, *Buying Time: Television Advertising in the 1998 Congressional Elections* (New York: New York University Law School, 2000).

40. Sabato and Larson, *The Party's Just Begun,* p. 77. On the effects of campaign finance reforms on the parties, see F. Christopher Arterton, "Political Money and Party Strength," in Joel L. Fleishman, ed., *The Future of American Political Parties* (Englewood Cliffs, NJ: Prentice-Hall, 1982), pp. 101–139; and Sorauf, *Inside Campaign Finance,* Chapter 7.

41. See Malbin and Gais, *The Day After Reform,* pp. 13–23.

42. The data on state campaign finance provisions are drawn from Harold W. Stanley and Richard G. Niemi, *Vital Statistics on American Politics, 1999–2000* (Washington, DC: CQ Press, 2000), Tables 2.2 and 2.3, pp. 84–87.

43. Zell Miller, "A Sorry Way to Win," *Washington Post,* Feb. 25, 2001, p. B7.

44. Wright H. Andrews (former president of the American League of Lobbyists), "Why This Lobbyist Backs McCain-Feingold," *Washington Post,* Mar. 19, 2001, p. A17.

45. For additional proposals for reform, see Green, *Financing the 1996 Campaign.*

PART 5

1. See John F. Hoadley, "The Emergence of Political Parties in Congress, 1789–1803," *American Political Science Review* 74 (1980): 757–779.

2. E. E. Schattschneider, *Party Government* (New York: Rinehart, 1942), pp. 131–132.

3. See the report of the Committee on Responsible Parties of the American Political Science Association, *Toward a More Responsible Two-Party System* (New York: Rinehart, 1950). The report also appears as a supplement to the September 1950 issue of the *American Political Science Review.*

4. Ian Budge and Richard I. Hofferbert, "Mandates and Policy Outputs: U.S. Party Platforms and Federal Expenditures," *American Political Science Review* 84 (1990): 111–131. See also

the discussion of this approach by Budge, Hofferbert, and others in "Party Platforms, Mandates, and Government Spending," *American Political Science Review* 87 (1993): 744–750.

CHAPTER 13

1. The Nebraska legislature is chosen in nonpartisan elections, although the partisan affiliations of its members are usually no secret. Of the 7,611 state legislators and the 535 members of Congress, only 33 were neither Democrats nor Republicans as of April 2000, according to the *Book of the States, 2000–01 Edition* (Lexington, KY: Council of State Governments, 2000), p. 70.

2. The view of leadership power as authority *delegated* to leaders by the party caucus is one of the cornerstones of the principal-agent conceptualization of Congress. In this view, the majority party is the principal, and its power to make policy is delegated to agents such as the leadership, the committees, the president, and even the bureaucracy. See D. Roderick Kiewiet and Mathew D. McCubbins, *The Logic of Delegation: Congressional Parties and the Appropriations Process* (Chicago: University of Chicago Press, 1991).

3. Even Cannon was constrained by the seniority rule in choosing committee chairs, however; see Eric D. Lawrence, Forrest Maltzman, and Paul J. Wahlbeck, "The Politics of Speaker Cannon's Committee Assignments," *American Journal of Political Science* 45 (2001): 551–562.

4. See Joseph Cooper and David W. Brady, "Institutional Context and Leadership Style: The House from Cannon to Rayburn," *American Political Science Review* 75 (1981): 411–425.

5. Quoted in Andrew Taylor, "A Senate of Singular Personalities and Possibilities," *CQ Weekly*, Jan. 27, 2001, p. 212.

6. On the Democratic Study Group, see Arthur G. Stevens, Arthur H. Miller, and Thomas E. Mann, "Mobilization of Liberal Strength in the House, 1955–1970: The Democratic Study Group," *American Political Science Review* 68 (1974): 667–681. For more on the reforms, see Leroy N. Rieselbach, *Congressional Reform: The Changing Modern Congress* (Washington, DC: CQ Press, 1994).

7. The rise of seniority as a principle for allocating committee positions in the House of Representatives can be traced to the period around the turn of the twentieth century, when House members became more likely to spend a long career in the chamber, and especially to the weakening of the Speaker after 1910. See Nelson W. Polsby, Miriam Gallaher, and Barry Spencer Rundquist, "The Growth of the Seniority System in the U.S. House of Representatives," *American Political Science Review* 68 (1969): 787–807.

8. See Gary W. Cox and Mathew W. McCubbins, *Legislative Leviathan: Party Government in the House* (Berkeley and Los Angeles: University of California Press, 1993), pp. 279–282. Once a few committee chairs had been stripped of their positions in 1975, the surviving chairs tended to become more solicitous of their committee and party colleagues. One study finds that the reforms increased party loyalty in roll-call voting among House Democrats who chaired committees or subcommittees or who were next in line to be a chair. See Sara Brandes Crook and John R. Hibbing, "Congressional Reform and Party Discipline: The Effects of Changes in the Seniority System on Party Loyalty in the U.S. House of Representatives," *British Journal of Political Science* 15 (1985): 207–226.

9. Steven S. Smith, "New Patterns of Decisionmaking in Congress," in John E. Chubb and Paul E. Peterson, eds., *The New Direction in American Politics* (Washington, DC: Brookings, 1985), pp. 203–233.

10. See, for example, Barbara Sinclair, "Evolution or Revolution? Policy-oriented Congressional Parties in the 1990s," in L. Sandy Maisel, ed., *The Parties Respond: Changes in Parties and Campaigns,* 3rd ed. (Boulder, CO: Westview, 1998).

11. There is a rich literature on party leadership in Congress. Among the best recent works are David W. Rohde, *Parties and Leaders in the Postreform House* (Chicago: University of Chicago Press, 1991); and Barbara Sinclair, *Legislators, Leaders, and Lawmaking: The U.S. House of Representatives in the Postreform Era* (Baltimore: Johns Hopkins University Press, 1995).

12. This account draws heavily from Rohde, *Parties and Leaders in the Postreform House*. Also see John H. Aldrich and David W. Rohde, "The Logic of Conditional Party Government: Revisiting the Electoral Connection," in Lawrence C. Dodd and Bruce I. Oppenheimer, eds., *Congress Reconsidered*, 7th ed. (Washington, DC: CQ Press, 2001), Chapter 12; and Sinclair, *Legislators, Leaders, and Lawmaking*.

13. See, for example, Vincent G. Moscardelli, Moshe Haspel, and Richard S. Wike, "Party Building through Campaign Finance Reform: Conditional Party Government in the 104th Congress," *Journal of Politics* 60 (1998): 691–704.

14. On Wright, see Rohde, *Party and Leaders in the Postreform House*, pp. 105–118; and Barbara Sinclair, "House Majority Party Leadership in the Late 1980s," in Dodd and Oppenheimer, eds., *Congress Reconsidered*, pp. 307–330. On the transition in styles from Wright to Foley, see Rohde, *Party Leaders in the Postreform House*, pp. 184–189.

15. Barbara Sinclair, *Unorthodox Lawmaking*, 2nd ed. (Washington, DC: CQ Press, 2000), pp. 103–106.

16. See Lawrence C. Evans and Walter J. Oleszek, *Congress Under Fire* (Boston: Houghton Mifflin, 1997); and Lawrence C. Dodd and Bruce I. Oppenheimer, "A House Divided: The Struggle for Partisan Control, 1994–2000," in Dodd and Oppenheimer, eds., *Congress Reconsidered*, 7th ed. (Washington, DC: CQ Press, 2001), Chapter 2.

17. Sinclair, "The New World of U.S. Senators," in Lawrence C. Dodd and Bruce I. Oppenheimer, eds., *Congress Reconsidered*, 7th ed. (Washington, DC: CQ Press, 2001), and *Unorthodox Lawmaking*.

18. Steven S. Smith and Gerald Gamm, "The Dynamics of Party Government in Congress," in Dodd and Oppenheimer, eds., *Congress Reconsidered*, Chapter 11.

19. Sinclair, "The New World of U.S. Senators," pp. 5–8.

20. The exceptions are some Southern states plus Nebraska, which is nominally nonpartisan. On parties in state legislatures, see Malcolm E. Jewell and Sarah M. Morehouse, *Political Parties and Elections in American States*, 4th ed. (Washington, DC: CQ Press, 2001), Chapter 8.

21. Jewell and Morehouse, *Political Parties and Elections in American States.*, pp. 234–235.

22. Jewell and Morehouse, *Political Parties and Elections in American States.*, pp. 236–238.

23. For more on parties and party leadership in state legislatures, see Keith E. Hamm and Robert Harmel, "Legislative Party Development and the Speaker System: The Case of the Texas House," *Journal of Politics* 55 (1993): 1140–1151; and Malcolm E. Jewell and Marcia Lynn Whicker, *Legislative Leadership in the American States* (Ann Arbor, MI: University of Michigan Press, 1994).

24. Thomas Stratmann, "Congressional Voting over Legislative Careers: Shifting Positions and Changing Constraints," *American Political Science Review* 94 (2000): 665–676.

25. See Barbara Sinclair, "Majority Party Leadership Strategies for Coping with the New U.S. House," *Legislative Studies Quarterly* 6 (1981): 391–414. On the favors leaders can bestow, see Roger Davidson, "Senate Leaders: Janitors for an Untidy Chamber?" in Lawrence C. Dodd and Bruce I. Oppenheimer, eds., *Congress Reconsidered*, 4th ed. (Washington, DC: CQ Press, 1989), pp. 225–252. On leaders' control of the floor through the Rules Committee and other devices, see Steven Smith, *Call to Order: Floor Politics in the House and the Senate* (Washington, DC: Brookings Institution, 1989).

26. See Larry J. Sabato and Bruce Larson, *The Party's Just Begun*, 2nd ed. (New York: Longman, 2002), Chapter 3; and Paul S. Herrnson, *Congressional Elections: Campaigning at Home and in Washington*, 3rd ed. (Washington, DC: CQ Press, 2000).

27. Julius Turner, *Party and Constituency: Pressures on Congress,* rev. ed., Edward V. Schneier, ed. (Baltimore, MD: The Johns Hopkins University Press, 1970), pp. 16–17.

28. The corresponding number of uncontested or "universalistic" votes, in which 90 percent of Congress votes the same way, conversely, increased steadily from the late 1940s to 1980. See Melissa P. Collie, "Universalism and the Parties in the U.S. House of Representatives," *American Journal of Political Science* 32 (1988): 865–883.

29. Barbara Sinclair, "The New World of U.S. Senators," p. 3.

30. Jeffery A. Jenkins offers a unique perspective on party influence on voting; he compares roll-call voting in the U.S. and Confederate Houses during the Civil War. See his "Examining the Bonding Effects of Party: A Comparative Analysis of Roll-Call Voting in the U.S. and Confederate Houses," *American Journal of Political Science* 43 (1999): 1144–1165.

31. To even out this "session effect," the data in Figure 13.2 are averaged across the two sessions of each Congress. The downturn in party voting in the even years, when House members stand for reelection, is seen as early as the 1830s.

32. Institutionalization is the term Polsby uses to characterize the development of a professionalized Congress with greater specialization of party and committee roles, established norms, deference to congressional experience, and greater longevity in office; see Nelson W. Polsby, "The Institutionalization of the United States House of Representatives," *American Political Science Review* 62 (1968): 144–168. By disaggregation, Burnham means a decline in the party-based linkage among candidates for various offices. See Walter Dean Burnham, *Critical Elections and the Mainsprings of American Politics* (New York: Norton, 1970), pp. 91–134.

33. See Dodd and Oppenheimer, "A House Divided," pp. 38–39.

34. Jewell and Morehouse, *Political Parties and Elections in American States,* p. 251.

35. Gary C. Jacobson, "Congress: Elections and Stalemate," in Michael Nelson, ed., *The Elections of 2000* (Washington, DC: CQ Press, 2001), pp. 204–205.

36. Rohde, *Parties and Leaders in the Postreform House,* especially Chapter 3. On changes in the South, also see Franklin D. Gilliam, Jr., and Kenny Whitby, "A Longitudinal Analysis of Competing Explanations for the Transformation of Southern Politics," *Journal of Politics* 53 (1991): 504–518; and M. V. Hood III, Quentin Kidd, and Irwin L. Morris, "Of Byrd[s] and Bumpers: Using Democratic Senators to Analyze Political Change in the South, 1960–1995," *American Journal of Political Science* 43 (1999): 465–487.

37. See Stephen Gettinger, "R.I.P. to a Conservative Force," *CQ Weekly,* Jan. 9, 1999, pp. 82–84.

38. A second Democratic House member also refused to vote for his party's candidate for Speaker, Minority Leader Dick Gephardt; his vote went instead to another Democrat.

39. For more on variations in presidential support in Congress, see Jon R. Bond and Richard Fleisher, *The President in the Legislative Arena* (Chicago: University of Chicago Press, 1990); Mark A. Peterson, *Legislating Together: The White House and Capitol Hill from Eisenhower to Reagan* (Cambridge, MA: Harvard University Press, 1990); and Cary R. Covington, J. Mark Wrighton, and Rhonda Kinney, "A 'Presidency-Augmented' Model of Presidential Success on House Roll Call Votes," *American Journal of Political Science* 39 (November, 1995): 1001–1024.

40. See Aage Clausen, *How Congressmen Decide* (New York: St. Martin's, 1973); and James M. Snyder, Jr., and Tim Groseclose, "Estimating Party Influence in Congressional Roll-Call Voting," *American Journal of Political Science* 44 (2000): 187–205. Political ideology also provides a powerful explanation of legislators' votes; some scholars have argued that it can account for most voting behavior in Congress. See Keith T. Poole, "Recent Developments in Analytical Models of Voting in the U.S. Congress," *Legislative Studies Quarterly* 13 (1988): 117–133; and Jerrold Schneider, *Ideological Coalitions in Congress* (Westport, CT: Greenwood Press, 1979).

41. See Jerome M. Clubb and Santa A. Traugott, "Partisan Cleavage and Cohesion in the House of Representatives, 1861–1974," *Journal of Interdisciplinary History* 7 (1977): 374–401; David W.

Brady and Philip Althoff, "Party Voting in the U.S. House of Representatives, 1890–1910: Elements of a Responsible Party System," *Journal of Politics* 36 (1974): 752–775; and Barbara Sinclair, "Party Realignment and the Transformation of the Political Agenda: The House of Representatives, 1925–1938," *American Political Science Review* 71 (1977): 940–953.

42. David W. Brady, "A Reevaluation of Realignments in American Politics: Evidence from the House of Representatives," *American Political Science Review* 79 (1985): 28–49, and *Critical Elections and Congressional Policy Making* (Stanford, CA: Stanford University Press, 1988).

43. Paul Allen Beck, "The Electoral Cycle and Patterns of American Politics," *British Journal of Political Science* 9 (1979): 129–156.

44. That the activity of Congress is organized around the election needs of its members is a view powerfully articulated in David R. Mayhew, *Congress: The Electoral Connection* (New Haven, CT: Yale University Press, 1974).

45. Warren E. Miller and Donald E. Stokes, "Constituency Influence in Congress," *American Political Science Review* 57 (1963): 45–57.

46. David Nather and Adriel Bettelheim, "Moderates and Mavericks Hold Key to 107th Congress," *Congressional Quarterly Weekly Report (CQ Weekly)*, Jan. 6, 2001, p. 49.

47. Membership turnover in state legislatures varies widely from one state to another; see *The Book of the States*, p. 72.

48. See Jewell and Morehouse, *Political Parties and Elections in American* States, pp. 212–215. On the activities of legislative leadership campaign committees, see Anthony Gierzynski, *Legislative Party Campaign Committees in the American States* (Lexington, KY: University of Kentucky Press, 1992); and Daniel M. Shea, *Transforming Democracy: Legislative Campaign Committees and Political Parties* (Albany, NY: State University of New York Press, 1995).

49. David Denemark, "Partisan Pork Barrel in Parliamentary Systems: Australian Constituency-level Grants," *Journal of Politics* 62 (2000): 896–915.

50. Party influence in the states should not be exaggerated, however. In one survey, state legislators were asked who made the most significant legislative decisions. A majority cited the party leadership in 67 of 99 legislative chambers, and the party caucus was important in 50 chambers, but committees were significant in 87. Of course, party leaders may have an indirect influence here, because the party leadership selects the committee chairs in many states. See Wayne L. Francis, "Leadership, Party Caucuses, and Committees in the U.S. State Legislatures," *Legislative Studies Quarterly* 10 (1985): 243–257.

51. Cox and McCubbins in *Legislative Leviathan* see the majority party as the prime actor in the House of Representatives. Other key works are Kiewiet and McCubbins, *The Logic of Delegation;* Rohde, *Parties and Leaders in the Postreform House;* and Sinclair, *Legislators, Leaders, and Lawmaking.*

52. U.S. Representative David E. Price offers a valuable insider's perspective on the role of party in Congress; see Price, *The Congressional Experience* (Boulder, CO: Westview, 1992).

53. Studies of legislative party voting in Britain and Canada suggest the parliamentary form is the main reason for the greater party discipline there than in the United States. On Britain, see Austin Ranney, "Candidate Selection and Party Cohesion in Britain and the U.S.," in William J. Crotty, ed., *Approaches to the Study of Party Organization* (Boston: Allyn and Bacon, 1968), pp. 139–168; and Gary Cox, *The Efficient Secret* (New York: Cambridge University Press, 1987). On Canada, see Leon D. Epstein, "A Comparative Study of Canadian Parties," *American Political Science Review* 58 (1964): 46–59; and Allan Kornberg, "Caucus and Cohesion in Canadian Parliamentary Parties," *American Political Science Review* 60 (1966): 83–92.

54. See Richard Fleisher and Jon R. Bond, "Polarized Politics: Does It Matter?" in Bond and Fleisher, eds., *Polarized Politics* (Washington, DC: CQ Press, 2000), pp. 195–200.

55. Even the *Contract with America* was created only by House Republicans, especially party leaders Newt Gingrich and Dick Armey, and not by the Republican Party organization, the Republican National Convention, or even Republican senators.

CHAPTER 14

1. On the Florida Supreme Court's decision, see David Von Drehle, Jo Becker, Ellen Nakashima and Lois Romano, "A 'Queen Kept Clock Running," *Washington Post,* Jan. 30, 2001, p. A1. On the U.S. Supreme Court, see David Von Drehle, Peter Slevin, Dan Balz, and James V. Grimaldi, "Anxious Moments in the Final Stretch," *Washington Post,* Feb. 3, 2001, p. A1.

2. This is the landmark case *Marbury v. Madison,* in which Federalist Chief Justice Marshall refused to order the new Jefferson administration to deliver a commission to Marbury that had been approved by the previous Federalist administration. In doing so, he claimed for the Supreme Court the power to judge congressional actions as to their constitutionality and used this power to rule that Congress had (wrongly) authorized the Supreme Court to exercise powers denied to it by the Constitution. This case is regarded as the key precedent for the Court's power of judicial review. See *Marbury v. Madison,* 1 Cranch 137 (1803).

3. See Clive Bean and Anthony Mughan, "Leadership Effects in Parliamentary Elections in Australia and Britain," *American Political Science Review* 83 (1989): 1165–1180.

4. Quoted in Adam Clymer, "Not So Fast: Suddenly Bush's Smooth Ride Turns Bumpy," *New York Times,* Sec. 4, Apr. 1, 2001, p. 1.

5. In this respect, presidents such as Clinton and Ronald Reagan follow in the footsteps of Franklin Delano Roosevelt, considered the consummate party leader as president in the twentieth century. On Roosevelt's legacy and its influence on later presidents, see Sidney M. Milkis, *The President and the Parties* (New York: Oxford University Press, 1993).

6. Philip Shenon, "Bush and His Cabinet Stepping In as Chief Fund-Raisers for G.O.P.," *New York Times,* Apr. 19, 2001, p. A1.

7. Adam Clymer, "Hints of Retiring in 2 Senators' Fund-Raising," *New York Times,* Aug. 8, 2001, p. A13.

8. Quoted in Edwin Chen and Janet Hook, "Bush Team Plays Role Fit for a Kingmaker," *Los Angeles Times,* Apr. 25, 2001, p. A13.

9. Roger G. Brown, "Party and Bureaucracy: From Kennedy to Reagan," *Political Science Quarterly* 97 (1982): 279–294.

10. Quoted in Joseph Califano, *Presidential Nation* (New York: Norton, 1975), p. 153.

11. On presidential coattails in U.S. House elections, see Randall L. Calvert and John A. Ferejohn, "Coattail Voting in Recent Presidential Elections," *American Political Science Review* 77 (1983): 407–419; John A. Ferejohn and Randall L. Calvert, "Presidential Coattails in Historical Perspective," *American Journal of Political Science* 28 (1984): 127–146; Richard Born, "Reassessing the Decline of Presidential Coattails: U.S. House Elections from 1952–80," *Journal of Politics* 46 (1984): 60–79; and James E. Campbell, "Predicting Seat Gains from Presidential Coattails," *American Journal of Political Science* 30 (1986): 164–183.

12. See James E. Campbell, "Presidential Coattails and Midterm Losses in State Legislative Elections," *American Political Science Review* 80 (1986): 45–63; and James E. Campbell and Joe A. Sumners, "Presidential Coattails in Senate Elections," *American Political Science Review* 84 (1990): 512–524.

13. See Edward R. Tufte, "Determinants of the Outcomes of Midterm Congressional Elections," *American Political Science Review* 69 (1975): 812–826; and *Political Control of the Economy* (Princeton, NJ: Princeton University Press, 1978), Chapter 5. Even more persuasive evidence of the relationship between presidential approval and midterm congressional outcomes may be found in Robin F. Marra and Charles W. Ostrom, Jr., "Explaining Seat Change in the

U.S. House of Representatives, 1950–86," *American Journal of Political Science* 33 (1989): 541–569.

14. Angus Campbell attributed this phenomenon to the absence in midterm elections of the short-term forces that had favored the president two years earlier. This in turn led to declines in turnout among those without strong partisan loyalties. See his "Surge and Decline: A Study of Electoral Change," in Angus Campbell, Philip E. Converse, Warren E. Miller, and Donald E. Stokes, eds., *Elections and the Political Order* (New York: Wiley, 1966), pp. 40–62.

15. Gary Jacobson offers an attractive "strategic politicians" explanation for this relationship. At the beginning of an election year, Jacobson suggests, many people who would be effective candidates for Congress are deciding whether or not to make the race. If a president of their party is high in popularity (and other promising conditions are present), then these prospective candidates might decide that this is a good year to run. The more of these experienced candidates who decide to run in a given year, the greater the likelihood that a party will do well in the fall election. See Jacobson's "Strategic Politicians and the Dynamics of U.S. House Elections, 1946–86," *American Political Science Review* 83 (1989): 773–793.

16. This translation of votes into seats, called the "swing ratio," is calculated by Edward R. Tufte in "The Relationship between Seats and Votes in Two-Party Systems," *American Political Science Review* 67 (1973): 540–554.

17. Samuel Kernell, "Presidential Popularity and Negative Voting: An Alternative Explanation of the Midterm Congressional Decline of the President's Party," *American Political Science Review* 71 (1977): 44–66. This negative voting thesis has been challenged by Richard Born, who concludes that it is the return of presidential defectors to their home party and not negative voting that accounts for the presidential party's loss of seats at midterm. See his "Surge and Decline, Negative Voting, and the Midterm Loss Phenomenon: A Simultaneous Choice Analysis," *American Journal of Political Science* 34 (1990): 615–645.

18. Dwight D. Eisenhower was long considered one such president. Fred I. Greenstein finds persuasive evidence, however, that President Eisenhower's public avoidance of partisan politics masked an abiding sense of partisanship and a commitment to strengthening the Republican Party. See his *The Hidden-Hand Presidency: Eisenhower as Leader* (New York: Basic Books, 1982).

19. On the role of the governor in party leadership, see Alan Rosenthal, *Governors and Legislatures: Contending Powers* (Washington, DC: CQ Press, 1990).

20. Victoria Allred, "Versatility With the Veto," *CQ Weekly,* Jan. 20, 2001, pp. 175–177.

21. See George C. Edwards III, "Measuring Presidential Success in Congress: Alternative Approaches," *Journal of Politics* 47 (1985): 667–685.

22. See Bruce Cain, John Ferejohn, and Morris Fiorina, *The Personal Vote: Constituency Service and Electoral Independence* (Cambridge, MA: Harvard University Press, 1987).

23. In *The End of Liberalism: The Second Republic of the United States* (New York: Norton, 1979), Theodore J. Lowi criticized Congress for delegating so much authority to the executive branch bureaucracy that they compromised the democratic nature of American politics. In their *The Logic of Delegation: Congressional Parties and the Appropriations Process* (Chicago: University of Chicago Press, 1991), D. Roderick Kiewiet and Mathew D. McCubbins defended these large grants of discretion by congressional "principals" to bureaucratic "agents" as reasonable and controllable exercises of majority party power.

24. In his *Building a New American State* (Cambridge, U.K.: Cambridge University Press, 1982), Stephen Skowronek shows how a federal regime dominated by political parties (through Congress and patronage) and the courts turned into government by a professional bureaucracy around the turn of the twentieth century. This change made the executive branch bureaucracy less responsive to the political parties but probably more responsive to the president.

25. Hugh Heclo, "Issue Networks and the Executive Establishment," in Anthony King, ed., *The New American Political System* (Washington, DC: American Enterprise Institute, 1979), pp. 87–124.

26. Dean E. Mann, *The Assistant Secretaries* (Washington, DC: Brookings Institution, 1965); and Brown, "Party and Bureaucracy."

27. Hugh Heclo, *A Government of Strangers: Executive Politics in Washington* (Washington, DC: Brookings Institution, 1977).

28. See Terry M. Moe, "The Politicized Presidency," in John E. Chubb and Paul E. Peterson, eds., *The New Direction in American Politics* (Washington, DC: Brookings Institution, 1985), pp. 235–271.

29. Joel Aberbach and Bert A. Rockman, "Clashing Beliefs Within the Executive Branch: The Nixon Administration Bureaucracy," *American Political Science Review* 70 (1976): 456–468.

30. Joel D. Aberbach and Bert A. Rockman, "The Political Views of U.S. Senior Federal Executives, 1970–1992," *Journal of Politics* 57 (1995): 838–852.

31. Donald R. Songer and Stefanie A. Lindquist, "Not the Whole Story: The Impact of Justices' Values on Supreme Court Decision Making," *American Journal of Political Science* 40 (1996): 1049–1063; Jeffrey A. Segal and Harold J. Spaeth, *The Supreme Court and the Attitudinal Model* (Cambridge: Cambridge University Press, 1993); and Robert A. Carp and Ronald Stidham, *Judicial Process in America* (Washington, DC: CQ Press, 1989).

32. See Randall D. Lloyd, "Separating Partisanship from Party in Judicial Research: Reapportionment in the U.S. District Courts," *American Political Science Review* 89 (1995): 413–420.

33. On judicial patronage, see Martin and Susan Tolchin, *To the Victor ...: Political Patronage from Clubhouse to White House* (New York: Random House, 1971), pp. 131–186.

34. Sheldon Goldman, "The Bush Imprint on the Judiciary: Carrying on a Tradition," *Judicature* 74 (1991), 294–306.

35. Sheldon Goldman, Elliot Slotnick, Gerard Gryski, and Gary Zuk, "Clinton's Judges: Summing Up the Legacy," *Judicature* 84 (2001): 244, 249.

36. An editorial in the *Washington Post* scolded both Clinton and the Senate, claiming that the confirmation system for the president's judicial nominations "serves to discredit both political parties, poses a threat to the independence and reputation of the judiciary, and badly needs to be reformed." (See "Avoiding the Senate," Dec. 31, 2000 p. B6.)

37. Daniel J. Parks, "Senate Judicial Nominations Spat Again Frustrates Appropriators," *CQ Weekly,* Oct. 20, 2001, pp. 2470–71. On party delays in confirming judicial nominees, see Sarah A. Binder and Forrest Maltzman, "Senatorial Delay in Confirming Federal Judges, 1947–1998," *American Journal of Political Science* 46 (2002): 190–199.

38. These data on judicial selection in the states come from the *Book of the States, 2000–01* (Lexington, KY: Council of State Governments, 2000), pp. 137–139. There is some overlap in these systems, as described in this volume.

39. On the political effects of different state selection systems, see Henry R. Glick and Craig F. Emmert, "Selection Systems and Judicial Characteristics: The Recruitment of State Supreme Court Judges," *Judicature* 70 (1987), 228–235; and Melinda Gann Hall, "State Supreme Courts in American Democracy: Probing the Myths of Judicial Reform," *American Political Science Review* 95 (2001): 315–330.

40. Data from a study conducted by Texans for Public Justice, reported in "Campaign contributions corrupt judicial races," *USA Today,* Sept. 1, 2000, p. 16A.

CHAPTER 15

1. David Nather, "Parties Push Together For Many Key Proposals of Bush's Education Plan," *Congressional Quarterly Weekly Report (CQ Weekly),* Apr. 7, 2001, p. 783.

2. See E. E. Schattschneider, *Party Government* (New York: Rinehart, 1942), pp. 131–132; and Austin Ranney, *The Doctrine of Responsible Party Government* (Urbana: University of Illinois Press, 1964).

3. Committee on Political Parties of the American Political Science Association, *Toward a More Responsible Two-Party System* (New York: Rinehart, 1950).

4. The distinguished British observer of American politics, Lord Bryce, long ago made the same complaint about American parties. See James Bryce, *The American Commonwealth* (New York: Macmillan, 1916).

5. See Ranney, *The Doctrine of Responsible Party Government,* Chapters 1 and 2, for an analysis of what party government presumes about democracy.

6. See the Committee on Political Parties, *Toward a More Responsible Two-Party System,* p. 15.

7. E. E. Schattschneider, *Party Government,* p. 208.

8. E. E. Schattschneider, *The Semi-Sovereign People* (New York: Holt, Rinehart, and Winston, 1960).

9. Pendleton Herring's *The Politics of Democracy* (New York: Rinehart, 1940) presented an early argument against the reformers. Also see Julius Turner, "Responsible Parties: A Dissent from the Floor," *American Political Science Review* 45 (1951): 143–152. The debate is effectively evaluated in Evron Kirkpatrick's "Toward a More Responsible Two-Party System: Political Science, Policy Science, or Pseudo-Science?" *American Political Science Review* 65 (1971): 965–990; and John Kenneth White and Jerome M. Mileur, eds., *Challenges to Party Government* (Carbondale: Southern Illinois University Press, 1992).

10. See Leon D. Epstein, "A Comparative Study of Canadian Parties," *American Political Science Review* 58 (1964): 46–59; Epstein's *Political Parties in Western Democracies* (New Brunswick, NJ: Transaction Books, 1980); and Austin Ranney, "Candidate Selection and Party Cohesion in Britain and the U.S.," in William J. Crotty, ed., *Approaches to the Study of Party Organization* (Boston: Allyn and Bacon, 1968), pp. 139–168.

11. See Malcolm E. Jewell and Sarah M. Morehouse, *Political Parties and Elections in American States,* 4th ed. (Washington, DC: CQ Press, 2001), p. 222; Morris Fiorina, *Divided Government* (New York: MacMillan, 1992), Chapter 3; and Fiorina's "Divided Government in the American States: A Byproduct of Legislative Professionalism," *American Political Science Review* 88 (1994): 304–316.

12. On the causes of divided government, see Gary Cox and Samuel Kernell, eds., *The Politics of Divided Government* (Boulder, CO: Westview, 1991); Gary Jacobson, *The Electoral Origins of Divided Government: Competition in U.S. House Elections, 1946–1988* (Boulder, CO: Westview, 1990); and Paul Allen Beck, Lawrence Baum, Aage Clausen, and Charles E. Smith, Jr., "Patterns and Sources of Split-Ticket Voting," *American Political Science Review* 86 (1992): 916–928.

13. James L. Sundquist, "Needed: A Political Theory for the New Era of Coalition Government in the United States," *Political Science Quarterly* 103 (1988): 613–635.

14. On the consequences of divided government, see Alberto Alesina and Howard Rosenthal, *Partisan Politics, Divided Government, and the Economy* (New York: Cambridge University Press, 1994); James E. Alt and Robert C. Lowery, "Divided Government, Fiscal Institutions, and Budget Deficits: Evidence from the States," *American Political Science Review* 88 (1994): 811–828; John J. Coleman, "Unified Government, Divided Government, and Party Responsiveness," *American Political Science Review* 93 (1999): 821–835; George C. Edwards III, Andrew Barrett, and Jeffrey Peake, "The Legislative Impact of Divided Government," *American Journal of Political Science* 41 (1997): 545–563; and Fiorina, *Divided Government,* Chapter 6. For a contrary view that divided government has not made much difference for federal policy-making, see David R. Mayhew, *Divided We Govern* (New Haven, CT: Yale University Press, 1991).

15. See Fiorina, *Divided Government,* Chapter 5. Also see Richard Born, "Split-Ticket Voters, Divided Government, and Fiorina's Policy-Balancing Model," *Legislative Studies Quarterly* 19 (1994): 95–115.

16. On ideology, see Vernon Van Dyke, *Ideology and Political Choice* (Chatham, NJ: Chatham House, 1995), and Kenneth R. Hoover, *Ideology and Political Life* (Monterey, CA: Brooks/Cole, 1987).

17. Otto Kircheimer, "The Transformation of the Western European Party Systems," in Joseph LaPalombara and Myron Weiner, eds., *Political Parties and Political Development* (Princeton, NJ: Princeton University Press, 1966), pp. 184–192.

18. On the consensus among Americans on the basic principles of politics, see Louis Hartz, *The Liberal Tradition in America* (New York: Harcourt, Brace, 1955).

19. Ian Budge and Richard I. Hofferbert have demonstrated that for the 1948–1985 period, important differences existed between the platforms of the two major American parties and the policies the parties enacted, as measured by federal expenditures when they controlled the presidency. See their "Mandates and Policy Outputs: U.S. Party Platforms and Federal Expenditures," *American Political Science Review* 84 (1990): 111–132, and the comments on their work in the same journal, 87 (1993): 744–750.

20. On the importance of racial issues in the changing nature of the party coalitions among both voters and political leaders, see Edward G. Carmines and James A. Stimson, *Issue Evolution: Race and the Transformation of American Politics* (Princeton, NJ: Princeton University Press, 1989).

21. Leslie Wayne, "Senate Shifts, So Lobbyists Must as Well," *New York Times,* June 9, 2001, p. A16.

22. See Geoffrey Layman, *The Great Divide* (New York: Columbia University Press, 2001).

23. Thomas B. Edsall, "Bush Deal Keeps GOP Stand on Abortion," *Washington Post,* July 1, 2000, p. A1.

24. See Dan Balz, "Bush Protects His Right Flank," *Washington Post,* Feb. 12, 2001, p. A1, and David S. Broder, "Party's Fault Lines Likely to Surface," *Washington Post,* Jan. 21, 2001, p. A22.

25. Quoted in William G. Mayer, *The Divided Democrats* (Boulder, CO: Westview, 1996), p. 1. On changes in party factionalism since the mid-1940s, see Nicol C. Rae, "Party Factionalism, 1946–1996," in Byron E. Shafer, *Partisan Approaches to Postwar American Politics* (New York: Chatham House, 1998), pp. 41–74.

26. Leading examples of the view that the American public alternates between different ideological postures are Arthur M. Schlesinger, Jr., *The Cycles of American History* (Boston: Houghton Mifflin, 1986); and Samuel P. Huntington, *American Politics: The Promise of Disharmony* (Cambridge, MA: Harvard University Press, 1981). For a systematic empirical analysis, see James A. Stimson, *Public Opinion: Moods, Cycles, and Swings* (Boulder, CO: Westview, 1991).

27. The seminal study is Philip E. Converse, "The Nature of Belief Systems in Mass Publics," in David Apter, ed., *Ideology and Discontent* (New York: Free Press, 1964), pp. 206–261. Also see Norman H. Nie, Sidney Verba, and John R. Petrocik, *The Changing American Voter* (Cambridge, MA: Harvard University Press, 1976), Chapters 7–9; John L. Sullivan, James E. Piereson, and George E. Marcus, "Ideological Constraint in the Mass Public: A Methodological Critique and Some New Findings," *American Journal of Political Science* 23 (1978): 233–249; and Russell J. Dalton, *Citizen Politics,* 3rd ed. (New York: Chatham House, 2002), Chapter 2.

28. For example, see Kathleen A. Frankovic and Monika L. McDermott, "Public Opinion in the 2000 Election: The Ambivalent Electorate," in Gerald M. Pomper, ed., *The Election of 2000* (New York: Chatham House, 2001), pp. 76–78 and 88–89.

29. For an excellent discussion of this point, see John Zaller and Stanley Feldman, "A Simple Theory of the Survey Response: Answering Questions versus Revealing Preferences," *American Journal of Political Science* 36 (1992): 579–616.

30. See Angus Campbell, Philip E. Converse, Warren E. Miller, and Donald E. Stokes, *The American Voter* (New York: John Wiley & Sons, 1960), 232–233. On ideological self-identification, see Pamela Conover and Stanley Feldman, "The Origins and Meaning of Liberal/Conservative Self-Identification," *American Journal of Political Science* 25 (1981): 617–645.

31. The survey results come from CBS News's "Millennium Poll," Dec. 1999, available from the Inter-University Consortium for Political and Social Research.

32. See Thomas Ferguson and Joel Rogers, *Right Turn: The Decline of the Democrats and the Future of American Politics* (New York: Hill and Wang, 1986), especially Chapter 1; and Paul R. Abramson, John H. Aldrich, and David W. Rohde, *Change and Continuity in the 1984 Elections* (Washington, DC: CQ Press, 1986), Chapter 6.

33. See Frankovic and McDermott, pp. 73–91.

34. Marc J. Hetherington, "Resurgent Mass Partisanship: The Role of Elite Polarization," *American Political Science Review* 95 (2001): 619–631; and Richard Fleisher and Jon R. Bond, "Evidence of Increasing Polarization Among Ordinary Citizens," in Jeffrey E. Cohen, Richard Fleisher, and Paul Kantor, eds., *American Political Parties: Decline or Resurgence?* (Washington, DC: CQ Press, 2001), pp. 58–67.

35. David Butler and Donald Stokes, *Political Change in Britain* (New York: St. Martin's, 1969), Chapter 9; and Philip E. Converse and Roy Pierce, *Political Representation in France* (Cambridge, MA: Harvard University Press, 1986), Chapter 4.

36. See, for example, Paul Sniderman, Richard Brody, and Philip Tetlock, *Reasoning and Choice* (New York: Cambridge University Press, 1991).

37. See Herbert McClosky, Paul J. Hoffman, and Rosemary O'Hara, "Issue Conflict and Consensus among Party Leaders and Followers," *American Political Science Review* 54 (1960): 406–427; Robert S. Montjoy, William R. Shaffer, and Ronald E. Weber, "Policy Preferences of Party Elites and Masses: Conflict or Consensus?" *American Politics Quarterly* 8 (1980): 319–344; John S. Jackson III, Barbara L. Brown, and David Bositis, "Herbert McClosky and Friends Revisited: 1980 Democratic and Republican Party Elites Compared to the Mass Public," *American Politics Quarterly* 10 (1982): 158–180; Warren E. Miller and M. Kent Jennings, *Parties in Transition* (New York: Russell Sage Foundation, 1986), pp. 189–219; and Denise L. Baer and David A. Bositis, *Elite Cadres and Party Coalitions* (New York: Greenwood Press, 1988), pp. 100–107. Evidence that party activists have become even more polarized ideologically is found in John M. Bruce, John A. Clark, and John H. Kessel, "Advocacy Politics in Presidential Parties," *American Political Science Review* 85 (1991): 1089–1105; and John H. Aldrich and David W. Rohde, "The Logic of Conditional Party Government: Revisiting the Electoral Connection," in Lawrence C. Dodd and Bruce I. Oppenheimer, eds., *Congress Reconsidered,* 7th ed. (Washington, DC: CQ Press, 2001), pp. 277–282.

38. On the use of ambiguity as a political strategy, see Benjamin Page, *Choices and Echoes in Presidential Elections* (Chicago: University of Chicago Press, 1978).

39. Anthony Downs discusses the tendency of general-election candidates to move toward the center in a two-party system; see Downs's *An Economic Theory of Democracy* (New York: Harper & Row, 1957). Rebecca B. Morton has shown that ideological candidates and parties will still diverge to some degree in spite of the pressures to converge; see her "Incomplete Information and Ideological Explanations of Platform Divergence," *American Political Science Review* 87 (1993): 382–392.

40. Recent research shows, however, that though survey respondents do see policy-based differences between the parties, they do not see a real difference in "process" concerns: the parties' vulnerability to organized interests, their affinity for negative campaigns, and their failure

to keep their promises. See John R. Hibbing and Elizabeth Theiss-Morse, "Process Preferences and American Politics: What the People Want Government to Be," *American Political Science Review* 95 (2001): 145–153.

41. Leon D. Epstein, "What Happened to the British Party Model?" *American Political Science Review* 74 (1980): 9–22.

42. Paul Allen Beck, "The Electoral Cycle and Patterns of American Politics," *British Journal of Political Science* 9 (1979): 129–156; and James L. Sundquist, *Dynamics of the Party System* (Washington, DC: Brookings Institution, 1983).

43. Beck, "The Electoral Cycle and Patterns of American Politics"; and Jerome M. Clubb, William H. Flanigan, and Nancy H. Zingale, *Partisan Realignment* (Beverly Hills, CA: Sage, 1980), pp. 155–188.

CHAPTER 16

1. This is a central theme of John H. Aldrich's *Why Parties?* (Chicago: University of Chicago Press, 1995).

2. For a systematic discussion, see Robert Harmel and Kenneth Janda, *Parties and Their Environments: Limits to Reform* (New York: Longman, 1982).

3. See Richard A. Brody, "The Puzzle of Political Participation in America," in Anthony King, ed., *The New American Political System* (Washington, DC: American Enterprise Institute, 1978), pp. 287–324; and Paul R. Abramson, John H. Aldrich, and David W. Rohde, *Change and Continuity in the 1996 Elections* (Washington, DC: CQ Press, 1998), pp. 79–90.

4. For example, multimember districts were once common in American state legislatures but their number has dwindled in recent years. See Richard Niemi, Simon Jackman, and Laura Winsky, "Candidates and Competitiveness in Multimember Districts," *Legislative Studies Quarterly* 16 (1991): 91–109; and Theodore J. Lowi, "Toward a More Responsible Three-Party System," *PS* 16 (1983): 699–706.

5. The extensive literature on the "decline of parties" during the 1960s and 1970s has been cited in earlier chapters. Most representative of these works are David S. Broder, *The Party's Over* (New York: Harper & Row, 1972); Alan Ware, *The Breakdown of the Democratic Party Organization: 1940–1980* (New York: Oxford University Press, 1985); and Martin P. Wattenberg, *The Rise of Candidate-Centered Politics* (Cambridge, MA: Harvard University Press, 1991).

6. These figures are taken from Harold W. Stanley and Richard G. Niemi, *Vital Statistics on American Politics 1999–2000* (Washington, DC: CQ Press, 2000), Tables 3.12 (on split-ticket voting, p. 133) and 1.13 (on split-district outcomes, p. 44).

7. See Bruce E. Cain, John Ferejohn, and Morris P. Fiorina, *The Personal Vote: Constituency Service and Electoral Independence* (Cambridge, MA: Harvard University Press, 1987).

8. Jeffrey E. Cohen and Paul Kantor, "Decline and Resurgence in the American Party System," in Jeffrey E. Cohen, Richard Fleisher, and Paul Kantor, eds., *American Political Parties: Decline or Resurgence?* (Washington, DC: CQ Press, 2001), pp. 255–257.

9. See Paul Allen Beck, "The Electoral Cycle and Patterns of American Politics," *British Journal of Political Science* 9 (1979): 129–156.

10. On the argument that recent signs of realignment do not meet the conditions traditionally required of a realignment, see Martin P. Wattenberg, "The Hollow Realignment: Partisan Change in a Candidate-Centered Era," *Public Opinion Quarterly* 51 (1987): 58–74; and Paul Allen Beck, "Incomplete Realignment: The Reagan Legacy for Parties and Elections," in Charles O. Jones, ed., *The Reagan Legacy* (Chatham, NJ: Chatham House, 1988), pp. 145–171. In *Critical Elections and the Mainsprings of American Politics* (New York: Norton, 1970), Chapter 5, Walter Dean Burnham contends that antiparty political reforms probably keep present or future realignments from becoming as complete as past realignments.

11. On information sources in American campaigns, see Robert Huckfeldt and Paul Allen Beck, "Contexts, Intermediaries, and Political Activity," in Lawrence C. Dodd and Calvin Jillson, eds., *The Dynamics of American Politics: Approaches and Interpretations* (Boulder, CO: Westview Press, 1994), Chapter 11. On the other hand, organized interests have become more polarized by party since the Reagan years; see Jack L. Walker, Jr., *Mobilizing Interest Groups in America* (Ann Arbor: University of Michigan Press, 1991), Chapter 8.

12. Larry M. Bartels, "Partisanship and Voting Behavior, 1952–1996," *American Journal of Political Science* 44 (2000): 35–50.

13. Such skepticism about the ability of the new "service" party to restore the party organization to its earlier prominence is best expressed in John J. Coleman, "The Resurgence of Party Organization: A Dissent from the New Orthodoxy," in Daniel M. Shea and John C. Green, eds., *The State of the Parties: The Changing Role of Contemporary American Parties* (Lanham, MD: Rowman and Littlefield, 1994), Chapter 20.

14. See Cornelius P. Cotter, James L. Gibson, John F. Bibby, and Robert J. Huckshorn, *Party Organization in American Politics* (New York: Praeger, 1984); Xandra Kayden and Eddie Mahe, Jr., *The Party Goes On* (New York: Basic Books, 1985); David E. Price, *Bringing Back the Parties* (Washington, DC: CQ Press, 1984); Larry J. Sabato and Bruce Larson, *The Party's Just Begun*, 2nd ed. (New York: Longman, 2002); and Joseph A. Schlesinger, "The New American Political Party," *American Political Science Review* 79 (1985): 1152–1169.

15. For a good summary, see Cohen and Kantor, "Decline and Resurgence in the American Party System," pp. 245–247.

16. Sabato and Larson, *The Party's Just Begun*, pp. 2–4.

17. On the greater sophistication and politicization of Western electorates and the resulting decline of "blind" party loyalties, see Ronald Inglehart, *Culture Shift* (Princeton, NJ: Princeton University Press, 1990), especially Chapters 10 and 11. See Kay Lawson and Peter H. Merkl, *When Parties Fail: Emerging Alternative Organizations* (Princeton, NJ: Princeton University Press, 1988), on the growing strength of competitors to the parties throughout the Western world.

18. Marjorie Randon Hershey, "If 'The Party's in Decline,' Then What's That Filling the News Columns?" in Nelson W. Polsby and Raymond E. Wolfinger, *On Parties* (Berkeley, CA: Institute of Governmental Studies, 1999), pp. 257–278. Doris A. Graber discusses media treatment of politics in *Mass Media and American Politics*, 5th ed. (Washington, DC: CQ Press, 1997).

19. On the centrality of the organization in these working-class parties, especially the British Labour Party, see Leon D. Epstein, *Political Parties in Western Democracies* (New York: Praeger, 1967), Chapter 11.

20. The only American parallels to the party organization's domination of campaign techniques are found in the few states that give public financing to the party organizations, not the candidates, and in the (now dwindling) coverage television networks give to the national party conventions.

21. See Paul S. Herrnson and John C. Green, *Multiparty Politics in America* (Lanham, MD: Rowman & Littlefield, 1997); and Steven J. Rosenstone, Roy L. Behr, and Edward H. Lazarus, *Third Parties in America*, 2nd ed. (Princeton, NJ: Princeton University Press, 1994).

22. Burnham, *Critical Elections and the Mainsprings of American Politics*, p. 133.

23. Willis D. Hawley, *Nonpartisan Elections and the Case for Party Politics* (New York: Wiley, 1973).

24. A slight socioeconomic status bias of the decline in turnout in recent decades is described in Ruy A. Teixeira, *The Disappearing American Voter* (Washington, DC: Brookings Institution, 1992), Chapter 3. Broader studies of voter participation in the United States and elsewhere demonstrate the importance of the political parties for mobilizing lower-status groups into politics. See Steven J. Rosenstone and John Mark Hansen, *Mobilization, Participation, and Democracy in America* (New York: Macmillan, 1993), especially Chapter 8; and Sidney

Verba, Norman H. Nie, and Jae-On Kim, *Participation and Political Equality* (Cambridge, U.K.: Cambridge University Press, 1978).

25. Together with colleague Bruce Larson in *The Party's Just Begun*, see especially Chapters 6 and 7.

26. Sabato and Larson, *The Party's Just Begun,* pp. 156–157.

27. John Mintz, "Everybody Can Get Into the Act With Issue Ads," *Washington Post,* Sept. 19, 2000, p. A1.

Index

Page numbers followed by *italicized* letters *f* and *t* indicate figures and tables, respectively